Essential Criminology

Essential Criminology

Second Edition

Mark M. Lanier
University of Central Florida

Stuart Henry
Wayne State University

A Member of the Perseus Books Group

Mark dedicates this book to Luke and Jessi
Stuart, to Lee and Jasmine

Copyright © 2004 Mark Lanier and Stuart Henry
Published in 2004 in the United States of America by Westview Press, 5500 Central Avenue, Boulder, Colorado 80301-2877, and in the United Kingdom by Westview Press, 12 Hid's Copse Road, Cumnor Hill, Oxford OX2 9JJ.

Library of Congress Cataloging-in-Publication Data

Lanier, Mark.
  Essential criminology / Mark Lanier, Stuart Henry.—2nd ed.
    p. cm.
  Includes bibliographical references and index.
  ISBN 0-8133-4089-6 (alk. paper)—ISBN 0-8133-4090-X (pbk. : alk. paper)
  1. Criminology. I. Henry, Stuart. II. Title.
HV6025.L25 2004
364—dc22

2003021961

The paper used in this publication meets the requirements of the American National Standard for Permanence of Paper for Printed Library Materials _Z39.48–1984.

10   9   8   7   6   5   4   3   2   1

Contents

v

Tables and Figures

Preface and Acknowledgments

The idea that "the only constant is change" has been around at least since the time of Heraclitus in 500 B.C. Since we wrote the first edition of this book in 1997, the world has certainly changed. It has become more globalized and we are more interconnected with others. The nature of crime has changed to include environmental and financial harms from multinational corporate crimes, global political terrorism, and violence at home, work, or school, all of which have become more significant than the threat from strangers on the street. The threat of terrorism affects everyone, everywhere. New vulnerabilities have appeared. The means we use to communicate and converse have changed and opened up opportunities for new types of white-collar fraud and identity theft. The business community has been racked by one scandal after another, eroding confidence in our economic systems. The nature of war has also changed from nation-to-nation fighting to ongoing conflicts between ethnic and sectarian groups. These changes, coupled with many suggestions from the readers and users of the first edition, led us to revise and update *Essential Criminology*. Most of all, we revised this book in the spirit of social philosopher Eric Hoffer (1902–1983), who said that "in times of profound change, the learners inherit the earth, while the learned find themselves beautifully equipped to deal with a world that no longer exists."

On the surface, this is still a book about crime and criminality. It is about how we study crime, how we explain crime, how we determine what is—and is not—criminal, and how we can reduce the harm caused by crime. It is also a book about difference. Crime is something we all know about—or do we? You may see crime differently from the way your parents or even your peers see it. You may see your own behavior as relatively acceptable, apart from a few minor rule violations here and there. But real crime? That's what others do—criminals, right? You may change how you view crime and criminals after reading this text.

As authors, we reflect difference; Stuart was raised in working-class South London, England. Mark traces his ancestry to southern plantation owners. Stuart was educated to traditional, long-tested, yet very narrow British standards; Mark, in a unique multidisciplinary U.S. program. Stuart seriously questions the utility of scientific methods (positivism); Mark relies on them daily. Stuart rarely does anything outdoors, except watch an occasional rock concert. Mark rides Harleys and is an active wakeboarder and surfer who loves outdoor life. Despite these differences we found common ground for our analysis of crime and criminality. Our differences provide for a balanced analysis of crime.

We see crime as complex, political, and harmful to victims and perpetrators. We also acknowledge the difference between people, culture, and regions. Thus we embrace conflict as not only inevitable but positive. Conflict promotes contemplation and understanding of others, including their culture, education, experience, and worldview. Conflict also prompts change and thus provides the opportunity for improving our social world. It presents the opportunity to confront our dissatisfactions and search for a better way.

Most Americans and many Europeans are dissatisfied with how we handle crime and criminals. This dissatisfaction raises questions. Is crime caused by individuals—criminals? Is it caused by the way society is organized? By rule makers? By poverty? Drugs? All of the above? Something else? Is crime even caused at all? We also question how to deal with crime. Should crime be handled by the criminal justice system? By social policy? By public health officials (did you know that the Centers for Disease Control now track homicides)? By you and other citizens ("take back the streets" and "neighborhood partnership" programs have become a significant part of community crime control)? Conflict over these issues and the need for a good, (relatively) short criminology text contributed to our desire to write this book.

At first we decided to write *Essential Criminology* as a concise introductory text that examines the nature and extent of crime and surveys the main theoretical perspectives on crime causation and criminal justice policy implications. The book is written in a clear, straightforward style and progressively builds students' knowledge. Much to our surprise, an analysis of programs adopting the text found it being used in graduate programs as well as freshman courses. Thus in this second edition we have tried to broaden the scope. We are glad the first edition had such broad appeal and we have tried to build on that.

After describing the scope of the subject, *Essential Criminology* guides students through the diverse definitions of crime and provides a brief treatment of the different ways crime is measured. It then turns to the major theoretical explanations for crime, from individual-level classical and rational choice through biological, psychological, social learning, social control, and interactionist perspectives. It explains the more sociocultural theories, beginning with social ecology, and moves on to strain/subcultural theory and conflict, Marxist, and anarchist approaches. We reorganized the final chapters to better reflect feminist contributions and the exciting new changes in postmodernism, peacemaking, and left realism. The conclusion examines the main arguments for and against integrative theories. Brief background information is provided on major theorists demonstrating that they are real people who share the experiences life offers us all. We have tried to cover the theories completely, accurately, and evenhandedly and have attempted to show how each is related to or builds on the others. Concerns about length mean that the student wishing to explore these connections in depth should consult more comprehensive theory texts. Ours provides the essentials.

Essential Criminology has several unique, student-friendly features. We begin each chapter with examples of specific crimes to illustrate the theory. The book includes an integrated "prismatic" definition of crime. This prism provides a comprehensive, multidimensional way of conceptualizing crime in terms of damage, social outrage, and harm. Our "crime prism" integrates virtually all the major disparate definitions of crime. Interestingly, when this first appeared we were encouraged to develop it further and the result was a journal article (Henry and Lanier 1998) and book-length treatment of the subject (*What Is Crime: Controversies over the Nature of Crime and What to Do About It* 2001). Throughout the text, we provide "equal time" examples from both white-collar ("suite") and conventional ("street") crime with the objective of drawing students into the realities of concrete cases. We make a conscious effort to include crimes that are less often detected, prosecuted, and punished. These corporate, occupational, and state crimes have serious consequences but are often neglected in introductory texts. We present chapter-by-chapter discussions of each perspective's policy implications, indicating the practical applications that the theory implies. Finally, summary concept charts conclude each chapter dealing with theory. These provide a simple yet comprehensive analytical summary of the theories, revealing their basic assumptions.

The book is primarily intended for students interested in the study of crime. This includes such diverse fields as psychology, sociology, political science, and history. We expect the book to be mainly used in criminology and criminal justice courses, but students studying any topics related to crime, such as juvenile delinquency and deviant behavior, will also find the book useful. Interdisciplinary programs will find the book particularly helpful.

Rarely is any book the product of one or two individuals. We drew on the talents, motivation, and knowledge of many others. Thus several people have earned our thanks and respect. In keeping with our title, however, we mention only key helpers. Jill Rothenberg was both patient and encouraging. Chrisona Schmidt's and Sharon DeJohn's copyediting added greatly to the book's clarity. We would particularly like to thank our graduate research assistants: Natalie Palchak, Jessica Stern, and Luann Brennan. We also thank two Wayne State University graduate library science students, Robert Graves and Jennifer Roth-Emkow, who provided research assistance for the book. Gregg Barak has always been at the forefront of recent theoretical movements and we are each indebted to him for his thought-provoking prose and friendship. We thank our colleague Dragan Milovanovic for continuing to provide cutting-edge critical theory that has moved the discipline beyond its narrow confines. Mark Lanier specifically thanks the teachers who first interested him in theory—William Osterhoff, Brent Smith, and John Sloan—as well as the teachers and peers who provided additional insight: Karol Lucken, Peter K. Manning, Bob Bohm, John Smykla, and Gene Paoline. He would also like to thank all the teachers outside the classroom: friends, students, deviants (bikers, surfers, and professors mostly), criminals, and police officers who broadened his view of crime. We would like to commend the external reviewers of this book, Mark Stafford of the University of Texas-Austin, and especially Martha A. Myers of the University of Georgia, who provided a thoroughly constructive commentary that made this book far better than it could have been. Finally, we would like to thank Rene van Swaaningen and Dragan Milovanovic for helpful suggestions pertaining to the book's revision.

Mark Lanier
Stuart Henry

1

What Is Criminology?
The Study of Crime, Criminals, and Victims

In the early part of the twenty-first century we have witnessed some surprising and shocking changes in the study of crime. Theoretically, the most significant change is the increased attention given to defining crime, not least because global terrorism has caused us to question the connection between politics, harm creation, and what kinds of actions should count as crime. Greater attention is being focused on crimes of the powerful, from governments to corporations, more generally known as white-collar crime. In practical terms the increasing severity and frequency of terrorism has altered our belief in the amount of freedom that individuals are prepared to sacrifice to government in exchange for state protection. Instead of security in the home to protect our private property, we are now more interested in "homeland security" to protect our energy resources, health network, water supply, communications system, and mass transportation facilities, including ports, airports, and trains. We are also strengthening public safety services: police, fire, EMS, and the National Guard. We are moving from decentralized and fragmented protective services to an integrated national system of security designed to protect the American "homeland." Fear in the minds of Western populations has shifted from burglars in the night to low-flying aircraft and bombs in movie theaters. The perceived vulnerability of Western civilizations stemming from the combination of openness and large population concentrations has reached a national crisis.

As a result of these changes, criminology is also undergoing major changes. Historically a discipline focused on explaining individual criminal motivations in relation to domestic institutions and social processes, it has become a multifaceted examination that links genetic disposition to political and global forces. What is this discipline, this study of crime? To contemporary criminologists, the scope of crime is much broader than

1

media portrayals of inner-city gang violence, child abductions, carjack-
ings, drive-by shootings, serial murders, workplace homicides, and drug
wars. Crime also includes a variety of misdeeds by governments, political
corruption, corporate fraud, employee theft, and offenses committed by
"ordinary" Americans.

Ever since the watershed of Watergate in the early 1970s, when it was
reluctantly realized that even a president could be a "crook," media coverage of crimes by those in positions of power has accelerated. For example, consider the harm caused by U.S. government radiation experiments
on unknowing citizens who subsequently developed cancer. Consider
also the 1930s syphilis experiments that were conducted on African
American men in Tuskeegee, Alabama. These infected men were diagnosed but deliberately not treated, even when penicillin was available as
a cure, in order for government doctors to study the long-term effects of
syphilis. Deceiving consumers through false advertising and price-fixing
by corporate giants like the Archer Daniels Midland Company (ADM)
(forcing consumers to pay above the market price by undermining competition) are just some of the crimes committed by corporations. Other
crimes of the powerful involve corporate executives deceiving investors,
as in the Enron, Worldcom, and Arthur Andersen scandals; Martha Stewart has made insider trading a household phrase. Corporate crime can
include manufacturers and hazardous waste companies that pollute the
environment, as well as the knowing manufacture of defective products,
as in the case of the Ford Pinto gas tank that exploded on low-speed rear
end impact; dangerous Firestone tires on Ford Motor Company automo-
biles (particularly its SUVs), with one of the poorest safety records on the
road; and unsafe food handling practices by meat processing companies
resulting in E. coli contamination of beef.

Also falling within the scope of criminology are the unsafe production
practices that result in death and injury in the workplace, such as the Imperial chicken plant in Hamlet, North Carolina, where twenty-five deaths
occurred when the factory caught fire. Imperial's owners had padlocked
the plant's fire exits to stop petty pilfering of chicken; each of the owners
received a ten-year prison sentence for nonnegligent manslaughter. Contemporary criminologists also study employees who steal from their
bosses, bosses who employ workers "off the books" to evade taxes, and
professionals (such as doctors) who defraud the government and rob the
public purse through Medicare and Medicaid fraud.

Finally, the United States has become the target of terrorist groups, as
evidenced by the 9/11 suicide hijackings of fully loaded passenger aircraft that were flown into corporate and government buildings and attacks on U.S. interests abroad, as in the USS *Cole* and the U.S. embassy in
Nairobi. What light can criminology shed on the political movements that

lead people to commit suicide bombings in furtherance of their cause? What global forces produce such widespread human suffering and what can we learn about the forces that prevent these devastating consequences?

Criminologists study not only the nature of this harmful behavior but also its causes and the systematic practices that produce patterns of harm in a variety of social contexts. For example, surfing may seem to be a crimefree activity, and generally it is. But in September 1995 at Laguna Beach, California, two surfers were videotaped beating another surfer who had ventured into their designated contest area. The two surfers were arrested and charged with felony assault. In court on December 20, 1995, the two surfers had their charges reduced through a plea bargain, and each was released on three years' probation. The videotape played a vital role in the case. Media coverage was vast and the case was featured on *Court TV*. That incident was followed by a flurry of similar cases involving surfers and violence. An article in *People* magazine (September 2, 2002) on the problem may further influence the prosecution of these violent surfers, or it may increase the violence. Indeed, the media have a significant role in shaping our conception of crime, especially through such celebrated cases as the police beating of a young teen in Inglewood, California, the Clarence Thomas–Anita Hill sexual harassment hearings, Kobe Bryant's rape charge, Michael Jackson's pedophilia charge, and the murder trials of O.J. Simpson and Michael Skakel (Barak 1994, 1996).

What do these various crimes have in common? What kind of cases grab media attention? Which do people consider more criminal? Which elicit the most concern? How does the social context affect the kind of crime and the harms suffered by its victims? How are technology and the media changing the face of crime? What do these events have to do with criminology? After reading this book, you should have a better understanding of these issues, if not clear answers.

In this first chapter, we provide an overview of criminology. We begin by looking at the scope of the discipline and how it overlaps other fields. Next, we introduce the variety of criminological theories, which we describe in more detail in later chapters. Finally, we conclude our broad introduction to criminology with an examination of victimology and the role of victims in crime events and criminal justice.

What Is Criminology?

At its simplest, criminology can be defined as the systematic study of the nature, extent, cause, and control of law-breaking behavior. Criminology is an applied social science in which criminologists work to establish knowledge about crime and its control based on empirical research. This research forms the basis for understanding, explaining, predicting, and preventing crime, as well as forming criminal justice policy.

Ever since the term "criminology" was coined in 1885 by Raffaele Garofalo (1914), the content and scope of the field have been controversial. Critics and commentators have raised several questions about its academic standing. For example, is criminology truly a science? Does its applied approach, driven predominantly by the desire to control crime, inherently undermine the value-neutral stance generally considered essential for scientific inquiry? Is criminology an autonomous discipline or does it rely on the insights, theory, and research of other natural and social science disciplines, and increasingly the media and public opinion? Which of the several theories of criminology offers the best explanation for crime? Answers to these questions are complicated by criminology's multidisciplinary nature, its relative failure to recommend policy that reduces crime, and its heavy reliance on government funding for research.

Criminology's subject matter is elastic. Unquestionable core components include (1) the definition and nature of crime as harm-causing behavior; (2) different types of criminal activity, ranging from individual, spontaneous offending to collective, organized criminal enterprises; (3) profiles of typical offenders and victims, including organizational and corporate law violators; (4) statistical analysis of the extent, incidence, patterning, and cost of crimes, including estimates of the "dark figure" of hidden or unreported crime, based on surveys of victims and self-report studies of offenders; and (5) analysis of crime causation. Less agreement exists about whether the scope of criminology should be broadened to include society's response to crime, the formulation of criminal laws, and the role of victims in these processes.

In the United States, the inclusive term "criminal justice" generally refers to crime control practices, philosophies, and policies used by police, courts, and corrections. However, those who study such matters are as likely to identify themselves, or be identified by others, as criminologists as are those who study criminal behavior and its causes. Criminology by contrast, concerns itself with the theoretical and empirical study of the causes of crime. The two areas are obviously closely related but a distinction is necessary.

Is Criminology Scientific?

Criminology requires that criminologists strictly adhere to the scientific method. What distinguishes science from nonscience is the insistence on testable hypotheses, whose support or refutation through empirical research forms the basis of what is accepted among scientific criminologists as valid knowledge. Science, then, requires criminologists to build criminological knowledge from logically interrelated, theoretically grounded, and empirically tested hypotheses that are subject to retesting. These theoretical statements hold true as long as they are not falsified by further research (Popper 1959).

Theory testing can be done using either qualitative or quantitative methods. Qualitative methods (Berg 2000) may use systematic ethnographic techniques, such as participant observation and in-depth interviews. These are designed to enable the researcher to understand what criminal activity means to the participants. In participant observation, the researcher takes a role at the scene of a crime or in the justice system and describes what goes on in the interactions between the participants. Criminologists using this technique study crime and its social context as an anthropologist would study a nonindustrial society. These methods have produced some of criminology's richest studies, such as Laud Humphries (1970) study of homosexuality in public rest rooms, entitled *Tea Room Trade*, and Howard Becker's ([1963] 1973) study of jazz musicians and marijuana smoking in his book *Outsiders*.

Quantitative methods involve numbers, counts, and measures that are arrived at via a variety of research techniques. These include survey research based on representative random samples and the analysis of secondary data gathered for other purposes, such as homicide rates or corporate convictions for health and safety violations. Criminologists using quantitative techniques make up the mainstream of academic criminology. Perhaps one of the most illustrative examples of quantitative research is the series of longitudinal studies of a cohort of 10,000 boys born in Philadelphia in 1945 and followed through age eighteen with respect to their arrests for criminal offenses (Wolfgang, Figlio, and Sellin 1972) and a second cohort of 27,000 boys and girls born in 1958 (Tracy, Wolfgang, and Figlio 1990). Each study seemed to indicate that a small proportion of offenders (6 percent), called "chronic offenders," accounted for over half of all offenses. Other quantitative research methods include the use of historical records, comparative analysis, and experimental research. Unfortunately, most quantitative research is not theory driven; it does not involve theory testing. A survey conducted in 1992 revealed that only 27 percent of the articles published over a period of twenty-eight years in the journal *Criminology* tested theory (Stitt and Giacopassi 1992). Apparently theoretically grounded research is lacking. This begs the question, Is criminology scientific?

Disciplinary Diversity

Although strongly influenced by sociology, criminology also has roots in a number of other disciplines, including anthropology, biology, economics, geography, history, philosophy, political science, psychiatry, and psychology (Einstadter and Henry 1995). Each of these disciplines contributes its own assumptions about human nature and society, its own definitions of crime and the role of law, its own preference of methods for the study of crime, and its own analysis of crime causation with differing policy implications. This diversity presents a major challenge to criminology's disciplinary integrity. Do these diverse theoretical perspectives, taken together when applied to crime, constitute an independent academic discipline? Are these contributing knowledges merely subfields, or special applications of established disciplines? Alternatively, is criminology interdisciplinary? If criminology is to be considered interdisciplinary, what is meant by this? Is "interdisciplinary" understood as the integration of knowledge into a distinct whole? If so, then criminology is not yet interdisciplinary. Only a few criminologists have attempted such integration (see Messner, Krohn, and Liska 1989; Barak 1998). There is sufficient independence of the subject from its constituent disciplines and an acceptance of their diversity, however, to prevent criminology being subsumed under any one of them. For this reason, criminology is best defined as multidisciplinary. Put simply, crime can be viewed though many lenses. This is well illustrated through an overview of its component theories, discussions of which form the bases of subsequent chapters in this book.

Criminological Theory

A precursor to scientific criminology was the rational thought and economic assumptions of the eighteenth-century Enlightenment philosophy of Cesare Beccaria (1735–1795) and Jeremy Bentham (1748–1832).

Founders of Classical Economic Theory

1764 Cesare Beccaria *Essay on Crimes and Punishment*
1765 Jeremy Bentham *An Introduction to the Principles of*
　　　　Morals

Individuals are said to choose to commit crime based on whether they will derive more pleasure from doing so than pain. Burglars, for example, weigh whether or not to invade someone else's property depending on the existence, among other things, of fences, locks, and guardians of property and whether they think they will get caught and, if so, seriously punished.

The idea that crime is chosen was challenged by the early anthropological and biologically based formulations of the Italian school of criminologists, including Cesare Lombroso (1835–1909), Raffaele Garofalo

(1852–1934), and Enrico Ferri (1856–1928), who believed crime was caused, not chosen. Analyzing convicted criminals and cadavers, these founding scientific criminologists claimed to show that crime was caused by biological defects in inferior "atavistic" individuals who were "throwbacks" from an earlier evolutionary stage of human development.

Founders of Biological Theory

1876 Cesare Lombroso *Criminal Man*
1884 Enrico Ferri *Criminal Sociology*
1885 Rafaele Garofalo *Criminology*

The idea that individual bodily differences can explain crime was developed in the late nineteenth century by U.S. criminal anthropologists, such as Ernest Hooton, who believed in the criminal man, and the constitutional theorist William Sheldon, who believed crime came from feeble minds and inferior physical constitutions.

Founders of Heredity and Constitutional Type Theory

1877 Richard Dugdale *The Jukes: A Study in Crime, Pauperism,
      Disease and Heredity*
1912 Henry Goddard *The Kallikak Family: A Study in the Hered-
      ity of Feeblemindedness*
1893 Charles Henderson *Introduction to the Study of Dependent,
      Defective, and Delinquent Classes*
1931 Ernest Hooten *Crime and the Man*
1939 Ernest Hooten *The American Criminal: An Anthropological
      Study*
1949 William Sheldon et al. *Varieties of Delinquent Youth*

One challenge to these theories came from the Freudian-influenced psychoanalysis popular in the early twentieth century. For thinkers such as Augusta Bronner, the root of crime lay in the failure of family socialization in a child's early years, resulting in a defective personality. Thus the antisocial delinquent act of vandalism might be explained by inadequate parenting leading to a failure to develop affective ties with others and therefore a lack of respect for their property.

Founders of Psychoanalytical Theory

1926 William Healy and Augusta Bronner *Delinquents and
      Criminals: Their Making and Unmaking*

Founders of Psychoanalytical Theory *(continued)*

1935 August Aichhorn *Wayward Youth*
1936 William Healy and Augusta Bronner *New Light on
      Delinquency and Its Treatment*
1947 Kate Friedlander *The Psychoanalytic Approach to Juvenile
      Delinquency*

Other challenges to early biologically based theories came from the ecologically influenced sociological approach, which viewed crimes caused more by location than by person. Thus the cultural ecologists of the Chicago school, such as Clifford Shaw and Henry McKay, argued that biology could not account for why certain geographical areas of a city showed consistent patterns of crime, even when their populations changed. Someone living in a dilapidated inner city, surrounded by prostitution, drug dealing, and vice, according to this theory, will be more likely to become criminal than someone living in a respectable suburban neighborhood with well-kept houses, tree-lined avenues, and well-funded recreational facilities.

Founders of Chicago School Ecological Theory

1925 Robert Park, Ernest Burgess, and Roderick McKenzie
      The City
1942 Clifford Shaw and Henry McKay *Juvenile Delinquency
      and Urban Areas: A Study of Delinquents in Relation to
      Differential Characteristics of Local Communities*

By the 1940s and 1950s, from these foundations, a variety of other sociological theories of criminal behavior emerged. For example, structural functionalist sociology was based on the anomie theory of nineteenth-century French sociologist Emile Durkheim. In a capitalist industrial society, founded on self-interested competition, the moral authority of communities would be undermined. Among people encouraged to aspire as individuals and to value self-interest over a concern for others, the resultant state of normlessness, or anomie, would lead to increased levels of crime and deviance. Robert Merton's 1938 adaptation of this idea for the United States in his version of anomie theory (which he called strain theory) placed the cause of crime on the failure of capitalist society's education and vocational opportunities to provide an adequate means for all those whose aspirations had been raised by advertising and the media to achieve the monetary success of "the American Dream." For Merton, crime was an attempt by some of the disadvantaged to go for that dream, even if they had to do so by illegitimate means. The neighborhood drug dealer buying a luxury SUV with drug profits is simply using illegitimate or unacceptable means to achieve the same ends as those sought by the Yuppie corporate executive and her BMW.

Founders of Sociological Structural Theory

1893 Emile Durkheim *The Division of Labor in Society*
1897 Emile Durkheim *Suicide: A Study in Sociology*
1938 Robert Merton "Social Structure and Anomie" *American Sociological Review*
1957 Robert Merton *Social Theory and Social Structure*

Edwin Sutherland ([1939] 1947), in contrast, took a more social-psychological view of crime causation. He was interested in how people learn to commit crime. His theory, called differential association, developed later with Donald Cressey (Sutherland and Cressey 1966), argued that criminal behavior, like any other behavior, is learned. It is learned in gangs from peers who are excessively invested in defining crime as acceptable behavior. Crime is thus a result of a differential association with criminal learning patterns. Youths continuously associating with peers who abuse OxyContin might learn the techniques, suppliers, and meaning of getting high, as well as how to rationalize this behavior as enjoyable, acceptable, and even normal.

Founders of Social Psychological Differential Association Theory

---

1939 Edwin Sutherland *Principles of Criminology*
1949 Edwin Sutherland *White Collar Crime*
1964 Donald Cressey *Delinquency, Crime, and Differential Association*
1966 Edwin Sutherland and Donald Cressey *Principles of Criminology*

Another sociological contribution that emphasized learning was Thorsten Sellin's (1938) culture conflict theory and the idea, later applied by Walter Miller (1958), that some people learn a different culture or a different set of core values that ultimately clash with those of the mainstream culture. Whether it is the justification of vengeance for ruining a daughter's virginity held by Sicilian immigrants or the prestige of street fighting among working-class Pittsburgh adolescents, the point is that what is conformity to one culture's norms can be lawbreaking to the wider society.

For other sociologists, cultural contexts did not just stem from class, race, or national differences but were multiple and even formed in reaction to aspects of the dominant culture. The 1950s subcultural theories of delinquency included Albert Cohen's (1955) theory of status frustration and Richard Cloward and Lloyd Ohlin's (1960) differential opportunity theory, according to which a person's place in a specific subculture, ethnic group, or economic class influences the options available and the choices made. Thus delinquents may form criminal or violent gangs precisely because their values have been rejected by the middle-class education system and they believe they can act better together than alone.

Founders of Sociological Subcultural Strain Theory

1955 Albert Cohen *Delinquent Boys*
1959 Richard Cloward and Lloyd Ohlin *New Perspectives on Juvenile Delinquency*
1960 Richard Cloward and Lloyd Ohlin *Delinquency and Opportunity*

The sociological contribution showed that crime was shaped by context, especially the context provided by sociocultural, structural, and organizational forces. Context means that the particular era in which one lives, the frames of reference one employs, and one's worldview all serve to selectively shape how one sees and interprets events such as crime.

The predominance of structural and cultural explanations in U.S. criminology began to be challenged in the 1960s by social-psychological influences. These emphasized that humans were not just passively molded by external forces but were actively involved in shaping their worlds and their own identities. From its roots in Gabriel Tarde's ([1890] 1903) imitation theory, social learning was established by Albert Bandura (1969, 1973) and Ronald Akers ([1977] 1985) as a major explanatory framework for violence. It went beyond B. F. Skinner's (1953) behaviorist operant conditioning model, in which one is conditioned to respond in a specific way (e.g., with violence).

Founders of Psychological and Social Learning Theory

1890 Gabriel Tarde *Gabriel Tarde's Laws of Imitation*
1971 B. F. Skinner *Beyond Freedom and Dignity*
1973 Albert Banduva *Aggression: A Social Learning Analysis*
1977 Ronald Akers *Deviant Behavior: A Social Learning Approach*

It also superseded both the criminal personality theory of Hans Eysenck ([1964] 1977), who asserted that some people were predisposed to being undersocialized because they were extroverted personalities, and the criminal thinking patterns theory of Samuel Yochelson and Stanton Samenow (1976, 1977), according to which people learned to think antisocially and then became locked into that way of thinking. Indeed, Bandura showed how children can learn to model violence not only from parents but also from television and film characters.

Founders of Psychological Personality Theory

1962 Gordon Trasler *The Explanation of Criminality*
1964 Hans Eysenck *Crime and Personality*
1976 Samuel Yochelson and Stanton Samenow *The Criminal Personality*

The rejection of "faulty mind" theories as a major explanation for crime was further encouraged by the 1960s neutralization and social control theories of David Matza, Gresham Sykes (1961), and Travis Hirschi (1969). Neutralization is the idea that although people may learn to behave conventionally, under certain circumstances they also learn that immoral behavior is sometimes acceptable. In other words, various excuses and justifications send them on a "moral holiday" where they drift between convention and crime, free from moral constraint. For example, employees in the workplace who justify their theft of company property and time with phrases like "Everybody does it" or "No one got hurt" or "Even the manager does it" are more likely to see their acts as perks than as stealing.

Founders of Social Control and Neutralization Theory

1940 Walter Reckless *Criminal Behavior*
1952 Fritz Redl and David Wineman *Controls from Within*
1953 Donald Cressey *Other People's Money*
1958 F. Ivan Nye *Family Relationships and Delinquent Behavior*
1964 David Matza *Delinquency and Drift*
1969 Travis Hirschi *Causes of Delinquency*

Travis Hirschi's (1969) control theory dealt with the failure of some people to form bonds to conventional society and values in the first place. Put simply, people who do not relate to a conventional parent or school system cannot identify with that person or institution, do not spend time doing conventional activities, and do not believe the existing society is worth much, are unlikely to refrain from breaking society's rules. This theory again played up the importance of adequate parental socialization if delinquency was to be avoided. However, it tended to ignore the role of peers; corrupt school and workplace practices; and the structural problems of society manifest in poor housing, inadequate employment possibilities, and bias in the justice system.

By the 1970s, U.S. criminology was addressing some of these issues through another social-psychological theory, called labeling, or new deviancy theory. Labeling theorists claimed that minor crime was actually made worse by criminal justice agencies' attempts to control it. This intensification resulted from the dramatic negative effect the system could have on individual self-identities. The new deviancy theory of Howard Becker ([1963] 1973), Edwin Schur (1965), and Erving Goffman (1961) showed how criminal and deviant careers were shaped progressively over time through interaction with significant others in meaningful social contexts. Adolescents who were constantly brought before the courts and told they were delinquents for engaging in liquor law violations, minor vandalism, and petty shoplifting eventually became professional career criminals because the label "delinquent" restricted their abilities to mature out of the associated behaviors, and limited subsequent career options.

Founders of Social Psychological Interactionist and Labeling Theory

---

1934 George Herbert Mead *Mind, Self, and Society*

1938 Frank Tannenbaum *Crime and the Community*

1951 Edwin Lemert *Social Pathology*

1961 Erving Goffman *Asylums*

1963 Erving Goffman *Stigma: Notes on the Management of Spoiled Identity*

1965 Leslie Wilkins *Social Deviance: Social Policy, Action, and Research*

1963 Howard Becker *Outsiders: Studies in the Sociology of Deviance*

In the early 1970s, conflict, radical, and critical criminology—reflected in the works of William Chambliss (1975), Richard Quinney (1974), and Ian Taylor, Paul Walton, and Jock Young (1973 1975)—was building on the early Marxist ideas of Willem Bonger ([1905] 1916). These theorists suggested that it was not just the agents of government who caused additional unnecessary crime, but that the whole capitalist system was criminogenic for valuing competition over cooperation and polarizing the rich and the poor. This "new criminology" argued that powerful social classes, and even the capitalist state, were committing more and worse crimes through corporate pollution, faulty product manufacture, bribery, fraud, and corruption. At the same time, the state was punishing the less powerful for expressing their resistance to the system, resistance often manifest through property and violent crimes against society.

Founders of Sociological Conflict and Radical Theory

1868 Karl Marx *Das Kapital*
1908 Georg Simmel *The Sociology of Conflict* and *The Web of Group Affiliations*
1916 Willem Bonger *Criminality and Economic Conditions*
1958 George Vold *Theoretical Criminology* (2d ed., 1979)
1959 Ralf Dahrendorf *Class and Class Conflict in an Industrial Society*
1969 Austin Turk *Criminality and the Legal Order*
1973 Ian Taylor, P. Walton, and Jock Young *The New Criminology*
1974 Richard Quinney *Critique of Legal Order: Crime Control in Capitalist Society*
1975 Ian Taylor, P. Walton, and Jock Young *Critical Criminology*

By the 1980s and early 1990s, it had become clear to many, and not least Carl Klockars (1980), that not only was the merit in these ideas limited— especially in their romantic call for socialism as the solution to the crime problem—but that criminology was uncertain about any of its particular theories, or at least not certain enough to discount any one of them. The result was a criminological "fragmentation" (Ericson and Carriere 1994) that spawned new research, new theoretical developments, and new empirical studies that tested the whole range of theories and resurrected and revised some of those previously discarded. Even radical theories were no longer uniformly radical. They were now more self-critical. For example, feminist critics argued that an overemphasis on boys, men, and class obscured important differences in gender and gender socialization. This produced an excessive control over young women through their sexuality and an excessive liberation of males to violence, materialism, and domineering competitiveness, resulting in men being 90 percent more seriously criminal than women. Anarchists challenged the value of all forms of power hierarchy, whether in corporations, government, or socialism, believing instead that decentralized democratic collectives practicing nonviolent peacemaking approaches to conflict resolution were the only way to transcend our self-destructive cycle of crime and violence (Pepin-sky and Quinney 1991).

Indeed, by the mid- and late 1990s several of these new perspectives were emerging from the fragmentation and forming new followings. The postmodernist criminological perspective, described as "constitu-tive criminology," embraced phenomenological sociology and social constructionism and cutting-edge ideas from chaos theory and Lacanian psychoanalysis. This theory argued that a critical synthesis of knowl-edge was needed since crime and its control were part of a continuum with society and if this was lost sight of, acts of crime would be intensi-fied through an endless discourse of crime talk that dominates public policy and popular culture (Henry and Milovanovic 1996, 1999). Others were inspired to call for an integrated critical theory of crime that would lead to comprehensive policy rather than knee-jerk law enforce-ment actions (Barak 1998). Yet others began to formulate theories about social justice and its relationship with crime and criminal justice (Arrigo 1999).

Founders of Varieties of Critical Theory

1976 Carol Smart *Women, Crime, and Criminology: A Feminist Critique*
1976 Harold Pepinsky *Crime and Conflict: A Study of Law and Society*
1977 Michel Foucault *Discipline and Punish: The Birth of the Prison*
1980 Larry Tifft and Dennis Sullivan *The Struggle to Be Human: Crime and Anarchism*
1985 Ray Michalowski *Order, Law and Crime*
1996 Stuart Henry and Dragan Milovanovic *Constitutive Criminology*
1997 Dragan Milovanovic *Postmodern Criminology*
1998 Gregg Barak *Integrating Criminologies*

Our purpose in this introduction is not to account for each of the recent theoretical developments, since we do that in subsequent chapters. Rather, we simply wish to emphasize through our overview of criminology's vast body of theory that it is rooted in and influenced by different disciplines and is a truly multidisciplinary enterprise. This is not to suggest that crim-inology is limited to theories of criminals and what causes their criminal activity. So far, we have said little about the victims of crimes, a closely re-lated area. Some recent theories, such as radical realism, have made victi-mology central to their approach. Before we turn our focus to the nature of crime (Chapter 2), let us complete our survey by looking at what might be called the underbelly of criminology: victimology.

Victimology

The scientific study of victimology is a relatively recent field, founded by Hans von Hentig (1948) and Benjamin Mendelsohn (1963), who claims to have coined the term in 1947. It is almost the mirror image or "reverse of criminology" (Schafer 1977, 35). Criminology is concerned mainly with criminals, criminal acts, and the response of the criminal justice system. Victimology is the study of who becomes a victim, how victims are victimized, how much harm they suffer, and what their role is in the criminal act. It also looks at victims rights and their role in the criminal justice system (Dorener and Lab 1998).

Victimology has been defined as "the scientific study of the physical, emotional, and financial harm people suffer because of criminal activities" (Karmen 2001, 9). This interrelationship has a long history. Prior to the development of formal social control mechanisms, society relied on individualized informal justice. Individuals, families, and clans sought justice for harms caused by others. Endless feuding and persistent physical confrontation led to what has been called the "golden age" (Karmen 2001), when restitution became the focus of crime control (see Chapter 3). With the advent of the social contract, individuals gave up the right to retaliation and crimes became crimes against the state—not the individual. The classicist social contract, simply put, says that individuals must give up some personal liberties in exchange for a greater social good. Thus individuals forfeited the right to individualized justice, revenge, and vigilantism. This creed is still practiced today. For that reason, O.J. Simpson's criminal trial was the state of California versus O.J. Simpson, not Goldman and Brown-Simpson versus O.J. Simpson, which was the realm of the civil trial. Advanced societies relying on systems of justice based on the social contract increasingly, though inadvertently, neglected the victims of crime. In the United States, "Public prosecutors . . . took over powers and responsibilities formerly assumed by victims. . . . Attorneys decided whether or not to press charges, what indictments to file, and what sanctions to ask judges to invoke. . . . When the overwhelming majority of cases came to be resolved through confessions of guilt elicited in negotiated settlements, most victims lost their last opportunity to actively participate" (Karmen 1990, 17).

Since the founding of victimology, there has been controversy between the broad view (Mendelsohn 1963) that victimology should be the study of all victims and the narrow view that it should only include crime victims. Clearly, if a broad definition is taken of crime as a violation of human rights (Schwendinger and Schwendinger 1970; Cohen 1993; Tifft and Sullivan 2001), this is more consistent with the broad view of victimology.

Only since the early 1970s has victimization been included in mainstream criminology. This followed Schafer's (1968, 1977) study and the flurry of victimization studies culminating in the U.S. Department of Justice annual national crime victimization survey, begun in 1972. Already, there are numerous texts on the field (see Doerner and Lab 1998; Elias 1986; Walklate 1989; Karmen 2001). We discuss some of the main findings of this research in Chapter 2.

Victimology has also been criticized for the missionary zeal of its reform policy (Fattah 1992; Weed 1995) as well as its focus on victims of individual crimes rather than socially harmful crimes, although there are rare exceptions to this in French victimology (Joutsen 1994). The more recent comprehensive approach considers the victim in the total societal context of crime in the life domains of family, work, and leisure as these are shaped by the media, lawmakers, and interest groups (Sacco and Kennedy 1996).

Summary

In this chapter, we saw that criminology has a much broader scope than simply studying criminals. There are few definitive "truths" in the study of crime. Controversy and diverse views abound. This is not without good reason. Criminology is perhaps the most widely examined (by the public, media, and policymakers) of the social sciences. As a result of nightly news, talk shows, and newsmagazine programs, crime and its control are topics in which everyone's interest is engaged and everyone has an opinion. Criminology is also policy oriented. The closely related criminal justice system is a significant source of employment and expenditures. In 1984, the state of California, for example, spent 14 percent of its budget on higher education and 4 percent on prisons (only one component of the criminal justice system). Ten years later, the prison system and education each consumed 9 percent of the total state budget (Skolnick 1995). The long-term implications of decreased emphasis on education and increased focus on punishment and incarceration are disturbing and the subject of much debate. Similar debate was lacking following the terrorist attacks against the United States. Government powers were increased dramatically following the events of September 11, 2001, with little or no debate.

Regardless of one's theoretical inclinations, preferred research tools, or policy preferences, dissension demands a clear articulation of one's position. Such articulation requires considerable thought in order to make convincing arguments and the insight to appreciate other positions. The end result is that criminology as a whole is strengthened.

We began this chapter by defining criminology and placing it in a historical context. We saw how criminology moved from philosophical speculation to scientific rigor and became theory driven and multidisciplinary. We introduced the basic ideas of criminology's different theories, from internal biological and psychological causes to the external influences of family, peer group, community, culture, and society. Criminology has evolved and will continue to expand and provide improved methods of study and more explanatory theories for understanding crime. The current direction seems to be toward a more inclusive criminology that considers crime as deprivation and harm—regardless of legislated law.

In the next chapter, we turn to the first building block of the criminological enterprise and examine how crime is defined. We look at how what counts as crime varies depending on who defines it, where it is defined, and when. We see how the definition is shaped by our personal experiences (whether we are victimized or victimizer); our social standing (whether we stand to benefit or lose from crime); and many other factors, such as the media, family, and friends. We introduce a way of taking account of most of the essential components of crime through a graphic illustration that we call the prism of crime.

2

What Is Crime?

Defining and Measuring the Crime Problem

In the prelude to the 2003 Gulf War gas prices soared to three dollars a gallon, although oil supplies were not disrupted. Was this a crime? Were the oil companies simply responding to anticipated shortages and increased demand? "That's criminal!" people often say when they feel they have been unjustly harmed. Others say, "That wasn't crime; it was just a response to difficult circumstances." Most people have a sense of what is criminal, but deciding precisely what is—or is not—criminal is not as obvious as it may seem. What for one person is deviance may for another be a crime. What is criminal to one person may be sharp business practice to another, such as when a corporate executive sells stock based on insider information. What is morally reprehensible to one group may be a lifestyle preference to another. For example, prostitution is condemned by the moral right yet celebrated by organizations for prostitutes such as COYOTE (Cast Off Your Old Tired Ethics). Like deviance, crime is a concept with elusive, varied, and diverse meanings.

As we argue elsewhere (Henry and Lanier 2001), if the definition of crime is too narrow, harms that might otherwise be included are ignored. This was the case for years with domestic violence, racial hate, and much of what now counts as corporate and white-collar crime. Conversely, if the definition is too broad, then almost every deviation becomes a crime. This was the case with the old concept of sin, where anything that deviated from the norm could be prosecuted by the church as an offense against God. But even where harm looks obvious, is such an act a crime? For example, in the aftermath of the 9/11 attacks the annual crime figures reported to the FBI for New York City *excluded* the 3,000 victims who died. These were victims of a terrorist attack, so why was this not seen as a crime by the FBI, and should it have been?

Is the obvious solution to the question of what is a crime to find out what the law says is criminal? Again, this is more complicated than it seems and "going to the law" as a solution leaves open many unanswered questions. In fact, since we first wrote this chapter there have been significant changes in the way both criminologists and the "law" look at what counts as "crime."

In the United States we asked scholars who had been debating different views about the issue to consider what they thought were the essential elements that makes a behavior or action "criminal," how crime should be defined, and how it was defined in law enforcement practice. This resulted in a published edited volume entitled *What Is Crime?* (Henry and Lanier 2001). In 2002, the highly respected Law Commission of Canada, a body that serves the Canadian Parliament, launched a project with a similar title, "What Is a Crime?" The commission hosted a series of meetings and conferences in Ottawa and Vancouver to reconsider the various issues of defining crime (Canadian Law Commission 2003), as well as sponsoring a nationwide student essay competition on the topic. Clearly the definition of crime is becoming a hotly debated topic at all levels of society.

Crime is contextual. Criminal harm takes different forms depending on the historical period, specific context, social setting, or situation in which it occurs. The written law might seem to provide an answer, but laws are open to interpretation. In this chapter, we look at the various definitions of crime, ranging from the legal definitions to those that take account of crime's changing meaning as social harm.

The definitions of crime arrived at by law, government agencies, and criminologists are used by others to measure the extent of what they have defined. Put simply, if this is the problem then how big is it? How much of it exists? Is there more of it in one part of the country than another, in the city rather than the country? Do different societies have different rates of this thing we have defined as crime? It is necessary to measure and define crime because several policy decisions concerning social control are based on a particular definition of crime: the selection of priorities in policing and what to police, budget allocations for measures such as crime prevention programs, how to "handle" offenders, and what a "crime-free" neighborhood actually looks like. For example, is a crime-free neighborhood one in which there are low rates of crimes known to the police, or one with a low incidence of serious harm? What is the real level of crime when the incidence of serious crime, such as homicide, burglary, rape, and aggravated assault, is low but the level of crimes that disturb the public, such as prostitution, vandalism, public drunkenness, and panhandling, is high? Should the public or community define crime or should this be a matter for legislators or the police?

Not only have criminologists and others been arguing about definitions for much of the past century but, as one commentator observed at century's end, "an appropriate definition of crime, . . . remains one of the most critical unresolved issues in criminal justice today" (Bohm and Haley 1999, 24).

We conclude this chapter with a description of the main measures of crime used by government agencies and criminologists. We also describe the major patterns of crime and discuss their historical trends. However, we do not provide current crime statistics, as this is more accurately and expediently accessed through the Internet. We suggest getting the most recent official crime data from the *Sourcebook of Criminal Justice Statistics*, on http://www.albany.edu/sourcebook.

Legal Definition

Since the eighteenth century, the legal definition of crime has referred to acts prohibited, prosecuted, and punished by criminal law (Henry and Lanier 2001, 6). Most commentators agree with Michael and Adler (1933, 5) that "criminal law gives behavior its quality of criminality." In other words, criminal law specifies the acts or omissions that constitute crime. Tappan's (1947, 100) classic definition is illustrative. He defined crime as "an intentional act or omission in violation of criminal law (statutory and case law), committed without defense or justification, and sanctioned by the state as a felony or misdemeanor." Tappan believed that the study of criminals should be restricted to those convicted by the courts. In fact, "most criminologists have traditionally relied on the legal conception, which defines crime as behavior in violation of criminal law and liable for sanctioning by the criminal justice system" (Kramer 1982, 34). And "most criminologists today act as if the debate is settled in favor of a 'legal' definition" (Bohm 1993, 3).

Other criminologists, however, argue that the legal definition is too limited in scope. First, it takes no account of harms which are covered by administrative law and are considered regulative violations. Edwin Sutherland (1949a) argued that as a result a strict legal definition excluded "white-collar crime." Suffering salmonella poisoning as a result of eating in a restaurant that systematically violates FDA regulations governing hygienic food preparation is no less criminal, according to Sutherland, than being robbed in the street. Both injure human life in the interest of profit. Sutherland argued for extending the existing legal definition of crime to take account of all offenses that are socially injurious or socially harmful and that repeat white-collar offenders deserve the label "habitual white-collar criminals." A second problem with a strict legal definition of crime is that it ignores the cultural and historical context of law. What is defined as crime by the legal code varies from location to location and changes over time. For example, prostitution is generally illegal in the United States but is legal in some places such as Nevada. Gambling is often illegal yet many states run lotteries to increase their revenue. Tappan (1947) acknowledged the cultural and historical variability of crime in society's norms but said this is why precision makes the law the only certain guide. Others have claimed that the law offers only a false certainty, for what the law defines as crime "is somewhat arbitrary, and represents a highly selective process" (Barak 1998, 21). Indeed, Barak notes with regard to crime, "There are no purely objective definitions; all definitions are value laden and biased to some degree" (1998, 21).

Consider, for example, the criminalization of substance abuse. During Prohibition, the production and distribution of alcoholic beverages in the United States was illegal. Today, the same acts are generally legal, although some counties still prohibit the sale of alcohol and some states regulate its sale more than others. In colonial Virginia, smoking tobacco was encouraged for medicinal purposes. In much of the twentieth century, smoking was celebrated as an aid to relaxation and social enjoyment. It is now illegal to smoke in many public places. In the 1920s, cocaine was promoted as a pick-me-up and was even included in the original formula for Coca-Cola. Today, such activity would result in a long prison sentence for drug dealing. Clearly, what counts as a crime at one time or in one culture may not be considered criminal at another time or in another culture. Nettler (1984, 1) summed up the relativity problems with a strict legal definition: "Because there are so many possible wrongs and because 'crime' denotes only a select sample of all disapproved acts, the definition of crime varies from time to time and from place to place and there is continuing controversy about what should or should not be called 'crime.'" In addition, relying on a legal definition of crime presents other problems related to who defines the kinds of behavior labeled crime.

Crimes are not produced by legislation alone. Judicial interpretation also determines what is or is not crime. Judicial decisions can also be appealed, overturned, and revised. Consider, for example, *Roe v. Wade*, the 1973 Supreme Court case that legalized abortion during the first three months of pregnancy (Fiero 1996, 684), and the more recent limitations that recriminalize certain aspects of abortion. Even where legislators make law, a significant problem is whose views they represent. Some critical criminologists argue that criminal actions by corporations often go unrecognized because those who hold economic power in society are, in effect, those who make the law. Legislators are influenced through lobbyists and donations from political action committees (PACs) set up by owners of corporations and financial institutions (Simon and Eitzen

1982). Their influence minimizes the criminalization of corporate behavior. This was at the heart of Sutherland's (1949a) original concern (discussed previously) to incorporate crimes defined by administrative regulations into the criminological realm. In short, relying on a strict legal definition for crime may be an appropriate study for police cadets but is sorely inadequate for students of criminology or the thinking criminal justice professional. The contextual aspects of crime and crime control require serious reflective study. A more comprehensive approach to the range of definitions is to divide them into one of two types depending on whether they reflect consensus or conflict in society.

Consensus and Conflict Approaches

Consensus refers to definitions that reflect the ideas of the society as a whole. It assumes that all agree on what should be considered crimes, such as homicide and rape. Consensus definitions constitute a set of universal values. Conflict refers to definitions of crime based on the belief that society is composed of different interest groups. These various groups compete with one another. This competition is often between the powerful and the powerless.

Consensus

Consensus theorists try to get around the problem of variations in the law by linking the definition of crime to social morality. They draw on the ideas of the nineteenth-century French sociologist Emile Durkheim ([1893] 1984), who believed that in the kind of integrated community that preceded industrialization, people were held together by common religious beliefs, traditions, and similar worldviews. These similarities acted as a "social glue" that bonded people in a shared morality. Thus the consensus position states that crimes are acts which shock the common conscience, or collective morality, producing intense moral outrage in people. Thus for Burgess (1950), "A lack of public outrage, stigma, and official punishment, attached to social action indicates that such action is not a violation of society's rules, independent of whether it is legally punishable" (quoted in Green 1990, 9). Current supporters of this position claim there is a "consensus," or agreement, between most people of all economic, social, and political positions about what behaviors are unacceptable and what should be labeled criminal. Echoing Durkheim, some recent commentators, such as Roshier (1989, 76), define crime "as only identifiable by the discouraging response it evokes."

Even this definition has problems, however. What at first appears as an obvious example of universally agreed-on crime—the malicious intentional taking of human life—may appear different when we take account of the social context. Closer inspection reveals that killing others is not universally condemned. Whether it is condemned depends on the social context and the definition of human life. For example, killing humans is regrettable yet acceptable in war. It is even honored. Humans identified as "the enemy" (as in the Persian Gulf War, or Desert Shield) are redefined as "collateral" and their death is described as "collateral damage." Governments that employ massive violent force to overthrow other governments that they define as "oppressive" consider themselves "liberators." As this was being written, American forces and a loose confederation of coalition forces liberated Iraq from Saddam Hussein. The deaths of civilians are not described as murder. Instead they are described as "regrettable" but "legitimate targets." Soldiers have followed "illegal" orders, taken lives, and avoided punishment and the stigma associated with crime. Also, pro-life advocates in the abortion debate define life as beginning with conception. They believe abortion of a fetus is murder. Pro-choice advocates, by contrast, do not believe life begins until birth, so abortion of a fetus is seen as an expression of women's right to choose; no more, no less.

Another major problem with the consensus view is the question of whose morality is important in defining the common morality. If harm affects a minority, will the majority be outraged? Is the conduct any less harmful if people are not outraged? Examples abound. Sexual harassment in the workplace, which was not previously defined as crime, was no less harmful to those forced to engage in sexual relations or subjected to sexual pressure under the threat of losing their job. Because men were the predominant employers and managers, women's needs were not addressed and their complaints were not heard. Sexual harassment and rape cases in the military provide a vivid illustration of this problem.

Clearly, understanding the social context is the first step toward defining crime. Consider sexual behavior as an example. Sexual intercourse with a minor, or statutory rape, is in the United States universally agreed to be a crime—until we consider the social context. On closer inspection, legally defined rape is not universally condemned. For example, sexually active boys and girls under the age of legal consent often do not consider themselves raped. In previous historical eras, adolescents of the same age were often married and shared the rights of adults. In this same historical era, husbands could not "rape" their spouses, though they could force themselves on unwilling wives. Under old German law an act of sexual intercourse with a woman would be considered "as rape only if it was committed against a respectable woman, but not a 'vagrant woman'" (Hinckeldey 1981, 107). Whether the physical act is condemned depends on the social and historical context and on the definition of rape.

For example, if parents give permission to marry, two sexually active teens are no longer committing "rape," though their physical actions (intercourse) and circumstances (age) are the same. Rape laws have historically had a gender bias as well. Young girls have traditionally been treated much more harshly "by the law" than are young boys (Edwards 1990). The social reaction to sexual activity and prowess continues to reflect gender bias.

Furthermore, whether an issue becomes publicly acknowledged as harm depends on a group's ability to turn private concerns into public issues (Mills 1959) and its skills at moral entrepreneurship (Becker [1963] 1973). This is the ability to whip up moral consensus around an issue that affects some individuals or a minority and to recruit support from the majority by convincing them it is in their interest to support the issue too. Creating a public harm often involves identifying and signifying offensive behavior and then attempting to influence legislators to ban it officially. Becker argued that behavior which is unacceptable in society depends on what people first label unacceptable and whether they can successfully apply the label to those designated "offenders." For example, prior to the 1930s smoking marijuana in the United States was generally acceptable. Intensive government agency efforts, particularly by the federal Bureau of Narcotics, culminated in the passage of the Marihuana Tax Act of 1937. This type of smoking was labeled unacceptable and illegal and those who engaged in it were stigmatized as "outsiders." In this tradition, Pavarini (1994) points out that what becomes defined as crime depends on the power to define and the power to resist definitions. This in turn depends on who has access to the media and how skilled moral entrepreneurs are at using such access to their advantage (Barak 1994; Pfuhl and Henry 1993). As the following discussion illustrates, for these and other reasons the consensus position is too simplistic.

Conflict Approaches

Conflict theory is based on the idea that people, instead of being similar, are different and struggle over their differences. According to this view, society is made up of groups that compete with one another over scarce resources. These resources could be broadly or narrowly defined. The conflict over different interests produces differing definitions of crime. These definitions are determined by the group in power and are used to further its needs and consolidate its power. Powerless groups are generally the victims of oppressive laws. For example, prison sentences for using crack cocaine, the form of the drug generally used by African Americans, are ten to fifteen years longer than sentences for using powder cocaine, favored mainly by the white middle and upper classes

(DeKeseredy and Schwartz 1996, 61; Tonry 1995). Orlando, Florida, recently passed a law banning sitting in downtown areas. Violation of the controversial ordinance results in a fine of $500 and sixty days in jail (Harris and Mathers 2002). An additional ordinance is being considered by the city council to limit group distribution of food to the homeless to four times a year. Presumably businesspeople will not be subjected to this law, while many homeless will.

In addition to wealth and power, groups in society form around culture, prestige, status, morality, ethics, religion, ethnicity, gender, race, ideology, human rights, the right to own guns, and so on. Each group may fight to dominate others. Approaches to defining crime that take account of these multiple dimensions are known as pluralist conflict theories. Ethnic or cultural conflict is a good example. From the perspective of culture conflict, different cultures, ethnic groups, or subcultures compete for dominance. According to Sellin's (1938) classic culture conflict theory, criminology should not merely focus on crime but include violations of "culture norms," that is, behaviors that are considered normal for a specific cultural group, such as Arab Americans or Asian Americans. Sellin describes two forms of conflict. The primary conflict occurs when a person raised in one culture is transposed into a different one. An immigrant may follow traditional cultural norms; for example, those of the Islamic faith see women who reveal bare skin as sexually promiscuous and available to be propositioned for sex. But acting on such assumptions may violate norms of the host country. Where these norms are expressed in law, criminal violation occurs.

Secondary conflict occurs between groups of people who live in specific geographic areas who create their own distinct value systems. Where these clash, conflict and norm violation occurs. An example of secondary culture conflict as crime is when the behavior of subgroups of society are targeted by laws. For example, some places specifically ban skateboarding and roller-blading—harmless recreational activities (sec. 18A.09, Orlando City Council 2002). In other places skateboarders are permitted and even encouraged. When power is determined by wealth, the conflict is considered class based. Analysis of this type of conflict is founded on principles outlined by the nineteenth-century social philosopher Karl Marx.

In Marxist conflict theory, the definition of crime focuses on conflicts that arise in capitalist society. Crime is rooted in the vast differences of wealth and power associated with class divisions. Groups that acquire power through political or economic manipulation and exploitation place legal constraints on those without power. A definition of crime based on economic interests emphasizes that "crime and deviance are the inevitable consequences of fundamental contradictions within society's economic infrastructure" (Farrell and Swigert 1988, 3). Crime is defined as the activities of those who threaten the powerful. Such a view explains why serious crimes are those of street offenders, whereas those of corporate or white-collar "suite" offenders are considered less serious, even though the financial losses from such white-collar crimes amount to at least ten times that from street crimes (Timmer and Eitzen 1989; Friedrichs 1996). Richard Quinney has expressed this position: "Crime is a definition of human conduct created by authorized agents in a politically organized society. . . .[It describes] behaviors that conflict with the interests of the segments of society that have the power to shape public policy" (1970, 15–16). In other words, the definition of crime is a political tool used to protect power, wealth, and position in a society. Not surprisingly, this power-and-wealth version of conflict theory has been termed critical criminology (Taylor, Walton, and Young 1975). This is because it criticizes the overall kind of society in which we live and suggests we replace it with a socialist system.

Critical criminologists also suggest that the harm of crime should become the main reason for law. Following Sutherland's ideas, they assert that the definition of crime should be expanded to include the socially injurious activities of powerful groups against the powerless as well as behavior that violates or intrudes into the human rights of others (Schwendinger and Schwendinger 1970).[1] Thus they argue that criminal harm can come not just from individuals but from the social contexts of conditions such as imperialism, racism, sexism, and poverty.

The idea of crime as a violation of human rights has become a major theme of critical humanist criminologists. As Quinney and Wildeman note, "The notion of crime as social injury, social harm, or a violation of human rights is, in effect, basic to those who strive to improve the human condition, for it provides the intellectual and practical tools for the reconstruction of society" (1991, 5; see also Cohen 1993). Other criminologists want to extend these rights to animals, arguing that harm to animals is a crime (Beirne 1994). This movement is gaining popularity among animal interest groups as well (e.g., PETA).

Marxist conflict theorists are farthest away from the view that law should define the content of crime. Instead, they argue that any behavior that causes harm is crime (Reiman [1979] 1995). Expanding Sutherland's (1949a) definition, Michalowski (1985) uses the term "analogous social injury," which includes harm caused by acts or conditions that are legal but produce similar consequences to those produced by illegal acts. For example, promoting and selling alcoholic beverages and cigarettes (described as "drug delivery systems"), although legal, still produce considerable social, health, and psychological problems. Other substances that are illegal, such as marijuana, may produce less negative consequences. The insidious injuries produced by the Johns-Manville asbestos company's knowing exposure of millions to deadly asbestos dust, in spite of the company's own research evidence showing that asbestos has carcinogenic effects (Calhoun and Hiller 1986), would be a good example of producing "analogous social injury."

Beyond Consensus and Conflict

Going beyond consensus, pluralist conflict, and critical Marxist theorists, other criminologists have begun to redefine crime more broadly. One such approach has pluralist leanings, but instead of seeing established groups as significant it sees the situational context and its constituent players as important. Crime is defined as a social event, involving many players, actors, and agencies. Thus crimes "involve not only the actions of individual offenders, but the actions of other persons as well. In particular, they involve the actions of such persons as victims, bystanders and witnesses, law enforcement officers, and members of political society at large. A crime, in other words, is a particular set of interactions among offender(s), crime target(s), agent(s) of social control and society" (Gould, Kleck, and Gertz 1992, 4; 2001). This broader view of crime highlights the complexities associated with defining crime by recognizing its socially constructed nature.

Another recent reassessment of the definition of crime that takes account of the total context of powerful relations and the situational context comes from postmodernist-influenced constitutive criminologists (Henry and Milovanovic 1996; Milovanovic and Henry 2001; Arrigo and Young 1996). Postmodernism is a perspective that rejects claims that any body of knowledge is true or can be true. Instead, its advocates believe that "claims to know" are simply power plays by some to dominate others. These theorists advocate an anarchy of knowledge giving the oppressed, marginalized, and excluded their own voice to define what harms them, rather than having others claim to know how to protect them. For example, consistent with the important place given to power, Henry and Milovanovic see constitutive criminology as "the framework for reconnecting crime and its control with the society from which it is conceptually and institutionally constructed by human agents. . . . Crime is both in and of society" (1991, 307). They define crime as an agency's ability to make a negative difference to others (1996, 104). Thus they assert, "Crimes are nothing less than moments in the expression of power such that those who are subjected to these expressions are denied their own contribution to the encounter and often to future encounters. Crime then is the power to deny others . . . in which those subject to the power of another, suffer the pain of being denied their own humanity, the power to make a difference" (1994, 119).

Perhaps the most dramatic call to expand the definition of crime comes from Larry Tifft and Dennis Sullivan (2001), who argue that the hierarchical structure and social arrangements of society produce harm that evades the legal definition and that these harms must be criminalized. They recognize that doing so will render many contemporary legal modes of production and distribution criminal, as will many responses of our criminal justice system to crime, based on the harms that they produce. They call for a "needs-based" system of justice based on the concept of equality of well-being as the objective.

It is clear that criminological approaches to crime have come a long way from the simplistic idea that crime is behavior defined by law. Recent ideas suggest that far more is involved than law. These ideas resurrect the central role of harm, the victim, and the context. Importantly, they even suggest that law itself can create crime, not merely by definition but by its use of power over others. Together, these definitions express the increasingly broad range of conceptions of crime that criminologists now share. Even though the division between consensus and conflict theory is helpful to gain an overall sense of different definitions, it does not present an integrated approach. But there is one attempt to define crime that, with modification, helps us overcome many of the difficulties so far identified. This approach has its beginnings in criminologist John Hagan's (1977, 1985) idea of crime as a continuous variable.

Hagan's Pyramid of Crime

From the previous discussion, it is clear that there is little agreement among criminologists about what constitutes crime. One very useful conception of crime, which takes account of several of the positions reviewed here, is provided by the Canadian criminologist John Hagan (1977, 1985) in his notion of crime and deviance as "a continuous variable." Explaining this concept, Hagan notes that rule breaking ranges from minor deviance from accepted standards of behavior, such as public drunkenness or dress code violations, to highly offensive acts that involve serious harm, such as urban terrorism or mass murder. He defines crime as "a kind of deviance, which in turn consists of variation from a social norm that is proscribed by criminal law" (1985, 49). His definition includes three measures of seriousness, each ranging from low/weak to high/strong. First is the degree of consensus or agreement, the degree to which people accept an act as being right or wrong. Most Americans believe that hijacking a plane and crashing it into buildings is very wrong. In contrast, few people consider a sixteen-year-old skipping school as seriously wrong (see Table 2.1). All crimes can be ranked on a scale of seriousness between these extremes. Hagan offers as the first measure of seriousness the degree of consensus or agreement about the wrongfulness of an act, which "can range from confusion and apathy, through levels of disagreement to conditions of general agreement" (1985, 49).

A second dimension of Hagan's approach is the severity of society's response in law. This may range from social avoidance or an official warning, through fines and imprisonment, to expulsion from society or ultimately the death penalty. Hagan argues, "The more severe the penalty prescribed, and the more extensive the support for this sanction, the more serious is the societal evaluation of the act" (1985, 49). Clearly, the sentencing to death of a convicted child murderer in Utah and the state's execution of the offender by firing squad would rank higher on the scale of social response than imprisonment of a small businessperson for tax evasion.

Hagan's third dimension is the relative seriousness of crime based on the harm it has caused. He argues that some acts, like drug use, gambling, and prostitution, are victimless crimes, which harm only the participants. Victimless crimes, or crimes without victims, are consensual crimes, involving lawbreaking that does not harm anyone other than perhaps the perpetrator (Schur 1965).[2] Many crimes, such as domestic violence, harm others, and some crimes harm more than one person at a time, as in the Beechnut Corporation's export of sugar water as 100 percent apple juice for babies or the export of infant formula that denied Third World babies necessary nutrients, exacerbating their malnutrition (Ermann and Clements 1984).

FIGURE 2.1   Hagan's Pyramid of Crime

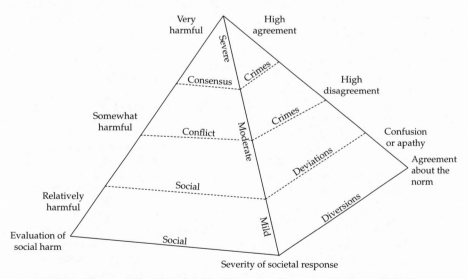

SOURCE: Hagan, *The Disreputable Pleasures*, Toronto: McGraw-Hill Ryerson (1977, p. 14). Used by permission.

TABLE 2.1 The Seriousness of Crimes

Conventional Crimes
Severity Score and Offense

72.1	Planting a bomb in a public building that explodes, killing twenty people.	15.5	Breaking into a bank at night and stealing $100,000.
52.8	A man forcibly rapes a women who dies from her injuries.	12.2	Paying a witness to give false testimony in a criminal trial.
43.2	Robbery at gunpoint during which the victim is shot to death.	12.0	Intentionally injuring a victim resulting in hospitalization.
39.2	A man stabs his wife who dies from the injuries.	10.5	Smuggling marijuana into the country for resale.
35.7	Stabbing a victim to death.	10.4	Intentionally hitting a victim with a lead pipe resulting in hospitalization.
33.8	Running a narcotics ring.		
27.9	A woman stabs her husband and he dies from the injuries.	10.3	Illegally selling barbiturates, such as sleeping pills, to others for resale.
26.3	An armed person hijacks a plane and demands to be flown to another country.	10.3	Operating a store that knowingly sells stolen property.
25.9	A man forcibly rapes a woman.	9.7	Breaking into a school and stealing equipment worth $1,000.
24.9	Intentionally setting fire to a building, causing $100,000 of damage.	9.7	Walking into a museum and stealing a painting worth $1,000.
22.9	A parent beats his young child with his fists and the child requires hospitalization.	9.6	Breaking into a home and stealing $1,000.
		9.4	Robbing a victim of $10 at gunpoint without physical harm resulting.
21.2	Kidnapping a victim.		
20.7	Selling heroin to others for resale.	9.3	Threatening to seriously injure a victim.
19.5	Smuggling heroin into the country.	8.5	Selling marijuana to others for resale.
19.5	Killing a victim by reckless driving.	7.9	A teenage boy beats his father with his fists resulting in hospitalization.
17.9	Robbing a victim of $10 at gunpoint, resulting in the victim being wounded.	7.5	Robbing a victim armed with a lead pipe without injury resulting.
16.9	A man drags a woman into an alley and tears her clothes but flees before causing further harm.	7.3	Threatening a victim with a weapon, receiving $10 with no harm to the victim.
16.4	Attempting to kill a victim with a gun, which misfires and the victim escapes.	7.3	Breaking into a department store and stealing $1,000 worth of merchandise.
15.9	A teenage boy beats his mother with his fists and she requires hospitalization.	7.2	Signing someone else's name on a check and cashing it.

(continues)

TABLE 2.1   *(continued)*

Conventional Crimes
Severity Score and Offense

6.9 Stealing property worth $1,000 from outside a building.	2.1 A woman engages in prostitution.
6.5 Using heroin.	1.9 Making an obscene phone call.
6.4 Getting customers for a prostitute.	1.8 A minor being drunk in public.
6.3 Failure to appear at court while on bail for a serious offense.	1.8 Being a knowing customer in a place holding illegal gambling.
5.4 Possessing heroin for personal use.	1.7 Stealing $10 worth of property from outside a building.
5.1 A man runs his hands over the body of a female victim, then runs away.	1.6 Being a customer in a brothel.
	1.6 A male over 16 has sexual relations with a willing female under age 16.
5.1 Using force to rob a victim of $10 but without causing injury.	1.6 Taking barbiturates without a prescription.
4.9 Snatching a handbag containing $10.	1.5 Intentional shoving or pushing without resulting injury.
4.8 A man exposes himself in public.	1.4 Smoking marijuana.
4.6 Carrying a gun illegally.	1.3 A consensual homosexual act.
4.4 Picking a victim's pocket of $100.	1.1 Disturbing a neighbor with noisy behavior.
4.2 Attempting to break into a home but leaving when disturbed by police.	1.1 Taking bets on numbers.
	1.1 Loitering after being told to move on by police.
3.8 Turning in a false fire alarm.	0.9 Teenager under 16 runs away from home.
3.6 Knowingly passing a bad check.	0.8 Being drunk in public.
3.6 Stealing property worth $100 from outside a building.	0.7 Teenager under 16 breaks curfew laws.
3.5 Running illegal gambling premises.	0.6 Trespassing in the backyard of a home.
2.5 Knowingly carrying an illegal knife.	0.3 Being a vagrant.
	0.2 Youth under 16 plays hooky from school.
2.2 Stealing $10 worth of merchandise from a department store.	

White-Collar Crimes
Severity Score and Offense

14.1 A doctor cheats on claims to a federal health insurance plan for patient service.	13.0 A factory knowingly gets rid of its waste in a way that pollutes a city water supply.
13.9 A legislator takes a bribe from a company to vote for a law favoring the company.	12.0 A police officer takes a bribe not to interfere with an illegal gambling operation.

(continues)

TABLE 2.1   *(continued)*

White-Collar Crimes
Severity Score and Offense

10.0	A government official intentionally hinders the investigation of a criminal offense.	6.5	An employer refuses to hire a qualified person because of the person's race.
9.6	A police officer knowingly makes a false arrest.	6.3	An employee embezzles $1,000 from the employer.
9.5	A public official takes $1,000 of public money for personal use.	5.4	A real estate agent refuses to sell a house to a person because of the person's race.
9.2	Several large companies illegally fix the retail prices of their products.	5.3	Loaning money at an illegally high interest rate.
8.6	Performing an illegal abortion.	4.5	Cheating on federal income tax.
8.2	Knowing that a shipment of cooking oil is bad, a store owner decides to sell it anyway, resulting in one person being sick and treated by a doctor.	3.7	A labor union official illegally threatens to organize a strike if an employer hires nonunion workers.
7.7	Knowing that a shipment of cooking oil is bad, a store owner decides to sell it anyway.	3.2	An employer illegally threatens to fire employees if they join a labor union.
7.4	Illegally getting monthly welfare checks.	1.9	A store owner intentionally puts "large" eggs in containers marked "extra large."

SOURCE: Adapted from Bureau of Justice Statistics, 1983.

Hagan illustrates the integration of these three dimensions on his "pyramid of crime" (see Figure 2.1). On the consensus dimension is the degree of agreement among people about the wrongfulness of an act. On the societal response dimension is the severity of penalties elicited in response to the act. Finally, on the third dimension is social evaluation of the harm an act inflicts on others. This can range from crimes of violence such as murder or terrorism at the peak down to victimless crimes at the base. Hagan claims,

> The three measures of seriousness are closely associated . . . the more serious acts of deviance, which are most likely to be called "criminal," are likely to involve (1) broad agreement about the wrongfulness of such acts, (2) a severe social response, and (3) an evaluation of being very harmful. However, the correlation between these three dimensions certainly is not perfect, and . . . in

regard to many acts that are defined as crimes, there is disagreement as to their wrongfulness, an equivocal social response, and uncertainty in perceptions of their harmfulness. (Hagan 1985, 50)

Although Hagan goes farther than most criminologists in attempting an integrated definition of crime, we believe that his analysis can be improved by adding three further dimensions and by configuring the pyramid display into a "crime prism." Let us see why.

From Hagan's Pyramid to the Prism of Crime

We suggest that Hagan's pyramid is incomplete because it neglects public awareness of crime—the realization that one has been a victim. Crime takes many forms, all of which involve harm, but not all of those harmed necessarily realize they have been victimized. We have already seen that participants in victimless crimes may claim that the criminal label is wrong. In the case of victims of government and corporate crimes, it is often a long time before the victims become aware that they have been harmed, and many never realize it! For example, the effects of environmental crimes may be so slow and diffused that no one notices any harm or change in the environment. Yet, over a period of years a particular area may become uninhabitable due to environmental crimes, as happened in the case of New York's famous Love Canal near Niagara Falls, in which the Hooker Chemical Corporation dumped fifty-five-gallon drums of toxic waste. When the area was subsequently developed by an unwitting school board and settled as a residential area, children and residents were, over several decades, exposed to noxious fumes and surfacing chemicals resulting in birth defects, liver disease, and emotional disorders (Mokhiber 1988). Such crimes can result in insidious injuries when the links between the causes and the effects are obscure, take a long time to appear, affect only a segment of the population, result in increased risk of injury or disease, and are widely dispersed through the population (Calhoun and Hiller 1986). Thus we argue that crime can range from being "obvious" or "readily apparent" to "relatively hidden" and, finally, so "obscure" that it is accepted by many as normal, even though it harms its victims (e.g., environmental crimes, racism, and patriarchy). Hagan acknowledges this but does not include the measure of obscurity as one of his dimensions.

A second missing, although implied, part of the pyramid of crime is the number of victims. If only one person is affected by a crime, this is certainly tragic and serious, as in the example of a person shot to death on the subway on the way home from work or by an intimate. But this crime is qualitatively different from, say, the Japanese terrorist religious cult that murdered many people in rush hour by intentionally setting off poisonous fumes in the subway system. These two additional dimensions, visibility and numbers harmed, are implied in surveys that depict the perceived seriousness of various acts (see Table 2.1). Note the difference in seriousness rating for different types of terrorism in the table. Absolute numbers of victims influence a society's perception of the seriousness of crime.

A third limitation of Hagan's pyramid relates to his dimension of seriousness of response. This dimension fails to capture the probability or likelihood that a convicted offender will receive a serious response even when the law sets such a penalty. Crimes of the powerless are far more likely to receive the full weight of the law than are crimes of the powerful. For example, the average prison term given for those convicted in the savings and loan scandal was 2.4 years and the average bank robber gets 7.8 years. Further, over 75 percent of the cases against these corporate executives, were dropped. Rarely are charges against bank robbers dropped (Calavita and Pontell 1993).

Another limitation of Hagan's analysis is in its visual structure. The way that it is laid out does not allow other elements (such as those we have noted) to be included. The pyramid suggests that crimes for which conflict exists about their criminality are only somewhat harmful. Some crimes may be extremely harmful, yet still not be seen as harms by society, not least because the media present them in a way that favors the perpetrators. Until recently, this was the case with crimes of gender, such as sexual harassment and date rape, in which the male offender was shown as having poor judgment but not intending harm.

It is clear to us that there is not always consensus about the seriousness of such actions as corporate crimes (such as pollution from toxic waste, deaths from avoidable faulty product manufacture, and deliberate violations of health and safety regulations). An obvious example is the padlocking of fire doors that resulted in the death of twenty-five employees in a North Carolina chicken plant fire in 1991.

We should be perfectly clear that corporate crimes can be extremely harmful. This is in spite of the moderate societal response to such acts and conflict between interest groups in society over the need for health and safety regulations and the like and whether their violation constitutes a crime. For example, corporations historically oppose health and safety regulations if they slow down production or add to cost. Corporations often consider such consumer or environmental protections as government interference in industry. Consumer protection groups such as Ralph Nader's Common Cause earn a living from disputing this point.

The Prism of Crime

To solve the problems with Hagan's pyramid, we have redesigned the visual structure of this depiction of crime by making it a double pyramid, or what we call the "crime prism" (see Figure 2.2). A further refinement of this concept appears in Henry and Lanier (1998). In our schema, we place an inverted pyramid beneath the first pyramid. The top pyramid represents the highly visible crimes that are typically crimes of the powerless committed in public. These include crimes such as robbery, theft, auto theft, burglary, assault, murder, stranger rape, and arson. These crimes are similar to many of what for years were called index crimes by the FBI, because their measure was seen as an index of the changing incidence of crime (see later in this chapter for an explanation of index crimes and the FBI's changing classification). The bottom, inverted pyramid represents relatively invisible crimes. These include a variety of crimes of the powerful, such as offenses by government officials, corporations, and organizations, as well as crimes by people committed through their occupations, for example, fraud and embezzlement, and even some crimes such as date rape, sexual harassment, domestic violence, sexism, racism, ageism, and crimes of hate. These are crimes typically conducted in private contexts, such as organizations and workplaces, that involve violations of trusted relationships. Together, crimes of the powerless and crimes of the powerful constitute the visible and invisible halves of our prism of crime. We use the term prism not only because of the visual appearance of the figure, but also because, just as a prism is used to analyze a continuous spectrum, so the crime prism can be used to analyze the spectrum of important dimensions that make up crime. Let us look carefully at these revised dimensions of the crime prism before explaining how they come together. The letters on the right side are used to provide illustrative examples. We begin with the dimension of agreement.

Social Agreement. The range of social agreement varies from the top of the crime prism, *a*, representing most agreement; through moderate agreement, *c*; down to the widest section of the pyramid, where there is apathy or disinterest, *e*. Social agreement then ranges through the lower half of the prism to crimes for which there is moderate disagreement, *i*, to those in which there is high disagreement or extreme conflict, *l*, at the opposite extreme. Beginning in the visible area (top half) of the prism, a planned murder might be placed at position *b*, whereas the crime of robbery at gunpoint would rank on the agreement scale at *c*. Acts of social deviance, such as wearing punk hairstyles or rings piercing various parts of the skin or engaging in a homosexual act, would rank at position *e*,

FIGURE 2.2   The Crime Prism

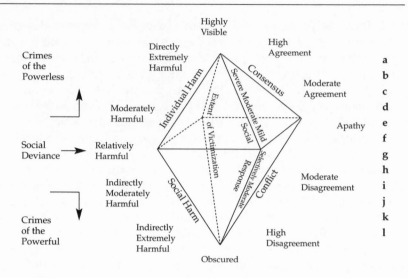

since these are acts about which many people are generally apathetic. Moving down to the invisible area, a doctor cheating on claims made to a federal health insurance plan for her patient would be placed at position *i*, whereas a factory discharging polluted waste in a way that results in pollution of the city water supply would rank around *k*. This is because people disagree about the need for government regulation, the intended or accidental nature of the action, and so on. Considerable conflict exists over these "invisible crimes" located in the lower half of the pyramid, such as whether workplace deaths and injuries resulting from accidents or criminal negligence of safety standards are crimes.

Probable Social Response.   The upper segment of this dimension runs from a high probability of severe sanctions for convicted offenders (e.g., death penalty or life in prison), *a*, through moderate sanctions (e.g., short prison terms, fines, probation), *b* and *c*, to a high probability of mild sanctions (community service, public condemnation), *d*. In our revision of Hagan's pyramid, this dimension now also extends from mild through selectively severe sanctions (e.g., fines, probation, restitution), *f*, and continues to symbolically severe sanctions at the lowest point, *j* through *l*. Symbolically severe refers to the low probability that severe sentences will be widespread and the recognition that these will often be reduced on appeal. For example, the ten-year imprisonment of Charles Keating for crimes in the 1980s savings and loans scandal provides one example of a symbolically severe sanction, since numerous similar offenders received much lower sentences, reduced sentences, and, in many cases, restitution orders for million-dollar offenses. Ivan Boesky agreed to pay a $100 million penalty (from his fortune of $200 million amassed from "insider trading") and served a three-year prison sentence. Michael Milken, found guilty of felony securities fraud and conspiracy, was sentenced to ten years but only served twenty-two months and agreed to pay a fine of $600 million from his billion-dollar fortune (Friedrichs 1996, 171–172). As DeKeseredy and Schwartz forcibly argue: "Poor people who accidentally kill bank tellers while attempting to rob them are labelled as murderers and are subject to harsh punishment. . . . Corporate executives who create unsafe working conditions are often exempt from both formal censure and prosecution, despite the fact that their decisions result in injuries and even death for thousands of people each year" (1996, 47).

Individual and Social Harm. For the upper section of the crime prism, the dimension of individual and social harm is also the same as in Hagan's analysis, except that in our crime prism it refers to direct individual harm, in which the offender has specifically targeted the victim. The most harmful crimes here include those whereby the victims are denied their life or become permanently injured and maimed, *a, b;* through crimes that are harmful through some temporary loss of capability, money, property, or position, *c;* to those that might offend moral sensibilities but do not directly result in personal loss, *e, f.*

The dimension of individual and social harm also reaches into the lower half of the prism to include, first, offenses creating moderate social harm (such as price-fixing that increases the costs of products to consumers), *h,* and then those social harms in which people have been physically injured and killed in the course of the general need to meet an organizational goal, as in the Union Carbide chemical factory disaster in Bhopal, India; two NASA space shuttle disasters; the Ford Pinto gas tank explosions, and Firestone tires causing SUVs to flip over, all of which might be located at *k* or *l.*

Extent of Victimization. The final dimension, extent of victimization, implied but not explicitly included in Hagan's measure of harm, represents the number of victims affected by a crime. Put simply, this spans a range from crimes in which numerous random victims result from highly visible individual crimes, *a,* through crimes in which several are affected by random crime, *b* and *c,* to crimes in which a few are affected, *d.* As this dimension extends into the lower prism of invisible crime, through *f* to *l,* more are affected, but now by being members of a particular "targeted" social category. For example, employees working with hazardous materials or in high-risk occupations, such as mining, construction, or chemicals; consumers buying a particular kind of faulty product; or residents living in an area where pollutants have contaminated the drinking water.

Integrating the Dimensions

Now that we have briefly illustrated the dimensions of the crime prism, let us discuss the spatial location of a few examples. Take the earlier example of terrorism. Here, crime is obvious, highly visible, extremely harmful, and noncontroversial with regard to the measure of consensus-conflict, as can be seen in Table 2.1. Smith and Orvis (1993) indicate that this kind of crime can be horrifying to the sensibilities of virtually all people, although directly harming relatively few (e.g., the Oklahoma City bombing). Societal response and outrage to this type of crime are immediate and pointed. Law enforcement agencies devote all available resources and form special task forces to deal with these crimes. Punishment is severe and can include the death penalty. As a result, such crimes would be placed on the top or very near the apex of the prism at point *a*. The more people harmed the greater the government and social response (e.g., September 11 tragedies). If fewer are harmed, and if the act is less visible, the ranking of the crime on the extent of victimization scale moves down.

Further down the prism, but still at its upper end, are violent acts of individual crime. These are also readily apparent as being criminal. They were traditionally called *mala in se*, meaning "acts bad in and of themselves," or inherently evil; they are universally recognized as crimes. Crimes of this type would include homicides, rapes, incest, and so on. Relatively few people are hurt by each act, yet societal reaction is severe and involves little controversy. Law enforcement considers these crimes its top priority. Sanctions are very severe, ranging from lengthy penal confinement to death. Beneath these come acts of robbery, burglary, larceny, and vandalism, perhaps at location *b* or *c*.

At the lowest levels of the upper segment is where Hagan (1985, 59) placed social deviations and social diversions. Deviance, the higher placed of the two, includes acts such as public drunkenness and juvenile status offenses (acts that if committed by an adult would be legal). It should be noted, however, that these are small-scale or low-value violations. Beneath the social deviations are what Hagan terms social diversions of unconventional lifestyles or sexual practices and so on. These offenses are relatively harmless and are met with confusion or apathy, a lack of consensus about their criminal status, and little formal law enforcement response. Examples would be certain "Goth" practices and skateboarding in public places. These will be located at *f* on the prism.

From this point on the inverted pyramid of our modified visual, it can be seen that the perception of criminality is relatively hidden. Offenses here are mildly responded to by law enforcement and often are merely subject to a variety of informal social sanctions or systems of internal social control.

As we move into the lower section of the prism and toward its lower point, the obscurity of the crime increases. Its harm becomes less direct. Conflict over its criminal definition increases and the seriousness of society's response becomes more selective. Acts that have been called *mala prohibita* are positioned here. *Mala prohibita* crimes have been created by legislative action (i.e., they are bad because they have been created or legislated as being bad). *Mala prohibita* definitions of crime necessarily involve a social, ecological, and temporal context. As we have seen, these acts may be criminal in one society but not criminal in another. Likewise, an act that is criminal in one county or state may be legal in another (e.g., prostitution). Such crimes also change over time. Crimes that do not reflect a consensus in society move toward the lower inverted part of the prism. In 1995 Calvin Klein was investigated by the U.S. Department of Justice for using underage models in an advertising campaign. The ads in question did not involve nudity but were apparently suggestive of child pornography. Many more people are harmed by similar acts, yet societal responses are moderate. The police exercise considerable discretion when dealing with these types of offenses. Often, fines and "second chances" are given to violators of these laws.

At a lower level, crime is unapparent (hidden) and indirect, yet hurts many people over an extended time period. For example, in 1987–1988, 11,319 savings and loan cases were referred to the Justice Department for possible criminal prosecution. It has been estimated that criminal activity was involved in 70–80 percent of the thrift institution failures (Calavita and Pontell 1993). Yet the impact of this type of crime is diffused and societal reactions diluted. Law enforcement is rarely equipped to handle it. As we mentioned earlier, over three-quarters of the cases were dropped. Prison sentences are rarely given; the more common sanctions are fines, restitution settlements, censure, and signs of disapproval. Regulatory agencies are responsible for law enforcement. Unless the offense is made public, corporations and their trade associations often handle these problems through their own disciplinary mechanisms. These offenses are located at point *i* on the prism.

At the final level, crimes are so hidden that many may deny their existence and others may argue as to whether or not they are crimes. Sexism, for example, is an institutionalized type of crime. It is patriarchal, subdued, and so ingrained into the fabric of a society as to often go unnoticed, yet the impact is very influential. Gary Condit lost his Republican

Senate seat due to the scandal with intern Chandra Levy; Bob Pack-wood was forced to resign his U.S. Senate seat as a result of sexual improprieties. Yet no criminal charges were filed. The law enforcement community generally scoffs at consideration of these crimes as criminal. These crimes are rarely, if ever, punished. Sanctions generally involve social disapproval (some groups will even voice approval) and verbal admonishment, although occasionally symbolically severe sentences are given.

Clearly the range of different crimes can be located on the crime prism. To better illustrate the prism, in the next section we consider how the concept applies to school violence.

Application of the Integrated Prism to School Violence

In the analysis of school violence, there is a tendency for commentators to narrowly define the scope of the problem. Typically they focus on interpersonal violence: among students toward each other, or by students toward their teachers. In terms of our prism, they focus on the visible harms between school students that would be located in the top half of the prism, but fail to see the broader dimension of the crimes that extend into the lower levels of the prism. We argue that the complexity of crimes like school violence defies such a simplistic framing. It fails to address the wider context of school violence, the wider forms of violence in schools, and the important interactive and causal effects arising from the confluence of these forces. What is demanded by this analysis is an integrated, multilevel definition of the problem that will lead to a multilevel causal analysis and a comprehensive policy response that takes account of the full range of constitutive elements. In our view the prism provides us with a conceptual framework to define the full dimensional scope of the problem.

The Scope of the Problem: The Paucity of the School Violence Concept?

Public analysis of social problems tends to be framed very narrowly. Violence is visible and manifest among school students, so it is assumed that they constitute the scope of the problem. Yet any analysis of school violence that simply looks at one factor, such as human fallibility, gun availability, or cultural toxicity, is in grave danger of missing the wider constitutive elements.

Violence is generally defined as the use of force toward another that results in harm. Simplistic versions limit the concept to "extreme physical force" (Champion 1997, 128; Rush 1994, 54), which may include intimidation by the threat of force (Bureau of Justice 1998). Omitted here are several critical elements of harm: (1) emotional and psychological pain that result from domination of some over others, (2) harms by institutions or agencies on individuals, (3) the violence of social processes that produces a systemic social injury, such as that perpetuated through institutionalized racism and sexism, and (4) the "symbolic violence" of domination (Bourdieu 1977) that brings coercion through the power exercised in hierarchical relationships.

In the school context, studies of violence typically refer to student-on-student and student-on-teacher acts of physical harm or interpersonal violence: "Violence refers to the threat or use of physical force with the intention of causing physical injury, damage, or intimidation of another person" (Elliott, Hamburg, and Williams 1998, 13–14).[1] This definition clearly refers to acts located in the upper half of our prism. However, considering the lower half of the prism is suggestive since it draws our attention to other hidden dimensions of the problem that we have described as the hidden crimes of the structurally powerful in society (Henry and Lanier 1998). It also sensitizes us to the symbolic social harms that deny humanity through violating human rights (see chapters by Milovanovic and Henry, Schwendinger and Schwendinger, and Tifft and Sullivan in Henry and Lanier 2001). In the school context these harms, located in the lower half of the prism, include harms committed by teachers on students, and by school administrators on both students and teachers. They also include the organization of schooling where this creates harm to both student creativity and the educational process. Conventional definitions of school violence, located in the upper half of the prism, neglect harmful institutionalized social and educational practices. These include acts and processes of institutionalized racism/sexism, discrimination, labeling and tracking (Yogan 2000), authoritarian discipline (Adams 2000), militaristic approaches to school security (Thompkins 2000; Pepinsky 2000), sexual harassment, and predation, all of which would be located in the lower half of the prism.

For example, gender discrimination has been shown to create harmful effects on female students' learning experience. When teachers favor male students over females, because of their seemingly extroverted classroom participation, they disadvantage females and oppress their potential development, which can lead to feelings of inadequacy, anger, and long-term depression. Such practices are not defined as violence but they are symbolically violent with long-term harmful consequences.

Consider, as further examples, a school administration that exercises arbitrary, authoritarian discipline or teachers who "get by" without their best effort and lack commitment to their students' education. Or the message conveyed to students about "trust" and "freedom" of educational thought when we deploy metal detectors, video cameras, identity tags, drug-sniffing dogs, and guards to "secure" that freedom (Adams 2000; Thompkins 2000). This "hidden curriculum" can have a significant negative impact on students' moral and social development (Yogan and Henry 2000).

At a broader level, consider the harm of inequitable school funding: one school receives better funding due to its location in a wealthy area, compared to a school located in a poverty-stricken urban setting. Finally, consider the harm created by celebrating competitive success while condemning academic failure; little wonder that "children who do poorly in school, lack educational motivation, and feel alienated are the most likely to engage in criminal acts" (Siegel 1998, 197–98). And this analysis does not even begin to address how competitive success corrupts the morality of the successful, driving them to win at all costs, regardless of the harm they cause to others in the process (Nicholson 2000; Staples 2000).

Toward an Expansive Integrated Concept of School Violence

Because of the omission of these broader dimensions of school violence we are missing much of the content and causes of violence in schools. We are blind to the part played by this wider context of violence in shaping the more visible forms of interpersonal physical violence manifest by some students. A more inclusive integrated concept of school violence is necessary.

With regard to the perpetrators of harm, the concept for those who exercise the power to deny others, conventionally described as "offenders," is limiting because it assumes that only individuals offend. Yet the manifestation of power that denies people their humanity can operate at many levels from individual to organization or corporation, community and society to nation-state. Further, the exercise of the power to harm, as mentioned earlier, can also be accomplished by social processes, such as sexism, ageism, and racism, which go beyond the individual acts of people. The exercise of power to deny others their humanity, by some agency or process, also takes place in a spatial social context. Even though the term "school violence" implies that the spatial location is the "school building, on the school grounds or on a school bus" (Bureau of Justice 1998), such a limited definition denies the interconnections between the school context and the wider society of which it is a part. It ignores the ways in which these acts of violence permeate social and geographical space. As a result, it fails to recognize that what may appear as an outburst in the school is merely one mani-festation of more systemic societal problems. These may begin in, or be modified by, activities in other spatial locations such as households, public streets, local neighborhoods, communities, private corporations, public or-ganizations, national political arenas, the global marketplace, or the wider political economy. As such, the social and institutional space of the school is merely one forum for the appearance of a more general systemic problem of societal violence.

The Pyramidal Analysis of Dimensions of School Violence

In this section we will relate school violence to the dimensions of the prism. How does the acknowledgment of multiple dimensions of defin-ing school violence affect our analysis? First is the dimension of relative seriousness of crime based on the harm it has caused. Some acts, like un-derage alcohol use and truancy, are victimless crimes in that they only harm the participants; others, such as the high-profile shootings in schools, harm more than one person at a time and the pain can extend to the victims' relatives, friends, and community (see Nicholson 2000).

Second is the degree of moral consensus or agreement about whether an act is right or wrong. This "can range from confusion and apathy, through levels of disagreement, to conditions of general agreement" (Ha-gan 1985, 49). Although there is consensus that drugs should not be in schools, the consensus is much greater against heroin and cocaine than against marijuana, and against all three compared to alcohol and ciga-rettes (see Venturelli 2000).

The third dimension is the severity of society's formal response. Sever-ity may range from social ostracism by school peers toward their fellow students, through informal reprimands by teachers, official warnings, ex-pulsion and exclusion from school, prosecution, or imprisonment, to the death penalty.

As we have seen, school violence takes many forms, all of which involve harm, but not all of those harmed necessarily realize they have been victimized. This relates to the visibility dimension of the crime prism. For example, it is difficult to see the negative effects of tracking, yet the tracking system has been shown to reinforce class and racial segre-gation; over time this practice operates as a crime of repression, limiting the intellectual, social, and moral development of those subject to it (Yo-gan 2000). The harmful effects of this practice are obscured and may take a long time to appear (in lowered expectations for self, poor self-esteem, etc.). Visibility of some aspects of school violence is an important dimen-sion because it is partly a reflection of the force of existing legal defini-tions, themselves shaped by powerful economic, political, and class interests. These interests, in turn, partly reflect the commercial interests of the mass media, which limit their framing of the crime question (Henry and Lanier 2001). In part, they reflect the popular culture's trivialization and sensationalization of direct interpersonal "true crimes" in preference to complex, diffuse social harms and injuries that have become institutionalized, compartmentalized, privatized, and justified via the legitimate goals of the organization.

In light of the pyramid discussion and analysis, an expansive integrated definition and reconception of school violence allows us to reframe our analysis. Types of school violence can be distinguished by the level of their perpetrators within the social structure, and these in turn reflect their positioning at different levels in the prism. Five levels of violence are identified, though the accuracy of the distinction between levels is less important than the range of levels addressed:

Level 1: Student on student, student on teacher, student on school

Level 2: Teacher on student, administrator on student, administrator on teacher, teacher/administrator on parents, parent on teacher/administrator

Level 3: School board on school/parent, school district on school/parents, community on school/parent, local political decisions on school and on parent

Level 4: State and national educational policy on school, state and national juvenile justice policy on student, media and popular culture on student and on administrator, corporate exploitation on students, national and state policies on guns and drugs

Level 5: Harmful social processes and practices that pervade each of the above four levels. Here social processes are the patterns of interaction that over time take on the appearance of a natural order or social reality existing above the individuals whose actions constitute that structure.

Discussion on school violence tends to be restricted to level 1 and some aspects of level 4. Even within level 1, some important distinctions can be made. In contrast to the excessive discussion of level 1 and some of 4, there has been virtually no discussion of levels 2, 3, and 5 which, given the interrelations between these types, represents a glaring deficiency.

Causal Implications of the Prismatic Analysis of School Violence

This expansive, integrated approach to defining school violence allows us to better identify different types of school violence. But it also raises the question of whether the different levels of violence manifest in the school setting are interrelated. Are the different levels of violence in school causally interrelated, such that invisible institutional violence at the level of, say administrators and teachers, are generative of visible violence among school students? Clearly this is an empirical question, and there is some evidence suggesting that this may be the case (Welsh 2000).

Although individuals may contribute to these social processes, it is the collective and cumulative repetition of actions by different people that creates harm to others. In the context of school violence these processes compose the practices and policies of the school, or what Welsh (2000) calls "school climate." It can include the policies and practices of school boards and their detrimental effects on school districts, and the local politics of communities. At a broader level, the collective actors can operate on the state and national level to include educational policy. An example would be a decision to expand prison building programs at the expense of school building, to hire corrections officers rather than schoolteachers, and even to submit to the apparent "economy of scale" that leads to building large schools over small ones, when all the evidence suggests that these are more alienating and more criminogenic.

While these collective and policy decisions may seem distant from the day-to-day activities of the school, their shadow and effects reach into the classroom and constitute part of the formative context for violence that is played out there. For example, Kramer (2000) distinguishes between three types of student violence: (1) predatory economic crimes, which involve the pursuit of material goals by any means, including violence, (2) drug industry crimes, which involve violent gang turf wars, and (3) social relationship violence by powerless angry youths who use acts of violence to resolve issues of humiliation resulting from their alienation (see also Staples 2000 and Cintron 2000). This third type may be a manifestation of the deeper social processes of harm in the lower level of our prism. In addition, we have argued that not all school students respond in the same way to the conditions that generate violence, even within level 1, and this has much to do with the influence of class, race, and gender (Henry and Lanier 2001).

Thus the prismatic definitional framework outlined above suggests that we need to take a much broader approach to examining the causes of school violence. Rather than operate simply on the individual analytic level that looks to psychological and situational explanations for why students act violently, we need to address the context of students' lives: their families, race, ethnicity, gender, and social class. We need to explore how these dimensions interconnect through social processes to shape and structure human thinking, moral development, and individual choices. We need to examine how these social forces shape school curriculum, teaching practices, and educational policy. At a deeper level we should be concerned to identify the way parents and schools themselves harm the lives of students, and the way they shape the content of young people's lives.

Finally, at the wider level we need to examine the ways in which the culture, comprising the economic, social, and political structure of American society, is reproduced and how it reproduces harmful processes. Although this level has been addressed through the discussions, analysis, and attempt to legislate against "toxic culture," this is an inadequate approach to macrolevel analysis. Discussion of cultural causes of school violence has focused on the role of violence in the media—in movies, videos, video games, and on the Internet—and on gun culture. The argument is that cultural violence amplifies aggressive tendencies in young males. It devalues humans into symbolic object images of hate or derision, trains youth to use violent skills, celebrates death and destruction as positive values, and provides exciting and colorful role models, who use violence as the solution to problems, glorifying the most powerful and destructive performances via news media infotainment. While this may be true it is not enough to simply blame toxic culture for poisoning kids' minds without also looking at the ways in which corporate America invests in the exploitation of violence for profit that feeds this cultural industry. A macroanalysis of "culture," therefore, has to connect that culture to the political economy of the society in which it is generated.

Policy Implications of the Prismatic Analysis of School Violence

The prismatic analytical framework to defining crime may allow us to identify the multiple interrelated causes of such violence, but this also has implications for policy and practice. Indeed, it affects the societal response dimension of the prism. Such an analysis is likely to provide for a more comprehensive approach to policy that reaches deeper into the roots of systemic violence than superficial quick-fix responses. It allows us to see the interconnections between different types of school violence and develop integrated policies designed to respond to them. An adequate policy response must be comprehensive, dealing simultaneously with each of the causes identified at each level of definition. It must penetrate the built-in protections of systems that conceal their own practice from analysis and change. It must be reflexive enough to recognize that policy itself can be part of the problem rather than the solution; policy should be self-critical and self-correcting. While this chapter does not allow us to expand on the immensity of the policy question called for by such an analysis, the question of "dispute resolution" can be indicative in illustrating how a restrictive versus an expansive definition of school violence would operate (see Adams 2000; Pepinsky 2000; Caulfield 2000; Nicholson 2000).

Dispute Resolution. A narrow approach to school violence prevention policy would begin by assuming a level 1 definition of the problem. For example, kids are violent in schools because they are taught to use violence to solve their problems or, at best, they are not taught nonviolent ways of dealing with conflict. The simplistic restrictive policy response suggests that dispute resolution training in techniques of nonviolent problem solving would be appropriate.

In contrast, an expansive definition and an integrated causal analysis would tie the use of violence by students to the use of symbolic and other forms of violence by adults, whether these are parents, teachers, administrators, or politicians. Instead of just implementing such training for students, it would argue for all school personnel, at every level, to undergo and practice nonviolent problem solving. Further, the school organization, curriculum, and educational processes would be subject to the same "violence cleansing" scrutiny to be replaced by what Pepinsky (2000) calls "educating for peace" rather than "educating about peace."

Viewed through the prism of crime the issue of school violence is not just about kids in schools; it is about the total coproduction of our society by each of its constituent elements. To approach school violence another way is not merely shortsighted but does more violence to those who have already suffered much pain.

Other Implications

Considering the location of crimes on the prism makes two things apparent. First, the positioning of crimes on the prism varies over time as society becomes more or less aware of the crime and recognizes it as more or less serious. For example, consider the changing position of domestic violence and sexual harassment, both of which have recently begun to move from the lower half to the upper half of the prism. In contrast, other acts that were once in the upper half have become so common as to be hidden, are relatively harmless, and evoke neither public outcry nor societal response. For example, Sutherland and Cressey (1966) pointed out that at different times it was a crime to print a book professing the medical doctrine of blood circulation, to drive with reins, to sell coins to a foreigner, to keep gold in the house, or to write a check for less than a dollar.

Second, the upper half of the prism (Hagan's pyramid) contains predominantly conventional crimes, or "street crimes," whereas the lower half of the prism contains the greater preponderance of white-collar crimes, or "suite crimes." Some have suggested that offenders committing the majority of the former crimes are relatively powerless in society, whereas those committing the majority of the latter hold structural positions of power (Balkan, Berger, and Schmidt 1980; Box 1983). A central question is, What does being powerful affect? Is it the type of crime that is committed or the ability to escape the effects of the law? Let us conclude our examination of definitions of crime by looking a little more closely at these two broad types of crime and what the criminological research about them reveals.

Crimes of the Powerless

Power can be considered on several dimensions, including class, gender, race, and ethnicity. Consider social class as an illustration. The original conception of crimes of the powerless was based on the accumulated evidence from data gathered by the criminal justice system. This showed that those predominantly arrested for conventional criminal activities were from lower- or working-class backgrounds. These street crimes of theft and personal violence, such as homicide, rape, aggravated assault, robbery, burglary, larceny, and auto theft, were committed by people holding relatively weak legitimate economic and political positions in society. For example, Balkan and her colleagues argued that street crime, "conventionally considered the most serious form of crime, is committed primarily by working-class persons" (1980, 340).

But the emergence of findings from numerous self-report surveys in which people are asked to anonymously report to researchers about the kinds of crimes they actually commit rather than those they are arrested for suggests that this view is inaccurate. Except for the most serious crimes, it was found that the proportions of street crimes committed by middle-class and lower-class youths are similar (Currie 1985; Elliott and Huizinger 1983). However, the lower-class offender is more likely to be arrested, charged, and convicted by the criminal justice system (Liska and Chamin 1984; Sampson 1986). Other dimensions of power, such as race or gender, are interlocked with the class dimension and can be subject to a similar analysis. Take race as an illustration. Self-report surveys found that African American and white offense rates were similar except for serious offenses, but African American arrest and conviction rates were higher (Elliott and Ageton 1980; Huizinger and Elliott 1987; Reiman [1979] 1995). Thus poor African Americans are more likely to be arrested than wealthy whites.

These findings show the importance of criminological research in shaping our thinking about crime. They suggest that we need to revise our conception of crimes of the powerless. Taking account of these data, "crimes of the powerless" refers to crimes for which those in relatively weak economic and political positions in society are predominately arrested. Powerlessness reflects qualities affecting not so much the commission of crimes but the ability to resist arrest, prosecution, and conviction.

Crimes of the Powerful

Crimes of the powerful are committed by people in relatively strong legitimate economic and political positions in society (Simon 2002). Again, let
us illustrate the argument on the social class dimension of power. Such
crimes include offenses by those in powerful occupational or political positions, such as business executives, professionals, lawyers, doctors, accountants, and politicians—crimes such as insider trading, tax evasion,
bribery and corruption, Medicare fraud, price-fixing, pollution, and so
on. Crimes of the powerful include much of what are called white-collar
crimes (Sutherland 1949a) because of the occupational position of those
who carry them out. They are also called suite crimes because they occur
typically in offices, corridors of power, and corporate boardrooms.

As with crimes of the powerless, it helps to understand the range of
crimes committed. These are not only offenses by individuals but also by
corporations, organizations, and agencies of government (Ermann and
Lundman [1992] 1996; Schlegel and Weisburd 1992) and government policies (Barak 1991). Thus we need to include (1) corporate crimes such as
faulty product manufacture, dangerous work conditions, price-fixing,
and consumer fraud; (2) government agency crime, such as systemic police corruption, subversion of regulatory enforcement, and violence (e.g.,
over 100 agents of the Bureau of Alcohol, Tobacco, and Firearms [ATF] in
Waco, Texas, in 1993 where senior agents altered written plans and tried
to cover up the fact after 73 Branch Davidians burned to death); and (3)
state crimes resulting from government policy such as violations of privacy rights, involuntary medical experimentation (e.g., radiation on unwitting subjects and the Tuskeegee syphilis study in which African
American males were not treated for syphilis so the government could
see the long-term effects of this disease), state monopolies and government subsidies, and crimes against other states.

It is also important to note, as with crimes of the powerless, that power
shapes not only the opportunity to commit crime but also the ability to resist arrest, prosecution, and conviction: "Crimes committed by the powerful are responsible for even greater social harms than those committed by
the powerless. The former have escaped public attention precisely because,
given the individualistic political-legal framework of capitalist society, it is
difficult to identify and prosecute the persons who are responsible for
crimes that take place within organizations" (Balkan et al. 1980, 145).

Considering our crime prism, the power of some to influence government, law, and the media; to obscure their harms; to resist arrest and prosecution; and to minimize sentences is why such crimes are located in the
bottom segment. They are very harmful but obscured, and they harm
their victims indirectly and diffusely, often without the victims realizing

who the offender is or perhaps even that they were victimized. The victims of these crimes are blamed for being stupid, careless, or unfortunate (as in the savings and loan fraud, injury and death in the workplace, and pollution and food poisoning). Only in recent years has social reaction begun to respond to these offenses and then only feebly, through selective regulatory control rather than criminalization. Until victims are clearly identified, crimes of the powerful are brought to public awareness, and governments are more democratically representative of the people rather than industry lobbyists, the location of these crimes on the crime prism will be low.

In the remainder of this chapter, we will look at the different kinds of data on crime and at how criminologists measure crime, determine its extensiveness, and establish crime trends.

Measuring Crime

On the surface, it might seem a simple matter to establish an objective measure of crime, but the reality of crime's harm is not readily reduced to factors and scales. Consider violence. The consequences or costs of violence include the pain and suffering experienced by injured crime victims and their families; their physical, emotional, and possibly also financial loss; their increased feelings of apprehension and insecurity; and their altered lifestyles. How do we measure this? Do we count how many violent acts there are and place a monetary value on their deprivations or do we ask the victims how they feel? Manning has suggested that criminologists should "study . . . the meanings of violence rather than its correlates" (1989, 1). A central problem for students of criminology is, however, whose meanings do we study and how are they constructed?

The many players telling crime stories with numbers include lawyers, politicians, police, corrections staff, victims, offenders, criminologists, dramatists, script writers, and journalists. Each one tells the numbers story somewhat differently. Our sense of the measure of crime is based on information generated by a combination of such accounts, filtered and selectively amplified by the media and interpreted via our personal past experience of harm and suffering (Surette 1997). Each piece presents part of an overall composite picture. In this section, we consider the manufacture of the data from which crime stories are produced. In the process, we pay close attention to the ways crime is measured and the methodological and philosophical problems associated with trying to measure crime.

Government Measures of Crime

In the United States, government agencies are responsible for measuring the extent of crime that our society experiences. Government data are also supplemented by "independent" measures produced by criminological researchers. Government measures are based on the legal definition of crime as an intentional act or omission that violates criminal law, is committed without justification, and is sanctioned by the state as a felony or misdemeanor. Independent appraisals of crime draw on measures and definitions of crime generated by academic researchers, who are based in universities or private research institutes.

The United States government routinely uses two measures of crime. The first measure, known as the official crime statistics, is published in the *Uniform Crime Reports (UCR)*. These are compiled annually by the FBI under the auspices of the U.S. Department of Justice (DOJ), based on data submitted by over 16,000 police agencies throughout the United States. The second government measure of crime is the National Crime Victimization Survey (NCVS), which is conducted by the Bureau of Justice Statistics (BJS), also for the DOJ.

Uniform Crime Reports

The *Uniform Crime Reports* is the oldest and best-known source of crime statistics. Starting in 1930, the FBI began recording the number of criminal offenses "known to the police." Crimes known to the police include those reported by victims or observed by officers or discovered by them through proactive policing and sting operations. By far the majority (over 90 percent) are crimes reported to the police. The number of offenses reported to the FBI by police agencies includes crimes for which no one is arrested.

The best-known summary data prepared from the *UCR* relate to the index crimes, which are also known as Part I offenses. They are called index crimes because changes in their number are used to indicate the level of crime in the nation. These data are used to produce a crime rate. The crime rate is the frequency with which given offenses occur in a certain place over a specific time period, usually one year. Index crimes include homicide and nonnegligent manslaughter, forcible rape, robbery, aggravated assault, burglary, larceny theft, motor vehicle theft, and arson.

In addition to index crimes, twenty-two other crimes are classified as Part II offenses. Interestingly, these nonindex offenses contain several of the white-collar crimes that some might consider very serious, including fraud, embezzlement, and forgery. They also include drug offenses, prostitution and vice, and some property offenses.

The FBI uses five main methods of presenting these data: (1) the actual number of crimes known by the police, (2) the percentage change for each crime from the previous year, (3) the crime rate per 100,000 of the population in a specified area, (4) the number of arrests for different offenses, and (5) the characteristics of offenders arrested.

The actual number of crimes known to the police has been around 14 million per year since 1990 (compare the early 1960s, when it was around 3.5 million per year). Arrest rate data are less helpful in assessing crime rates since their purpose is to document who police arrest. Consequently, they have been used to obtain characteristics of offenders. Those who are disproportionately arrested are young, male, and African American, but this tells us little about the characteristics of who commits these crimes since arrests are such a small proportion of crimes known to police.

The police provide the FBI with monthly data on the number of crimes "cleared by arrest." A cleared crime means that a person is arrested and charged with the crime or a suspect is identified but physical arrest is impossible (due to death, offender leaving the country, etc.).

Crime Rate and UCR Crime Trends

As mentioned previously, the crime rate is based on data provided in the UCR. A crime trend is the standardized measure of the crime rate plotted on a graph over a period of years. It is necessary to calculate crime rates and crime trends based on ratios of the population in a given area to ensure that crime counts do not increase or decrease solely as a result of changes in population in one year compared to another. If a certain area has a population expansion, the use of raw crime data is likely to result in recording more crime simply because there are more people in the area. Furthermore, without standardization it would be impossible to compare the crime rates of cities with each other or with the crime rates of rural towns and villages, let alone with the crime rates of different nations of various sizes. The solution to this problem is to work out the crime rate per unit of population; "100,000 people" has been selected for statistical convenience, since calculating the more conventional percentage rate would produce less than whole numbers. The standardized crime rate is then calculated by the formula:

$$Crime\ rate = \frac{Crimes\ known\ to\ the\ police \times 100,000}{Area\ population}$$

Unfortunately, once such data have been produced and graphically presented, the tendency is for speculation to begin. This speculation seeks to explain the changes and includes everything from climate, immigration, and changes in age cohorts (especially the baby boom generation) to crime control policies by various political parties. Nearly always forgotten in this process is the simple fact that the data represent crimes reported to the police. Since, as we shall see later, several factors affect people's propensity to report crimes and, at best, only a third of all crimes are reported, significant change in this crime rate can occur by changes to either reporting practices or police recording practices.

Problems with the UCR

Several methodological and conceptual problems with the UCR have been identified (Vito, Latessa, and Wilson 1988). First, the UCR only reflect crimes known to the police. Many crimes are never reported or discovered by police agencies. This unreported crime is commonly referred to as the "dark figure" or "hidden crime." There are many reasons why the police do not know about all crimes. Respondents to victimization surveys, which we shall examine later, reveal the following reasons for nonreporting: (1) private matter, (2) nothing could be done, and (3) victims may be embarrassed and not wish to notify the authorities (see Figure 2.3). For example, rape victims—male and female—not only feel the matter is private or personal but may be ashamed to admit to the violation or may feel that the police are biased. One study found that if victims were robbed and beaten as well as raped, the crime was seen as more serious and was more likely to be reported (Lizotte 1985). This study also found that in the case of women victims, victims who know the offender are less likely to report the offense, as are college-educated women. This is particularly relevant to the issue of date rape on college campuses, which also highlights the problem of the offenders' and victims' perceptions of rape.

Other victims who do not report offenses may not want to go through the trouble of negotiating the judicial maze. Some victims may feel that the police will be unable to recover property that was lost or apprehend the offender. Still others may fear retaliation from the offender. Some victims may know the offender or feel the person deserves a second chance. For these and other reasons, a considerable amount of crime will always remain unknown to the police.

Importantly, the nature of the victim also affects his or her propensity to report crimes. According to the NCVS, females are more likely to report crimes than males, those over thirty-five are more likely to make reports than those younger, and crimes involving homes having higher property values are more likely to be reported than those affecting homes with lower values (BJS 1993, 32). In general, the more violent the crime the more likely it is to be reported. Automobile theft is also a highly reported crime (probably due to the widespread use of insurance, which demands a police report to obtain compensation).

Another methodological problem with the *UCR* data is that police departments may use differing definitions of specific crimes. For example,

FIGURE 2.3   Why People Fail to Report Crimes to the Police

Crime	Most frequent reasons for not reporting to the police	
Violent Crime		
Rape	Private or personal matter,* 18% Police inefficient, ineffective, or biased,* 13% Offender unsuccessful,* 13%	‹ The most common reasons for not reporting violent crimes to the police are that the crime was a personal or private matter and that the offender was not successful.
Robbery	Object recovered, offender unsuccessful, 19% Lack of proof, 13% Police would not want to be bothered, 11%	
Aggravated assault	Private or personal matter, 22% Offender unsuccessful, 16% Lack of proof, 9%	
Simple assault	Private or personal matter, 26% Offender unsuccessful, 19% Reported to another official, 13%	
Theft		
Personal larceny with contact	Object recovered, offender unsuccessful, 25% Lack of proof, 22% Police would not want to be bothered, 11%	‹ The most common reasons for not reporting thefts are that the object was recovered or the offender was unsuccessful, the theft was reported to another official, and lack of proof.
Personal larceny without contact	Object recovered, offender unsuccessful, 28% Reported to another official, 18% Lack of proof, 11%	
Household Crime		
Burglary	Object recovered, offender unsuccessful, 24% Lack of proof, 11% Not aware crime occurred until later, 11%	‹ The most common reasons that victims of household crimes did not report to the police are because the object was recovered or the offender was unsuccessful, the police would not want to be bothered, and lack of proof.
Household larceny	Object recovered, offender unsuccessful, 31% Police would not want to be bothered, 12% Lack of proof, 11%	
Motor vehicle theft	Object recovered, offender unsuccessful, 36% Police would not want to be bothered, 10% Lack of proof, 7%	

*Estimate is based on about 10 or fewer sample cases.

SOURCE: Bureau of Justice Statistics (1993, p. 33).

Siegel (1995) reported one study finding that Los Angeles had a much higher incidence of rape than Boston. Figures for 1980 reveal that Boston had a rape rate of 29.0 per 100,000, whereas Los Angeles had a rate of 75.4 per 100,000. This higher rate resulted from the Los Angeles police department reporting rapes, attempted rapes, and sexual assaults, whereas Boston police recorded only completed rapes. By 1992, these data had dramatically reversed, with Boston reporting a rate of 93.7 and Los Angeles a rate of 51.8 per 100,000. Did this mean that Boston had become a city where a person is more than twice as likely to be raped as in Los Angeles, whereas the reverse was true twelve years earlier, or did the switch reflect changing definitions of crime used by the police?

In addition to definitional problems, different departments use various methods of recording crimes. Many police departments recorded a huge increase in the number of crimes once they began to rely on computerized record keeping. Obviously, the numbers of criminal acts did not increase as dramatically as the records indicated; the police simply became more accurate with keeping data. Conversely, it can be expected that errors will be made with recording and reporting crime data.

Third, a more sinister explanation for changes in crime rates is that police agencies may deliberately alter crime data to improve their department's reported clear-up rate. They can do this by failing to count ambiguous or lesser offenses, lowering the value of goods stolen below the level necessary for the offense to be counted as an index crime, and counting multiple offenses by single offenders as one offense. Indeed, if multiple crimes are committed during the same incident, the FBI only counts the most serious offense. Thus, if a person is abducted at knifepoint, raped, and then murdered, only the homicide will show up in the index crimes—assuming of course that the offenses are reported. Other problems associated with the UCR include the fact that not all police departments submit reports, that incomplete acts are counted as completed acts, that the FBI does not include federal crimes in its estimate (because these are not categorized as index offenses), and that the FBI uses forecasts in its total crime projection.

Finally, and seriously misleading, is that the UCR only report street crime or offenses that we earlier described as direct individual crimes. Crimes committed by white-collar criminals or collective indirect offenders are not recorded. Examples would include crimes by corporations, such as price-fixing; health and safety violations; and environmental, political, and state crimes. Perhaps for obvious reasons, crimes by governments are not recorded either, even though the victims can suffer serious injury and death, not to mention human rights and privacy violations.

As a result of these weaknesses, any attempt to equate the *UCR* crime index to actual crimes committed is subject to serious error. As Beirne and Messerschmidt ([1991] 1995, 38) note, "The UCR's 'Crime Index Total' actually misrepresents the crime rate in any given year. It is an FBI composite figure for public and media consumption [which] . . . misleads because no attempt is made to distinguish offenses by severity." The result is that an increase in serious crime, such as murder, could be offset by a decrease in larceny, yet "the Crime Index Total would show the 'crime rate' had remained constant" (1995, 38).

In 1989 the FBI modified the *UCR* in an effort to remedy some of the methodological problems (FBI 1992). Crime definitions were revised to be more accurate and uniform. The major change was a switch to the National Incident-Based Reporting System (NIBRS). This new system involves the reporting of each individual crime incident and each individual arrest. Furthermore, twenty-two crimes now make up what the FBI calls Group A offenses as opposed to the previous eight Part I offenses. Importantly, this group includes several white-collar offenses, such as bribery, counterfeiting and forgery, drug offenses, embezzlement, extortion and blackmail, fraud, and pornographic offenses. Group B offenses, the name given to a second group of crimes, are now much less serious than the old Part II crimes and include minor status offenses, such as curfew violations, runaways, liquor law violations, and so on. In addition, the hierarchy rule is also eliminated. Thus each offense committed is counted—not just the most serious one.

These changes represent the first major revision to the *UCR* in over fifty years. Unfortunately, partially due to the voluntary nature of police participation, many of the new changes have not been fully implemented. Furthermore, these changes do not address all of the serious problems listed previously.

The changes came about in part as a result of the success of victimization data, itself a response to "recurring criticism that offense data based on police records omit a 'dark figure' of crime that victims do not report to the police" (Blumstein, Cohen, and Rosenfeld 1991, 238).

Victimization Surveys: The National Crime Victimization Survey (NCVS)

The second official measure of crime is the National Crime Victimization Survey (NCVS). This study was first conducted in July 1972. It is a general survey of a representative sample of U.S. households designed to find out whether persons responding, or other persons in their household, have been a victim of a violent or property crime in the period covered by the survey. The National Academy of Sciences is responsible for evaluation, design, and sampling strategies, but the actual surveys are conducted by the DOJ and the U.S. Bureau of the Census.

The surveys are designed to provide a different way to measure crime in the United States. Unlike the *UCR*, which rely on data provided voluntarily by police agencies, this national survey tries to determine the proportion of crime victims among the general population and record their experiences. The specific research methodology employed is a "stratified multi-stage cluster sample" (Hagan 1993). This means that a sampling frame is developed from 2,000 primary sampling geographic areas (these are standard metropolitan statistical areas, counties, or small groups of contiguous counties). From these primary population areas, "clusters" are created based on size, density, population mobility, and other socioeconomic factors. A total of 376 clusters are created, covering the entire United States. Then one primary unit is chosen from each cluster, using a selection process whereby each unit has an equal chance of being selected. Next, every fourth household is selected from the chosen unit. Theoretically, using this sophisticated research design, every household in the country has an equal chance of being selected.

Once a household is selected for inclusion in the survey, it becomes part of a "panel." The annual sample of households has increased since the early surveys. One person from each of these households is interviewed at six-month intervals. Each month, around 10,000 households are interviewed. Each household remains part of the study for three years, but each month new households are added and three-year-old ones are replaced.

Once a household is selected, an interview is conducted by a person from the Census Bureau. These thirty-minute interviews include screening questions (to determine if victimization occurred) and incident reports. Usually, only one person from each household (anyone competent and over twelve years of age) is interviewed. After the first face-to-face interview, a combination of telephone and personal contact methods are used for the next three years.

As in the *UCR*, only certain crimes are measured by the NCVS. These are classified as either "personal" or "household" and include rape, robbery (personal), assault (aggravated and simple), household burglary, larceny (personal and household), and motor vehicle theft. Unlike the *UCR*, the NCVS also collects information on victim characteristics such as age, gender, race/ethnicity, education, and income.

One of the most interesting findings of the NCVS is who is most likely to be victimized (see Figure 2.5). Rather than the stereotypical fearful elderly white female, the reality is that teenage African American males are the most likely to be violently victimized; and elderly white females, the least. For personal theft, the highest victimization rates are for teenage white males and young adult African American males (BJS 1993, 20).

Perhaps most disturbing is that more than two in five African American males will become victims of violent crime at least three times over the course of their life, and the lifetime risk of homicide for African American males is 1 in 30, compared to 1 in 179 for white males, 1 in 132 for African American females, and 1 in 495 for white females (BJS 1988).

Finally, although the NCVS also cannot provide much information about the characteristics of offenders—especially for property crimes when no face-to-face contact occurs—it does give some insight on interpersonal violent crimes. The information shows that 60 percent of violent crimes were committed by strangers, but that in the nonstranger category 66 percent of offenders were related or well-known to the victim, with boyfriend/girlfriend and spouse/ex-spouse topping the list. Women are victimized by family violence at three times the rate of men. In most cases, victims of completed acts of violence are the same race as their offender, with 75 percent of white victims being victimized by whites and 86 percent of African Americans being victimized by African Americans (BJS 1994, 290).

Similar results on victimization have been found internationally and, although not directly comparable to the situation in the United States, help place victimization data in a wider context (Joutsen 1994).

What the *UCR* and NCVS Tell About Crime Trends

Comparing the *UCR* and NCVS data provides an instructive exercise about how statistical information on crime can be misleading. Part of the explanation for this discrepancy stems from the considerable variation between research methodologies employed by the *UCR* and NCVS. There is also an ongoing debate among criminologists as to whether the *UCR* and NCVS reflect similar trends in crime rates (see Blumstein, Cohen, and Rosenfeld 1992; McDowall and Loftin 1992). Two primary differences are that the NCVS crime rates are higher and reflect greater covariance (McDowall and Loftin 1992). Despite this variation and the higher rates reported by the NCVS, some similarities exist. Some researchers have argued that for certain offenses, "a strong correspondence between *UCR* and NCVS crime rates that persists over time suggests that both series may indeed be indicators of a single underlying crime phenomenon, whose year-to-year fluctuations are reflected in annual deviations from trends that are similar for the two series" (Blumstein et al. 1991, 257).

FIGURE 2.4   Proportion of Crimes Reported to the Police

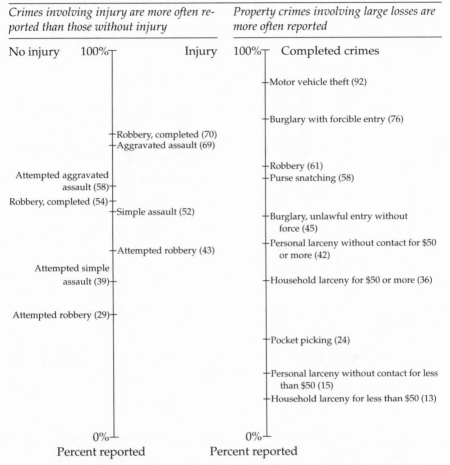

Crimes involving injury are more often reported than those without injury	*Property crimes involving large losses are more often reported*

NOTE: For some types of violent crime, 1992 reporting percentages were not available by whether or not the victim was injured. By definition, attempted assaults are without injury. In 1992, 53% of all rapes were reported to the police.

SOURCE: Bureau of Justice Statistics (1993, p. 31).

Other research has found weak or even inverse relationships (Menard and Covey 1988; Messner 1984).

Divergence between the NCVS and *UCR* suggests "the possibility of substantial bias in one or both of the measures" (McDowall and Loftin 1992, 131). In part, this possibility led to the development of alternative crime measures.

FIGURE 2.5   Likelihood of Victimization by Age, Race, and Sex

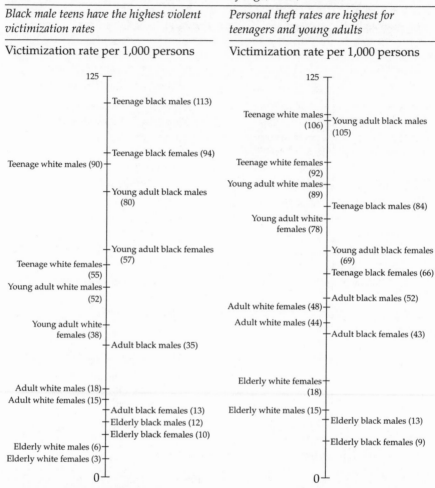

Black male teens have the highest violent victimization rates	*Personal theft rates are highest for teenagers and young adults*
Victimization rate per 1,000 persons	Victimization rate per 1,000 persons

NOTE: Teenage = age 12–19
          Young adult = age 20–24
          Adult = 35–64
          Elderly = age 65 and over

SOURCE: Bureau of Justice Statistics (1993, p. 20).

Problems with the NCVS

Like the *UCR,* the NCVS also has faults. Ironically, one deficiency lies with the use of respondents. Blumstein and colleagues (1992, 116) noted, "The measurement processes at work in NCVS rates are located primarily within respondents: their identification of some events as crimes, their ability to recall crime events accurately, and their willingness to report those events to the survey staff." Thus the results of victimization surveys can be contaminated by the respondent exaggerating the crime, being mistaken about it, or forgetting information. One common memory problem involves recalling the time the crime was committed, which can result in telescoping. This occurs when events happening over a longer time frame are collapsed into a shorter one. There is also a class bias shown by respondents, some of whom who may not relate well to middle-class interviewers or surveys in general (Sparks 1981).

Critics of victimization surveys also raise several other conceptual and methodological problems with their ability to measure crime, which can lead to under- or overestimates of crime, especially corporate and white-collar crime. Four categories of omission can lead to underestimates: (1) victimless crimes are omitted because the offenders are the victims and will not likely report on themselves; (2) underage victims are omitted because children under twelve, who may be subject to child abuse and other domestic violence, are not interviewed in the survey; (3) abstract victims such as the state and the general public may be victimized but no individual will report this as a personal or household crime; and (4) unknowing victims such as corporations subject to employee embezzlement or individuals or the general public subject to corporate fraud, faulty product manufacture, price-fixing, or pollution are unlikely to report these, not least because collective organizations or groups are not the unit of analysis. Internationally, the French victimization survey is the only one to move the scope of victimization beyond traditional crimes to include "abuse of power, collective victimization or the victims of 'modern' offenses (such as environmental crime and economic crime)" by covering businesses and the abuses resulting from the violation of employment regulations and consumer law (Joutsen 1994, 6; Zaubermann et al. 1990).

Data on corporate and government crime are available from official sources such as federal regulatory agencies and are another source of crime measures that supplement those we have already discussed (Beirne and Messerschmidt [1991] 1995, 48; Clinard and Yeager 1980). Other official agencies also compile victim data, such as the Centers for Disease Control (CDC), a government-sponsored public health organization.

Independent Crime Measures

So far, we have only discussed official measures of crime. Much of our knowledge about crime, however, comes from independent researchers in diverse disciplines. University researchers have a long history of measuring crime patterns and rates. The dominant methods employed are self-report surveys; participant observation studies; and unobtrusive measures using historical, documentary, and comparative data. Several problems confront researchers using any one of these measures to study crime, not least because the subjects wish to keep their crime a secret.

Self-Report Studies

With self-reports, researchers invite a random sample of the general population to voluntarily and anonymously describe any criminal or deviant acts in which they have participated during a set time frame, typically in the "last year" or in the "last month." The idea is to get people to admit to offenses that they have committed. The most common method of acquiring this information is through anonymous questionnaires, although person-to-person interviews are also used. The classic self-report study was conducted by James Wallerstein and Clement Wyle (1947), who asked a sample of 1,698 New Yorkers whether they had ever committed any of forty-nine offenses listed in a questionnaire. The subjects were screened to exclude any with prior criminal records, and still 99 percent admitted to at least one of the offenses. Although this study was crude, it unveiled the fact that rather than being committed by a small minority, crime was prevalent among the whole population. Self-report data have subsequently indicated that most adults have committed acts for which they could be incarcerated. Some of the more commonly reported offenses are larceny, indecency, and tax evasion (Gabor 1994).

Most self-report studies have been conducted on youths, typically with sample sizes of 500 to 3,000. The overriding conclusion of these studies is that upward of 90 percent of juveniles admit to delinquent and criminal activities. Martin Gold, one of the founders of the self-report method for delinquency, pointed out that "if social science demonstrates empirically that almost everyone sometimes breaks the law, but there are wide differences in how frequently and seriously individuals do so, delinquency should be recognized as a matter of degree" (1970, 4). In a composite review of all the previous studies, Empey and Stafford (1991) report that 60 percent of youths admit committing petty property crimes and 20 percent admit to more serious ones, with boys admitting to committing twice as many offenses as girls. (This compares with official *UCR* data on arrests that suggest a male-female ratio of 8 to 1.) When subjects were asked if they had committed property crimes in the past year, the proportion falls considerably but the ratios stay the same. With violent offenses, a similar pattern exists, although there are fewer offenses. Interestingly, the more serious the offense, the greater the difference between males and females.

One of the best executed self-report studies is that conducted annually since 1975 by the University of Michigan's Institute for Social Research (ISR) on drug use by U.S. high school students (ISR 1994). These data are complex and involve the extent to which youths will admit to using some substances rather than other ones. This depends on the prevailing climate of "moral panic" depicted in the media over specific types of drug use (Surrette 1997). The figures are also complicated by the substitution of substances about which nothing is known for those about which much is known. Thus increasing or decreasing drug use trends might reflect changes in publicly expressed attitudes toward certain substances or changes in use between documented and undocumented substances. Use at higher frequencies, in larger quantities, and of "harder" drugs is much more common among incarcerated youths (Lanier and McCarthy 1989), and this pattern is consistent in diverse geographic locations (Lanier, Di-Clemente, and Horan 1991).

Like victimization surveys, self-report studies have several methodological weaknesses. They are only conducted on individuals, generally in specific areas, and largely with youths. One of the few national surveys is Elliott and Ageton's (1983) National Youth Survey. Because the various surveys have different origins and purposes, their results are difficult to compare. Other questions concern self-report studies' replication, reliability, and validity, such as their accuracy in measuring crime. They suffer similar problems to those of victimization surveys in that they also may involve exaggeration, lying, forgetfulness, invention, and telescoping. These difficulties are made more likely by the practice in some studies of paying participating youths for their time and trouble!

Some self-report studies use a cross-sectional research design. This means that the study is conducted at one point in time with one sample of the population. Other self-report surveys use what is known as a longitudinal design. The National Youth Survey, which uses a panel design whereby the same respondents are interviewed at several points in time, is an example of a longitudinal study. Another example of this technique is the cohort study.

Cohort Studies

One of the most expensive and time-consuming research techniques used by independent researchers is known as the cohort study. It is a longitudinal study in which the same group of individuals is followed until a certain age. During the research period, the participants are regularly surveyed about either the crimes they commit or their victimization experiences. One of the best examples of a cohort study is the one by Wolfgang and colleagues (1972), a study of 9,945 Philadelphia boys born in 1945. At eighteen years of age, 35 percent of these boys had been arrested at least once for an offense more serious than a traffic violation. Importantly, of those with at least one arrest, 54 percent had been arrested for two or more offenses. Replications of these studies have revealed similar results (Tracy, Wolfgang, and Figlio 1985, 1990).

Obviously, the results of these studies have implications for criminal justice policy, but the studies are not without their critics. Again, because the studies focus on individuals, their scope is severely limited; more emphasis is needed on corporate crime. Some indication of how much emphasis is necessary can be seen in Sutherland's (1949b) original finding. Of the seventy largest industrial and merchandising corporations that he studied, all had at least one law violation over the "life careers of the corporations," and 83 percent were responsible for 252 adverse decisions on charges of restraint of trade; indeed, he argues, "three fourths of large corporations are habitual white collar criminals" (1949b, 514). A similar finding in a more recent, rigorous study (Clinard and Yeager 1980, 119) revealed that "small corporations accounted for one-tenth of the violations, medium-sized for one-fifth, and large corporations for almost three-fourths of all violations" and for 72 percent of the most serious ones. This shows that the chronic offender label applies to more than individuals.

Qualitative Studies:
Ethnography, Participant Observation, and Interviews

Participant observation is a method whereby researchers immerse themselves in the world of the criminal to study criminal activities and their meaning as an anthropologist studies a nonindustrial society. This type of research, which is one kind of ethnography, has a rich tradition, and many important insights have been gained through this technique. It is not, however, as commonly conducted as quantitative crime studies (the distinction between qualitative and quantitative methods was discussed in Chapter 1). Part of the explanation for this scarcity of ethnographic research may be that "qualitative research takes much longer, requires greater clarity of goals during design stages, and cannot be analyzed by running a computer program" (Berg 1989, 1). In spite of the observation that "criminology would benefit from theoretically informed ethnographies" (Manning 1989, 22), this methodology has been more popular for studies of deviant behavior than in criminology (e.g., Humphries 1970; Douglas and Rasmussen 1977). Noteworthy earlier ethnographies of crime exist, including Ditton (1977), Mars (1982) on occupational crime, and Henry's ([1978] 1988) study of the hidden economy of amateur fencing. Moreover, in answer to Manning's question, "Where are the detailed ethnographies of murder in Detroit, of drug dealing terror in Miami, of gangs in Los Angeles?" (1989, 5), we can now point to Meiczkowski's (1992) studies of drug dealing in Detroit, Williams's (1989, 1992) ethnography of the crack house, and Hagedorn's (1988, 1994) study of Milwaukee gangs.

Criminology benefits from ethnography because it provides an insight into the ways in which those who harm others and themselves construct their world as meaningful contexts in which to live. If these experiences can be understood to the extent that generalizations can be made and trends can be identified, then policies can be enacted to reduce the harms that the actions cause. This logic justifies not only in-depth studies of street criminals but also in-depth studies of corporations and executive decision making among "habitual white-collar corporate offenders" and corruption in agencies of government.

Importantly, qualitative studies of crime also include standard interviews and unstructured "dramaturgical interviews," in which the researcher scripts, acts, and plays a role encounter with offenders to gather sensitive information through an interactive social performance. "Dramaturgy . . . involves the elements and language of theater, stagecraft and stage management" (Berg 1989, 14–15). Illustrative of these studies are Katz's (1988) study of the excitement of crime and his revelatory notion of murder as "righteous slaughter" and, by way of contrast, Clinard's (1983) study of the business ethics of those engaged in corporate crime.

Finally, the qualitative in-depth interview can focus on a single individual and has been the basis for several classic criminological biographical case studies, including Sutherland's original *The Professional Thief* (1937), and Klockar's (1974) and Steffensmeier's (1986) case study approach to ethnography of the professional fence, a person who deals in stolen property.

Summary

We began this chapter by discussing the legal definition of crime and its limitations in accounting for the variability of crime across time and cultures. We then looked at how consensus theorists tied crime to societal agreement about universal morality. We went on to discuss the criticisms of this approach by those who saw division and conflict in society. We saw how conflict theorists disagreed in their ideas about the basis of division in society and how their differences produced definitions of crime highlighting different issues, not least of which is the nature of harm itself.

After exploring some social constructionist and postmodernist alternatives, we explained Hagan's crime pyramid and then offered a modified version through our prism of crime. The prism aimed at integrating the range of different approaches previously discussed. We then applied the prism concept to the case of school violence. We concluded the definitional section by briefly outlining the two kinds of crime emerging from this discussion: those of the powerful and the powerless. We noted empirical research suggesting that power not only shapes the opportunity to commit crime but also a person's likelihood of getting arrested and convicted for one kind of crime rather than another. Clearly one's definition is ideologically based. Despite this we do have fairly accurate measures of crime and the means to measure crime. However, several commentators have made the point that measuring crime is neither simple nor straightforward, not least because "crime statistics seldom, if ever, speak for themselves. They require interpretation" (Hagan 1985, 146). Indeed, "crime data depend, to a certain extent, on the assumptions of our theories" (Beirne and Messerschmidt [1991] 1995, 55). In this chapter, we have seen that although harms against others can be quantified, this alone does not enable us to draw conclusions without considerable caution.

This chapter illustrated the difficulties associated with defining and measuring crime. Official government statistics, relying on quantitative methods, provide one view of crime. This view depends on victims and police officers reporting crime accurately. Aside from the methodological problems, this approach to measuring crime is limited in that no understanding of the social context is provided; nor is a description of the interactions between target (victim), assailant, and the physical environment. Ethnographies, in contrast, provide a more complete view of crime. This research method often presents crime from the perspective of the criminal. Ethnographies have a problem, however, in that it is difficult to generalize from them. What occurs in one study cannot be said to be typical of other offenders, even of offenders of the same type. Cities vary, people are different, times change, and so on. Thus the context and meaning of one ethnographic study are not completely applicable to other people, locations, or times. Ethnographies are superior for delineating causality. In the next chapter, we turn our examination to theories about crime causation and examine the ideas and analysis of those who seek to explain why persons commit crimes.

Notes

1. See also Cohen 1993, 98–101; Lea and Young 1984, 55; Michalowski 1985; Reiman 1979); Von Hirsch and Jareborg 1991.

2. Unfortunately, when examples are given of so-called consensual crimes, such as personal drug use, prostitution, gambling, and so on, the role of power in the structural context in which the offender-victim eventually "chooses" the behavior is ignored.

3

Classical, Neoclassical, and Rational Choice Theories

Classical theory was prevalent prior to "modern" criminology's search for the causes of crime, which did not begin until the nineteenth century. Classical theory did not seek to explain why people commit crime but was a strategy for administering justice according to rational principles (Garland 1985). It was based on assumptions about how people living in seventeenth-century Europe, during the "Enlightenment era," began to reject the traditional idea that people were born into social types (e.g., landed nobility and serfs) with vastly different rights and privileges. Classical thinkers replaced this bedrock of the feudal caste system with the then-radical notion that people are individuals having equal rights.

Prior to the Enlightenment era, during a period of absolute monarchies, justice was arbitrary, barbarous, and harsh. Rulers used torture to coerce confessions, and corporal punishments such as whipping, flogging, and pillorying were common. The death penalty was applied to numerous offenses, including petty theft, deception, and poaching. However, even by 1520 reformers began to recognize that not all who violated society's norms should be subject to harsh and arbitrary punishments. While the poor and unemployed who stole to survive were treated harshly by today's standards, in England and Belgium for example, a distinction was made between the deserving and undeserving poor.

By the seventeenth century a major change was taking place. Utilitarian philosophers recognized the gross injustices of the legal and political system and saw much of the problem as resulting from the enormity of church and state power. Their solution was legal and judicial reform, which was consistent with emerging ideas about human rights and individual freedom. They sought philosophical justification for reform in the changing conception of humans as freethinking individuals. People were reinvented as rational and reasoning beings whose previously scorned individuality was now declared superior. These ideas about the "new person" built on the naturalist and rationalist philosophy of Enlightenment scholars such as Hutcheson, Hume, Montesquieu, Voltaire, Locke, and Rousseau.

Classical theory was originally a radical rather than a conservative concept because it opposed traditional ways, challenged the power of the state, was heretical to the orthodoxies of the Catholic Church, and glorified the common people (Williams and McShane 1988). However, it was also conservative in that it sought to expand the scope of disciplinary punishment (although not its severity), having it apply to everyone, while ignoring the social conditions of the crime problem (Beirne and Messerschmidt 2000, 72; Garland 1997).

The original concepts and ideals presented by the social philosophers Cesare Beccaria and Jeremy Bentham included such now familiar principles as innocent until proven guilty, equality before the law, due process procedure, rules of evidence and testimony, curbs on a judge's discretionary power, the right to be judged by a jury of one's peers, individual deterrence, and equal punishment for equal crimes. These ideas were prevalent when the U.S. Declaration of Independence and the U.S. Constitution were written. They laid the basis of the modern U.S. legal system, shaping the practices of law enforcement and the operation of the courts. Thus anyone working in the criminal justice system needs to understand the origin of these principles and why they were deemed necessary.

In this chapter, we outline the central theoretical ideas of classical theory and illustrate how classicism applies to contemporary crime and justice. Later in the chapter, we discuss theoretical extensions of classicism. These include early-nineteenth-century French neoclassicism, which revised the original ideals to take account of pragmatic difficulties, and the late-twentieth-century postclassical developments of the justice model, together with administrative criminology's theories of rational choice, situational choice, and routine activities. Finally, we consider the empirical support for classical and rational choice assumptions. Does research indicate that classical ideas are effective in practice? In our evaluation of this perspective, we examine the empirical support for three key areas: (1) research on the deterrent effect of legal punishments, including the death penalty, (2) the extent to which offenders make rational choice decisions prior to committing crime, and (3) the extent to which rational choice precautions by potential victims affect the probability of subsequent victimization.

The Preclassical Era

To fully appreciate classical thought, it is necessary to understand the historical context in which it developed and, in particular, how humans viewed each other before the onset of classical thought. By the sixteenth century, several European societies had undergone considerable transformation from the feudal era. Political power was consolidated in states whose monarchical rulers aspired to total domination. Many rulers claimed to have special relations with deity, and they conducted their affairs with limited interference from representatives of the people (Smith 1967). People were born into positions of wealth and power, positions that they claimed as their natural right. The law was the will of the powerful applied to the lower members of society. The administration of justice was based on inflicting pain, humiliation, and disgrace to those accused of offenses. This occurred in spite of a growth in scientific knowledge throughout Europe and was validated by the Church.

Although the political and religious order of life in pre-seventeenth-century Europe sounds fundamentally different from U.S. society today, some similarities were beginning to emerge. If still a class-based society, post-Renaissance Europe had broken from the rigid feudal order of the "ancient regime," in which a person's birth determined his or her place in life. By 1650, many governments adopted the new mercantile system of trade, especially colonial trade monopolies, and this paved the way for upward (and downward) mobility. Humans (meaning men) were now seen as capable of making a difference to their life and situation through acts of will. The concept of "the individual" was thus born, with the highly revered qualities of rationality and intelligence.

In sixteenth-century England, for example, the middle classes enjoyed considerable economic and social advancement. The state had divested feudal families of their land and middle-class land speculators were rewarded with land for their loyalty to the monarchy. As a result, the emerging middle class, or bourgeoisie (meaning those beneath the aristocracy), of merchants and traders rose to form a new power elite. This was at the expense of farmers, artisans, laborers, and the poor, many of whom became beggars and thieves. This polarization between wealth and poverty was caused by a combination of events, including government-decreed fixed wages for the lower classes at a time of massive price inflation; the decline of arable farming and the shift to animal husbandry, particularly sheep farming; and the enclosure of common lands, which converted cropland to pasture, enabling quicker profits. The Acts of Enclosure deprived common people of their traditional right to use the land and declared such use to be the crimes of poaching and theft. At the same time, urbanization was accelerating and cities were growing, but also becoming crowded with the dispossessed poor. Families were often forced to share single-room houses.

Urban dwellers who could not survive the lack of work, hunger, and insecurity roamed from town to town as homeless vagabonds; others were forced, by sickness or misfortune, into an impoverished life of debauchery, begging, and theft. So grew a population that the rising merchant class and gentry referred to as "savages," "beasts," and "incorrigibles," in need of harsh discipline. This attitude contrasted to, and indeed conflicted with, the nonpunitive relief policies of the medieval monasteries.

The problem of vagabondage as a constant feature of social life all over England had existed since 1520, but was especially rampant in the towns (Salgado 1972, 10). During this time the "idle and dangerous classes" swarmed into the towns in search of food and shelter. Hospitals and houses giving relief to the poor were seen as breeding grounds for those who became beggars, thieves, and drunkards. Rookeries of thieves among the slums threatened to envelop the metropolis in vice and crime: "Citizens found themselves besieged in their streets by the leper with his bell, the cripple with his deformities and the rogue with his fraudulent scheme" (O'Donoghue 1923, 137).

The growth in street crime was not slowed by the pervasive corruption in the criminal justice system. Officials whose job was to control common crime actually encouraged it by accepting bribes. The absence of effective organized law enforcement at a time when informal social and kinship network ties had been broken was another factor facilitating the growing crime problem. The lackadaisical manner in which laws were enforced compounded the problems associated with the existing laws. "Justice" was questionable, since the judicial system operated arbitrarily and unpredictably. Juries were corruptible and witnesses sold their evidence. Indeed, the term "straw man" referred to "witnesses" who wore a piece of straw in their shoe buckles indicating that they could be bought (Hibbert [1963] 1966). Secret accusations and private trials were not uncommon. Justice was anything but blind, and the economically and socially disadvantaged were held accountable to different standards, since the legal system reflected the interests of the wealthy.

Concern for the poor soon became mixed with fear of a threat to public order. "Respectable" citizens—and especially the new merchant classes—wanted "to protect themselves from the unscrupulous activities of this vast army of wandering parasites" (Salgado 1972, 10), and demanded that city streets be made safe for the conduct of business. In response to the rising fear of crime, European parliaments passed harsher penalties against law violators. In England alone, during the sixteenth century, over two hundred crimes warranted the death penalty and many persons died during the torture used by governments to extract their confession. Yet there were already stirrings of change. By the middle of the sixteenth century, English reformers were calling for a clear distinction between the respectable deserving poor and the disrespectable undeserving poor.

The *respectable poor* included those suffering from sickness and contagious diseases, wounded soldiers, curable cripples, the blind, fatherless and pauper children, and the aged poor. They were seen as the responsibility of the more fortunate and would be segregated by their class and condition, given immediate assistance, including shelter, treatment, adequate maintenance, and, in the case of the children, education and training, in a variety of houses and hospitals around the city. Such "respectable" citizens, who had fallen on hard times through no moral fault of their own, by reason of failure in business, ill health, or other misfortunes, were given weekly pensions and might be employed in clearing the church porches of beggars.

In contrast, the *disrespectable poor*, which included vagabonds, tramps, rogues, and dissolute women—described as worthless—were punished with imprisonment and whipping before being trained for honest work (O'Donoghue 1923, 139–140). For this group was proposed a prison, the Bridewell, which should also be a house of work, with opportunities for character improvement. The premises would also be used to train poor and resistant children into various trades. Most vilified was the "robust beggar," whose presence among beggary was seen as a choice for a soft and easy life. The "stubborn and foul" would be set to make nails and to do blacksmith's work; the weaker, the sick, and the crippled might make beds and bedding. Bridewell, established in 1556, was intended "to deal with the poverty and idleness of the streets, not by statute, but by labor. This was the first 'house of corrections': The rogue and the idle vagrant would be sent to the treadmill to grind corn, but the respectable poor— whether young, not very strong, or even crippled—would be taught profitable trades, or useful occupations" (O'Donoghue 1923, 151–152). The justification was that enforced labor would permanently cure begging and thievery, where statutes of law had failed. By the middle of the eighteenth century, the target of reform was the law and justice itself.

The Classical Reaction

The combination of a rising propertied middle class and a rising crime rate led the philosophical leaders of the classical movement to demand double security for their newfound wealth. They needed protection against the threat from below, the "dangerous" classes symbolized by the growing crime rates. They also wanted protection against threats from above, the aristocracy that still held the reins of governmental power and legal repression. The middle classes saw a solution to their dilemma in a reformed legal system "that would defend their interests and protect their 'rights and liberties' against the arbitrary power hitherto wielded exclusively by the landed classes and the Crown" (Young 1981, 253). Indeed, to be free to move up the class hierarchy, reformers needed a new legal concept of humans that would limit the power of the old aristocratically run state and liberate the freedom, safety, and security of the individual to create and keep wealth. This emerged in the concept of universal rights to liberty and freedom that would apply equally to all people (though many classes beneath the middle classes were excluded). Universal rights demanded predictability and calculability, neither of which was present in the existing system of arbitrary justice.

Thus the primary focus of utilitarian philosophers was to transform arbitrary justice into a fair, equal, and humanitarian system. They sought to do this by aligning the law and its enforcement and administration with logical and rational principles. These principles were consistent with the emerging concept of humans as individuals and were most eloquently expressed by the philosophers Cesare Beccaria and Jeremy Bentham, although several others contributed.

Cesare Beccaria

Perhaps the most influential protest writer and philosopher of the period was the Italian marquis, Cesare Bonesana, Marchese di Beccaria (1738–1794) or as he is more popularly known, Cesare Beccaria. Beccaria's ideas were molded by his friends the Milanese political activist brothers, Pietro and Alessandro Verri. These intellectuals formed a radical group called "the academy of fists," which was "dedicated to waging relentless war against economic disorder, bureaucratic petty tyranny, religious narrow-mindedness, and intellectual pedantry" (Paolucci 1963, xii).

With considerable prodding and much editorial help from Pietro Verri, in 1764, at age twenty-six, Beccaria published a small book on penology translated into English as *On Crimes and Punishment*. It gained much notoriety after the pope banned it for what he alleged to be highly dangerous, heretical, and extreme rationalism (Beirne 1991). Anticipating just such a reaction, Beccaria published the book anonymously. His modest work became highly influential, first in Paris and then worldwide. By 1800, it had appeared in twenty-three Italian editions, fourteen French editions, and eleven English editions. The book justified massive and sweeping changes to European justice systems. The founding fathers of the United States relied on it. Thomas Jefferson used it as "his principal modern authority for revising the laws of Virginia" (Wills 1978, 94). The writers of the U.S. Constitution and the Bill of Rights utilized it as a primary source.

In addition, its impact remains very clear in contemporary U.S. judicial and correctional policy.

What caused so much reaction to this book? Certainly Beccaria's motivation for writing the book was rooted in the resentment he felt toward the authoritarian aristocracy into which he was born. It was fueled by his friends' radical ideas about the state of Italian society and particularly the abuse and torture of prisoners. Arguably, the book drew together, in a readable, poetic way, all the main intellectual ideas of the era, providing an exemplar for change. Expressed alone, these ideas had little force. Expressed together, as part of a logical framework, they were revolutionary.

Beccaria challenged the prevailing idea that humans are predestined to fill certain social statuses. Instead, he claimed, they are born as free, equal, and rational individuals having natural rights, including the right to privately own property. They also had natural qualities such as the freedom to reason and the ability to choose what is in their own best interests. Drawing on the ideas of Hobbes' (1588–1679) and Rousseau's (1712–1778) "social contract" and Locke's (1632–1704) belief in inalienable rights, Beccaria believed that government was not the automatic right of the rich. Rather, it was created through a social contract in which free, rational individuals sacrificed part of their freedom to the state to maintain peace and security on behalf of the common good. The government would use this power to protect individuals against those who would choose to put their own interests above others. As a contemporary example, we give up the right to drive where and whenever we want at whatever speed we want and submit to government traffic laws designed to promote rapid and safe transportation. Some individuals are tempted to disregard these laws. When they do so the government, through its agents of enforcement, punishes or removes these individuals so that we may all travel with relative predictability and peacefulness. Indeed, government maintained individual rights to ensure that it did not become excessively powerful and that citizen voices were always represented.

Taken together, these assumptions led to the principle of individual sovereignty (Packer 1968). This means that individual rights have priority over the interests of society or the state. This was especially important in the exercise of law to protect individuals. Thus Beccaria opposed the practice of judges making laws through interpreting their intent. Instead, he insisted that lawmaking and resolving legal ambiguities should be the exclusive domain of elected legislators who represented the people. He believed that the wisest laws "naturally promote the universal distribution of advantages while they resist the force that tends to concentrate them in the hands of the few." He argued that laws should always be designed, like government itself, to ensure "the greatest happiness shared by the greatest number" (Beccaria [1764] 1963, 8).

Beccaria also shifted the focus of what counted as crime. Rather than offenses against the powerful, he saw crimes as offenses against fellow humans and thus against society itself. He believed crimes offended society because they broke the social contract, resulting in an encroachment on the freedom of others.

It was in the administration of justice that Beccaria saw individual sovereignty most at risk, so he sought reforms that would guarantee justice. He argued that the law, the courts, and especially judges have a responsibility to protect the innocent from conviction and to convict the guilty, but to do so without regard to their status, wealth, or power. The only basis for conviction was the facts of the case. This led to the principle of the presumption of innocence (Packer 1968), designed to protect individual rights against excessive state power or corrupt officials. Several procedural elements were necessary for a system of justice to ensure this protection. These included (1) procedural restraint over arbitrary power, (2) protection of the accused defendant against abuses and error, and (3) minimizing discretion or arbitrariness by rules that limit police power and govern what is acceptable evidence.

Beccaria also believed that individuals were best protected through an adversarial trial in which the accused had the right to be represented and was ensured equality of inquiry and equality before the law. Moreover, this trial should not be judged by the government but by a jury of the accused's peers (but he also believed that half the jury should be of the victim's peers) and the procedures should provide the accused the right to appeal to an independent body.

When it came to the issue of crime prevention, Beccaria did not believe that the best way to reduce crime was to increase laws or increase the severity of punishment, since doing so would merely create new crimes and "emboldens men to commit the very wrongs it is supposed to prevent" (Beccaria [1764] 1963, 43). Instead, he argued, laws and punishments should be as restrictive as necessary to deter those who would break them by making it not in their interests to do so.

To maximize the possibility of justice and deterrence, Beccaria believed that punishments should fit the crime in being proportionate to the harm caused. Thus the severity of the harm determines the level of punishment. Punishment should not affect others or influence their future offending. General deterrence, which means using the punishment of one individual to discourage others from committing crime, should, according to Beccaria, be replaced by specific or individual deterrence, which encourages each individual to calculate the costs of committing the crime. The level of punishment would be assessed by relating punishment to what an offense deserves. This is the principle of "just deserts": convicted offenders deserve punishment commensurate with the seriousness of the harm they caused through the specific offense they committed. This punishment cannot be for any other reason, such as to teach others a lesson or because they had committed other crimes in the past and so might be more likely to repeat them in the future.

To be an effective deterrent in individual calculations, punishments should also be certain, argued Beccaria. "The certainty of punishment, even if moderate, will always make a stronger impression than the fear of another which is more terrible but combined with the hope of impunity" ([1764] 1963, 58). Certainty means a high chance of apprehension and punishment. Beccaria believed it was more important for potential offenders to know certain punishment would follow a crime than to merely associate crime with severe sanctions. If the severity of punishment is high but the likelihood of apprehension and punishment low, then people are still likely to commit the act. This was dramatically illustrated at the public executions of pickpockets in London, which attracted large crowds of spectators whose pockets were picked by the clearly undeterred pickpockets among them.

Finally, for punishment to appear as a cost to potential offenders it must also occur swiftly after apprehension (with celerity), for as Beccaria ([1764] 1963, 55) wrote, "The more promptly and the more closely punishment follows upon the commission of a crime, the more just and useful will it be."

Jeremy Bentham

An influential social philosopher and a supporter of Beccaria's ideas was the Englishman Jeremy Bentham (1748–1832). Bentham expanded on Beccaria's initial contribution by offering the notion of the "hedonistic, or felicity calculus" as an explanation for people's actions. This calculus states that people act to increase positive results through their pursuit of pleasure and to reduce negative outcomes through the avoidance of pain. Bentham's conception of pain and pleasure was complex, involving not just physical sensations but political, moral, and religious dimensions, each of which varied in intensity, duration, certainty, and proximity (Bentham [1765] 1970; Einstadter and Henry 1995, 48).

Bentham believed that people broke the law because they desired to gain money, sex, excitement, or revenge. Like Beccaria, Bentham saw the purpose of law as increasing the total happiness of the community by excluding "mischief" and promoting pleasure and security. For individuals to be able to rationally calculate, he believed that laws should ban harmful behavior, provided there was a victim involved. Crimes without victims, consensual crimes, and acts of self-defense should not be subject to criminal law because they produced more good than evil. Laws should set specific punishments (pain) for specific crimes in order to motivate people to act one way rather than another. But since punishments were themselves evil mischief, the utility principle (the idea that the greatest good should be sought for the greatest number) only justifies their use to exclude a greater evil and only then in just sufficient measure to outweigh the profit of crime and to bring the offender into conformity with the law (Bentham [1765] 1970).

Bentham argued that punishments should be scaled so that an offender rationally calculating whether to commit a crime would choose the lesser offense. For example, if rape and homicide were both punished by execution, the rapist might be more inclined to kill the victim. Doing so would reduce the risk of identification and execution. But if more severe punishment resulted from murder than rape, the offender would be more likely to refrain from the more harmful crime.

In contrast to Beccaria, Bentham believed that in the case of the repeat offender it might be necessary to increase the punishment to outweigh the profit from offenses likely to be committed. Also, Bentham introduced the notion that different kinds of offenses required different types of punishment, ranging from confinement for failure to conform to the law, such as nonpayment of taxes, to enforced labor in a penal institution for those guilty of theft. Like Beccaria, he rejected the death penalty because it brought more harm than good and therefore violated his utility principle. Instead, Bentham preferred fines and prison. Judges could equalize fines and stage them in progressive severity. Similarly, prison allows judges to vary the time served and set terms at different levels for different offenses. Indeed, Bentham was responsible for designing the ultimate disciplinary prison, known as the Panoptican (all seeing), designed "to control not only the freedom of movement of those confined but their minds as well" (Shover and Einstadter 1988, 202; Foucault 1977). Bentham's prison was a circular structure organized so that a guard in the center could see into each cell without being seen by the prisoner, with the result that prisoners would believe they were under constant surveillance. He also believed that this disciplinary system should extend to factories, hospitals and schools. None were built in England, although Pennsylvania and Illinois constructed Panoptican-type prisons.

Limitations of Classical Theory

Although radical and influential for their times, the ideas discussed here were not without certain contradictions. First and foremost was the assumption that people were equal. What could this really mean? Were all people equal? Did equality include people of different intellectual ability? What about children? What about the insane? Did equal mean to the classicists that men and women were equal? Second, how could a system designed to allow some people to create more wealth than others, and therefore to become materially unequal, maintain that in law all persons were formally equal? How could there be equal punishments for equal crimes without taking into account differences in wealth? Third, why do some people commit more crimes than others, if they are all equally endowed with reason? It soon became necessary to revise classical ideas to fit emerging realities.

Neoclassical Revisions

The first significant legislation based on classical concepts was the famous French Code of 1791. Following the successful French Revolution of 1789, the victors focused on equality and justice. In seeking fairness and the elimination of discriminatory misuses of justice, the French code of 1791 treated all offenders equally—regardless of individual circumstances. But the French soon recognized that justice required some discretion and latitude. Pure classicism took no account of individual differences. Yet differences were obvious. For example, should children receive the same penalties as adults? What should happen to those with limited mental facilities? What about women who had long been denied equal status to men?

In 1819, the French revised the code of 1791 to permit judges some discretion. This neoclassical position recognized "age, mental condition and extenuating circumstances" (Vold and Bernard 1986, 26). Despite these changes, the basic underlying assumptions—that humans are rational, calculating, and hedonistic—remained the cornerstone of criminal justice policy.

Thus fifty-five years after Beccaria first presented his original thesis, an actual justice system incorporated the new revisions. These changes have remained virtually the same since. But the growth of scientific criminology in the nineteenth and early twentieth centuries led to a considerable slippage, since the focus of criminal justice shifted away from the criminal act and how equal individuals chose it toward what kinds of individuals would choose such acts and why other kinds would not.

We shall discuss the rise of scientific criminology in the next chapter, but it is important here to recognize certain parallel histories that led to the resurrection of a version of neoclassicism, or postclassicism, that has become known as contemporary rational choice theory. Crucial in this history is the emergence of modernism, science, and progress during the nineteenth and twentieth centuries. This is the notion that scientific laws, the development of rational thought, and empirical research could help society progress into a better world. Harnessing the forces of science and incorporation of its discourse into government policies served to legitimate government domination and control. The application of scientific methods to all fields, including criminal justice, combined with a political climate in which government grew in its responsibility to serve the public, soon translated into more power for the state and more discretion for its institutions.

There was a growing observation that modern (i.e., scientific) solutions, while producing massive changes in technological development, also brought untold human suffering and increased rather than reduced social problems, resulting in a questioning of faith in science. Nowhere was this more apparent than in the failure of scientific principles applied to the problems of crime and justice. These had brought a considerable abandonment of the principles of equality of the individual before the law as increased discretion was used in courts and by judges to adjust sentences to fit the particular needs of individual offenders.

Against this background, by the 1970s a familiar call was being heard from those challenging the power and growing discretion of the state in matters of justice. These postclassicists were calling for a return to equality standards, protesting that discretion based on the dubious claims of science and social science had gone too far. Two developments in this regard were particularly important. The first is justice theory and related developments toward a conservative "law and order" approach to crime control, and the second is rational choice theory and its extension, routine activities theory.

Criminal Justice Implications: The Move to "Justice" Theory

By the 1960s, classical theory had become little more than a footnote to scientific and sociological theories of crime. In the decades following 1859, Darwinist evolutionary ideas, science, and technology promised to liberate humankind from the philosophical speculations of the Enlightenment era. The scientific search for the causes of crime (which we discuss in detail later) displaced the armchair philosophers of rationality and reason. The new scientific method relied on the manipulation of variables, observation, and measurement and employed specific rules that had to be followed. It forced criminal justice policy to take account of individual and social differences, especially differences in sentencing practices. In attempting to address individual differences, criminal justice returned to discretionary sentencing, which some saw as similar to the policies existing prior to the classical movement. But instead of arbitrary justice, scientific evidence justified disparate sentences based on offender "needs." Offenders were diagnosed as having specific problems and were deemed to need sentences (treatment) based on their diagnosed problems. Thus reliance on the scientific method, diagnosis, and rehabilitation shifted the emphasis from deterrence to treatment under what was termed "rehabilitative justice."

The outcome, however, was the same as before. Convicted offenders received different sentences for similar crimes and different treatments depending on the diagnosis of cause. For example, one juvenile offender might get sent to a detention center, another to probation, and a third to boot camp, all for the same offense, because a social worker's report claimed that each individual offender had different needs.

By the 1970s, critics raised two central problems. First, for all the effort at rehabilitation, did it work? The rehabilitation skeptics answered, "Nothing works." Martinson (1974, 25), an advocate of rehabilitation, concluded that with few and isolated exceptions "rehabilitative efforts . . . have had no effect on recidivism."

The second charge against rehabilitative justice was that it was unfair. In the context of the slide from classical principles, some called for the "rehabilitation of punishment." Bottomley (1979) argued that rehabilitative justice "culminated in the entire notion of the indeterminate sentence coming under attack for its therapeutic pretensions in a situation where not only was hard evidence of therapeutic effectiveness lacking . . . but where indeterminacy created unacceptable tensions for prisoners and their families, providing further scope for discretionary decision-making by the executive and instruments of control within penal institutions" (1979, 127).

Justice theorists pointed to a tendency for rehabilitation and treatment to drift toward discretion and inconsistency. They claimed that in spite of its advocates' emphasis on understanding and concern, rehabilitation often inflicted more cruelty than the punitive approach. They despised the "discriminatory use of penal sanctions" and the "wide margins of discretionary power in the hands of police, district attorneys, judges, correctional administrators, parole boards, and parole agents" (American Friends Service Committee 1971, 124). This position has a similar ring to Beccaria's earlier criticisms about preclassical punishment. These new critics argued that allowing prosecutors and judges the flexibility to plea-bargain, to grant concessions, or to pass harsh sentences based on individual circumstances resulted in "a system of wide disparities in charging and sentencing similarly situated individuals, a system that has lost sight of its goals in its eagerness to dispose of cases" (Heumann and Loftin 1979, 393).

In response to these problems, a move back toward policies based on classical principles developed. From the ashes of rehabilitation skepticism rose the justice model, or just deserts model (Fogel 1975). This model reflected many of the original principles presented by Beccaria and Bentham. The justice model contained four key elements: (1) limited discretion at all procedural stages of the criminal justice system, (2) greater openness and accountability, (3) punishment justified by the last crime or series of crimes (neither deterrence goals nor offender characteristics justify punishment), and (4) punishment commensurate with the seriousness of the crime, based on actual harm done and the offender's culpability.

The move back to justice gave priority to punishment "as a desirable value and goal in its own right"; this was different from the traditional justification of penal goals, such as deterrence or rehabilitation (Bottomley 1979, 139).

An application of these revised classical principles was a renewed emphasis on equal punishment for equal crimes. This required replacing the broad range of sentences available for particular classes of felonies with a "tariff system" of determinate sentences. Each punishment was a fixed sentence with only a narrow range of adjustments allowed for seriousness or mitigating circumstances (Fogel 1975, 254). Perhaps the best example of a tariff system is the parking fine or speeding ticket for which each offender, regardless of circumstances, receives the same penalty, and the penalties increase by fixed amounts for offenses of increasing seriousness.

The Conservative Law and Order Turn

Instead of the neoclassical influence waning, as many predicted, it continues to exist today and as one commentator says, its "demise is greatly exaggerated" (Schmalleger 1999, 163). Combined in a conservative or "law and order approach" to crime control, the prevailing just deserts model holds that crime is freely chosen and rewarding and, therefore, it demands both deterrent and retributive responses. This is not only because of the harm done, but also because the offender knew the consequences before committing the crime. Although this position alters the original classical principles (see Einstadter and Henry 1995 for a discussion of the differences between classical theory and conservative theory), it is popular with politicians and, as Schmalleger points out, "is now in its ascendancy" (1999, 163). The conservative distortion of neoclassical thought provides a formidable and popular election platform, when combined with other law and order elements such as "boot camp" for juvenile offenders, "incapacitation" (the idea of removing an offender's ability to commit further offenses), mandatory sentencing (which fixes the mini-mum sentence for various crimes), truth in sentencing (requiring judges to state the actual sentence that will be served), three strikes and you're out laws (requiring three-time felony convictions to serve long sentences, typically life without the possibility of parole), and the death penalty as a general deterrent. However, the reality of criminal justice is often differ-ent from the rhetoric and the result of failed conservative policies, and the accumulated evidence on the ineffectiveness of some of the key elements is beginning to lead to a rethinking during the early part of the twenty-first century. Below we look at four of these: determinate sentencing, inca-pacitation, three-strikes laws, and the death penalty.

Determinate Sentencing

Determinate sentences are designed to make justice "fair" and to make potential offenders aware of what sentences they can expect for commit-ting specific crimes. Several questions remain, however. Does determi-nate sentencing reduce the sentencing disparity between those sentenced for similar types of crimes? Does it increase levels of incarceration? Does any increase in incarceration from determinate sentencing result in early release of more serious offenders? Finally, does determinate sentencing increase the tendency for alternative systemic discretion, such as plea bargaining?

Evidence from research on state-level sentencing reform shows that the policy of determinate sentencing reduces sentencing disparity (Blumstein et al. 1983; Tonry 1988) and increases prison populations at both state (Kramer and Lubitz 1985; Goodstein and Hepburn 1986; Hepburn and Goodstein 1986; Bogan 1990) and federal institutions (Mays 1989). One exception seems to be in Minnesota. The effects of Minnesota's determi-nate sentencing reform show overwhelmingly that the policy of sentenc-ing guidelines has reduced sentencing disparity, but it has done so without producing increased prison populations (Blumstein et al. 1983; Miethe and Moore 1985). When judges are concerned about prison over-crowding, however, they are motivated to circumvent the guidelines. In doing so, they shift the burden of incarcerating offenders to the local level, resulting in increases in jail incarceration rates (D'Alessio and Stolzenberg 1995; Miethe and Moore 1989).

Michigan Abandons Mandatory Sentencing
for Drug Offenses after a 23-year Experiment

On Christmas Day 2002, in one of his last acts before leaving office, Governor John Engler signed a bill that brought an end to Michigan's inflexible mandatory minimum sentencing laws for drug convictions.

During the 1970s, following New York's lead, several states, including Michigan, enacted tough laws that mandated a minimum sentence for people convicted of major drug offenses. A 1978 law mandated minimum sentences of 20 years to life without parole, even for a first offense, for possession of 650 grams (23 ounces) of certain "hard" drugs such as cocaine and heroin. The laws were passed during a time when there was much concern about crack cocaine epidemics in the nation's cities and fear that well-organized armed and violent gangs, such as Detroit's Young Boys Inc, were overtaking the streets. The tough mandatory sentencing laws were seen as a way of removing "drug Kingpins." The effects of the law were to incarcerate lower level young offenders. The prisons became overcrowded and there seemed to be little effect on the drug problem.

In response, the judicial system began to look for ways around the sentencing laws. "Many prosecutors now reduce charges through plea-bargaining to avoid what they see as excessively harsh penalties, said Michigan Department of Corrections spokesperson Russ Marlan. Judges also use an option that permits them to depart from mandatory-minimum sentences if they can find compelling reasons to do so" (Heinlein 2002, p. 9A).

By 1998 Michigan's lawmakers slightly relaxed the mandatory minimums for non-drug offenses but by December 2002, the Michigan Legislature repealed the mandatory drug sentencing laws completely, allowing judges' full discretion. Under the new law tough sentences are possible but judges will be able to use their discretion to not only order shorter sentences but also give alternatives to punishment, such as drug treatment. The Michigan legislation leads the nation in reforming drug laws, placing the sentences for drug offenses back in the indeterminate sentencing guideline structure.

Adapted from Gary Heinlein, "Michigan Eases Drug Sentences: Judges' Discretion Replaces Mandatory Terms for Offenders," *Detroit News and Free Press*, December 29, 2002, A1.

At the federal level, Lanier and Miller (1995) found several other problems with determinate sentencing. Most of these have to do with plea bargaining, which results in over 90 percent of criminal defendants pleading guilty to lesser charges in exchange for having the more serious charge (and therefore sentence) dropped. Any plea bargaining necessarily circumvents the principles of classical theory and the intentions of determinate sentencing guidelines. A major question therefore becomes, does determinate sentencing increase the use of plea bargains? Several commentators predicted that when judges could no longer select from a wide variety of sanctions, the prosecutor's discretion would increase (Sarat 1978; Horowitz 1977). Research has confirmed that in spite of formal compliance with mandatory laws, where both judges and prosecutors consider the required penalties to be too harsh, they circumvent the guidelines. Thus they can avoid mandatory minimum sentences by dismissing charges or acquitting defendants (Cohen and Tonry 1983). The logical solution seems to be to eliminate plea bargains, which would also prevent any tendency for police to "overcharge" on the assumption that a plea bargain will occur. The recommendation has a long history (National Advisory Commission 1971), but so far only one state (Alaska) and a few county jurisdictions have implemented it.

Simply put, policies that mandate justice and equity do not guarantee equal justice unless the realities of the system as a whole are taken into account. These total system effects are further complicated by the fact that sentence length is also affected by other considerations such as probation officers' presentence reports (see Lanier and Miller 1995).

In conclusion, the introduction of mandatory sentencing, although theoretically consistent with the ideals of classical theory, is ultimately faced with the realities of a system that has its own inertia. The U.S. justice system is so vast and so encumbered with the institutional practices associated with other correctional ideologies that changes to any part of it that do not take account of the whole are unlikely to succeed. Moreover, in spite of reformers' intentions to improve justice and equity, they are more likely to produce unintended effects that may even counter those objectives. In summary, the existence of judicial discretion, whether through plea bargains, reduced sentences for circumstances, or parolee's early release, seriously undermines neoclassical principles, but so too does the selection of some dimensions of the classical principles, such as certainty of punishment and deterrence, without also incorporating the others, such as minimal and proportionate punishment. Nowhere is this more evident than the politically popular extension of the mandatory prison sentence idea known as "three-strikes" laws.

Three-Strikes Laws

It might seem strange that a nation as complex and sophisticated as the United States would formulate a corner of its criminal justice policy on a baseball analogy, but that is precisely what three strikes and you're out laws offered. As another attempt to embody the classical principle of "certainty of punishment," three-strikes laws were introduced in the early 1990s largely in response to the drug problem. More consistent with Bentham's idea that repeat offenders should receive greater sentences to outweigh the profit from offenses likely to be committed, this concept resulted in long and harsh sentences for persons convicted of three felonies, even if these were nonviolent drug offenses and even if the third offense was less serious than the previous two (even purse-snatching and shoplifting count as a strike). These laws, a variation of the mandatory minimum sentence laws, imposed stiff penalties for the third conviction, such as twenty-five years to life under the 1994 California law. In 1995 thirteen states had three-strikes laws and Georgia even had a two-strikes law that resulted in a life sentence without parole (Rush 2000, 321).

Here again we see the distortion of classical principles, exaggerating one element (higher punishment for repeaters) at the expense of the others (e.g., proportionate punishment for the crime related to the harm committed). The objective again was deterrence; the reality was again different. Consider the case of Jona Rottenberg, arrested in MacArthur Park for possession of less than one gram of cocaine. Under California law she faces twenty-five years to life (Pape 1999); a man who shoplifted $153 worth of children's videos from Kmart will be imprisoned until 2046, and another man who stole three golf clubs worth $400 was convicted for life. Critics argue that not only is three-strikes punishment excessive and unnecessary, but it also contributes to the problem of clogged courts and prison overcrowding, as well as increasing the determination of third-time offenders to avoid being caught (Schmalleger 1999, 138–139). The likely effect is quite the reverse of the classical principle that offenders choose the lesser offense; rather, they will calculate that it is in their interests to choose additional and more serious offenses to avoid apprehension and conviction. Moreover, the policy was seriously questioned by the empirical evidence on its effectiveness at incapacitating the most serious offenders (CECP 1997). Indeed, while advocates claim that crime in some states, such as California, has gone down 40 percent since the three-strikes laws were implemented in 1994, critics, such as the Sentencing Project, argue that other states have shown a similar crime reduction but do not have three-strikes laws, such as New York (41 percent), Massachusetts (33 percent), and Washington, D.C. (31 percent), questioning the contribution of three-strikes (Kasindorf 2002, A3).

By November 2002 the Supreme Court was considering the case against a Court of Appeals ruling that California's three-strikes law was unconstitutional because it violated the Eighth Amendment ban on cruel and unusual punishment, which had ruled, consistent with original classical principles, "that the punishment for a third-strike crime cannot be grossly disproportionate to the offense committed" (Kasindorf 2002, 3A). One of the main justifications for three-strikes laws is their incapacitation effects: Criminals who are locked away for twenty-five years are not going to victimize their communities. Let us examine this element in the conservative distortion of classical thought.

Incapacitation

Incapacitation or "containment," as it is also called, is the penal policy of taking the offender "out of circulation" by a variety of means, the most common of which is the use of confinement in prison, which is designed "to deny offenders the opportunity to commit additional offenses and further victimize society for the duration of their incarceration" (Hussey 1997, 120). Incapacitation policy related to penal confinement asserts that putting adjudicated offenders "in prison" stops them from practicing criminal behaviors and the "outside world" is correspondingly safer, albeit temporarily. It is based on a set of questionable empirically derived assumptions such as the finding that 50 percent of all crimes are committed by 6 percent of the population of some cities (Wolfgang, Figlio, and Sellin 1972), and that a five-year sentence for any felony would reduce the rate of crime by 15 percent (Greenwood 1983; Murray 1997). Some critics see this "actuarial" approach as a "new penology" that is less interested in the lives of offenders than in risk management and case processing, in short, "techniques of identifying, classifying and managing groups sorted by levels of dangerousness" (Carrabine 2001, 147; Feely and Simon 1992). For others, incapacitation is an illusion in its claim of removing offenders from the rest of the population. As Milovanovic and Henry (2003) point out, the costs of prison affect everyone, and the imprisonment exerts an impact on the families of the convicted, their communities, and race relations, since a disproportionate number of those convicted are African American. They point out that we pay the economic cost of the massively expanded prison programs, 2 million incarcerated in our state and federal prisons and jails in 2002, compared to less than 200,000 in the 1970s. And this is for a relatively small reduction in the actual crime rate of 5 percent, which itself is only questionably attributable to the policy of incapacitation (Currie 1998). Moreover, the "new penology" of incapacitation has accentuated the issue of race in American society, since one in three African American males between twenty and twenty-nine are in prison, on probation, or on parole (Mauer 1997). This permeates the mind-set of some African Americans outside of prison who withdraw support for society's formal institutions, especially from government and law enforcement.

Deterrence and the Death Penalty

From the criminal justice policy perspective, unless offenders think rationally before committing their crimes there is little point to the deterrence argument. A second related issue is that unless the meaning of the gain or satisfactions to the offender can be measured, there is no precise way to design punishments that will counter the potential gain. A third issue in deterrence theory is the extent to which potential offenders using rational thought processes perceive the same risks and severity in punishments set by the legal system and how well they know its penalties (Geerken and Gove 1975). Indeed, this is a pillar of classical theory. If people's perceptions of sanctions are more different than they are similar, the issue becomes one of scientific criminology (i.e., to determine how and why they are different). A related issue is what makes perceptions of sanctions different? If the answer has to do with differences between people rather than differences in information, then the focus again should be on what causes individual differences. Not surprisingly, classical (and rational choice theories, which we look at later) assume that individual differences are "relatively much less significant in accounting for variations in criminal action between different individuals, different groups and over different time-periods than are variations in the control exercised by perceived incentives and disincentives" (Roshier 1989, 74).

Illustrating the idea of deterrence is the contemporary example of capital punishment. Despite the link between classical theory and deterrence, it is important to remember that classical theorists, as we saw earlier, were actually opposed to the death penalty (Beccaria supported it in the extreme case of attempting to overthrow the state). Furthermore, although U.S. public opinion consistently supports the use of the death penalty—the 1990s shows the highest numbers since the 1950s at 79 percent in favor of death for convicted murderers (BJS 1996: 181; Bohm 1991)—virtually all the empirical research evidence shows that execution does not have a deterrent effect on crime or murder.

Research by the economist Isaac Ehrlich (1975) linked an offender's decision to commit crime to his or her perception of the risk of being executed; Ehrlich claimed that every additional execution would save seven or eight victims from murder. A replication study by Bowers and Pierce (1975) refuted Ehrlich's findings, however, and went on to show that executions actually increase the homicide rate (Bowers and Pierce 1980). They found that over a period of fifty-seven years the homicide rate in New York state went up by two for each additional execution. This is known as the "brutalization" thesis, first put forward by Beccaria and empirically documented by Dann (1935) and Forst (1983). The argument is that the more violence people see by legitimate government, the more numbed they become to its pain, and the more acceptable it becomes to commit violent acts, including murder. The brutalization effects of capital punishment are supported by global research showing that a decline in homicide rates in countries around the world followed the abolition of the death penalty. Bailey and Peterson (1989) found that executions do not deter criminal homicides. However, Cochran and Chamlin (2000) in a more sophisticated analysis divided homicide into two types: nonstranger felony murders (murder between intimates and acquaintances) and argument-based homicides between strangers. They found that state executions were positively related to the brutalization hypothesis (homicides may actually increase) yet deterrence was effective at reducing nonstranger murders.

Some of the best studies on the deterrence effect of punishment have been conducted by Ray Paternoster. Paternoster and his colleagues (Paternoster et al. 1983, 1985) show that the perceived risk of certainty of arrest is not constant but declines with experience in committing offenses. Indeed, a study on recidivist property offenders shows that although they may use the rational thought process, their perception of sanctions did not deter them because they thought that they would not get caught, that any prison sentences would be relatively short, and that prison was non-threatening (Tunnell 1992).

Paternoster (1989), in researching the effects of certainty and severity on decisions by high school students to offend, found that certainty of punishment had more impact than severity of punishment (which had no significant impact on the delinquency decision). Moreover, he found that the greatest effect came from the perceived certainty of informal sanctions from peers or parents rather than any sanctions from the legal system, a finding supported by others (Hollinger and Clark 1983; Grasmick and Bursik 1990; Williams and Hawkins 1989). However, Pogarsky (2002) found severity to have more effect than certainty with "deterrable" university students. As Akers (1994, 57) points out, traditionally conceived deterrence from legal sanctions, even if these are a catalyst to informal social sanctions, is undermined by such evidence. Indeed, in a review of the overall evidence, Akers concludes:

> Studies of both objective and perceptual deterrence often do find negative correlations beteen certainty of criminal penalties and the rate or frequency of criminal behavior, but the correlations tend to be low. Severity of punishment has an even weaker effect on crime. Neither the existence of capital punishment nor the certainty of the death penalty has ever had a significant effect on the rate of homicide. . . . The empirical validity of deterrence theory is limited. (1994, 54)

Not only is the deterrence effect of capital punishment highly questioned, and its brutalization effect agreed on, but, like incapacitation, capital punishment disproportionately impacts races, with 50 percent of those on death row being from minority groups; although African Americans account for only 12 percent of the U.S. population, they make up 40 percent of those executed. Finally, serious questions were raised in the late 1990s about how many innocents have been executed, as DNA evidence was found to exonerate numerous convicted death-row inmates, resulting in a moratorium on the death penalty by Illinois Governor George Ryan.

Critics of deterrence theory argue that it is founded on a narrow view of humans and the reasons for their actions. They argue that "we need to develop a considerably more sophisticated theory of human behavior which explores the internal and external checks on why people do or do not engage in criminal activity. This theory must also recognize that there are a bewildering number of motivational states, rational and irrational, that lead to the commission of criminal acts" (McLaughlin 2001, 88). Some criminologists believe they have begun to do just that.

Redefining Rational Choice: Situational Factors and Routine Activities Theory

Political and philosophical backlash against the rehabilitation models of the 1960s created a second development that had less to do with the administration of justice and more to do with how offenders decide to commit a crime. This was a renewed and more refined interest in classical economic ideas of rational choice. A principal advocate of this renewed idea was Ronald Clarke, who at the time was head of the British government's crime research unit. Clarke and his colleague Derek Cornish (Clarke and Cornish 1983; Cornish and Clarke 1986) developed a more sophisticated understanding of how people make rational choices about whether to act—and about whether to commit crime. They spawned a whole new direction in postclassical contemporary criminological research that looked at the situational factors that influence offenders to choose to commit crime. In the United States, Marcus Felson and Lawrence Cohen (Cohen and Felson 1979; Felson 1986) were working on similar ideas, although they were looking at how the regular daily patterns of citizens' behavior create or inhibit the opportunities for offenders to commit crime. Clarke and Felson would eventually collaborate together at Rutgers University, where Clarke became the dean of criminal justice. Let us explore their ideas in more detail.

Rational choice theories explain how some people consciously and rationally choose to commit criminal acts. Consider the example of burglary. Beyond the monetary motive as a factor that leads to burglary, research shows that burglars decide to commit their offenses through a variety of rational decisions (Walsh 1980; Bennett and Wright 1984). These are based on situational circumstances, including their mood (Nee and Taylor 1988). Consider the questions a burglar might ask: Which area offers the best burglary targets—middle-class suburban housing or wealthy residential areas? Does it matter if the occupant is at home? Is burglary likely to be more successful during the day when people are out on short trips, when they are away on vacation, or at night when they are home? Do neighbors watch each other's houses? Will the method of entry to the property attract undue attention and is there a system of surveillance? Once entrance to the residence has been gained, what kinds of goods will be taken—jewelry, antiques, electronics, or cash? Are there two entrances so that one can serve as an escape route? What means are available to dispose of the goods? These are just some of the questions a burglar might ask in his or her rational choice approach to the crime.

Some "professional" burglars specialize in certain property and plan their entry into a target house over a period of time, whereas others are occasional opportunists. One study found that the most important environmental factor in target choice was the existence of two escape routes, one at the front and another at the rear of the building, especially where the rear exit has vegetation obscuring visibility (Nee and Taylor 1988). Dogs and alarms are only conditionally a deterrent. Occupancy in the day is checked, typically by knocking on the front or rear door and, if someone answers, making up an excuse about needing directions. But some burglars actually prefer the residents at home and asleep because there usually is more cash, jewelry, and checkbooks available (Nee and Taylor 1988).

According to rational choice theorists, then, potential offenders consider the net benefits gained from committing crime. Offenders, as in the burglar example, use free will and weigh the perceived costs against the potential benefits. This weighing is called choice structuring. Offenders choose to engage in criminal acts if their rough calculation suggests the action might result in net gain. As we can see, circumstances, situation, and opportunities affect their decision, since these are factors to be considered when calculating the cost/benefit estimations of risk.

Contemporary rational choice theory differs from classical ideas in the degree of rationality attributed to offenders. Both rational or situational choice theory (Clarke and Cornish 1983 1985) and routine activities theory (Cohen and Felson 1979; Cohen and Machalek 1988) emphasize the limits of rational thought in the decision to commit crime. They claim that criminal decisions are neither fully rational nor thoroughly thought through. A variety of individual and environmental factors affect the choices made. Instead of pure rational calculation, offenders exercise "limited rationality" (Clarke and Cornish 1983, 49–50). Offenders, like everyone else, vary in their perception, motives, and skills and their abilities to analyze a situation and to structure choices toward a desirable outcome (Cornish and Clarke 1987; see Figure 3.1).

Conceptual and Empirical Limitations: What the Research Shows

Both the rational or situational choice and routine activities theories make some dubious assumptions. They claim the benefits of one type of crime are not equally available from another or from the same crime in another place. Criminologists call this the problem of "crime displacement."

FIGURE 3.1   Cornish and Clarke's Reasoning Criminal

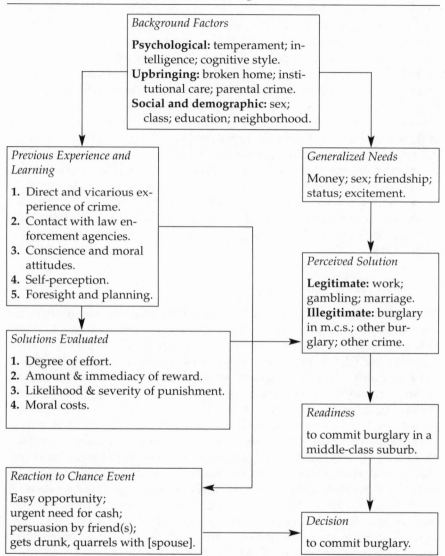

SOURCE: Derek Cornish and Ronald Clarke (eds.). 1986. *The Reasoning Criminal.*
New York: Springer-Verlag, p. 3. Reprinted with permission of the publisher.

Consider, for example, whether a shoplifter is likely to become a robber if he or she reasons that this will reduce the chance of success. Similarly, would a shoplifter at a high-security store switch to a low-security store? Indeed, Cornish and Clarke (1987, 935) admit that the readiness to substitute one offense for another depends on whether "alternative offenses share characteristics which the offender considers salient to his or her goals and abilities." As many people living in areas surrounding former drug neighborhoods have learned, however, one neighborhood's cleanup can become another's crime problem. As we shall see later, there are other problems with rational choice theories as evidenced by empirical research.

We can evaluate the contribution of classical and rational choice theories to criminology at several levels. Space precludes an extensive review and critique (for these, see Akers 1990, 1994). It is necessary, however, to briefly summarize the evidence in relation to (1) rational choice in the motivation to commit crime and (2) the extent to which rational choice precautions by potential victims affect the probability of subsequent victimization.

Evidence on the Rational Choice Decisionmaking Process

The central issue in rational choice theory is whether potential offenders use a rational thought process in their decision to commit crime. We have already argued that rational choice, even as proclaimed by its advocates (Cornish and Clarke 1986), involves a limited notion of rationality ("partial rationality" or "soft rationality") and that any theory assuming "pure" rationality "has virtually no empirical validity" (Akers 1994, 58). Studies focusing on part of the process in committing a crime, such as target selection by burglars (Maguire and Bennett 1982; Bennett and Wright 1984; Rengert and Wasilchick 1985), "provide considerable empirical support for a 'limited rationality' view of decision making by lawbreakers" (Gibbons 1994, 124). For example, Nee and Taylor's (1988) interviews with fifty convicted residential burglars support the view of the offender as a "rational" agent, making decisions under a variety of prevailing circumstances. Similarly, Bennett's (1986) study of rational choice by opiate users challenges the arguments about crime displacement, because he shows that their original motivation is the particular opiate drug culture and that in its absence alternative subcultures may not be as appealing. Finally, Vaughan's study of rational choice decisionmaking by corporate organizations in the case of NASA's fatal decision to launch *Challenger* leads her to conclude that the rationality of corporate officials is a complex process, affected by a corporate organizational bias toward taking risky decisions and differing little from the rationality of robbers and burglars in its "bounded" nature (Vaughan 1998).

As Akers (1990; 1994, 60) points out, however, when other factors that constrain rationality are factored into the decisionmaking process (such as affective ties to parents, moral beliefs, and peer influences) it is questionable whether what is being supported is rational choice or the other theories that assume nonrational factors, such as social learning theory (Chapter 6) or social bonding theory (Chapter 7).

Evidence on Routine Activities and Crime

In addition to rational thought processes and the deterrent effects of sanctions, a third factor in the equation of the criminal event is the coincidence of these in time and place. According to routine activities theory, the presence of motivated offenders and suitable targets in the absence of capable guardians is more likely to lead to crime. Leaving aside the question of what makes a motivated offender, empirical research has focused on targets and guardians. The main findings suggest that certain areas, known as "hot spots," account for most victimizations and that people who go out to these places, such as bars, dances, parties, shopping centers, and so on, at night are more vulnerable to being victimized than those who stay home (Messner and Blau 1987; Kennedy and Forde 1990a, 1990b). In the case of property crimes such as burglary, however, victims' absence may seem more conducive to crime than their presence. For example, the more people are absent from home, as happens when both parents are working, the more likely they are to be victimized. O'Shea found that "ten of eleven predictors of burglary victimization reflected the efficacy of security measures" (2000, 162). Robinson (2000) found further support for altering physical and social environments to reduce risk of victimization.

Some studies however have been criticized for relying too much on stereotyped conceptions of crime and of the different kinds of offender (Nee and Taylor 1988) and ignoring hidden crime and gender issues. Indeed, because of the link between intimates and violence (see Chapter 2), those who stay at home may be more likely to be victimized (Messner and Tardiff 1985; Maxfield 1987). In particular, DeKeseredy and Schwartz (1996) point out that women actually suffer a greater likelihood of personal victimization in the home from husbands and partners than from going out. Furthermore, they argue for a feminist routine activities theory that explains why college campuses are dangerous places for women, whose susceptibility to sexual attack is increased by alcohol and socializing with sexually predatory men in the absence of capable guardians. Again, the explanation of why men are sexually predatory has more to do with nonrational choice theory, since it relies on notions of socialization into peer subcultures supportive of sexual exploitation and on the social construction of masculinity (see Chapter 11).

Policy Applications of Rational Choice and Routine Activities Theories

Rational choice theorists suggest there are differences in the circumstances or the situations in which offenders select their crimes. As we have seen, these different situations can affect the criminal's choice of target (Clark and Cornish 1983, 49). In short, these theories emphasize crime as the outcome of "choices and decisions made within a context of situational constraints and opportunities" (Clarke and Cornish 1983, 8). Thus a central policy issue becomes identifying the environmental triggers that facilitate criminal action.

A major element in the preventive policy of rational choice is to manipulate the opportunity structure in a particular environment to reduce the likelihood that offenders will choose to commit crime. In the case of the burglar, more than one car in the driveway and several lights on in the house might indicate more than one person is at home and not asleep. Observant neighbors might also act as a deterrent. Moriarty and Williams (1996) found the absence of homeowners between 6:00 P.M. and 11:00 P.M. made the residences most likely to be victimized. Manipulation of the environment, then, is designed to make the choice of crime more difficult and costly (Clarke and Cornish 1983, 48; Cornish and Clarke 1987). This leads to a variety of situational crime prevention strategies. The practice, known as "target hardening," decreases the chance that someone or something will be a victim of crime. Target hardening requires the potential victim to be more active in the process of crime control by taking steps to secure their poroperty. Target hardening has been particularly prominent in the related theory of routine activities (Cohen and Felson 1979, 589).

We have seen that routine activities theory considers how everyday life brings together at a particular place and moment potential offenders, crime targets, and vulnerability. As is clear from the burglary example, the presence of guardians is a key factor affecting vulnerability (Felson 1987, 911; Cohen and Felson 1979; Felson and Cohen 1981; Felson 1986). Therefore, increasing the presence of capable, caring, intimate guardians (such as friends, relatives, and neighbors) of potential victims reduces the probability of victimization. Walking with another person to a parking lot at night offers more protection against a solitary robber than walking alone. Another strategy is for potential victims to change or vary their routine activities, behavior, and lifestyle. This makes them less vulnerable to personal crimes. Farrington and Welsh (2002) conducted a meta analysis on the effects of street lighting and found mixed results in the United States. However, when research from Britain was included, improved street lighting led to reductions in crime.

One major study (Weisburd 1997) suggests that many additional environmental manipulations show how a school may reduce its vulnerability to crime. These include access control, offender deflection, facilitator control, entry/exit screening, formal surveillance, employee surveillance, natural surveillance, and rule setting. While each practice involves empirical research on why offenders choose to refrain from, rather than commit, crime, it is clear that since the 1990s in the case of schools, the increase in serious violence has led many schools adopt such environmental measures under "safe school" programs. The critical question is, have such environmental manipulations transformed schools into institutions more like prisons (Crews and Tipton 2002)? In the process have we undermined the very purpose that the institution was designed to serve such that the controls are more destructive than the original problem (Hinkle and Henry 2000)?

Characteristics of Security in American Educational Institutions and the Penal System

American Public School	*American Correctional System*
Metal Detectors	Metal Detectors
Identification Badges	Identification Badges
Uniforms or Clothing Standard	Uniforms
Surveillance Cameras	Surveillance Cameras
Searches	Searches
(Personal Property, Lockers, etc.)	(Personal Property, Housing Units)
Teachers Use of 2-Way Radios	Correctional Personnel Use 2-Way Radios
Panic Button in Classrooms	Correctional Officer Panic Button

Characteristics of Security in American Educational Institutions and the Penal System

American Public School	*American Correctional System*
Locked Perimeter Doors	Locked Perimeter Doors
School Resource Officers	Correctional Officers
Controlled Movements	Controlled Movements
In-School Suspension/ Detention	Solitary Confinement/ Protective Custody

---

SOURCE: Gordon A. Crews and Jeffrey A. Tipton, *A Comparison of Public School and Prison Security Measures: Too Much of a Good Thing?* (2002).

This kind of response to the fear of crime has created considerable controversy. Critics, particularly feminists, argue that routine activities theory blames the victim. This is especially true for rape victims. In effect, potential male rapists are forcing women to change behavior, lifestyle, and even appearance. The policy approach of this theory appeals to those favoring cost cutting and simplistic technical solutions to crime. The perspective may lead to a siege mentality, however, as society increasingly orients itself "to ever-increasing oversight and surveillance, fortification of homes, restrictions on freedom of movement, and the proliferation of guns for alleged self-defense" (Einstadter and Henry 1995, 71).

In spite of its theoretical and empirical limitations, the idea that criminals choose to commit crime reflects the U.S. public's psyche. The consequential strategy of denying an offender the opportunity to engage in crime by manipulating the physical environment through target hardening, environmental design, and other measures gives people a sense of control over their fear of crime. Regardless of its effectiveness, rational choice theory is valuable on these grounds alone. A fundamental question remains, however, of whether crimes by the powerful should also be subject to rational choice analysis and environmental manipulation.

Policy and Crimes of the Powerful

Should we place surveillance cameras in corporate boardrooms and corridors of power? It is not just individuals who use rational thought processes to satisfy their goals without regard for the harm caused to others, but corporations also do this, often with deadly results. For example, there is no question that rational choice decisionmaking affects the decisions in cases of corporate crime, but rational choice theory is rarely focused on this issue.

An excellent illustration of the priority of rational cost/benefit calculation in corporate fraud is found in the case of the Ford Pinto. In the 1970s, the Ford Motor Company, under President Lee Iacocca, was trying to reclaim its lost car market from foreign competition. Both Volkswagen and Japanese carmakers had been successfully selling subcompact cars at relatively low prices. To compete, Ford designed and developed the Pinto to sell for less than $2,000. From its introduction in 1970, the Pinto soon became the fastest-selling domestic subcompact. Unfortunately, preproduction crash tests showed the vehicle's fuel tank was easily ruptured during rear-end collisions at speeds over 25 miles per hour.

However, as fatal fiery crashes began to occur involving the Pinto's inadequate gas tank, Ford made the rationally based decision not to replace it. An indication of the decision process involved that supports rational choice assumptions is available from an investigative news report of the time (Dowie 1977). This showed that the cost of making each car safe would be $11. But when multiplied by the number of cars, the sum was more costly than the expected liability from injury suits: "Although the company calculated that eleven dollars per car would make the car safe, it decided that this was too costly. They reasoned that 180 burn deaths and 180 serious burn injuries and 2,100 burned vehicles would cost $49.5 million (each death was figured at $200,000) but that recall of all the Pintos and the eleven-dollar repair would amount to $137 million" (Simon and Eitzen 1982, 99). Moreover, evidence obtained from a Ford memorandum titled "Fatalities Associated with Crash-Induced Fuel Leakage and Fires" laid out these rational calculations. As one commentator noted, "This cold calculation demonstrated Ford's lack of concern for anything but profit" (Green 1990, 129).

Deaths from dangerous gas tanks on the Pinto (and the Mercury Bobcat) were estimated by 1977 to number 500 to 900 (Dowie 1977; Box 1983, 24). In 1978, Ford was indicted by a grand jury in Indiana on three counts of reckless homicide for the deaths of three teenage girls in a fiery rear-end collision, but the company was acquitted of this criminal charge in 1980 (Cullen, Maakestad, and Cavender 1987). The Elkhart, Indiana, county prosecutor, Micheal Consentino, felt corporations, like individuals, should be held accountable for their actions (Becker, Jipson, and Bruce 2002). Also in 1978, the U.S. Department of Transportation ordered a recall of all 1971–1976 Pintos. Only then, after months of vehement denials of the problem, did Ford comply. As Green (1997, 68–69) states:

> . . . occupational violations (unlike rape, assault or drug use) are most often the result of calculated risks that seek to increase financial benefits. The vast majority of persons who commit occupational crimes seem to do so after considering the certainty, celerity, and severity of formal and nonformal consequences . . . almost all persons who plan to commit an occupational crime . . . are potentially deterrable. . . . Occupational criminals should receive a greater severity of punishment for their offenses than do street criminals because occupational offenders usually have more investment in the social order (job, respectability, education, career) and therefore perceive that they have more to lose if caught.

If rational choice theory has a place in criminology, it certainly needs to be applied to all forms of criminal harm. Policies that emerge from the theory need to go beyond the individual to include organizational and even state levels of rational choice decisionmaking (Henry 1991; Barak 1991). Consumers and clients need to develop ways to avoid their routine vulnerability, such as avoidance of relying on expert knowledge of professionals, developing cynicism over commercial and industrial processes (e.g., food production and waste disposal), and avoiding relations with corporate and government systems that use and abuse power. Fortunately some criminologists are aware of this and have begun applying both rational choice and routine activity theory to corporate and white-collar crime (Paternoster and Simpson 1993; 1996; Shover and Wright 2001; Vaughan 1998).

Summary and Conclusion

Classical theory has been credited with enhancing democracy and with reforming harsh, arbitrary, and brutal techniques of crime control, including the elimination of torture (Einstadter and Henry 1995), but its limits were soon recognized. It is overly idealistic. It proved almost as unjust to treat people the same who were clearly different as to treat people differently arbitrarily and capriciously, as had pre-Enlightenment justice. A society that celebrates individual achievement produces disparities of wealth, status, and social standing. Any attempt to provide equal punishments that ignores this reality simply provides those who can afford punitive fines or an adequate legal defense with a license to commit crime. The result of such a system is that it proves to be "more just" for some than it is for others: "For whereas the rich offender may be cushioned by his or her wealth, the poor offender, with the same sentence but little to fall back on, is punished in fact disproportionately" (Young 1981, 266). Jeffery Reiman ([1979] 1995) aptly proclaimed this in his book *The Rich Get Richer and the Poor Get Prison.*

Policy implications based on rational choice premises have both positive and negative effects on an individual's or a group's calculation. The U.S. system of criminal justice employs these principles in the due process model, but criminal justice deals with the issue very narrowly. Originally, classicists assumed that if punishment was certain, swift, and sufficiently severe the potential offender would be less likely to commit the crime. Contemporary versions of classical thoughts have reintroduced several of these ideas. Mandatory sentences and limited discretion are logical extensions of the tradition. However, determinate sentencing policies deny consideration of individual circumstances and any need for rehabilitative corrections. Advocates also do not apply the same principles to offenders who are convicted of more than one offense. Selecting some aspects of the classical model (deterrence and certainty) while ignoring others (proportionality) can lead to law and order distortions of the classical position that produce outrageous injustices (life in prison without parole for small-scale property offenses).

Should corporations that act criminally be subject to mandatory sentences and limited discretion? Alternatively, are corporations sufficiently different that these differences must be recognized when dispensing justice? And what about corporate rehabilitation?

Rational choice and routine activities theorists focus on the design, security, and surveillance measures that potential victims may take to frustrate potential offenders. The goal is to increase the difficulty, risk of apprehension, and time involved in committing crime. These same theorists, however, rarely consider applying such environmental disincentives to crimes of the powerful. Should they do so? One ramification of adopting such practices is that potential criminals may seek other, less vulnerable targets.

A further criticism of classical justice is that setting punishments equally, or even proportionately, takes no account of differences in offenders' motivation, in their ability to reason, or in their perception of the meaning and importance of punishment. It also fails to consider irrational behavior, spontaneous crimes (e.g., violent crimes committed in "the heat of the moment"), or the role of peer groups and their different effects on rationally calculating individuals. As soon as these differences are acknowledged, we are no longer dealing with a classical rational choice model. Indeed, recognition of these deficiencies coupled with scientific advances (in research methods, biophysiology, psychology, sociology, etc.) led criminologists to focus on a variety of "causes" of criminal behavior. The following chapters explore these scientific criminologies in more detail.

Summary Chart: Classical, Rational Choice, and Routine Activities Theories

Basic Idea: Essentially an economic theory of crime captured in the idea that people are free to choose crime as one of a range of behavioral options.

Human Nature: Assumes that humans are freethinking, rational decisionmakers who choose their own self-interests by weighing pleasure against pain and choosing the former. Their choice is goal-directed and aimed at maximizing their sense of well-being, or utility. Utility depends on wealth, and life is evaluated primarily in monetized terms and can include the value and use of time. Rational choice and routine activities theorists acknowledge a limited or conditional rationality.

Criminals: Rational, hedonistic, free actors no different from noncriminals except that they broke the law. Lawbreakers are those who choose to limit the freedom of others as defined by law.

Social Order and Law: A consensus around a highly stratified hierarchy based on a social contract assumed between free individuals who choose to sacrifice a part of their freedom to the state so that they may enjoy the rest in security. Some economists, however, see order as a situation of conflict over interests. Law preserves the individual's freedom to choose. Crime is defined by the legal code such that there is no crime without law. There is a preference for statutory law.

Causal Logic: Free choice, lack of fear of punishment, ineffective criminal justice system, available unguarded targets, opportunistic situations. Crime is the outcome of rational calculation. Offenders act on their perception, rather than reality, that the benefits of crime outweigh the costs. Recent theorists recognize this, arguing that a low perception of the probability of both apprehension and punishment together with the belief that punishment will be of uncertain, negotiable, or low severity combined with a relatively low expectation of gains from legitimate work and high expected gains from illegitimate work, in a context where moral reservations are absent, will lead to criminal activity.

Criminal Justice Policy: Social function of policy is to administer justice fairly, based on equal treatment before the law, in order that individuals will accept responsibility for their offending and choose not to offend. Increased efficiency of criminal justice is desired, especially enforcement, making it visible, certain, and swift. Later policy also includes reducing the opportunities for crime to occur. Due process model: (1) sovereignty of individual, (2) presumption of innocence, (3) equality before the law and between parties in dispute, (4) restraint of arbitrary power, (5) protection of defendant against abuses and error, (6) no discretion or arbitrariness but rule-based system (rules limiting police procedure and power and governing what is acceptable evidence), (7) adversarial trial (ensuring equality of inquiry), (8) right to be represented, (9) efficiency and fairness in protecting rights of individual, (10) certainty of detection and more efficient police preferred to simple presence of police, (11) trial by peers, (12) right to appeal to independent body.

The policy involves (1) retribution, (2) just deserts, (3) individual deterrence, and (4) prevention. Penalties to be only so severe as to just deter. Equal punishments for equal crimes, preferably by determinate or mandatory sentences. Punishment based only on the crime committed. Proportionality of punishment, so that potential offenders choose lesser crime. Increase security, reduce opportunity, and harden targets. Ensure legitimate wages, job creation, and job training. Raise perceptions of the value of gains from legitimate system and devalue those from illegitimate system.

Criminal Justice Practice: Fines because they can be equalized and staged in progressive severity; prison because time served can be adjusted and staged at different levels for different offenses; death penalty only as the ultimate sanction for serious offenders; and environmental manipulation and adjustments of routine activities of potential victims to avoid crime.

Evaluation: Explains the decisionmaking involved in white-collar and corporate crime and some street crime. Any crime with a pecuniary or even an instrumental motive is explainable, such as some theft and burglary. Ignores inequality of structure and assumes formal equality is perceived the same way irrespective of social class; difficult to achieve in pure form; fails to account for irrational behavior or spontaneous crimes; fails to consider the role of peer groups and their different effects on the rational calculus; allows those who can afford punishment to buy license to crime. Policies are only applied to crimes of the powerless, not to those of the powerful.

4

"Born to Be Bad"

Biological, Physiological, and Biosocial Theories of Crime

The idea that crime is "in the blood," that certain criminal behaviors are inherited, is the hallmark of the biological approach to criminological explanation. Contemporary bioethicists argue that with biotechnology we have the ability to manage high-risk populations. The term "biogovernance" (including using biotechnology to manage potential deviants) is used already in connection with the Human Genome Project, reproductive technologies, cloning, genetically engineered foods, hybrid animals, gene therapy, DNA profiling, and data banking (Gerlach 2001). Science and criminal justice are linked as never before with DNA and data banks containing considerable information—at a minimum, fingerprints. Proponents argue that "developments in biotechnology and knowledge have opened up discussion and debate about biology, crime and social control in an unprecedented way. People have always linked criminality to heredity to some extent, but we are much closer to scientifically legitimating that link and developing strategies for doing something about it" (Gerlach 2001, 113).

What if we could predict violence in advance? Consider the case of twenty-five-year-old Charles J. Whitman, who in 1966 killed his mother and wife and the next day shot sixteen people to death and wounded another thirty from a 307-foot tower on the campus of the University of Texas at Austin. Going up into the tower, he also killed a receptionist by hitting her in the back of the head. After Whitman was killed by police sharpshooters, an autopsy revealed a walnut-sized malignant tumor in the hypothalamus region of Whitman's brain. This type of tumor is known to cause irrational outbursts of violent behavior, which Whitman had reported experiencing in the months prior to the mass murders. According to thirty-two medical experts and scientists, the tumor "was the probable cause of his criminal actions" and the primary precipitating factor in the mass murder (Holman and Quinn 1992, 66–67). The note Whitman left next to his wife's body contained chilling insight into his medical abnormality. Parts of it read:

> I have been a victim of many unusual and irrational thoughts . . . overwhelming violent impulses. . . . After my death I wish that an autopsy would be performed on me to see if there is any visible physical disorder. I have had some tremendous headaches. . . . I decided to kill my wife. . . . I cannot rationally pinpoint any specific reason. (www.popsubculture.com/pop/bio project/charles whitman.html)

Could this murder spree have been prevented through "modern" biotechnology? Is it true that "a systematic predetection . . . to prevent risky individuals and groups from becoming manifestly dangerous" (Gerlach 2001, 97) is now a reality? If the violence is the result of genetic inheritance, tumors, or changes in body chemistry, can the subject be held responsible?

Biological explanations of crime have appeared since the sixteenth-century "human physiognomy" (the study of facial features) of J. Baptiste della Porte (1535–1615), who studied the cadavers of criminals to determine the relationship between the human body and crime (Schafer 1976, 38). In the 1760s, Johan Caspar Lavater (1741–1801) claimed to have identified a relationship between behavior and facial structure (Lilly, Cullen, and Ball [1989] 1995), and in 1810 Franz Joseph Gall developed a six-volume treatise on "craniology" or "phrenology." According to Gall, crime was one of the behaviors organically governed by a certain section of the brain. Thus criminality could be ascertained by measuring bumps on the head (Savitz, Turner, and Dickman 1977). The biological explanation for crime did not become fully established, however, until the late 1800s.

Following the 1930s there was a historical aversion to biological explanations among many criminologists (Wright and Miller 1998). This changed with the publication of E. O. Wilson, *Sociobiology: The New Synthesis* (1975). In the past fifteen years there has been a huge increase in the numbers of studies dealing with genetics, personality traits, and behavior, with even some criminology textbooks taking a pro-sociobiological evolutionary perspective (Ellis and Walsh 2000). By the early 2000s there had been significant advances in the search for biological causes due to more sophisticated diagnostic procedures. We now know, for example, that "various kinds of brain injuries and cerebrospinal disorders can be related to severe personality changes and emotional problems, which, in their turn, can be paired with maladaptive behavior . . . also viral infections such as the Borna disease virus are often linked to neurobehavioral and 'emotional' disturbances" (Martens 2002, 172).

In this chapter, we present the basic premises of this search for the causes of crime, outline the historical context under which it evolved, provide illustrative examples of the early and contemporary studies, evaluate findings and assumptions, and provide policy implications.

Biological and Positivistic Assumptions

To understand biological theories, it is necessary to grasp the underlying assumptions about humans that biological criminologists make. The major emphasis of this applied science of criminology is that humans have unique characteristics, or predispositions, that under certain conditions lead some to commit criminal acts. In other words, something within the individual strongly influences his or her behavior but this will only emerge in certain environments. For example, some people seem to behave perfectly normally most of the time, but when they get behind the wheel of a car the slightest inconvenience sends them into an angry rage (James and Nahl 2000). Without the automotive environment, they do not manifest anger. According to biological theory, the same can be true for offenders. For some, perhaps Winona Ryder, who on November 6, 2002, was convicted of shoplifting over $5,500 of merchandise, department stores provide an environment that results in shoplifting when combined with their personal predispositions. The setting and act together provide a thrill, which according to biological theorists might satisfy an abnormal need for excitement. For others, the environmental trigger to crime might be alcohol, drugs, or being subjected to authority.

For early biological criminologists, the classical philosophers and jurists' view of crime was unscientific speculation. Any serious examination of criminal behavior cannot assume humans are essentially all the same (rational thinkers). Rather, they argue, looking at individuals' unique characteristics and differences would reveal the underlying causes of criminal tendencies. The key to understanding crime, biologists believed, was to study the criminal actor, not the criminal act. Criminologists should study the nature of criminals as "kinds of people" (Cohen 1966) who would commit such acts.

Of central importance to these founding biological criminologists was how to study the criminal. Accurate study of human features demands rigorous methods and careful observation. The approach these pioneers of scientific criminology adopted is called the positivist method. It is defined as the "application of the scientific method to the study of the biological, psychological, and social characteristics of the criminal" (Vold and Bernard 1986, 45). Its detailed direct observation, experimentation, and use of controlled samples allowed criminologists to identify individuals with a predisposition for crime. This method of research is still very prevalent today and forms the basis of most contemporary criminological theory, regardless of its disciplinary roots. As Rafter (1992, 1998) points out, however, unlike contemporary positivists, early positivists also accepted folk wisdom, anecdotes, and analogies to lower forms of life as part of their empirical data.

Criminal anthropologists were the first to take an interest in this approach. They believed that criminals could be explained by physical laws that denied any free will (Rafter 1992, 1998). They claimed it was possible to distinguish types of criminals by their physical appearance. The physical features most often studied were body type, shape of the head, genes, eyes, and physiological imbalances. Although their methods were crude and later shown to be flawed, an understanding of these founding ideas is instructive. As Martin, Mutchnick, and Austin (1990) have noted, we need a few good "bad" examples to help show us which way to go in science.

The Social Context of Criminal Anthropology

Evolutionary biology heralded a different way of looking at human development. In 1859, the Englishman Charles Darwin (1809–1882) presented his theory of evolution *On the Origin of Species* ([1859] 1968), in which he argued that the development of any species proceeds through natural variations among offspring. The weakest strains fail to adapt to their environment and die off or fail to reproduce, whereas the strong survive, flourish, and come to dominate the species at a more advanced state.

Cesare Lombroso (1835–1909), a professor of forensic medicine, psychiatry, and later criminal anthropology, together with his students Enrico Ferri and Raffaele Garofalo, applied these ideas to the study of crime. This "holy three of criminology" became known as the Italian School (Schafer 1976, 41). Their position was radically opposed to Italian classicists such as Beccaria, whom they saw as overemphasizing free choice at the expense of determinism (Ferri's dissertation was on the problem of free will). Rather than seeing humans as self-interested, rational individuals possessing similar abilities to reason, the Italian School criminologists believed humans differ and some are more prone to crime than others. As Young (1981, 267) has pointed out, their approach was the mirror image of classicism: "Free-will disappears under determinacy, equality bows before natural differences and expert knowledge, and human laws that are created become scientific laws that are discovered." If classicism is the language of logical deduction, traditional opinion, and abstract reasoning, wrote Ferri (1901, 244), "We speak two different languages."

The new scientific criminology, founded on positivist assumptions, valued the "experimental method" as the key to knowledge based on empirically discovered facts and their examination. This knowledge was to be achieved carefully, over years of systematic observation and scientific analysis. The task of the criminologist was to apply the appropriate scientific apparatus, the calipers, dynamometer, and aesthesiometer, to measure and chart the offender's deformities (Rafter 1992). Only then would we discover the explanation for crime and for what would become known as the "born criminal."

The Born Criminal

To appreciate the revolutionary nature of these early biological and physiological theories, it is necessary to recall that in the late nineteenth century, science was viewed as a sort of "new religion," a source of knowledge and a solution to problems such as disease, starvation, unemployment, and—of interest to us—crime. Lombroso is widely recognized as the most influential founding scholar to rely on the scientific method to study crime and is often called the "father of modern criminology." With Ferri and Garofalo and later his daughter Gina Lombroso-Ferraro, he explored the differences between ordinary, "noncriminal" people and those who committed criminal offenses; therein, he argued, would be found the secret to the causes of crime.

Lombroso's theory of atavism, explained in his 1876 book *The Criminal Man*, was founded on Darwinian ideas about humanity's "worst dispositions," which were "reversions to a savage state" (Darwin 1871, 137). Atavism (meaning "derived from ancestor") is the reappearance of a characteristic in an organism or in families after it has been absent for several generations. According to this theory, criminals were hereditary throwbacks to less-developed evolutionary forms. Since criminals were less developed, Lombroso felt they could be identified by physical stigmata, or visible physical abnormalities, which he called atavistic features. These signs included such characteristics as asymmetry of the face; supernumerary nipples, toes, or fingers; an enormous jaw; handle-shaped or sensile ears; insensibility to pain; acute sight; and so on.

Possessing five of the eighteen stigmata indicated atavism and could explain "the irresistible craving for evil for its own sake, the desire not only to extinguish life in the victim, but to mutilate the corpse, tear its flesh and drink its blood" (1911, xiv). Not all criminals, however, fell into the atavistic category. By the fifth edition of his book, Lombroso recognized four main classes of criminals. The first, referred to as the "born criminal," was atavistic, responsible for the most serious offenses, and recidivist. This group made up about a third of the criminal population and was considered by Lombroso to be the most dangerous and incorrigible. The second class, criminals by passion, commit crime to correct the emotional pain of an injustice. Third, the insane criminal, could be an imbecile or have an affected brain and is unable to distinguish right from wrong. Fourth, the occasional criminal included four subtypes: (1) the criminaloid, who is of weak nature and easily swayed by others; (2) the epileptoid, who suffers from epilepsy; (3) the habitual criminal, whose occupation is crime; and (4) the pseudo-criminal, who commits crime by accident (Martin et al. 1990, 29–32).

Eventually Lombroso conceded that socioenvironmental factors, such as religion, gender, marriage, criminal law, climate, rainfall, taxation, banking, and even the price of grain, influence crime. By the time his last book, *Crime: Its Causes and Remedies* ([1912] 1968), was published, he had shifted from being a biological theorist to being an environmental theorist, but not without forcefully establishing the idea that criminals were different from ordinary people and especially the powerful. Even though his main ideas were disproved and his research found to be methodologically unsound, the search for the biological cause of crime was inspired by his work (Goring 1913).

Lombroso's student at the University of Turin, Enrico Ferri (1856–1928), was even more receptive to environmental and social influences that cause crime, but he still relied on biological factors. Ferri studied statistics at the University of Bologna, Italy. Later in Paris he was influenced by the ideas of the French lawyer and statistician A. M. Guerry (1802–1866) and the Belgian mathematician and astronomer A. Quetelet (1796–1874). Ferri used his statistical training to analyze crime in France from 1826 to 1878. Ferri's (1901) studies suggested the causes of crime were (1) physical (race, climate, geographic location, etc.), (2) anthropological (age, gender, psychology, etc.), and (3) social (population density, religion, customs, economic conditions, etc.). This view was obviously much more encompassing than Lombroso's and is not dissimilar from modern ideas about multiple causality.

Ferri's anticlassicist ideas cost him his university position. They also affected his views on criminal justice and policy, which he was invited to implement in Mussolini's fascist regime (and which were eventually rejected for being too radical). He reasoned that since causes needed scientific discovery, juries of laypeople were irrelevant and should, he believed, be replaced by panels of scientific experts, including doctors and psychiatrists. Not surprisingly, since he rejected the idea that crime was a free choice, Ferri also believed it was pointless to retributively punish offenders, preferring instead the idea of prevention through alternatives (which he called substitutions). His idea was to remove or minimize the causes of crime while protecting the state. He advocated "hygienic measures" such as social and environmental changes and, consistent with his socialist politics, favored the state provision of human services. He also advocated "therapeutic remedies" that were designed to be both reparative and repressive and "surgical operations," including death, to eliminate the cause of the problem (Schafer 1976, 45). Ferri's primary contribution was to offer a more balanced, complete picture of crime relying on scientific methods.

Raffaele Garofalo (1852–1934), also a student of Lombroso trained in the law, was of Spanish noble ancestry, although he was born in Naples. He saw crime as rooted in an organic flaw that results in a failure to develop both altruistic sensibilities and a moral sentiment for others. Garofalo presented a principle called adaptation that was based on Darwin's work. He argued that criminals who were unable to adapt to society and who thereby felt morally free to offend should be eliminated, consistent with nature's evolutionary process. This should be accomplished through one of three methods: death, long-term or life imprisonment, or "enforced reparation" (Vold and Bernard 1986, 44).

These theories have been relegated to the status of historical artifacts, although each contains some resonance of truth. The research methods employed were simplistic or flawed, revealed a racist bias, and have not stood up to empirical verification. The theories are important because they chart the course of later theories and also point out the importance of using scientific principles. Many of the research methods associated with the perspective of the Italian school persist into the twentieth century.

Early U.S. Family-Type and Body-Type Theories

Shortly after the conclusion of the American War between the States in 1865, it was widely believed that there were basic differences between individuals and between ethnic groups and that certain families could be mentally degenerate and "socially bankrupt." This notion has to be understood in historical context. U.S. society was undergoing rapid transformation with the abolition of slavery and massive immigration of Europeans of various ethnic groups, who, like the freed slaves, were largely poor and unskilled. These immigrants moved into the rapidly growing cities, where, living in crowded conditions, they presented a threat of poverty and disease to established Americans. Since the 1870s some Americans had been calling for eugenics measures, according to which a nation could save its stock from degeneration by rejecting the unfit, preventing their reproduction, and encouraging the fit to procreate (McKim 1900; Rafter 1992).

Richard Dugdale's work was consistent with these views. In his book *The Jukes: A Study in Crime, Pauperism, and Heredity* ([1877] 1985) Dugdale found that a family, which he called the Jukes (from the name of the family of illegitimate girls that a Dutch immigrant's sons had married), had criminals in it for six generations. Dugdale concluded that "the burden of crime" is found in illegitimate (unmarried) family lines, that the eldest child has a tendency to be criminal, and that males are more likely than females to be criminal. Obviously his conclusions are subject to varying interpretations.

Following Dugdale's degenerative theory, European criminal anthropology became available in the United States through a variety of works (e.g., MacDonald 1893; Boies 1893; Henderson 1893; Drahms 1900; Lydston 1904; see Rafter 1998 for an overview). These authors were the first U.S. criminal anthropologists to claim that their approach was a new science studying the criminal rather than the crime, just as medicine studies disease. Rafter (1998) states that the central assumption of this new science was that the physical body mirrors moral capacity and criminals were, as Boies (1893, 265–266) argued, "the imperfect, knotty, knurly, worm-eaten, half-rotten fruit of the human race."

After the turn of the century, science was still viewed as the solution to most human problems. Social science research became more rigorous and improved research methods, such as larger sample sizes and control groups, became important. For example, in 1939 E. A. Hooton, a Harvard anthropologist, published *The American Criminal: An Anthropological Study*, based on his research comparing 14,000 prisoners to 3,000 noncriminals. His results indicated that "criminals were organically inferior" and that this inferiority is probably due to inherited features, including physical differences such as low foreheads, compressed faces, and so on.

Hooton's methods have been criticized on several grounds. First, his control or comparison group included a large percentage of firefighters and police officers who were selected for their jobs based on their large physical size. Second, the differences he found were very small, and furthermore there was more variation between prisoners than between prisoners and civilians. Finally, his methods have been called tautological, meaning that they involved circular reasoning. For example, some people are violent so there must be something wrong with them; find out how they are different and this explains their violent behavior.

Ten years later, in spite of a general decline in the idea of a correspondence between the human body and moral behavior, the physician William Sheldon and his colleagues sought to explain the relationship between the shape of the human body and temperament. The most complete statement on this typology and crime was *Varieties of Delinquent Youth* (Sheldon, Hastl, and McDermott 1949). Using somatyping (classifying human bodies) Sheldon observed three distinct human body types. The first, endomorphs, were of medium height with round, soft bodies and thick necks. Mesomorphs were muscular, strong-boned people with wide shoulders and a tapering trunk. The final group, ectomorphs, had thin bodies and were fragile, with large brains and developed nervous systems. Sheldon recognized that no "pure" type existed and that each person shares some of all the features. Each type had a different personality and favored a different kind of criminal activity.

Endomorphs, motivated by their appetite, were tolerant, extroverted, sociable, and inclined to delinquency and occasional fraud. Ectomorphs had sensitive dispositions and were tense, thoughtful, and inhibited. They could become occasional thieves. Mesomorphs lacked sensitivity and were assertive, aggressive, and prone to habitual violence, robbery, and even homicide. Some of these results were confirmed in the 1950s studies on delinquency by Sheldon and Elinor Glueck, whose study of 500 incarcerated persistent delinquent boys compared with 500 nondelinquent boys found that although only 31 percent of the noncriminal comparison group were mesomorphs, 60 percent of the delinquents had a mesomorphic body type. When other factors were considered, however, such as parenting practices, the Gluecks found that body type was only one of several factors contributing to delinquency (Glueck and Glueck 1956). Other controlled studies claim stronger correlations, one finding that 57 percent of delinquents were mesomorphic compared to 19 percent of nondelinquent controls (Cortes and Gatti 1972).

Fishbein (1998, 92) points out that "early 'biological criminology' was eventually discredited for being unscientific, simplistic and monocausal." The early studies suffered serious methodological weaknesses, including poor sample selection, inadequate measurement criteria, and the failure to control for factors including unreported delinquency, social class, and criminal justice agency bias. In addition, they tend to reinforce class, gender, and especially racial stereotypes. For these reasons a conference funded by the National Institute of Health (NIH), Genetic Factors and Crime, was canceled as recently as 1992. By excluding hidden crime, crimes by women, occupational crimes, and crimes of the powerful and by often relying on samples of convicted offenders, body-type theories tell us more about who is likely to be processed through criminal justice agencies than about what causes crime. These theories were sufficiently tantalizing, however, to inspire a new generation of inquiry into the nature of what was inheritable. This new era of biosocial criminological theory is more sophisticated and deserves serious consideration, not least because it is built on new knowledge about the human brain and the multidisciplinary insights gained from genetics, biochemistry, endocrinology, neuroscience, immunology, and psychophysiology (Fishbein 1998, 92).

Contemporary Biological Perspectives

In spite of earlier methodological shortcomings, biological theory and scientific methods remain popular in criminology in the twenty-first century. Improved technology, computerization, and advanced statistical techniques have allowed more precise measurement and improved data collection, especially with regard to detailing the genetic process and mapping genes. Genes, called the "atoms of heredity," were discovered by Mendel in 1865 and reinvigorated again in the 1920s as essential elements in chromosomes. The 1952 discovery of the chemical constitution of genes as an explanation of how "like begets like" fueled the new genetic era of biology. By 1959, genes were being used to explain every aspect of individuals, every variation of their personality, yet as Fishbein (1998, 95) points out, while "numerous studies have attempted to estimate the genetic contribution to the development of criminality, delinquency, aggression and anti-social behavior . . . it is difficult to isolate genetic factors from developmental events, cultural influences and housing conditions." First among the contemporary approaches was twin and adoption studies.

Twin Studies and Adoption Studies

A major boost to the genetic theory of crime came with evidence from twin studies and adoption studies. Put simply, if crime is the outcome of some genetically conveyed heritable factor (e.g., impulsivity, low arousal to pain, sensation seeking, or minimal brain dysfunction), then we would expect to find more crime in the twin partners of identical twins—where one twin is criminal—than in fraternal twins or between siblings. This is because fraternal, or dizygotic (DZ), twins occur when two separate eggs are fertilized at the same time and as a result share around 50 percent of the same genes. Genetically, they are no different from two separate eggs being fertilized at different times, as with other siblings. The other and more rare type, monozygotic (MZ) twins, results from fertilization of a single egg. These identical twins share all of the same genes from their parents. This explains why MZ twins are always of the same gender whereas DZ twins may be a male and female. Researchers have compared twins of each type and claim to find that there are greater similarities in criminal convictions between identical (MZ) twins than between fraternal (DZ) twins, which lends support to the genetic basis for crime.

The most comprehensive study of this type was conducted by Karl Christiansen (1977; Mednick and Christiansen 1977), who studied 3,568 pairs of Danish twins born between 1881 and 1910. He found that 52 percent of the identical twins (MZ) had the same degree of officially recorded criminal activity, whereas only 22 percent of the fraternal twins (DZ) had similar degrees of criminality. These findings persisted even among twins who were separated at birth and raised in different social environments. Moreover, in an overview of all previous twin studies Mednick and Volavka (1980) found the same basic relationship, with identical twin pairs being two and a half times more likely to have similar criminal records when one of the pair is criminal than are fraternal twin pairs. Similar results for aggression have since been found by others (Rowe 1986; Ghodsian-Carpey and Baker 1987).

This apparently consistent finding has been criticized for its methodological inadequacy. Factors criticized include dependence on official crime statistics (especially conviction records), unreliable processes for classifying twins, errors resulting from the pooling of small samples, failure to take account of the similar environmental upbringing of identical twins compared with fraternal twins, and the inability of genetics to explain "why the majority of twin partners of criminal twins are not themselves criminal" (Einstadter and Henry 1995, 94). However, an Ohio study based on self-reports rather than official crime statistics found both greater criminality and greater criminal association among identical twins where one twin admitted delinquency compared with fraternal twins (Rowe 1986). Yet, several others, including Christiansen himself, argue that the higher-quality twin studies are less clear about the genetic contribution (Hurwitz and Christiansen 1983; Walters 1992). Indeed, controlling for the mutual behavioral influence of twins on each other (Carey 1992) and for other environmental effects has been found to render the differences between the two types of twins insignificant (Dalgard and Kringlen 1976).

Adoption studies seem to offer a way out of some of the environmental confusion plaguing twin studies. Adoption studies look at whether children adopted at birth carry their biological parents' criminality with them. If some biologically heritable predispositional factor is involved in criminality, we would expect that the biological children of convicted criminals would have criminal records more consistent with those of their natural fathers than with their adoptive fathers. Barry Hutchings and Sarnoff Mednick (1975) studied adoptees born between 1927 and 1941. They found that if boys had adoptive parents with a criminal record but their natural parents had no criminal record, then 11.5 percent of the adoptive sons were also criminal. This was little different from cases where neither natural nor adoptive parents have a criminal record (10.5 percent). But where boys had noncriminal adoptive parents but criminal natural parents, 22 percent of the adoptive sons were found to be criminal. Moreover, these effects seem additive; where both fathers were criminal, 36 percent of adoptive sons were found to be criminal.

Reporting more recent studies with larger samples and looking at both parents, the authors found similar although less pronounced results with 15 percent of boys having criminal records where their adoptive parents also had a criminal record and their natural parents did not, compared to 20 percent where the biological parents had a criminal record but their adoptive parents did not (Mednick, Gabrielli, and Hutchings 1987, 79). This finding was confirmed between adoptive girls and their mothers (Baker et al. 1989) and has been supported by other studies (Crowe 1975; Cadoret 1978), in particular those examining the effect of a biological parent having alcohol and antisocoial tendencies on the likelihood that their adopted off-spring would also have these problems, relative to the adopted offspring of noncriminal biological parents (Cadoret et al. 1995). Mednick and his col-leagues (Mednick et al. 1987) conclude that these data force them to accept the strong likelihood that genetic factors influence criminal behavior. More recently, Martens found that adoption and twin studies show that genetics and environment have a measurable impact on antisocial personality disor-der (1997, 2000). Martens feels the justice system should rely more on sci-ence, arguing that "unfortunately the administration of justice often shows only minimal consideration for the neurobiological correlates and/or ge-netic determination of immorality and crime" (2002, 178).

In spite of proponents' claims, critics have raised several questions about adoption studies. A major problem is "selective placement," whereby the adoption agency may match the adoptive home with the natural home in terms of social class and physical characteristics (Kamin 1985; Walters and White 1989; Walters 1992). Another problem is whether the effects being measured reflect prenatal or perinatal factors. Deborah Denno (1985, 1989) has questioned whether something happens to the mother during pregnancy, such as malnutrition or drug or alcohol abuse, that changes the fetus and results in later developmental problems, espe-cially problems related to intellect. In addition, since up to 40 percent of children spend time with their biological parents, with foster parents, and in institutions before adoption, the effects of early parenting need to be controlled for (Walters 1992). For one thing, children who spend more time in institutions show higher evidence of criminality in later life. Denno also points out that the adoption relationship surprisingly affects property crime but not violent crime, yet most violent offenders are also property offenders. She argues that the supposed genetic effect could be an artifact of the way we collect data, especially when we fail to take ac-count of hidden crime, occupational crime, and corporate crime.

Overall, then, what at first seemed to offer solid and consistent scientific evidence of a heritable genetic predisposition to crime turns out to raise more questions than it answers. This has not stopped various biological processes being identified as causal candidates for explaining crime.

TABLE 4.1   Some Claimed Biological Causes of Crime

Predisposing Cause	Basic Idea
XYY chromosomes	Having an extra male chromosome produces super-males who are more crime prone and more represented in prisons.
Defective genes	Some patterns of genes carry forward qualities, such as low emotional arousal and impulsivity, that affect the brain and conditionability, so that under certain environmental conditions criminal behavior is more likely.
Biochemical, endocrinal, and hormonal imbalances	Certain glands in the body produce hormones that affect the brain and the temperament. In men, high levels of testosterone are associated with aggression; in women, premenstrual syndrome (PMS): Changes in women's hormone levels prior to menstruation produce emotional disturbances, irritability, and violent rages.
Low intelligence or IQ, learning disabilities, attention deficit disorder	Low IQ and hyperactivity are seen as heritable qualities that affect children's ability to learn conventional morality.
Brain chemistry disorders, low arousal of autonomic nervous system, neurotransmitter imbalance	Those with low arousal of the autonomic nervous system need greater stimuli from the environment and can achieve this through crime, drug taking, and other risk-producing, highly stimulating activities. Those with low levels of the neurotransmitter serotonin are more likely to become violent.

Biosocial Criminology:
A Developmental Explanation of Crime

Since the 1950s, researchers have received media attention for various "discoveries" that they claim may explain the biological causes of crime (Nelkin 1993; Nelkin and Tancredi 1994). The cover of *U.S. News and World Report* (April 21, 1997) carried a similar title to that of this chapter, "Born Bad?" and dealt with biological causes of crime. Table 4.1 summarizes the main biological processes that have been claimed as possibly related to crime.

Before examining illustrative examples of these processes, we need to understand the logic used by the biosocial criminologists to explain crime. Biosocial criminology was founded on the ideas of E. O. Wilson (1975), whose book *Sociobiology* marked a resurrection of the role of biological thinking in social science. The basic idea is that the genetic makeup of humans controls their direction in life as their "selfish genes" strive to reproduce themselves through whatever means is necessary, including crime, if committing crime will expand their ability to procreate and expand their gene pool. As Ellis and Walsh express it:

> All versions of this gene-based theory of evolution have converged on a simple but powerful idea: To the degree that a particular characteristic is prevalent in a population, it is likely to have contributed to the reproductive success of the ancestors of the individuals currently living. Increasingly this fundamental principle has been applied to the study of behavior . . . including criminal behavior. (1997, 232)

Thus human development—through family, social, and organizational environments—interacts with the human gene machine and is adapted, even coopted, to enhance the human organism's ability to dominate others. These environmental contexts, together with each human organism's unique biology, shape subsequent behavior patterns.

All serious advocates of genetic explanations for crime agree that genes alone do not determine behavior and that there is no "crime gene" (Ellis and Walsh 1997). Rather, criminal behavior is seen to result from the combination of hereditary factors interacting with environmental ones. Together, these affect the brain and cognitive processes, which in turn control behavior (Jeffery 1994; Ellis 1988; Ellis and Walsh 1997; Fishbein and Thatcher 1986; Wilson and Herrnstein 1985; Hurwitz and Christiansen 1983). As Fishbein (1998, 94) explains, "Behavior (criminal or otherwise) is not inherited; what is inherited is the way in which an individual responds to the environment. Inheritance provides an orientation, predisposition, or tendency to behave in a certain fashion." For this reason, some researchers prefer the term maladaptivity rather than criminality, since it includes a wider range of problem-causing behaviors stemming from a combination of predispositions and environment (Fishbein 1998).

In addition to the interaction between genetic predispositions and environment, contemporary biological theorists, unlike their forerunners, do not abandon the notion of free will. Instead, they prefer the concept of conditional free will. In this approach, various factors restrict and channel an individual's decision to act and each "collaborates internally (physically) and externally (environmentally) to produce a final action" (Fishbein 1998, 104–105):

> The principle of conditional free will postulates that individuals choose a course of action within a preset, yet changeable, range of possibilities and that, assuming the conditions are suitable for rational thought, we are accountable for our actions. . . . This theory . . . predicts that if one or more conditions to which the individual is exposed are disturbed or irregular, the

individual is more likely to choose a disturbed or irregular course of action. Thus, the risk of such a response increases as a function of the number of deleterious conditions.

Unlike earlier deterministic biological theory, biosocial criminology proposes an interactive gene-based developmental theory of crime over the life course that integrates rather than opposes these classic notions of free will versus determinism. Yet even this advance on the age-old debate may be moot if Rose is correct in stating, "traditional dichotomies of sociological thought—free will versus determinism, society versus biology—are not very helpful in understanding the relationships of power, knowledge, ethics and subjectification that are taking shape within these new practices of control" (2000, 25).

Chromosomes, Nervous System, Attention Deficit Disorder, Hormones, and the Brain

As can be seen from Table 4.1, the list of causal candidates for the predispositional side of this interactive equation is long, and growing. None have captured the imagination more than those based on aspects of genetic theory. For example, in the 1960s a chromosomal theory of crime attributed violent male criminality to an extra Y chromosome. This extra chromosome created what was termed a "supermale," who was excessively violent. This theory was initially supported by the finding that 1–3 percent of male inmates had an extra Y chromosome compared to less than 1 percent of the general population of males (Jacobs et al. 1965; Telfer, Baker, and Clark 1968). Further research revealed, however, that incarcerated inmates with an extra Y chromosome were less likely to be serving a sentence for a violent crime. Moreover, the XYY chromosome pattern was more prevalent among prison officers than prisoners (Sarbin and Miller 1970; Fox 1971). Consequently, the XYY theory has now been largely discarded, except for a few stalwart supporters (Ellis and Walsh 2000).

Another candidate used to explain the intergenerational transmission of criminality is the autonomic nervous system (ANS), which controls emotions. The argument here is that people who are not easily emotionally aroused are less responsive to conditioning, whether punishment or rewards. Consequently, they resist socialization processes and are more likely to break the law without fearing the consequences (Mednick 1977; Eysenck [1964] 1977). Lykken (1995) found that antisocial individuals had an inborn central nervous system defect. Other evidence for this is inconclusive.

Attention deficit disorder (ADD) has also been targeted as a possible heritable factor in criminality (Moffitt and Silva 1988). Rose predicts that ADD finds a high likelihood of "genetic screening of disruptive schoolchildren, with pre-emptive treatment a condition of continuing schooling" (2000, 23). ADD is already a relatively common diagnosis for children having difficulty in school, with up to 12 percent of U.S. schoolboys in 1996 diagnosed with ADD. This condition is said to contribute to crime by reducing the ability of ADD children to do well in conventional activities, especially schooling. Children with ADD are more likely to be involved with the criminal justice system. ADD causes them to be less successful and less accepted in the mainstream school environment and they seek notoriety in more criminal ways. Their lack of success in school also results in a lack of marketable job skills and decreased employment opportunities. But critics argue that ADD is no more than a device to legitimate the medical control of unruly children and help teachers maintain order in the classroom (Box 1977).

Hormones have also been claimed as causative agents in criminality. Hormones are biochemical substances produced by human cells that are transported via the blood to other cells, which they stimulate by chemical action. Higher than normal levels of testosterone in men have been linked to aggression and violence (Rushton 1995; Booth and Osgood 1993; Olweus 1987; Rubin 1987; Rada, Laws, and Kellner 1976). Dabbs, Riad, and Chance (2001) found testosterone to be related to "familiarity and intent for homicide" but not for other violent crimes such as assault, robbery, or sex offenses. Zuckerman (1994, 175) found that sensation seeking was linked to "low levels of monoamine oxidase, cortisol and high concentrations of gonadal hormones." In some women, a reduction in the hormone progesterone that precedes menstruation and arguably produces premenstrual syndrome (PMS) has been said to cause sufficient stress and irritability that under certain circumstances they are irresponsible and prone to violent actions (Dalton 1961; Taylor and Dalton 1983). But reviews of the evidence suggest that neither hormonal explanation has adequate research support; some have even argued that hormonal changes "may be the product rather than the cause of aggression" (Curran and Renzetti 1994, 73; Katz and Chambliss 1991; Horney 1978).

The Importance of Neurotransmitters in Relation to Depression and Aggression

The role of neurochemical processes, particularly neurotransmitters, is increasingly seen as important. These are chemicals (e.g., serotonin and dopamine) released by electrical signals given off by nerves that transmit information to receptors in the brain. The brain then instructs the body to adjust various behaviors, including aggression, in relation to the human organism's environment. Serotonin in humans or animals inhibits aggression, and having relatively low levels of this substance released by neurotransmitters results in a failure to inhibit violent and impulsive behavior

(Fishbein 1989). In contrast, dopamine is an excitatory transmitter that offsets the effects of low serotonin. As Fishbein (1998, 99) says, dopamine "operates as the 'fuel' while serotonin provides the 'brakes' for behavioral responses." For example, studies of monkeys and apes show that serotonin is associated with various kinds of aggression (Rubin 1987) and that low levels of serotonin are linked to impulsive aggression. Dolan (1994) also found an association between low serotonin (5-hydroxytryptamine, 5-HT) function and aggressive behavior. Morover, the effects of dopamine go a long way to explain the high among "cocaine" users. Ingested cocaine (free-basing "crack" cocaine is a rapid way to do this) has the effect of attaching itself to dopamine that has been released from neurotransmitters on its way toward receptors. The modified dopamine is prevented from returning home to the transmitter with the result that more dopamine is released by the transmitters to correct the apparent deficit. It is this excessive production of dopamine that gives cocaine users their "high." Importantly, it is not the cocaine that makes for the excitement but its ability to trick the brain's own drug production system.

Unfortunately, since dopamine is only half of the equation, when the other half, serotonin, kicks in the situation of "tolerance" occurs. Over time, in response to the higher levels of released dopamine, the brain produces higher levels of serotonin, which depresses the effect of dopamine. Once this occurs the experience is of normality, rather than a high, and more cocaine is needed to reach a high than previously. However, now serotonin is being produced when dopamine is not, with the effect that in the absence of cocaine, the drug user experiences intense "lows" and needs cocaine just to reach a normal, balanced mood.

As with hormones, however, it is uncertain whether changes in serotonin and dopamine are the outcome of changes in environment or the reverse (Gibbs 1995). For example, some primate research indicates that dominant males do not have low serotonin levels before they move to the top of their social organizational hierarchy, but the level drops after they achieve their dominant position. Similarly, research on the placebo effect suggests that neurochemical processes can be induced by human expectations rather than by actual drugs. This suggests not only that biological factors may result from behavioral and environmental ones, but that the biological factors are not immutable and can be altered by changes in behavior and environment.

Recent Directions in Biosocial Criminology: The Work of Lee Ellis

Related to these new developments is a biocriminological theory that is increasingly seen as tying together many of the earlier findings. Lee Ellis (1987, 1990, 1995; Ellis and Walsh 2000) has become one of the leading advocates in this field and has contributed significantly to its development following his early Wilsonian influenced diatribe predicting the death of sociology (which he compared to astrology) and its replacement with biosocial theory (which he compared to astronomy). While Ellis's prediction has not come true, his biocriminology has grown to command a significant place in criminological thinking. Ellis has several dimensions to his theory (Ellis and Hoffman 1990; Ellis and Walsh 1997; Ellis and Walsh 2000).

In his sensation seeking/arousal theory, Ellis has argued that under normal environmental conditions as a result of low levels of dopamine and dopamine-like neurotransmitters called endorphins some people have lower than average emotional arousal. (This is similar to the discussion of cocaine tolerance above, but Ellis is arguing that for some the "low" is a predisposition.) Whereas most people are excited by a wide range of stimuli found in their daily environment, dopamine depressed people are easily bored. To raise their level of arousal and to bring back normal, or even accentuated levels of arousal, such individuals engage in superchallenging or intensely stimulating activities. Some of us surf in hurricanes, others street race, yet others turn to crime. Indeed, such sensation seeking is "strongly linked to other antisocial traits such as impulsiveness, recklessness, irresponsibility, and criminality" (Martens 2001, 174). Criminal behavior provides this "on the edge" stimulation for such "sensation seekers" (Ellis 1995; Zuckerman 1979).

Ellis argues that we can expect a higher level of criminality from sensation seekers than from those with normal sensitivities to stimulation. Evidence has accumulated supporting the idea that sensation seeking, risk taking, and impulsivity are biologically determined (Knoblich and King 1992; Magnusson, Klinteberg, and Stattin 1992), and studies of convicted offenders reveal that a key motivational factor is a neurophysiological "high" experienced in the course of committing an offense (Wood, Gove, and Cochran 1994; Gove and Wilmoth 1990). This high is similar to the intrinsic pleasure experienced from drugs and alcohol; it results from a similar external stimulation of internal opiates known as endorphins (Wood et al. 1995; Fishbein 1990; Fishbein and Pease 1988). As Barak (1998) observes, Ellis's theory of arousal may also explain corporate and white-collar crime. Corporations have been shown to seek precisely the kind of executive motivated to maximize sensations through risk taking, and it is just such a profile that is associated with corporate crime (Gross 1978; Box 1983).

More disturbing is Ellis's cluster of biocriminological theories based on the reproductive drives of the selfish gene, which he uses to explain behavior from rape, spousal assault, child abuse, and male sexual promiscuity to theft (Ellis and Walsh 1997). The common theme underlying these explanations is the idea that it is in men's reproductive interest to behave in these ways. For example, r/K theory assumes that rates of reproduction vary along an evolutionary continuum from r to K. Persons at the r end reproduce prolifically and do not need to care much for their offspring as there will be many and some will survive. In contrast those at the K end produce a small number of offspring in which they invest much time and energy to ensure their survival, and are generally more caring and nurturing. Criminals and psychopaths are expected to be at the r end, to come from large families, begin sexual activity early, and produce many offspring. Ellis acknowledges the racist inferences that could be drawn from such an idea and states, "whichever racial/ethnic groups or social strata exhibit r-related traits to the greatest degree will also exhibit high rates of crime and psychopathy" (Ellis and Walsh 1997, 257).

Related to these ideas, "cheater theory" argues that some sexually aggressive men seek to dominate as many women as possible and employ deception to appear like the high-investing males that women seek. They use illegal and violent means to acquire the resources for multiple sexual access to females. Yet others, when women resist their cautious mating behavior, will use force, including rape, which Ellis and Walsh (1997, 255) refer to as "forceful copulatory tactics," to overcome the tension between the sexes. These authors recount a similar line for spousal assault, which is seen as "associated with maintaining exclusive copulatory access," and they predict that "spousal assaults should be most common in populations in which infidelity is most common" (256).

These biological explanations not only show "that evolutionary theories of criminal and antisocial behavior have in fact reemerged during the past two decades" (Ellis and Walsh 1997, 260) but also embody racism and sexism that resonates with the discredited nineteenth-century biological criminology. One can only hope that the genuine contribution that biosocial knowledge can make to our understanding of crime is not swept away by the broom of reaction to these applications of its insights. Indeed, such controversy is already stirring. In general, Platt and Takagi (1979) called the trend toward biological criminology "scientific racism." Their claim has some basis in past government practices and, as we illustrate below, some merit.

Biosocial Theory and the Racism Controversy

Perhaps the most controversial theory links biology, race, and crime. At the forefront of this movement is J. Phillippe Rushton (1995, 1999). Rushton argues that races with lower intelligence are more crime prone. For example, African Americans are 12 percent of the population in the United States but account for 50 percent of violent crimes and 67

percent of robberies; three-quarters of the women arrested for homicide
are black. Meanwhile, Asians are dramatically underrepresented in
crime statistics. Lynch (2000) counters that "Rushton is able to prove his
claim of an association between race and crime by selectively focusing
on one category of crime, street crime, to the exclusion of crimes that are
more likely to be committed by Whites, corporate crime." Lynch and
Neopolitan (1998) debunk each of Rushton's arguments and highlight
his misuse of the scientific method. Finally, races are influenced by
human evolution and adaptation over a long period of time. From this
biological and evolutionary standpoint whites and Hispanics are virtually identical, yet Hispanics are five times more likely to commit street
crimes. Since Rushton discounts cultural explanations, his findings
cannot be explained by the race and crime hypothesis (see Lynch 2000
for a more complete critique).

Future Directions in Biosocial Criminology

Interestingly, it is always the newest discoveries in the biological search
for crime that hold the most promise. The very latest idea, genetic antici-
pation theory, based on dynamic gene mutations, will offer a new direction to criminologists, since these challenge Mendel's classic law of
heredity. Genetic researchers have discovered that new gene mutations—
called triplet repeat mutations—are not stable but change each time they
are passed from parent to child (Sutherland and Richards 1994; Randall
1993). The mutation occurs in a repeat form in certain nucleotides at a certain part of the gene. All individuals have some of these "repeats," but
persons with certain known genetic diseases have as many as 1,000.
Moreover, when the repeats are passed down a generation they become
highly unstable and amplify, resulting in greater chances of the disease
and its earlier onset. So far, this theory has only been applied to specific
diseases and some forms of mental retardation, but if history is a predictor it will not be long before this theory is being applied to criminal families and even used to explain changing crime rates!

In summary, it is clear from this brief survey of the range of contemporary biological theories that these approaches are difficult to assess in
terms of the certainty of their contribution to criminal behavior. For some
critics, the relevance of biology to criminology has more to do with crime
control and is more related to genetic discrimination in insurance, employment genetic risk management, and quasi-consensual treatment of
offenders (Rose 2000). As the list of biological factors grows, so does the
refutation from accumulated studies. Researchers have so far found little
support for connections between aggression and physiology, brain chemistry, and hormones (Gibbs 1995), although sensation seeking/arousal

theory may have some support. There are several conceptual and empirical limitations for this that we briefly explore next.

Conceptual and Empirical Limitations

We have already discussed several limitations in research methodology with regard to the early biological theories. Even though contemporary genetic studies use far more sophisticated methodology, they too are fraught with numerous difficulties. One problem stems from the nature of criminal behavior itself as a legal rather than a behavioral category and one that comprises different behavioral types. For example, because rape is defined as a violent criminal offense, does this mean all rapists are similarly motivated? Some are motivated by sexual desire, others by opportunity (e.g., date rape), and others by power; others are rapists due to the age of their willing partner. If biological theory is to explain rape or violence— or whatever—researchers should disaggregate "behaviors that are reflective of actual acts that can be consistently and accurately measured and examined" (Fishbein 1998, 98). Accordingly, "genetic studies that focus on criminal behavior per se may be inherently flawed; as criminal behavior is heterogeneous, genetic effects may be more directly associated with particular traits that place individuals at risk for criminal labeling" (1998, 98).

A second and related problem is that researchers rarely distinguish between those with an occasional criminal behavior pattern, whose actions might be the result of situational factors, and those whose criminal offending is more long-term and repetitive, whose actions may be more explainable by inherent predispositions (Fishbein 1998, 98).

Even if behavior is disaggregated, since no single gene has been associated with most behavior, research on antisocial behavior suggests multiple combined effects that are difficult to isolate, not only from each other but especially from developmental events, cultural influences, early experiences, and housing conditions (Fishbein 1998, 94).

In spite of these limitations, the new multidisciplinary direction in biosocial research focused on the relative interaction between biological, psychological, and social factors seems to offer the best hope for the future. Meanwhile, contemporary theorists continue to suggest—if with caution—criminal justice policy implications based on their limited evidence. As we shall see in the next section, this approach has a dangerous track record.

Criminal Justice Policy Implications

At its simplest, the policy of biological theory is the medical model, which involves identification, prevention, and treatment. Under this model, if inheritable predispositions, such as genes, chromosomes, hormones, or imbalances in brain chemistry, are the causes or at least the predisposers of crime, then preventive policy should involve identifying those individuals potentially predisposed prior to their creating harm. Darwin's first cousin Francis Galton coined the term "eugenics" in 1883. He used the term to mean "purely born" and the betterment of the human species by planned breeding (Garland 2001). If the criminal is "sick," a cure is more appropriate than punishment. Sentences should reflect this by being designed to meet whatever is diagnosed as the "cause" and this should be determined by expert scientific rather than judicial analysis. Thus indeterminate sentences are designed for each individual offender, based on needs, with treatment length dependent on the time taken to cure the cause.

We have described how early anthropological biocriminologists proposed invasive criminal justice policy and practice to deal with offenders. Suggested measures ranged from drug treatment and surgery to segregation and elimination through negative eugenics (forced sterilization) and even death for those who could not be "cured." In the United States we involuntarily sterilized over 60,000 institutionalized people prior to the 1960s (Garland 2001). These ideas have raised fears because of their racist and sexist connotations, and because of politicians' inclinations for simple technological fixes based on apparently objective science to absolve them from dealing with more complex issues (Nelkin 1993; Nelkin and Tancredi 1994; Sagarin and Sanchez 1988). Civil rights and invasion of privacy issues involved in enacting policy on the basis of questionable evidence that affects some groups in society more than others have created considerable opposition that has resulted in canceled conferences and withheld federal research funds (Williams 1994). Some contemporary biocriminologists have suggested screening clinics, early diagnosis, and preventive treatment as part of policy solutions. C. Ray Jeffery, for example, suggested that "crime prevention programs including pre- and post-natal care, early help for under-weight infants, well baby clinics, nutritional programs, neurological examinations for brain injuries, examinations for lead contamination in children, examinations for learning disabilities and hyperactivity, and other public health projects, would be of great value to the black community" (1993, 8).

In his book *Born to Crime: The Genetic Causes of Criminal Behavior* (1984), Lawrence Taylor suggested genetic screening and offered justifications for several "prophylactic" policies designed to protect society against a three-year-old diagnosed as a future criminal or others genetically diagnosed as potentially dangerous but who never committed a crime. These measures include execution, preventive isolation based on future risk ("before he or she commits the statistically probable crime"), medical treatment with chemical or hormonal therapy, prefrontal lobotomies ("destruction of the amygdala or prefrontal lobes"), genetic splicing for violent conduct ("no reason why a 'bit of cut-and-sew work' could not be employed"), and for the general population, routinely administering some substance to the water supply to counter criminal tendencies (1984, 147–154). Taylor supports abortion "if the fetus is found to have 'bad' genes" and raises again the possibility of sterilization "for any person genetically capable of transmitting aberrant genes to offspring" (1984, 157–158).

Interestingly, and contrary to critics' expectations, not all biocriminologists have summoned such a totalitarian specter. Some of the leading contributors suggest that in addition to being illegal and against due process rights, invasive treatments are not even the most appropriate. Instead, the gene-environment interaction thesis suggests that the environment of potential offenders can be manipulated to prevent their manifesting crime, including improving prenatal and perinatal care and, in the case of sensation seekers, providing alternatives that are less harmful but still exciting and challenging (Mednick 1985; Fishbein and Thatcher 1986). Indeed, as Wood and colleagues (1994, 75–76) note, "An effective crime control system would create conditions which minimize the likelihood that persons would commit crimes. . . . The key to preventing some crime may depend on finding alternative activities that both produce a neurophysiological 'high' and which are symbolically meaningful to the persons performing the crimes." This might include competitive sports and Outward Bound programs as well as activities such as skydiving, bungee jumping, surfing, rock climbing, wake boarding and similar kinds of risky, thrilling, nonharmful activity. On this basis, we might speculate that states such as North Dakota and Montana have low crime rates because of the large proportion of their male population who are hunters!

Summary and Conclusion

The early biological hereditary theories have been discredited because their findings have not been confirmed by later studies. Despite the reliance on careful observation and the scientific method, these early studies had serious methodological problems, including the failure to adequately define crime, reliance on official crime statistics, and failure to control for environmental factors, that render the results suspect. The early theorists stimulated research into the biological and environmental causes of crime, however, and they also promoted use of the scientific method. This was an improvement over the "armchair" classical philosophers who used logic and reason to develop their theories of crime.

Contemporary biological theories also have mixed validity. The search for causes of crime has become more sophisticated, in large part due to improved technology. Particularly important has been the research with genetics. Furthermore, modern biological theories do not state that biological defects alone produce criminal acts, but that biological factors in conjunction with certain environmental or social factors limit choices that result in criminality. But the modern studies still have questionable validity due to the research methods employed. At best, biological factors are viewed as indirect causes. The most recent neurophysiological studies (explaining the relationship between brain processes and behavior) seem to offer the best hope for the future of this perspective. However, to date their studies have not ruled out the possibility that physical and chemical changes in the brain are the result rather than the cause of criminal behavior.

The policy implications affiliated with biological positivism are also very troublesome. One objective is to identify potential criminals before they commit a crime. But trying to "cure" someone who has not committed a crime is unethical. Even after a crime is committed, the interventionist treatment policies associated with biological positivism have ethical problems, as is illustrated in the discussion of "voluntary" chemical castration. The less invasive alternatives involving environmental manipulation may seem preferable, but these theorists seem naive about society's willingness to accept policies that provide better options to those identified as potential criminals than to those predicted to be noncriminals.

The best role for the biological contribution to our understanding of crime seems to be as a contributing part to some overall integrated theory (Fishbein 1998; Barak 1998). So far, the theories most conducive to such a mix are the psychological, social learning, and social environmental theories that we explore in the next four chapters.

Summary Chart: Biological Theory

Basic Idea: Some are "born criminal" with a predisposition to crime. Theorists believe that human behavior is influenced by biological forces that in some manifest as crime under certain environmental conditions.

Human Nature: Humans inherit biological and genetically determined attributes that make people different. Attributes are randomly distributed; genetic variation makes each person unique. Most people possess a similar normal range of attributes and capabilities. Extremes of this distribution include those who are exceptional, either positively or negatively. Human behavior is an outcome of the mix of the biologically inherited qualities and their environment.

Society and the Social Order: A consensus is implied. Law is a reflection of the consensus of society. Crime is a deviation from normal behavior that is prohibited by law. Science can measure what is normal and therefore aid in law creation, crime detection, and crime treatment.

Criminals: Break laws naturally and will break norms and laws in any society.

Criminals are different from noncriminals in being defective. The predisposition to crime emerges under certain conditions.

Causal Explanation: Defective biological attributes make some people predisposed or prone to deviate, under certain environmental conditions. This is because they (1) are impelled to anger, (2) are impulsive, because of low levels of serotonin, (3) have impaired learning ability limiting their capacity for socialization, (4) are unable to control their behavior, and/or (5) are sensation seekers suffering from low arousal of the autonomic nervous system due to low production of dopamine or excessive production of serotonin, each of which might also result from environmental factors, including substance abuse. Early theorists believed that defects were reflected in physical appearance (physical stigmata or body types), somatypes such as mesomorphs being more crime prone, and that science could discover the cause of crime by examining appearance of criminals compared to "normals." Recent work has concentrated on genetic theory, and the evidence from twin and adoption studies show a consistent relationship suggesting hereditary factors. Specific inheritable defects have included physical inferiority, XYY chromosome pattern, brain disorders or dysfunction, mental deficiency, feeblemindedness, low IQ, learning disabilities (especially hyperactivity), hormonal imbalance, low or high levels of serotonin, low levels of dopamine, defective genes resulting in a slow autonomous nervous system, blood chemistry disorders, and ecological stimuli or deficiencies such as excessive sugar consumption, allergens, or vitamin and mineral deficiencies.

Criminal Justice Policy: Treat the defect and protect society from the untreatable. This is achieved through the medical model of criminal justice, which involves (1) information collection, (2) individualized diagnosis, (3) discretion, (4) experts as decisionmakers, (5) prediction, (6) treatment presumption, (7) treatment selection, and (8) indeterminate sentencing.

Criminal Justice Practice: Treatments include surgery or drugs, incapacitation, eugenics for the untreatables, genetic counseling, environmental manipulation, and alternative environmental sources of stimulation.

Evaluation: May be useful for explaining some forms of crime resulting from insanity or delinquency resulting from attention deficit disorder (ADD), some aggressive offenses, and some addiction. Contradictory support for twin study and adoption data. The theory does not consider the majority not caught for offenses. Genetic defects are found in only a small proportion of the offenders. Tendency to medicalize political issues, and potential for being used by governments as a harsh form of social control.

5

Criminal Minds

Psychiatric and Psychological Explanations for Crime

Some seventy years before Eric Harris and Dylan Klebold shot up Columbine High School on April 20, 1999, America's worst case of school violence occurred in Bath, Michigan. On May 18, 1927, fifty-five-year-old elected school board member and anti-school tax campaigner Andrew Kehoe killed his wife by bashing in her skull, blew up their farm, and then blew up the village school using 1,000 pounds of dynamite that he'd secretly planted and wired while working as a school custodian: "Maniac Blows Up School and Kills 42, Mostly Children," ran the headline in the *New York Times* of May 19, 1927 (Gado 2002; Ellsworth 1927). Thirty-eight children and seven teachers were killed that day, in addition to Kehoe's wife, and numerous horses and other animals were burned alive on Kehoe's farm when he blew it up. Also killed outside the school (when Kehoe fired at more dynamite in his truck) was school board president Emory Huyck, with whom Kehoe had been feuding for years, the village postmaster who unfortunately was with Huyck, and Kehoe himself, whose body parts were later found in a nearby garden. Interestingly, found wired to a fence at Kehoe's demolished farm was a sign that read: "Criminals are Made Not Born." Was Kehoe insane, as the newspapers suggested, or was he rational, focused, and determined? He certainly exhibited rationally planned behavior: purchasing and testing explosives on his farm (he was known locally as the "dynamite farmer"), laying out and concealing the wiring for the explosions over a considerable period of time, earning respect as a handyman, and exhibiting a well-articulated debate against raising taxes for schools. Yet his mass homicide that day drew attention to the extremes of his traumatic past: as an abused stepchild of fourteen, Kehoe watched (some speculate, caused) his stepmother burn to death from a malfunctioning stove, suffered a traumatic head injury from a fall at age twenty-nine, was impatient and intolerant of criticism, and refused to pay his mortgage. His strange, compulsive behavior had him changing clothes many times a day in order to always appear neat and clean. Was Kehoe a biological defective or was there a process in his development that led to this tragic outcome? Had Kehoe lived, could he have invoked the insanity defense?

In 1982, John Hinckley successfully used an insanity defense to avoid prosecution for attempting to assassinate President Ronald Reagan. In 1994, Lorena Bobbitt argued that an "irresistible impulse" caused her to slice off her husband's penis with a kitchen knife while he slept. She was found not guilty by reason of "temporary insanity," based on her state of mind following an alleged abusive sexual assault by her husband. On Monday, December 8, 1980, John Lennon was fatally shot in front of the Dakota Hotel in New York City. His killer, Mark David Chapman, "suffered delusional paranoid schizophrenia. He had attempted suicide twice, and during 1979 became increasingly fixated on both Holden Caulfield (the fictional hero of J.D. Salinger's *The Catcher in the Rye*) and John Lennon. In the end, Chapman believed he was living a life that mirrored that of Holden Caulfield and mirrored the unreal superstar life of John Lennon. Chapman was confused and paranoid about who he really was, and perhaps in (the) killing of John Lennon, he was trying to kill himself" (www.lennon-chapman.com). Chapman pled guilty to murder, against the strenuous objections of his attorneys. They, together with nine psychiatrists, felt that Chapman would be found not guilty by reason of insanity. These four exceptional, but widely publicized cases illustrate the importance of psychiatry and psychology as a criminal defense and as an explanation for aberrant behavior that is accepted by the courts.

Criminal law requires two things for a crime to be proven: (1) criminal intent, or mens rea—"a guilty mind" and (2) actus reus, voluntary participation in overt willful behavior (Severance, Goodman, and Loftus 1992). The U.S. Supreme Court ruled in *In re Winship* (1970) that these mental and behavioral elements must each be proven beyond a reasonable doubt. Thus, if defense attorneys can establish that their client is, or was at the time of the offense, mentally ill, criminal responsibility and therefore culpability based on mens rea cannot apply.[1]

Even in the most heinous crimes, juries are reluctant to accept the insanity defense. Attorneys for Jeffrey Dahmer, the serial killer who drugged young gay men before strangling them, having sex with their corpses, and eating them, were unable to convince the jury that their client was insane. Dahmer was convicted of murder and sentenced to prison, where he was murdered by a fellow prisoner in 1994. John Salvi, who in 1996 argued the insanity defense for murdering abortion clinic personnel, was also found guilty; he committed suicide in prison. These cases show the typical outcome: Juries more often than not choose to reject criminal defenses relying on insanity or temporary insanity based on the expert opinion of psychiatrists and psychologists (Maedor 1985). Promoted by disproportionate media attention to certain kinds of lurid or bizarre crimes, a popular misconception prevails, however, that many criminals are "crazy" or "sick"—that something in their mind motivated their crime (Holman and Quinn 1992, 83; Pallone and Hennessy 1992).

In addition to the popular imagery and the legal dimension, there are other reasons why psychiatry and psychology are important components of criminological knowledge. There was an enormous growth of interest in forensic psychology during the 1990s (Arrigo 2000; Bartol and Bartol 1994). Psychological principles are applied in several criminal justice settings. For example, the apprehension of serial killers and rapists relies on psychological profiling.

Profiling techniques are developed by the Behavioral Science Unit of the FBI located at its training center in Quantico, Virginia. Psychology has led to the development of many screening, diagnostic, and analytical measures used in profiling. For example, Mark David Chapman was examined and found to have an IQ (intelligence quotient) of 121, well above average. Profiles are composite characteristics of the personalities and behavioral attributes of the typical offender for different types of crimes. They involve building specific profiles based on the early crime scene evidence in cases being investigated by the police. They are psychological identities parallel to the police artist impressions of an offender. Psychological profiles are used not only to apprehend offenders but also to predict future strikes by an offender and protect victims.

Yet the "Unabomber" crimes had nothing to do with the profile created. Theodore Kaczynski, a former math professor, was eventually caught after seventeen years, when his brother recognized his writing style. Likewise, the two African Americans arrested for the 2002 sniper killings in the Maryland area were far from the single, white, intelligent male in a white van profiled by the FBI. Despite these failures, criminal profiling holds great interest to many professionals and students. Movies like *The Silence of the Lambs* fuel this interest. Profiling does have a legitimate scientific base as we show in this chapter, yet psychologist Curt Bartol (1999, 5) states that "profiling is at least 95 percent an art based on speculation and only 5 percent science." Not surprisingly, it profiles "street" rather than "suite" offenders.

Finally, offenders and victims have been diagnosed with posttraumatic stress disorder (Riggs, Rothman, and Foa 1995), which can result in violence when someone's mind returns to a prior situation of stress. Criminal offenders have been diagnosed as having a wide range of mental disturbances. Both victims and offenders can require diagnosis and treatment based on psychological concepts. For these reasons, students of criminology need to understand the underlying assumptions of the psychological perspective, together with its study methods and policy implications and the limitations of this approach to criminal behavior. In this chapter, we outline the search for the psychological factors in crime causation, present the basic premises, describe some illustrative contemporary studies, and critique the findings and assumptions.

From Sick Minds to Abnormal Behavior

The human mind has long been considered a source of abnormal behavior and this connection is sustained by the media linking mental illness to incidents of violence (Monahan 1992). Since crime is seen as abnormal behavior, it has been subject to psychiatric and psychological analyses. English psychiatrist Joseph Pritchard used the term "moral insanity" to explain criminal behavior in 1835 and another psychiatrist, Henry Maudsley (1835–1918), argued that crime was a release for pathological minds that prevented them from going insane. Like Maudsley, Isaac Ray (1807–1881) believed that pathological urges drive some to commit crime. These early psychiatric explanations were founded on the assumptions that psychoses were biologically based and were, therefore, variations of the biological theories discussed in the previous chapter. More important, as Barak (1998, 127) points out, "Like the theories of a 'born criminal' the theories of a 'sick criminal' are just as fallacious" in that those diagnosed as mentally ill are no more likely to commit crimes than those seen as mentally healthy. Indeed, over sixty years ago Reckless (1940, 104) observed, "It cannot be shown that the general run of adult offenders are alarmingly more psychotic than the non-delinquent population." Recent extensive reviews of the evidence confirm that "offenders with mental disorders were no more criminally prone or violent than offenders without mental disorders" and, moreover, were found to be "less likely to recidivate than nondisordered offenders" (Bartol 1999, 141; Bonta, Law, and Hanson 1998). There is one exception: the subtype of mental disorder known as antisocial personality disorder, also known as psychopaths and sociopaths (see pages 137–138). A useful way to think about the mind is to distinguish between differential psychology and process psychology:

> *Differential psychology* takes as its province the illumination of differences between people that result in variant behavior between different behavers . . . *process psychology* . . . focuses on the process by which criminal behavior is

emitted, construing that process as a dynamic interchange between the person and environment—between intraperson propensities . . . and situational cues and variables which . . . seem to invite, permit, or tolerate certain ways of behaving. (Pallone and Hennessy 1992, 4–6)

From the process perspective, it is not so much that sick minds cause crime but that certain psychological processes in any mind may produce criminal behavior. The science of psychology is a way to examine these processes. Psychological theories of crime explain abnormal behavior as the result of mind and thought processes that form during human development, particularly during the early years. Several different approaches may be taken by psychologists examining the mind, and most share certain common assumptions.

Shared Psychological Assumptions

Psychological explanations for crime, like biological theories, look for differences that might explain some people's predisposition toward crime. They look for either differences between individuals (differential psychology) or differences in the situation and emergent environment (process psychology). The view commonly held by those adopting psychological explanations is that humans are formed through socialization and developmental processes rather than being biologically predetermined. It is widely accepted that humans develop through a series of necessary mental, moral, and sexual stages. When this development is abnormal (usually beginning in early childhood) or subject to traumatic events, personality disorders and psychological disturbances may become part of the individual's personality characteristics, or may be constructed as an appropriate behavioral response under a particular set of circumstances. These disorders and disturbances reside within the mind of the individual, but may be latent. Many psychologists agree that social or environmental factors may trigger erratic or criminal behavior in those psychologically predisposed. Dysfunctional process or traumatic experiences may also produce antisocial personality tendencies. This implies differences in mental functioning that may cause those affected to commit crimes. In this context, crimes are only one form of "aggressive or antisocial behavior" that "violates certain social norms" or legal norms (Shoham and Seis 1993, 5; Fishbein 1998).

Psychologists, especially those taking a differential approach, rely heavily on scales, inventories, and questionnaires to identify and classify the differences between individuals who suffer from psychological disturbances and those who do not. Measurement is thus a very critical component, since what is "normal" must be differentiated from what is "pathological." Hoge (1999) and others (Zhang, Welte, and Wieczorek 2002) have outlined many of the scales and their application. These scales include measures of personality: Basic Personality Inventory, Jesness Inventory, Millon Adolescent Personality Inventory, and the Minnesota Multiphasic Personality Inventory (MMPI); behavioral measures include the Revised Behavior Problem Checklist, the Behavior Assessment System for Children, and the Child Behavior Checklist; there are also scales that measure antisocial behavior, the Self-reported Delinquency Scale, Psychopathic States Inventory, and Drug Use Screening Inventory. Finally, there are attitudinal measures, measures of environmental factors, risk classification measures, and interview schedules. The Rorschach (inkblot) test is often used to assess aggressive and psychopathic personalities (Gacono and Meloy 1994).

Since criminal behaviors are said to stem from abnormal developmental processes affecting the mind, some form of psychological treatment intervention is necessary to correct or counteract those with criminal predispositions or to change the process whereby these personalities are formed. Beyond these similarities, psychological approaches have important differences. We consider seven different theoretical approaches evident in the literature and briefly describe each (see Table 5.1).

The development of psychological theory in relation to crime can be seen as a movement. It began with the idea of uncovering hidden unconscious forces within the individual's mind. It progressed to an increased recognition of the role of family influences on learning and led to a growing acknowledgment that the human learning process is not simply passive-reactive but involves complex, creative interpretation and analysis of information and that this is itself interrelated with the psychophysiology of the brain's function. It reached the stage where cognition is shaped by interaction of the mind with the wider social environment. We begin our analysis of this movement by looking at the pioneering work of Sigmund Freud and the various subtheories that emerged from his approach.

The Psychoanalytic Approach

The Viennese psychiatrist Sigmund Freud (1856–1939) is most responsible for establishing the role of the unconscious mind in shaping behavior. Although Freud himself wrote little on crime, his theory has been applied by others of the Freudian psychoanalytic school (Aichhorn 1935; Healy and Bronner 1926, 1936; Alexander and Healy 1935; Bowlby 1946; Abrahamsen 1944, 1960; Friedlander 1947; Redl and Wineman 1951, 1952; Redl and Toch 1979). The psychoanalytic approach is a relatively complicated theory of behavior based on several unproven, and arguably unprovable,

TABLE 5.1   Psychological Theories Compared

Theory	Basic concept	Key Theorists
Psychoanalytical • Attachment Theory • Frustration- Aggression Theory	Disfunctional mind formed by inadequate childhood development processes producing buried conflicts Failure to form attachment with mother produces insecurity and lack of empathy for others Aggession as an adaptive mechanism to relieve stress	Sigmund Freud, August Aichhorn, Kate Friedlander John Bowlby John Dollard, William Healy and Augusta Bronner, Seymour Halleck
Trait Based • Personality Type • Self-control	Differences in personality traits/drives produce different behavioral responses; low self control produces crime prone behavior	Hervey Kleckley Hans Eysenck
Evolutionary	Mind is an epiphenomenon of evolutionary desire for genetic proliferation; selfish gene	William Rushton Lee Ellis
Behavioral Learning Theory	Behavior depends on the rewards and punishments it received	Ivan Pavlov B.F. Skinner
Social Learning and Modeling Theory	Learning to behave by imitating and modeling the behavior of others, from groups or in media images	Gabriel Tarde Albert Bandura Ronald Akers
Cognitive Theory	The mind is made up of patterns of thinking that develop through interactive experiences and can be underdeveloped and/or destructive	Jean Piaget, Lawrence Kohlberg, Aaron Beck, Stanton Samenow
Constructivist and Ecological Theory	People construct the meaning of their world from experiences with the broad social environment, particularly their community	George Kelly J. Rappaport

assumptions about how human minds develop and function. The basic argument is that crime is an expression of buried internal conflicts that result from traumas and deprivations during childhood. Traumatic events that occur during childhood affect the unconscious component of the human mind.

Freud assumed that the mind was composed of conscious and unconscious components. The conscious personality he termed the ego. The ego is concerned with reality and attempts to rationally mediate between the conflicting demands of unconscious desires. The unconscious is divided into two parts. The id is the source of basic biological and psychological drives present from birth, including the libido, or sexual energy, Eros, the "life instinct," and Thanatos, the destructive "death instinct." The id follows the pleasure principle—"If it feels good, do it."

Opposing the id is the superego, the "moral police," or conscience, internalized from socialization into the norms of a society and containing moral and ethical restraints on behavior. The superego reflects each person's social experiences and becomes a source of self-criticism based on the production of guilt. The id and superego compete with each other to control behavior. The ego balances the desires of the id and superego.

A basic conflict for individuals involves guilt: "The individual experiences all sorts of drives and urges coming from the id, and feels guilty about them because of the prohibitions of the superego" (Vold and Bernard 1986, 112). Freud identified two primary ways people handle guilt. First, in *sublimation* the desires and drives of the id are diverted to actions that meet the approval of the superego (e.g., aggression may be directed toward athletic events). A second reaction is *repression*, which occurs when the drives of the id are denied. This results in various abnormal reactions. Reaction formation is one manifestation of repression. In this case, a person with repressed sexual drives would be very prudish about sex. Another reaction to repression is projection, whereby people see their own desires and urges in others.

These basic conflicts occur in different stages of an individual's life. Freud says that during childhood, basic drives are oriented around oral, anal, phallic, latent, and genital drives that seek to be satisfied. These sequential stages of development cause problems when a person remains "fixated," or stuck at one stage, because of experiencing a denial of satisfaction or a traumatic event. Freud argued that if the guilt associated with the various stages was not satisfactorily handled by the ego, then the personality of the individual would be negatively affected later in life. For example, Abrahamsen (1973, 9–10) argues,

> Murder emerges from the intensity of death wishes that co-exist with our life saving emotions. . . . Homicide . . . is released by the intensity of inner conflicts. . . . Murderers were intensely tormented. Deep down, they felt beset, trapped in an intense conflict growing out of a struggle between their sexual and self-preserving feelings on the one hand and their surroundings on the other. . . . The conflict I refer to is due to serious traumatic situations, primarily experienced in earliest childhood, before the child is one or two years old.

Freud (1915, 1950) further argued that one outcome of the unconscious guilt complex is crime. This can occur in several ways. It can result from a fear of authority and an overdeveloped superego. Lawbreaking can allow persons feeling guilt to draw punishment on themselves and thereby temporarily relieve their guilt. This has been used to explain burglars who leave obvious clues to their identity and shoplifters who take few precautions to cover their acts.

Blaming the Mother: Attachment Theory

For other post-Freudians, if the parental upbringing was important in forming a healthy personality, then the role of the mother (who at that time was seen as spending most of her time nurturing children) was crucial. As Aichhorn (1935) argued, for some children inadequate or faulty upbringing may result in a weak or underdeveloped ego and superego, in which state the child either is unable to control his or her riotous id or suppresses these instinctual desires, resulting in "latent delinquency" (Friedlander 1947). This failed developmental process is also found in Abrahamsen's (1944, 1960) concept of damaged superego, Bowlby's (1946) notion of the "affectionless character," and Friedlander's (1947) "anti-social character," each of which pointed to "maternal deprivation" or maternal mishandling of the child. One of the enduring theories from this approach has become known as *attachment theory* and emphasizes the importance of forming a secure emotional base for subsequent personality development. John Bowlby (1951, 1988) argued that children who have frequent breaks in relations with their mother in their early years up to the age of eight or have factors that mitigate against secure maternal bonding, such as child abandonment, foster care, and child abuse, develop anxiety and have difficulty forming relationships with others. Part of that difficulty may be a maladaptation that prevents them from getting involved with others in order to avoid the emotional pain of being hurt. In particular, these affectionless children lack the ability to empathize with others and do not see or feel the pain that harm may cause them.

Maladaptive Coping Strategies: Frustration-Aggression Theory

For Healy and Bronner (1936), thwarted desires and deprivations cause frustration. When this frustration is combined with the failure of parenting to provide nondelinquent channels for compensatory gratification, affective ties to conventional adults fail to form and the result is a weak superego that is unable to protect against delinquency. John Dollard and his colleagues (1939) argued that frustration emerges as a natural course of living but that most people are able to find socially acceptable outlets, such as sport, or listening to rock or rap music, or playing video games. For some, however, the frustration may be displaced onto other people who have nothing to do with the cause of the frustration, but this still serves as a release.

Indeed, there are similarities here to Alfred Adler's (1931) idea of the inferiority complex: Those whose style of life fails to provide them a sense of superiority or status may compensate through abnormal forms of compensatory behavior. As both Adler (1931) and most recently Halleck (1971) have argued, those who feel the world is against them may turn to crime as a means of satisfying their creativity and autonomy. Halleck's theory of displaced aggression, enabling one to survive frustration with dignity, is echoed in the voices of Katz's (1988) delinquents who saw murder as "righteous slaughter." Thus the ego develops defense mechanisms in the form of excuses and justifications to rationalize harmful actions. This kind of psychoanalytical approach may explain theft from the workplace, which is found to be committed by those who express intense job dissatisfaction and frustration with their employers (Hollinger and Clark 1983). It may even explain the loner who commits violence against an employer (Fox and Levin 1994).

Limitations and Policy Implications of Psychoanalytical Theory

The psychoanalytic approach has been largely discredited by most contemporary criminologists. One frequent criticism is that it is tautological: the theory implies in its premise what is then made explicit in the conclusion, making it repetitious rather than explanatory. For example, Akers notes, "It is only the interpretation of the therapist that determines when the independent variables of unconscious urges and impulses are present. Psychoanalytic interpretations, therefore, tend to be after the fact, tautological, and untestable" (1994, 85). The lack of testability stems from the fact that rather than being a formal theory the psychoanalytic approach is more a set of interrelated concepts that in combination provide a plausible explanation for human behavior, but one that defies empirical measurement (Vold and Bernard 1986; Martin et al. 1990). Indeed, since these key concepts are located in the individual's unconscious, it is impossible to confirm or deny their existence. Moreover, psychoanalysts frequently disagree about the diagnosis of a problem. Another difficulty with evaluating this approach is that most research has focused on a small number of subjects in a clinical setting. Thus controlled comparisons with a larger healthy population have not been conducted. Finally, psychoanalysis is gender biased, assuming women are inherently abnormal (Klein [1973] 1980; Naffine 1987). Yet other aspects, such as the parental deprivation thesis (not specifically maternal) in the work of post-Freudians has been supported by empirical findings (Cerncovich and Giordino 1987; Farrington and West 1995).

In spite of its limitations, there are several policy implications of psychoanalytical theory. According to this approach, a criminal offender is not necessarily responsible for his or her actions. Rather, the offender is sick and needs a cure. (Punishment may actually make the illness worse, since it could tend to heighten feelings of guilt.) Since the sickness is located in the subconscious, treatment must address underlying emotional disturbances. Treatment involves evaluation and analysis to help the offender uncover the childhood root causes. Since repression is the root cause of so many dysfunctional reactions, it is important for repressed experiences and desires to be recognized and handled. To explore the subconscious, Freud developed the therapeutic technique of psychoanalysis, in which patients are asked to relax and talk about whatever comes to mind. Connections, or associations, are then made, and the patients can recognize and understand the unconscious and gain a degree of control over their actions.

Freud also relied on the process called transference, which is based on the assumption that past relationships (e.g., with one's mother) influence current relationships. As the therapist becomes increasingly important to the patient, the patient will replay the earlier relationship with the therapist (the therapist assuming the role of the earlier problem-generating person). Treatment, then, consists of the therapist correcting the current relationship between herself and the client, which simultaneously resolves the earlier problem relationship.

The ultimate value of psychoanalytic therapy should be in helping individuals overcome their "problems." But it has been shown that patients who receive these treatments do no better than those who receive no treatment (Schwitzgebel 1974). At best the theory has a heuristic or sensitizing value (Shoham and Seis 1993), highlighting the importance of mental processes in producing behavioral outcomes. In spite of its limitations, it also established psychology as a scientific academic discipline.

Since Freud, psychology has taken divergent directions. One direction, the *trait-based perspectives* founded on the work of Gordon Allport (1937; 1961), sees human development leading to distinctive personality types based on learned traits. Another direction, *behavioral and situational learning* theories, based on both Ivan Pavlov's ([1906] 1967) and B. F. Skinner's (1953) theories of operant conditioning, see current behavior as the result of accumulations of responses resulting from past learning. These two approaches have been combined in several applications to criminology, including Eysenck's ([1964] 1977; Eysenck and Gudjonsson 1989) criminal personality theory, examining the role of extroversion and neuroticism as factors in criminal and psychopathic personalities. Eysenck combined trait theory and conditioned learning theory. Zuckerman's (1989) theory of criminal personality incorporated the traits of impulsivity, aggressiveness, and irresponsibility. Wilson and Herrnstein's (1985, 44) "eclectic" integrated theory, incorporating "both genetic predispositions and social learning," is "built on modern behavioral psychology." Let us look in more detail at trait-based theory.

Trait-Based Personality Theories

Trait-based personality theories differ from the psychoanalytic approach in that abnormal behavior is said to stem from abnormal or criminal personality traits rather than unconscious causes. Traits "represent consistent characteristics of individuals that are relevant to a wide variety of behavioral domains" (Caspi et al. 1994, 165). Allport (1937, 48) defined personality as the dynamic organization of an individual's psychophysical systems of predispositions in response to certain environmental triggers. One task of trait-based theory, then, is to measure these various, frequently occurring traits to see how they are assembled differently in different people and with what effects.

Several varieties of trait-based personality theory are applied to criminality. All share the view that criminal behavior is a manifestation of an underlying trait-based problem. Generally, criminological applications of trait theory look at personality characteristics such as impulsiveness, aggressiveness, extroversion, neuroticism, psychoticism, thrill seeking, hostility, and emotionality. As we saw in the previous chapter, these have also been tied to biological and neurological processes.

One of the first theorists to adopt a trait-based personality approach to crime was psychiatrist Hervey Cleckly (1941) in his book *Mask of Insanity.* Cleckly laid the foundation for what would be an enduring composite description of what he called a psychopath, or what others call a sociopath, and what most recently has become known as "antisocial personality disorder." Not only has the core of Cleckly's original observations found its way into the DSM *(Diagnostic and Statistical Manual of Mental Disorders)* but it is also found in the World Health Organization's classification of mental disorders. The composite set of traits from all these sources describes someone with self-obsessed personality who is disconnected from others and finds herself in conflict with the social world (see Table 5.2). The extreme version of this aberrant personality, the psychopath, "is an asocial, aggressive, highly impulsive person, who feels little or no guilt and is unable to form lasting bonds of affection with other human beings" (McCord and McCord 1964, 3). Psychopathy is also linked with an inability to delay gratification or learn from experience, sensation seeking, and superficial charm (Zhang, Welte, and Wieczorek 2002). They are also callous and unemotional (Caputo, Frick and Brodsky 1999). The term "antisocial personality" (Lykken 1995) has largely replaced the term "psychopath." The fundamental question that remains is whether these traits are simply a

---

Table 5.2 Core traits of an Antisocial Personality
(Sociopath or Psychopath)

Self

    Intelligent
    Self-centered/egoistical/
       selfish/arrogant
    Shameless
    Guiltless
    Impulsive
    No life-plan
    Intolerant

Relations with others

    Superficial
    Disconnected
    Impersonal
    Unreliable
    Disloyal
    Deceptive/liar
    Lack of empathy toward/
       unable to love
    Unresponsive to
       interpersonal relations
    Unable to sustain
       enduring relations
    Blames others for problems

Relations to society

    Disregard for norms/rules/obligations

---

description of someone who repeatedly commits offenses or whether they actually explain why a person possesses the traits.

One of the first to attempt to explain personality traits of offenders was Hans Eysenck ([1964] 1977), who, like Cleckly, tried to establish a criminal, or psychotic, personality. Drawing on Carl Jung's ideas of introversion and extroversion and Pavlov's learning theory, Eysenck claimed to show that human personalities are made up of clusters of traits. One cluster produces a sensitive, inhibited temperament that he called introversion. A second cluster produces an outward-focused, cheerful, expressive temperament that he called extroversion. A third dimension of personality, which forms emotional stability or instability, he labeled neuroticism; to this schema he subsequently added psychoticism, which is a predisposition to psychotic breakdown. Normal human personalities are emotionally stable, neither highly introverted nor extroverted. In contrast, those who are highly neurotic, highly extroverted, and score high on a psychoticism scale have a greater predisposition toward crime, forming in the extreme the psychopathic personality. Eysenck explained that such personalities (sensation seekers) are less sensitive to excitation by stimuli, requiring more stimulation than normals, which they can achieve through crime, violence, and drug taking. These people are impulsive, being emotionally unstable. They are also less easy to condition and have a higher threshold or tolerance of pain. Low IQ can affect the ability of such personalities to learn rules, perceive punishment, or experience pain, as in biological theory.

A major contribution made by the trait-based personality theorists is their reliance on relatively sophisticated diagnostic devices. For example, Starke Hathaway (1939) developed the Minnesota Multiphasic Personality Inventory (MMPI) to detect deviant personality patterns. The MMPI uses several scales to measure personality traits such as depression, hysteria, psychopathy, and compulsiveness; 550 true/false statements aid with diagnosis. These statements are grouped into ten separate scales measuring different personality traits (e.g., depression, hysteria, etc.). The MMPI has "received considerable attention in the determination of criminal offender personality typology" (Carmin et al. 1989, 486). For example, using this scale Glaser, Calhoun, and Petrocelli (2002) were able to classify personality by type of offense committed by a group of juvenile offenders. Another common personality measure is the California Psychological Inventory (CPI). The CPI is used to determine if a person has traits such as dominance, tolerance, and sociability. Recent research using yet another scale, the Multidimensional Personality Questionnaire (MPQ), correlates personality and delinquency, finding that "male and female delinquents exhibited convergent personality profiles characterized by impulsivity, danger seeking, a rejection of traditional values, aggressive attitudes, feelings of alienation and an adversarial interpersonal attitude" (Caspi et al. 1994, 176–177). Caspi and colleagues argued that crime proneness is correlated to multiple psychological components, particularly negative emotionality, such as experiencing states of anger, anxiety, and irritability, and by weak or low constraint, meaning a difficulty in controlling impulses, making these individuals "quick on the draw."

Others seeking to measure personality traits associated with crime have focused on specific offender types. Caputo and colleagues (1999) examined juvenile sex offenders and found sex offenders to have high levels of callous and unemotional traits. In another example, Myers and colleagues (1995) set out to study the diagnostic, behavioral, and offense factors in juvenile homicide and to identify profile characteristics of homicidal juveniles. They found:

> The juvenile murderer is typically a disruptive behavior-disordered youth with family and school problems who has been raised in a violent environment and abused by one or more caretakers. He has prior evidence of

difficulty controlling aggressive urges toward others and has been arrested for earlier offense(s). . . . In spite of diagnosable psychiatric disorders in 96% of these youths, only a few (14%) had ever received any mental health care. . . . The high frequency of neuropsychiatric vulnerabilities in this sample, primarily a history of psychotic symptoms (71%) and serious past head trauma is not an unusual finding in juvenile murderers. Such vulnerabilities are postulated to be contributory factors in the etiology of violence. (1995, 1487)

Sutherland and Shepherd (2002) examined 13,650 English youth and found that lack of self-control and low self-esteem predict violence. In an even more comprehensive study, Miller and Lynam (2001) conducted a meta-analysis of personality traits and antisocial behavior. They found strong empirical support and were able to distinguish personality traits of antisocial individuals (hostile, self-centered, spiteful, jealous, and indifferent). They also provide a comprehensive description of various personality theories and relationships to crime. Given that such traits can be found in child and adolescent murderers, the critical question becomes, What is the causal relation of these traits to the crime and what are the policy implications of these types of causal analysis? If we are born with certain traits, they are based on generation-to-generation transmission. This process may go back millions of years and involves evolution.

Evolutionary Psychology

A relatively new psychological area of inquiry involves evolutionary psychology (EP) (Thornhill and Palmer 2000; Barkow, Cosmides, and Tooby 1992). This version of psychology stresses that behavior is either directly or indirectly related to inherited mechanisms that increase survival odds while dealing with natural selection. As we saw in the previous chapter, the first to apply this idea to criminology via what they describe as r/K selection theory were the evolutionary biosocial criminologists Lee Ellis (1987; Ellis and Walsh 2000) and J. Philippe Rushton (1990, 1995). Evolutionary psychologists strongly dispute the idea that the mind is a general learning-solving apparatus. Instead the mind/brain is the result of millions of years of evolutionary processes meeting environmental challenges, which led to "specific cognitive functions to meet those challenges through the process of natural selection and sexual selection" (Ellis and Walsh 2000, 147). Our brain is composed of specific "modules" or areas that are geared to solving different adaptive problems. Evolutionary psychology is well illustrated by Thornhill and Palmer's argument (also argued by Ellis 1989, in his book *Theories of Rape*) that rape is best understood in the context of mate selection and adaptive processes.

Males and females faced quite different sexual-selection problems in the Pleistocene period. More specifically, for females selecting a mate was a major decision as they typically invested long periods of time in bringing up their young. Therefore, selecting a male who was likely to invest his resources in her children was critical to ensuring their survival. Women evolved to choose their mates extremely carefully and placed a premium on traits such as reliability, kindness, and high status (i.e., access to more resources). Because males were typically more eager to have sex than females, it was possible to choose from a range of possible mates. However for males, sex was a low-investment activity, all they had to contribute was a small deposit of sperm and a few minutes of their time. In addition, finding a mate was an intensely competitive process with high quality males likely to dominate the sexual arena and secure exclusive sexual access to females. Therefore, males with the highest status and most resources were more likely to obtain sexual access to females, thereby increasing the chances that their genes would be passed on and their offspring survive (Ward and Siegert 2002, 151).

Other males were left to forcibly take their mates in order to pass on their genes. Having sex with as many women as possible further increased the male's chances of reproductive success (see Ellis's "cheater theory" of crime in the previous chapter). Males acquired multiple partners because women conceive internally and males could never be certain of their paternity. Under the EP paradigm, people are just another form of animal. This perspective has understandably been criticized (Ward and Siegert 2002) and is especially challenging to the feminist perspective (discussed later).

The Limitations and Policy Implications of Trait-Based and Evolutionary Psychology

A major limitation of trait-based personality theories is that, like psychoanalytical approaches, they are tautological (rely on circular reasoning). By definition, lawbreakers have defective personalities and this is used to classify them: Stealing may be taken as an indicator of impulsiveness and impulsiveness given as the reason for stealing. Similarly committing offenses against others is seen as evidence of a lack of empathy, yet lack of empathy is seen as a trait to explain offending. Thus a recurrent criticism of trait-based theories is that they represent correlational rather than causal connections. In other words, do the traits develop in advance of criminal behavior or as a result of it or its implications? Moreover, Akers has noted, "The concept of the psychopathic personality, for instance, is so broad that it could apply to virtually anyone who violates the law" (1994, 87).

In addition to these theoretical and methodological flaws, results of research into the effects of personality traits have been mixed. One of the first comprehensive reviews reported that most previous studies did not find significant differences between delinquents and nondelinquents (Schuessler and Cressey 1950). A review of the more sophisticated studies did find significant differences, however (Waldo and Dinitz 1967). The empirical research on Eysenck's theory provides a good illustration. Studies report little relationship between crime and the major dimension of extroversion, although some support was found for the dimensions of psychoticism and neuroticism (Cochrane 1974; Burgess 1972; Passingham 1972; Feldman 1977). But Eysenck's theory is empirically and methodologically so flawed that it is even discounted by sympathetic psychologists (Bartol 1999).

The implication of trait-based personality theory for policy is that if traits exist, then they may be measured and used to predict and prevent future delinquency and crime. Thus if traits can be identified in potential offenders at an early age, treatment should begin then, even before antisocial behavior has emerged. The traits may be counteracted through various therapeutic programs designed to compensate for them. Eysenck ([1964] 1977, 213) sees psychiatry as a practical intervention aimed at the "elimination of antisocial conduct." Similarly, one of the objectives of the study by Myers and colleagues (1995) was to identify profiles fitting juveniles who may be homicidal. There are obviously serious moral questions about screening children for personality traits, defining them as "at risk," and giving them "preventive" treatment.

Overall, the trait-based approach is limited by its narrow focus, which excludes cognitive and social learning factors. Both cognitive and social learning theory grew out of a disenchantment with the limits of behaviorism.

Evolutionary psychology has been criticized on a number of grounds (Ward and Siegert 2002). First, it does not consider other competing theories. The modal thesis of how the brain is organized has not been proven or is incomplete (Gilbert 1998). Further research on rapists shows that they view women differently than nonrapists—a learned behavior (Ward, Keenan, and Husdon 2000). Ward and Siegert also question whether the rapist during the Pleistocene era would be harmed or killed by the female's relatives. Empirical research shows that many rapists have difficulty with erections and fail to ejaculate—further damaging the EP argument. Finally, humans can modify their behavior and learn from their mistakes. It is unclear what policies would fit with EP. Presumably, equal access and opportunities would, over millions of years of evolutionary process, lead to the diminishing need for rapists to rape.

Behavioral, Situational, and Social Learning Theories

Early learning theories assumed a passive model of individuals whose past experiences and associations led to their present actions. These theories evolved to a more active view of humans as making various judgments about current actions based on their interpretations of past and present experiences.

Behavioral Learning Theory

The passive behavioral version of learning theory, rooted in the work of Pavlov and Skinner, saw crime as the outcome of learning that under certain circumstances, certain behavior will be rewarded. Pavlov ([1906] 1967) discovered what has become known as classical conditioning. He argued that stimuli will consistently produce a given effect. In his classic example, a dog will always salivate when presented with meat. This is a passive learning approach, since the person learns what to expect from the environment. A slightly more active version was developed by Skinner (1953, 1971) with his notion of operant conditioning. In this case, behavior is controlled through manipulation of the consequences of previous behavior. This model of learning is more active because the individual learns how to get what she or he wants from the environment rather than passively waiting for it to materialize.

A central idea of operant conditioning is reinforcement, which involves strengthening a tendency to act in a certain way. Such strengthening can be in the form of positive reinforcement, whereby past crimes are rewarded. An example would be a corporation that wins competitive bids by consistently undercutting the competition's costs through the manufacture of defective products. Negative reinforcement occurs when an unpleasant experience is avoided by committing crime (e.g., taking illegal drugs to avoid painful low self-esteem). A manufacturer's violation of health and safety laws would be an example of negative reinforcement if such action reduced declining productivity. In spite of popular misunderstanding, punishment itself is not negative reinforcement because it is designed to weaken rather than strengthen a tendency to do something. But taking action to avoid anticipated punishment reflects the consequences of negative reinforcement.

Social Learning and Modeling Theory

A more complex and active approach called social learning theory gets close to the active learning of cognitive theory (see later discussion). Originating in the work of Gabrial Tarde (1843–1904) on imitation and developed by

Albert Bandura (1969, 1973, 1977; Bandura and Walters 1963), social learning is initially based not on reward and punishment but on the idea that individuals are complex beings who do not simply respond mechanically but observe and analyze situations before they decide to act. Part of the learning process involves role modeling based on identification with others, either real or represented, such as persons or images portrayed in the media, on television, in the movies or in video games. In social learning, we watch others and decide which patterns of behavior to imitate. These may be real-life heroes, celebrities such as recording artist Marilyn Manson, or fictional or even cartoon characters such as Beavis and Butthead, or the children of South Park. No specific reinforcement is necessary for this modeling to occur. However, Bandura says that once modeled such patterned responses may be triggered by events or adverse situations in a person's life. Once acquired, however, the prospect or practice of the learned behavior may be goal directed toward a rewarding outcome, which then may become reinforced by its outcome if this is met by the desired result. The enactment of learned patterns thus can become self-rewarding and thereby reinforced.

A particularly good example of role modeling from video games is seen in the arguments of former military officer Dave Grossman, who has coined the term "killology" for his Web site (http://www.killology.com) and is explored in his book, *Stop Teaching Our Kids to Kill: A Call to Action Against TV, Movie, and Video Game Violence* (Grossman and DeGaetano 1999). Grossman argues that video games incorporate the very same elements that the military uses to train soldiers to kill the enemy, and they provide the rationalizations and practice mechanisms to train teenagers to engage in school and other violence:

> In the military, you are immediately confronted with a role model: your drill sergeant. He or she personifies violence and aggression. Along with military heroes, these violent role models have always been used to influence young, impressionable minds . . . Today the media are providing our children with role models. We get copycat, cluster murders that work their way across America like a virus spread by the six o'clock news. No matter what someone has done, if you put his picture on TV, you have made him a celebrity, and someone, somewhere, will emulate him . . . when the images of the young killers are broadcast on television, they become role models. The average preschooler in America watches 27 hours of television a week. The average child gets more one-on-one communication from TV than from all her parents and teachers combined. The ultimate achievement for our children is to get their picture on TV.
>
> *(Grossman 1998; http://www.killology.com/art_trained_video.htm)*

In short, social learning theory says that the observation and experience of poor role models produce imitation and instigation of socially undesirable behaviors. In this way, violent behaviors can be seen as acceptable behavioral options, as in the case of spouse abuse modeled on the way the abuser's parents interacted when dealing with conflict. Longitudinal research on the television programs watched by children in the 1970s shows that those who watched the most violent programs were more likely to be violent in adult life than those who did not watch such shows (Huesmann et al. 2003). Using follow-up interviews, interviews with friends and relatives, and criminal justice records, the research was conducted on 329 adults between 1992 and 1995, who were initially surveyed as children in 1977–1978. The study found that those ranked in the top 20 percent for watching the most violent television shows (such as *Starsky and Hutch,* the *Six Million Dollar Man,* and even the Roadrunner cartoon) were more than twice as likely to act aggressively toward their spouse than those with less violent television viewing as children. Men were more likely to push, shove, hit, or slap and women were more likely to have thrown something at their spouses. Those children in the original study who identified with the characters and who believed they depicted real life were those found to be more violent in later life. Importantly, those who watched such programs with their parents, who were able to mediate the violence portrayed, were not as violent as those who watched the programs alone (Huesmann et al. 2003). This research provides major support to Bandura's theory of social learning through behavior modeling. Several criminologists have incorporated these different versions of learning into their theories, most notably Ronald Akers (1985, 1998), and we shall examine these more fully in Chapter 6, on learning criminal behavior.

Limitations and Policy Implications of Learning Theory

There are several limitations to learning theory, central to which is why only some of those exposed to negative learning patterns, role models, and reinforcement actually adopt them, whereas most know the difference between fiction and reality. Clearly, some people are more open to influence than others. As the more sophisticated of these arguments suggest, most are endowed with or also learn "protective factors," such as believing in other values that serve as intervening variables limiting the enactment of the negative patterns. Social learning theory is also unable to easily explain gender, age, or racial differences in behavior, unless it incorporates a notion of identification with specific role models having significance to the social learner. However, as soon as this is conceded, the theory moves beyond simple modeling into cognitive theory, which we discuss below.

The policy implication of behavioral and learning models is to reward conventional and positive behavior. Ellis and Walsh (2000, 346) observe:

"Social learning theory is impressive in terms of the number of treatment programs it has helped to inspire. The most unique feature of [these] programs ... is a heavy emphasis on rewarding prosocial ('good') behavior rather than trying to punish antisocial behavior." As a result, in the Skinnerian behavioral approaches, the role of discipline in home and school is important, particularly focusing on the practices of parents and teachers. Thus the social learning version of the theory involves varieties of resocialization, individual and family counseling, development of new behavioral options, and the provision of new "proper" role models (Patterson 1997). In summary, the policy argues for strengthening the family to encourage children to make noncrime choices, teaching appropriate parental socialization of children into responsible moral behavior, and teaching children right from wrong, which are all part of positive reinforcement. In terms of policy, social learning and modeling theory imply a heavy monitoring of media and developing societal mechanisms to control and filter the kind of television children watch and for restricting the kind of video games that they are allowed to play. The cognitive learning perspective, which we turn to next, is less mechanistic than simple learning theory and goes beyond the modeling patterns of social learning theory to consider how social learning is a creative activity.

Cognitive Theories

Founded on the ideas of Wilhelm Wundt (1832–1920), William James (1842–1920), and the Swiss child psychologist Jean Piaget (1896–1980), cognitive psychology captures the idea that human reasoning processes shape the way humans act and orient them to behavior. There are several kinds of cognitive theory relevant to criminology, notably those by Lawrence Kohlberg, Aron Beck, and Todd Friedberg.

Piaget's ideas are seen in the notion of progressive moral development outlined by Lawrence Kohlberg (1969). Here cognitive theory has as its major theme how mental thought processes are used to solve problems— to interpret, evaluate, and decide on the best actions. These thought processes occur through mental pictures and conversations with ourselves. The assumption is that individuals' future orientation to action and their environment will be affected by the knowledge they acquire and process. For Piaget ([1923] 1969, [1932] 1965, [1937] 1954), children develop the ability to use logic, construct mental maps, and eventually reflect on their own thought processes. He argued that this cognitive development occurred in stages, with each new stage of intellectual development emerging as a resolution to the contradictions between different and competing views of the same events.

Kohlberg (1969) applied Piaget's ideas to moral development, finding that children develop through six stages. They progress from a premoral stage, in which morality is heavily influenced by outside authority, through levels of convention in which decisions about right and wrong are based on what significant others expect, to full social awareness combining a sense of personal ethics and human rights. Most people never make it to the last stage.

Cognitive theory emerged in criminology, noticeably the work of Yochelson and Samenow (1976, 1977; Samenow 1984), whose explanation of the criminal personality integrated free will, rational choice, and thinking patterns. These clinical psychologists, who had to abandon all their clinical training (Freudian and behaviorist), argued that faulty learning produces defective thinking, which results in criminal behavior choices. Yochelson and Samenow developed a theory rejecting the idea of determinism, arguing, "The essence of this approach is that criminals choose to commit crimes. Crime resides within the person and is 'caused' by the way he thinks, not by his environment. Criminals think differently from responsible people" (Samenow 1984, xiv). Criminal thinking is different from a very early age. In general, criminals think concretely rather than abstractly; are impulsive, irresponsible, and self-centered; and are motivated by anger or fear. These characteristics describe a person with a "criminal personality" who is difficult to change or rehabilitate. These underlying psychological emotions lead criminals to view themslves as being worthless and to feel that others may come to see them the same way and that the condition is permanent. Criminals thus commit crimes to avoid reaching this state and to avoid having their worthlessness exposed. The fear that it might be exposed produces intense anger and hatred toward certain groups, who may be violently attacked for not recognizing the individual's inflated sense of superiority or for injuring his or her sense of pride.

A second line of cognitive theory applied to the criminology of violence is by Aaron Beck (1999), who is seen as the father of modern cognitive therapy. In his book *Prisoners of Hate,* Beck links human thinking processes and emotional and behavioral expressions. Put simply, the way we think shapes our feelings and actions. Beck argues that extreme forms of violence from verbal abuse, domestic violence, rape, and hate crimes to terrorist bombing and genocide are exaggerations of patterns of everyday thought. These dysfunctional patterns of thinking Beck calls "hostile framing." They are the fundamental ways in which humans both see themselves as morally right and classify others with whom they are frustrated and in conflict as "less than us," as "dangerous, malicious and evil" (Beck 1999, 8). Once negatively framed, the other's past and present words and actions are seen as challenging, hurtful, and demeaning, and produce anger and hostility as we perceive ourselves the victim of the other's attack. We deal with these problems by further dehumanizing the other into an exaggerated caricature of negative aspects, which leads to an endless cycle of disrespect, resulting in a desire for preemptive elimination of the other. Beck, like the other cognitive theorists, sees patterns of thinking developing over time and says that those of us who employ "hostile framing" are at an early stage that he calls "primal thinking." Once locked into these patterns, we become a prison of reaction to the image we have constructed of the other rather than to the person: "They mistake the image for the person. . . . Their minds are encased in 'the prison of hate'" (Beck 1999, 8). This would explain hate crimes against targeted and stereotyped groups like gays.

A related approach that relies on cognitive analysis is found in the work of Shoham (1979) and Katz (1988). These authors are concerned with understanding how individuals strive to make a meaningful world when confronted with strong feelings of fear, anxiety, and alienation. Unlike Beck, who sees primal thinking as one stage in a sequence, Shoham sees it as emanating from a specific event: birth, which is seen as a cosmic disaster leading to ego formation and ego identity. Deviance is an attempt to deal with the trauma of birth separation through the negation of ego identity. Katz, in particular, was concerned with identifying how offenders make their world meaningful in ways that provide the moral and sensational attractions leading to crime. But both authors recognized that these approaches lack empirical verification and point only to vague policy objectives such as participatory democracy (Shoham and Seis 1993; Faust 1995, 56). In yet another interesting and fruitful endeavor DeCoster and Heimer (2001) have integrated symbolic interactionism (discussed later) and psychology. They show that depression and law violation are not only related, but are the interactive product of social-structural-psychological mechanisms (e.g., stressful events, family relationships, reflected appraisals). At this point, it is questionable whether these various cognitive "psychologies" are not just as arguably social constructionist sociologies.

In the previous chapter we showed that most serious biosocial theorists consider biological organisms to be in an interactive relationship with their environment. In this chapter we have increasingly seen how psychologists have moved from a trait-based to a learning and ultimately a cognitive-environmental view of the mind. A recent development in psychology that could have important implications for the psychological study of crime attempts the interrelationship of brain-mind-environment. In his book *Altered Egos: How the Brain Creates the Self*, neurologist and psychiatrist Todd Feinberg (2001) shows that the physical workings of the brain's various and separate biological functions can produce a synthesis or unified self that produces meaning, purpose, and a sense of being from the world around it. He argues that the self and mind emerge from the many parts of the material (physical) brain. He says that the "self can be understood as a nested hierarchy of meaning and purpose" (Feinberg 2001, 138) where the levels of self, and the many parts of the brain that contribute to the self, "are nested within all the other levels of the hierarchy" (Feinberg 2001, 149). The implications of this approach are to recognize the irreducibility of mind to biology or to see the functions of the brain as disconnected from the mind.

Limitations and Policy Implications of Cognitive Theory

Cognitive theory has received some empirical support but also has some inherent weaknesses. Some psychologists have developed instruments to measure the different "thinking styles" thought to be associated with serious criminal activity (e.g., Psychological Inventory of Criminal Thinking Styles; see Walters 1995). Others, such as Blatier (2000), examined locus of control, stability, self-esteem, and controllability in a study of convicted offenders. She found support for cognitive theory. Not surprisingly, the longer one is incarcerated the lower one's self-esteem and the more powerless one feels (Goldstein and McKenzie, 1984). This has policy implications since a higher self-esteem is related to a lower rate of recidivism. Similarly, a study by Henning and Frueh (1996) found that treatment intervention involving a "cognitive self-change program" designed to correct "criminogenic thinking errors" among incarcerated offenders supported the value of such therapeutic intervention.

However, as with several of the psychological theories we have examined so far, cognitive theorists such as Yochelson and Samenow do not explain why some offenders think criminally and others do not. They also used no control groups in their evaluation and provide little evidence of systematically gathered data. Perhaps most important, they overgeneralize from a highly selected group of problem-suffering clients or hospitalized hard-core adult criminals and serious juvenile offenders to the general population of offenders (Vold [1958] 1979, 155).

At a broader level, cognitive theory has been criticized for ignoring psychobiological explanations, disregarding the effects of emotions, and the same circular reasoning that was seen as a defect in trait-based theory: "It seems that behaviors are taken to indicate cognitive processes, and that in turn, the cognitive processes are given as explanations for the behaviors" (Faust 1995, 54).

Consistent with their assumptions about "stinking thinking" leading to crime, cognitive-oriented theorists' policies for crime control involve the identification and elimination of dysfunctional thought processes or reasoning ability. For example, Yochelson and Samenow's (1977) interventions were designed to identify and destroy current destructive criminal patterns of decisionmaking by confronting offenders directly and by creating new thought processes. Yochelson and Samenow believe that criminals can be confronted with their behavior as victimizers of society in an attempt to increase feelings of guilt and self-disgust that eventually deter their criminal thinking. But these theorists also claim to teach the suppression of criminal thoughts and substitution of noncriminal ones. Thus, Samenow (1984, 257) argued, "We are as we think. It is impossible to help a person give up crime and live responsibly without helping him to change what is most basic—his thinking."

For these theorists, "The criminal must learn to identify and then abandon thinking patterns that have guided his behavior for years. He must be taught new thinking patterns that are self-evident and automatic for responsible people but are totally foreign to him" (1984, 6–7). To do this, Yochelson and Samenow got criminals to write down their day-to-day thinking and report it to a group. Then, the therapists would point out the errors in this thinking and suggest how to correct it. They claim that eventually those treated developed new patterns of thought and behavior and discovered the rewards of behaving responsibly, without deception or intimidation.

Similarly, Beck's cognitive therapy concentrates on correcting biased thinking patterns in order to "reframe their negative images" (Beck 1999, 8). Unfortunately, Beck also celebrates the work of those, such as Dodge (1993), who screen kindergarten children in high poverty areas for aggressive behavior and subject them to social and cognitive skill training from first through tenth grade. Clearly there are serious moral questions about preventative intervention, which we looked at in the last chapter.

In the next section we look at how far psychologists have come toward embracing a broader social perspective, by considering those who focus on the environment as a significant factor in shaping the mind.

Ecological Psychology

Ecological psychology is the study of how environmental factors, such as unemployment and social settings, prevail on a person's mind to affect behavior. Ecological psychology developed as a reaction against the narrow clinical approach to treatment and a disenchantment with psychotherapy, and it is considerably more eclectic in its assumptions. Ecological psychologists argue that psychotherapy has not demonstrated its effectiveness. Traditional psychology is accused of using a medical model with "a passive help giver who waits for the client to define his or her own need and then to request help" (Levine and Perkins 1987, 36).

The focus of ecological, also called community psychology, is not to find out what is wrong with the individual. Rather, the emphasis is on looking at what is right with the person and his or her fit with the culture and environment (Rappaport 1977). Thus, this approach is much more encompassing than traditional psychological clinical approaches. Several factors that reflect the changing social context led to the development and growth of the perspective.

The social context of the mid–1960s was one of turbulence and change. First, the Kennedy-Johnson War on Poverty stimulated attention to many related social problems, such as crime, unemployment, poor education, mental retardation, and welfare inequities. Community psychology was one way of welding these problems into one cohesive mass. Second, with the large deinstitutionalization of mental health patients in the 1960s, it was recognized that new service delivery models were needed. This recognition was spurred on in part by the efforts of President Kennedy (who had a mentally challenged sister). Furthermore, the recognition of the inability of the mental health community to keep pace with the demands society places on it called for a greater emphasis on prevention. Finally, empirical research documented that emotional problems are much more severe in areas (communities) of social disorganization (Levine and Perkins 1987). As a result, in 1961 President John F. Kennedy's Joint Commission on Mental Health suggested (1) there should be a broader definition of who could deliver mental health services, (2) early intervention was critical, and (3) intervention should occur in the community. Ecological psychology is also called community psychology because it actively seeks out those who require help in their own environment or community.

According to Levine and Perkins (1987, 95), the people and settings within a community are interdependent. First, change occurs in a whole social system and not just in an individual, and thus a variety of different problem definitions and solutions are possible in any situation. Second, community systems involve resource exchanges among persons and settings involving commodities such as time, money, and political power. Third, the behavior that we observe in a particular individual always reflects a continuous process of adaptation between that individual and his or her level of competence and the environment, with the nature and range of competence it supports. Adaptation can thus proceed by changing the environment as well as the person. Finally, change occurs naturally in a community, as well as by intentional design, and change represents an opportunity to redefine and reallocate resources in ways that facilitate adaptation by all populations in the community.

Limitations and Policy Implications of Ecological Psychology

Ecological psychology has been faulted for "lack of a well-articulated, widely shared conceptual model or set of theoretical principles" (Levine and Perkins 1987, 63). It has also been criticized for being more sociological than psychological. But as with the other theories we have examined, this has not stopped the formulation of policy.

Ecological psychology advocates a policy of manipulating environmental factors, specifically by making resources available. According to Levine and Perkins, "In the ecological perspective, human behavior is viewed in terms of the person's adaptation to resources and circumstances. From this perspective, one may correct unsuccessful adaptations by altering the availability of resources. Thus new services may be created, or existing strengths in social networks may be discovered and conditions created to enhance the use of such resources" (1987, 5). Community psychology also recognizes that "before any individual appears his society has had a specific social life organized and systematized, and the existence of this life will exercise a tyrannical compulsion on him" (Saranson 1981, 832). Although the individual may need specialized attention, the preventive objective is to reduce the incidence of individuals requiring such attention. Ecological psychologists are thus concerned with neighborhood-level preventive interventions. Providing material, educational, and psychological resources to help people fit in diverse or different societies is the objective.

One strategy is community policing. Using an approach based on ecological psychology, basic components of any theory must be identified, operationalized, and tested using psychometric procedures. For example, among the stated objectives of community policing are to reduce fear of crime and increase community cohesion, in part through decreasing physical and social disorder. Thus scales, or instruments, were developed to measure cohesion, disorder, and fear of crime (Lanier and Davidson 1995). The next step would be to implement community policing and evaluate the impact using psychometric measures. The lack of resources is a major problem with this approach, however. It is difficult to make resources available to those in need when the political climate does not support such efforts.

Summary and Conclusion

The psychological perspective has added a rich and important dimension to criminological theory. In spite of mixed empirical support, it has raised serious questions with both the mechanical determinism of biological theories and the open vistas of individual freedom claimed in classical models. It has sensitized criminology to the importance of individual development, unconscious processes, and the consolidation of behavioral characteristics during childhood development. Most important, it has explored the way the human mind engages its environment toward self-preservation or destruction. Differences between the various psychological approaches have also enriched our understanding of how the environment may be translated into both constructive and destructive behavior. Ultimately, psychological criminology has provided a window to our mind and an opening to individualized treatment. Its attention to therapy has fostered understanding of the nature of our actions and the consequences of past relationships on future behavior, and how we may intervene at the individual level to make a difference to our relational world.

Summary Chart: Psychological Theories of Crime

Basic Idea: People have personalities formed through parental socialization. Some are inadequately socialized or are traumatized during development and form crime-prone personalities or behavioral tendencies or criminal-thinking patterns.

Human Nature: Humans are seen as biological entities but with personalities that are shaped by childhood developmental experiences in the family. Humans therefore are malleable. Their behavior reflects a combination of biological attributes and early socialization experiences that are mediated through cognitive processes of the "mind." Psychoanalytical theory claims the key to the mind is its unconscious process. Behaviorists believe human minds are a blank slate. Trait-based approaches fall somewhere between the two, seeing adult personality formation emerging from socialization with distinct traits. Social learning and cognitive theories assume perception, self-identity, and rational decision making. Existential and phenomenological approaches assume the importance of socially constructed meanings, emotions, and feelings absent in the behavioral learning models. Finally, ecological psychology is concerned with identifying the fit between individuals and their environment, seeing how the latter can shape an individual's mind.

Society and the Social Order: Generally seen as a consensus, with the exception of social learning theory, which sees conflicting social norms. Law is seen as the rules designed to protect the ongoing development of society. Crime is one form of abnormal behavior manifested by those with personality problems or defective personalities. Psychologists prefer the nonlegal definition of crime as aggressive or antisocial behavior reflecting norm violation rather than law violation. Criminals, especially in trait theory, differ from noncriminals. Criminals, according to cognitive theory, are those who have learned incorrect ways to think or behave in society.

Causal Logic: Most attribute cause to defective socialization by primary groups, principally the family, although some recognize modeling on significant others or even images of significant groups or role models. Specific causes vary depending on the variety of psychological theory: (1) Psychoanalytic theory argues that offensive behavior or antisocial behavior is the outcome of early childhood frustrations. Primitive drives of the id combine with weak ego and superego development because of (a) failed parental socialization, (b) unconscious guilt, (c) oedipal conflict, and (d) aggression. The result is frustration, and an unconscious search for compensatory gratification leads to aggression and delinquency. Weak superego and riotous id cause breach of social controls; overdeveloped superego or damaged ego can also cause crime. (2) Behavioral learning theory sees crime as the outcome of learning that under certain circumstances it will be rewarded. A key concept is operant conditioning, whereby behavior is controlled through manipulation of the consequences of previous behavior. A central idea is reinforcement, which can be positive, in cases where past crimes are rewarded for their commission, or negative, where punishment or other consequences are avoided by committing the offense. (3) Trait-based personality theory argues the development of a criminal or psychotic personality is sometimes a result of extroversion or low IQ affecting ability to learn rules, perceive punishment, or experience pain, as in biological theory. (4) Social learning theory says observation and experience of poor role models produce self-reinforcement of observed deviant behavior, leading to imitation and instigation of the same. Violent behaviors are seen as acceptable behavioral options, and the imitation of others' criminal behavior is experienced as rewarding. (5) Cognitive interpretive processes explain why criminals and noncriminals behave differently, even when they have similar backgrounds. Applied to crime, the theory argues that faulty learning produces defective thinking, which produces criminal behavior. Existential and phenomenological variants of the theory focus on individual construction of meaning that triggers criminal activity. (6) Environmental or community-based psychology looks at the fit between individuals and environment and attempts to manipulate the environment to prevent offending.

Criminal Justice Policy: Depends on version, but most involve prediction and prevention and some kind of therapeutic intervention, assisted by drugs to correct and control traits.

Criminal Justice Practice: Psychoanalytic theory involves evaluation and treatment to help offenders uncover the childhood root causes, bring these to the conscious, and train to effectively control or correct problems of parental or "maternal" deprivation. Behavioral models require rewarding conventional behavior and not rewarding deviant behavior; the role of discipline in the home and school is important. Social learning theory involves varieties of resocialization, individual and family counseling, development of new behavioral options, provision of new, "proper" models. Cognitive theory involves learning new ways to think and replacing destructive thought processes with constructive ones. The environmental approach involves manipulation of community resources to prevent problems arising from the outset. The various intervention techniques are largely focused at the individual level of treatment and include psychoanalysis, group therapy, counseling, family therapy, drug treatment, and environmental manipulation.

Evaluation: Psychoanalytical theory is criticized for being male oriented and seeing females as inherently abnormal. The theory is difficult to test, and ideas about "basic instincts" and "unconscious forces" cannot be verified or falsified. Trait theory provides an alternative to Freud and behaviorism; it promoted empirical research to find personality traits but ignores situational structuring of traits and so is too narrow. Both theories have problems of circular reasoning. Behavioral approaches oversimplify the learning process by excluding cognitive processes such as interpretation, memory, and perception. Behaviorism based on stimulus-response is too mechanical. Cognitive theory also suffers from circular reasoning: Behavior is taken to indicate cognitive processes and the processes are taken as explanations for the behavior. Phenomenological approaches lack scientific verification and policy implications. Environmental psychology does not deal with the wider political structures that shape the environment. Overall, psychological perspectives tend to do better explaining sexual and violent crimes. But the approach has important implications for the way we discipline children and the public consumption of media messages, as in sex and violence on TV. This approach fails to explain individual differences in response to learning and provides only weak causal connections between factors.

Notes

1. There are four legal bases for the insanity defense. The M'Naghten Rule (1843) requires that it be proved that the accused either did not know the illegal act was wrong or did not know its nature because of defective reasoning resulting from disease of the mind. The Durham Rule (1871) is broader in that it allows an accused to escape criminal responsibility if the illegal act was the product of mental disease or defect, a definition that permits greater input by psychiatric expert witnesses. The Irresistible Impulse Test requires evidence to prove that the defendant could not control his or her behavior because of mental illness. Finally, the Substantial Incapacity Test says a person is not criminally responsible if at the time of the illegal act a mental disease or defect resulted in a lack of substantial capacity to appreciate the wrongfulness of the conduct or to conform to the law. Several states have established a compromise guilty but insane plea in which the person is first sent to a secure hospital or psychiatric center for treatment and when cured completes the remainder of the sentence in prison.

6

Learning Criminal Behavior
Social Process Theories

What we call human nature in actuality is human habit.
—Jewel [Kilcher] (1994)

Military and vampire cultures appear to be at the opposite end of the moral and behavioral spectrum. The military represents discipline, uniformity, respect for authority, high ethical standards, hierarchical status, and the promotion and protection of American values. Goth and vampire (or "vampyre") cults represent anarchy, individualism, disregard for authority, minimal ethical development, and challenge the most deeply held religious and social values. Each, however, can socialize their members into crime. Consider first the case of William Calley and then the case of Charity Keesee.

On March 16, 1968, in Vietnam, as many as 500 men, women, and children were killed by U.S. Army platoons in what became known as the My Lai massacre. A squad sergeant from one of the platoons testified, "We complied with the orders, sir" (Calley 1974, 342). Lieutenant William Calley, who gave the order for his squad to "get rid of 'em" (1974, 347), reasoned: "Well everything is to be killed. . . . I figured 'They're already wounded, I might as well go and kill them. This is our mission'" (1974, 342). Dead Vietnamese were part of a GI's "body count." As Calley explained, these people were not seen as human beings: "We weren't in My Lai to kill human beings really. We were there to kill ideology that is carried by—I don't know. Pawns. Blobs. Pieces of flesh, and I wasn't in My Lai to destroy intelligent men. I was there to destroy an intangible idea. To destroy communism" (1974, 343). Calley did not learn this on the street in a criminal gang but in U.S. schools, being brought up as a "run of the mill average guy." As he explains:

I went to school in the 1950s remember, and it was drilled into us from gram-
mar school on, "Ain't is bad, aren't is good, communism's bad, democracy's
good. One and one's two," et cetera: until we were at Edison High, we just
didn't think about it. . . . The people in Washington are smarter than me. If
intelligent people told me, "Communism's bad. It's going to engulf us. To
take us in," I believed them. I had to. . . . Personally, I didn't kill any Vietnamese that day: I mean personally. I represented the United States of America. My country. (Calley 1974, 342–344).

Prior to her incarceration Charity Lynn Keesee gained notoriety by be-
longing to a vampire cult that resulted in the notorious "Vampire Clan
killings," which have been the topic of several books, movies, and television documentaries. Although vampire cultism does not typically result
in violence and death, more than 4,000 are estimated to practice it. Unlike most, Charity's cult committed one of the most publicized crimes of
the twenty-first century. The leader of her cult and her boyfriend, Roderick (Rod) Ferrell, 16, and Scott Anderson, 17, broke into the home of cult
member Heather Wendorf and beat her parents to death with a crowbar.
Cigarette burns in the shape of a "V" were found on the victims. Charity,
Heather, and Dana Cooper, 19, were across town visiting with friends
during the attack. After the brutal, satanic murder Ferrell and Anderson
stole the family SUV and picked up the girls. After successfully eluding
the police for days, Charity phoned her mother from a hotel in
Louisiana. According to Charity, she had her mother notify the authorities as to their whereabouts (personal correspondence, November 2002).
Others dispute this explanation, stating that she was simply seeking
funding. In either case, this phone call resulted in the arrest of the group
in Baton Rouge. On June 15, 1996, Charity Lynn Keesee was convicted of
being an accessory to first degree murder and sentenced to fifteen years
in Florida correctional institutions. By the start of 2003 Charity had been
incarcerated for seven years. After meeting with her numerous times,
Mark Lanier had the impression that she was still in many ways a lost
sixteen-year-old. She was shy, sweet, and very open about her life and
activities. She was very willing to please, anxious to improve her life,
and looking forward to an education. There was also an undercurrent of
strength, anger, and defiance. While not criminal, Charity seeks refuge
through self-mutilation. Her recollections of her problems go back to
1995 as a culmination to a traumatic upbringing. In May 1995 Charity
Keesee was fifteen years old and a runaway from rural Kentucky. She
weighed ninety-five pounds and was pregnant. She was a lonely, shy
girl, intelligent but rebellious. She was also a member of a group of kids
who belonged to a vampire cult. Charity describes her entry and life into
the world of "darkness and evil."

I don't know exactly where to start in where I went wrong. I used to blame it on my parents, but now realize I can't do that. I was my own person. I was a bad girl.

My rebellionsness [sic] started out with my stepfather and mother. My step-father, Harold, started sexually abusing me when I was seven years old. My mother worked the night shift at a communications company, which left me home alone with Harold from the time I got out of school until about one in the morning. The sexual abuse went on for a few months short of five years.

When I was twelve I finally told my grandparents what he was doing to me, despite Harold's threats if I ever told anyone. My mother told me I was lying, but later after Harold admitted to her what he had been doing she said I asked for it. Later that year a judge gave my mother a choice: have her child in the house with her, or have Harold. She chose Harold.

I was sent to Kentucky to live with my father. I wanted to stay with my dad because I know I'd be spoiled, but I still resented my mother because I felt like she abandoned me.

When I got to Kentucky my mind was a swirl of confusion. I trusted no one. Not even my father. All men were a threat to me. I would shrink away if my father got too close or if he even tried to hug me.

Daddy was gone a lot in those days, which left me home alone in our country house fifteen miles out of town. I didn't have many friends—by my own choice—and the ones I did have were all a few years older.

I met Rod that year. At the time he was a kindred spirit; a victim of sexual abuse himself, as well as someone with as many resentments as I had. Maybe more.

Rod wasn't always around. He would disappear sometimes for a week at a time. I was very lost and alone when he wasn't there. I was hurting inside and could find no way to stop it. Then I found a way. I would find razor blades in my dad's auto shop out back and slice my skin for hours. The phys-ical pain and sight of blood made me forget that I was hurting inside. Dad was rarely home, so he'd never notice.

When I was thirteen Rod bought some acid, weed, and other drugs to my house. I was hooked. I discovered with acid I didn't have to think. Didn't have to feel. I was numb. Nothing mattered.

When I was fifteen, I started spending most of my time at Rod's apart-ment. Of course my father didn't know that, but what could he have done even if he found out? Nothing. I was out of control.

Rod and I started using heroin that year. It made him very violent. I would sit quietly, but inside the burning flames of rage were overtaking me. I was tired of life. I was tired of hurting. I found out I was pregnant in June. I told Rod, and he only said he was going to literally kill me. He didn't want a child. We had a fight and I left. I didn't see him for two weeks after that. Later that month Rod came out to my house. He was crying saying he de-cided he wanted the baby and ordered me to stop my current drug spree. He didn't stop though.

In September, a week after my birthday, I came back to the apartment later than Rod thought I should, and wearing clothes he said were too tight—too revealing. He met me at the door at the top of the stairs and beat me. Then proceeded to knock me down two flights of stairs. I lost the baby.

After that I really didn't care anymore. Life didn't mean anything. My drug habit worsened. I skipped school, and when I did go I was high. I couldn't get away from Rod either, despite that I hated him more than I'd ever hated anyone.

Right before my sixteenth birthday, Rod started talking about how he wanted us to come to Florida. We were going to pick up his friend Zoey (Heather), and the three of us would run away to New Orleans. I don't know how he intended us to survive there—all of us were under eighteen, from another state, knew no one there, and I was pregnant. Again.

I'm not going to go into the details about what happened once we got to Florida. All I will say is there was two murders, a burglary, and a weeks worth of running from the cops. We did make it to New Orleans; however, we didn't stay.

That was seven years ago. I can't say I've changed completely. I still can't stand to be alone in a room with any man. Even my father. I still tend to try to cover up my inner pain with physical. However, I have figured out that if I've made it this far, there isn't anything that's going to tear me down now.

January 27, 2003 (Mark Lanier, personal correspondence)

Following her abuse Charity found relief through self-mutilation. She also became an active participant in role-playing games such as Dungeons and Dragons and Masquerade. Over time, she increasingly sought refuge with what she calls "kindred spirits"—similarly abused youth who were into the Goth scene; her particular band, however, went further than most.

In contrast to Charity, William Calley grew up the 1950s as a privileged white male in a segregated patriarchal society. Calley represented America, discipline, success, and honor. Charity Keesee belonged to "gen X" and was an abused, powerless, rural girl. She was an individualistic rebel outside the mainstream. Yet they participated in two of the most publicized crimes of our times. Is there a common bond that could explain these very different types of crimes and types of people? What do Lieutenant William Calley and Charity Keesee have in common?

Like William, Charity belonged to an organized, hierarchically structured group. Cults and clans, while less formal than the military, follow specific rituals, demand allegiance, and promote "values." Like Calley, Charity complied with whatever her "commander" demanded. Goths and vampire cults, like the military, dress in a uniform of sorts. Despite their professed desire to be unique, they all wear black, have pale skin, and follow Victorian clothing styles (one of the author's current students makes fake fangs for vampires in Orlando and Virginia Beach and has a thriving business). Goths look alike. The fantasy role-playing games and obedience to authority practiced by many self-proclaimed vampires is not so different from small children who play soldier and carry toy guns, as Calley did during childhood. Also like the military, Goths are law-abiding citizens the vast majority of the time. They work, eat, and pay bills like everyone else. Occasionally they "drift" into crime. They also learn justifications that excuse their behavior. The same can be said of the military.

These two different examples illustrate the central theme of this chapter: Ordinary human beings can become criminal offenders as a result of social processes through which they learn harmful behaviors and attitudes and rationalizations that excuse or justify harm to others. Whether they are conforming to the code and conventions of vampire cults or to the military objectives of the government, what they learn can result in criminal harm. In this chapter, we examine several perspectives on social learning—social process theories—that explain how this comes about. "Social process theories hold that criminality is a function of individual socialization. They draw attention to the interactions people have with the various organizations, institutions and processes of society" (Siegel 1998, 196).

This chapter and the next one mark a transition from the individually oriented rational choice, biological, and psychological principles (microlevel theories) outlined in the previous chapters. We will now move our understanding of crime and criminality toward the cultural, sociological, and structural principles (macrolevel theories) that follow in the rest of the book. The two social process theories considered in this chapter, (1) differential association and (2) neutralization and drift, each in its different way addresses the important contribution of social interaction in the process of becoming criminal. But they each make different assumptions about humans and the role of socialization in learning. In the next chapter, we consider two more social process theories, labeling theory and social control theory, that in many ways are mirror images of the theories examined here. As we shall see, differential association theory views crime and delinquency as the outcome of normal learning processes whereby youths learn the "wrong" behavior, whereas labeling theory sees crime and deviance as a reaction to learning processes that focus on and distort negative values and behavior. Neutralization and drift theory view delinquency and crime as a result of juveniles learning to excuse, justify, or otherwise rationalize potential deviant behavior (which allows them to be released from the constraints of convention and drift into delinquency). Social control theory argues that they are never sufficiently committed to convention in the first place. Let us look at the first two of these social process theories in more detail.

Common Themes and Different Assumptions

In the previous chapter, we discussed psychological explanations of how human minds learn to think criminally and develop "criminal" personalities. Several sociological theorists, notably Edwin Sutherland and his colleague Donald Cressey (1966), in their theory of differential association, rejected the psychological analysis that criminals were different; instead they argued that delinquents and criminals are no different from noncriminals. Criminals do not have different personalities and do not think or learn differently. Criminals learn to commit crimes just as they learn any other behavior and just as anyone else learns any type of behavior. Learning comprises "habits and knowledge that develop as a result of the experiences of the individual in entering and adjusting to the environment" (Vold and Bernard 1986, 205). The primary learning mechanism occurs in association with others. Most responsible for learning are those we are in close association with, usually through informal small groups, such as parents, family, friends, and peers.

We learn through our interactions with these significant others and adapt to their social conventions, as the examples provided by Charity Keesee and William Calley illustrate. What is crucially different between lawbreakers and law abiders is the content of what is learned. Both law abiders and lawbreakers are socialized to conform to social norms. The norms that law abiders learn are those of conventional mainstream society, whereas the norms learned by delinquents and criminals are those of a delinquent subculture with values opposed to the larger society.

Some sociologists, such as David Matza (1964) and Gresham Sykes (Sykes and Matza 1957; Matza and Sykes 1961), in their theory of neutralization and drift, argued that social learning theory presented an overly simplistic picture that was also too deterministic. First, the theory assumed that humans are passive social actors, or blank slates, to be filled in with good or bad knowledge about how to behave. Second, it drew too stark a contrast between conventional mainstream values and delinquent subcultural values. Instead of being separate, these values are interrelated; delinquency forms a subterranean part of mainstream culture. Instead of being immersed in and committed to either convention or delinquency, individuals are socialized to behave conventionally but can occasionally be released from the moral bind of law to drift between these extremes. Charity, for example, comes across as sweet, conforming, and innocent—most of the time. However, she belongs to one of the most ostracized of all social groups. Calley belonged to the highly trained, disciplined U.S. Army. Ultimately, individuals are able to exercise their own will to decide whether or not to act.

We begin our analysis of these two perspectives by considering the work of Edwin Sutherland, who has been described as "the leading criminologist of his generation" and "the most prominent of American criminologists" (Martin et al. 1990, 139).

Sutherland's Differential Association Theory

Edwin Hardin Sutherland (1883–1950) was the son of a Baptist college president. He earned a doctorate from the University of Chicago, with a double major in sociology and political economy, and eventually went on to chair the sociology department at Indiana University. He first presented his theory of differential association in the third edition of his textbook *Principles of Criminology* (1939). He subsequently revised and developed the theory and presented the final version in the next edition, published in 1947.

Sutherland discounted the moral, physiological, and psychological "inferiority" of offenders (Jacoby 1994, 78) and rejected "internal" psychological theories (Martin et al. 1990). His perspective explained crime by learning in a social context through interaction and communication (influenced by the symbolic interactionist tradition discussed later). Differential association is short for "differential association with criminal and anticriminal behavior patterns" (Martin 1990, 155; Cressey 1962). Its central concept parallels Gabriel Tarde's ([1980] 1903) ideas that behavior is imitated in proportion and intensity to the social closeness between people.

According to Vold and Bernard (1986) there are two basic elements to understanding Sutherland's social learning theory. First, the content of what is learned is important. This includes the specific techniques for committing the crime, motives, rationalizations, attitudes, and especially evaluations by others of the meaningful significance of each of these elements. Second, the process by which learning takes place is important, including the intimate informal groups and the collective and situational context where learning occurs. Reflecting aspects of culture conflict theory (discussed in Chapter 8), Sutherland also saw crime as politically defined. In other words, people who are in positions of power have the ability to determine which behaviors are considered criminal. Thus Sutherland said we have "the differential implementation of the laws" (1949b, 513). More importantly for our present purposes, he argued that criminal behavior itself is learned through assigning meaning to behavior, experiences, and events during interaction with others.

The systematic elegance of Sutherland's theory lies in nine clearly stated, testable propositions:

1. Criminal behavior is learned.
2. Criminal behavior is learned in interaction with other persons in a process of communication.
3. The principal part of the learning of criminal behavior occurs within intimate personal groups.

4. When criminal behavior is learned, the learning includes (a) techniques of committing the crime . . . (b) the specific direction of motives, drives, rationalizations, and attitudes.
5. The specific direction of motives and drives is learned from definitions of legal codes as favorable and unfavorable.
6. A person becomes delinquent because of an excess of definitions favorable to violation of law over definitions unfavorable to violation of law.
7. Differential associations may vary in frequency, duration, priority, and intensity.
8. The process of learning criminal behavior by association with criminal and anti-criminal patterns involves all of the mechanisms that are involved in any other learning.
9. Though criminal behavior is an expression of general needs and values, it is not explained by those general needs and values since noncriminal behavior is an expression of the same needs and values (Sutherland 1947, 6–8).

The core of differential association is found in proposition 6, which states that learning an excess of definitions favorable to committing crime over those that are unfavorable results in people choosing the criminal option. As Martin and colleagues have noted, "The situation most conducive to the development of criminality is that in which there is association with criminal behavior patterns and an absence of association with anti-criminal patterns" (1990, 157–158).

Both criminal and anticriminal associations can be affected by (1) priority of learning: how early this is learned in life; (2) frequency: how often one interacts with groups encouraging the behavior in question; (3) duration: the length of exposure to particular behavioral patterns; and (4) intensity: the prestige or status of those manifesting the observed behavior. If each of these four aspects is favorable toward law violation, then there is a high probability of the person choosing criminal behavior.

A final aspect of Sutherland's theory is the shift from the concept of social disorganization to differential social organization. Social disorganization theory (discussed more fully in Chapter 8) says that those who become criminals are isolated from the mainstream culture and are immersed in their own impoverished and dilapidated neighborhoods, which have different norms and values. Differential social organization suggests that a complex society comprises numerous conflicting groups, each with its own different norms and values; associations with some of these can result in learning to favor law violation over law-abiding behavior. A good illustration of this is how Sutherland explains crimes by businesspersons, those he termed white-collar criminals:

Respectable business men who violate the law are seldom in poverty and seldom manifest the social and personal pathologies. The General Motors Corporation does not violate the law because of an Oedipus complex, the General Electric Company because it is emotionally unstable, the Anaconda Copper Company because of bad housing conditions, Armour and Company because of a broken home, the Standard Oil Company because of a lack of recreational facilities or any of them because of poverty. . . . We should attempt to explain white collar crimes and any other crimes in terms of processes that are common to both of them. These common factors are to be found in the "laws of learning" and in the modern social organization, with its specificity of cultural relations. (Sutherland 1949b, 514)

Sutherland argued that illegal practices which increase profits are diffused within business groups that are in conflict with others in society. This conflict is particularly strong in relation to specific practices, described as "just doing business." These practices within business groups are accompanied by definitions favorable to the violation of certain laws that are restrictive of business. At the same time, businesses are "isolated from and protected against definitions which are unfavorable to such crime" (Sutherland 1949a, 247). For example, being raised in a home where honesty is a virtue does not carry over to the specific cultures of corporations.

Empirical Support and Limitations of Differential Association Theory

The biggest problem with the original version of differential association theory was that some of the central concepts were not clearly defined and depended on a simple, passive definition of social learning. We saw in Chapter 5 how cognitive theorists show that learning is a creative and active process. Indeed, by focusing on learning in small groups, Sutherland ignored what the social learning theorist Albert Bandura (1977) found to be significant modeling of images glorified in the media. Early on, Sheldon Glueck (1956) raised another concern by asking if all criminal behavior is learned from others or if some people invent their own criminal behavior. If not, how does criminal behavior begin? Differential association may explain why some people in high-crime areas commit crime. Indeed, several research studies have illustrated this. But it does not explain how behaviors originate or who started them. Nor does it explain how some individual crimes are committed without associates. It does not explain what counts as an excess of definitions. Nor does it explain irrational acts of violence or destruction. It does show how patterns of criminal behavior can persist over time, however, and how social and organizational groups of both the powerful and the powerless can sustain these.

Methodologically, research on differential association has been criticized on several counts. Glueck (1956) questioned the ability to test differential association, although others argue that it is testable (DeFleur and Quinney 1966) and considerable empirical research on the theory would seem to support this.

A further criticism is that most studies rely on asking subjects about their relationships with significant others. This method does not determine causality, and thus researchers are unsure if differential associations cause deviant behavior or result from deviant behavior. In addition, most of the studies rely on cross-sectional rather than longitudinal samples, which makes it impossible to know whether learning came before criminal behavior or during it.

Research on differential association has generally not been able to empirically validate the claims made, although it has received some support. Short (1960) was able to identify a connection between membership in a delinquent group and criminal acts. Orcutt (1987) linked marijuana use to peer influence, but Johnson, Marco, and Bahr (1987) found little support for differential association, in that adolescent drug use is influenced by drug use itself rather than attitudes and definitions of close peers, and hardly at all by parents. Indeed, the general conclusion of this research is that peer influence in general increases with age during adolescence and especially in relation to drug use and delinquent behavior (Gorman and White 1995). Baier and Wright (2001) conducted a meta-analysis that examined the effects of religion on criminal behavior. Based on concepts from differential association, religion should provide an excess of definitions unfavorable to crime through "social selection and socialization" (Wright et al. 1999). Their reanalysis of 60 prior studies found that religious practices and belief do show a significant, moderate inhibiting effect on crime commission. However, in another study Costello and Vowell (1999) stated that "a major reconceptualization of differential association theory would be necessary" (1999, 829) for doubts to be removed about its efficacy.

Modifying Differential Association: Differential Reinforcement Theory and Differential Identification Theory

In an attempt to overcome some of the early limitations of Sutherland's original theory, C. Ray Jeffery (1965) and Robert Burgess and Ronald Akers (1966; Akers [1977] 1985, 1998) developed versions of differential reinforcement theory of crime based on a combination of Skinner's ideas of operant conditioning and Sutherland's ideas of differential association. Jeffery's version of differential reinforcement argues that individuals have differences in their reinforcement history with respect to being rewarded and punished; for some being rewarded for minor rule breaking can lead to more serious law violation. He also points out that for others, being punished may be interpreted as "attention receiving," and that rather than reducing the tendency to crime, punishment can actually increase it. Moreover, Jeffery (1965) claims that once a criminal behavior is learned it can become self-reinforcing.

Rather than seeing a simple mechanical relationship between stimulus and response, Burgess and Akers (1966; Akers [1977] 1985), like Bandura, see a more complex relationship that depends on the feedback a person receives from the environment. Akers explains how people learn criminal behavior through operant conditioning and argues that people evaluate their own behavior through interaction with significant other people and groups. Burgess and Akers (1966) present a revised version of the propositional statement of Sutherland:

1. Criminal behavior is learned according to the principles of operant conditioning.
2. Criminal behavior is learned both in nonsocial situations that are reinforcing or discriminative and through social interaction in which the behavior of other persons is reinforcing or discriminative for criminal behavior.
3. The principal part of the learning of criminal behavior occurs in groups that make up the individual's major source of reinforcement.
4. The learning of criminal behavior (including specific techniques, attitudes, and avoidance procedures) is a function of the effective and available reinforcers and the existing reinforcement contingencies.
5. The specific class of behaviors that are learned and their frequency of occurrence are a function of the reinforcers that are effective and available and the rules or norms by which these reinforcers are applied.
6. Criminal behavior is a function of norms that are discriminative for criminal behavior, the learning of which takes place when such behavior is more highly reinforced than noncriminal behavior.
7. The strength of criminal behavior is a direct function of the amount, frequency, and probability of its reinforcement. These interactions rely on norms, attitudes, and orientations.

Burgess and Akers were particularly interested in the role of punishment and who provides it. They saw punishment as "positive" when it follows a behavior causing it to decrease and as "negative" when it takes the form of a reduction or loss of reward or privilege. Burgess and Akers argued that differential reinforcement occurs when the rewards are given to two behaviors, but one is more highly rewarded than the other. This differential rewarding is particularly influential when it comes from others who are significantly identified with, such as parents, teachers, peers, and so on. Furthermore, in his version of social learning theory, Akers, like Bandura, acknowledges that modeling can arise based on the rewards one sees others getting. Daniel Glaser (1956) called this identification with others, particularly the generalized characteristics of favored social groups or reference groups, differential identification theory.

Empirical research has extensively tested differential reinforcement theory. Several large-scale studies (Akers et al. 1979; Krohn et al. 1985) have found it to be supported. Sellers and colleagues (2000), however, criticize narrative studies, stating that "the theory appears to have attracted a great deal of consensus on its predictive accuracy. This conclusion, however, has been based primarily on narrative reviews of numerous, widely disparate empirical tests of the theory," which can be compromised by subjective factors. Nevertheless, their own meta-analysis summarizing 140 other studies confirmed this support (Sellers et al. 2000).

In spite of empirical efficacy, this theory does not explain how people rewarded for conventional behavior (e.g., economically affluent youths) still commit crimes. Akers, like Sutherland, does not explain where the values transmitted through differential reinforcement come from in the first place, although he does point out that the social environment one is exposed to contains different content, some more conducive to illegal behavior than others. In a more recent work he develops the macrolevel social structural side of this argument, proposing that environments impact the individual through learning (Akers 1998, 302). The greatest merit of social learning theory is that it draws together the psychological process components examined in the previous chapter of learning by role modeling and reinforcement of that learning, but "most significant, Akers contended that definitions and imitation are most instrumental in determining initial forays into crime" and that "continued involvement in crime, therefore, depends on exposure to social reinforcements that reward this activity. The stronger and more persistent the reinforcements . . . the greater the likelihood that the criminal behavior will persist" (Lilly, Cullen, and Ball 2002, 46), and the more conducive the social environment to providing this reinforcement, the more likely are such structures to contribute to such criminogenesis (Akers 1998). As Sampson (1999, 438) states in an evaluation of Aker's latest magnum opus, "Heir apparent to Sutherland's differential association theory, Ron Akers long ago made his mark in criminology. . . . There is also little doubt that social learning theory is one of the titans battling it out for supremacy in the etiology of delinquency wars."

Policy Implications of Social Learning Theory

The policy implications associated with differential association theory are relatively straightforward. If socialization in small groups provides an excess of definitions favorable to law violation, the implication for prevention is to keep young, suggestible people away from such groups and train them to resist their messages. For those already influenced, treatment involving resocialization is consistent with the theory's general principles. Specific prevention programs that follow from this theory include peer-led interventions, resistance skills training, and personal and social skills training. In a review of research on such programs, however, Gorman and White (1995, 149) noted that these "were shown to be of minimal effectiveness and conceptually limited in that they fail to address the complexity of the relationship between group associations and delinquency." Gorman and White argued that because the relationship is reciprocal it is insufficient to intervene at the adolescent peer group level since doing so ignores the parent–child interaction in earlier years that leads to involvement with antisocial peers in the first place. They suggested that family-based and community programs seem to be more conceptually consistent with differential association theory than the school-based skills programs, but the effectiveness of such programs has not yet been adequately demonstrated.

Also overlooked in the policy arena is the role of the law and public policy in influencing definitions favorable or unfavorable to law violation. For example, clearer and simplified laws provided by the dominant mainstream culture are indicated. A related policy would be to publicly proclaim the law and reasons for following it; the media may provide an effective format for delivering this message. Recognizing the role of words and messages in affecting delinquency motivation is an area expanded and developed first by Sutherland's student and colleague Donald Cressey (1953) and then by Gresham Sykes and David Matza (1957) in what became known as neutralization theory.

Neutralization Theory:
Learning Rationalizations as Motives

One very important element of the behavior learned in intimate social groups and considered by Sutherland was the rationalizations that accompany behavior. These rationalizations are related to Sutherland's ([1939] 1947) idea about how law violations can be defined as favorable or unfavorable, and they were especially important to Donald Cressey. In a study of the "respectable" crime of embezzlement, Cressey (1953,

1970) found that three key elements were necessary for a violation of financial trust to occur: (1) a nonsharable financial problem (meaning a problem the offenders feel embarrassed to tell others about, such as gambling debts); (2) the perception of their legitimate occupation as a solution to the problem, typically through using funds to which they have access; and (3) verbalizations, or words and phrases that make the behavior acceptable (such as "borrowing" the money and intending to pay it back). It is this third element and the possibility that such words and phrases may be found in the common culture that makes the crime possible. As Cressey (1970, 111) said: "I am convinced that the words and phrases that the potential embezzler uses in conversations with himself are actually the most important elements in the process that gets him into trouble."

For Cressey, verbalizations were not simply rationalizations occurring after the fact of crime to relieve an offender of culpability. Instead, they were words and phrases that could, as C. Wright Mills (1940) argued earlier, be "vocabularies of motive." These could inhibit someone from engaging in a criminal act by showing the potential offender that using such excuses or justifications after a criminal act might not be honored as acceptable. Alternatively, the excuses and justifications could be honored by future questioners, allowing the potential offender a sense of "freedom" that it might be acceptable to violate the law under the particular situation or circumstances described. The most sophisticated development of these ideas came from David Matza (1964) and Gresham Sykes (Sykes and Matza 1957; Matza and Sykes 1961) in their studies of juvenile delinquency.

Drifting In and Out of Delinquency: Matza and Sykes's Neutralization Theory

In 1957, while at Princeton University, Gresham Sykes teamed up with his former student David Matza to develop a new theory of delinquency that extended Sutherland's learning theory (Sykes and Matza 1957). The analysis originated in Sykes's studies of prison inmates and guards learning to rationalize rule breaking (Martin et al. 1990). Matza (1964) argued that existing theories, whether biological, psychological, or sociological, were too deterministic. These theories presented the adolescent as either committed to convention or committed to delinquency. Matza felt that this was an overstatement that left out the classicist element of the choice to commit crime. He argued that existing theories predict too much crime. Most juvenile delinquents do not continue their criminal behavior into adulthood. If a biological or psychological factor "caused" crime, why would its influence diminish after adolescence? If delinquent subcultures were so compelling at socializing youths to define crime as acceptable, then what accounts for their maturational reform—the tendency for juvenile delinquents to relinquish their delinquency as they age into their twenties and thirties? Matza sought to combine these observations to explain most delinquency (which he called mundane delinquency), arguing,

> the image of the delinquent I wish to convey is one of drift; an actor neither compelled nor committed to deeds nor freely choosing them; neither different in any simple or fundamental sense from the law abiding, nor the same; conforming to certain traditions in American life while partially unreceptive to other more conventional traditions; and finally, an actor whose motivational system may be explored along lines explicitly commended by classical criminology—his peculiar relation to legal institutions. (1964, 28)

Matza sought to combine these many orientations, in part, by making a case for soft determinism. According to Matza, positivistic criminology (the scientific study of crime that had prevailed since the late nineteenth century, as discussed in Chapter 4) "fashioned an image of man to suit a study of criminal behavior based on scientific determinism. It rejected the view that man exercised freedom, was possessed of reason, and was thus capable of choice" (1964, 5). Conversely, soft determinism argues "that human actions are not deprived of freedom because they are causally determined" (Matza 1964, 9). The amount of freedom each person has varies. Some are more free than others and have a greater range of choices available. Moreover, this freedom varies according to circumstances, situations, and context.

Most important to understanding Matza and Sykes's argument is the concept of "subculture of delinquency," which they prefer to the idea of "delinquent subculture." As traditionally conceived, delinquent subcultures are considered separate and oppositional; their norms and values are different from those in the mainstream culture. The gang is the best example. For Matza and Sykes (1961), however, this was a false distinction. Most delinquents, they argue, are not full-fledged gang members but "mundane delinquents," who express remorse over their actions. Many admire law-abiding citizens. Furthermore, most differentiate between whom they will victimize and whom they will not. Finally, delinquents are not exclusively criminal; they also engage in many noncriminal acts. These factors suggest that delinquents are aware of the difference between right and wrong and are subject to the influence of both conventional and delinquent values.

Rather than delinquency and mainstream culture being separate, argue Matza and Sykes, mainstream culture has an underbelly of "subterranean values." These exist side-by-side with conventional values. Consider the example of sensation seeking: "Kicks, big time spending and rep have immediate counterparts in the value system of the law abiding" (Matza and Sykes 1961, 717). A good illustration of subterranean values can be found in the school setting.

When a teacher presents social studies materials she or he teaches the knowledge content of the subject; when the teacher employs favoritism, using gender or racial bias, or emphasizes grades as more important than understanding, she or he simultaneously sends a different message. Students learn how society works. They learn that there are public statements and private practices; they learn that beneath the rhetoric, what matters is getting ahead by whatever means, including cheating if necessary. This is useful, albeit informal, knowledge. When these students get to the workplace, they will encounter formal rules and informal rules, such as the company policy on health, safety, and hygiene, as well as the preferred unspoken practice, which may be to cut corners and suspend rules in order to make a profit, regardless of who gets hurt. This kind of knowledge does not require the exclusivity of a gang of delinquents; it is there beneath the surface of every formal institution, policy, and practice. It is part of the subterranean subculture of delinquency.

This subterranean subculture of delinquency makes it unnecessary for adolescent youths to join gangs or other subcultural groups to learn delinquent values. Instead, simply by learning and being socialized into conventional values and norms, adolescents are simultaneously socialized into the negation of those values. Nowhere is this more evident than in legal codes.

Legal codes are inconsistent and thus vulnerable. As Matza (1964, 60) wrote, "The law contains the seeds of its own neutralization. . . . Criminal law is especially susceptible of neutralization because the conditions of applicability and thus inapplicability, are explicitly stated." This means people can claim various kinds of exemptions in the belief that they are, under certain mitigating circumstances, not bound by the law. The classic example is "self-defense." Another example is the idea that criminal intent (mens rea) must be present for an act to be criminal; Lorena Bobbitt, among others, used this rule to her advantage, as we demonstrated in Chapter 5. Not only is this ambiguity present in the law, but in U.S. society it is reflected in contradictions resulting from trying to balance freedom of the individual and the collective interests of society. Take the example of speeding laws. It seems that only in the United States would the law ban speeding while allowing the sale of radar detectors; these detectors are even sold by police at auctions of unclaimed recovered stolen property! Consider the laws in many states prohibiting gambling—yet Native Americans can run casinos and the states can run lotteries. Little wonder, then, that the ordinary Joe asks, "Why shouldn't I be able to utilize my local bookie to place bets? Why is that any different from the state-run lottery? I can afford it and do so to relax."

Such legal contradictions and the implicit claims for exemption that follow from them allow the possibility for choice and freedom because they render juveniles and others intermittently free to choose to commit delinquent acts. Whether youths break the law depends not so much on their being in a delinquent subculture but, first, on whether they are freed into a state of drift and released from the larger culture's moral bind, and, second, on whether they then exercise free choice: "Drift stands midway between freedom and control. Its basis is an area in the social structure in which control has been loosened. . . . The delinquent transiently exists in a limbo between convention and crime, responding in turn to the demands of each, flirting now with one, now with the other, but postponing commitment, evading decision. Thus he [or she] drifts between criminal and conventional action" (Matza 1964, 28).

This "loosening" of control, or release from moral convention into a state of drift, may initially be accidental, and it occurs through neutralization. For Matza, neutralization comprises words and phrases that excuse or justify lawbreaking behavior, such as claiming an action was "self-defense." Unlike rationalizations, which come after an act to avoid culpability and consequences, and verbalizations that come after contemplating an act to allow oneself to commit it, neutralizations come before an act is even contemplated. Thus for Matza they are "unwitting," something that occurs to an actor that results from the unintended duplication, distortion, and extension of customary beliefs relating to when and under what circumstances exceptions are allowed: "Neutralization of legal precepts depends partly on equivocation—the unwitting use of concepts in markedly different ways" (Matza 1964, 74; Taylor 1972). Neutralization frees the delinquent from the moral bind of law so that he or she may now choose to commit the crime. Crucially, whether or not a crime occurs no longer requires some special motivation.

Sykes and Matza (1957) classified excuses and justifications that provide a moral release into five types, which they called "techniques of neutralization":

1. Denial of responsibility (e.g., "It's not my fault. I was drunk at the time."). Offenders may list reasons such as alcohol, peer pressure, bad neighborhood, and so on that caused them to commit the act.
2. Denial of injury (e.g., "No one got hurt."). Offenders may deny that anyone or anything was harmed by their action. For example, shoplifters might claim that stores have so much money and insurance that "They can afford it" or employee thieves may claim their company wastes so much "They'll never miss it."

3. Denial of victim (e.g., "They had it coming to them."). Some of- fenders may claim that although someone got hurt, he or she de- served it. For example, corporations may treat their employees badly, paying them too little or instituting a stringent dress code. Employees may pilfer goods out of resentment "to get back at the company," saying they are the real victims of the corporation's abuse. Women who harm physically or psychologically abusive spouses may claim that the "victim" was actually an offender who had therefore forfeited his rights to victimhood, and was finally getting what he deserved.

4. Condemnation of the condemners (e.g., "Everybody's crooked."). Offenders may reject the people who have authority over them, such as judges, parents, and police officers, who are viewed as be- ing just as corrupt and thus not worthy of respect: "Even ministers steal from the collection box." The ongoing revelations of sexual abuse of children by Catholic priests and the cover-up by the Catholic Church provided considerable fuel for the denial of their moral authority to judge others.

5. Appeal to higher loyalties (e.g., "I didn't do it for myself."). Many offenders argue that their loyalties lie with their peers (homeboys, fellow gang members, fellow employees, etc.) and that the group has needs that take precedence over societal demands. Female em- bezzlers claim to have stolen for their families and mothers have committed arson to provide work for their unemployed firefighter sons. Drug users' higher loyalty may be to the complete fulfillment of the human spirit.

Since Matza and Sykes's original studies on delinquency, researchers have applied neutralization theory to adult crime, especially to offenders who maintain a dual lifestyle and are both part of the mainstream and yet also engage in crime, as in employee theft (Ditton 1977; Hollinger and Clark 1983; Hollinger 1991) and buying and selling stolen goods (Klockars 1974; Henry 1978). As a consequence, at least four additional types of neu- tralization have been discovered (Henry 1990; Pfuhl and Henry 1993):

1. Metaphor of the ledger (e.g., "I've done more good than bad in my life."). This was used by Klockars (1974) to show how the profes- sional fence believed himself to be, on the balance of his life, more moral than immoral ("Look at all the money I've given to charity and how I've helped children. If you add it all up, I've got to come out on the good side.").

2. Claim of normality (e.g., "Everyone is doing it."). This suggests that the law is not reflecting the popular will and since everyone

engages in, say, tax evasion, pilfering from the office, extramarital sex, and so on, then such acts are not really deviant and therefore not wrong.

3. Denial of negative intent (e.g., "It was just a joke."). Henry (1990; Henry and Eaton 1999) found this was used by college students to justify their use of explosives on campus, among other things ("We were only having some fun."). The neutralization is partial denial, accepting responsibility for the act but denying the negative consequences were intended.

4. Claim of relative acceptability (e.g., "There are others worse than me."). Unlike condemning the condemners, this appeals to the audience to compare the offender's crime to more serious ones and can go so far as claiming to be moral. For example, LAPD officers claimed that the beating of the African American Rodney King, after being stopped on a traffic violation, helped prevent him being killed by nervous fellow officers (Pfuhl and Henry 1993, 70).

The important point about these techniques of neutralization is their timing. All could be used as techniques or devices (1) *after* an illegal act to seek to reduce blame or culpability, or (2) *before* committing the act while contemplating it in order to seek self-conscious approval that it is acceptable to go ahead. But for Matza and others (Taylor 1972; Henry 1976), the critical point is that they can also occur (3) *before contemplating the act*, releasing the actor to be morally free to choose the act. In the latter case, the context, situation, and circumstances provide a neutralizing discourse that removes the moral inhibition, releasing a person to commit criminal acts, as they would any other act, should they choose to do so.

Limitations and Policy Implications of Neutralization Explanations

The critical issue when evaluating neutralization theory is whether or not offenders are committed to conventional values and norms in the first place. If they are not committed, neutralization is unnecessary, a point made by control theory, which we discuss in the next chapter. Even Matza accepted that not all delinquents were committed to conventional values, since a minority were compulsive in their behavior, committed to unconventional values, and differed from the majority of mundane "drifters" (Taylor, Walton, and Young 1973, 180–181).

Early empirical research found little support for the idea that delinquents share mainstream values (Ball and Lilly 1971). Indeed, Michael Hindelang (1970, 1974) found that delinquents are committed to different values from those held by nondelinquents. Moreover, in an overview of the studies, Agnew (1994) found most research showing that delinquents are more likely to accept techniques of neutralization than are nondelinquents. A self-report study by Landsheer, Hart, and Kox (1994) found that some delinquents viewed their acts as unacceptable yet did them anyway, which tends to support neutralization theory, since this scenario requires some means for the delinquents to deal with their own moral objections.

Research on neutralization theory also faces a causality problem, particularly in establishing when the neutralizations occur—before or after the criminal act. For Hamlin (1988), neutralizations are produced after the act as motives attributed to behavior in response to questions about why it happened. But Agnew's (1994, 572) analysis of the National Youth Survey longitudinal data suggests that neutralization preceding violent acts "may be used as both after-the-fact excuses and before-the-fact justifications," and "has a moderately large absolute effect on subsequent violence."

Ultimately, like Sutherland's theory of differential association, neutralization theory does not explain how neutralization originates or who invents the extensions of the words and phrases that are learned.

Many of the studies that find relationships between neutralizations and delinquency suffer from methodological problems, such as using cross-sectional rather than longitudinal data that does not allow the researcher to know whether neutralization preceded or followed the act. Other "supporting" research has sampling problems. For example, W. William Minor (1981), whose research provided limited support, relied on college criminal justice students for his sample. In an earlier study using a better sample, he could not support neutralization theory, concluding that in many cases, "neutralizations and rationalizations are simply unnecessary" (Minor 1980, 115). Other studies have failed to distinguish neutralization from unconventional beliefs. By contrast, from his longitudinal study Agnew (1994, 573) found that, at least in relation to violent acts, the majority of respondents disapproved of violence and "accept one or more neutralizations for violence." However, as one commentator recently stated, "as with techniques of neutralization, drift theory does not have a solid foundation in empirical research, and this is a serious drawback" (Moyer 2001, 148). Part of the problem with Matza's drift theory, says Moyer, is that it has not been possible to develop a good operational definition, and this has inhibited research. Perhaps nothing captures the concern more than the lecture given at Cambridge University in 2003 by Shadd Maruna entitled "Excuses, Excuses: What Have We Learned in 50 Years of Testing 'Neutralization Theory'?"

Policy Implications of Neutralization Theory

Although neutralization theory explains certain kinds of criminal behavior, it also presents difficult policy questions. It suggests that contradictions in the dominant culture, injustice, and double standards need to be elimi-nated to lessen the possibility of people being able to neutralize. Cressey ([1965] 1987) was one of the few writers to specify the policy implications of this theory at least at the level of institutional control. He suggested that to reduce the probability of verbalizations allowing embezzlement, employers should adopt educational programs that allow employees to discuss emerging financial problems from losses and that phrases used to excuse and justify such behavior should be repeatedly corrected to reveal their harm and crime. Some retail stores have begun to implement this suggestion through weekly meetings with sales staff, pointing out to them the precise losses from internal theft and how the company suffers. The aim is to undermine any neutralizing use of "denial of injury" by em-ployees tempted to steal from the store.

Others have shown that it is not just the words and phrases that need constant monitoring and replacing but the conditions that give rise to them. Take, for example, the finding that employee resentment is highly correlated with employee theft and that high levels of job satisfaction are inversely correlated with employee theft (Hollinger and Clark 1983). Re-search by Greenberg (1990) has shown that although rates of employee theft typically rise if wages are cut, this can be avoided if employers use words and phrases to explain why the cuts are necessary and if they in-volve and inform the employees about what is happening. This way, the neutralizing effect of "denial of victim" is preempted and that justifica-tion for employee theft is undermined. Of course, whether such a policy would be effective depends on whether the theory is correct. Indeed, Maruna (2003) states, "Nowhere is the influence of this theory more ap-parent than in correctional practice, where the notion that habitual ex-cuse-making promotes criminal behavior is largely taken for granted. Interventions as diverse as cognitive-behavioural therapy and restorative justice conferencing are all premised explicitly on overcoming rationalisa-tions and encouraging offenders to take responsibility for their behaviour. Yet, does the research on neutralization theory over the last 50 years jus-tify the faith in this theory?"

It was against neutralization theory that Travis Hirschi (1969) devel-oped his oppositional ideas about bonding and social control, one of the most frequently discussed and tested criminological theories (Stitt and Giacopassi 1992). We turn to an examination of this and control theories generally in the next chapter.

Summary and Conclusion

In this chapter, we have focused on theories that examine the interactive social processes involved in learning and becoming criminal. We moved from theories offering a passive model of human nature to one in which people learn criminal behavior from others. We explored the various elements in the learning process and in particular, looked at the importance of learning words and phrases that form excuses and justifications that can serve to neutralize the moral inhibition to crime, releasing people into a state of drift in which crime becomes simply a behavior to choose, like any other. These theories, in spite of their relatively different empirical validity, offer some insight and have implications for parenting children and minimizing the impact of negative social practices on their development.

Summary Chart: Social Process Theories

1. Differential Association/Social Learning Theory

Basic Idea: People learn to commit crime as a result of exposure to criminal behavior, ideas, and rationalizations that are favorable to violating the law.

Human Nature: Humans are social blanks until socialized into healthy social roles by families, education, and society. No difference between offenders and nonoffenders. All seen as rule following; which rules they follow depends on which groups socialize them.

Society and the Social Order: Society is seen as a conflict of values. Law consists of behavioral prohibitions. Criminals are those who learn that under certain circumstances law violation is acceptable.

Causality: Sutherland's version: Individuals participate in both conventional and criminal groups and use the same process to learn behavior in both. In these groups or learning situations, they learn patterns of conventional and criminal behavior and the rationalizations that accompany them as well as the skills to carry them out. Learning an excess of definitions favorable to committing crime over those unfavorable results in people being free to choose crime. Akers version of social learning considers the importance of psychological learning by modeling and operant conditioning in a facilitative social environment.

Criminal Justice Policy: Keep children away from bad influences; publicly and frequently proclaim the law and reasons for following it; challenge all excuses and justifications; rehabilitate through reeducation and resocialization of offenders; segregate offenders.

Criminal Justice Practice: Preference for restitution and reparation and social rehabilitation; group therapy and counseling for children of immigrants to provide them with coping skills needed to survive clash of cultures; clearer and simplified laws provided by dominant culture; greater flexibility of law when dealing with other or lower-class cultural contexts; parental skills training; decreased policing of streets; a tariff system that can be negotiated down in exchange for guilty pleas.

Evaluation: Explains why some people in high-crime areas commit crime but does not explain how behaviors originate or who started them; does not explain individual crimes committed without associates in group; does not explain what counts as an excess of definitions; does not explain irrational acts of violence or destruction; does not explain why those rewarded for conventional behavior, such as middle-class youths, commit crimes; does not explain why some delinquent youths do not become adult criminals, despite being rewarded for crime. Assumes a passive and unintentional actor who lacks individuality or differential receptivity to criminal learning patterns.

2. Drift and Neutralization Theory

Basic Idea: Crime can become a behavioral option for people when their commitment to conventional values and norms is neutralized by excuses and justifications that render them morally free.

Human Nature: Humans are rational actors who choose behavior out of free will in a context of more or less commitment to convention and are capable of much moral ambiguity. Rules and acceptable behavior are open to interpretation.

Law: Contains both the imperatives for action and the principal exceptions— "seeds of its own neutralization"; law is thus ambiguous.

Criminals: No different from noncriminals; all are subject to neutralization by context and circumstance and on those occasions all excuse or justify lawbreaking. Criminals may have highly developed abilities for neutralizing or may have learned words and phrases by which they can convince themselves that whatever they want to do is justified.

Causal Logic: Youths (and others) learn ways to neutralize moral constraints in the company of others, but these are not phrases absent from the wider society or words unique to delinquent subcultures; rather they form a subculture of delinquency throughout the whole society. Invocation of words and phrases can occur in many circumstances. Timing is critical. Simply excusing or justifying after the act is not neutralization but merely rationalization; doing so before the act is committed (as in Cressey's verbalization) is motivating through removal of inhibition (even if by design). Crucial for Matza is the unwitting extension and distortion of excuses and justifications before contemplation of the act, such that it simply appears morally justified (e.g., working for an unfair boss builds up the neutralization of denial of victim). Neutralization releases the individual to a "moral holiday," free to choose or drift into delinquency. Neutralization occurs through use of several techniques: (1) denial of responsibility, (2) denial of injury, (3) denial of victim, (4) condemnation of condemners, (5) appeal to higher loyalties, (6) metaphor of the ledger, (7) claim of normality, (8) denial of negative intent, (9) claim of relative acceptability.

Criminal Justice Policy: Prevention to clarify property ownership and identify how people are harmed.

Criminal Justice Practice: Public exposure and declaration of excuses and justifications; education into ethics and how we deceive ourselves into honest dishonesty.

Evaluation: Explains why delinquents undergo maturational reform; explains why people can participate simultaneously in both conventional and unconventional behavior; explains how people can maintain illegal, self-destructive behavior. Difficult to test since it cannot easily be established whether neutralization occurs before or after law violation. Does not explain why some people drift and others do not.

7

Failed Socialization
Control Theory, Social Bonds, and Labeling

"An abandoned child manifests evil instincts in his early childhood."
—Jean-Paul Sartre

Jack Henry Abbott, convicted murderer and author of the book *In the Belly of the Beast* (1981), spent most of his childhood in foster homes. At the age of twelve he was committed to a juvenile penal institution in Utah for "failure to adjust to foster homes." Released after five years, he was again incarcerated, this time in the Utah state penitentiary for issuing a check against insufficient funds. By age twenty-nine, he had killed one inmate, injured another, escaped, and committed a bank robbery. After spending twenty-one of his thirty-seven years in prison, he was released on parole in 1981, only to murder an actor in a barroom argument. Abbott's history, taken from his own account, serves to illustrate the escalating and combined consequences of inadequate socialization, the failure to bond with convention and institutional labeling:

> He who is state raised—reared by the state from an early age after he is taken from what the state calls a "broken home"—learns over and over and all the days of his life that people in society can do anything to him and not be punished by the law. . . . After a certain age you are regarded as a man by society. . . . Gradually your judgement is tempered. Your experience mellows your emotions because you are free to move about anywhere, work and play at anything. . . . You are taught by the very terms of your social existence, by the objects that come and go from your intentions, the nature of your own emotions—and you learn about yourself, your tastes, your strengths and weaknesses. You, in other words, mature emotionally. A prisoner who is not state-raised tolerates the [prison] regime because of his social situation prior to incarceration. He knows things are different outside prison. But the state-

raised convict has no conception of any difference. He lacks experience and
. . . maturity. His judgement is untempered, rash; his emotions are impulsive,
raw, unmellowed. . . . At age thirty seven I am barely a precocious child. . . .
Can you imagine how I feel—to be treated as a little boy and not as a man?
And when I was a little boy, I was treated as a man—and can you imagine
what that does to a boy? . . . The state-raised convict's conception of man-
hood . . . is a fanatically defiant and alienated individual who cannot imagine what forgiveness is, or mercy or tolerance, because he has no experience
of such values. (Abbott 1981, 11–14)

In February 2002 Jack Henry Abbott, 58, was found hanged in his cell
with a bedsheet and a shoelace; accompanying him was a suicide note.

As shown by Abbott's case, criminologist Travis Hirschi (1969) rejects
the idea discussed in the previous chapter, that everyone is socialized into
conformity from which some are occasionally released from the moral
bind of law, to offend. In contrast, Hirschi, in his theory of bonding and
social control, believed that some people are not socialized adequately in
the first place. He argued that law abiders and lawbreakers are the
same—all are potential offenders. What distinguishes us is how effectively we are socialized not to break the law. Hirschi claimed that inadequate socialization processes in children and youths allow, or even foster,
the formation of unconventional attitudes that can result in crime and
delinquency. When socialization works adequately, a tie or bond is created with conventional society that prevents law violation by insulating
people from temptation. Learning self-control is a crucial element in the
process of resisting the impulse to law violation. What affects socialization most are the social bonds of attachment, commitment, involvement
and belief formed between children and conventional others, such as
teachers and parents. If these bonds are weak or do not form, children
will lack self-control and will be free to violate the law.

The astute reader will note that this bonding/social control view of crime
causation can be related to Sutherland's differential association theory. Indeed, some researchers empirically compare and test the two theories
(Costello and Vowell 1999). Where Sutherland focused on learning criminal
activity, bonding and control theories examine the connections and controls
that link people to conventional society. These connections must be established, and Hirschi (1969) describes several ways this occurs. Thus these
theories are compatible with the learning processes explained in differential association theory and allow us to consider the "missing" half of
Sutherland's theory: exposure to conventional, legal norms and behavior.

This chapter also deals with the effect that society's agents of social control, such as police, schoolteachers, social workers, and probation officers,
have on creating crime and criminals. Author Mark Lanier first met Nick

during his sophomore year in college. He stood out in a class of over 100 due to his happy, friendly disposition. He came from a prominent, well-educated family in South Florida. Though bright, studying was not Nick's forte. This nineteen-year-old was on the five-year plan toward his criminal justice major and a career in law enforcement and never skipped class. The previous year, Nick became involved in a minor barroom altercation, which he did not start, with another drinking patron—an off-duty police officer. Nick was arrested for "assaulting a police officer." The officer walked away laughing with his friends. Nick pled guilty rather than notify his parents and accepted the small fine and probation. The unanticipated long-term effects have been serious, however. Nick was arrested three more times before he graduated from college. Most recently, he was at a rugby team "keg" party where underage females were present. Either a neighbor called the police or they decided to drop in on the party during a routine drive-by. The police proceeded to check everyone's identification. Of the forty people present, only Nick was arrested, despite the fact that he was compliant and it was not his house, keg, or female friends. He is convinced that when his arrest record was pulled by the officers on the scene and "assaulting a police officer" appeared, he was singled out for "special treatment." Needless to say, Nick's's dreams of working in law enforcement have ended. He now works in landscaping. His family is still wondering what happened. Nick represents a case of how minor rule-breaking behavior can produce a stigma that amplifies the original deviance to have life-changing effects; in extreme cases these effects can be full-blown criminal careers.

Labeling theorists are concerned with the failure of socialization. Instead of focusing on bonds, they examine the social reaction component of interaction. For labeling theorists, adequate socialization occurs when youthful indiscretions and minor rule violations are tolerated. Labeling theorists argue that society—specifically through persons in powerful positions—creates deviance by overreacting to minor rule breaking. This results in negative socialization that undermines a person's sense of self-worth and fosters a commitment to deviance. Labeling theorists, such as Edwin Lemert (1951, 1967) and Howard Becker ([1963] 1973), also argued that social interaction with others is important in shaping whether or not people become offenders. Humans are not passive but are actively engaged with others in the construction of their own social identities. Not all others are equally significant in this interactive process, however. Those more significant are members of powerful groups and significant individuals who seek to ban certain behavior through passing laws and having these enforced via social control agents. So powerful is the impact of these agents that otherwise minor rule breaking is magnified through criminal justice processes to have a significant impact on perpetrators. The impact of these meaningful encounters can transform fragile social identities into criminal careers. While Nick has not become a serious criminal, his life has been dramatically altered by this exact process. Others, such as Jack Henry Abbott, have become the violent actor that their label projected; whether this would have occurred without the labeling is the central question that labeling theorists address. Let us examine each of these theories of failed socialization in more detail.

Control Theory: Learning Not to Commit Crime

Whereas Sutherland's ([1939] 1947) learning theory seeks to explain how some people are introduced to and adopt lawbreaking behavior, control theory, also called social control theory, assumes a universal motivation to crime and deviance (like classical theory) and instead asks why most people conform (Hirschi 1969). Control theorists answer that attachment and commitment to conforming people, institutions, and values produce a loyalty that protects against the temptation to deviate. Thus control theory "assumes consensus on certain basic values codified in criminal law and views delinquency as infraction of legal norms resulting from weakened commitment to conformity" (Kornhauser 1984, 23).

Broken Bond Theory

Two general kinds of control theory can be differentiated on the basis of when attachment and commitment occur and how they are weakened. Most control theories assume that socialization into convention occurs from an early age, but something breaks or weakens the bonds to convention, freeing a person to deviate. This type of control theory can be called broken bond theory. For example, the neutralization of the moral bind of law discussed in the last chapter has been considered a version of this type of control theory (Akers 1994, 114). Another example of broken bond theory is social disorganization or social ecology theory (discussed in the next chapter), which argues that the isolation and breakdown of communities can undermine a person's commitment to conform to the dominant or mainstream culture (Kornhauser 1984).

Failure to Bond Theory

The second kind of control theory, which is the one considered in this chapter, assumes that the very creation of a commitment to convention is problematic. Persuading humans to conform to socially approved norms and values is very difficult and requires the investment of time and energy and considerable maintenance (Box [1971] 1981). Inducing conforming social behavior requires certain kinds of socialization and can easily go wrong: "Differences in nurturing account for variations in attachment to others and commitment to an ordered way of living" (Nettler 1984, 290). Without this attachment and commitment forming in the first place, humans are more likely to deviate and break the law. We call this type of control theory failure to bond theory.

One of the earliest versions of failure to bond theory is John Bowlby's idea, also known as "attachment theory" (see Chapter 5). Bowlby (1951) conducted research on forty-four juvenile delinquents who were referred to his child guidance clinic (which he compared to 44 controls). He found that children whose relationship with their mother was frequently interrupted during the early years of their development (up to the age of eight) or who have factors that mitigate against secure maternal bonding, such as child abandonment, foster care, or child abuse, develop anxiety and have difficulty forming relationships with others. Consequently they become "affectionless characters" who lack the ability to empathize with others and, as a result, do not see or feel the pain that harm may cause others. The desirable state, according to Bowlby's revised theory of attachment, is "secure attachment." It requires a responsible, lovingly responsive, and sensitive mother figure who is empathetic and able to satisfy childhood needs for emotional and physical security. In contrast, those like Jack Henry Abbott represent the failure of the attachment process: "Attachment theory predicts that the most problematic individuals will be those who were abandoned at an early age, who experienced multiple placements (in foster homes and so on), who had to deal with the early absence of one or both parents, and who faced traumatic conditions in early childhood (physical, sexual or other abuse)" (Schmalleger 2002, 186).

Several other early versions of social control theory exist, however. Drawing on Reiss's (1951) ideas about offenders' failure to internalize personal self-control and the absence of direct external social controls such as law and informal social control, F. Ivan Nye (1958) distinguished between three kinds of controls: (1) direct control from the threat of punishment; (2) indirect control, which protects youths from delinquency through their wish to avoid hurting intimates, such as parents; and (3) internal control, which relies on an internalized sense of guilt.

Another early version of failure to bond theory was Walter Reckless's ([1950] 1973, 1961) containment theory. He argued that adolescent youths are motivated toward delinquency by "pushes" from the pressures and strains of the environment and "pulls" provided by peers. Juveniles will violate the law unless protected by both internal and external controls, which he called inner and outer containments. Outer containment comes from parents and school discipline, whereas inner containment comes from a strongly developed sense of guilt and a positive self-concept. The interplay of these forces could produce more or less delinquency. In particular, positive self-concept can be enhanced by external social approval, and this in turn binds the youths to the community and to conventional behavior. Conversely (and anticipating labeling theory, discussed in the next section), negative reaction from society would result in a negative self-concept through which a reciprocity of disrespect leads to a failure to adopt conventional behavior.

Ruth Kornhauser summarized how both internal and external controls and rewards influence acts of conformity: "Social controls are actual or potential rewards and punishments that accrue from conformity to or deviation from norms. Controls may be internal, invoked by self, or external, enforced by others" (1984, 24). Kornhauser added, "Social bonds vary in depth, scope, multiplicity, and degree of articulation with each other" (1984, 25). Travis Hirschi has been celebrated for developing an elaborated version of the failure-to-bond version of control theory. Hirschi drew on several dimensions of these earlier theories to develop his social control theory.

Hirschi's Social Control Theory

Hirschi's (1969) book *Causes of Delinquency* is most often associated with recent social control theory, and his version of failure to bond theory has stimulated the most research. Like the early control theorists, Hirschi draws on an idea developed by Jackson Toby (1957), who argued that the key to forming commitment was developing an investment in convention, which he called a "stake in conformity." Once invested, the cost of losing this stake serves as a barrier to law violation. The underlying assumption in Hirschi's argument is that all people would break the law if they did not fear the damage and consequences of getting caught. Ties or bonds to conventional parents, school, friends, employers, and so on make crime too much of a risk for most people.

For Hirschi, the "social bond" consists of several components: attachment, commitment, involvement, and belief, each of which has a very precise meaning, different from its conventional or even psychological understanding. *Attachment* is defined as caring about others, including respecting their opinions and expectations, and is based on a mutual trust and respect that develops from ongoing interactions and intimate relations with conventional adults. *Commitment* refers to the individual's investment in conventional behavior, including a willingness to do what is promised and respecting the expectations others have that it will be done. Commitment implies that "the interests of most persons would be endangered if they were to engage in criminal acts" (1969, 21). In other words commitment involves a cost benefit analysis of what degree of previous investment or "stake in conformity" would be lost if one were to participate in the act. *Involvement* is the time and energy of participation in conventional activities. This can be interpreted as a simple ratio. Since time and energy are limited, the more time spent doing conventional activities, the less time is available for deviant acts. Finally, the bond is solidified by *belief* in the moral validity of conventional norms and on the child's respect for the authority of those limiting their behavior. This is a fundamental and explicit assumption of control theory, which "assumes the existence of a common value system within the society or group whose norms are being violated" (1969, 23). More broadly, belief refers to an ongoing conviction that conventional behavior and respect for its underlying principles, norms, and values is important and necessary. Finally, the elements of bonding in Hirschi's theory are interrelated such that "the chain of causation is thus from attachment to parents, through concern for persons in positions of authority, to the belief that the rules of society are binding on one's conduct" (1969, 200).

By way of illustrating Hirschi's theory, let us consider the example of two college seniors, Trevor and Shantell, who have fallen in love, feel like soulmates, spend a lot of time together, respect each other, and plan to get married after graduation. In a new criminology class, Trevor meets an attractive sophomore, Donna, who "just wants to have fun." The opportunity arises for a date during which Trevor would be tempted to cheat on his longtime girlfriend, Shantell. How do Hirschi's key concepts explain what might unfold? Strong attachment means that Trevor would not go on the date, because he knows it would be disrespectful toward Shantell, who would feel upset and betrayed. Strong commitment means that Trevor has led Shantell to trust in him. Such a date, especially with Donna, would be cheating on his relationship. This would undermine the trust between Trevor and Shantell and risk the breakup of the relationship and cancellation of their planned marriage. Strong involvement in the relationship with Shantell would mean that Trevor was so busy doing activities with her that there literally would not be time for anyone else. Finally, strong belief in their relationship would include reference to certain values such as honesty, safety, monogamy, stability, security, and maybe even the belief that taking risks is unwise.

In short, Hirschi's bonded conventional student, Trevor, would probably reject the date, recognizing that it threatened his valued relationship with Shantell. Of course, if he justified the act to himself with the arguments that the date with Donna would be a onetime kind of thing, that his steady would not know about it, and she would be working anyway, he would not be a Hirschi-bonded student, but a Matza-neutralizing drifter off on a moral holiday, free to date Donna, at least on this occasion!

Hirschi's bonding theory, which stands alone as a viable explanation for crime, raised the question of whether the reason some people failed to form connections with conventional others had to do with their capacity for self-control, itself affected by parental socialization practices. These questions led Hirschi to a further refinement of control theory, *self-control theory*, which we consider next.

Self-Control Theory

In 1990, with his colleague Michael Gottfredson, Travis Hirschi wrote *A General Theory of Crime*. This book has enjoyed wide circulation. Cohn and Farrington (1998) found that the book had the second most citations of all books published in the 1990s. In this text, Gottfredson and Hirschi moved away from the four-component version of social bonding theory to focus on self-control or the lack of it that results in impulsive behavior. They identify juvenile delinquency as just one of a wide range of crimes, including embezzlement and fraud, that can be explained not so much by the absence of bonds as by a lack of self-control on the part of the offender, especially in circumstances of increased opportunity and heightened situational temptation. Criminals lack self-control, according to Gottfredson and Hirschi, because they have been poorly trained as children, as a result of low parental investment in child rearing, poor monitoring, and disciplining practices. This explains "the differential tendency of people to avoid criminal acts whatever the circumstances" (Gottfredson and Hirschi 1990, 87).

The underlying assumption about human nature here is the same as in control theory: All people are motivated to break rules and make a rational choice decision whether or not to do so. The difference is in the ability to suppress or restrain such urges and drives and in the need for excitement, risk taking, and immediate gratification. Most people do not engage in criminal acts because they have been effectively socialized by parents to exercise self-control over their behavior. Those who are not properly socialized have a lack of control that can also be related to "low self-esteem." Pratt and Cullen (2000, 932) add that this "increases the likelihood that individuals will be unable to resist the easy, immediate gratification that crime and analogous behaviors seductively, and almost ubiquitously, present in everyday life." For some people the socialization process, then, is defective, providing little protection against committing crime. Their socialization is defective not because of something biological or psychological within the individual but because the parents have failed to use adequate child-rearing practices. In early childhood this lack of self-control is manifested as "conduct problems" (Pratt and Cullen 2000). Matt DeLisi succinctly outlined Gottfredson and Hirschi's position:

> Abject parenting nullifies successful childhood socialization. The outcome, in persons exposed to such an environment, is low self-control. Persons with low self-control (a) prefer immediate gratification of desires, (b) pursue simple tasks rather than activities that require tenacity, (c) value physical rather

than verbal or cognitive experiences, (d) enjoy quick returns instead of long-term commitments such as marriage or occupational and educational careers, (e) are employed in low-skilled versus academic endeavors, and (f) are self-centered and generally insensitive to the feelings of others. (DeLisi 2001, 1)

Developing Gottfredson and Hirschi, Harold Grasmick and colleagues (1994) constructed a character profile of those with low self-control:

Grasmick's Characteristics of Low Self-Control

Is impulsive

Seeks instant gratification

Has low levels of diligence, tenacity, and persistence

Seeks sensation and excitement

Prefers simple physical tasks over complex intellectual tasks

Is self-centered

Is insensitive to the needs of others

Has low tolerance to frustration

Addresses conflict though confrontation

Let's look in more detail at the parental failings that produce these lack of self-control characteristics.

Parenting includes three functional components, which we call (1) surveillance, (2) labeling, and (3) punishment. Surveillance refers to parents or guardians monitoring children's behavior. Monitoring can be reduced because of lack of care, lack of time, or the periodic physical absence of the child from her parents, for example, due to hospitalization of the child or parental work commitments. Labeling refers to the parent's or guardian's conception of the norms, rules, and laws of society and their readiness to label behavior as consistent with or deviant from these. Parents may not label behavior for several reasons, including the popular child-rearing philosophy that this practice is harmful for healthy child development (we discuss labeling theory in more depth in the last section of this chapter). Finally, even if they watch and label, parents may not provide effective punishment for deviant behavior or adequate rewards for conforming behavior. Together, inadequate surveillance, inappropriate labeling, and ineffective punishment result in dysfunctional child rearing. This has a serious impact on children through their formative years (ages six to eight) and reduces the effectiveness of other socialization through formal schooling or informal peer groups.

Overall, social control theory has been one of the most tested of all theories. As Rankin and Kern (1994, 495) have noted, "Among the various social control perspectives, Hirschi's (1969) version is probably most responsible for developments in family and delinquency research. It is relatively explicit, well developed, and amenable to empirical tests." The bonds Hirschi outlined have been extensively studied. Costello and Vowell found the bonds to have "important direct effects" (1999, 815). One commonly identified element of the bond is religion. Baier and Wright conducted a meta-analysis of sixty studies examining religion and delinquency and concluded that "religious behavior and beliefs exert a significant, moderate effect on individuals' criminal behavior" (2001, 12).

Similarly, studies of low self-control have produced considerable support. One of the more robust means of assessing theory quantitatively is through the use of meta-analysis (a summary and comparison of all the previous studies). When Pratt and Cullen conducted a meta-analysis of twenty-one research studies on low self-control, they found that self-control, or lack thereof, is a strong predictor of crime (2000). Likewise, DiLisi (2001), Vazsonyi and colleagues (2001), and Hay (2001) found self-control to be inversely related to criminal offending. Those who exhibited low self-control were indeed found to be impulsive and risk takers, and were more serious criminals (DiLisi 2001). Overall, the research on self-control theory is fairly conclusive. In another summary of existing studies, Hay found that "with few exceptions, these studies indicate that low self-control, whether measured attitudinally or behaviorally, positively affects deviant and criminal behavior" (Hay 2001, 707).

Evaluation, Limitations, and Policy Implications of Control Theory

While research has revealed much support for the various versions of this theory, it has also exhibited some flaws. Krohn (1991) has pointed out that Hirschi's original bonding theory fails to adequately distinguish between different elements of the bond and is unclear about the causal direction of bonding. Thus, although a lack of parental attachment can affect delinquency, delinquency can also affect parental attachment (Liska and Reed 1985). Social control theory doesn't explain whether some parents fail to bond with their children because the children themselves are the problem: "No recognition is given to evidence that children come into the world with different personalities and temperaments, and in so doing affect the behavior of parents from a very early age" (Ellis and Walsh 2000, 326). LaGrange and White (1985) pointed out that the strength of the bond to convention varies based on a number of factors, particularly age.

Others have criticized control theory for failing to explain gender differences in delinquency: "why parents, schools, and churches throughout the world would socialize children in ways that make males form weaker bonds and have less self-control than females" (Ellis and Walsh 2000, 326). Nor does the theory gain as much support for serious adult crime, which is at its best explaining delinquency.

The parental controls that feature so prominently in Gottfredson and Hirschi's (1990) self-control theory can counteract the effects of bonding and can work in different and complex ways (Wells and Rankin 1988; Rankin and Wells 1990). Akers (1994, 123) has argued that self-control theory is untestable because it is tautological: "Propensity toward crime and low self-control appear to be one and the same thing." Pratt and Cullen disagree, arguing that "the charge of tautology does not apply to studies that measure self-control with attitudinal scales that were developed to assess self-control independently of criminal behavior" (2000, 945). Further, as with social bonding theory, self-control theory is limited by gender "because it more robustly predicts delinquency among males than among females" (DeLisi 2001, 3).

Finally, control theory seriously ignores the insight of Matza and Sykes concerning the subterranean values of conventional society. As a result, the theory ignores the finding that effective bonding to convention and self-control do not protect against serious deviance. When those who have leading roles in conventional society, including parents, also indulge in unconventional behavior, from drug use to corporate fraud, then being bonded to "convention" can also mean being bonded to crime. Those who engage in pleasing the conventional employer, from former U.S. presidents (e.g., Richard Nixon) to corporate presidents (such as Pharmor's Mickey Monus or Enron's Kenneth Lay) may come to realize that their commitment to convention necessarily involves a commitment to crime and deviance. Recognizing the value of their "stake in conformity" as an instrument of compliance was clearly expressed by Richard Nixon's comment about loyalty allowing moral and criminal laws to be broken: "Catch them by the balls (high salaries, high mortgages, investment in kids' college) and their hearts and minds will follow" (meaning they'll do any risky or immoral behavior that you ask of them).

Curran and Renzetti (1994) observe, not surprisingly, that the narrow range of white-collar crimes Gottfredson and Hirschi examined for their general theory of crime, relying on low self-control explanations, omits the majority of crimes committed in corporate entities and government structures by executives and managers who are loyal to conventional values. Like Lieutenant Calley in the My Lai massacre described at the beginning of the previous chapter, these persons believe they are supporting conventional values as they commit their crimes.

Policy Implications

Control theory implies policy interventions based on preventive social-ization designed to protect and insulate individuals from pushes and pulls toward crime. Part of this protection comes from supervision, sur-veillance, and control. The major focus on preventive policy, according to control theory, lies in the informal control of children by their parents, not control provided by the formal criminal justice system, which should re-main as the punitive last resort. This implies strengthening bonds to con-vention through developing more effective child-rearing practices. Early intervention programs include parent training and functional-family therapy that seek to reduce family conflict through dispute settlement and negotiation, reduce abuse and neglect, promote positive parent–child interaction, and teach moderate discipline (Morton and Ewald 1987). When family problems cannot be resolved, it has been suggested that youths be placed in surrogate families and group homes with trained "teaching parents" (Braukmann and Wolf 1987; Agnew 1995b). Based on the studies of religion cited above, deepening religious belief should also be explored as a policy means of reducing crime.

A second level of intervention for some control theorists is directed to-ward those "at risk" of engaging in antisocial activities. Policy here can fo-cus on providing counseling and problem solving and social skills training (Goldstein, Krasner, and Garfield 1989; Hollin 1990), especially in the school context. Gottfredson and Hirschi (1990) argue that unless this kind of inter-vention occurs early in the child's development, it is already too late to make much difference. Indeed, a RAND study shows that both parent-based and school-based programs are more cost-effective in prevention than reliance on incarceration (Greenwood 1996). The study compared crime prevention programs that (1) sent child care professionals into homes of children prior to their birth up to the age of two to monitor their behavior and provided four subsequent years of day care, (2) provided parent train-ing and therapy to families of children between ages seven and eleven who showed signs of aggressive behavior, (3) provided disadvantaged high school children aged fourteen to eighteen with cash incentives to graduate, and (4) provided twelve- and thirteen-year-olds special counseling and su-pervision programs. The study found that high school graduation incen-tives were the most cost-effective, followed by parent training programs, with delinquency supervision programs and prison being less cost-effec-tive. Interestingly, the least cost-effective was early childhood intervention, although this did cut child abuse by 50 percent (Greenwood 1996).

These kinds of interventions also have serious moral implications that go beyond economics to raise questions about the relationship between the state and the family that would need to be resolved before any such programs could be implemented on a wide scale. One obvious question is, Why are children who do not succeed in school (but do exercise adequate self-control) unable to get a general equivalency diploma (GED), help, or financial support (e.g., loans)? How far might intervention programs providing benefits work as an incentive for otherwise law-abiding children to commit fraud in order to get the benefits?

Labeling Theory: A Special Case of Failed Socialization?

Like the theorists we have just examined, labeling theorists believe that social interaction with others is important in shaping whether or not people become offenders. But where social control and bonding theory see clear moral labeling of behavior as important, labeling theory views this as the problem. The issue is not so much what we learn or how we bond to others but how our sense of self-identity is built on the views that others have of us and how this identity can be negatively impacted through other people's reactions to our behavior. Again, Nick's drama mimics what has happened to countless students who were on their way to conventionally defined success as college graduates until agents of social control intervened.

Another student, a senior with a 4.0 GPA, was enjoying his final spring break. He was sharing a room with five or six of his fraternity brothers in Daytona Beach, Florida. A few had small quantities of marijuana. Someone smelled the burning cannabis and notified police. Hours later, when this student returned from the beach alone, he entered the room and the police closely followed. They searched the room, put all the small bags of pot into one big pile, thereby greatly increasing the weight, and charged the student with a felony due to the (now) large quantity. Had a drug detecting test been administered, the student would have been found drug free. Unfortunately, like Nick, he did not notify his parents and handled it himself, greatly hurting his case. His friends all left and he remained in jail for several days. His lifelong dream of working in federal law enforcement ended abruptly.

We discover self-identity through symbolic communication in interaction and role-play with others in social contexts. For adolescent youths, what their peers think of them and what image they project to others are of utmost importance, resulting in a concentration on style, body image, and so on. Many people define themselves, and are defined by others, according to how they appear. Look around you in class and you can readily identify the Greeks who always wear their letters on clothing, purses, and cars, and wear T-shirts displaying significant parties and socials. Observe too the Goths with their pale skin and dark hair, the Surfers with their golden hair, board shorts, flip-flops, and deep tans. You may even have some bikers with their tattoos, Harley shirts, chains, and boots. Can you identify the ROTC students in your class? The athletes or jocks? Do the students who dress differently from one another make eye contact, sit by and speak to each other? Who did you sit by on the first day of class? Many of us love the academic environment because of this broad diversity of experiences; students unfortunately often take this for granted as part of the social landscape, without recognizing the serious consequences of the social labels they live by. Yet the impact of these labels can be destructive and deadly. The spate of school violence and homicides of 1994–1999 were fueled if not directly caused by the negative stereotypes applied to vulnerable children who were seen as "geeks" or "nerds" before their frustration from bullying exploded into violence such as occurred at Thurston High in Springfield, Oregon, and Columbine High in Littleton, Colorado (Hinkle and Henry 2000; Lawrence 1998). Instead of understanding the labeling process and its destructive effects, social control agents created a moral panic to seek out these nonconforming oddball killers, labeled by jocks as the Trench Coat Mafia in what John Katz (1999) described as "geek profiling." He relates how these marginalized "teenagers traded countless stories of being harassed, beaten, ostracized and ridiculed by teachers, students and administrators for dressing and thinking differently from the mainstream. Many said they had some understanding of why the killers in Littleton went over the edge." Consider the following account of "Jay" from Katz's (1999) Web site, Voices from the Hellmouth:

> I stood up in a social studies class . . . and said I could never kill anyone or condone anyone who did kill anyone, but that I could, on some level, understand these kids in Colorado, the killers. Because, day after day, slight after slight, exclusion after exclusion, you can learn how to hate, and that hatred grows and takes you over sometimes, especially when you come to see that you're smart and different, or sometimes even because you are online a lot, which is still so uncool to many kids! After class I was called to the principal's office and told that I had to undergo five sessions of counseling or be expelled from the school as I had expressed ?sympathy? with the killers in Colorado, and the school had to be able to explain itself if I "acted out." (Katz 1999, http://slashdot.org)

The social interaction of observing differences in others, negatively stereotyping them and then excluding, taunting, bullying, and teasing those who display these attributes (e.g., clothing, speech, and diction) is the subject of labeling theory. This theory of how social selves, self-esteem, and social identity are formed itself is based on symbolic interactionist theory rooted in social psychology.

According to symbolic interactionists, we see ourselves through the mirror of others, as they react to what they see in us. Charles Horton Cooley (1864–1929) called this the "looking glass self" ([1902] 1964). To the symbolic interactionist ideas of George Herbert Mead (1863–1931), who devised the notion of the social self, or generalized other (1934), Mead's student Herbert Blumer added that humans are actively engaged with others in the construction of their own social identities (Blumer 1969).

Once formed, these identities are not fixed but continually reformed and reinterpreted. Not all others are equally significant in this interactive process, however.

The most significant others are powerful groups who ban certain behavior through passing laws, and social control agents, such as police, courts, social workers, psychiatrists, school administrators, teachers, counselors, and so on, who enforce these laws. Agents of social control exert such a powerful impact, according to labeling theorists, that otherwise minor rule breaking or difference is magnified through criminal justice processes to have a significant effect. The impact of these officially sanctioned meaningful encounters can transform fragile social identities into criminal careers through a process Frank Tannenbaum (1938, 19–20) originally referred to as the "dramatization of evil." Either punishment or reform, argued Tannenbaum, can lead to the very "bad behavior it would suppress," such that "the person becomes the thing he is described as being" (1938, 19–20). The key to this process, according to Tannenbaum, was the "tag," or label, attached to the rule breaker. Most recently, skateboarders have been singled out by government as being an undesirable element. Many youth have bumper stickers stating that "skateboarding is not a crime." Clearly, a nonharmful recreational activity should not be criminalized in the view of the participants.

During the 1950s, the early ideas of labeling theorists lay dormant because of the dominance of social and structural explanations (Shoemaker 1996, 191). By the 1960s, the social and political climate became open to the view that humans are malleable. Consistent with the general criticism of tradition and established institutions of control, labeling theorists found a resonance in the idea that excessive control inhibited the potentially free human spirit striving to be different. Along with other protest movements for women and civil rights, labeling theory, or, as some called it, the "new deviancy theory" (Taylor et al. 1973), seemed, at times, to romanticize if not celebrate the lawbreaker.

Founding figures in this "radical" movement were Edwin Lemert (1951, 1967), Howard Becker ([1963] 1973), and Erving Goffman (1961); major contributions also came from Lofland (1969), Schur (1965), Mankoff (1971), and Young (1971). Space precludes extensive coverage here, but you can gain a good understanding of the central ideas of this perspective by examining the ideas of the early theorists.

Lemert's Primary and Secondary Deviance

Edwin M. Lemert (1951, 1967) argued that crime begins not with the activities of the rule breaker but with the social audience that passes laws banning certain behavior as immoral or criminal. He argued that rather than deviance leading to social control, "social control leads to deviance" (1967, v). Laws and their enforcement by control agents within society are responsible for escalating minor rule violations into a more serious activity for a person's identity, or "psychic structure." Orlando, Florida, "the city beautiful," is a tourist Mecca. Recently the city government become concerned with the image that the many homeless people present. These downtrodden unfortunates do not fit the Disney image. Consequently many new ordinances have been passed aimed at this "problem." No longer can you lie on a park bench or splash water on your face from a fountain. You cannot even stand still in certain places. It is a safe bet that businessmen in suits and tourists with their children are not arrested for splashing water on their faces. Once arrested, a person is much more likely to be rearrested. (For a compelling look at the plight of the homeless in America, see Gregg Barak's award winning *Gimme Shelter* [1991b]).

Lemert called spontaneous, sporadic, minor rule violations primary deviance. Primary deviance may stem from many different sources. Secondary deviance, in contrast, refers to behavior that results after authorities, particularly social control agents of the criminal justice system, react to primary deviance. Secondary deviance is rule-breaking behavior that emerges from a person's social identity. This occurs partly as a result of having to deal with labeling by others and partly because of who the person has become as a result of the social reaction to the primary deviance. This reaction produces stigmatization.

Everyone engages in forms of primary deviance, and alone it has little consequence for a person's social identity, provided that the person has a strong self-image. For example, employees who steal office equipment, use the telephone for personal calls, or overclaim expenses rarely think of themselves as "employee thieves," or embezzlers. Those who are uncertain of their identity as a result of a weak self-image are vulnerable to what others think of them, however. The homeless described above would fit into this category, as would the high school "geeks" so heavily criticized by those around them for being different.

Repeated, forceful negative definition of their identity can raise serious questions for them about who they are and result in "identity transformation" through self-labeling. They come to see themselves as a deviant type and engage in subsequent deviance because of the stigmatized deviants they have become. They sometimes join groups of similarly labeled deviants (e.g., "Trenchcoat Mafia"), forming a deviant or criminal subculture

in which the members provide support for each other. Some gay and lesbian groups, juvenile gangs, groups of drug abusers, and prostitute collectives may be formed through such a process. In such subcultures,
members normalize one another's behavior through role adjustments
(Becker [1963] 1973; Sagarin 1969). In some cases, through a process of delabeling and relabeling, group associations may result in the abandonment
of the original deviant behavior—although not the problem created by the
stigma, as in the case of alcoholics and narcotics users or the obese (Trice
and Roman 1970; Robinson and Henry 1977; Pfuhl and Henry 1993).

Becker's Interactionist Theory: Social Reaction and Master Status

Howard S. Becker was a student of the interactionists Herbert Blumer and
Ernest Burgess and Everett Hughes at the University of Chicago. Becker
began participant observation studies (living in the daily lives of the group
being studied) in graduate school by keeping a diary on barroom musicians at the Chicago tavern where he played jazz (dance) piano (Martin et
al. 1990, 350; Debro 1970, 159). His major book on deviance, *Outsiders*
([1963] 1973), was begun in 1954, just after Lemert's early works were written but without knowledge of them (Debro 1970, 165). Becker combined a
theoretical analysis with the early case studies of musicians and marijuana
users. He found that the effects of an activity were a consequence of how a
person interprets his experience. Although this work has become a classic
in the field (*Outsiders* is the top-selling book on crime and delinquency by
a sociologist, selling over 100,000 copies; see Gans 1997), Becker himself
admits to being only marginally involved in the study of deviance and
then just as a diversion from his studies of occupations, education, and
more recently the social organization of art (Debro 1970, 167).

Becker ([1963] 1973, 9) shifts the causality of rule breaking from the actor
to the audience, arguing that "deviance is not a quality of the act a person
commits but rather a consequence of the application by others of rules and
sanctions to an 'offender.'" He suggests that rule breaking is the outcome
of a three-stage process: Social groups create deviance by (1) "making the
rules whose infraction constitutes deviance," (2) "applying those rules to
particular people," and (3) "labeling them outsiders." The deviant actor is
the product of this process, "one to whom that label has been successfully
applied; deviant behavior is behavior that people so label."

The first stage of Becker's labeling process may involve actors engaging
in behavior that an audience finds offensive, such as drug use, but it need
not. Some people, such as minority youths, may be arrested on suspicion
by police for minor rule-breaking behaviors such as "loitering," or DWB
(driving while black). What is crucial is that the audience selects a behavior
that it defines as offensive. As we saw in Chapter 2, this can be a very

arbitrary decision and shows considerable variation culturally and historically. Importantly, Becker recognized that what becomes defined as deviant
behavior and what may be criminalized depend on power and interests.

Becker coined the term "moral entrepreneur" to refer to those with
more power who shape the law with their own ideas of what is offensive.
This is one reason why the offenses of adolescents become labeled "delinquency," yet the offenses of corporations and governments often remain
"administrative violations."

The second stage in the deviance process, in which control agents select
people whose behavior is offensive and label their behavior, also depends
on power. The process involves identifying some people's behavior as
different, negatively evaluating it as offensive, finding the appropriate offense category, and supplying an interpretation of why the person's behavior is an example of that category. As Becker said in an early
interview, "The whole point of the interactionist approach to deviance is
to make it clear that somebody had to do the labeling. It didn't just happen. . . . The court labeled him or his parents labeled him or the people in
the community" (Debro 1970, 177).

In the third stage, the contested definition over the meaning of signi-
fied behavior depends on who has the greater power to influence the labeling process and whether an accused has the power to resist the
application of a deviance label. Young, lower-class, urban, minority
offenders typically do not have the resources for resistance. In contrast,
middle- and upper-class offenders are typically able to redefine their
activities as acceptable. Chambliss (1973), for example, found that although middle-class adolescents engage in similar delinquent activities
as their lower-class counterparts, they are able to do so in greater secrecy
and even when caught are protected because of their demeanor and family or community connections.

Once successfully labeled, a person is subject to the negative effects of
the label itself, which provides what Becker called a "master" status. Being caught and publicly labeled as an offender "has important consequences for one's further social participation and self-image" (Becker
[1963] 1973, 31). The status of "deviant" highlights certain characteristics
of the person as central to his or her identity while diminishing others.
This interaction with others, wrote Becker ([1963] 1973, 34), produces a
"self-fulfilling prophecy" that "sets in motion several mechanisms which
conspire to shape the person in the image people have of him [or her]."
Part of this process involves closing off legitimate forms of activity, which
restricts the opportunities for the labeled offender to behave differently.
The label also leads others to engage in retrospective interpretation.

Retrospective interpretation occurs when a review of a person's past
activity highlights previous instances that can be reinterpreted as con-

sistent with the new deviant master status. Such actions further lead to a new, narrow focus by the audience, now with heightened sensitivity toward the labeled individual. This in turn results in more deviance being discovered. Wilkins (1965) and Young (1971) describe this as "deviancy amplification," since it leads to even more secrecy and interaction with similarly defined others. Deviancy amplification may eventually result in an individual accepting the label, adopting a deviant or criminal career, and joining in an organized deviant group (Becker [1963] 1973, 37).

For Becker, then, the central issue was not the normal rule breaking that everyone sometimes engages in as part of human freedom and curiosity. Rather, when others transformed that activity into a negative, restricted force, new and additional offenses resulted. In clarifying his account, Becker ([1963] 1973) argued that the secret deviant, who on the surface seems to contradict his idea that deviance does not exist until it is labeled (Gibbs 1966), actually refers to evolving definitions of behavior. Becker noted that at one point in time the powerful do not provide the procedures for determining a behavior's standing, yet at a subsequent time they do so.

If the work of Lemert and Becker sensitized us to the power of the definition process, Erving Goffman led us to the force of stigma and spoiled identities that can result from institutionalization.

Goffman's Stigma and Total Institutions

Erving Goffman (1922–1983) was a sociologist in the interactionist tradition of Mead. He used his fieldwork on a Scottish island community to write his doctorate at the University of Chicago, where a fellow student was Howard Becker (Martin et al. 1990). Although most of his work described and analyzed everyday, face-to-face interaction in a variety of noncriminological settings, his work on stigma and mental hospital institutionalization has direct relevance to criminological discussions of labeling theory. Goffman uses the metaphor of drama: The world is a stage and we are all players performing and demonstrating our strategic gamesmanship to the audience. His book *Stigma* (1963) distinguishes between the physical, moral, and racial forms of stigma, each of which is based on identified differences that others negatively evaluate and construct into "spoiled identities." The person affected by disabilities or schizophrenia would be an example of a spoiled identity. Through interactive situations, individuals classify others into categories, some of which may be stigmatized ones.

Once people are classified, we treat them as a spoiled or "virtual" identity rather than as who they actually are. For example, those with physical or mental disabilities are seen as blemished and treated as though they have numerous other deficits—and as less than human. Similarly, those racially or ethnically different from a dominant group are typically treated as deficient and inferior. Consider our discussion in Chapter 5 of immigrants to the United States from Europe around 1900 and how they were seen as paupers and degenerates. Finally, those whose behavior may indicate a character flaw, such as criminal offenders, are treated as morally bankrupt, dishonest, evil, and so forth. As a consequence of this process, the stigmatized are uncomfortable with their classifiers, who they feel have unjustly exercised social and political power to deny them their full humanity.

Applied to inmates of mental hospitals or correctional settings, it is clear that the stigma process reduces the ability of those stereotyped as "spoiled" to return to a mainstream or noncriminal life (Goffman 1961). The result may be an effort by the stigmatized to conceal their physical and socially constructed defects by constructing a "front" in order to pass as "normal," that is, as persons appearing to have no defects. For example, consider men who abuse their wives in the privacy of their home but appear charming in public.

Goffman's notion of "total institutions," which was formulated in his study of a mental hospital, *Asylums* (1961), has had considerable impact on labeling theory generally and especially on understanding the way prisons dehumanize the inmate. A total institution is a place where similarly classified people are forced to live, work, and play together around activities consistent with the goals of the institution. This takes place under formal supervisory control governed by strict rules and procedures and within a restricted environment. The inmates in total institutions are separated formally and socially from the staff and have no input into decisionmaking about their activities or outcomes. According to Goffman, this process is designed to force inmates to fit the institutional routine. When continued over time, the process results in dehumanization and humiliation. As a result of the adaptive behaviors inmates have to adopt in order to cope, their behavior patterns become solidified. This changes their moral career and renders them unfit for a return to life outside the institution (1961, 13). Goffman argues this results in a "mortification" of the self. How permanent such identity change is has been subject to controversy, but unquestionably Goffman's work adds to our understanding of the impact of social and institutional effects on the labeling process.

In light of the theories discussed in this and the previous chapter, labeling demonstrates the dangers inherent in attempts to intervene to change people. This is most pronounced when punitive interventions are falsely presented as reform programs that suggest a "spoiled identity."

Braithwaite's Reintegrative Shaming

John Braithwaite is an Australian criminologist who studied white-collar crime in the pharmaceutical industry. He is one of the most recent contributors to the labeling perspective, agreeing that the kind of stigmatization Goffman described is certainly destructive. In his book *Crime, Shame, and Integration*, Braithwaite (1989) defines this negative stigmatization as disintegrative shaming and argues that it is destructive of social identities. It morally condemns people and reduces their liberty yet makes no attempt to resolve the problem by reconnecting the accused/convicted to the community. Braithwaite describes a second, positive kind of stigmatization, which he calls reintegrative shaming. This is actually constructive and can serve to reduce and prevent crime. Reintegrative shaming, while expressing social disapproval, also provides the social process mechanisms to bring those censured back into the community, reaffirming that they are morally good—only a part of their total behavior is unacceptable. Braithwaite believed this explains why numerous different communitarian societies, such as Japan, that use a positive reintegrative form of shaming have low crime rates, whereas those that use disintegrative shaming have high crime rates. In the latter cases, offenders are cut off from the mainstream society and are free from informal controls to recidivate.

Although labeling processes are a major component of Braithwaite's analysis, several commentators (Akers 1994; Gibbons 1994; Einstadter and Henry 1995) see his ideas as an integrated theory linking several of the social process theories we have discussed in this and the previous chapters (learning, control, differential association, and labeling) with those we shall discuss in the next two (cultural, subcultural, and strain). We shall briefly return to these again in Chapter 12.

Limitations and Policy Implications of Labeling Theory

Labeling theory, with its commonsense truth of a "self-fulfilling prophecy," has been controversial. It suggests, seemingly outrageously, that attempts to control crime can actually make it worse. The first major criticism was that the theory does not explain why people engage in primary deviance and why some people engage in more of it than others (Gibbs 1966). Second, if deviance is only a product of public labeling, why do some, such as white-collar offenders, employee thieves, embezzlers, and so on, and some violent offenders, such as abusive husbands, engage in careers of crime without ever being publicly labeled (Mankoff 1971)? One study found that the label applied by parents was strongly related to conceptions of delinquency, a factor that may explain more than the "official" labels that are applied. Moreover, if the effects of labeling are so strong on vulnerable identities that such persons become locked into criminal careers, how do some reform? The question ultimately is, how resilient is the label and is it only a coping strategy for the institutionalized?

Some critics even contest that control agents arbitrarily select offenders (Akers 1968; Wellford 1975). One researcher (Jensen 1972a, 1980) has found that the label applied differentially affects youths based on race or ethnicity. Whites accept the labeling consequences of official sanctions more than African Americans.

Finally, why does labeling theory tend to focus largely on the agencies of social control and on certain labeled groups—"nuts, sluts, and perverts" (Liazos 1972)—but ignore the wider structure of society and the power of the state and corporate interests in shaping public policy of agencies that enforce the labeling (Taylor et al. 1973; Young 1981)? The empirical evidence largely fails to offer support for the theory, although some question the validity of these studies (Plummer 1979; Paternoster and Iovanni 1989).

A major feature of this research is the relative lack of support for the notion that being labeled produces a negative self-image among those labeled (Shoemaker 1996). As a result, as one of its founding critics observes, it became far less dominant in the 1970s, has little to distinguish it, has lost its influence, and "no longer generates the interest, enthusiasm, research and acceptance it once did as a dominant paradigm two or three decades ago" (Akers 1994, 137).

In spite of these criticisms, labeling theory has had a considerable impact on criminal justice policy, especially with regard to juveniles. It has even impacted popular culture through the use of person-preserving politically correct terms such as a "person with disabilities" as opposed to a "disabled person" and "visually challenged" rather than "blind" and "metabolically challenged" rather than "fat."

With regard to criminal behavior, since the central tenet of labeling theory is that social reaction to minor rule breaking creates extra deviance and crime, the policy is clear. If repeated negative definition by official social control agencies transforms ambivalent social identities into criminal ones, the policy must involve reducing social reaction. This will minimize the production of secondary (or extra) rule breaking and, in particular, prevent minor rule breakers from entering criminal careers. Edwin Schur (1973) defined this overall approach as "radical nonintervention." Einstadter and Henry (1995, 220–223) summarize four policy components of this perspective identified in the literature: (1) decriminalization, (2) diversion, (3) decarceration, and (4) restitution or reparation.

Decriminalization is the legalization of crimes involving consent—victimless crimes (Schur 1965) that include activities such as drug use, homosexuality, gambling, and prostitution (see Chapter 2). Not only is banning these activities morally questionable (Duster 1970), but their illegality in the face of a wide public demand for them provides a basis for organized crime, gang activity, police corruption, and bribery, together with the accompanying violence necessary for "market" protection (Schur and Bedau 1974; Curran and Renzetti 1994).

Diversion is a policy that redirects those engaged in minor law violations, especially status offenses such as truancy, runaways, and curfew violation, away from the courts through informal processes leading to noncorrectional settings. The approach is credited with being responsible for the existence of the parallel system of juvenile justice, separate from and less formal than the criminal justice system for adult offenders. Juvenile justice is designed to be less stigmatizing. It involves settlement-directed talking, such as conflict resolution, mediation, and problem solving, rather than punishment.

Decarceration attempts to deal with the stigma effects of total institutions by minimizing their use and releasing numerous people, such as those convicted of substance abuse offenses, on alternative sentences such as probation or electronic tethers. Instead of calling for more prisons, this strategy involves stopping prison building and stopping the sentencing of offenders to prison terms for nonviolent offenses. In particular, juveniles in institutions such as reform schools and training schools were deinstitutionalized into community-based programs (Akers 1994, 131–132).

Restitution and reparation are designed to make the offender responsible for the crime by repaying or compensating either the victim (restitution) or the community or society (reparation) for the harm done. This can involve working to pay back the offender or forms of community service.

Finally, we need to consider the policy implications from Braithwaite's (1989) analysis of reintegrative shaming. This involves providing both public exposure of harmful behavior and informal rehabilitation programs designed to bring the accused back as acceptable members of society. Like programs for recovering alcoholics, these programs can be used as an example of how problems can be worked through (see Henry and Milovanovic's [1996] notions of the "recovering subject" and "replacement discourse," discussed in Chapter 12, for a similar kind of analysis). Braithwaite (1995) described this as a move toward new forms of "communitarianism" that are a social movement and that focus on the family. Finally, his ideas are consistent with the notion of "restorative justice," which involves bringing together offenders and victims in mediation programs designed to reintegrate both into the community and allow both a participative role in determining what is the appropriate level of restitution or reparation. Restorative justice will be discussed further in the policy section of the next chapter, since it is an emerging policy for how communities are coping with juvenile crime.

In many ways, the policy implications of labeling theory are very radical and are not acceptable to most Americans, who have been fed a media diet of punishment and the quick fix ("Three strikes and you're out") from politicians. As a result, the practice of such measures as stopping prison building is confronted with the reality of massive prison-building programs. Mandatory prison sentences for first-time drug dealers, however, such as college students occasionally selling cocaine to friends, who then get eight years in prison, with all that involves to their potential identity, suggests that labeling theorists may have a point, especially in the case of some kinds of offenders.

Summary and Conclusion

In this chapter, we have looked at two social process theories that present a mirror image of the two we examined in the previous chapter. Social control theory rejects the neutralization idea that interactive communications may release us from the moral bind of law and instead suggests that what is important is that bonds form in the first place. Failure to bond to convention produces low self-control and allows deviance to go unchecked. For labeling theorists, fear of the diversity of human behavior may lead to social processes of control that limit the assumed creativity of human lives, bringing about and sustaining careers focused on the very acts the controllers wish to prevent. Thus learning the wrong values is not the issue; nor is bonding to convention or being released from it. For labeling theorists, the issue is how difference is reacted to. Indeed, how deviants are rejected and labeled is most devastating to their future sense of self, leading them to acquire deviant identities.

Although all these theories sensitize us to the importance of adequate socialization and symbolic interaction, they disagree about what is helpful and what is not. Moreover, they do not offer an understanding of the wider cultural and structural forces that shape the contexts in which these social relations take place. We turn to these theories in the next chapter.

Summary Chart: Control Theory and Labeling Theory

1. Control Theory

Basic Idea: Explains why we do not all commit crime; claims we do if the controls never form or are worn away.

Human Nature: Humans are seen as rationally calculating, self-interested, and selfish actors (as in classical theory) whose behavior is limited by connections and bonds to others who are significant reference groups for them.

Society and the Social Order: Consensus. Law is an expression of the rules of the conventional society. Criminals are those for whom bonds of care for others never formed or are removed. We are all potential criminals.

Causal Logic: Crime results when people are not socialized into a bond with society and do not develop a stake in conformity. Social bonding consists of four elements: (1) attachment to teachers, parents, friends, etc. and the desire not to lose them or hurt them; (2) commitment to conventional behavior, with a willingness to do what one has expressed in trust; (3) involvement in conventional activity, especially school related; and (4) belief in the need to obey conventional rules and in the institutions of society.

Criminal Justice Policy: Ensure an adequate level of bonding between youths and conventional society through intensive socialization in traditional and conventional values.

Criminal Justice Practice: Prevention and rehabilitation through increased bonding; strengthened families and increased commitment to conventional occupations by work-training schemes; reinforced participation in conventional activities at school.

Evaluation: Explains crime by all social classes; has been empirically tested and has highest level of support of all theories of crime causation, but fails to explain differences in crime rates or whether a weakened bond can be strengthened; does not distinguish relative importance of different elements of the bond; does not explain how those highly bonded to convention commit crime or how bonding can actually be used as leverage to coerce offenders who are committed to the high rewards of their jobs and will do anything to keep them; does not explain ethnic and class influences on beliefs or school performance; does not consider role of delinquent peers and subcultures in breaking bonds.

2. Labeling Theory

Basic Idea: As a result of negative labeling and stereotyping (especially by society's control agents), people can become criminal; crime, then, is a self-fulfilling prophecy rooted in the fear that people might be criminal.

Human Nature: Humans are malleable, pliable, plastic, and susceptible to identity transformations as a result of interactions with others and based on how others see them. Human behavior is not fixed in its meaning but open to interpretation and renegotiation. Humans have a social status and humans are inextricably social beings who are creative and free to interact with others but when they do so become subject to their controls.

Society and the Social Order: A plurality of groups dominated by the most powerful, who use their power to stigmatize others less powerful. Law is the expression of the power of moral entrepreneurs and control agents to determine which behaviors are criminalized and which are not. Rules are made that impute ancillary qualities to the deviator. Conflict over legal and public definitions of crime and deviance. Crime is a status. Criminal is a socially constructed public stereotype or "master status" for those who control agents identify as breaking the rules of those in power. We can all become criminals if we have the misfortune to become subject to processing by the criminal justice system.

Causal Logic: Social control agents cause crime by their dramatizing of it and by their excess reaction to people's expression of individuality. Powerful groups ban behavior and then selectively enforce the ban through control agents, such as the police, psychiatrists, social workers, etc. Some people's banned behavior is seen as significant, is reacted to, and is made subject to official agency processing. Lemert distinguishes between primary and secondary rule breaking, or deviance. Primary deviance is the incidental and occasional rule breaking that we all do; selective application of rules to some offenders produces stigma, which Goffman describes as a spoiled identity and a master status; this results in a deviant and negative self-image. Others engage in "retrospective interpretation," perceiving the actor as having always been deviant and reinterpreting past behavior for "signs" and "cues" of current status. Attempts at stereotypical designation may initially be negotiated or bargained over, as in psychiatric assessments or police discretion, but if the designation is pursued to formal processing the result is individual role engulfment in a deviant career. Secondary deviance is the repeated rule breaking that comes from us believing that we are now the people that we have been labeled. "Deviancy amplification" comes from the expansion of deviant behavior as we now engage in other deviance in order to conceal our deviant identity and commit acts because we are not that person governed by this master status and committed to a criminal career.

Criminal Justice Policy: Social function of existing system is seen as moral degradation of offender's status; the alternative is to prevent the condemnation and degradation of the defendant by limiting social reaction through radical nonintervention. The perspective is critical of this process, of the shaming and social degrading of defendants as morally inferior, and of agents' control over the process. Preferred alternatives are (1) participant control over process, (2) victim-offender interaction, (3) mediation and conciliation, and (4) action taken against defendants is to be influenced by their past relationships with others.

Criminal Justice Practice: Radical nonintervention; tolerance to replace moral indignation; restitution, reparation, and rehabilitation. Minimalist approach: (1) decriminalize victimless crime, (2) diversion programs to avoid stigmatizing adolescents, (3) stop building prisons, (4) decarcerate prison population, especially nondangerous offenders, (5) develop alternative programs that allow offenders to be rehabilitated from the label, and (6) imprison only the most serious offenders.

Evaluation: Does not explain primary deviance; does not explain how in spite of labeling attempts some never perceive self as stigmatized; does not explain perpetuity of the label (how long does it last?); does not spend enough time on the reasons for banning behavior in first place; some policy implications are impractical; overemphasizes relativity of rules and laws; does not explain common law crimes; does not explain differences between groups or individuals in same stigmatized category.

8

Crimes of Place

Social Ecology and Cultural Theories of Crime

Two Edward James Olmos movies, *The Family: Mi Familia* and *American Me*, provide stirring documentaries of Hispanic gang life in California. In East Los Angeles, there have been Hispanic "gangs" for a number of years. These gangs are often generational in nature; current members typically have relatives who were members of the same gang in years past. The gangs have a strong affiliation with certain neighborhoods, staking out turf lines that coincide with neighborhood boundaries. To their members, the gangs serve a function in the "hood." They preserve the ethnic quality and supposedly provide "rites of passage" for young males entering adulthood. Studies of California gangs and those in New York, Washington, D.C., and Milwaukee also show that gang members are variably involved in irregular employment in the drug economies of the area. These produce an income ranging from $300 to $3,700 per month in areas of cities that have little formal employment (Fagan 1991; MacCoun and Router 1992; Hagedorn 1994). But some "homeboys" desire a conventional U.S. lifestyle. They want to settle down in a conventional job, live with a wife and kids, and, most of all, leave the street life (Hagedorn 1994, 211). Ecological theorists seek to explain why such patterns of criminal activity occur in specific geographical areas and why they persist over time, even when original members move out, mature to legitimate work, are incarcerated, or die.

Paul Bellair summarized this phenomenon, stating, "the concentration of crime within a small number of urban communities is an unfortunate, yet enduring, social fact" (2000, 137). Criminologists like Bellair, who examine the connection between crime and geographical space, are known as social or human ecologists (from *oikos*, the Greek word for "household" or "living space"). Their criminology is based on the idea that the way plant and animal species colonize their environment can be applied to the

way humans colonize geographical space. As a criminological theory, social ecology involves the study of "criminal" places. Certain neighborhoods, homes, and places remain crime problem areas for years,
regardless of the particular people who live there. These places gain bad
reputations (e.g., "Sin City") and are known as areas with high levels of
street crime, such as robbery, drug dealing, and prostitution. People know
better than to walk there alone at night, park their car there, or look lost or
confused when passing through. Omitted from the commonsense and
media accounts, however, are explanations of the economic and political
forces that work to create and maintain these criminal areas. In this chapter, we look at the main themes of social ecology as well as the related cultural theory, each of which contributes to understanding how crime
becomes spatially concentrated. We also examine the recent developments in social ecology and cultural theory that make a more critical
analysis of its driving forces.

Social ecology theory examines the movements of people and their concentration in specific locations. In Western nations, the most significant
transformation of populations occurred when agricultural workers
moved into the cities during eighteenth- and nineteenth-century industrialization (see Chapter 3 for more discussion of population migrations).
This flow of people to the city and its tendency to be associated with areas
of criminal activity was first described by nineteenth-century social reformers such as Henry Mayhew and Charles Booth, who provided rich
descriptions of the criminal areas of London known as "rookeries" (Mayhew [1861] 1981). The Belgian mathematician-astronomer Adolphe
Quetelet and the French lawyer-statistician Andre Michel Guerry of the
"cartographic school" were the first to gather quantitative data on the residential addresses of delinquents and showed how these were associated
with locality. During the late nineteenth and early twentieth centuries, the
U.S. economy, like that of Europe, was shifting from agriculture to industry, and consequently cities like Chicago were growing at a rapid and unprecedented rate. In the fifty-seven-year period from 1833 to 1890
Chicago grew from 4,100 residents to 1 million and just twenty years later
had reached 2 million, largely fueled by waves of immigration from Europe, the South and rural areas (Lilly, Cullen, and Ball 2002, 32, citing
Palen 1981). Chicago faced exaggerated growth, social opportunities, and
prosperity, but also mushrooming poverty and social problems. These
changes, coupled with the presence of the first U.S. sociology department
(established in 1892 at the University of Chicago) made Chicago a natural
laboratory for sociological research in what became known as the
"Chicago School." James Short, a sociologist from the University of
Chicago, has described the department and many of its members, themes,
and contributions (Short 2002). Chicago sociologists gathered both statis-

tical and qualitative data that seemed to demonstrate that crime was a "social product" of urbanism. This shifted the theoretical focus from an emphasis on individual pathology (biological and psychological differences) as the cause of crime to the social, cultural, and structural forces accompanying the massive social changes taking place (social pathology). We will discuss the Chicago School's contribution in more detail after examining the core themes and assumptions that characterize the overall position of social ecology.

Common Themes and Assumptions

Social ecologists see humans as social beings shaped by their dependence on one another, their dependence on the resources of their environment, and the functions that they perform for the system within their localized communities. Within these constraints, humans make rational choices, but their choices are "environmentally structured" (Einstadter and Henry 1995, 126).

Social ecology holds both a conflict and a consensus view of the social order. Individuals make up community and neighborhood units competing with each other for scarce resources. This results in conflict. Yet these different units also exist in a symbiotic balance with each other and with the society as a whole. Nowhere is this more evident than in the notion of a dominant or "mainstream" culture, implying a consensual U.S. culture containing a diversity of ethnic subcultures. Humans conform to their own groups and subcultures as these form in certain areas, yet they also conform to the U.S. cultural identity in terms of ideology and law. Early social ecologists believed that the driving forces of social change bringing together different groups in the cities would subside and that the dominant or mainstream culture would absorb the diversity of differences. The failure of this to happen and the permanence, rather than transience, of criminal areas led to later revisions in the theory to account for this tendency.

Sociologist Rodney Stark has provided a helpful summary of the main themes of social ecology in answer to his fundamental question, "How is it that neighborhoods can remain the site of high crime and deviance rates despite a complete turnover of their populations?" He believed that "there must be something about *places* as such that sustain crime" (Stark 1987, 893; emphasis in original). Concentrations of population, argued Stark, lead to increased population density, which brings people from different backgrounds together. This coming together increases the level of moral cynicism in a community as private conflicts become public knowledge and poor role models become highly visible. Dense neighborhoods have crowded homes resulting in a greater tendency for people to congregate in the street and in other public places, which raises the opportunities for crime. Crowding also lowers the level of child supervision, which in turn produces poor school achievement and a reduced commitment to school and increases the tendency for conflict within the family, which further weakens children's commitment to conformity. High-density neighborhoods also tend to mix commercial and residential properties, with the former threatening to take over the latter.

Sampson and Wilson (1993; Wilson 1996) show that changes in economic patterns produce inequality and an "underclass" of the poor. The more successful move out to the suburbs, leaving the least able concentrated and isolated in the inner city, where they increasingly fail to achieve common values (what Kornhauser 1978 referred to as "attenuated culture") and may develop values that oppose those of mainstream culture (Anderson 1999).

Mixed-use neighborhoods that evolve, unlike those planned for gentrification, increase the opportunities for those congregating on the street to commit crime. Such neighborhoods, partly because of the commercial property ownership and partly because of the creation by residential property owners of cheap, run-down, dilapidated rental property, have high transient populations, which in turn further weakens family attachments in the community, undermines informal and formal control, and reduces levels of surveillance. This produces neighborhoods further stigmatized by visibly high rates of crime and deviance that people want to leave. Residents' commitment to their neighborhood is further reduced when the most successful flee and conventional, successful role models fail to replace them. As Bursik and Grasmick have argued, in addition to isolation and a lack of integration and organization, crime becomes "an alternative means of gaining economic and social sustenance from the environment" (Bursik and Grasmick 1993b, 266), an observation first made by the human ecologist Amos Hawley (1950). This results in a concentration of those who have failed to leave, who become demoralized and more vulnerable as victims. As formal policing gives up on the defeated neighborhood, moral cynicism further increases, together with crime and deviance, which draws in more people who are looking to participate in crime. The outcome is even more crime, with consequences including higher levels of fear, criminal victimization, and involvement of family members with the criminal justice system. All of these developments normalize crime as part of everyday life, as a visible and "normal" way of succeeding in the inner city (Stark 1987).

For Wesley Skogan (1986), a similar pattern can begin from a series of fear-driven events that cause people to withdraw from community life, which weakens informal social controls. Fear also produces a reduction in organizational life and business activity.

Three major dimensions left undeveloped in early social ecology theory but taken up in recent theorizing are (1) the political-economic forces that cause populations to concentrate in the first place, (2) the dynamics of these forces within a neighborhood, and (3) how these forces impact the systemic relationships between neighborhood networks, extracommunity networks, and social control. We discuss these issues later in this chapter. First, we review the contribution of the Chicago School researchers who developed what has been described as "one of the most ambitious data collection projects ever attempted in the United States," and whose "key innovative aspect . . . was the interpretation of the spatial patterns within the context of human ecology and social disorganization theoretical frameworks" (Bursik and Grasmick 1995, 108).

The Chicago School

Robert Park, a newspaper reporter who became a sociologist and chair of the University of Chicago's department of sociology, made some important initial observations. First, he deduced that like any ecological system a city did not develop randomly. Park (Park and Burgess 1920; Park 1926; Park, Burgess, and McKenzie 1925) believed that the distribution of plant and animal life in nature held important insights for understanding the organization of human societies. Just like plant and animal colonies, a city grows according to basic social processes such as invasion, dominance, and accommodation. These produce a "biotic order" that comprises competing "moral orders." The second major contribution by Park and his colleagues was the argument that social processes are best understood through careful, scientific study of city life. Park's students and contemporaries built on these two themes and developed the very influential Chicago School.

Among Park's most important followers were Clifford R. Shaw and Henry D. McKay, two researchers employed by a child guidance clinic in Chicago. Shaw and McKay ([1942] 1969) used an analytical framework developed by Ernest Burgess (a colleague of Park's) to research the social causes of crime. This framework is known as concentric zone theory. Burgess (1925) used five concentric zones, each two miles wide (see Figure 8.1) to describe the patterns of social development in Chicago. He argued that city growth was generated by the pressure from the city center to expand outward. Expansion threatened to encroach on the surrounding areas and did so in concentric waves, or circles, with the center being the most intense, having the highest density and highest occupancy. These concentrations become progressively less intense and of lower density with greater distance from the center.

At the heart of a city was Zone 1, composed of the central business district (in Chicago this was known as the "Loop" because it was where the

FIGURE 8.1   Concentric Zone Theory

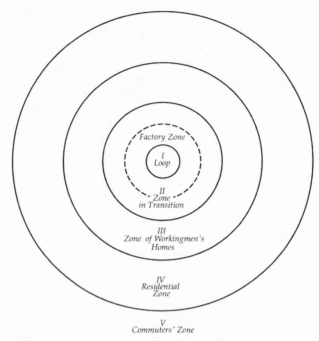

SOURCE: Burgess (1925, p. 51).

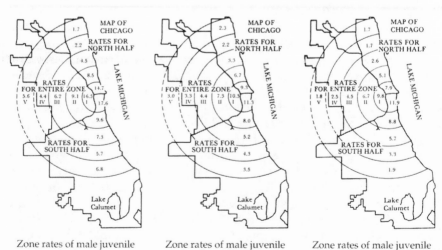

Zone rates of male juvenile
delinquents, 1900–1906 series

Zone rates of male juvenile
delinquents, 1917–1923 series

Zone rates of male juvenile
delinquents, 1927–1933 series

SOURCE: Shaw and McKay ([1942] 1969, p.69

commuter trains turned around). This was a commercial area that had valuable transportation resources (water and railways). Zone 2 was a transitional zone because it was an area of previously desirable residences threatened by invasion from the central business district and industrial growth. The residences, which were already deteriorating, were allowed to further erode by slum landlords who were waiting to profit from increased land values. They did not want to invest money in repairing their property, however, and only attracted low-income renters, those least able to afford a place to live. These were typically newly arrived immigrants and African Americans from the rural South, who found it convenient to live close to factories in the hope of obtaining work. This zone was an area of highly transient people, and those who were able to move up and out to more desirable homes did so. Zone 3 was made up of workers' homes. Most of these people had "escaped" from Zone 2 and were second- and third-generation immigrants. Zone 4 was a residential suburban area of more expensive residences. Zone 5 contained the highest-priced residences and was called the commuter zone. This zone contained single-family dwellings and was most desirable because of its distance from the hustle of downtown, pollution from factories, and the poor. The most influential white middle- and upper-income residents lived here and were imbued with the dominant mainstream culture and values.

According to social ecology theory, these concentric zones were based on patterns of invasion and dominance common among plants. Each zone or circle comprised specific defined areas, or natural neighborhoods, each with its own social and ethnic identity: African American, German, Irish, Italian, Polish, Chinese, and so on. How could this ecological analogy explain crime?

In nature, order is stable in settled zones and unstable in transitional areas, where rapid changes to the ecostructure take place. Applying this observation to the social ecology of the city, Shaw and McKay's ([1942] 1969) primary hypothesis was that Zone 2, the transitional zone, would contain higher levels of crime and other social problems such as drug abuse and alcoholism, suicide, tuberculosis, infant mortality, and mental illness. This would be the case regardless of which racial or ethnic group occupied the area, independent of its economic impoverishment, and primarily because of its level of "social disorganization."

Social Disorganization

Social disorganization was a concept first coined by W. I. Thomas and Florian Znaniecki (1920) to explain the breakdown of community among second-generation Polish immigrants to Chicago. They defined it as the "decrease of the influence of existing social rules of behavior on individual members of the group" (1920, 1128). More generally, social disorganization refers to a situation in which there is little or no community feeling, relationships are transitory, levels of community surveillance are low, institutions of informal control are weak, and social organizations are ineffective. Unlike an organized community, where social solidarity, neighborhood cooperation, and harmonious action work to solve common problems, socially disorganized neighborhoods have several competing and conflicting moral values. Immigrant children in these areas can become increasingly alienated from their parents' ethnic culture as they adapt more rapidly to aspects of the dominant culture, which in turn weakens parental control over the children. A further problem associated with social disorganization is the conflict in these impoverished areas between various ethnic groups over scarce resources. Finally, delinquency patterns themselves become a competing lifestyle as a means of surviving and as a way of obtaining income, intimacy, and honor. As Frederick Thrasher (1927), another Chicago School sociologist, demonstrated in his classic study *The Gang*, gang membership provides a substitute for the disorganized and fragmented community, one that develops its own values and traditions of loyalty and support for fellow gang members. Once formed, these gangs are self-sustaining as a source of "conduct, speech, gestures, and attitudes," from whose members a child "learns the techniques of stealing, becomes involved in binding relationships with his companions in delinquency, and acquires the attitudes appropriate to his position as a member of such groups" (Shaw and McKay [1942] 1969, 436).

Given Edwin Sutherland's presence at the University of Chicago during this period, it is not surprising that there are parallels between this gang research, pointing to the transmission of criminal behavior patterns, and Sutherland's ([1939] 1947) differential association theory (discussed in Chapter 6). The argument is that the environment provides the context for not only the transmission of criminal behavior patterns but also the failure to transmit conventional behavior patterns (the central point of control theory, discussed in Chapter 7). Social disorganization within certain areas of a city creates the conditions for crime to flourish, independent of the individuals who live there or their ethnic characteristics. The lack of community integration and social control together with the presence of contradictory standards and values allows residents the freedom to choose crime (Walker 1994).

Initial Empirical Support

To test their hypotheses, Shaw and McKay (1931, [1942] 1969) examined 56,000 official court records from 1900 to 1933 and created "spot maps" based on 140 square-mile areas. On these maps, they located the residences of juveniles (aged 10 to 16) who were involved in various stages of criminal justice adjudication. They then created other maps, or overlays, that showed community factors such as demolished buildings and the incidence of tuberculosis and vagrancy. Rate maps were then constructed indicating the rate of male delinquency for each zone. The final step was to create zone maps. These confirmed that community problems were concentrated in the zone of transition (i.e., Zone 2).

Shaw and McKay's research showed that official crime rates were greatest in Zones 1 and 2 (in the 1927–1933 series ranging from 7.9 to 11.9 percent in Zone 1), declining with distance outward from the city (being as low as 1.7 to 1.9 percent in Zone 5). The pattern persisted over forty years, no matter which ethnic group or nationality moved into the area during each new wave of immigration.

Shaw and McKay also found that official delinquency rates varied within a zone. For example, Zone 3 (working-class homes) was 2.6 percent on the North Shore side of Chicago, but was nearly double at 5.7 percent on the South Side. Subsequent research confirmed the same patterns in eighteen other cities (Shaw and McKay [1942] 1969) and over a period of sixty years has demonstrated that "official rates of delinquency decline with movement away from the inner city" (Shoemaker 1996, 80).

As some commentators have observed, the fact that delinquency areas persisted after the immigration waves of the 1930s subsided eventually caused Shaw and McKay to change their explanation of delinquency. They subsequently emphasized the importance of economic pressure and the response to "strains experienced by economically deprived people in a society that encouraged all citizens to aspire to [monetary] success goals" (Gibbons 1994, 30; Finestone 1976). This anticipated Merton's strain theory, which we discuss in the next chapter. Nevertheless, the Chicago School of sociology moved criminology away from individual pathology and personality traits and toward social pathology and the view that "crime and deviance were simply the normal responses of normal people to abnormal social conditions" (Akers 1994, 142).

Limitations and Policy Implications of the Chicago School's Theory

Despite the Chicago School's considerable impact on criminology and U.S. social policies (discussed later), there are several notable criticisms. For example, Alihan (1938) argued that the use of plant ecology was based on a series of false analogies that resulted in the fallacious error of using aggregate-level data to explain individual action. This criticism questions the entire theoretical basis of the ecological theory of the Chicago School. Known as the ecological fallacy, this major defect involves making assumptions about individuals based on group characteristics. The Chicago School primarily relied on aggregate, group-level data to explain deviance.

Another major criticism is the Chicago School's failure to show that residents of low-crime, desirable areas were more organized than their counterparts in high-crime areas (Kobrin 1971). However, subsequent research has offered support in this regard. Sampson and Groves (1989), in a study of 10,000 respondents to the British Crime Survey, found that structural factors such as low socioeconomic status, low levels of heterogeneity, high residential mobility, and family disruption increased social disorganization and produced weakened friendship networks, low participation in community organizations, and unsupervised teens. Crime rates were higher in such areas than in organized areas (See also Lowenkamp, Cullen, and Pratt 2001; replication study cited in Lilly et al. 2002).

Kobrin (1971) pointed to the weakness of some of the data concerning the claims that a delinquent cultural tradition resulted from conflicting moralities. A related criticism is the tautological (circular) nature of Shaw and McKay's logic in which neighborhoods with a high rate of delinquency are the result of the existence of a tradition of delinquency (Bursik 1988).

A further methodological criticism leveled at Shaw and McKay is their reliance on official police and court records to document delinquency rates (Robison 1936). No account is taken of self-report data or victimization data. A self-report study by Johnstone (1978) reveals that most delinquency was found in Chicago among lower-class adolescents living in better-class neighborhoods rather than in the transitional areas. Furthermore, white-collar and corporate crimes conducted in corporate offices in the inner city or the residences of the outer zones were not included, begging the question of what kind of crime counts as real crime (Henry and Lanier 2001).

Shaw and McKay also argued that different racial and ethnic groups would experience similar rates of delinquency if subjected to the same physical environment. Yet contemporaneous research found that "Oriental" residents had lower rates of delinquency (Hayner 1933; Jonassen 1949). Conversely, and perhaps most important in terms of crime and its control, "was the inability of the model to account for the existence of highly stable, well-organized neighborhoods that appear to have fairly uniform and consistent cultural systems yet have traditionally high rates of delinquency" (Bursik and Grasmick 1995, 111; Schwartz 1987). This problem has also been raised by research on cities outside the United States (DeFleur 1967; Ebbe 1989), which suggests that, at best, Shaw and McKay's research may only apply to the structure of U.S. cities.

The policy implications associated with the Chicago School's social ecology theory are massive in nature and would require dramatic changes in economic structuring to be fully implemented. To their credit, members of the Chicago School, especially Clifford Shaw, applied their theories to reducing delinquency by attempting to strengthen the sense of community and increasing the levels of social organization in disorganized neighborhoods (Kobrin 1959).

In 1932, Shaw developed the Chicago Area Project (CAP) to assist with developing social organizations through involving neighborhood residents in setting up local groups and clubs for youths. Adults in the affected communities ran these groups (to prevent imposing a dominant alien middle-class culture), and through them the programs attempted to combat neighborhood disorganization in several ways. First, they organized recreational activities such as athletic and youth leagues and summer camps. Then they sought to reduce physical deterioration in the neighborhoods. CAP staff members also tried to help juveniles who came into conflict with the criminal justice system. Finally, they provided curbside counseling to troubled residents. The objective was to allow local residents to organize activities that would reduce crime at the local level.

The Chicago Area Project met with mixed success. Because the project was not subject to controlled empirical evaluation, scientific verification was impossible. Schlossman and his colleagues (1984) provided a comprehensive evaluation, however, which concluded that the project had been successful in reducing reported delinquency, although other evaluations of similar projects have found little success (Miller 1962).

Overall, a major limitation of Shaw and McKay's research was their unwillingness or inability to act on the economic and political realities of inner cities. The same business owners who drove the engine of environmental deterioration sat on the Chicago Area Project board and contributed financially to the project (Curran and Renzetti 1994, 141; Snodgrass 1976). Similarly, the "natural" areas of the city were actually planned for and governed by statutes and ordinances (Suttles 1972). This suggests that any ecological criminology has to account for the role of economic and political power in order to explain how environment causes crime. What is needed—and to some extent has been provided by recent contributions to social ecology theory—is a political economy of urban ecology. As Shoemaker (1996, 89) has observed, "The theory of social disorganization, as principally developed by Shaw and McKay, has merit in that it has pointed to social causes of delinquency that seem to be located in specific geographical areas. . . . The theory would appear to be generally accurate, but incomplete." More recent developments in social ecology theory have attempted to address this deficit.

The New Social Ecology Theories

Since the 1960s, social ecology theory has taken three distinct but related new directions. The first, which we call *design ecology*, relates to the issue of space and design. The second direction, which we call *critical ecology*, tries to take account of the political and economic forces in creating and shaping the space that is used to facilitate crime. The third direction we call *integrated* and *systemic ecology*; it suggests that what is required is a systemic approach that focuses on the way ecological theory interrelates with biological, social learning, routine activities, rational choice, and cultural theories. A related version focuses on the regulatory capacities of relational networks in neighborhoods and between them. Let us look briefly at each of these new directions in ecological theory.

Design Ecology

During the 1970s, several criminologists claimed that the physical design characteristics of urban neighborhoods could be manipulated in a way that would reduce street crime (Jeffery 1971). A notable contribution to this literature came from Oscar Newman (1972, 1973), an architect and city planner from New York who argued that crime prevention should be part of the architect's responsibility. He believed that crime prevention should create areas of "defensible space." Newman argued that preventing crime requires enhanced feelings of territoriality among neighborhood residents, which in turn leads the residents to protect their neighborhoods through self-policing. His planning and design strategies are aimed at reassigning "ownership" of residential space to reduce the amount of common, multiple-user, open space because residents cannot assert responsibility for these areas, leaving them open to crime and vandalism (Newman 1996). Newman claims to demonstrate that physical environment can be used to define zones of influence, clearly separate public from private zones, and provide facilities with zones to meet occupants' needs. Re-creating a sense of ownership by dividing areas and assigning them to individuals and small groups to use and control isolates criminals because their turf is removed (Newman 1996). To achieve this aim, city architects and planners should include a significant component of physical security elements, such as restricted pedestrian traffic flow, single rather than multiple entrances, regulated entry, and clear boundary markers. Newman maintains that physical design can also be used to improve surveillance through better windows, lighting, and altered traffic flow. Planning safe residential zones next to other safe facilities adds to the overall effect of crime reduction. Finally, according to Newman (1973), distinctiveness of design, such as height, size, material, and finish, can reduce the stigma of a neighborhood.

The impact of the defensible space theory has been enormous, and it has recently been merged with rational choice and routine activities theories (Gardiner 1978; Clarke and Mayhew 1980), which we discussed in Chapter 3, to become a major movement: crime prevention through environmental design (CPTED). Research in this area suggests that crime and the fear of it can be reduced by paying attention to four key sets of physical features: (1) housing design or block layout, (2) land use and circulation patterns, (3) resident-generated territorial features, and (4) physical deterioration (Taylor 1988; Taylor and Harrell 1996; Weisel and Harrell 1996).

Each can "influence reactions to potential offenders by altering the chances of detecting them and by shaping the public vs. private nature of the space in question" (Taylor and Harrell 1996, 3). But the evidence leaves researchers unable to distinguish whether crime reductions result from physical changes or from the social and organizational changes that accompany the effort at redesign. Moreover, design ecology takes no account of the political and economic forces that create and sustain existing environmental contexts.

Critical Ecology

A second new direction taken in the social ecology literature, which we call critical ecology, tries to take account of the political and economic forces in creating and shaping the space that is used to facilitate crime. Research has revealed that three kinds of political decisions affect the formation of criminal areas: (1) local government planning decisions, (2) local institutions, and (3) public policing decisions. Local government can exacerbate social disorganization by concentrating problem residents in older, less desirable housing, which results in delinquent areas (Morris 1957; Gill 1977). Other studies, however, show that the concentration of problem families, even in new and well-maintained privately owned but subsidized "Section 8" housing, can also result in criminal areas (Weinstein et al. 1991). Such low-income housing becomes a refuge for drug trading, associated criminal activity, high levels of domestic violence, and child neglect. But this concentration is not simply a natural development, for "without the forces of political economy and state, those affected most by economic transformations would remain relatively dispersed" (Weinstein et al. 1991, 54).

Local institutions can also impact the extent of collective efficacy, social capital, and thereby social control. Schools and churches that are mistrusted will not be able to run effective after-school programs. Communities that do not take the political initiative to develop coordinated action between their businesses, schools, and voluntary organizations to develop alternative programs for youth run the risk of allowing gangs to flourish, which creates further fear that undermines collective efficacy. (Markowitz, Bellair, Liska, and Liu 2001). Research has also shown that in these disorganized neighborhoods the presence of features such as a concentration of alcohol outlets, which reflects business power, correlates with increases in violent crime (Costanza, Bankston, and Shidadeh 1999; Peterson, Krivo, and Harris 2000). This supports the assertion proposed by concentic zone theory that the further one moves from the city core, the weaker the relationship between alcohol availability and violent crime (Costanza et al. 1999). It also supports the critical ecology argument that business decisions which are not regulated by community planners can result in increased crime problems.

Finally, as well as informal social control, communities need the resources of public formal control, which means an effective police presence. Research has shown that in the absence of adequate levels of formal policing, criminal gangs and drug operations can readily locate in a neighborhood (Klinger 1997). As Siegel points out,

> The police presence is typically greatest when community organizations and local leaders have sufficient political clout to get funding for additional law enforcement personnel. . . . In more disorganized areas, the absence of political power brokers limits access to external funding and protection. Without money from outside, the neighborhood lacks the ability to "get back on its feet." In these areas there are fewer police and those that do patrol the area are less motivated and their resources are stretched more tightly. These communities cannot mount an effective social control effort. (2004, 189)

Clearly the critical ecological perspective suggests that a combined effort by local political leaders is necessary to make a difference to the ability of effective social control.

Integrated and Systemic Ecology

A third development attempts to bring together various aspects of previous developments in social ecology theory. One version, integrated ecology, is an attempt to integrate ecological, biological, social learning, routine activities, rational choice, and cultural theories. This began with Cohen and Machalek's (1988) evolutionary ecological theory and was extended by Bryan Vila (1994). Like early social ecology, it looks at human adaptation to the environment but pays particular attention to cultural traits based on socially learned information and behavior, the evolution of which can be "guided." This approach enables criminologists to "integrate ecological factors that determine what opportunities for crime exist, micro-level factors that influence an individual's propensity to commit a criminal act at a particular point of time, and macro-level factors that influence the development of individuals in society over time" (Vila 1994, 312). We consider this and other integrated theory in the Conclusion of this book.

Systemic ecology moves away from the idea that social disorganization demands a policy response of social organization and instead suggests that what is required is a "systemic model that focuses on the regulatory capacities of relational networks that exist within and between neighborhoods" (Bursik and Grasmick 1995, 107–108; see also 1993a, b). We call this systemic ecology, and it draws heavily on the idea of "social capital." Systemic theory focuses on ecological dimensions of social order (Capowich 2003). Under this theory, the composition of a neighborhood can help or hinder the development of "social networks" (Bellair 2000). Systemic social disorganization impacts control at the neighborhood level "through its effects on the private (primary relationships among family), parochial (informal networks of friends and acquaintances), and public (neighborhood links with public agencies) dimensions of social order" (Capowich 2003, 41). The systemic crime model (Bellair 2000) is shown in Figure 8.2.

Figure 8.2 Bellair's Systemic Crime Model

Social Networks --------+-----------Informal Control------ - ------Street Crime

---

Drawing its theoretical framework from Walter Buckley's (1967) systems theory, Robert Bursik and Harold Grasmick (1995) note four components of their expanded social ecology of neighborhood-based networks and crime. First, they argue that it is necessary to take into account the totality of complex interrelations between individuals, groups, and associations that make up a community. We must consider (1) how these networks and ties serve to integrate residents into intimate, informal, primary neighborhood groups that operate to privately control behavior (Bursik and Grasmick 1993b) and (2) how a parochial level of control operates to signal external threats and supervise neighborhood children in a general way and through community organizations.

Second, Bursik and Grasmick argue that the degree of systemness will vary across social structures in a community depending on factors such as size and density of the networks, with many-member small-location networks tending to have lower crime rates; scope (closure) of crosscutting ties, with increased ties across different cultural, ethnic, and racial groups helping to reduce the crime level; reachability, or the real ability of network members to meet; content, or nature of the network ties; durability, or the length the network has existed; intensity of the obligation of network members; and frequency with which members use the network (Bursik and Grasmick 1995, 115–116). The hypothesis is that neighborhoods with large, dense networks, minimal barriers between groups, and members who meet regularly and have intense mutual obligations will have the highest level of crime control and the lowest rates of crime. In other words, areas with high social capital will be areas of low crime rates.

Third, the system components of a community can change without destroying the network of relations, for they exist in a larger system of relationships that "bind them into the broader ecological structure of the city" (Bursik and Grasmick 1995, 117). This component of the theory allows, in contrast to Shaw and McKay's ([1942] 1969) earlier work, consideration of the wider transformation of cities through the "urban dynamics" of postindustrial societies, including the effects of economic polarization.

Fourth, like critical ecology, systemic ecology does not ignore the forces that create these "unfortunate" movements of industry and the resultant concentrations of poverty and power. It takes an open systems approach, allowing for external factors including the political, social, and economic contexts in which the communities are embedded (Bursik and Grasmick 1995, 118; Bursik 1989). Drawing on Hunter (1985), these authors refer to the effect of such forces on the "public level of control . . . the ability to secure public and private goods and services that are allocated by groups and agencies located outside the neighborhood" (Bursik and Grasmick 1995, 118) and the effects this ability has on a community's regulatory capacity.

Sampson, Raudenbush, and Earls (1997) further developed the idea of the failure of a community to enact informal social control building on their notion of "collective efficacy." This is a measure of social cohesion among residents and their willingness to act to control unacceptable behavior. The degree to which neighborhood residents intervene in response to unacceptable behavior by others in their community, whether by personally stepping in or calling authorities for assistance, varies. Sampson and colleagues say that it depends on the extent to which neighbors trust one another. A variety of structural and cultural factors (such as population stability/instability, economic advantage/disadvantage) affect whether there is a high degree of trust that leads to a high level of social capital (networks of connected neighbors), which in turn results in a high degree of collective efficacy and thereby informal social control. As Lilly and colleagues (2002, 43) state, collective efficacy is distinctive because of its "focus not merely on the degree of neighborhood disorganization but also the willingness of neighbors to activate social control . . . 'efficacy' implies not merely a state of being socially organized but rather a state of being ready for *social action.*" Indeed, Bursik (1999, 86) defines social organization as "the regulatory capacity of a neighborhood that is imbedded in the structure of that community's affiliational, interactional and communication ties among the residents."

The problem with the existing system model is that it is predominantly designed around structural organizational factors. Barbara Warner (2003) argues that we need to consider *both* structural and cultural weakness that work together to reduce informal social control, freeing residents to engage in varieties of law-violating behavior. She states that cultural weaknesses (attenuated culture) affect social control because residents do not perceive their neighbors as holding conventional values, do not see themselves as similar, and therefore do not see their neighbors intervening to control crime. Her model incorporating both structural and cultural components and how they affect social control is shown in Figure 8.3.

Figure 8.3   Warner's Integrated Cultural Attenuation System Model

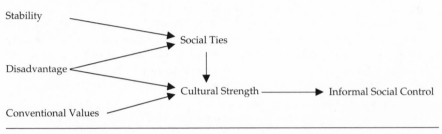

Source: Warner (2003: 87)

Systemic Ecology Policy.   The systemic ecology of Bursik and Grasmick, Sampson and colleagues, and Warner draws on considerable existing research, but many of its new ideas remain to be tested. In one recent analysis Capowich (2003) examined eight Chicago neighborhoods and found empirical support. It has significant policy implications that go beyond early social ecology theory, particularly at the level of public control. Importantly, the development of crime-preventive networks is related to the perceived effectiveness of crime control and the relations between local community representatives and law enforcement agencies. Bursik and Grasmick argue that "the development of extracommunity networks for the purposes of crime control presupposes at least a minimal set of private, parochial, and public control structures that can familiarize local residents with the operations of public and private agencies and can represent the community to these constituencies so that the relationship can be developed" (1995, 120–121). Where these do not exist because of past police action or lack of trust between police and neighborhood residents (typically found in economically deprived, low-class minority neighborhoods), then higher rates of crime can be expected. Law enforcement agencies have recognized this and have also embraced the idea that social and physical disorder can result in crime. Wilson and Kelling (1982) first presented this "broken windows" thesis in 1982. As visible disorder increases, so do fear and isolation (Kelling and Coles 1996). Eventually more serious forms of crime will grow in these areas (Cordner 1981, 1998).

Also crucial to the development of crime-preventive networks are the solicitation of other resources, such as those for public works, those providing financial and mortgage activity conducive to residential improvement and mobility, and those affecting daily services such as garbage collection, sewer repair, environmental protection, and so on, all of which improve the physical ambience of neighborhoods (e.g., Kennedy 1996; Weisel and Harrell 1996). Organized neighborhoods that fail to integrate into the wider political, social, and economic systems may well be vulnerable to high crime and delinquency. This can only be counteracted through fostering intracommunity linkages and networks among constituencies of heterogeneous neighborhoods and paying attention to how resources can be channeled to them. Finally, Warner (2003, 94) argues that "building stronger communities will require, not only strengthening the structural arrangements therein, but also strengthening the culture . . . creating opportunities for residents of all neighborhoods to live out conventional values such that those values are visible and alive within the community."

Under the Clinton presidency the U.S. government supported several programs that meet the criminal justice policy implications of the new social ecology theory for a more coordinated community-based approach to crime prevention (Conly and McGillis 1996). Through the Office of Justice Programs, funding has been provided to communities to bring together government officials, service providers, businesspeople, and residents to identify crime-related problems and mobilize a broad spectrum of community resources (Robinson 1996). For example, Project PACT (Pulling America's Communities Together) has been established in four states to "empower local communities to address youth violence by developing broad-based, coordinated anti-violence strategies" (1996, 5). Another community-based program, SafeFutures, operating in six sites, includes components such as after-school mentoring, family-strengthening programs, mental health services, and gang prevention intervention and suppression for schools (Robinson 1996, 5; Conly and McGillis 1996). The Justice Department has even promoted experiments in transforming the criminal justice system toward the concept of restorative justice, or community justice.

Restorative justice (discussed in more detail Chapter 12) holds the offender accountable to the victim who has been harmed and the community that has been disrupted: "Restorative Justice seeks not to punish for punishment's sake but to right the wrong, to repair the damage to the extent possible, and to restore both the victim and the community" (Robinson 1996, 6). It combines the philosophies of restitution, which involves making the victim whole, and reparation, which is compensating the community, typically through some form of community service. In some cases, these sentences are determined by trained community boards; in others, they are the outcome of citizen dispute settlement programs; and elsewhere, they involve a "family group conference" designed to shame the offender's behavior (rather than the offender as a person) and explain the full impact of the crime on the victim and the community (Robinson 1996, 7).

This latter development draws on Braithwaite's (1989) concept of reintegrative shaming: Offenders are made to feel guilty for their offense but brought back into the community instead of being ostracized or rejected by it. Community-based approaches to justice include victim-offender mediation, in which victims and offenders discuss the impact of the crime and a means of reparation (Umbreit 1994), as well as the more familiar community policing (Skogan 1996; Trojanowicz and Bucqueroux 1995). The experimentation in transforming criminal justice in some cities also involves neighborhood district attorneys, community defenders, community courts, and community corrections, all of which were first suggested by Danzig (1973) in his seminal paper on community justice.

Neighborhood district attorneys are engaged in community prosecutions designed to reflect the specific concerns of residents and businesses for safety and to devise alternative ways to use the law. These include civil remedies and bringing people together to negotiate and solve problems. The neighborhood district attorney also acts as an advocate for the community (Boland 1996). Community defenders represent people from a community who cannot afford lawyers via a team-based approach focusing on the whole experience for the offender, not just the trial (Stone 1996). Community courts involve citizens actively participating in the judgment of offenders (Rottman 1996; see also Fisher 1975). Finally, community corrections involves an orientation to the "place" where the offender lives and working with the offender in that place (Clear 1996).

Let us now turn to cultural theory, which in many ways grew out of early social ecology and, as we have seen from the previous discussion, intersects and interrelates with later versions, particularly through the integrated systemic ecological theory.

Cultural Deviance Theories

Ecological theorists argue that environmental conditions in certain places create or encourage crime. Cultural theorists observe that people from different origins and ethnic groups have distinct cultural heritages. One group may numerically or economically dominate, and that culture is then considered "normal" or mainstream. Members of a "minority" culture may have values and cultural norms that are in conflict with the dominant culture. Sometimes these behaviors are criminalized by the dominant culture, making criminals of people who are doing what they would normally do: conform. For example, some southwestern Native Americans have traditionally used peyote, a cactus containing a hallucinogen, in their religious rites. The state of California legislated against "peyotism," arguing that "it seemed to threaten the Indians' relationship to larger society" and "to be a reversion to uncivilized practices, wholly out of place in modern times" (Morgan 1981, 162).

The norms and behavior patterns of each culture are taught by a process of socialization and social learning in the manner we described in Chapter 6. Thus people are seen as being born equal and are thought to acquire behavioral patterns through learning from others in their culture. Regardless of whether a culture is dominant or subordinate, the means of learning behavior are the same.

Sellin's Culture Conflict Theory

The first substantial culture conflict theory was presented by the Swedish-born criminologist Thorsten Sellin in 1938. As we have already seen, in this period the United States was being urbanized and saw an influx of many immigrants from southern and eastern Europe. These new arrivals had very different cultures from previous immigrants to the United States. In *Culture Conflict and Crime* (1938) Sellin argued that legal definitions are relative, changing over time as a result of changes in conduct norms. Conduct norms are associated with a culture and define some behavior as acceptable and other behavior as unacceptable. These norms regulate an individual's daily life and behavior. But different cultural groups have different ideas about what behaviors are appropriate or inappropriate, what is acceptable or unacceptable, and what should be considered criminal. In other words, conduct norms are different for different cultures.

In U.S. society, behavior defined as criminal by those sharing conduct norms of the majority culture is legislated against by its members, who dominate the legislature and the institutions of government. The differences in culture norms between the dominant and subordinate cultures create conflict. Conflict occurs when following the norms of one's own culture causes a person to break the legislated conduct norms of the dominant culture. In this theory, then, crime is not a result of deviant individuals but of conforming individuals who happen to belong to cultures with norms that conflict with the dominant ones. Religious cults, such as the Branch Davidian cult in Waco, Texas, which in 1993 ended with the death of ninety adults and seventeen children after a three-month standoff with ATF officers, provide excellent illustrations of culture conflict theory.

Sellin distinguished between two types of culture conflict: primary and secondary. In primary culture conflict, the norms of the subordinate culture are considered criminal in the new (dominant) culture. In secondary culture conflict, segments within the same culture differ as to the acceptability of conduct norms. In other words, one social group defines something as deviant or criminal, yet others in the same culture consider this behavior normal and noncriminal. Sellin argued, "The more complex a culture becomes, the more likely it is that the number of normative groups which affect a person will be large, and the greater is the chance that the norms of these groups will fail to agree, no matter how much they may overlap as a result of a common acceptance of certain norms" (1938, 29). We consider secondary culture conflicts and subcultures as causes of crime in the following chapter.

Limitations and Policy Implications of Cultural Theory

Insofar as crime is the result of cultural or subcultural conformity, policies based on deterrence are unlikely to be effective, since individual members of these groups perceive their actions as being proper and appropriate based on their cultural or subcultural values. Vold and Bernard provided a succinct description of the problem: "Cultural theories suggest that there are at least some normative differences among groups about rules for expected behavior in specific situations. But groups with norms are necessarily low-power groups, or they would protect and defend their norms in the processes of the enactment and enforcement of criminal law" (1986, 295). For these reasons, Sellin argued that criminologists should reject legal definitions. Instead, they should base their definition of crime on the breaking of any conduct norm. Indeed, he argued that criminologists should construct their own scientifically based classification of norms into universal categories. Little has come of this idea, perhaps not least because, like criminal laws, conduct norms are likely to be constantly changing (Gibbons 1979, 67). With regard to empirical testing, very little has been done. Research has been conducted on subcultural theory, which we consider in the next chapter.

To date, the policy for dealing with culture conflict has been through a process of assimilation. Over time—sometimes generations—a subculture or different culture assimilates the values and behaviors of the dominant culture. In the past, immigrants to the United States learned to speak

English and ultimately, at least by their second and third generations, "behaved" like Americans as they assimilated. Some research has started to suggest that ethnic subcultural gangs, such as Chinese gangs, are now becoming more criminogenic than earlier generations (Chin 1990). This observation is explained in Chapter 10.

A more proactive policy alternative to natural assimilation is to speed or assist the process of integration into U.S. culture. This entails cultural socialization in schools and community. Some also claim that clearer and simplified laws are required for the dominant culture and these must be taught to the other cultural groups. But this approach is culturally hege-monic and is likely to result in alienation and isolation of the very diver-sity that enriches U.S. culture.

New Cultural Theory of Crime

There are three developments in the cultural theory of crime. One is Wal-ter Miller's (1958) idea that lower-class cultures develop that are opposi-tional to the dominant culture. A second approach focuses primarily on the "subculture of violence" (Bennett and Flavin 1994, 363). Parker (1998), for example, examined homicides in a cultural context. Building on the classic Wolfgang and Ferracuti (1982) study of the development of favor-able attitudes toward the use of violence in the slums or urban areas, sev-eral commentators have provided detailed descriptions of the values of inner-city neighborhoods. Elijah Anderson (1990, 1999) examined the key features of "street culture" and found that some youth whose families are cut off from conventional culture, suffering from a range of economic and social problems and inconsistently monitored and disciplined, become alienated from the mainstream society that they have little hope of join-ing. A central theme of these youth is to elicit respect from others through a "street reputation" for toughness, mediated by a code that demands a violent response to any challenge to their reputation and any act of disre-spect, however slight. This code prevails in the urban environment and applies to all who live there, even those who are not alienated and are from morally decent backgrounds. If they do not follow the code, they be-come victims. Others, such as Jeff Ferrell and Clinton Sanders (1994), de-scribe a similar set of conditions that lead to a cultural abandonment of the mainstream in favor of cultural values of erotic excitement and cheap fun that can lead to destructive behaviors which annoy the guardians of the mainstream, such as graffiti signing. This in turn can indicate and cel-ebrate more sinister elements, such as the presence of ethnic gangs.

Cultural theories of crime are not restricted to slum neighborhoods. Cultural theory also explains crime in the wider society. Research by Ger-ald Mars (1982) applies the insights of anthropologist Mary Douglas

(1970, 1978) to workplace crime. Using Douglas's grid-group analysis, Mars shows that occupational subcultures place different constraints on the opportunities for crime in the workplace. Put simply, the grid dimension is the extent to which a culture imposes categories and role expectations on its members and fixes their behavior. In occupations, grids impose constraint based on autonomy, insulation, reciprocity, and competition. Strong-grid jobs are those that allow the incumbent limited freedom. In these jobs, the tasks and expectations are highly structured; there are many rules, different functions, and uniforms. These features allow little room for an official to offer or receive favors and little control over other employees. A typical high-grid job would be a supermarket checkout person or a bank security officer. Weak-grid jobs have few of these constraints and provide their incumbents with much autonomy to deal and negotiate; they include professional jobs such as doctors, lawyers, accountants, as well as traveling salespeople.

The group dimension is the extent to which a culture collectively constrains an occupational role incumbent through face-to-face interaction with its other members. This dimension contains several components not dissimilar to those discussed under the systemic social ecology theory. They include the frequency of face-to-face contact, mutuality of contacts between members of the network, the scope or extensiveness of contacts, including the number and types of levels on which these contacts are made, and, finally, "boundaries," or the extent to which meetings among workers are formal or informal. High-group occupations have many face-to-face contacts among employees doing similar tasks on various levels in different settings and are typically informal. High-group occupations include waiters and waitresses and teamwork jobs such as mining. Weak-group jobs would have little group constraint and include business owners, artists, and university professors. Combining these dimensions of grid and group produces four types of occupations: (1) strong grid–weak group, called Donkeys, (2) strong grid–strong group, or Wolves, (3) strong group–weak grid, or Vultures, and (4) weak grid–weak group, called Hawks.

Mars's analysis shows that cultural considerations shape occupational positions and structure the opportunities for workplace crime. It is not that some occupations have crime and others do not; rather, the kind of crimes workers can commit depends on the strength of their occupational culture. Hawks are more free to engage in complex individual frauds and financial swindles, such as Medicare fraud and tax evasion. Donkeys are restricted to simple time theft (such as calling in sick when not or taking extended breaks), sabotage (deliberately damaging equipment to stop production), and cash thefts or petty pilfering of company products. Wolves are doubly constrained but collectively are able to protect their members most against external controls, whereas Vultures are free to steal from employers and customers while enjoying the collective peer support of those in their network.

Mars argues that unless corporations and organizations understand the kind of cultural constraints operating on employees, simple punitive responses to workplace crime are likely to be ineffective and to create increased conflict, resulting in increased crime. In contrast, an understanding of grid-group dynamics allows policies that directly address the opportunities for crime by increasing constraints that make it less available or desirable.

Although no one has yet integrated the new cultural theory of grid-group analysis into social ecology theory, Bennett and Flavin (1994) have used it to analyze the fear of crime in cities of different cultures (Newark, New Jersey, and Belize). Ultimately, any systematic analysis of city crime would need to show how this new cultural theory explains the interactive effects of different cultural constraints from informal organizations, as well as those of the diverse community subcultures. It may well be that different ethnic cultures in a city are subject to different grid-group constraints and that any crime-preventive organizational networks, such as those suggested by Bursik and Grasmick (1993b), need to take account of those differences if they are to be effective.

Summary and Conclusion

In this chapter, we moved from the notion that crime is a product of individual choices, causes, or processes to the idea that places, networks, and cultural adaptations create criminal opportunities. We saw how economic and political forces can produce massive social changes and population movements, which can result in highly volatile concentrations of people that accentuate their problems. Once formed, these patterns are self-sustaining and reinforcing.

The political and economic forces that shape specific areas can also provide the context for the learning of behavior (as we discussed in connection with differential association theory) and the formation or lack of attachments (discussed previously under bonding theory). Regardless of the "causality" (perhaps learning or bonding) of individual effects, the downward spiral of certain places can carry with it those who are unable to escape, who may violate laws simply by conforming to their culture or subculture or in order to survive the hardships of their neighborhood. Once the process begins, fear and limited resources undermine a community's ability to control its own members, which results in further crime and more fear. This leads to the departure of those best able to escape, leaving behind those least able to cope. Angry with their situation but politically rudderless, some form gangs that compete with each other for survival.

Although preventive efforts and ideas have become increasingly sophisticated, one of the major omissions from social ecology and cultural theories of crime is what drives the movements that makes places criminal. In the next chapter, we look at one of the ways sociologists have tried to fill this gap by examining structural forces and how these shape cultural and subcultural responses.

Summary Chart: Social Ecology Theory and Culture Conflict Theory

1. Social Ecology Theory

Basic Idea: Rooted in geography and notions of space, population movement, and density and how these are shaped by the physical environment; crime is a product of the geopolitical environment found in certain areas of a city.

Human Nature: Human actions are determined by major social trends that affect the physical and social environment. The choices and moral sense they have emerge in environmentally structured contexts. People are seen as conformist and act in accordance with values and norms of groups with which they self-identify.

Society and the Social Order: Early theories emphasized consensus yet implied group conflict and the plurality of values and norms that are found more explicitly in later theories. Law is taken for granted but reflects the norms and values and interests of the dominant culture. Criminals are those who are in a state of transition through fragmented social organization; criminality is not a permanent state.

Causal Logic: Social change, such as immigration, rural-urban migration, high social mobility, and growth of cities, undermines traditional coping behaviors and especially traditional control institutions: family networks destroyed, extended family fragmented, ethnic culture lacks authority. This produces social disorganization in which people compete rather than cooperate as a community. At the same time, these neighborhoods are insulated from values of the dominant culture. Parents lose the respect of their children, who are in conflict with them over mixed value systems, and this results in a loss of parental control over children. Social disorganization leads to personal disorganization. This leads to crime, delinquency, and mental illness, especially suicide. Insulated from dominant culture and alienated from parents, some immigrant youths form their own new primary subcultures, or gangs. Gangs develop their own delinquent traditions, which are passed on to new members. The areas where this disorganization is most intensely felt are inner-city zones of transition where property values are low but rising and slumlords neglect properties while waiting for rise in value. These low-income housing areas have the highest numbers of immigrants. Some immigrant subcultural groups, such as the Chinese, are able to resist the wider disorganization of neighborhood by maintaining their original strong culture and tradition. Some argue that disorganized areas are not all the same but may have as many as three or more subareas of disorganization.

Criminal Justice Policy: Some in the 1930s felt areas would eventually improve as immigration stopped and the city stabilized, so little need be done. Others argued that it was necessary to move those most affected by disorganization to new geographical areas. Yet others argued for strengthening community organization. More recent theorists believe in a systemic or integrated approach to strengthen both internal informal networks and their connection with wider political, social, and economic networks and resources.

Criminal Justice Practice: Structural and institutional changes, community mobilization (e.g., Chicago Area Project), facilitation of the process of assimilating both immigrants and the disorganized into mainstream society.

Evaluation: Explains some inner-city street crime and why crime rates are highest in cities and slums. Undermines argument of biological and psychological theories, since they would predict more random occurrence of crime geographically. Criticized for accepting official crime statistics as valid, ignoring white-collar crime in suburbs, ignoring excessive policing of inner cities. Fails to explain corporate crime, fails to explain insulation of some youths in the inner city from delinquency, and fails to account for how people in disorganized areas disengage from crime as adults.

2. Culture Conflict Theory

Basic Idea: Some people have cultural heritages that differ from those of the dominant culture and they are often in conflict with it; they become criminal simply by following their own cultural norms.

Human Nature: Humans are seen as equal, sociocultural blanks that are socialized into norm- and rule-following actors.

Society and the Social Order: Divided by culture into dominant and a diversity of subordinate or ethnic minority cultures, which are in conflict. Law is the rules of the dominant groups of a particular society. Criminals are those caught breaking another culture's laws; no different from noncriminals, in that both are rule following, except that they follow different rules.

Causal Logic: Socialization into the norms of another culture through the family produces three ways lawbreaking may occur: (1) In Sellin's version, the other culture is the native country of the immigrant, and when its norms are followed and they clash with norms of dominant culture, this "normal" behavior is defined as criminal and punishment may result; (2) when immigrant parents enforce standards of behavior of their native country on their children, who react because of their indoctrination in the adoptive country, the resulting strife and alienation may cause delinquency; (3) because complex societies have multiple social groups and a pluralism of subcultures, including corporate culture, norm and law violation can result when the behavior of one group or subculture conflicts with that of the dominant culture.

Criminal Justice Policy: Some argue that crime will melt away when the United States becomes "one culture" after assimilation of immigrants into the mainstream, so we need to do very little. Others believe we need acculturation programs and policies.

Criminal Justice Practice: Education and cultural socialization in schools and community; increased opportunities for assimilation and changing values of diverse ethnic groups; counseling for children of immigrants to provide them with coping skills needed to survive clash of cultures; clearer and simplified laws provided by dominant culture; greater flexibility of law when dealing with other or lower-class cultural contexts; decreased policing of streets.

Evaluation: Useful to explain minority and ethnic crime and recent Chinese, Cuban, Haitian, Vietnamese, and Hispanic gangs. But does not explain why offender cannot compromise cultures or hold dual values and norms. Does not explain adult crime in lower-class neighborhoods or middle- and upper-class crime.

9

The Sick Society
Anomie and Strain Theory

Phil was an economically disadvantaged yet ambitious young man who aspired to all the trappings of middle-class success: two cars, meaningful employment with benefits, status, and prestige. Most of his peers were from middle- or upper-class families and he was exposed to their lifestyle. Unfortunately, his family was unable to provide him with much economic support. He shared a two-bedroom trailer with five others and had little hope of financing a college education. Being resourceful and attuned to the drug culture, Phil began selling marijuana. Four years later, he was a senior in college, financed by two greenhouses where he grew his product, and was aspiring to achieve middle-class goals. At this point, he brought his high school-age brother into the "business." The younger brother was less discreet and bragged about their "business" success, which resulted in a raid by the police. The older brother received a ten-year sentence in the state penitentiary. Phil illustrates the main themes of the sociological ideas of strain theory: He accepted U.S. society's cultural goals and objectives for success (high monetary rewards, good job, etc.). He did not, however, use normatively accepted means (student loans, hard work, delayed gratification) to achieve those goals, but instead innovated with illegitimate means to achieve them.

Strain theory is not restricted to explaining conventional street crime; nor is it confined to the lower reaches of the social structure. It has also been applied to corporate and organizational crime, as the following analysis illustrates:

> Corporations, like all organizations, are primarily oriented towards the achievement of a particular goal—profit—at least in the long run. . . . This defining characteristic . . . makes a corporation inherently criminogenic, for it necessarily operates in an uncertain and unpredictable environment such that its purely legitimate opportunities for goal achievement are sometimes

limited and constrained. . . . The contradictions between corporate goal-achieving behaviour and . . . environmental uncertainties create a strong strain towards innovative behaviour. . . . Examples [include]: espionage, arson, patent copying; bribery and corruption to influence those in new and expanding markets, such as government officials in developing economies . . . refusal to make work conditions safe or properly inspected/maintained . . . fraudulent advertizing, misleading sales behavior; false labelling of products; manufacture and distribution of dangerous products. (Box 1983, 35–37)

In this chapter, we begin to consider the ideas of theorists who argue that the structure of society (i.e., how society is organized) can affect the way people behave. In particular, we examine the idea that "some social structures exert a definite pressure on certain persons in the society to engage in nonconforming conduct rather than conformist conduct" (Merton 1938, 672). We examine the theories of the sociological functionalists, principally Emile Durkheim and Robert Merton, who argued that the organization of industrialized societies produces divisions between people and between groups based on social position in a hierarchy and occupational role within the system (known as the division of labor). Functionalist sociologists believe that social roles become specialized and work interdependently to serve the system as a whole.

Emile Durkheim first presented the basic components of this functionalist analysis of crime in 1893, when he was trying to explain how society could change from the stability of its preindustrial order to the potential chaos that the capitalist industrial system could produce. He argued that in times of rapid change the moral regulation of behavior is undermined by the structural divisions and by a cult of the individual, which promotes unlimited aspirations, some of which involve criminal behavior ([1893] 1984). In the twentieth century, these ideas were applied to the United States by Robert Merton (1938, [1957] 1968), who examined society after the Great Depression and found that its culturally defined goals, such as "the American Dream," could be met by illegal means by those denied access to approved means. These approved means would include legitimate opportunities such as formal education and economic resources. Development and extension of these ideas included the seminal work of Albert Cohen (1955) and Richard Cloward and Lloyd Ohlin (1960) on collective rather than individual adaptations by working-class populations to societal strain; Robert Agnew (1992 1995a) on strategies of avoiding the frustration and anger produced by strain, based on a variety of social-psychological variables; and most recently Steven Messner and Richard Rosenfeld's (1994) ideas about the role of U.S. economic institutions in dominating other social values and undermining strong social controls. Before we explore the different forms anomie (or strain) theory has taken and its criminal justice policy implications, let us look at the core underlying assumptions.

Assumptions of Strain Theory

Anomie theory, more recently called strain theory, has gone through several transitions in its hundred-year development and has proven remarkably resilient at explaining crime in changing societies. During this process, many of its underlying assumptions have remained constant, although others have changed and become subject to disagreement. All versions of strain theory agree that deviant behavior is a normal response to abnormal conditions. Furthermore, humans are socialized to behave in often predictable ways. Strain theorists may disagree over what the specific goals are, but they agree that seeking goals is a normal human trait. Finally, strain theorists agree that society and culture cause strain by their organization, the goals they prescribe, and the allocation of resources; more recent theorists disagree about the extent that individual behavioral characteristics can mitigate these forces. Let us consider these assumptions in greater detail, first looking at their similarities and complementary aspects and then looking at how they diverge.

All strain theorists assume that crime is a normal reaction to abnormal social conditions. Strain theory emphasizes "the problem-solving functions" served by nonconforming, antisocial, delinquent, and criminal behavior (Brezina 1996, 39). Strain theories link macrolevel variables, such as the organization of societies (especially capitalism), to the microlevel behavior of individuals. In other words, strain theory "links the macrostructural organization of society to the micro-social choices of its individual members" (Holman and Quinn 1992, 217). Thus it is often termed a mesolevel explanatory framework (or what Merton [(1957) 1968] called a theory of the "middle range").

Taken as a whole, strain theory describes the interplay between social structures, cultural context, and individual action. Different strain theorists disagree over some fundamental dimensions of their theory, however, and therefore emphasize different aspects of its components. For example, Durkheim's original theory of anomie assumes a view of humans born with insatiable appetites to be "heightened or diminished by the social structure" (Einstadter and Henry 1995, 149). Thus his theory has much in common with control theory (discussed in Chapter 7) but goes beyond it in its attention to structural conditions. In contrast, versions of strain theory in the Merton mold assume individual appetites are "culturally rather than structurally induced" (Einstadter and Henry 1995, 149) but societal strain comes from differential opportunities in the social structure that have not met the culturally raised appetites.

Individual appetites also include an instrumental component (Orru 1990). This means that crime is seen as an instrumental act of goal seeking. Whether committed by individuals or corporate entities, crime serves a purpose. Mertonian theory assumes that humans act rationally and have self-serving motivations for their behavior, "not in the utilitarian sense of having 'free will,' but as actors whose choice of behavior is influenced by societal structures, cultural definitions, and interactive processes" (Einstadter and Henry 1995, 148–149). Mertonian conceptions of a structured human choice also reflect the results of socialization in families, in schools, and particularly through the media. These are the ways that cultural values are communicated.

Combining the ideas of Merton and Durkheim in a formulation known as traditional strain theory reveals a key issue to be goal-oriented, achievement-directed behavior and the way the social structure and culture shape this. For Mertonians, the culture, most vividly expressed through the mass media, encourages people to achieve certain goals such as monetary success: "Go for it!" express "No fear!" and "Have it all!" At the same time, the culture fails to place limits on acceptable means of achievement, and the structure does not provide real opportunities for all to achieve societal goals. Such a society is described as suffering strain because of (1) a dysfunctional mismatch between the goals or aspirations it sets for its members and the structure of opportunities it provides for them to achieve these goals (Merton 1938), (2) an unleashing of individual aspirations without a corresponding provision of normative or moral guidelines to moderate the level of raised aspirations (Durkheim [1897] 1951), and (3) the failure to match people's skills and abilities to the available positions in the society (known as a "forced" division of labor) (Durkheim [1893] 1984). A society experiencing such structural strain is unable to retain a meaningful sense of moral authority with regard to normative controls on behavior and is referred to as being in a state of anomie, or normlessness (Durkheim [1897] 1951). In a word, the society is "sick."

Societal strain can affect people, groups, and organizations in different ways as they seek to adapt to solve the problems that strain creates. One of these adaptations is crime, whereby people attempt to achieve societal goals regardless of the means used (as in the example of dealing drugs presented at the start of this chapter) to achieve money, material success, and social status. In short, they cheat. Crime, then, is one way of both responding to the strain and realizing common goals espoused by the larger dominant culture.

The Durkheim-Merton tradition of strain theory seems useful for explaining property crimes among the economically disadvantaged, who may experience greater personal stress as a result of structural strain, as Merton pointed out. But Merton ([1957] 1968) also recognized that the theory explains how the economically powerful commit economic crimes using illegal or unethical innovations, illustrated by the analysis of corporate crime at the start of the chapter. Indeed, "If 'success' is far more heavily emphasized in the higher strata of society, and if its measurement is virtually open-ended in these strata, then Merton's theory of anomie is even more applicable to white-collar crime than it is to conventional crime" (Friedrichs 1996, 232; Cohen 1995; Waring, Weisburd, and Chayet 1995). This too is what led Durkheim ([1897] 1951) "to focus on the top social stratum as the primary location of anomie, for it was power not poverty that facilitated too easily the personal achievement of socially inculcated cultural ambitions" (Box 1983, 40). Nowhere is this better illustrated than in the 1980s insider-trading crimes linked to the "unbridled pursuit of pecuniary rewards" (Lilly et al. [1989, 67] 1995). Also shown in the earlier corporate illustration are the numerous illegal strategies corporations use to achieve goals of financial profit that they are unable to achieve legitimately (Vaughan 1983; Passas 1990). Moreover, as Passas (1990) argues, the commission of crimes by the wealthier sections of society, combined with their immunity from prosecution, produces a cynicism among the population. Such cynicism feeds the general state of anomie as those in less privileged positions become confused about what moral rules really apply (Friedrichs 1996, 232).

Newer versions of strain theory, such as Agnew's (1985) revised strain theory, may be less compatible, since Merton's notion of goal-seeking actors is partially replaced by a view of humans invested in behavior designed to follow a particular rule of justice. For example, adolescents may be more concerned with the fairness of a process of job hiring than whether they get the job. Moreover, this response can be modified by individuals' different cognitive and behavioral attributes. Those who have doubts about their identities and capabilities may be more satisfied with less than those without such doubts, who may become more frustrated with injustices and choose crime to escape their frustrations. As we will see later, differences in the assumptions made about humans are some of the main features that distinguish the different versions of strain theory.

Another assumption over which strain and revised strain theorists disagree is the extent to which a consensus exists on societal goals, their nature, and diversity. Since Durkheim's original anomie theory, the types of goals have increased. In the most recent theoretical revisions the goals held by people are very different, depending on their social influences, peer groups, gender, race, and age. Let us examine in more detail the ideas of the specific versions of strain theory that have emerged over the past hundred years.

Founders of Strain Theory

In this section, we consider the ideas of the founding theorists in the strain theory tradition. We begin with Durkheim's anomie theory and then look at Merton's adaptation of these ideas to the twentieth-century United States before discussing how their approaches were supplemented by the research of Merton's students Albert Cohen and Richard Cloward.

Durkheim's Original Concept of Anomie

The French sociologist Emile Durkheim (1858–1917) was one of the three founders of sociology who at the turn of the century sought to explain the transformation that was taking place as societies changed after the Industrial Revolution (Max Weber and Karl Marx, whose ideas we discuss in the next chapter, were the other two founders). Durkheim's view of humans was not unlike that of the classical philosopher Hobbes and the later control theorists (discussed in Chapter 7). He believed people were born with potentially insatiable appetites, which can be heightened or diminished by social structure. In a well-ordered society, a cohesive set of values and norms regulates the levels of aspiration and expectation. As a result, levels of crime are relatively low.

For Durkheim ([1895] 1950), crime was any action that offends collective feelings of the members of society—that shocks their common conscience. He believed that some level of crime is normal and necessary for several reasons. First, even in a well-ordered society (even a society of saints), crime is necessary (functional) to remind the community of its values and standards. Second, crime serves to create a sense of solidarity among law-abiding citizens; the criminal or crime presents an occasion to bring people together to celebrate their values by denigrating those they oppose. Third, society can make moral messages about which rules are most important by adjusting the severity of punishment. Fourth, the punishments given to criminals help to force compliance with the law; fear of shame, humiliation, and lack of liberty, motivate people to obey the laws. Finally, and important for Durkheim, was the idea that crime functioned to warn a society that something may be wrong with the overall way it operates—its social structure. Crime is the pain of a sick society. It serves as a stimulus for innovation and social change.

For Durkheim, some level of crime was inevitable, if only because of those he saw born as biological and psychological misfits (Taylor et al. 1973, 84). Crime is inevitable because of "the incorrigible wickedness of men" ([1895] 1982, 98). But Durkheim also saw excessive levels of crime as a result of change from the small-scale, face-to-face society with a low division of labor and everyone doing similar tasks and shared common (religious and traditional) values to a large-scale industrial society with a high division of labor and diverse beliefs. In modern industrial society, people become highly specialized in their tasks. Moreover, they are encouraged to act as individuals rather than as members of a common

group in pursuing their differential occupational roles and to aspire to individual rather than social desires (which he called egoism).

Under these circumstances, the moral authority of the collective conscience loses much of its force and people aspire to positions and levels
for which they are ill suited and that do not satisfy them. Their "greed is
aroused" and opens up an insatiable "thirst for novelties, unfamiliar pleasures and nameless sensations, all of which lose their savor once known"
(Durkheim [1897] 1951, 256). Such a society is in a state of anomie: a
"breakdown in the ability of society to regulate the natural appetites of
individuals" (Vold and Bernard 1986, 185), "a situation in which the unre-
stricted appetites of individual conscience are no longer held in check"
(Taylor et al. 1973, 87). In a condition of anomie, rates of all kinds of non-
conformity increase, including crime and suicide, as "individuals strive
to achieve their egoistic desires in a way that is incompatible with social
order and incommensurate with their biologically given abilities" (Taylor
et al. 1973, 85).

These ideas formed Durkheim's contribution to current concepts of
strain. He drew attention to changing social structures (e.g., feudalism to
capitalism) that generated the social pressure that Merton later called
strain. The impending eruption of crime and suicide from this misalignment could, however, be avoided. Durkheim's solution was not to go
back to a face-to-face society but to advocate new secular values that
would acknowledge the rise in individualism but provide appropriate
constraints on aspirations. He saw this secular morality as being built
around occupations but did not thoroughly address how conflicts between these moralities would be resolved.

Merton's Instrumental Anomie and Differential Opportunity Structures

Robert K. Merton, the sometimes delinquent son of eastern European
Jewish immigrants, whose father was a carpenter and truck driver in
South Philadelphia, rose from part-time magician to a leading contemporary sociologist at both Harvard and Columbia Universities (Martin et al.
1990). He presented the first contemporary anomie theory in 1938. Although relying heavily on Durkheim and his concept of anomie, Merton
made different assumptions about humans and society. In contrast to the
class-stratified structure of Durkheim's nineteenth-century France, twentieth-century U.S. society was founded on a supposed equality between
people, an ethic in which hard work and innovation were rewarded, and
an overall utilitarian ideology. In Durkheim's France, it was normal for
people to be told, "You must go no further"; in Merton's United States the
cultural motto was, "Never stop trying to go further" (Passas 1995,
94–95). Merton appropriately shifted the emphasis of anomie from a

breakdown of or a failure to develop adequate moral or normative regulation to "differential access to opportunity structures" that, combined with the egalitarian ideology, produced relative deprivation (Box [1971] 1981, 97–99; Merton [1957] 1968; Passas 1995).

Relative deprivation is the condition in which people in one group compare themselves to others (their reference group) who are better off and as a result feel relatively deprived, whereas before the comparison no such feeling existed. Merton ([1957] 1968) used reference group theory to explain why some people in anomic situations did not resort to deviance whereas others did (Shoemaker 1996, 96).

Unlike Durkheim, Merton argued that human "appetites," or desires, are not natural. Rather, they are created by cultural influences (Passas 1995). For example, in the United States heavy emphasis is placed on monetary and material success, such as owning one's own home and car(s). Societal institutions, such as parents, families, schools, government, and the media, impose this pressure to succeed. This is known as the "American Dream." In the United States, people with money and wealth are generally held in high esteem. In other cultures, different characteristics are valued, for example, old age or religious piety. Merton pointed out that he was only using monetary success as an illustration, and in his later arguments he asserted that "cultural success goal" could be substituted for money with the same results (Merton [1957] 1968; 1995, 30). It is "only when a system of cultural values extols, virtually above all else, certain common symbols of success for the population at large while its social structure rigorously restricts or completely eliminates access to approved modes of acquiring these symbols for a considerable part of the same population, that antisocial behavior ensues on a considerable scale" (1938, 680).

In the United States, as in other capitalist societies, the approved modes of acquiring success symbols are the institutionalized means used for achieving society's goals. These means are emphasized in the "middle-class values" of saving, education, honesty, hard work, delayed gratification, and so on, but the means are not evenly distributed. This is because the society is divided into a class hierarchy in which access to the approved means is restricted for most of the population; it is "differentially distributed among those variously located in the social structure" (Merton 1938, 679).

It is this mismatch between "certain conventional values of the culture" and "the class structure involving differential access to the approved opportunities for legitimate, prestige bearing pursuit of the cultural goals" that "calls forth" antisocial behavior (Merton 1938, 679). This condition, or disjunction, creates the strain that produces anomie. The resolution of this strain can include deviance and crime.

Thus, in contrast to Durkheim's original conception, Merton's anomie "is used to clarify the contradictory consequences of an overwhelming emphasis on the monetary success-goal coupled with the inadequacy of the existing opportunity structure" (Orru 1987, 124). Nor are these contradictions restricted merely to class divisions, since, as Merton argues, the structural sources of differential access to opportunity "among varied social groups (not, be it noted, only social classes)" are "in ironic conflict with the universal cultural mandate to strive for success" in a "heavily success-oriented culture" (1995, 11).

When individuals are socialized to accept the goals of material wealth and upward social mobility but, due to their disadvantaged economic position, are unable to obtain the resources (means) to achieve these goals, they may cope in several ways, some of which involve crime. Merton emphasized that the differential opportunity structure (not merely confined to economic opportunities) is the cause of strain, rather than the cultural goals (1995, 27–28).

Merton identified five ways in which individuals respond or adapt to "selective blockage of access to opportunities among those variously located in the class, ethnic, racial, and gender sectors of the social structure" (1995, 12). These five adaptations—conformity, innovation, ritualism, retreatism, and rebellion (see Table 9.1)—are based on an individual's attitudes toward means and goals.

The conformist accepts the goals of society and the legitimate means of acquiring them, including delayed gratification, hard work, and education: "'The American Dream' may be functional for the substantial numbers of those with the social, economic, and personal resources needed to help convert that Dream into a personal reality" (Merton 1995, 16). Illustrative of this adaptation are people from economically disadvantaged families and those against whom considerable institutional discrimination exists who succeed due to extra effort or education. Actual success is not necessary, so long as the conformist continues to make the effort and plays by the rules: "Access need not mean accession" (Merton 1995, 8).

Merton claims, however, that the dream "may be dysfunctional for substantial numbers of those with severely limited structural access to opportunity . . . and under such conditions it invites comparatively high rates of the various kinds of deviant behavior—socially proscribed innovation, ritualism, and retreatism" (Merton 1995, 16). Innovators accept the goals but significantly reject or alter the means of acquiring the goals; put simply, they cheat. They innovate and seek alternative means to success—often illegitimate. This mode of adaptation accounts for the majority of the crime explained by strain theory. Persons who want, say, wealth and status but lack legitimate means of acquiring them may find new methods through which wealth can be acquired. Crime is one option. Some common examples of this mode of adaptive behavior are theft, drug dealing, white-collar crime, and organized crime. A good illustration of white-collar innovation

TABLE 9.1   Merton's Individual Modes of Adaptation

	Cultural Goals	*Institutionalized Means*
I. Conformity	+	+
II. Innovation	+	−
III. Ritualism	−	+
IV. Retreatism	−	−
V. Rebellion	±	±

SOURCE: Robert K. Merton. 1938. Social Structure and Anomie, *American Sociological Review* 3: 672–682. p. 676.

NOTE: (+) signifies acceptance, (−) signifies elimination or rejection, and (±) signifies rejection and substitution of new goals and standards. Replacement represents a transitional response that seeks to institutionalize new procedures oriented toward revamped cultural goals shared by the members of society. It thus involves efforts to change the existing structure.

is the case of the prospective graduate students who in 1996 paid $6,000 to be part of a scam to take the Graduate Record Examination (GRE). The test was taken on the West Coast after expert test takers had taken the same test three hours earlier on the East Coast and phoned the correct answers to the West Coast, where they were inscribed on pencils given to the cheating students.

The third type of adaptation to structural strain is ritualism. Ritualists reject societal goals but accept the means. These people recognize that they will never achieve the goals due to personal inability or other factors. The bureaucrat who becomes obsessed with the rules but loses sight of the objectives of the organization is one example of a ritualist. University department chairpersons who routinely hold pointless meetings simply for the sake of meeting provide a classic example. Another is the "terminal student" who has no expectation of ever finishing college but continues to take courses. Merton argues that this action is deviant because the culture demands striving to get ahead, not accepting failure or only doing enough to get by.

Retreatism is an adaptation whereby the individual rejects both the goals of society and the legitimate means to attain them. This mode of adaptation is most likely to be chosen when the socially approved means are perceived as being unlikely to result in success and the conventional goals are seen as unattainable. Retreatism becomes an escape device for such people. Examples of retreatist behavior include chronic alcoholism, drug abuse, and vagrancy, behavior that reflects giving up the struggle. The retreatist is "in society but not of it" and may even go on to commit suicide (Merton 1964, 219).

The final mode of adaptation is rebellion. Rebels not only reject the goals and means but replace them with new ones. Members of street gangs and motorcycle gangs may fit into this category, as do right-wing militia groups. Another form of rebellion can be seen among members of religious orders who seek certain states of consciousness and reject material gain and members of religious cults such as Heaven's Gate, whose core members committed mass suicide in 1997.

There have been some notable criticisms of Merton's version of strain theory: It falsely assumes a universal commitment to materialistic goals; it ignores violent, passionate, or spontaneous crime; it cannot explain middle-class, corporate, or white-collar crime; it relies on official crime statistics; and it fails to differentiate between aspirations (desired goals) and expectations (probable accomplishments) (Adler and Laufer 1995). These have been addressed by recent developments and extensions, as we show next.

Cohen: Status Frustration and Delinquent Subcultures

Albert Cohen, a student of Merton's and Sutherland's, went on to integrate Chicago School ideas on culture, differential association, and crime with Merton's anomie theory. He used Merton's theory to answer the criticism of differential association, that it fails to explain how patterns of delinquent behavior originate (discussed in Chapter 6). But he criticized Merton for overemphasizing the individual dimension of adaptation to strain. Cohen (1955) observed that most delinquent behavior occurs in interactive group or gang settings and also originates there. Each member stimulates the others into behavior they would not commit individually: "Deviant as well as non-deviant behavior is typically not contrived within the solitary individual psyche, but is a part of collaborative social activity, in which the things that other people say and do give meaning, value and effect to one's own behavior" (Cohen 1965, 8). He also observed that most of this collective action among juvenile delinquent boys was "non-utilitarian, malicious, and negativistic" in nature (Cohen 1955, 25). He criticized Merton's individualistic version of anomie theory for failing to explain the nonutilitarian nature of delinquency. He argued that lower-class male delinquent behavior was the result of a collective adaptation or adjustment to the strain caused by the disjunction between culturally induced goals and differential opportunity structure.

Cohen claimed that for juvenile boys the central value was achievement or success that brought social status. The socially approved context for this was the school, which provides status based on the middle-class values of accomplishment, display of drive and ambition, individual responsibility and leadership, academic achievement, deferred gratification, rationality, courtesy, self-control over violence and aggression, constructive use of leisure time, and respect for property (Hagan 1994; Shoemaker 1996). But many lower-class adolescents, prior to entering school, have low ascribed status (which is conferred by virtue of one's family position). Nor do they have the socially relevant means and background skills to legitimately achieve status by accomplishing the goals that would bring success in the school setting. Such youth are judged by middle-class standards and typically cannot measure up to their middle-class counterparts. This places lower-class adolescents under severe strain, from which they experience status frustration. This is a psychological state involving self-hatred, guilt, self-recrimination, loss of self-esteem, and anxiety. To resolve their status frustration lower-class juveniles seek achieved (aspired) status, but since they are unable to achieve this by legitimate means they collectively rebel (as in Merton's fifth mode of adaptation to strain) through a process that Cohen calls reaction formation.

Reaction formation involves "(1) redefining the values among similarly situated peers; (2) dismissing, disregarding, and discrediting 'school knowledge'; and (3) ridiculing those who possess such knowledge" (Einstadter and Henry 1995, 164). These youths rebel against middle-class values by inverting them and thereby creating their own peer-defined success goals, which form the basis of the delinquent subculture. Thus, argues Cohen, these oppositional values are often negative and destructive, involving behavior such as fighting, vandalism, and any acts that provide instant gratification. For Cohen's delinquent boys, "middle-class standards are not only to be rejected, they are to be flouted. Thus, 'good' children are to be terrorized, playgrounds and gyms are to be taken over for aimless use, golf courses are to be torn up, library books are to be stolen and destroyed and so on" (Shoemaker 1996, 106). Status for conducting such activities is achieved among like-minded peers, ultimately in gang membership. In the gang context, others who hold the same negative values respect the deviant lawbreaker. Cohen argues that "the delinquent's conduct is right by the standards of his subculture precisely because it is wrong by the norms of the larger culture" (1955, 28).

Cohen recognized that his theory was not all-inclusive and did not explain all juvenile crime, particularly crimes by females. He also argued that, as well as the delinquent subculture, there were two other collective responses, the nondeviant "college boy" subculture, whose members struggle against all odds to achieve conventional success, and the dropout "corner boy" subculture. The corner boy parallels Merton's individual retreatist in that he is unable to succeed and believes he is destined to fail at school. But instead of suffering his fate alone, he joins collectively with others for emotional support and engages in marginally deviant activities, which are driven by fatalistic motives rather than the rational goal-directed ones of the delinquent subculture. Subsequent theorists used this as a transitional point and examined these groups.

Cloward and Ohlin: Differential Opportunity Structures and Alienated Youths

Like Cohen, Richard A. Cloward and Lloyd Ohlin saw collective rather than individual action as a key feature of delinquent behavior. In contrast to Cohen, however, their major insight was the notion that rather than rejecting middle-class values, working-class males are rational, goal-seeking, and oriented toward these values, particularly economic success. They also added an important new dimension that involved differential access to success—goals by illegitimate means. This implied the parallel existence of an illegitimate opportunity structure (Cloward 1959), an idea first appearing in Cloward's doctoral dissertation on military prison completed under Merton and Ohlin at Columbia University. In 1960, Cloward and Ohlin presented their classification scheme to explain the formation of three types of delinquent gangs, showing how these varied depending on the illegal opportunity structures.

Gang formation was rooted in the alienation of adolescents who were unjustly denied access to legitimate means to succeed in conventional society. Gangs formed as a result of interaction with other similarly affected juveniles. The way they formed depended on the neighborhood characteristics. Reflecting Chicago School ideas (discussed in Chapter 8), opportunity was also ecological in nature. Different neighborhoods had different resources and opportunity structures available—both legitimate and illegitimate. Concepts central to differential association were vital because youths identify with neighborhood role models and pattern their behaviors after these significant others. Cloward and Ohlin's explanation successfully integrated the ecology theories of the Chicago school, Sutherland's ([1939] 1947) differential association, and Merton's anomie.

Like Merton, Cloward and Ohlin agreed that strain and anomie exist because of a "discrepancy" between aspirations and opportunities. Their view, more consistent with Merton's than Cohen's, was that crime may be the result of "differential opportunity structures." Cloward and Ohlin argue that lower-class youths are "led to want" "conventional goals" but find these actually unavailable. Because of the "democratic ideology . . . espousing equality of opportunity and universally high aspirations for success" (Cloward and Ohlin 1960, 108) and "faced with limitations on legitimate avenues of access to these goals, and unable to revise their aspirations downward, they experience intense frustrations; the exploration of nonconformist alternatives may result" (1960, 86). Moreover, these frustrations are likely to be more intensely felt among those at social positions where the discrepancy causing the frustration is most acute (1960, 108).

What further distinguishes Cloward and Ohlin from Cohen is that the frustration produced by the differential opportunity systems is not interpreted by adolescents as their own fault or failing. Rather, they perceive their failure as the fault of the system: "It is our view that the most significant step in the withdrawal of sentiments supporting the legitimacy of conventional norms is the attribution of the cause of failure to the social order rather than to oneself" (Cloward and Ohlin 1960, 111). Thus youths viewed their failure not as a "reflection of personal inadequacy" but the result of "unjust or arbitrary institutional arrangements" (1960, 111). Although such youths do internalize conventional goals, they do not internalize the failure to accomplish them as the result of their own inadequacy but as a result of an unjust cultural and social system.

For Cloward and Ohlin, the strain producing frustration does not lead automatically to collective delinquent solutions but depends first on alienation. Whether this alienation from the conventional system converts into subcultural delinquency depends on the outcome of a complex interactive and dynamic evolutionary process among peers. Indeed, those who aspire to economic success are more likely to take part in serious criminal conduct than those who aspire to a middle-class lifestyle (Hoffmann and Ireland 1995, 248–249). Anticipating subsequent renditions of control and neutralization theory (discussed in Chapters 6–7), Cloward and Ohlin argued that before delinquent subcultures can form, four conditions must be met: "First, they [youths] must be freed from commitment to and belief in the legitimacy of certain aspects of the existing organization of means. . . . Secondly, they must join with others in seeking a solution to their adjustment problems rather than attempt to solve them alone. Thirdly, they must be provided with appropriate means for handling the problems of guilt and fear. . . . Finally, they must face no obstacles to the possibility of joint problem-solving" (1960, 110).

Cloward and Ohlin identified three primary types of deviant subcultures that form in response to the shared perception of injustice. They argued that subcultures develop in relation to the legitimate and illegitimate neighborhood opportunities in which young people grow up. Members of the criminal subculture are primarily interested in crimes that bring material gain: theft, drug dealing, numbers rackets, and so on. These groups are likely to form in neighborhoods where there is a connection between both conventional activity and theft and various money-making rackets. This mutual interdependence provides a relatively stable illegal opportunity structure. Here, adult criminal role models exemplify an alternative career path and appropriate criminal skills for the juveniles who, like Merton's innovators, are goal-directed instrumentalists rather than impulsive, irrational actors (Shoemaker 1996, 113). The members of these gangs avoid irrational crimes involving violence because such acts would threaten their criminal careers.

In contrast, conflict subcultures form where stable organized criminal activity fails to develop. This is because of a variety of ecological factors, including a transient population, few adult role models, and isolation from conventional opportunity structures. Conflict subcultures have parallels with Merton's rebellion and Cohen's delinquent subcultures. Members of conflict subcultures are involved in violent or "expressive" crimes essentially motivated by an angry war against society for the injustice and humiliation it bestowed on them. These subcultures may be gangs who fight to preserve territorial boundaries and honor. Here, self-worth, or "rep," is developed through establishing oneself as a risk taker, hard, being cool, and having a violent macho image. Being "quoted," or beaten by gang members as an initiation rite, illustrates this value. Part of the reason for this alternative status/honor hierarchy is the absence of stable legitimate opportunity structures.

Finally, retreatist subcultures are composed of dropouts involved with excessive alcohol and drug use, sexually promiscuous behavior, and survival activities such as pimping. Members of these subcultures are deemed "double failures" since they have also failed in other types of gangs (criminal and conflict) as well as with conventional society. The retreatist reflects the important point of blockage by both the legitimate and the illegitimate opportunity structures.

Limitations and Policy Implications of Classical Strain Theory

Most criticisms of Merton's original strain theory have been addressed by subsequent theorists such as Cohen and Cloward and Ohlin, but several have proved resilient. These include (1) the omission of major segments of the population whose social characteristics lead them to not share in dominant cultural goals of economic success, notably women (Leonard 1982) and minorities (LaFree, Drass, and O'Day 1992); (2) confusion over the definition of goals and means (Sanders 1983); (3) oversimplification of the process of gang formation, gang types (Spergel 1964; Campbell 1984), and what motivates gang members (Katz 1988; Hagedorn 1988); and (4) failure to allow for humans being creative and interpretive enough to overcome the social structure and transform it (Suchar 1978). Although it is now recognized that Merton's theory has been "reborn" as "a viable and promising theory of delinquency and crime" (Farnworth and Leiber 1989, 273), primarily because of recent attempts to develop and extend it (discussed later), even these new ideas are subject to challenge.

The empirical evidence for strain theory demonstrates conditional support, although support is growing for the various revised versions of the theory. The incorporation of the dimensions of other theories improves the likelihood of empirical support. Thus the ecological ideas of Cloward and Ohlin about neighborhood organization and gang formation are better supported. But the balance of evidence suggests that both Cohen's and Cloward and Ohlin's theories are not generally supported by the empirical data, especially Cohen's idea of juveniles joining with others to commit offenses in opposition to middle-class values as a result of school failure. Nor has Cloward and Ohlin's notion that lower-class youths blame the system for their failures or their typology of gangs received much empirical support (Shoemaker 1996, 111, 114–115, 120).

The policy implications of traditional anomie/strain theory vary depending on which version is followed. Since all relate the source of crime to the strain produced by structural (means) and cultural (goals) contradictions, crime control policy must attend to removing or reducing these strains or improving the legitimate ways that those affected cope.

Policy Implications

There are two broad policy approaches addressing the structural-cultural causes of strain. First, the raised cultural aspirations emphasizing monetary acquisition produced by a society can be tempered. Second, the unequal opportunity structure can be addressed. By far the majority of policy suggestions and implementations from traditional strain theories have attempted to increase access to legitimate opportunities. We will see later that one version of the new strain theory attempts to deal with the cultural question.

At the macropolicy level of dealing with problems of differential opportunity structure, it is clear that if juveniles lack the means to achieve "middle-class" success, then the means should be provided to them. Programs such as Head Start help disadvantaged children from an early age to succeed in the school setting. Providing resources and mobilizing disorganized communities are also suggested by strain theorists. Unlike many criminological theories, these policies have been implemented—although not completely and not with much success.

In the early 1960s, Robert Kennedy was appointed attorney general of the United States by his brother, President John F. Kennedy. Robert Kennedy had read Cloward and Ohlin's book and as a result asked Ohlin to help devise a new federal policy for dealing with juvenile delinquency. The Juvenile Delinquency Prevention and Control Act of 1961 was designed to provide employment and work training for disadvantaged youths. The Act also directed resources to social services and community organizations. Despite good intentions, the Act is generally considered to have failed, in part, according to some, because it did not go far enough.

For example, Ohlin advocated strikes against schools and lawsuits against landlords as a means of promoting change. The Act was much less ambitious, incorporating only piecemeal solutions. But it was the forerunner of Lyndon Johnson's War on Poverty, announced in 1964, including the Office of Economic Opportunity (Gilsinan 1990; Sundquist 1969). From the Kennedy and Johnson administrations emerged numerous social engineering programs, such as Mobilization for Youth, Head Start, Job Corps, Vista, Neighborhood Legal Services, and the Community Action Program (Dallek, 2003). Some have argued that the $6 billion spent on these programs between 1965 and 1968 was a gross underfunding given the magnitude of the problems and claim that up to $40 billion would have been more appropriate (Curran and Renzetti 1994, 170; Empey and Stafford 1991).

Others argued that the programs underestimated the extent of political resistance reflected in the fact that those that challenged the political and economic structure of their communities saw their funds withdrawn (Empey and Stafford 1991). The outcome was more certain: "Contrary to expectations, the crime rate, rather than decreasing appeared to increase. Moreover, as legitimate opportunities seemed to expand, the demand for even greater opportunity increased ... and urban riots became a commonplace spectacle on the nightly news" (Gilsinan 1990, 146). By the 1980s, most of Johnson's War on Poverty programs had been dismantled (Curran and Renzetti 1994, 172).

In summary, classical versions of strain theory have drawn attention to the interplay between structural/cultural forces and individual/collective adaptations to the misalignment of these and the deviant/criminal outcomes that result. Policy suggestions have been implemented with some success, if limited resources. What has been omitted from the theory and the policy is an analysis of increasingly diverse social values, variation among individuals' perceptions, and the contribution from institutions to these developments. The various revisions to strain theory attempt to fill these gaps and begin to make policy recommendations but as yet have received only limited empirical evaluation.

Recent Revisions to Anomie/Strain Theory

Several contemporary criminologists have presented revised versions of traditional strain theory. For example, while retaining the core elements of strain theory, Elliott and his colleagues (Elliott, Ageton, and Canter 1979; Elliott, Huizinga, and Ageton 1985) asserted that juveniles have varied goals that differ between individuals and groups. Moreover, juveniles may hold multiple goals that they consider important. These may include having an active social life, being a good athlete, getting good grades, and having a good physical appearance and an attractive personality (Agnew

1984; 1995a, 114–115). However, like the original versions of strain theory this version has a very limited scope since it only examines the behavior of delinquent boys in urban environments (Broidy 2001).

Passas (1995, 101) extended the original formulation by arguing that anomic trends apply "at all levels of the social structure" and shows especially how they apply to corporate deviance (Passas 1990, 1993). He pointed out that in "achievement-oriented societies" where people are encouraged to compete "they do not compete for the same things." Thus we do not necessarily need comparisons between different classes; comparisons can occur with more successful peers, which may be upsetting and "generate frustrations and bring about a breakdown of normative standards" (Passas 1995, 101–102). Perhaps the most visible contributor to the revised strain theory is Robert Agnew (1985, 1992, 1995a, b), who also argued for a general strain theory able to explain crime and middle-class delinquency, and has sought to identify the conditions that cause strain (Agnew 2001) and the interrelation between personality traits or "negative emotionality" and strain (Agnew et al. 2002).

Agnew's General Strain Theory

Whereas Merton sought to explain how macrolevel influences produce strain that bear on individual choices, Robert S. Agnew's (1992) general strain theory argued that microlevel stresses emanate from negative interpersonal, peer group or familial relationships that produce strain and that these forms of strain may be more important. For example, Agnew argued that juveniles not only seek goals but exercise pain-avoidance behavior. But legitimate avenues of avoidance may be blocked: "Adolescents who are abused by parents, for example, may be unable to legally escape from home. Or adolescents who are harassed by teachers may be unable to legally escape from school. This inability to escape from painful situations, or this blockage of pain-avoidance behavior, [is] another major type of strain" (Agnew 1995a, 115–116; 1985; 1989). In other words, Agnew focuses on social psychological variables instead of social structure (Broidy 2001). To Agnew, strain triggers negative emotions that necessitate coping strategies.

Agnew (1992, 47) presents four sources of strain: (1) "strain as the actual or anticipated failure to achieve positively valued goals" (e.g., failure to get into college); (2) "strain as the actual or anticipated removal of positively valued stimuli" (e.g., being kicked off the high school basketball team or thrown out of a rap group); (3) "strain as the actual or anticipated presentation of negatively valued stimuli" (e.g., experiencing domestic violence or being subject to school bullying); and (4) the strain produced by the "failure of achievements to meet expectations" (e.g., failing to meet a conspicuously desirable boyfriend or girlfriend or getting into an average college but not the top college that friends have achieved). Strain resulting from each of these sources manifests in negative emotions such as anger and frustration, which "creates pressure for corrective action, with delinquency being one possible response" (Agnew 1995a, 116; Brezina 1996). Delinquency operates as one way of coping with "negative social relations" and their resultant psychological states (e.g., anger and frustration) (Agnew 1995a, 113). More recently Agnew refined this by arguing that vicarious and anticipated strain are also important (Agnew 2002). Vicarious strain "refers to the real-life strain experienced by others around the individual. . . . The individual may directly witness the strain experienced by these others (e.g., such as an assault), may hear these others experience of strain (e.g., gunshots, screams), or may hear about the strain of these others (e.g., from victims or in the media)" (2001, 604). Anticipated strain is the person's expectation that the current strain will continue into the future. Agnew also posits that some types of strain will not be related to crime (Agnew 2001).

What Agnew contributed, then, is an analysis of the psychological processes that convert structurally induced frustrations and negative emotions (especially anger) into delinquent action, focusing on cognitive, behavioral, and emotional coping strategies (Agnew 1995b, 63). Put simply, he argued that the unique contribution of strain theory is its essential insight "that if you treat people badly, they might get mad and engage in delinquency" (Agnew 1995a, 132; 1995b, 43). They are more likely to get mad if they have personality traits that include ineffective problem-solving skills, emotional sensitivity, low tolerance to adversity, and poor self-control (Agnew et al. 2002). Recently Agnew (2001) specified which of the wide range of potential strains are most likely to be responsible for crime and delinquency: (1) strain perceived as being unjust (e.g., being "picked on" for punishment by a teacher for behavior that others get away with); (2) strain of high magnitude (e.g., consistently experiencing abuse at home or continually witnessing parents fighting; (3) strain accompanied by low social control (e.g., being abandoned by a beloved father and having to accept a hated stepfather); and (3) strain creating pressure to engage in criminal coping (e.g., viciously fighting back against a bully or retaliating against those who allow bullying to continue, such as teachers and other students).

Limitations of Revised Strain Theory

As a result of its focus in psychological, behavioral, and cognitive processes, Agnew's revised strain theory is seen by some as reductionist, undermining the major structural tenets of the original theory (Farnworth and Leiber 1989, 272; Shoemaker 1996, 96). Agnew (1995b) himself argues that his revision is not intended to displace the structural dimension but to complement it.

While the basic tenets of general strain theory are supported by recent empirical research (Brezina, Piquero, and Mazerolle 2001; Piquero and Sealock 2000), it is also quite robust and allows extension and modification. Walsh (2000), for example, applies behavioral genetics and biology to explain individual behavior based on strain theory. Capowich, Mazerolle, and Piquero examine situational anger and the role of social support networks (2001). Aspects of Agnew's general strain theory concerning the negative effects of multiple sources of strain on social bonds and increased delinquent peer associations have also received some empirical support. Overall, "there is consistent empirical evidence that exposure to strain increases the likelihood of criminal offending" but "less support for the idea that adaptations to strain are conditioned by a range of other factors" yet "some evidence that the combination of strain and anger increases the risk of criminal conduct" (Lilly, Cullen, and Ball 2002, 61).

A major methodological difficulty in many of the empirical studies, however, is the failure to take account of the difference between public and private crimes when measuring differences between youths of school age and what happens when they go to work. Without taking account of the crimes inside the privacy of the workplace such as employee theft, which has been shown to be highest among male youths (Hollinger and Clark 1983), it is impossible to determine whether committing crime goes up or down with increased employment opportunities and reduced pressures of school. What may be happening is a substitution of street crime with the less risky occupational crime rather than a decrease in crime per se (Foster 1990).

Policy Implications

Not surprisingly, the revised strain theories (like those of Agnew) see the problem in social-psychological terms and therefore prefer the microlevel, individual policy solutions. Since Agnew (1995b) reduces the problem of strain to treating people badly—they get mad and commit crimes—he not surprisingly sees policy suggestions as relatively straightforward. First, "reduce the likelihood that people will treat one another badly" by introducing family, school, and peer group programs that teach people "prosocial skills so that they will be less likely to provoke negative reaction from others." Second, "reduce the likelihood that people will respond to negative treatment with delinquency" by providing them with social support and teaching them better coping skills (Agnew 1995b, 43).

In particular, Agnew provides five concrete policy proposals for juveniles: (1) Reduce the adversity in youths' social environment by providing them with more participation in the decisions that affect their lives. This will increase their sense of "distributive justice." (2) Provide academic and social monitoring, support, and rewards for prosocial behavior while helping them overcome adverse environments, whether this involves changing schools or families. (3) Provide social skills training programs to reduce adolescents' likelihood of provoking negative social reactions in others. (4) Provide social support such as advocates or counselors and mediation programs to increase youths' ability to solve problems legitimately, particularly in stressful times of transition. (5) Increase social skills training and problem-solving and anger control programs to increase the ability of juveniles to cope with adversity without resorting to delinquency (Agnew 1995b, 64).

It is important to point out, as Agnew did, that none of these coping strategies remove the forces causing strain in the larger environment and influencing the success or failure of particular programs. As he acknowledged, "It is difficult for parent training programs to be successful, for example, when parents face multiple stressors such as the lack of good jobs, poor housing, and neighborhoods plagued by a host of social problems" (Agnew 1995b, 61). Agnew left this level of policy intervention to others. There could be no better complement than the recent work of Messner and Rosenfeld (1994), who combine broad social-structural processes and, in particular, examine the shift toward an extreme emphasis on material goals and the impact this has on institutions of social control.

Institutional Anomie Theory

Messner and Rosenfeld's (1994) book *Crime and the American Dream* presented the idea of institutional anomie to explain the unique U.S. obsession with crime. This revised interpretation of Merton's strain theory included elements of control theory not dissimilar to Durkheim's original argument. It focused, however, on what the authors claim is the unique character of U.S. culture, the "American Dream" and the relationships between U.S. economic institutions.

Rosenfeld and Messner (1995b, 164) defined the American Dream as "a commitment to the goal of material success, to be pursued by everyone in society, under conditions of open, individual competition." The American Dream promotes never-ending individual achievement as a measure of social worth. It emphasizes winning over the way we play the game and is described as a dysfunctional anomic imbalance. Messner and Rosenfeld argued that social institutions, such as schools and the family, perpetuate the economic status quo, failing to stimulate alternative means of self-worth, and as a result are unable to tame economic imperatives: "In short the institutional balance of power is tilted toward the economy" (Rosenfeld and Messner 1995b, 170).

Rosenfeld and Messner stated that this economic dominance over social organizations is manifest in three different ways: "(1) in the devaluation of noneconomic institutional functions and roles; (2) in the accommodation to economic requirements by other institutions; (3) in the penetration of economic norms into other institutional domains" (1995b, 171). For example, in U.S. culture, education becomes a means to jobs rather than an end in itself; educational curricula reflect accommodations to economic needs. Educational practice is penetrated by economic norms reflected in grading schemes, individual learning, and program assessment. Similarly, occupational roles are seen merely instrumentally as a means to economic rewards. Even the political institutions are reduced from their role of setting collective goals to facilitating ways to obtain material possessions. This is well captured in the political campaign slogan on what is the priority issue: "It's the economy, stupid!"

Institutional anomie theory "holds that culturally produced pressures to secure monetary rewards, coupled with weak controls from non-economic social institutions, promote high rates of instrumental criminal activity" (Chamlin and Cochran 1995, 413). This is because under the particular insatiable demands of the American Dream no amount of money obtained from legal sources is ever enough: "Illegal means will always offer further advantages in pursuit of the ultimate goal. There is a perpetual attractiveness associated with illegal activity that is an inevitable corollary of the goal of monetary success" (Rosenfeld and Messner 1995b, 175). Moreover, the authors argue that the negative effect of anomie is ameliorated by the strength of noneconomic social institutions, but without the breaks of social networks, crime knows no bounds (Messner and Rosenfeld 1994).

Rosenfeld and Messner's institutional anomie theory has particular relevance for explaining crime in a postmodern society where there is a celebration of the "culture of consumption." As they said, the American Dream is fulfilled through consumption that is often not possible without crime: "The consumer role is the principal structural locus of anomic cultural pressures in modern market societies" (Rosenfeld and Messner 1995a, 2). Whether or not the anomic tendencies of the consumer role lead to crime depends on the embeddedness of consumption. In community-based societies such as Japan, the anomic pressures are subdued in market relations with strong noneconomic content and control. Market relations "are embedded in noneconomic institutional domains" that foster trust and networks of interpersonal relations (Rosenfeld and

Messner 1995a, 6). In postmodern societies such as the United States, where the economic "bottom line" pervades all institutional arenas and social standing and personal worth are defined primarily in terms of individual material acquisition, anomic pressures to engage in crime are stimulated. This point is nicely illustrated by Siegel. In discussing institutional anomie theory, he states that "economic language, standards, and norms penetrate into noneconomic realms. Economic terms become part of the vernacular. People want to get to the 'bottom line'; spouses view themselves as 'partners' who 'manage the household'; we 'outsource' home repairs instead of doing them ourselves. Corporate leaders run for public office promising to 'run the country like a business'" (Siegel 2004, 195).

Limitations of Institutional Strain Theory

Messner and Rosenfeld's contribution can be said to revert to the economic reductionist argument focusing on the centrality of the materialist American Dream, but Merton (1995) rejected this view as too limited. Indeed, focusing on the formal economic institutions of society as the dominant shaping forces of U.S. culture and formal social institutions as ameliorators ignores the force of the often differently focused informal institutions and informal and hidden economies (Robinson and Henry 1977; Henry [1978] 1988, 1981; Ferman, Henry, and Hoyman 1987). That these informal institutions focus on social support and reciprocity as central organizing themes of their members and exist as part of the subculture of U.S. society has hardly been addressed by strain theorists (Cullen 1994).

However, institutionalized strain theory has received some empirical support. Jukka Savolainen used data from the World Health Organization to show that economic inequality is related to homicide in nations with weak collective institutions of social protection. Specifically, "the positive effect of economic inequality on the level of lethal violence is strongest in nations where the economy dominates the institutional balance of power" (2000, 1026). As we argue in the next chapters, this may also support conflict and radical theory, but Savolainen prefers an explanation based on institutional anomie and strain. Nonetheless social structure is clearly related to crime. Similarly, Cernkovich, Giordano, and Rudolph (2000) found that white Americans in particular who believed in the American Dream but failed to achieve economic success were more crime prone than whites who have achieved success, whites who didn't believe strongly in the American Dream, and African Americans who have lower expectations because of their unique history. Bernburg (2002) and Deflem (1999) add excellent commentary on this.

Policy Implications

With regard to policy questions, theorists have rarely suggested addressing the cultural problem of raised aspirations. Rosenfeld and Messner do
just that. As they observe, "Americans . . . live in a society that enshrines
the unfettered pursuit of material success above all other values. . . . Reducing these crimes will require fundamental social transformations that
few Americans desire and rethinking a dream that is the envy of the
world" (Rosenfeld and Messner 1995a, 176–177). Thus, although the following are antithetical to U.S. cultural values of individualism and material gain, stressing them would reduce or eliminate the insatiable desire to
pursue instrumental goals: the values of cooperative activity; social rather
than instrumental relations; sharing rather than consuming; humility and
satisfaction with the inner self as opposed to monetary success, physical
beauty, and material trappings.

Some have suggested shifting the culture toward increased social support at the very time when it appears to be moving away from this value
(Currie 1985; Cullen 1994). Currie (1997) argues that where the market is
allowed to predominate over other social institutions and norms that
have historically sustained families and communities, high rates of violent crime are found and are to be expected. The "competitive con-
sumerism" of the market economy withdraws public support and
undermines informal networks that might otherwise cushion the deprivation and disadvantages of those who struggle to make it.

Indeed, evidence suggests that in capitalist nations that provide a
safety net of welfare, pensions, and health care, extreme economic deprivation is avoided and crime rates are lower (Savolainen 2000). However,
addressing the pervasiveness of market principles, instead of simply providing welfare, would require a massive restructuring of capitalist society. For example, Einstadter and Henry pointed to one aspect of what
such a policy might entail:

> limiting the extent to which we create a demand for unnecessary consump-
> tion through advertising in the mass media. Controls might include laws
> minimizing advertising to informational claims, reducing the length of ad-
> vertisements to one or two line announcements as currently occurs on Public
> Broadcasting Service sponsorship, and vigorously controlling any "hyping"
> of product that is not substantially supported by independent consumer re-
> search. (1995, 172)

Ultimately, of course, this kind of approach begins to challenge the very
foundation of capitalist society, and as we shall see in the next chapter, that
is precisely what some feel it should do. Indeed, critical theorists, beginning with Marxists, argue that the ultimate failure of the strain approach is

that it is reformist; the system is rigged and no amount of adjustment is going to remove the strain that stems from its basic inequalities.

Summary and Conclusion

In this chapter, we examined the ideas that a society's culture, combined with its social organizational structure, sets the conditions for human behavior. Under certain circumstances, these structural forces present some sections of the population with problems to which they have to adapt. The results of these forces, experienced as anger and frustration, are dealt with either individually or collectively. We examined the several individual and collective ways—often criminal—that people, particularly juveniles, react to these forces and the different patterns of behavior that emerge. We went on to examine recent revisions to these ideas that expand their breadth and provide a more detailed analysis of their social-psychological components. We also presented extensions of strain theory to corporate and white-collar crime. We explored how the U.S. capitalist system represents an extreme version of institutional anomie that might account for its having the highest violent crime rate among industrialized nations. We explored the policy implications of these theories and evaluated their theoretical and empirical adequacy, concluding that the more recent revisions tend to be more supported than the original statements. Perhaps most significantly, anomie/strain theorists have contributed considerably to our understanding of social and structural forces in shaping the context for individual actions. However, they have been less helpful in explaining why societies put up with the maladaption, malintegration, strain, and stresses of social structure and have been more inclined to accept the conditions as inevitable. In the next chapter, we examine theories observing the same trends by advocates who believe that the solution is to eliminate the inequitable social conditions that create crime: capitalism itself.

Summary Chart: Anomie/Strain Theory

Basic Idea: The way a society is organized, particularly the nature and distribution of occupational roles, opportunities, and the means to obtain them, can contradict its cultural goals. The resulting strain created by differential opportunity structures creates problems, frustration, and anger for people whose adaptive solutions may include illegitimate behavior. Subcultural versions argue that strain is adapted to collectively rather than individually by the formation of groups that may have different values from the wider society from which the individual defects; through "peer pressure" new members learn behavioral patterns, skills, and rationale/justification for committing crime.

Human Nature: Humans are born as rational beings with the ability to learn and be socialized into goals and values and have the capacity to learn the necessary norms and skills to achieve those values; they have a tendency toward conformity. Subcultural version emphasizes youthful susceptibility to "peer pressure" and "pressure of the group" in the socialization process.

Society and the Social Order: A moral consensus on class hierarchy as well as goals and values, although later versions recognize the diversity of goals. Law for Durkheim is an expression of a society's collective conscience; for Merton it serves the function of integrating the members of the society and maintaining order necessary for the smooth functioning of occupational mobility. Criminals for Durkheim appear as four types: (1) biological, (2) egoistic (those subject to unbridled emphasis on satisfying selfish ends/goals), (3) anomic (those without moral guidance who are "rudderless"), and (4) rebellious (those who show structure is in need of change). For Merton, most criminals are no different from us all. They have followed society's success goals but have been frustrated in their attempt and so have adapted. Subcultural versions see some criminals learning different oppositional values and norms that replace those of dominant culture; they are various kinds of defectors rather than defectives.

Causal Logic: For Durkheim, the cause of crime is a combination of (1) the breakdown of traditional moral regulatory structures of the family, kinship networks, the community, and traditional values coexisting with (2) a "forced" division of labor (rather than "spontaneous"); (3) celebration of the individual, or the "cult of individualism," raising aspirations to insatiable levels; and (4) the failure to adapt the social structure fast enough to accommodate rapid social change. For Merton, there are four modes of deviant adaptation to the fundamental cause, which he sees as structural strain and the maladaption of cultural goals and values in society to the means available to achieve them. A society shares and promotes common values and goals; in the case of the United States this is captured by the notion of the American Dream, meaning acquisition of wealth and display of material (money) success. Unequal access to the legitimate means to achieve these goals expressed by unequal access to education or other credentials and unequal availability of good jobs places strain on conformity to the legitimate goals-means package. Individuals adapt to this strain in different ways. Merton identifies four nonconforming modes of adaptation: (1) innovation—rejecting the legitimate means but maintaining the same societal goals, which explains lower-class property, white-collar, and even corporate crime; (2) ritualism—rejecting the goals by giving up the attempt to achieve more than one has but conforming to the legitimate means, which explains some petty bureaucratic deviance; (3) retreatism—rejecting both goals and means, which explains some dropout forms of deviance, such as vagrants and drug and alcohol abusers; (4) rebellion—rejecting prevailing values and the legitimate means and substituting new goals and using new means, which explains terrorism, revolutions, and even political crimes. In subcultural versions, the American Dream is combined with inadequacies of lower-class socialization and preparation for claimed educational meritocracy, which leaves lower-class youths with impaired ability to compete with middle-class counterparts and decreased achievement against middle-class educational standards. For Cohen, this leads to loss of self-esteem and "status frustration" as the failure within the dominant middle-class system is reacted to, rejected, or replaced by a negative subculture. Identification with those in the same situation results in the formation of a "delinquent subculture" with inverted values of dominant classes: versatile, malicious and negativistic, nonutilitarian behavior and the desire for immediate rather than deferred gratification. Two other responses are those of the "corner boy," who makes the best of the existing situation, and the "college boy," who strives to achieve middle-class standards despite adverse conditions. In the case of Cloward and Ohlin, the situation of the American Dream and blocked opportunities produces alienation that is perceived as injustice. If the adolescent blames him/herself, then solitary solutions and dropping out result; if the system is blamed, support for it is withdrawn and it is replaced by one of three subcultures, depending on neighborhood conditions: (1) a criminal rationalistic subculture that emphasizes illegitimate means to achieve societal goals, such as drugs trading, numbers running, burglary; (2) a conflict subculture emphasizing violence and protest; or (3) a retreatist subculture escaping into drug use. Agnew's revised version of strain introduces strategies for avoiding the pain of strain, based on a variety of social-psychological variables. Messner and Rosenfeld centralize Merton's concept of the American Dream, showing the importance of the dominant role of U.S. economic institutions undermining strong social controls.

Criminal Justice Policy: Change the social organization of society to better integrate members to socioeconomic roles available; do not overpromote goals or raise people's aspirations beyond their capabilities; reduce the sources of strain; balance the overemphasis on market principles at the expense of other values.

Criminal Justice Practice: Provide economic opportunities for lower classes; create jobs, education, welfare, and child care programs, War on Poverty, Head Start programs; organize local communities to have an investment in conventional society; create community and youth-participation programs; include programs to accept more wide-ranging skills and knowledge in the educational system; draw schoolteachers from a broader social base; teach legitimate social and coping skills but also provide legitimate opportunities at school and workplace; have group discussion on change and growth for youths.

Evaluation: Points out how the organization of society can affect individual behavior; supported by studies of better integrated societies with high family values having low crime rates, such as Japan and Switzerland; shows how strain can create criminal solutions in anyone; explains both lower-class crime resulting from strain and middle- and upper-class crime. Fails to explain why people choose particular crime patterns and fails to explain violence and senseless acts. Subcultural version shows how conditions of inequality of opportunity can produce frustration and crime; explains violent behavior and destructive acts; indicates how people become involved in different types of crimes. Cohen's version has received inconclusive empirical support; ignores rational profitable delinquency and does not explain middle-class crime. Cloward and Ohlin's version also fails to account for middle-class crime (unless middle classes see selves as relatively deprived) and subcultural specialization argument is contradicted by evidence. Later versions apply to corporate and white-collar crime. Agnew's revised general strain theory has empirical support. Messner and Rosenfeld's institutional anomie theory is gaining support.

10

Capitalism as a Criminogenic Society
Conflict, Marxist, and Radical Theories of Crime

Capitalism is a system of economic production in which power is concentrated in the hands of a few, with the majority existing in a dependency relationship to the powerful. This class-based economic order is maintained by a criminal justice apparatus that serves the interests of the wealthy at the expense of the poor. Those who challenge this system of production are destined for social control, especially if they are seen as a serious threat to the system. Certain minorities form the lower classes but are also considered "dangerous." They are kept in their marginalized status by agencies of law enforcement that use a variety of control practices, one of which is racial profiling. Racial profiling is at the forefront of any critical examination of police practices. The journal *Police Quarterly* (2002) has devoted an entire issue to the topic.

In recent times profiling had become a frowned upon, ignored, denied, and vilified practice. However, since the terrorist attacks on September 11, 2001, profiling has enjoyed increased support. Much like the Japanese Americans who were detained during World War II due solely to their racial profile and perceived threat, the new "ethnic" threat to America—those who came to the United States from the Arab world and are Muslim—are receiving attention. Although ethnic profiling enjoys a strong degree of popular support among the majority of European Americans, its use in law enforcement reflects the way agencies of government reinforce institutionalized social divisions that reflect a threat that these populations pose to its system of production and to the dominant economic and political class.

Clearly racial profiling is nothing new. It began to receive attention following the Civil War in the 1860s when African Americans were the target of increased police attention. This is not just a perception. Research shows that African Americans and Hispanics are stopped more often, searched more often, and issued more tickets than whites (U.S. Bureau of Justice Statistics 2001). The practice continued with the profiles for drug couriers in the 1980s and 1990s and now has shifted toward terrorist threats.

Many people of color feel victimized by this practice and have coined the term "driving while black" (DWB) (Meehan and Ponder 2002, 400). As Smith and Petrocelli noted, "historically, minorities, particularly African Americans, have had physical force used against them or have been arrested or stopped by police at rates exceeding their percentage in the population" (2001, 5). While African Americans are 12 percent of the total population, they are arrested for nearly a third of all crimes. Hispanics are stopped by police even more often than African Americans (Smith and Petrocelli 2001). Law enforcement officials often counter, "well, they commit more crime!" In fact, "many law enforcement officers view racial profiling as an appropriate form of law enforcement" (Barlow and Barlow 2002, 337). The issue is not so black and white, however. Social standing may also play a role. Meehan and Ponder noted that "disparate treatment by the police may not be the product of race alone—the racial and class composition of a neighborhood influences police behavior" (2002, 400). Thus the stage is set for conflict between the two groups and the advocates of each. Surprisingly, there has not been a theoretically driven explanation for racial profiling. After an extensive literature review of research on the topic, Engel, Calnon, and Bernard (2002) found no theoretically informed study. They then proceeded to illustrate how several different theories could be used to explain profiling.

Radical and conflict theorists provide a theoretical explanation, since they are concerned with social inequity, class and racial differences, and the power used by the ruling class through its criminal justice apparatus to impose white supremacist standards on a minority population while claiming that their judgments are neutral, legitimate, and grounded in the Constitution (Schwendinger and Schwendinger 2001). In short, racial profiling is part of the apparatus of mystification of the real power, which results in many people of color being victimized by profiling practices and by the institutionalized discrimination that subordinates people of color and the economically marginalized (Meehan and Ponder 2002, 400).

Conflict, Marxist, and radical theorists consider how the state (government), dominated by political elites and a social structure reflecting a capitalist organization of production, impact human behavior. As the profiling example illustrates, certain disempowered groups are targeted, feel resentment toward, as well as alienation from, a system that excludes them, and eventually solidify in a social or political movement that leads to either social change or crime. Martin Luther King harnessed such resentment and effectively channeled it into social change. Fidel Castro utilized peasant resentment to overthrow the Cuban government.

Radical theorists are also interested in corporate and government crimes because they bring out features of the structural causes of crime that are not immediately apparent when criminologists look at conventional street crime. These theorists suggest that crime is not simply an individual but a societal phenomenon, affecting all levels of society. Their theories reflect how law, crime, and law enforcement are often political acts rooted in the conflict between groups or classes in society. Conflict, Marxist, and radical theorists see the root of crime in the conflict that stems from the inequalities produced by capitalist society (Schwendinger and Schwendinger 2001).

Although some use the terms "conflict," "Marxist," and "radical" interchangeably, others make a clear distinction. Yet "there are many forms of Marxism, and . . . many Marxists disagree with one another" (Matthews 2003, 1). There is no one "radical" or "conflict" view of crime, and "no firm consensus or precise definition of radical criminology, either with respect to its key concepts or its primary theoretical emphasis" (Lynch and Groves 1986, 4). We feel it is useful to differentiate between conflict and Marxist and radical theories based on their different conceptions of inequality (Bohm 1982; Vold and Bernard 1986; Einstadter and Henry 1995).

In general, conflict criminologists draw their analysis from the ideas of the nineteenth-century German sociologists Max Weber (1864–1920) and Georg Simmel (1858–1918). Conflict theorists see inequality based on differences in wealth, status, ideas, religious beliefs, and so forth. These differences result in the formation of interest groups that struggle with each other for power. Some criminologists even reject the need in society for any form of power/control regardless of its basis, since power is seen as the source for difference and domination. As a result, they adopt an anarchistic approach, even rejecting the need for government.

Marxist and radical criminologists draw on the ideas of the German social theorist Karl Marx (1818–1883); they believe that the fundamental conflict is economic. This conflict is between capitalists, or propertied classes (the bourgeois), who own the "means of production" (land, buildings, factories, plants, machines, etc.) and wage earners, or nonpropertied classes, who own only their labor (the ability to work), which they sell to make a living. The result is a class-divided society, with those in the lower classes (wage earners) being exploited by those in the upper classes (owners of capital). Radical theorists argue that the conflict over economic inequality is at the root of all other conflicts in society.

Not only does capitalist society generate vast inequalities of wealth, but those who own the wealth, who control large corporations and financial and

commercial institutions, influence those who political power (former business leaders work for government and former politicians are retained by
corporations). As we saw in Chapter 2, both conflict and radical theorists reject the restricted legal definitions of crime because these take power for
granted. Indeed, "the role of power in the definition of crime is the central
focus of conflict criminology" (Vold and Bernard 1986, 267; Muncie 2000).

Shared Assumptions and Differences: Conflict, Marxist, and Radical Theories

Conflict, Marxist, and radical theorists share a view that humans are active,
creative agents who invest their energy in building the social structure. Conflict theorists see individuals cooperating with like-minded others to form
groups, which then compete in the struggle over resources, ideas, ideologies, and beliefs. There are also similarities between conflict and radical theories over the cause of crime. Each views crime as the result of the economic
and political organization of society. Both conflict and radical views share a
macrolevel perspective. Thus each looks to structural causes of crime in the
conflict within society; most crime is seen as the result of large forces (e.g.,
economic, form of government, etc.) rather than individual pathologies.

Conflict and radical perspectives share a concern with who holds
power and closely examine "law creation, interpretation and enforcement" (Holman and Quinn 1992, 289; Chambliss 1989). Consistent with
their ideas about society, however, conflict theorists see law as a social
control mechanism, a resource and weapon in the struggle for power intended to help those who capture it to maintain or increase that power
(Turk 1969). Conflict theorists also recognize that law has a symbolic role,
publicly representing the social standing of the ideas of those in power
(Gusfield 1963). They argue that groups who have power over others
(whether economic, social, ideological, moral, or religious) typically define which behaviors are criminal and which are not. Thus laws reflect the
values and interests of the dominant group(s). As a result, laws mainly
criminalize crimes of the powerless, leaving harms caused by the powerful (such as corporations and government) as lesser administrative or regulative offenses. Similarly, the powerful organize the system of criminal
justice to benefit those with money. The sanctions given to powerful offenders are usually civil or restitutive in nature. Although severe prison
sentences are given on rare occasions to the powerful who commit exceptional crimes and corporations are sometimes given large fines, the majority of such offenders receive relatively little punishment. For example, the
average corporate fine is the equivalent of $10 for a person earning
$35,000 per year (Ermann and Lundman [1992] 1996, 40).

Despite these similarities, there are also some important differences. Conflict theorists view human nature as amoral rather than good or bad. Marxists and radicals view human nature in a more positive light: People are born with a "perfectible" nature, but forces shape them into imperfect, deviant, and criminal ways. If humans behave badly, therefore, it is not their doing alone, but how their nature is shaped by the social structure, particularly "the ways in which capitalism itself creates the conditions in which crime is likely to occur" (Matthews 2003, 3). Humankind is assumed to be basically good and the structure of society is what created or caused evil people. Marx thus believed human nature is "perfectible," but perfection requires a society that celebrates social connections over individuality.

Marxists and radicals also see humans as social beings who use their energies to transform the world. They are thus purposeful. In the course of transforming the world, they are themselves shaped and formed. As Marx insightfully observed, "Humans are both the producers and products of history" (Young 1981, 295; Marx [1859] 1975); Marx also believed people are shaped more by their society's economic organization than by their own individuality.

Although both versions see the idea of consensus as a myth, their ideas about the nature of conflict differ. Conflict theorists recognize that society is composed of many different groups, which have differing, and often competing, interests, values, and norms. They acknowledge a plethora of interest groups (women vs. men, ethnic group vs. ethnic group, rich vs. poor, liberal versus conservative, Greek students versus non-Greek, etc.) and issues (more government versus less government, anti-abortion versus pro-choice, etc.). Since there are limited resources (both material and social) available in any given society, competition between these different groups for resources inevitably results in conflict—students compete for grades with the other students even if they don't desire to do so.

More conservative conflict theorists (Simmel [1908] 1955; Coser 1956; Dahrendorf 1959) believe the competition among interest groups produces a balance and compromise that can actually prove functional to society; others believe that some groups emerge as dominant and that such domination can be destructive (Vold [1958] 1979). In particular, those who control the resources and those who have authority positions have power in society (Turk 1966, 1969). This is because over time humans in subordinate positions learn to follow those who dominate them.

Based on Marx's analysis, radical theorists offer a more dichotomous view of the sources of conflict rooted in economic inequalities. Those who own and control the "means of production" (capitalists) are in conflict with and control the lives of those who do not—the labor providers (workers). The radical analysis therefore is primarily focused on economic structure and class stratification (Taylor et al. 1973; Quinney 1974), with all other conflicts being an outcome of the basic economic struggle between the capitalist and working classes.

Radical theorists take one of two views. One view believes that the state, and through it the law, represents the machinery of capitalist repression, directly controlling those who challenge the economically powerful (Quinney 1975b, 1977). This is known as the "instrumentalist view" because the state is an instrument of the ruling class: "Instrumentalists see little state autonomy, as the policies of the state are manipulated in favor of the interests of powerful segments of society" (Matthews 2003, 6). The second Marxist view holds that the state (and the law) is an ideological device that mystifies the power of the dominant classes by pretending to be neutral in its protection of individuals, regardless of their power (Young 1981). This is known as the "structuralist" view that sees the state as semiautonomous and exists "to resolve the inherent contradictions of the capitalist system" (Matthews 2003, 6).

Radical criminologists define crime more broadly than do established legal definitions to include all acts that create harm, including those that violate human rights. Consequently, crimes of domination such as "imperialism, racism, capitalism, sexism, and other systems of exploitation" are defined as criminal by those sharing a radical perspective (Platt 1974, 6; Schwendinger and Schwendinger 1970; Quinney and Wildeman 1991; Muncie 2000; Henry and Lanier 1998, 2001).

Methodologically, "radical criminologists are more specific than conflict theorists in their identification of the explanatory variables that presumably account for crime" (Bohm 1982, 566). Radicals look to the political and economic structure of society, whereas conflict theorists consider a much wider basis of stratification as the culprit. Radicals see the capitalist structure as forcing humans into competitive hostility with one another rather than helping people to be cooperative partners. Crime is the outcome of this competition and an expression of the anguish exploitation imposes on the powerless (Engels [1845] 1958; Bonger [1905] 1916). As a result, some crime is also an expression of political protest towards the capitalist system (Taylor et al. 1973), while other crime is the result of greed. Let us now explore these differences in more detail, first by examining conflict criminology.

The Roots of Conflict Criminology

Social conflict is present in all societies and occurs at all levels, from individuals to groups. It has been defined as "a struggle over values or claims to status, power, and scarce resources, in which the aims of the conflicting parties are not only to gain the desired values but also to neutralize, injure, or eliminate their rivals" (Coser 1968, 232). In Chapters 2 and 8, we discussed Sellin's (1938) ideas of culture conflict and saw that culture conflict is an integral part of conflict theory's intellectual roots. Here, we are concerned with the ideas of those who look at crime as resulting from structural rather than cultural differences, although the two are clearly interrelated (see Ferrell 2003). Early ideas about broad notions of structural conflict can be found in the work of Max Weber.

Weber's Class, Status, and Party

Max Weber (1864–1920), a German lawyer and sociologist, is considered one of the three founders of sociology and a major contributor to the understanding of the sources of conflict. At age thirty-four, he suffered acute depression that lasted for five years. Weber did not present a theory of crime causation, but he did identify the sources of conflict.

Weber's discussion of conflict emerges in his analysis of the role played by charismatic leaders in the transition from traditional society to modern capitalist society (Weber [1922] 1966). Weber identified three important dimensions of inequality: (1) power, represented by party; (2) wealth, which relates to economic position, represented by class; and (3) prestige, which is attached to those in high-status groups. Conflict, according to Weber, is most likely to occur when these three major kinds of stratification coincide—when those who have wealth also have status and power. Conflict is also likely when only a few are allowed access to positions of privilege or when social mobility to these positions is highly restricted. Such a merger produces tension and resentment among those without power, prestige, and wealth who engage in conflict with the privileged group.

Those excluded also become receptive to charismatic leaders who organize conflict groups to challenge traditional authority (Turner 1986, 146–149). This new challenge may simply create another form of traditional authority, thereby producing a new privileged group. This depends on whether a rational-legal bureaucratic system is instituted or not.

A rational system establishes authority based on formal rules applied equally to all without taking account of privilege and allows social mobility based on performance and ability. According to Weber, the increasing rationalization of society prevents conflict by freeing the individual to pursue personal goals, but this comes at a price: "Rationalization of life brings individuals a new freedom from domination by religious dogmatism, community, class, and other traditional forces; but in their place it creates a new kind of domination by impersonal economic forces, such as markets and corporate bureaucracies, and by the vast administrative apparatus of the ever-expanding state" (Turner 1986, 149).

Simmel's Functions of Group Conflict

Like his friend Max Weber, Georg Simmel (1858–1918) was a German sociologist, but he was far more optimistic about the nature of modern society and the role of conflict. For most of his life, he taught at the University of Berlin, becoming a professor only four years before his death. Simmel was one of the first sociologists to explain conflict as a common and stable form of interaction. Conflict to Simmel was one of several patterns of reciprocal relations, along with competition and cooperation, that underpin complex social behavior. Unlike Weber, Simmel looked at the interrelationships between individual meanings attributed to social action and the transpersonal meanings that people construct. His major contribution to conflict theory was a short but influential essay in which he argued that conflict is both inevitable and functional in its ability to resolve contradictions and leads to a unity of the systemic whole (Simmel [1908] 1955). Simmel believed that biological differences were natural and were exacerbated by differences of interest but could also be placated by harmonious relations. Simmel believed that conflict was a variable phenomenon and that some levels of less violent conflict served a functional "tension-reducing" process that "promoted the solidarity, integration and orderly change of systems" (Turner 1986, 140). Simmel saw violent conflict occurring where different groups have a high degree of harmony, emotional involvement, and solidarity among their members and where the nature of conflict is beyond the members' individual interests. The violent actions of some right-to-life groups who define abortion as murder provide a clear contemporary crime illustration. Recently caught (June 2003) abortion clinic bomber Eric Rudolph provides an example of how conflicting ideas can lead to homicidal actions. But the history of the abortion conflict seems to undermine another of Simmel's arguments: that as specific goals of interest groups become clarified, violence is replaced by other (political) means to achieve the same ends.

Dahrendorf's Dialectical Conflict Perspective

Ralf Dahrendorf, a sociologist who taught at the University of Hamburg and Stanford University and later became director of the London School of Economics, went into politics and was named a British lord. In a critique of functionalism, which he saw as utopian and unrealistic, Dahrendorf (1959) presented a "pluralistic" version of conflict in which he showed two faces of society, both consensus and conflict, existing in a dialectical relationship. This is based on Hegel's notion that a society produces contradictions (seen here as conflicts between opposing forces) whose resolution results in a new organization different from its original (seen here as consensus) (Balkan et al. 1980, 336).

By examining conflict between economic interest groups and a variety of groups that compete for authority, Dahrendorf incorporated Weberian ideas, although some say as a result he ultimately reproduces a conservative-consensus perspective (Taylor et al. 1973, 238; Turner 1986). Dahrendorf describes groups as having an organization of social roles whereby some people exercise power over others whom they can coerce to conform. Thus people exist in relations of domination (possessing authority) and subordination (subject to authority). But these relations of domination and subjugation need not mean people are totally dominated because they may hold different positions in different groups or organizations: "Since domination in industry does not necessarily involve domination in the State or a church, or other associations, total societies can present a picture of a plurality of dominant (and conversely, subjected) aggregates" (Dahrendorf 1959, 171). Dahrendorf argued that such power relationships become accepted by members as legitimate authority (1958, 1959). Simultaneously, power and authority are seen as resources to be won and over which subgroups within the organization fight. Those who acquire power coerce groups without power to conform. This creates two basic types of social groups, each contesting authority: the rulers and the ruled, the former trying to preserve their power, the latter trying to redistribute it. Should those who are dominated take control, the whole cycle repeats, resulting in further polarization around new interests, followed by further conflict and resolution (Dahrendorf's dialectical process of social change). Thus conflict is continually coming and going as conflicting groups first win control and then stabilize before again reverting into conflictual relations.

For Dahrendorf, conflict is not a matter of a particular underlying inequality of economic interests but can be based on any kind of difference. For him, the existence of inequality is inevitable because humans evaluate each other as different rather than equal. Therefore, some will always be dominant over others in terms of a rank-ordered social status. Inequality, then, is a function of organizational processes that produce legitimate authority roles of domination and subordination. Like some other founding conflict theorists, Dahrendorf did not specifically address crime, but his ideas greatly influenced later conflict criminologists, particularly Austin Turk, as we shall see later.

Vold's Group Conflict Theory

George Vold (1895–1967) was one of the first criminologists to systematically apply the conflict ideas presented by Weber, Simmel, and Dahrendorf to the study of crime. Vold, who taught at the University of Minnesota and was a contemporary of Dahrendorf, published his highly respected *Theoretical Criminology* in 1958. Later editions of this book are still much in use today and the work has become a standard text on criminological theory (Vold [1958] 1979; Vold and Bernard 1986; Vold, Bernard, and Snipes 1998). Vold was especially influenced by the work of Simmel. He presented a view of certain crimes being caused by conflict and argued that it was absurd to explain these acts by individual-level theories. He pointed out that humans are group-involved beings and that society is a continuity of group interaction "of moves and countermoves, of checks and cross-checks" (Vold [1958] 1979, 283). Society exists in a state of equilibrium and relative stability, not because of consensus among all its members but because of "the adjustment, one to another of the many groups of varying strengths and of different interests" (Vold [1958] 1979, 284), in other words, conflict between rival groups. Vold argued that groups come into conflict because of overlapping interests and encroachments over territory that lead to competition. Group members must protect against the danger of being taken over or replaced. Members of groups are invested in defensive activity, which they express through acts of identification, loyalty, and self-sacrifice, each intensified by conflict. In the conflict between groups, the weak are generally overwhelmed and absorbed, whereas the strong may increase their power, be vanquished, or meet with compromise.

Applying these ideas to crime, Vold argued that in the conflict between groups each seeks the support of the state to defend its rights and protect its interests, with the result that "the whole political process of law making, law breaking, and law enforcement directly reflects deep-seated and fundamental conflicts between interest groups and their more general struggles for the control of the police power of the state" (Vold [1958] 1979, 288). Those who win dominate the policies that define crime. With regard to crime, Vold noted a prevalence of group involvement, from organized crime to delinquent gangs, each fighting for turf, markets, and social honor in ways that are in conflict with those of organized society.

The group also defines member behavior as acceptable, even honorable. Vold described how much criminal activity is a product of the clash of interests between groups and their members' attempts to defend against challenge to their control. Obvious examples are violence as a result of disrespect or turf infringements by members of different gangs, violence between rival organized drug distribution networks, and violence protesting dominant systems of justice, as in the 1990s Los Angeles race riots following the police beating of the African American Rodney King or the more recent violence against alleged police brutality in Cincinnati, Ohio, (2002, 2004) and Benton Harbor, Michigan (2003). This latter kind of protest represents a more general case of crime as a political expression against the dominant groups in society. Vold concluded, "There are many situations in which criminality is the normal, natural response of normal, natural human beings struggling in understandably normal situations for the maintenance of the way of life to which they stand committed" (Vold [1958] 1979, 296).

Contemporary Conflict Criminology

Since Dahrendorf and Vold, others have sought to develop and extend the ideas of these founding conflict theorists to crime and the law (Box [1971] 1981; Hills 1971; Chambliss and Seidman [1971] 1982; Krisberg 1975; Pepinski 1976; Reiman [1979] 1995; Schwendinger and Schwendinger 2001). Here we focus on two illustrative contributors: Austin Turk (1969), whose ideas closely follow those of Dahrendorf, and Richard Quinney (1970), whose theory was more derived from Vold's approach. We then look at anarchist criminology as an extension of conflict theory.

Turk and the Criminalization of Resisting Subordinates

Austin Turk's major contribution to conflict criminology, *Criminality and the Legal Order* (1969), was deeply indebted to Dahrendorf's dialectical conflict theory of society. Turk (1966, 1969) attempted to show how people in subordinate positions of authority are subject to the values, standards, and laws of those in authority positions. Unless the subordinates learn to be deferential to authority, their behaviors will be defined as criminal and they will be given the status of criminals. Turk argued that people continually learn to interact with each other as holders of superior or inferior social status. The learning is never complete or stabilized but is in constant adjustment and conflict because of individual differences. Turk defined the norms learned in this process as norms of domination and norms of deference. He argued that the extent to which a person relates to norms of domination is related to sociocultural factors such as age, race, and gender. "Norm resisters" are relatively unsophisticated in the "knowledge of patterns in the behavior of others which is used in attempts to manipulate them" (1966, 348). For Turk, crimes are the acts of those who have not been "conditioned to accept as a fact of life that authorities must be reckoned with" and it is such conditioning that underlies social order in all societies (1969, 44).

Turk identified the conditions that make conflict between authorities and subjects over different norms and values more likely: (1) when cultural values and social actions of authorities are in close agreement and a similar congruence exists in the case of subjects, (2) when authorities and subjects are organized, and (3) when authorities or subjects are less sophisticated. He then described the conditions under which conflict will lead to people being criminalized. Again three major factors are involved: (1) when law enforcers and the courts agree on the serious nature of the offenses, (2) when there is a large power differential between enforcers and resisters, and (3) when conflict moves designed at imposing norms or resisting their imposition are unrealistic. The Schwendingers (2001) use student protest and the government's response as an excellent illustration of this argument.

In his later work, Turk (1976 1982) suggested that over time the authority–subject relationship becomes less coercive and more automatic, as new generations of people are born into the existing set of laws, rules, and definitions of reality, which they are less likely to contest.

Quinney's Social Reality of Crime

A contemporary of Austin Turk's in the University of Wisconsin sociology department, Richard Quinney has been one of the most prolific critical theorists in criminology. Although beginning as a functionalist in the anomie/strain mold, Quinney metamorphosed through interactionism, social constructionism, conflict theory, and instrumental and structural Marxist theory and eventually reached a spiritualist-informed peacemaking approach (discussed in the next chapter). During each phase, he wrote one or more passionately committed books on the perspective (Martin et al. 1990). His contribution to conflict sociology came with his 1970 book *The Social Reality of Crime*. Drawing on several of the conflict traditions discussed previously, particularly Simmel's and Vold's, Quinney saw humans as rational, purposeful actors subject to an unequal distribution of power that produces inevitable conflict. This conflict is between competing groups or "segments" of society, whose members' actions are designed to maintain or advance their position (Quinney 1970, 8–14).

Segments of society share norms, values, and ideology, but unlike Vold's interest groups, they need not be organized (Vold [1958] 1979, 302). Those who have the power to shape public policy act through authorized agents in society (such as legislators and judges) to formulate definitions of crime that contain, or control, the behaviors of members of those segments with whom they are in conflict. Recall our opening discussion of racial profiling. The conflict need not be organized political struggle but can consist of individual acts of resistance by members of powerless segments. Criminalization is done with a view to maintain the current balance of power or increase a segment's position of control.

Definitions of crime are not merely legislated but become part of the public psyche and popular culture as a result of their dissemination through the mass media. In other words, some rather than other meanings of a crime have social reality because they are defined, illustrated, elaborated, and sensationalized in the media. For example, bank robbers are demonized as violent criminals whereas corporate criminals are presented as engaging in "financial irregularities."

Quinney further argued that criminal definitions are then applied by the authorized agents (police, judges) of those segments of society having power. This is done in relation to the degree of threat that the powerful perceive from the powerless and in proportion to the degree of visibility of their crime(s). Thus crimes most visible and most threatening to the powerful are those most subject to criminal processing. In response, those who are relatively powerless develop patterns of behavior in relation to the definitions imposed on them (Quinney 1970, 15–23). For example, African Americans may avoid taking shortcuts through affluent white neighborhoods because they fear being stopped, searched, and ticketed. From this, Quinney concluded that the social reality of crime in a politically organized society is a political act designed to protect and perpetuate a particular set of interests over others.

We conclude the review of conflict theory by considering the extreme suggestion that power is the cause of conflict and thereby of crime. This implies that the only solution to crime is to remove the conflict, which means removing all sources of power. This is precisely the position taken by anarchist criminology.

Anarchist Criminology as a Version of Conflict Theory

The anarchist theory argues that crime is caused by structures of power and domination. Thus the anarchist criminologist spends more time trying to replace structures of power than developing analyses of how these actually cause crime.

Anarchy means a society without rulers. It is not a society without order, although that is often assumed in the pejorative use of the term. Anarchism refers to those who oppose organizational and institutional authority. It has its intellectual roots in the nineteenth-century writings of Pierre-Joseph Proudhon (1809–1865), Mikhail Bakunin (1814–1876), and P'etr Kropotkin (1842–1921) (Woodcock 1963, 1977). Proudhon believed that authority and power in any form are oppressive and that they are rooted in the private ownership of property, which he saw as theft. Bakunin, like Proudhon, vehemently opposed Karl Marx's communism, believing that his ideas for a dictatorship of the proletariat would simply result in another form of domination and re-create the state in a new form (history has provided support for this view). He argued that privilege makes humanity depraved and can only be removed by destroying all forms of hierarchy. Kropotkin demonstrated, in contrast to Darwin, that successful societies are founded on cooperation and mutual aid rather than competition and that the government is unnecessary and destructive. These anarchists take the view that cooperative interactive relations are a natural human form that will emerge, provided people are allowed to engage in free and open interaction. Structures of power, whatever their form, are based on inequality and hierarchy, which create conflict and destroy the freedom necessary for constructive cooperation. More recently, these ideas have been applied to criminology through the works of Larry Tifft, Dennis Sullivan, Hal Pepinsky, and Jeff Ferrell.

Anarchist criminologists (Pepinsky 1978; Tifft and Sullivan 1980; Ferrell 1994) believe that hierarchical systems of authority and domination should be opposed. As Ferrell (1994) argued, nothing is more formidable than the unchallenged supremacy of centralized authority structures that feed off of divisions of class, gender, and race. Recent anarchist criminology relates crime as a meaningful activity of resistance to both its construction in social interaction and "its larger construction through processes of political and economic authority" (Ferrell 1994, 163). Anything that fragments the state from its seamless hierarchies of authority and power is desirable. Thus anarchists believe existing structures of domination should be replaced by a "fragmented and decentered pluralism" that "celebrates multiple interpretations and styles" (Ferrell 1994, 163). Like the postmodernists we examine in chapter 12, anarchists believe that knowledge and information is a structure of domination to be discredited and replaced by embracing "particularity and disorder."

State justice should be replaced by a decentralized system of negotiated, face-to-face justice in which all members of society participate and share their decisions (Wieck 1978; Tifft 1979, 397), a system of "collective negotiation as a means of problem solving" (Ferrell 1994, 162). This is designed to bring the individual to accept responsibility for his or her behavior by reminding offenders of their connectedness to other members of the society. The aim is to restore the wholeness of social existence to the collective after it has been breached by a person's failure to accept responsibility and connectedness. In the anarchist view, crime and deviance may be no more than indicators of difference. Such a view demands an "anti-authoritarian justice" that "would entail respect for alternative interpretations of reality" but would oppose "any attempt to destroy, suppress, or impose particular realities" (Ryan and Ferrell 1986, 193) and would encourage "unresolved ambiguities of meaning" (Ferrell 1994, 163). Clearly, the logic of the anarchist criminologist's position is that if power is the source of domination and thereby the source of crime, it is power and structures of power that should be removed, as we shall see below in looking at policy implications of conflict theorists.

Limitations of Conflict Theory

Conflict theory has been criticized on a number of grounds, some coming from conflict theorists themselves. For example, Quinney's theory has been criticized both by others (Taylor et al. 1973) and by himself (Quinney 1974). One primary criticism is that the theory is overly pluralistic and fails to acknowledge that powerful segments are actually economically powerful classes. Taylor and colleagues (1973, 266) criticized Turk for accepting "the retrenchment of existing orders of domination and repression" and criticized conflict theory generally for being limited to exposing ruling-class interests in the criminal justice system while ignoring how law and the crimes of the poor and rich are connected to the structure of capitalism. As Lynch and Groves (1986, 40) pointed out, in contrast to the pluralistic ideas of conflict theorists, radicals "emphasize structured inequalities as they relate to the distribution of wealth and power in capitalist society, and hence define power in terms of class affiliation, rather than diffuse interest groups or segments."

In spite of these criticisms, one recent commentator points out that "there is a considerable body of research supporting the conflict view. Criminologists routinely have found evidence that measures of social inequality, such as income level, deteriorated living conditions, and relative economic deprivation are highly associated with crime rates" (Siegel 2004, 257).

Policy Implications

The policies advocated by conflict theorists range from reform to transformation, and in their anarchist version they advocate revolution. Of all the conflict theorists, Austin Turk has most clearly detailed the changes to criminal justice that remain consistent with the essence of conflict theory. With regard to policy, Turk is to be commended for at least specifying the concrete measures about which most conflict and radical theorists are silent. In a 1995 paper, "Transformation Versus Revolution and Reformism: Policy Implications of Conflict Theory," Turk identified five general principles on which he based his program for structural transformation: (1) policymaking is a political process aimed at minimizing human casualties, not merely the application of technical fixes; (2) reducing crime and criminalization requires changing structural relationships, not merely persons; (3) policies must fit within a broad strategy of change rather than being piecemeal programs and reforms; (4) policy should recognize "field controls" emphasizing environmental changes rather than "command" proclamations and moral invectives and threatening punishment; and (5) policy should aim for a more viable rather than a more docile society (Turk 1995, 18–21). Based on these five principles, Turk identified eleven concrete measures to reduce crime, and we have added examples that move toward his suggested measures:

1. Establish a public information resource center on crime and justice to organize research favoring structural transformation. For example, the establishment of the National Center for Research on White Collar Crime in West Virginia.

2. Establish gun control nationwide. For example, lawsuits against gun manufacturers for making dangerous products, which is likely to result in a form of gun control.
3. Abolish capital punishment. For example, some states, such as Michigan, do not have the death penalty, and others have it but don't use it.
4. Indefinitely incarcerate heinous violent offenders. For example, three-strikes laws and truth in sentencing have made this a reality.
5. Stop building prisons. For example, declining state budgets and shorter sentences for less serious offenders during the early twenty-first century made this a reality.
6. Create paid part-time community service jobs for all young people. For example, Peace Corps.
7. Decriminalize drug possession and use, returning control to medical authorities. For example, marijuana possession has been made legal and treatment options, in some cases, increasingly are preferred over prison for drug offenders.
8. Decriminalize all consensual sexual activities. For example, the Supreme Court upheld sodomy as legal in the privacy of the home.
9. Decriminalize all forms of recreational gambling. For example, increasingly liberal laws on gambling as many states now allow casinos and run lotteries.
10. Declare a moratorium on all mandatory sentencing. For example, some states, such as Michigan, have repealed mandatory sentencing laws.
11. Establish community policing and community development. For example, most police agencies have community policing. (Abridged from Turk 1995, 21–24)

In addition, Turk proposed more radical and less likely policies including the establishment of national commissions to oversee every level of government, meet the health and economic needs of families, promote educational excellence, develop communities, promote progressive and eliminate regressive taxation, and encourage socially conscious economic and technological development. These policy proposals and practices are designed to eliminate the structural barriers "that pit classes and groups against one another" and to minimize "the conflicts among them" (Turk 1995, 26). However, if Turk's version of radical reform sounds unlikely, even more so are the ideas behind anarchist calls to abolish the state.

There are similarities between the anarchist call to dismantle the state and its system of justice and the more limited calls of radical abolitionists that focus on dismantling penal institutions as a way of dealing with crime. Abolitionism has its roots in the criminology of the Norwegians Thomas Mathiesen (1974, 1986) and Nils Christie (1977, 1981) and, more recently, in the work of the Dutch criminologists Herman Bianchi and Rene van Swaaningen (1986) and Willem de Haan (1990). Abolitionism is rooted in the notion that punishment is never justified. It is a movement not merely to reform prisons but to get rid of them entirely and replace them with community controls and community treatment. Not only are prisons seen to fail to control crime and fail to prevent recidivism, but they are viewed as an inhumane mechanism used mainly for controlling the least productive members of the labor force. Abolitionists point out that the "cultural values embedded in the conception of prisons reflect a social ethos of violence and degradation. When prisons are expanded, so too are negative cultural values symbolizing acceptable strategies for resolving interpersonal conflict" (Thomas and Boehlefeld 1991, 242).

For abolitionists, social control should not be about inflicting pain but reducing pain. To achieve this, it should be decentralized and broken up into democratic community control and new concepts such as "redress" should be adopted (de Haan 1990). These concepts are based on redefining crimes as undesirable events, problems to be solved. For example, Knopp (1991) points to the complete failure of the current system of punishment and argues for a system of "restorative justice" (see also Chapters 9 and 12) founded "on social and economic justice and on concern and respect for all its victims and victimizers, a new system based on remedies and restoration rather than on prison, punishment and victim neglect, a system rooted in the concept of a caring community" (Knopp 1991, 183).

Like anarchism, abolitionism has been criticized, even by sympathizers, for its romantic idealism, lack of conceptual clarity, failure to develop a well-grounded theoretical analysis of its opposition to punishment, and the absence of concrete practical strategies for dealing with dangerous offenders (Thomas and Boehlefeld 1991).

Rooted in a similar humanistic concern, some of the founders of conflict theory, Richard Quinney and Hal Pepinsky, and the founders of anarchist criminology, Dennis Sullivan and Larry Tifft, have gone on to develop one of the most promising new developments in critical criminology through their advocacy for peacemaking criminology and restorative justice, which we consider in Chapter 12.

Before examining these ideas and those of other critical criminologies, let us first see if Marxist and radical theory has something further to offer.

The Roots of Radical Theory: Marx's Analysis of Capitalist Society

The German Jewish philosopher, sociologist, and historian Karl Marx (1818–1883) is one of the most influential social thinkers of all time. Entire governments and social systems have been developed from his ideas. Marxist theory has also been one of the major frameworks of study in all the social sciences. It is therefore surprising for students to learn that Marx wrote very little about crime! Marx and his colleague, the cotton mill owner Friedrich Engels (1820–1895), wrote about the economic class conflict that exists in capitalist societies and, they believed, would ultimately result in the downfall of capitalism. Their analysis was based on the concept of *historical materialism*, which is a method of study and explanation for understanding how past empirical events shape future social systems, and in turn shape the actions of people within them. Unlike the German philosophical idealist Georg Hegel (1770–1831), who believed that humans created the world from their own thoughts and ideas, Marx and Engels adopted the opposite, materialist view that human consciousness was created by the concrete conditions of productive work (labor). But Marx's notion of materialism was not the traditional one that saw humans laboring as isolated individuals but a new "historical" materialism that recognized the social relations of productive activity in different historical eras (Carver 1987, 105). Thus, in one of Marx's most frequently quoted passages, he argued:

> In the social production of their existence [hu]men[s] inevitably enter into definite relations, which are independent of their will, namely relations of production appropriate to a given stage of development of their material forces of production. The totality of these relations of production constitutes the economic structure of society, the real foundation, on which arises a legal and political superstructure and to which correspond definite forms of social consciousness. The mode of production of material life conditions the general character of the social, political, and intellectual life. It is not the consciousness of [hu]men[s] that determines their existence, but their social existence that determines their consciousness. At a certain stage of development, the material productive forces of society come into conflict with the existing relations of production. . . . Then begins an era of social revolution. (Marx [1859] 1975, 425–426)

Marx argued that different historical periods typically have a dominant or characteristic mode of production (e.g., slavery, feudalism, capitalism, socialism). This is a particular combination of the forces or means of production (e.g., technology, resources, tools, energy, knowledge, and skills) and the relations of production that compose "the network of social roles encompassing the use and ownership of productive forces and of the products that emerge" (e.g., employer, worker, investor, dependent) (Carver 1987, 109). Curran and Renzetti helpfully translate this nineteenth-century terminology: People "make a living" through a productive process that we call the economy. Economies can be of different types in different periods of history depending on the resources, technology, and environment in which they operate and the relationships they enter into in order to do productive work. (We are now shifting from a service-based economy to an information-based economy that is referred to as "postindustrial," just as the economy previously went from agricultural to industrial to service.) The important point Marx makes is that "people do not make their living in isolation, but rather in association with other people. . . . The production process is not just physical or material, it is also social" (1994, 25).

According to Marx, throughout history the relations of production have been class relations and the history of existing society is a history of class conflict. In capitalist society, these social relations exist between owners of the means of production and those who only own their labor. Conflict is rooted in the contradictions of the capitalist system, which at its heart is a system of economic exploitation. One simplistic, yet insightful summary of this conflict is that it is "inherent in the nature of social arrangements under capitalism, for it was capitalism that generated the vast differences in interests and capitalism that gave the few at the top so much power over the many at the bottom" (Lilly et al. [1989] 1995, 134). Class conflict is based on the inequality of wealth whereby those capitalists who own the means of production (capital, plants, equipment, machinery) exploit workers who own their labor, which they must sell to capitalists for a wage in order to make a living. The providers of labor, whom Marx called the proletariat, sell their labor to the capitalists, who prosper through paying the laborers less than the value of their work and keep the difference as profit.

To enable profit to be made, it is necessary to keep wage levels low. This is achieved by retaining a "surplus population" of unemployed to be drawn on whenever the competition between employers increases the cost they have to pay for workers. This surplus population or *lumpen proletariat*, as Marx described them, occupies the lowest strata of society: underemployed or unemployed persons who do not contribute to society in any meaningful way other than as a reserve source of labor should capitalist business require it (Lynch and Groves 1986, 10). Capitalism's need for keeping a reserve labor force that will gladly work for low, rather than no, wages also produces the contradiction of poverty, disease, and social problems as these people struggle to survive on very little. To live, some of the lumpen proletariat devise nefarious and tenuous means, including begging, prostitution, gambling, and theft. They thus form "criminal classes" that, while necessary, are seen as a danger and a threat to the capitalist system. From this point of view, crime is an inevitable product of the inherent contradictions of capitalism.

It may be asked, why do the masses of underemployed remain complacent? Why don't they riot against the capitalist system? For that matter, why don't exploited workers strike or revolt if they are so exploited? On many occasions they did just that but were suppressed by police. For Marx, one answer was ideology, which among other meanings "is a process whereby beliefs, deriving from real social relationships, hide or mask the precise nature of such relationships . . . masking from exploited classes the nature of their oppression and its precise source" (Beirne and Messerschmidt [1991, 342] 1995). Marx described this as false consciousness and said it results in part from capitalist society's superstructure. One's awareness or consciousness is shaped in a way that is consistent with one's class position. Institutions of society's superstructure (i.e., political institutions, legal institutions, church, educational system) instill into people certain values and ideas. For example, most religions teach that it is good to be humble and accept your position in life because you will be rewarded in the afterlife. Marx called religion the "opium of the masses" ([1844] 1975, 175) for this reason. Education in capitalist societies stresses delayed gratification and hard work as the means to monetary and emotional reward. One of the most important ideological components of the superstructure is provided by law.

The capitalist system of law, "bourgeois legality," as a part of the superstructure, reflects the particular mode of production of capitalist society. Bourgeois law serves the capitalist power holders, or *bourgeoisie*, who use it and other means to retain or increase their power and control. This is not used simply as a coercive instrument of power but as ideological domination in which workers are both controlled and defined by law. People are simultaneously "protected" by law from the dangerous classes and from extreme excesses of exploitation created by the capitalist system. Law therefore controls by the assent of the majority. As Young pointed out, state law under capitalism exists in a dual relation. It limits excessive exploitation but allows the system of exploitation to remain, it controls all of the population but exercises greater control over some classes than others, and it provides the freedom for the worker to sell his or her labor while preventing the worker from owning the means of production (1981, 299).

In addition to the crimes committed by the lowest strata, Marx and Engels also recognized that the capitalist system of production was criminogenic (crime prone) overall because of the way it impoverished all those within it. One way it does this is through alienation. According to Marx ([1844] 1975), alienation refers to the way the capitalist system of production separates and isolates humans from their work, its products, each other, and themselves. It estranges (separates) them from (1) the products of their labor since they only contribute to a part of the production process, the outcome or products of which they have no ownership or control over (the Harley Davidson company recognized this and now has a group of three workers completely build each of its Sportster model motorcycles); (2) their own work process, which loses all personal ownership and intrinsic worth as it is sold to owners and carried out under their control; (3) their own unique creativity and intellectual possibilities, which are lost to the instrumental purpose of work; and (4) other workers and capitalists, with whom they are set in conflict and competition. Thus workers in a capitalist society "in their alienation from the product of their labor, from their capacity to freely direct their own activities, from their own interests and talents, from others and from human solidarity—are alienated from their deepest human needs, that is, their needs for self-determination and self-realization" (Bender 1986, 3). This impoverishment by capitalism renders humans "worthless." Through the alienated work process they learn to view one another as isolated individuals and potential enemies rather than social beings with mutual interests (Jaggar 1983, 58). This leads to a lack of human care and concern for others. Alienation therefore makes the harm of crime more tolerable to the society and to those who may offend.

Engels argued that crime also emerged as a reflection of the inherent strains and pressures capitalism creates (Engels [1845] 1958). One way the conditions of crime are created by the capitalist system is through its use of technology. As technology is improved and production is made more efficient, there is less need for workers and they are replaced by machines, a process that intensifies their feelings of worthlessness.

Another way criminogenic conditions are generated is from capitalist competition, which serves to further disempower members of the working class since they must "not only compete with the capitalist over working conditions, but are forced to compete with each other for a limited number of jobs and a limited livelihood. Consequently, Engels viewed crime as the result of competition over scarce resources" (Lynch and Groves 1986, 52). Engels viewed crime as a result of the brutalization, impoverishment, and dehumanization of workers by the capitalist system. They turn to crime because capitalism undermines their morality to resist temptation; crime is an expression of their contempt for the system that impoverishes them and an exercise in retaliatory justice. As Engels pointed out, when everyone looks to his or her own interests and fights only for him- or herself, whether "he [or she] injures . . . declared enemies is simply a matter of selfish calculation as to whether such action would be to his [or her] advantage or not. . . . In short, everyone sees in [his or her] neighbor a rival to be elbowed aside, or at best a victim to be exploited for [his or her] own ends" (Engels [1845] 1958, 145–146).

Finally, Marx and Engels also saw crime, like any other activity, as sustained and exploited by the capitalist system while at the same time being a productive aspect of it. Marx pointed out that in addition to the ideological function, crime actually served those who live parasitically off the crime industry: "The criminal produces not only crime but also the criminal law . . . the professor who delivers lectures on this criminal law, and even the inevitable text-book in which the professor presents his lectures. . . . The criminal produces the whole apparatus of the police and criminal justice, detectives, judges, executioners, juries, etc." (Marx [1862] 1964, 158–160). The increasing numbers of students majoring in criminal justice programs is further evidence of this insight, as is the huge numbers of people employed by the criminal justice apparatus, especially in the United States.

Marx and Engels' criminological contribution was, as we have noted, tangential to their analysis of the capitalist system. The first systematic Marxist consideration of crime was attempted by the Dutch criminologist Willem Bonger.

Bonger's Criminality and Economic Conditions

Willem Bonger (1876–1940) built on Marx's and particularly Engels' concern about the impoverishment that capitalism brings to society. This impoverishment sets the economic and social conditions for crime. But whereas Marx and Engels focused on the conditions conducive to working-class crime, Bonger extended the analysis to include crime at all levels of society. This included crime among the capitalist classes and a wide range of other crimes, including sex offenses, crimes of vengeance, and political crimes. Bonger saw crimes as the acting out of a "criminal thought." People are more likely to have criminal thoughts when a society promotes egoism rather than altruism. In a notion somewhat reminiscent of Durkheim's anomie theory, Bonger suggested that altruism was a predominant theme in traditional precapitalist societies. In these societies, the process, shared conditions, and problems of living promoted a sense of community among the people, "a uniformity of interest" that "obliged them to aid one another in the difficult and uninterrupted struggle for existence" (Bonger [1905] 1916, 35). The result of altruism was to suppress the criminal thought. The change in the mode of production to capitalism brought with it not only the misery of impoverishment, a condition that was demoralizing and dehumanizing, but it also promoted egoism, which for Bonger meant individual greed, selfishness, and fervent excitement. The climate of egoism favors the criminal thought. The fragmentation of community brought by the capitalist system has a diminished capacity to curtail this destructive thought. The capitalist celebration of egoism is not reflected in official crime rates, argued Bonger, because the upper economic classes determine the shape of the criminal law to legalize the crimes of the rich and criminalize those of the poor.

In spite of Bonger's attempt to bring Marx's work alive in criminology, his ideas and those of Marxism generally did little to stimulate criminologists until the advent of radical criminology some sixty-five years later.

Contemporary Radical Criminology

In revising Marxist criminology in the 1970s, radical criminologists such as Richard Quinney, William Chambliss, Steven Spitzer, Raymond Michalowski, Ian Taylor, Paul Walton, and Jock Young developed a composite critique of the criminogenic nature of capitalist society that has continuities with earlier conflict and Marxist theories. The reason for the reappearance of radical criminology cannot be divorced from the historical period of growing social conflict and unrest.

The 1960s were a turbulent era in the United States. Radicals prospered in the climate of revolution and change. There were many legitimate social grievances, such as the war in Vietnam, the sexual revolution, the civil rights movement, the women's movement, and so on. University faculty members and students at Berkeley, California, were at the forefront of the protest movement. The most notable Marxist movement in criminology occurred at the University of California at Berkeley. Many U.S. Marxists and radicals were taught there or served as faculty members. Herman and Julia Schwendinger have written on this and are currently preparing a book on the topic. Since radicals advocate social change and action (praxis) rather than just passive empirical observation and measurement (like most positivist criminologists), they actively and aggressively spearheaded a social movement. It is not insignificant, then, that funding for the School of Criminology was eliminated by Governor Ronald Reagan as a consequence of their ideas. The demise of the school for political reasons is a fascinating story and illustrates several principles (or lack thereof), such as academic freedom (see Geis 1995). The abolition of this academic program by the state of California was interpreted by some as confirmation of these critical arguments that the state supports the interest of capitalists. By way of a summary, let us look at the basic ideas of these contemporary radical theorists.

Central Themes of Radical Criminology

Radical criminologists reject individual-level theories of crime that place humans apart from their society and thereby fail to take account of the structural context of human action. They also reject reformist structural-functionalist theories that inadequately account for capitalism's criminogenic nature. The primary impetus here came in the book *The New Criminology* by the British criminologists Ian Taylor, Paul Walton, and Jock Young (1973), which was eventually translated into twenty languages. This devastating criticism of all previous "positivist" criminology and even the early "interpretive" and conflict criminology marked a resurgence of radical Marxist criminology. The authors called for a "new" criminology adequate for grasping the connection between the capitalist "society as a totality," its system of inequality, the class conflict within it, the crime resulting from this conflict, and the social reaction to crime from its structures of power expressed in law (1973, 278).

They argued that, caught in a "dialectic of control and resistance to control," humans are simultaneously "creatures and the creators of a constraining structure of power, authority and interest" in which they weave a diverse range of responses, consciously making choices "freely chosen albeit within a range of limited alternatives" (Taylor et al. 1973, 248). A new criminology must account for this duality of freedom and constraint, not by separating humans from the political economy that forms the social structure but by bringing the parts together that form the dynamic social whole. As these authors acknowledged, "This 'new criminology' will in fact be an old criminology, in that it will face the same problems that were faced by the classical theorists" (1973, 278). Indeed, for this reason, "It is perhaps more accurate to refer to the emergence of radical criminology as a renaissance rather than a 'New Criminology'" (Bohm 1982, 569). Together, these authors did not develop the radical theory beyond their critique, although separately, and with others, they have done so (Taylor et al. 1975; Taylor 1981; Young 1981). The central ideas we summarize now.

1. Capitalism shapes social institutions, social identities, and social action. The mode of production, facilitated by the ideology promulgated through social institutions, shapes the character of the institutions through which it operates; encourages divisions of class, race, and gender; and shapes identities and the activities of the individuals subject to it (Michalowski 1985).

2. Capitalism creates class conflict and contradictions. Capitalist society forces humans into class conflict based on the inequalities of ownership and control of the means of production (Spitzer 1975; Quinney 1977). These classes are divided since the capitalist owners and employers want to maintain the existing power relations or improve them in their favor by increasing profits, whereas workers want to change the system and increase their share of the fruits of production by increasing wages. These desires produce two fundamental contradictions. The wages, profits, and consumption contradiction requires workers to have sufficient income to make purchases and thereby increase economic growth. Too much growth, however, is undesirable as profits and investment possibilities are undermined. The wages–labor supply contradiction requires that a surplus population of unemployed workers be maintained to keep labor costs down but these people are not so impoverished that they create problems and costs for capitalism (Chambliss 1988).

3. Crime is a response to capitalism and its contradictions. Crime is a rational response to the objective conditions of one's social class (Chambliss 1975, 1988). Capitalism creates crime directly through generating and maintaining a surplus labor force of the unemployed and underemployed, or "underclass" (resulting from technological replacement), who are necessary for keeping wages low but may commit crimes to survive (Spitzer 1975; Chambliss 1988). Capitalism creates problems indirectly through education, necessary for managing increased technology, but with the unintended consequence of raising consciousness (Spitzer 1975). Predatory crimes of theft, robbery, and burglary and violent crimes such as murder, assault, and rape are the result of the oppressive conditions of capitalism to which those exploited have to accommodate. Crimes such as sabotage and political violence are the result of resistance to and even rebellion against capitalist domination. Crimes of both accommodation and resistance may be more or less politically conscious acts (Quinney 1977; Michalowski 1985; Taylor et al. 1973). Crimes among the dominant economic classes also result from capitalists attempting to resolve the contradiction of wages, profits, and consumption by cheating to get illegally what they cannot get legally, such as price-fixing, bribery, and health and safety violations (Chambliss 1988).

4. Capitalist law facilitates and conceals crimes of domination and repression. Capitalist law as part of its methods of domination inflicts harms on those subject to control, including violence and violations of human rights. As well as such "crimes of control," capitalism facilitates "crimes of government," including corruption and graft; "crimes of economic domination" such as corporate fraud, price-fixing, dangerous production methods and products, and toxic pollution, which are undertaken in response to its basic contradictions; and social harm or injury to human rights resulting from institutionalized racism and sexism, which are reflective of the hierarchy of domination in the capitalist system as a whole (Quinney 1977).

5. Crime is functional to capitalism. Crime provides work for the surplus population and for others in the crime control industry, mystifies the capitalist exploitation of workers (Chambliss 1975), and justifies the need for the very law that maintains that system of exploitation (Young 1981).

6. Capitalism shapes society's response to crime by shaping law. The ruling economic class defines the content of criminal law in order to control the subordinated classes, which threaten or create problems for capitalism's accumulation of wealth and its system of domination (Chambliss 1975; Spitzer 1975; Quinney 1977). These problems include threats to the capitalist system of ownership of the products of work (e.g., theft), threats to the production process

(e.g., unemployment, vagrancy, drug use, mental illness), threats to the system of distribution and consumption (substance abuse, theft), threats to the system of reproduction of workers (truancy, homosexuality), and threats to the institutions promoting the dominant ideology (alternative schools, cooperatives). For the purpose of management, these threats fall into one of two problem populations: the relatively harmless "social junk," which has to be carried by the system, and the relatively dangerous "social dynamite," which must be controlled and undermined (Spitzer 1975).

Many of these concepts have been addressed by contemporary researchers. The role of the state or government in relation to the management of crime resulting from the contradictions of capitalism has led to two divergent radical positions, which we now explore.

The Capitalist State and Crime Control: Instrumental Versus Structural Marxism

Radical theorists have taken two directions, identified as instrumental and structural Marxism, the difference between them having to do with the role of state in relation to capitalism (Beirne 1979). Instrumental Marxists see a direct and crude relationship between the ruling economic classes and the government (Chambliss 1975; Quinney 1974; Krisberg 1975); the political administration is dominated by, and serves the will of, the economically powerful. Instrumental Marxists argue that the law and criminal justice system are coercive "instruments" used to control the lower classes. This control serves to maintain the existing social, political, and economic system. Members of the dominant capitalist ruling class make laws and devise a criminal justice system that promotes their own economic interest. Instrumental Marxists see two major classes: a capitalist elite and the mass of the proletariat.

In contrast, structural Marxists see a much more autonomous role for government, which acts on behalf of the long-term interests of capitalism rather than in the short-term interests of powerful corporations (Kinsey 1979; Young 1981; Greenberg [1981] 1993; Chambliss and Seidman [1971] 1982; Chambliss 1988). They view the instrumental perspective as being too simplistic. For example, "If law and justice were purely instruments of the capitalist class, why would laws controlling corporate crimes, such as price fixing, false advertising, and illegal restraint of trade, have been created and enforced?" (Siegel 1995, 248). Furthermore, instrumentalists suggest a single "homogeneous capitalist ruling class" when it is clear, even in Marx's original analysis, that capitalists compete with each other and undermine each other (Chambliss and Seidman [1971] 1982).

Structural Marxists argue that "the functions of the state are presumed to be determined by the structures of society rather than by the particular people who occupy positions of state power or by individual capitalists" (Bohm 1982, 576; Michalowski 1985). The contradictions of capitalist society create a force of disturbance that needs to be contained. In light of these contradictions, criminal law cannot exclusively represent the interests of a ruling elite to repress the lower classes. If it did so, it would risk revolt and would need to divert wasteful energy into social control. Thus, in order to retain ideological dominance rather than use coercive dominance, it must enact and enforce laws that also benefit the less powerful. Furthermore, "legislation is designed to prevent any single capitalist from dominating the system. . . . One person cannot get too powerful at the expense of the economic system" (Siegel 1995, 248).

The Limits and Policy Implications of Marxist Criminology and Radical Theory

Earlier, we saw that conflict theorists have been criticized for having a limited view of the structural causes of conflict and for failing to show the precise links between crime, conflict, and capitalism. We also saw how instrumental Marxists were criticized for their crude, overly deterministic conception of class structure. Much of the criticism of radical theory is really a criticism of instrumental Marxism, not structural Marxism. When radical Marxists are criticized for lacking realism, for being imprecise, for misrepresenting reality, for making untestable claims, and for being insufficiently supported by empirical evidence (Klockars 1980; Mankoff 1978; Turk 1980), what we are seeing is further criticism of instrumental rather than structural Marxism. When Klockars argues that the state empowers oppressed people and provides them with genuine rights they otherwise would not have, this too is part of the structural Marxist critique. Similarly, radicals are criticized for demanding controls on crimes of repression and domination, since that would only serve to increase the state's power and control, not lead to a "withering away of the State" (Lynch and Groves 1986, 30). But this was a call from conflict theorists rather than Marxists, who, as we have seen, want to change the social structure, not criminalize more behavior.

Criticisms by Klockars and others—that the class divisions of capitalist society, rather than being harmful, can actually be helpful and that interest groups allow valuable connections across class boundaries—applies to both structural Marxism and conflict theory. A further criticism offered by Klockars to both versions of Marxist criminology is that radicals romanticize the freedom from crime under socialism while ignoring the relative freedom from crime enjoyed in capitalist countries like Switzerland and Japan. If capitalism is criminogenic, why are these capitalist societies relatively crime free? Recent events such as the dramatic increase in organized crime in Russia since the introduction of free market capitalism and the revelations of massive corporate and government corruption in Japan tend to weaken this criticism, however. So too does the observation that both Japan and Switzerland are very strong collective societies.

As we have already seen, the structural Marxist critique of crude instrumental Marxism is perhaps the most devastating, and it has recently been supplemented by the arguments of left realists. We discuss their theoretical position in Chapter 12 but point out here that left realism is rooted in former radical criminologist Ian Taylor's (1981) "practical socialism" and Jock Young's (1979, 1987) critique of the "left idealist" versions of radical theory. Weiss (1983) pointed out that structuralism itself has problems and tends toward a "superdeterminism" that denies and confines the contribution of human ability to social action and the structures that emerge from it.

The policy implications of radical theory are clear. If social structure is the cause of conflict resulting in exploitation and crime, the only solution is to change the social structure. Criminal justice cannot be the focus because this "does little to alter the fundamental economic inequalities which structure social relationships" (Lynch and Groves 1986, 108). Instead, it is necessary to change the system of capitalist production to another that does not reproduce the conditions that generate crime. This involves revolution.

Marx and Engels thought that the masses would eventually recognize their plight as an oppressed class and revolt. As Marx and Engels wrote in *The German Ideology* ([1845] 1964), revolution is necessary because "the ruling class cannot be overthrown in any other way, but also because the class overthrowing it can only in a revolution succeed in ridding itself of all the muck of ages and become fitted to found society anew" (Tucker 1978, 193). For Marx and Engels, this revolution would be followed by a period of state-run socialism before arriving at a final stage of communism. In this final stage, the private ownership of property would be abolished and humanity would be emancipated from exploitation. As Engels put it, where all people have their basic material and spiritual needs satisfied, where hierarchy ceases to exist, "we eliminate the contradiction between individual [hu]man and all others, we counterpose social peace to social war, we put the axe to the root of crime" (Engels [1845] 1958, 248–249).

Many contemporary radical theorists are also convinced that socialist revolution is the only solution to the crime problem. Illustrative is Quinney's (1975a, 199) statement: "Only with the collapse of capitalist society and the creation of a new society, based on socialist principles, will there be a solution to the crime problem." In his most recent writings, however, Quinney has abandoned this call for revolutionary socialism in favor of a spiritual peaceful revolution. The policy solutions advocated by radicals have also been criticized as utopian and unrealistic. These criticisms have led to the development of various revisions by leading radicals that we consider in Chapter 12.

New Developments in Marxist Criminology

The radical criminology of the 1970s spawned many developments that have become known as critical criminology, and we explore them in the remaining two chapters of this book. Since the mid-1990s Marxist and radical criminology has seen a resurgence of interest by theorists who believe that the emergence of new critical criminologies, such as postmodernism, "creates an obstacle to the development of a truly critical criminology." In other words, a Marxist criminology prioritizes a theory of the state and the economy and advocates social transformation (Russell 1997, 61, 86). Similarly Hil (2002) has argued that critical criminology has been left "battered and bruised" by "an endless array of revisions, renewals, mea culpas, altered perspectives, paradigm shifts and ajured [sic] theoretical positions." As a consequence Marxist criminologists have "reconvened" their perspective. Not insignificantly, in 1998 *New Criminology Revisited* was published (Walton and Young 1998), which reaffirmed the ideas of the 1973 original and pointed out how state governments continue to fund criminological research that supports the society's powerful interests. Indeed, such a refocusing of intellectual analysis seems crucial, given what some see as "the deepening crisis of late twentieth-century capitalism, marked by increased inequality and poverty (both in the United States and globally)" (Matthews 2003, 12). Some have pointed out that political protest against capitalism has reached global proportions since the 1999 protests in Seattle, Washington, and 2004 protests in Miami, Florida, as antiglobalization protesters now regularly disrupt economic summit meetings of international economic leaders demanding that trade agreements respect human rights and protect the environment. Indeed, Hil (2002) argues for a reconfiguration in light of "contemporary global transformations and government practices" and "specific socioeconomic and political changes that are occurring across the world" toward "those social movements that actively pursue social justice and human rights." Similarly, Rene van Swaaningen (1997) argues that we need to undermine the hegemonic risk-based approaches to law and order to a criminology linked to social justice, the changing relations between the state and the global marketplace, and the culture of corporate capitalism. The question arises as to whether a Marxist-based radical criminology is best equipped to transcend its nineteenth-century shackles, or whether one of the newer critical criminologies will present the way forward in the new millennium.

Summary and Conclusion

The summary chart provides the key elements in the assumptions and arguments of conflict and radical theories. Their major contribution is to force criminologists to look beyond simple individual behaviors to the deeper causes of crime contained in the social structure of society—particularly capitalist society. Although we have presented here three somewhat different approaches (conflict, instrumental, and structural Marxist), the disagreements between them may be less problematic for critical theory than they may seem at first. A resolution may be found in the recognition that each theoretical model, including the functionalist model (strain theory) examined in the previous chapter, may actually represent a snapshot of a different stage in the dialectical historical development process of capitalism. Roberto Unger (1976; Collins 1987) has suggested a cyclical development process in which conflict and "legitimacy crisis" are recurrent stages between various more stable states. Thus we begin with the elite domination model (described by instrumental Marxists) relying on coercive domination that was characteristic of early capitalism, followed by a legitimacy crisis and a breakdown into conflicting interest groups. This is succeeded by the dual-power model (described by structural Marxists) in modern capitalism as the state becomes more autonomous. As we shall see in Chapter 12, the implications of this kind of historical analysis are that the crisis of legitimacy for modern capitalism and the relative increase in societal conflict it has seen herald a move from modern capitalist society to advanced capitalist and even postmodernist society that requires further revisions to the critical framework.

Summary Chart: Conflict Theory and Radical Theory

Basic Idea: The structure of capitalism involving the private ownership of property and vast differences in inequality creates conflict and contradictions that provide the conditions for crime. Conflict theorists see the source of conflict in different group interests; radicals (Marxists) see the source of conflict in the class structure of capitalism's exploitative system of economic production.

Human Nature: Humans are basically a social species, connected to others and shaped by their social structural contexts as well as their own human agency. They can join with others depending on their interests (conflict theory) or their objective class position (radical theory).

Society and the Social Order: Conflict theory sees divisions and competition based on a variety of different interests (class, status, power, gender, race, etc.). Radical theorists see a major conflict in capitalist society based on class interests between owners of wealth and owners of labor. The instrumental version sees the state as a tool of the ruling economic class. The structuralist version sees the state as semiautonomous, protecting the long-term interests of society against threats from particular interests, whether powerful or powerless. Conflict between the two major classes (owners and workers) is repressed either by coercive (instrumental Marxist) or ideological (structural Marxist) means of domination.

Law: Conflict theorists see the law as rules enforced by the powerful to maintain their economic, political, and social positions. Content of law and what counts as crime are set by the powerful. Instrumental Marxists see law as a coercive instrument of repression used by the dominant classes. Structuralists see the law as both a protector of the capitalist system and an ideological vehicle mystifying class exploitation and building consensus for capitalism by providing genuine rights and protections.

Criminals: Those who challenge the powerful (conflict theory) and threaten the capitalist mode of production, especially the surplus labor population or underclass (radical theory). There is no difference between criminals and noncriminals except that the latter are better able to get around the criminal justice system and can steal through quasi-legal means. Criminals are rationally responding to their objective situation of exploitation and see crime as a solution.

Causal Logic: Conflict theory argues that capitalism is criminogenic because it intensifies differences in positions of domination and subordination and produces the conditions for humans to commit crime: the demoralization of human cooperative spirit and the celebration of egoistic tendencies over those of altruism, which free the criminal thought. Radical theory sees capitalism as criminogenic because it produces fundamental contradictions, the resolution of which includes crime. Capitalism causes inequality; division of labor; specialization; and the alienation of humans from themselves, the products of their labor, the labor process, and their own species. Demoralization, brutalization, and dehumanization result in crime as an unconscious expression of anger and revolt against those who dominate politically and economically. Law and the criminal justice apparatus add to frustration through their use to repress legitimate expressions of injustice. They facilitate crimes by the powerful in the course of repressive control as both capitalists and workers attempt to overcome its inherent contradictions.

Criminal Justice Policy: Conflict theorists want to reduce the causes of conflict and restructure the society to be less conflicting and more cooperative. Radicals want to reduce conflict born of inequalities of wealth by removing or considerably reducing economic inequality in society.

Criminal Justice Practice: Restructure the distribution of wealth and ownership; move ownership to the employees; create a world in which people are concerned with each other's welfare; create and enforce laws equally against wealthy and poor; and decriminalize consensual crimes, minor property theft, and drug offenses. Structural change needed to prevent crime in the future involves revolution and move to socialist or communist society.

Evaluation: Analysis of law and injustice related to social structure helpful but criticized for being unrealistic, idealistic, and assuming crime does not occur in socialist countries. Some capitalist countries have very low crime rates and this is not explained. Criticized for a lack of practical concern for current crime victims.

11

Patriarchy, Gender, and Crime
Feminist Criminological Theory

Ramos, an undergraduate at Placebo University, felt forced to leave the school as a result of the gossip, protest, and outrage that followed an accusation that he had raped a fellow student. Ramos had left his dorm room to visit a friend across the corridor. In his friend's room, he found a female student passed out in the bed. There was evidence of drinking and vomit on the floor. The female student awoke, approached Ramos, and began to undress him. Ramos returned to his dorm room, but the female student followed. She kissed him and continued her advances. She asked him if he wanted to have sex and told him to put on a condom. The next morning, the female awoke and talked at length with Ramos. She also gave him her phone number. Six months later, Ramos was charged with rape. The Placebo University women's organizations argued that Ramos was guilty of rape because he took advantage of someone clearly under the influence of alcohol who was not in control of her full senses. Ramos claims he had consensual sex after being pursued by the female to his own room. It was clearly seen as consensual the next morning when the young woman gave Ramos her phone number. Much later, Ramos was accused of rape and arrested. This is a case, argue women's groups, where "yes" means "no," and they believe Ramos took advantage of the female student. Do you think he is guilty of rape?

The Ramos case illustrates the way some feminists and women's groups interpret crimes against women that for years have been concealed as acceptable sexual conduct. It is also an excellent illustration of critical theory (see Chapter 12), since it argues that the law and cultural norms are gender biased (among other biases), allowing victimization of the powerless, especially women and minorities. The ongoing sex scandal at the U.S. Air Force Academy presents another example. The 12 percent of female cadets who experienced rape at the academy matches the number generally reported in traditional university settings.

Women have traditionally been portrayed as more empathic and caring then men. The types of crimes they commit reflects this, being less violent. When they are violent, it is often a response to repeated abuse by men. However, examples of callous crimes by women exist. For example, while driving home, Chante Mallard, a twenty-seven-year-old nurse's aide, hit thirty-seven-year-old Gregory Biggs, who was walking along a freeway in Texas. Rather than stop to render aid, she drove home with him lodged in her windshield. Once home, she closed her garage door and left him in the windshield, where he bled to death over the next few hours. The next day she had two male friends dump his body in a park. They then burned the passenger seat of her car to conceal the crime. When one of the two men told his girlfriend of a "caper they had gotten away with," she called the police. On June 26, 2003, a Texas jury found Mallard guilty. She received a fifty-year sentence for murder and ten years for tampering with evidence. She will be eligible for parole in twenty-five years under Texas state law. She accepted responsibility for her actions but blamed drugs and alcohol for her poor judgment. She had been drinking, smoking pot and had taken one ecstasy pill prior to driving home that fateful day. How do criminologists explain crime by women, as opposed to crime against women? How do they explain patterns of crime by women and their relatively low rates of arrest and conviction compared with men?

In this chapter, we consider the contribution of feminist theory to the explanation of crime. Feminist theorists seek to explain why actions like those by Ramos and some Air Force cadets are crimes in terms of the silent harms they inflict. They also explain why women like Mallard engage in serious crime and why most violent crime is committed by men. Importantly, they seek to explain some interesting recurring patterns of crime. Why, for example, when some men decide to commit suicide do they kill their wife first, but when women decide to commit suicide they almost never kill their husband, although they may kill their children (Polk 2003)? Why are few serial killers or mass killers female? Why do some men kill their female partner out of jealousy, yet women almost never do? Why do some men feel compelled to use lethal force to defend their honor or resolve disputes, whereas "women almost never feel that they must use exceptional violence to defend their sense of honor. And . . . they rarely employ lethal violence as way of resolving . . . personal conflicts" (Polk 2003, 136). As we shall see, feminist scholars believe that traditional mainstream criminology is unable to explain these patterns of behavior because it ignores the structuring of society by gender that results in patriarchy. In contrast, as Jody Miller has argued, "Feminist criminology . . . situates the study of crime and criminal justice within a complex understanding that the social world is systematically shaped by relations of sex and gender" (Miller 2003, 15).

Basic Assumptions of Feminist Criminology

According to Kathleen Daly and Meda Chesney-Lind's (1988) seminal article on feminist criminology, there are five key aspects that distinguish it from mainstream criminology and they relate to the nature of gender: (1) gender is a social, historical, and cultural construct built on biological sex differences and reproductive capacities; (2) gender and gender relations are fundamental organizers of social institutions and social life; (3) gender relations and the social constructs of masculinity and femininity are based on assumptions that men are superior to women and this is reflected in male dominance in social, economic, and political institutions; (4) what is taken for granted as knowledge of the natural and social world is men's knowledge, the production of which is gendered; and (5) women should be at the center of intellectual inquiry and not function as peripheral, invisible appendages to men (1988, 504). Failure to acknowledge the politics of gender has resulted in a myopic view of crime and criminal justice that fails to address some of its most distinctive features.

A major criminological finding that has remained consistently unexplained by mainstream criminologists is that although women do occasionally commit serious, and especially violent, crimes, they generally commit far fewer than men do and are rarely arrested or convicted for their crimes (Cain 1989). Indeed, "gender—specifically being male—is one of the strongest correlates of criminal offending. This is especially the case, the more serious and more violent the crime in question" (Miller 2003, 17). Some simple statistics demonstrate the point. In the United States, according to the *UCR* data, annually around 80 percent of all people arrested are men, and men make up 95 percent of inmates in state and federal correctional facilities. Similarly, victimization data reveal that the offender was male in 85 percent of single-offender victimizations. As Polk says, "across many different countries and in many research studies, official crime, especially violent crime, involves mostly male offenders. In the case of homicide for example, typically males make up between 85 and 95 percent of known offenders" (Polk 2003, 133). Even in the case of crimes typically associated with women, such as sexual offending, women are less frequently convicted. For example, in Canada 4,545 inmates were convicted of sexual offenses in the early 1990s; only 19 were female (Syed 1996).

What does this preponderance of male offenders say about the causes of crime? Is crime caused by something to do with being a man, differences between male and female hormones, or by the socially constructed identity of masculinity? If so, is this identity rooted in the legal historical content of Western societies or in biological, cultural, or structural forces? Or is crime created by those who make the laws? Recent research suggests that gender differences for certain types of crime (e.g., drug offenses and some violent crimes) do not vary significantly between men and women (Alarid, Burton, and Cullen 2000). Further, the small group of offenders who commit the most crimes do not vary significantly by gender (Piquero 2000). Some self-report data also suggest less distinct levels of offending (Campbell, Muncer, and Bibel 1998; Chesney-Lind 1997). However, serious violent crime is consistently a male activity.

Responses to observations about gender differences in both levels of crime and arrest rates by feminist criminologists began with critical works by Dorie Klein ([1973] 1980), Rita Simon (1975), Freda Adler (1975), and Carol Smart (1976). But the feminist perspective in criminology did not become firmly established until the 1980s and did not appear in textbooks on theory until the 1990s. Part of the explanation for this omission and delay was that mainstream criminology was really "malestream" (i.e., dominated by men). These theorists were very slow to respond and tended to marginalize feminist contributions and exclude them (Menzies and Chunn 1991; Messerschmidt 1986). Also, as Simpson (1989) pointed out, some of the early accounts by women were less involved with developing their own theoretical position than with criticizing the lack of attention by male criminologists to women and gender issues (e.g., Leonard 1982). Jeanne Flavin postulates that "many criminologists' dismissal of feminism stems as much from ignorance and misinformation as deliberate, ideological resistance" (2001, 271).

Early feminist criminologists argued that the history of criminological theory is a history of the study of men behaving badly: criminology has been "gender blind." Omitted has been significant research or discussion on women as victims or offenders (Morris 1987; Gelsthorpe and Morris 1988). Criminological research, for the most part, has been about males, and criminology has been shaped by a male view of the world (Leonard 1982; Heidensohn 1985).

Traditional criminological theories also neglect "gender-related factors such as patriarchal power relations" (Alarid, Burton, and Cullen 2000, 172). Criminological theory "has either ignored women—focusing exclusively or implicitly on explaining male participation in crime and defining females as unimportant or peripheral—or has ignored gender" (Miller 2003, 16). Further, as Gaarner and Belknap note, "traditional theories of crime causation, which tend to be based on male models of crime and behavior, cannot adequately explain the experiences of delinquent girls" (2002, 482) or, for that matter, those of criminal women. Applying theories of male crime to women but not applying theories of women's crime to men makes "women a subcategory of men" (Miller 2003, 16). Mainstream constructions of "the female offender" embody the traditional stereotype that "women's greater emotionality, passivity and weakness . . . account for both their involvement (or lack thereof) in crime and the nature of their criminal activities" (Miller 2003, 17).

Recent research on female murderers challenges this view of the "passive woman" and suggests that biased portrayals in the media, law, and even feminist discourse that present women murderers as victims denies their agency and freedom to be human (Morrisey 2003). As Carol Smart (1976) observed thirty years ago, as a result of gender-biased criminology women are denied not only their individuality through subordination but also their criminality and their victimization. Through rape, prostitution, and domestic battering, women are seen to "deserve" or "ask for" their problems. Indeed, victimization studies reveal that some of the previously most hidden victims of men's harm are women. Studies show that violence toward women and rape has been, until relatively recently, grossly underreported (Brownmiller 1975). Self-report studies have also shown that women are not merely passive accomplices of men but actively participate in similar deviant and criminal acts.

The crimes of women are not restricted to status offenses, sex offenses, shoplifting, and poisonings, as in the typical media stereotype. They include robbery, violence, child abuse, drug abuse, drug dealing, and gang activity (Campbell 1984, 1993) as well as white-collar crime, as illustrated by the Martha Stewart case. But the data on such crimes have been largely gathered from studies of men, which means any differences of gender are disregarded and generalizations are less about crime and more significantly about masculinity (Daly and Chesney-Lind 1988; Leonard 1982; Messerschmidt 1993).

In seeking alternative explanations, some feminist writers have suggested that there are different "pathways to crime" for women. Certain events or life experiences increase the risk of offending (Heimer and De Coster 1999). Pathways research suggests that child neglect, as well as physical and sexual abuse of young girls, is often related to their incidence of "doing" crime (Gaarder and Belknap 2002). Also, developmental pathways may significantly affect the ways girls and boys respond to situational triggers. Heimer and De Coster (1999) note that direct family controls, such as supervision and coercive discipline, are gender structured, with young girls being more likely to be subject to indirect controls, such as emotional bonding, while boys are subject to direct controls. Similarly, they argue that boys are more likely to associate with peers who are risk takers and have a favorable view of violence.

The "pathways" approach also explains that the crimes of men and women have a foundation in different childhood development processes.

In the years following the initial critiques, feminist criminology moved into several different theoretical strands and is currently moving toward a reintegration of its diverse positions. What are the areas of crime and justice that feminist scholars have focused on and what are the different ways their scholarship theorizes the causes of crime by both men and women?

Jeanne Flavin (2001) described three directions that most scholarship and practice involving women has taken. First, feminist criminology criticizes the mainstream omission of women: "most . . . scholarship focuses on men or extends theorizing based on men's experiences to women without offering any reconceptualization" (273). This is simply adding women to the mix and "stirring." Miller (2003) describes this as the "generalizability approach," which she says cannot explain men's disproportionate involvement in crime (known as the gender ratio of offending), and also ignores the confluence and amplification effects of class, race, and gender.

A second movement of feminist scholarship has been to focus on crimes that adversely affect women more than men. Domestic violence is given as a prime example, though sexual violence is also commonly studied in this manner. This type of research is also guilty of treating men as the norm and women as anomalies, according to Flavin. Other feminists have criticized this approach for assuming the concept of a "universal woman," and thereby not accounting for the different experiences of women, such as those affected by race and class, that lead to different outcomes of offending and victimization (Miller 2003, 22–23). Finally, feminist scholars are beginning to study women "on their own terms" and recognize a "multiplicity of factors and offer a richer contextual analysis" (Flavin 2001, 273). As part of this trend, feminist scholarship has also moved toward a more general analysis of gender and difference that is more inclusive of other differences, experiences, and inequalities (Smart 1990; Caulfield and Wonders 1994; Schwartz and Milovanovic 1996; Daly and Maher 1998).

An important contribution made by feminist theory is the concept of "blurred boundaries" (Daly 1992; Daly and Maher 1998). This points to an overlap between women as victims and women as offenders (e.g., abused women who kill their partners or women who escape violent homes only to pursue street survival strategies, including drug use and prostitution). The term "blurred boundaries" suggests that patterns of past victimization can result in future violent offending. The emphasis on gendered victimization as a cause of future offending is a special case of the pathways approach discussed earlier. However, simply using past abuse and economic stresses may not fully capture the etiology of female offending since it again presents a passive view of women and ignores their intentionality and resistance (Gaarder and Belknap 2002; Maher 1997; Miller 2003).

Before examining recent theoretical developments such as the integration of a variety of feminist ideas in gendered theory, we briefly survey the differences between the four main feminist positions that developed in the 1980s and 1990s: liberal feminism, radical feminism, Marxist feminism, and socialist feminism (Jaggar 1983; Daly and Chesney-Lind 1988; Simpson 1989; Alleman 1993; Tong 1998). As we explore these varieties of feminist theory, it is important to consider how gender relations shape crime and criminal justice and how patriarchy (a society whose organization is dominated by men and masculine ideas and values) is as powerful a force as class and race.

Liberal Feminism

In response to the core question, "What causes crime?" liberal feminists answer, gender socialization. They argue that the subordinated position of women and the criminal tendencies of men result from the way boys and girls are socialized into different masculine and feminine identities and from male discrimination against feminine identities. Men are socialized to be risk-taking, self-interested individuals and to use coercive power to win; women are socially controlled. For example many young males are encouraged to engage in physically demanding sports such as hockey, football and wrestling. Young girls more often play soccer, volleyball, or softball. Newer forms of recreation such as wakeboarding, snowboarding, and surfing are much less gender specific and many young women excel at these sports. Increasing numbers of women are participating in traditional male activities like motorcycling. At "bike week" in Daytona Beach, Florida, and at the annual Sturgis, South Dakota, motorcycle rally, women once were relegated to riding on the back of the bike. But now many own and ride their own Harley Davidsons. Ten years ago women accounted for only 1 percent of Harley Davidson sales; today they exceed 10 percent. Does this mean that women will engage in the newer forms of crime (e.g., computer crimes, credit card fraud) equally with males? Will women begin to engage in more violent forms of crime as equality is realized?

The official arrest data on crime and gender show that women's crime also results from social and cultural factors. Liberal feminists reject the traditional claims of Lombroso and Ferrero (1900) that women are biologically averse to crime or their criminality is the product of a flawed person (Klein [1973] 1980). Nor is women's participation in certain kinds of crimes, typically petty property offenses, shoplifting, check fraud, welfare fraud, and embezzlement, a result of their "deceptive" and manipulative sexuality, as Pollak (1950) claimed, or of their pathological sickness or hormonal imbalances. Rather, liberal feminists believe that the difference between men's and women's rates of crime is a result of differences in (1) sex role expectations, (2) socialization, (3) criminal opportunities, (4) sex roles in recruitment to delinquent subcultures, (5) the way crimes are defined, and (6) the way males and females are socially controlled (Hoffman-Bustamente 1973). Social changes that reduce these distinctions and remove discrimination also mean that women's crime rates will inevitably increase. Let us look at this hypothesis.

The argument that women's crime rates reflect their changing social position began with two books: Freda Adler, *Sisters in Crime: The Rise of the New Female Criminal* (1975) and Rita Simon, *Women and Crime* (1975). When these books were written, the media had noted the "alarming" statistic that women's official rate of crime was increasing from 10 percent of all crime to 15–20 percent. Adler and Simon explained this by the liberation or emancipation thesis, which is based on women's social masculinization.

This thesis proposed that as a result of the 1960s women's movement, women were becoming socially and culturally more like men, competing with men, working more, encountering more economic opportunities, and fighting as aggressively as men to establish themselves (Adler 1975). Experiencing strain similar to that encountered by men would produce similar patterns of crime and higher female crime rates—which would eventually reach the levels of men's crime rates (Adler 1975; Figueira-McDonough 1980). In short, increasing women's criminality was seen as a consequence of social masculinization and a cost of liberation.

In another twist to the liberation-causing-women's-crime argument, Hagan, Simpson, and Gillis (1987) combined patriarchy and class in relation to gender role socialization in what they refer to as power-control theory. They suggested that class relations in the workplace and gender relations in society come together in the family and produce two basic types of families with different consequences for female crime. Where the husband/father works in a powerful authority position and the wife/mother stays at home, this patriarchal family reproduces a sexual division of labor in their children, with daughters becoming homemakers and sons being active in the labor force. In contrast, when both parents work and share domestic chores, this egalitarian family produces daughters and sons equally prepared to work. Daughters of egalitarian families, unlike those in patriarchal families, are socialized to be greater risk takers and are just as likely to be involved in crime as are the sons.

Liberal feminists are concerned with working within the mainstream arguing for equal rights for women. They believe discrimination and oppression can be reduced by social and legal reforms to the existing system designed to increase opportunities for women in education, employment, and politics and reduce gender role socialization.

Limitations

Liberal feminists have come under attack for such liberation-causes-crime arguments, both from mainstream theorists and other feminists. In an analysis of official crime rates of property offenses between 1965 and 1977, Steffensmeier (1978, 1980) found that increases in female crime occurred prior to the women's movement of the late 1960s. He also found that the subsequent increase was a result of increases in traditional women's crimes of shoplifting and check and welfare fraud and not in new crimes of opportunity suggested by the liberal feminists. Nor are women's rates catching up with those of men (Messerschmidt 1986).

Carol Smart (1979) rejected both the liberal feminist argument and Steffensmeier's interpretation. She argued that the biggest increase is in violent crime, which is not a traditional area, and that any comparative increase is misleading because of the small absolute figures. For example, a 500 percent increase in murder can occur when the figures go from one to five, but that need not be as significant as an increase in absolute figures from 1,500 to 2,000, which is 500 more murders but only a 25 percent increase in the murder rate (a point also made by Steffensmeier). Smart pointed out that data from earlier decades, such as 1935–1946 and 1955–1965, show a more rapid increase in women's crime than does the time of the women's movement. Finally, she argued that official crime arrest statistics are biased. They overrepresent the working class and minorities, and they are affected by changes in police and prosecution policy, including the attitudes of police officers.

According to the *chivalry hypothesis*, in the past women have been less likely to be featured in the official crime statistics not because they are less criminal but because of "knightly virtue" and kindly treatment of women by police, district attorneys, and judges, most of whom have typically been male. In recent years, this has changed because greater numbers of women entering criminal justice professions are less likely to treat women offenders lightly. Also, attitudes toward women as active agents are changing. As Smart (1976) argued, the recent increase in women's crime rates is a product of women's liberation insofar as liberation makes enforcers such as police, social workers, and judges believe in liberated women, and they are prepared to arrest them, charge them, and sentence them. This is particularly true for women's violent offenses (Box 1983). In short, the pattern of female criminality is an artifact of the selectivity shown by the police and courts and other agencies toward women, which is based on sexist assumptions and perceptions (Campbell 1981; Box and Hale 1983; Morris 1987). In certain types of crimes, sentencing results in women getting tougher sentences (Chesney-Lind 1986; Chesney-Lind and Sheldon 1992). This is particularly true for single women, who compete with men for jobs, challenging the male-dominated (patriarchal) society's gender norms. Not least of these norms is patriarchy's need to control young single women. As a result, young women, whose status offenses include running away from home to avoid victimization, can be doubly victimized, first by their male caretaker abusers and second by the criminal justice system, which may unwittingly return these daughters to abusive parents, compounding their harm.

Similarly, the more recent power-control thesis, which implies that a mother's liberation explains increases in her daughter's crime, has been criticized for falsely "assuming that working in an authority position in the labor market translates into power and authority in the home" (Beirne and Messerschmidt [1991] 1995, 549). Power-control versions of liberal feminism have also been criticized on the basis that they are not supported by the evidence. Although women's participation in work has increased, all measures of female delinquency show stability (Chesney-Lind 1989, 20).

Finally, socialist feminists have argued that any real increase in property crime is due to women's economic marginalization in a patriarchal society, not that liberation leads to increases in crime among women. This means more women are either unemployed or employed in insecure, part-time, unskilled, low-paid jobs, at a time when welfare is increasingly cut back, "so they are less able and willing to resist the temptations to engage in property offenses as a way of helping solve their financial difficulties" (Box 1983, 198–199; Box and Hale 1983).

Because of the weaknesses in the liberal feminist analysis, other feminist criminologists argue that it is not enough to pursue equality for women through reform—what is needed is systemic change away from patriarchy. Most vigorous in this criticism are the radical feminists, whose position we examine next.

Radical Feminism

Radical feminists such as MacKinnon (1987, 1989) criticize liberal feminists for attempting to change the law to bring about equality, as well as liberal and Marxist feminists (discussed later) for buying into male culture. They argue that liberal feminist attempts at legal reform miss the central problem of patriarchy and, worse, leave it intact under the veil of formal equality. They also argue that prioritizing the economic sphere (as in Marxist feminism) is accepting male standards of what is important, while doing nothing about patriarchy.

According to radical feminists, the explanation for the gender ratio in crime is self-evident. Crime is men's behavior, not women's. It is in men's biological nature to be aggressive and dominate. Crime is simply an expression of men's need to control and dominate others. This occurs in numerous forms, including imperialism, racism, and class society, but most of all men seek to dominate women, forcing them into motherhood and sexual slavery (Barry 1979). Men are born to be sexually dominant and it is this biological difference that directly causes their criminality (Brownmiller 1975). Thus rape is the ultimate expression of women's subordination because it is "an act of aggression in which the victim is denied her self-determination" (Griffin 1979, 21) and through which all men keep all women in a state of fear (Brownmiller 1975, 5).

A distinguishing feature of radical feminism is its focus on patriarchy and human reproduction and how this is used as a basis to force women into subordination (Jaggar 1983). Women are subordinated to men through a sexual division of labor in which women are assigned all the work necessary to rear children and the "sexual division of labor established originally in procreation is extended into every area of life" (Jaggar 1983, 249).

The sexual division of labor is reinforced by male aggression, which is used to define and control the culture and institutions of society, including (1) the state and its institutions of government, (2) employment (where men's ideas dominate industry and commerce) and especially work relationships, and (3) social institutions, especially the family, which provides the root of this "law of the father." In each of these arenas, men control women through psychological, economic, sexual, and physical abuse and manipulation, often linked to controls over their sexuality and reproduction. In addition, the male-constructed law has limited consideration of the ways women's bodies and activities are controlled through the law and the state, both of which are male dominated, in ways far more repressive than the laws affecting men. Not surprising, women's culture reflects their servile status and fosters an attitude of self-sacrifice.

There is an interesting parallel between the radical feminist analysis and the biological/evolutionary psychology perspective we discussed in Chapter 4, which argues that male violence contributed to successful human evolution by ensuring that the most able and successful males reproduce with the best suited females.

Radical feminists believe that they can only be free from male domination by liberating themselves from male definitions of reality and from women's roles and place in society, particularly in the family. Since male domination shapes the state and its laws, if they hope to advance their cause women must take power from men in these institutions (MacKinnon 1989). This means replacing men in powerful positions, particularly in the law and the courts and other institutions of criminal justice. Furthermore, women should become sexually autonomous in reproduction and involve themselves in women-centered and women-only organizations, developing their own values and culture rooted in women's traditional hidden culture. It is because radical feminists want to exclude men from social life that they are also referred to as separatist feminists (Young 1995, 287). Radical feminists believe that once women have obtained power the objective is to abolish gender, hierarchy, and the distinction between the public and private spheres of society (Jaggar 1983, 254–255). Ultimately, argue radical feminists, patriarchy must be replaced by matriarchy (rule of mothers), "a society in which production serves the interests of reproduction; that is, the production of goods is regulated to support the nurturance of life" (Love and Shanklin 1978, 186). Only then will crime—men harming others—diminish.

Among modern-day matriarchal societies, such as the Minangkabau people of West Sumatra, Indonesia, it is not so much that the women rule, even though their power extends into economic and political realms of the society and women control land inheritance (Sanday, 2002). Rather men and women are seen as complementary, with social emphasis placed on nurturing growth and on the maternal in daily life. "While we in the West glorify male dominance and competition, matriarchy in this society is about making the maternal the center, origin, and foundation, not just of life but of the social order as well" (Sanday 2003). Most importantly, Sanday describes a peaceable, almost violence-free Minangkabau society of 4 million people.

Limitations

Criticism of the radical feminist agenda has come from numerous sources, including other feminists (Danner 1991; Messerschmidt 1993; Munro 2003). One of the primary objections is that it assumes a biological determinism in which men are destined to be harmful, aggressive, and controlling. Catharine MacKinnon, a leading radical feminist, has been particularly criticized on deterministic as well as essentialist issues (Munro 2003). Research suggests men's abuse of women is not always motivated by control. Second, radical feminism ignores differences among men and among women, perceiving gender as a "sex caste." This "assumes a universality and commonality of women's subordination that does not exist. Important power differentials among women are ignored" (Danner 1991, 52). Third, the argument about men controlling women through physical force and violence in the best interests of societal evolution fails to explain how the criteria of being successful have changed, such that those who are most successful "in the competition for resources in fact are the least likely to employ serious forms of violence as a tactic in their interpersonal negotiations, including dealing with competitors either for economic resources or in terms of the reproductive capacities of women" (Polk 2003, 138). Fourth, in its instrumental conception of the state as a means to power, radical feminism assumes that men are the sole problem, rather than power itself being problematic. In attempting to use the state to protect women against male violence, radical feminists risk increasing the power of the male state against women (Pitch 1985; Currie 1989; Smart 1989). Furthermore, by ignoring the construction of differences among people, radical feminism presents a naive view that women in institutions would be able to create a nurturing society devoid of power relations. For many, particularly Marxist and socialist feminists, the radical position is inadequate without a more profound analysis of social structure and the state.

Marxist Feminism

The Marxist feminist perspective emerged in the late 1960s as an attempt to explain women's oppression using Marxist analysis (Messerschmidt 1993). Marxist feminism, like radical feminism, sees society structured as a patriarchy but argues that this patriarchy is rooted in the kind of economy a society has, particularly its class relations of production. Historically, capitalist societies based on private ownership of the means of production and male inheritance have created class-divided societies in which men dominate. Gender differences are used as a means to subordinate and exploit women as a "reserve army of labor"; they are used as free domestic labor to keep capitalist wage costs down. As Engels (1884) argued, women's place in the family is based on the master–slave relationship, which exploits women through their subordinate and dependent relationship to men. Their role, and the role of the family, is to reproduce/socialize compliant workers who will sell their labor to capitalists. Although capitalist class society oppresses the majority, "women are doubly oppressed through their tie to a domestic sphere that is inconsequential in terms of its power and influence. . . . The essence of the Marxist-feminist position, therefore, is that women, like men, are oppressed economically but, unlike men, women are once again enslaved by their domesticity" (Alleman 1993, 27).

Thus it is the double oppression of women, argue Marxist feminists, that leads to both their victimization and their criminality. In contrast to radical feminists, Marxist feminists see male crime against women not as the result of inherent qualities of male nature but as a product of men's molding to exploitative relations by a capitalist system. Men see others as competitive threats that need to be controlled in order to retain their own position of relative power and to keep women economically dependent. It is for this reason that men rape women, a phenomenon not typically found in noncapitalist societies, and women feel guilt, blaming themselves for being raped (Schwendinger and Schwendinger 1983; Sanday 1981).

The class patriarchy analysis also explains spouse battering, which victimizes women at three times the rate of male victimization (BJS 1993, 25). This is explained as men's attempt to control women, who are trying to liberate themselves from economically dependent domesticity (Saunders 1988).

The relative lack of women's criminality and the nature of women's crimes are also explained from the Marxist feminist perspective. Their control of economic exploitation explains why women, like slaves, commit very few crimes. Moreover, the crimes women do commit reflect their class-defined dependency or attempts to break from it. For example, women, unlike men, typically commit embezzlement to help solve economic problems facing their family for which they alone feel responsible; virtually anything justifies maintaining the welfare of their husband, children, or parents (Zietz 1981). Similarly, unlike men who kill women intimates, "women who kill their partners typically do so only after years of enduring various forms of physical, sexual, and psychological abuse. Typically, these women have used up all available forms of social support, perceive that they cannot leave their abusive relationships, and fear for their lives" (DeKeseredy and Schwartz 1996, 291; DeKeseredy 1993; Dobash et al. 1992). Other petty property crimes are also the result of women's oppressed position in a capitalist economic system that attaches them to the subordination of family servitude (Balkan et al. 1980).

Given the priority of class over patriarchy in Marxist feminist analysis, it is not surprising that their solution involves changing the capitalist class structure to involve women as full and equal independent productive members of society. This means eliminating male-dominated inheritance of property, paying women for housework, and providing house care and child care services. This would only be possible if the capitalist system were replaced with a democratic socialist one (Daly and Chesney-Lind 1988).

Limitations

The major criticism of Marxist feminists comes from socialist feminists who disagree with the priority given to class over patriarchy. In particular, Marxist feminism has been criticized for explaining women's domestic labor in relation to capital but not in relationship to men (Messerschmidt 1993, 52). Instead, socialist feminists address the class patriarchy relationship, as we show in the next section.

Socialist Feminism

Socialist feminism is an attempt to merge Marxist feminism and radical feminism (Jaggar 1983; Danner 1991; Einstadter and Henry 1995; DeKeseredy and Schwartz 1996). It examines the interrelated and interdependent forces of capitalism and patriarchy that lead to men's crime and women's oppression, subordination, and dependency. It does this without prioritizing one over the other (Eisenstein 1979; Hartmann 1981).

A major statement from a socialist feminist on the cause of crime came from James Messerschmidt, a criminologist at the University of Southern Maine. In his book *Capitalism, Patriarchy, and Crime* (1986), Messerschmidt argued that relationships between owners of capital and workers result in the exploitation of the workers by the owners (based on class inequality). Intertwined with class oppression is a system of "relations of reproduction." Through these relations, men exploit women's labor power and control their sexuality in order to reproduce the existing social order (including its sex role divisions and hierarchy of power relations). The relatively powerful position of men gives them greater opportunities for crime and a greater ability to create harm. In contrast, women's relatively subordinate position affords them less opportunity to offend, just as it affords them less opportunity to benefit from legitimate opportunities. In short, class patriarchy not only creates crime but subordinates women.

Whereas the other versions of feminism see women's subordination resulting from one or another determining force (evolutionary, liberal socialization, radical biology, Marxist–capitalist class relations), socialist feminism sees humans as shaped and transformed by cooperative productive activity "in which human beings continuously re-create their physiological and psychological constitution" (Jaggar 1983, 303). As Jaggar (1983, 304) noted, "Socialist feminism's distinctive contribution . . . is its recognition that the differences between men and women are not presocial givens, but rather are socially constructed and therefore alterable."

The policies advocated are based on the idea that if cooperative productive activity creates differences, then it can also be used to change the differences between men and women. Thus, socialist feminists see the solution to women's subordination as replacing capitalism with a collective political and legal order based on equality between class and gender. They want to expose and eliminate male-dominated power hierarchies, the wage-based capitalist system, and its fostering of male attitudes and behaviors. In short, they want to abolish both class and gender. Socialist feminists believe that of central importance in any new order is reproductive freedom (i.e., women's control over whether and under what circumstances they bear and rear children) and sexual freedom. They also believe that there should be an end to compulsory motherhood. They believe in the availability of paid maternity leaves and of publicly funded, community-controlled child care. These policies are designed to liberate women from alienated motherhood and allow them the freedom to be economically independent of men. But the socialist-feminist collective order requires more than an absence of hierarchy. As Einstadter and Henry (1995) argued, it requires an equality based on the recognition of differences of experience, while at the same time not discriminating on the basis of these differences.

Limitations

Socialist feminist analyses have been subject to criticism, again largely from other feminists. Some claim the theory is still essentially Marxist and deterministic in that the double vision for patriarchy and capitalism leaves no room for the meaningful construction of human action (Smart 1987). Radical feminists criticize both Marxist and socialist feminism for failing to explain why capitalism requires women to be subordinate. Furthermore, they argue that there is no guarantee that a socialist revolution would liberate women (Hartmann 1981).

Another serious criticism comes mainly from those who see the focus on capitalism and patriarchy as exclusionary. For example, Brown (1988) argues that the concept of patriarchy fails to recognize the historical variation within women and within men. Others find the concepts of patriarchy and gender to be racist and ethnocentric since they are based on the experiences of white women and exclude women of color (Ahluwalia 1991; Barrett and McIntosh 1985; Mama 1989; Rice 1990). See also Hood-Williams (2001) for a critique of "masculinity" in general and of Messer-schmidt's theory in particular.

In response to some of these charges, recent versions of socialist feminism have shifted toward analyzing the interconnections between all dimensions of hierarchy and acknowledging the concept of difference: "The crux of the socialist-feminist concern with the intersection of gender, class, and race is the recognition of difference. . . . Patriarchy cannot be separated from capitalism, neither can racism, imperialism or any other oppression based on 'otherness'" (Danner 1991, 53). This shift to "difference" rather than particular structural forms occurs in two new directions; one is postmodern feminism and the other is the emergence of gendered theory, which we consider first.

Gendered Theory

Although the approaches to feminist analysis discussed above have differences (Caulfield and Wonders 1994), they are united around the need to "develop a gendered theory of crime, that is a theory that explicitly takes into account the effects of gender and more significantly, gender stratification, on women's lives and development . . . [and] the recognition that people's perceptions, opportunities and experiences are shaped not only by the mode of production under which they live, but also by the form of gender relations dominant in their society" (Curran and Renzetti 1994, 272).

One of the implications of gendered theory is that we consider how both women's femininity and men's masculinity are formed by their experiences. In this context, Messerschmidt has revised his socialist feminist position toward one of structured action theory, arguing, "Crime by men is a form of social practice invoked as a resource, when other sources are unavailable, for accomplishing masculinity" (Messerschmidt 1993, 85). This is almost like saying that crime is the result of blocked opportunities to be a man. Messerschmidt argues that the concept of patriarchy obscures real variations in the construction of masculinity. He notes that there are differing masculinities, just as there are different femininities. Committing crimes depends on class, age, and situation but is an example of "doing gender" (the social construction of gender), or building masculinity or femininity. In other words, doing crime is part of manliness (Polk 2003).

Epistemological Issues and Postmodern Feminism

Epistemology is "theories of what knowledge is, what makes it possible, and how to get it" (Harding 1991, 308; Flavin 2001). Epistemology is how we create knowledge. As such it involves the methods we employ. Part of the difficulty confronted by gendered theory is that the available social science methodology is based on male culture's definitions and ways of obtaining knowledge and truth through positivism; in other words, our commonsense knowledge and "ways of knowing" are gendered (Hatty 2000). Such approaches are arguably incapable of appreciating the diversity of gender constructions. In contrast, some feminist theorists have developed an alternative research method called "standpoint epistemology," which claims that "the construction of knowledge requires many voices; especially those that have been marginalized by racism, sexism or class privilege. No one standpoint is given greater honor over others; together they give a rough understanding of the many ways to grasp the incredible complexity and ever-changing patterns of social life. Standpoint epistemology . . . reveals a neglected or forgotten point of view, it empowers those excluded" (Young 1995, 730). Flavin adds that "standpoint feminists try to construct knowledge from the perspectives of the persons being studied on the grounds that the perspective of the oppressed or marginalized tends to be less distorted" (2001, 274).

This attention to a diversity of experiences, multiple knowledges, and the social construction of difference has led some to the view that a new, nonexclusionary paradigm is necessary. One such approach is postmodernism (which we discuss in detail in the next chapter). Briefly, postmodernism "emphasizes the importance of alternative discourses and accounts and frequently takes the form of examining the effects of language and symbolic representations" (Flavin 2001, 274). Postmodern feminists who write about crime, law, and social control, such as Carol Smart (1989), Alison Young (1990, 1996), and Adrian Howe (1994), go further than the standpoint feminists, although their positions may at first seem similar. Both celebrate the legitimacy of discounted knowledges. Standpoint feminism wants to replace male truths with truths based on the diversity of women's experiences. Postmodern feminists prefer multiple knowledges rather than new truths because these tell different stories. This continuing diversity offers resistance to any domination, particularly from identities formed in hierarchical contexts that tend to reproduce further domination (Smart 1990; Grant 1993). Postmodern feminists reject notions of class, race, and gender and note that the early white Western feminist notions of the universal subordination of women neglect differences among women, particularly women of color, Third World women, lesbian women, and others. The notions of "woman" and "women" themselves have been questioned as inadequate by feminist postmodernism (Howe 1994, 167; Smart 1992; Bordo 1990). The assumption that each person has one fixed sex, one sexuality, and one gender is replaced by crosscutting sex, sexuality, and gender constructs that capture the complexity of gendered experience (Lorber 1996). Postmodernism criticizes early feminist criminology for taking for granted assumed gender distinctions between men and women, masculine and feminine, without questioning these (Brown 1990). Consideration of alternative discourses is thus critical.

A third way of creating knowledge is through traditional social science methods: positivism. While most feminists have rejected this methodology, some have embraced it. For example, Campbell, Muncer, and Bibel (1998) conducted a sophisticated statistical analysis on the female evolutionary perspective (1998). This type of researcher/theorist is called feminist empiricist, and this position is considered "the most conservative" feminist approach (Flavin 2001).

Conclusion

In this chapter we reviewed the contribution of dominant feminist theories and theorists. We conclude by noting that feminist criminology has shown that "gender inequalities exist in society and that these inequalities should be addressed" (Flavin 2001, 272). We have shown how feminist scholarship has focused on core issues that highlight the importance of the difference between men's and women's patterns of crime and victimization. We showed how feminist theory moved from a liberal critique of differences and a call for equality, through radical, Marxist, and socialist forms before reintegrating around a set of issues having to do with the gendering of crime and justice, and of crime as an exercise in "doing gender." Several social policies have been examined in this vein, each offering a way in which gender, together with race and class, needs to be incorporated into justice in order to correct the deficits of a male dominated theoretical tradition. In the next chapter we extend this "critical" discussion and focus on postmodernism, peacemaking, and left realism. As you read the next chapter, you will note that it is really an extension of the basic critical assumptions that began this chapter on feminism, but we have framed it in the wider context of global change.

Summary Chart: Feminism

Human Nature: Humans are (1) in liberal feminism, social blanks socialized into gender roles through family, media, education, and work; (2) in radical feminism, biologically determined—men are aggressive and competitive, women are cooperative and nurturing; (3) in Marxist feminism, human differences exploited for class interests create artificial divisions and accentuate competitive male characteristics; (4) in socialist feminism, "gendered identities"—gender, like race and ethnicity, comprises socially constructed categories imposed on biology that create women as secondary, marginal beings, a view reinforced by socialization.

Society and the Social Order: Represents male interests in its structure, organization, institutions, and operation and excludes women's interests: (1) in liberal feminism, hierarchy with unequal opportunity for women; (2) in radical feminism, patriarchy with male gender dominating all institutions of power, including state; (3) in Marxist feminism, class hierarchy based on inequalities of wealth in which women are dependent and reproductive of male labor; (4) in socialist feminism, class-based patriarchy with coalescing inequalities of class, gender, and race, with state seen as relatively autonomous.

Crime: Crime is men's domination and control over women, who are devalued; in socialist feminism, doing crime is doing masculinity.

Law: Law reflects male definitions: (1) in liberal feminism, law upholds inequalities; (2) in radical feminism, law is an extension of male power; (3) in Marxist feminism, law reflects capitalist interests and works to maintain dominant class interests, which are male; (4) in socialist feminism, law bolsters male supremacy and reinforces appearance of women's inferiority as natural but also affords women some protection. Criminals manifest the gendered identity of masculinity.

Causal Logic: (1) in liberal feminism, women's liberation as women becomes more androgynous; (2) in radical feminism, male aggression, dominance, and control; (3) in Marxist feminism, class exploitation and subordination of women leave them dependent, weak, and vulnerable; (4) in socialist feminism, interaction of forces of class and gender subordinates women, creating them as a category of "otherness" that is part of a general social construction of difference; masculinity is used by some to dominate others through patriarchy. Feminist empiricism accepts traditional models of causality.

Criminal Justice Policy: (1) in liberal feminism, seeks to end gender discrimination through changes to law increasing women's opportunities and fights for equal treatment in law; (2) in radical feminism, seeks to replace patriarchy with matriarchy in which production serves reproduction and nurturance and sees state as major resource to be captured; (3) in Marxist feminism, seeks to replace capitalist class hierarchy with socialist society; (4) in socialist feminism, seeks to replace class patriarchy with decentralized socialism providing equal control over decisionmaking to the disempowered (women, minorities etc.), to eliminate power based on difference and allow women to define themselves, and to demystify gender constructions of masculinity and femininity to show diversity within.

Criminal Justice Practice: Encourage increased reporting of violence against women at home and at work; pass new laws banning sexual harassment, stalking, date rape, pornography, and so on: (1) in liberal feminism, acquire more control over men's power through stronger police force, stricter laws, and regulating men's violence; (2) in radical feminism, replace men in institutions of power with women; (3) in Marxist and socialist feminism, decentralize democratic institutions of justice and replace rational male principles with women's principles of care, connection, and community.

Evaluation: Radical feminism criticized for assuming biological determinism and sex castes composed of dominant men and subordinated women; liberal and radical feminism accused of strengthening power of the male state and denying entry points for women to make change. Radical feminist view of men as criminal/women as victim ignores women as offenders, reinforces view of women as passive and men as active. All criticized for being blind to race and ethnicity, for ignoring unique qualities of persons of color.

12

Criminologies for the Twenty-First Century

Globalization, an Issue of War or Peace?

In this chapter we consider whether the world in which we live has changed so fundamentally that traditional ways of theorizing about crime and our response to it need dramatic revision. What theories address crime in the twenty-first century? For most of the twentieth century, crime and violence were seen as problems to be confronted within nations by their systems of criminal justice and social policy. Individuals or groups, largely male, within society and especially within cities but also within homes, organizations, and workplaces, were seen as committing acts of harm against their family, their neighbors, their fellow workers, or their communities. As we have seen throughout this book, the theories about why they commit these acts have ranged from individual choice and opportunity, through individual biology and personality development, through varieties of social survival and adaptation, to political conflict and resistance. Only strain theory (anomie) and critical criminology (conflict, Marxist, radical, or feminist), which we examined in the previous three chapters, see the crime problem as related to the culture and structure of societies. For the most part, societies have framed crimes as disconnected from one another, acts that threaten our security that can be controlled, eliminated, treated, or otherwise removed from society.

The common approach to the crime problem viewed it as a disease or an enemy on which society must wage war. During the late twentieth century a "war" rhetoric expanded into the social fabric and was used by politicians and government to frame a whole range of social problems, from the "War on Poverty," the "War on Drugs" (Johns 1992), the "War on Crime" to, most recently, the "War on Terrorism." However, the war rhetoric approach, which creates an "us" versus "the enemy" division, is contradicted by the reality that defies such a simplistic analysis. The last years of the twentieth century witnessed fundamental changes in societies which demonstrate the increasing connections among humans, not just nationally but globally—that the security of any one of us is connected with the security of all others, and that we must think about problems and issues (e.g., crime) locally, nationally, and *globally*.

More important, if we are to increase our sense of security we need to approach problems in a way that reduces the total conflict/harm, rather than adding to it through criminal justice responses that create and add their own level of harm and deprivation under the guise of "punishment" and "just deserts." Instead, argue proponents of these new theories, we need to address problems in ways that take a peacemaking rather than a harm-creating or a war-making approach. Recognizing our interconnection requires us to think beyond national boundaries, disciplinary knowledge, and simplistic solutions. In dealing with complex problems such as crime, we need approaches, analysis, and policy that are holistic, interdisciplinary, and comprehensive.

Six fundamental changes can be identified that demonstrate the changed nature of our world toward increasing interconnection and interdependence: (1) globalization, (2) the communications revolution, particularly the Internet, (3) privatization/individualization, (4) the global spread of disease, (5) changing perceptions of conflict and national security, (6) the internationalization of terrorism.

Globalization

Globalization is a process whereby people act and react to issues in terms of reference points beyond their own society. These reference points are material and cultural issues that affect the globe, such as environmental issues (e.g., global warming, global pollution) or commercial issues (e.g., fast food, McDonald's, Levis; one take on this development has been to describe it as McDonaldization, as McDonald's fast food restaurants spread throughout the world's economies). Globalization also relates to an international universalism, whereby events happening in one part of the world affect those in another; conversely, it relates to the way people in different societies identify with values that cut across nations and cultures, yet it also relates to the recognition of the diversity of experience among different cultures: "'Globalization' refers to all those processes by which peoples of the world are incorporated into a single world society, global society" (Albrow 1990, 9).

The global society has, by implication, a global economy that relates to the increasing multinationalization of corporations, which produce on the "global assembly line" (Ehrenreich and Fuentes 1994). The result is that "economic goods, services, and personnel flow back and forth across national, hemispheric and continental boundaries" such that "economic, social, political and environmental events in one part of the world have significant impacts in other parts of the world . . . beyond the ability of any one society to control" (Soroka and Bryjak 1999, 176). This has occurred simultaneously in many parts of the globe with "balkanization, the opposite of globalization . . . the breakup of nation-states into ethnic entities. Many ethnic groups are striving for independence and sovereignty denied to them when they were incorporated into larger nation-states . . . [where they] had to abide by laws and customs that were not of their own choosing and had to suppress their own languages and cultures. Now they are searching for identities, territories, and criminal justice systems of their own" (Adler, Mueller, and Laufer 1995, 365). Yet in many ways, the balkanization of society is itself a part of the globalization phenomenon, whereby ethnic identities and religious affiliations transcend both political and geographic boundaries. As Schmalleger says:

> On a global scale, there appears to be a shared agreement that society is experiencing a period of unprecedented change. Both the substance and the pace of change are fundamentally different from what has occurred in past decades and centuries. No longer are sequences of events occurring in relative isolation over longer patterns of time. No longer are discrete groups of people affected by each change; rather, there is a greater simultaneity of occurrence, swifter interpenetration, and increased feedback of one set of changes upon another. (2002, 480)

A classic example of the interconnection and inability of individual societies to influence/control the crime/harm created by globalization is the case of the worst industrial accident in the world: the toxic gas leaking from Union Carbide's insecticide plant in 1984 in the Indian town of Bhopal, killing between 4,000 and 15,000 and injuring up to 600,000 (Beirne and Messerschmidt 2000, 494–495):

> What is most frightening about Bhopal is . . . the way people are routinely treated by corporations. . . . Cancer-causing pesticides banned in the West are freely sold to farmers in Latin America, Eastern Europe and Asia. Native American Nations are bribed to accept nuclear waste . . . Malaysian hill people are killed or run off their land so Japanese companies can cut down their forests to make chopsticks. Leaded gasoline, banned in the West because of its devastating health effects on children, is sold to Thailand, Mexico and India. This kind of corporate violence is repeated in every corner of the Earth. (Cohen 1998, 3; cited in Beirne and Messerschmidt 2000, 494–495)

Some, such as Nikos Passas (2000), have argued that the process of globalization, including the spread of capital, labor, management, news, and information across national borders, is itself criminogenic, since it provides motivation and opportunities for corporate deviance at the same time as it leads to less effective control systems (Robinson 2004).

The Globalization of Communications

Prior to 1985 global communication was largely restricted to the affluent. The advent of the personal computer and the development of the Internet (World Wide Web) transformed the way we communicate. Now people connect daily with others all over the world at next to no cost. They exchange ideas, performances, propaganda, ideologies, and technical information. Using Internet search engines such as Google and Dogpile, they can draw on knowledge from any part of the globe. Global communications via the Internet means that people from any society anywhere can read newspapers and opinions, engage in chat room discussions, and take university courses via online programs in any country. No longer are people limited to what their own mainstream ideology and/or culture feeds them, which paradoxically can lead to expanded knowledge and perspectives or reinforcement for any idea or view, however strange or outrageous it may seem. This means that we are increasingly interconnected with the world in both positive and negative ways. What affects people in one part of the globe can affect us immediately in another.

At the same time, global communications have led to a massive shift of jobs from manufacturing into service, communications, and information (called the Postindustrial Society). Because information jobs require higher education and training, increasing numbers of people are becoming underemployed or unemployed on a global scale. The result of these changes is growing worker anxiety and job stress among those who have "not yet been 'bumped,' 'deselected,' 'surplussed,' 'vocationally relocated,' 'dehired,' 'decruited' or otherwise done away with" (Soroka and Bryjak 1999, 180). Work-related stress leads to increased competition, "backstabbing," isolation, detachment, and alienation as well as increased family and workplace violence. In addition, the effects of increased global communication have brought a rush of new crimes that use the computer, such as Internet fraud and identity theft, drug smuggling and bomb making. The growing dependence on global communications has also made national infrastructures and government vulnerable to varieties of Internet terrorism through hacking and computer viruses.

Privatization and Individualization

Two trends related to globalization and global unemployment have produced a reduction in our concern for others, despite enhanced interconnectedness. We have already mentioned increasing competition in the workplace, the attitude of everyone looking out for themselves. This is in contrast to the collective movement around trades and professions that culminated in unionization and collective action during the middle of the twentieth century. Increasingly we are seeing the "death of society" in the sense of the decline in collective actions and social policy requiring some to give up part of their wealth to help the less fortunate or to increase the public good. Instead, partly because of government fiscal crises and partly because of conservative ideology, the twenty-first century has witnessed a growing privatization of government, particularly in the areas of welfare and social programs. Privatization reinforces the individualization of human actions, as well as allowing major policy decisions to be made in terms of what maximizes profit for corporate shareholders, not public or social interests. Thus the 1980s and 1990s saw massive deregulation and privatization of everything, including transportation, communications, energy, welfare, and even law enforcement.

Increasingly, family members tend to stay at home, not as families but as appendages to technology such as television, computers, and computer games. The result is the impersonal society, in which people live in isolation from other real people (or "bowling alone," as Putnam [1995] termed it), where media images and Internet game characters become interspersed with real people (others) who are seen as superficial, objectlike caricatures. The impact of globalization on the economic structures of societies has been to polarize rich and poor, with numerous groups being excluded from the mainstream (Young 1999). In their relatively impoverished state they are vulnerable to harming each other increasingly, through violence in their homes and neighborhoods.

Globalization of Disease

Black death or plague, smallpox, and polio have demonstrated throughout human history that disease can be a global phenomenon. However, the systemic use of hygienic practices, including clean water, effective sanitation, and sewerage and the discovery and use of antibiotics and other drugs meant that for much of the twentieth century the global spread of disease was seen as a thing of the past, or as limited to underdeveloped countries. But by the end of the twentieth century, through the advent of increased global travel, the terror of disease on a global scale was given new meaning, first with HIV/AIDS, then with "mad cow disease," West Nile virus, and most recently SARS (severe acute respiratory syndrome). Worse, terrorists could potentially introduce disease such as smallpox or anthrax on a global scale as part of an attack against people or governments. Like the previous developments, the dual effect was on the one hand to render people increasingly fearful of contact, especially intimate contact with strangers, tending to undermine interpersonal relations, while on the other, increasingly showing how interconnected we have all become.

The Changing Nature of Global Conflict

During the twentieth century, each generation faced a significant war or warlike threat to their survival, including World War I and II, the Korean War, the Vietnam War, and the Cold War. In these twentieth-century global conflicts it was possible to clearly identify the enemy posing the threat, and to come together as nations to wage war to defeat the threat. However, in the twenty-first century it is becoming increasingly clear that for many nations "the enemy" is multiple, diffuse, and interwoven into the fabric of each society.

Nations on the continent of Africa, for example, face serious threats on several fronts (e.g., starvation, HIV/AIDS, and numerous civil wars). Civil wars in African nations such as Sierra Leone, Rwanda, Ethiopia, and Mozambique have killed millions of innocent people. In the twentieth century former colonial powers would step in and multinational peacekeeping forces, such as United Nations, NATO, provided both clarity and stability. However, in the twenty-first century these bodies seem reluctant to intervene everywhere violence occurs. Part of the explanation may be that the "international community is increasingly reluctant to provide peacekeeping forces for difficult, expensive and politically unrewarding operations" (Brayton 2002, 304).

Another part of the explanation is the changing nature of war and conflict. The two superpowers of the Cold War, the United States and the Soviet Union, no longer square off. The United States has emerged as the world's dominant military power and as a result, "America has reduced the military role of its European allies in NATO to that of its strategic reserve, to be used where the job is relatively easy, requires less capable forces, and where such tasks require long-term commitment of troops and peacebuilding rather than fighting duties" (Cilliers 2003, 112). The role of allies and multinational organizations such as NATO and the United Nations is changing. Consequently, the nature of war is also changing. Today, "to an extent unprecedented in modern times, entities other than nation-states wage war across multiple physical and ideological boundaries. The Cold War's clear dichotomies and array of proxy wars have devolved into myriad intrastate conflicts and cross-border wars of uncertain and shifting ideological foundation" (Brayton 2002, 305).

There were twenty-five major armed conflicts in 2000, yet only two were between nation-states, according to the Stockholm International Peace Research Institute 2001 (cited in Brayton 2002). If nation-states are not waging war, and if major powers are not intervening in conflict resolution (except of course when oil is involved), how are these conflicts being resolved?

In the poorest countries and regions, they are not. In more affluent areas, armies are for hire; mercenaries fight for pay. Increasingly, small countries, and some large ones, are finding themselves unable to "protect the political, military, economic social and cultural life of their citizens" (Brayton 2002, 303). Papua New Guinea provides an illustrative example. In 1997, the Bougainville Revolutionary Army (BRA) seriously threatened the regime of Prime Minister Sir Julius Chan. As a result of this conflict the Panguan copper mine was closed—the source of 30 percent of the country's export income. Chan hired the mercenary force Sandline International for $36 million. The Sandline corporation recognized the economic advantages of opening and protecting this mine. Chan was able to obtain the military assistance he needed. What is wrong with this practice? Some argue that "in proffering security to collapsing, mineral rich states . . . multinational corporations accentuate the international exploitation and marginalization of the states in question" (Brayton 2002).

Increasing numbers of large, well-organized private armies have alarmed the United Nations, which views them as a "threat to sovereign equality, political independence and territorial integrity." There are dozens of these huge corporate armies for hire. The "peacekeeping" role of these corporations is based on profit and armed conflict. While national conflicts have become decentralized, global conflicts have become dispersed. Rather than nations facing off, terrorists are employing tactics once used by anarchists and fringe radical groups to make war for a variety of causes from anti-abortionists to Muslim extremists.

Global Terrorism

The single most feared event and, according to surveys of public opinion, the "crime" considered most serious is a terrorist attack. Since September 11, 2001, the occasion of the New York World Trade Center and Pentagon suicide airliner bombings, the threat of terrorism on a global scale has become part of the daily fear of populations around the world, not least because these events are instantly communicated to everyone, everywhere, as they happen. No longer restricted to the tactics of a few extreme radical or fringe groups in certain nations, terrorism has become the method of war for any ethnic or religious group lacking the power to succeed politically. It has been facilitated by developments in communication, transportation, and technology that have enabled explosives and other weapons to become smaller and more lethal. Clearly terrorism has become a global threat, whether this takes the form of an interconnected web of terrorism around fundamentalist Muslim religious extremism, such as that claimed by followers of Osama bin Laden and al Qaeda, or an Arab-led terrorist movement opposed to Western culture, or more specific actions such as those in Northern Ireland by IRA and splinter groups against the Protestants and the British government, or in Indonesia or Bali against supporters of the West.

Terrorist tactics are used in a way that exploits the systems of interconnection spawned by globalization, whether transportation, communication, energy, or immigration/democracy. Theories based on particular assumptions of biology or psychology, or those based on the sociology of particular societies, are inadequate to deal with the global dimensions of twenty-first-century crime.

How do societies reconfigure their vision of crime to deal with its global dimensions? Should acts of terrorism and acts of war be considered crimes? What about the actions of states that abuse human rights? Are there new criminologies that are able to confront these more integrated global-level forms of harm creation? In this chapter and in the conclusion we consider several new criminologies that attempt to address crime from a wider, more holistic perspective. Some of these—postmodernism, chaos, constitutive theory, and peacemaking—build on the critical perspectives that we examined in the previous two chapters, while others, known more generally as integrative theory, bring together mainstream and critical theories. Let's begin with postmodernism, which starts out as an approach that acknowledges the interconnectedness and the global transformation that we have been discussing.

Postmodernism

Postmodernism is more a movement than a theory. It is much larger than crime, criminal justice, and criminology (Kraidy 2002), encompassing among other things art, architecture, literature, and social movements. It has only recently been applied to the study of crime and crime control. The concept of postmodernism is inherently abstract, broad, and multifaceted. Postmodern ideas mark a major break from those we have so far examined. As one commentator recently noted, "postmodernism and poststructuralism are difficult to both define and comprehend" (Bohm 1997a, 134). Thus it is important to consider their contribution to our understanding of crime at the outset.

What unites all these different disciplines under postmodernism is the "idea of making space for different ways of knowing and being" (Longstreet 2003, 11). Put simply, postmodernist theory alerts us to the socially constructed (and thus somewhat arbitrary) nature of social rules, norms, and values. Further, "postmodernism rejects the possibility of an agreed upon version of objective reality . . . and it postulates instead that all accounts of reality are in fact interpretive" (Mason 1995). A postmodernist view of crime would include not only legal definitions but also the total society as a source of crime. As we saw in Chapter 2, a postmodernist definition of crime involves a much wider range of harms than a legal or even a sociological definition, in that it includes harms created by the routine practices of our society's institutions, such as work, bureaucracy, government, law, and family (this will be further elaborated later).

Furthermore, unlike previous theories, which identify a causal force, whether at the level of individual, family, institutions, community, culture, or social structure, postmodernism sees the "cause" of crime in the interplay of all of these elements as expressed through prevailing ways of describing our world, called discourses. Finally, postmodernism agrees with the Greek philosopher Heraclitus, who observed that you can't step in the same river twice. Things are in a state of flux and change—we elaborate on this point later when we discuss chaos theory. Postmodernism also is consistent with Werner Heisenberg's uncertainty principle—reality is affected by the observer, even in subatomic particles, such that what is real and true is less certain, less decidable.

The policy implications (unlike those of other theories) do not involve changing individuals, institutions, or central features of society such as structural features. Rather, they involve changing our whole set of societal practices and our mode of current discourse to replace this with other, less harmful discourses. In short, it "is not this or that" which is wrong with modern industrial society but the way we approach everything. We can only fix it by changing it all, together. Let us look at this approach in more detail, remembering our caution about complexity.

Postmodernism refers to a school of thought that has emerged out of a period of intense skepticism with science. Scientific method and rational thought were, as will be recalled from Chapters 3–4, an outcome of the eighteenth-century Enlightenment that prevailed until the late twentieth century. Science assumes that rational and objective methods can be used to discover knowledge and truth, which can then be used to solve society's problems and control nature. The concept of scientific "progress" characterized the "modern era." Disenchantment with modernism, linked to the suffering that its hierarchies, divisions, and exclusions have brought to many (through imperialism, sexism, racism, and class oppression), together with its increasing inability to solve society's problems (e.g., pollution, poverty), has led to a questioning of its values, particularly the value of scientific analysis and rational thought (Hunt 1991; Best and Kellner 1991; Borgmann 1992) as well as the source of that knowledge.

Many modern problems have been exacerbated by science and technology, for example, the threat of nuclear devastation, germ warfare, pollution, ozone depletion, and the Holocaust. The creators of this technology have also been subject to examination: "communities that were custodians of that knowledge were called into question as well. A shift away from the dominance of scientific knowledge, largely controlled by military, industrial, and governmental communities, occurred in favor of a plurality of different communities. Many of these communities were avowedly unscientific and subjective. Indeed, they frequently interpreted the claims to objectivity and the universality of science as a subterfuge giving power to a military, industrial, and institutional complex that was anything but objective" (Longstreet 2003).

Postmodernists see rational thought as a form of elite power through which those who claim to have special knowledge earn the right to decide the fate of those who do not share this knowledge. Postmodernists fundamentally disagree that there is such a thing as objective truth. Instead, all knowledge is subjective, shaped by personal, cultural, and political views. Whereas feminism's standpoint epistemology believed that many oppressed versions of truth are valid, postmodernists argue instead that all knowledge is made up simply of "claims to truth" (Foucault 1977, 1980). They believe that knowledge and truth are "socially constructed." This means that there is no independent reality outside the minds and practices of those who create and re-create it. Knowledge is artificial, an outcome of humans making distinctions and judging one part of any distinction as superior to another, one set of ideas as superior to another, and so on. These distinctions are conceptual and are made through communication, particularly but not exclusively written or spoken language, referred to by postmodernists as discourse (Manning 1988; Arrigo 2003).

One of the major causes of conflict and harm in societies, according to postmodernists, results from people investing energy in these "discursive distinctions," believing in their reality and defending them and imposing them on others. Distinctions made in discourse result in categories that exclude and marginalize. For example, the gender distinctions "men" and "women" exclude the differences within these categories and preclude connections between them; so too with "black," "brown," "tan," and "white" distinctions based on race that exclude others. As a result, postmodernists point to the centrality of language in shaping social reality (Arrigo 2003).

Postmodernists reject the self-evident reality of distinctions. They reject the idea that distinctions should be made between different kinds of knowledge, especially between "scientific knowledge" and "common-sense knowledge." One of their principal tools of analysis is to expose the soft, socially constructed "belly" of privileged knowledge through what they call critique. This is different from criticism, which involves arguments against a particular position and policy suggestions to arrive at a solution. Critique is a continuous process of challenge to those who claim to know or hold the truth; it uses deconstruction (Derrida 1970, 1981) to expose the socially constructed rather than real nature of truth claims. Postmodernists adhere to an "aura of unmaking the old—decentering, deconstructing, demystifying" (Longstreet 2003).

Deconstruction is a method of analysis that seeks to "undo" constructions and demolish them, in a way that exposes how they are built and why they appear to be real (Rosenau 1992; Cohen 1990). As T. R. Young explained, "Whereas modern science privileges objectivity, rationality, power, control, inequality and hierarchy, postmodernists deconstruct each theory and each social practice by locating it in its larger socio-historical context in order to reveal the human hand and the group interests which shape the course of self-understanding" (1995, 578–579).

Arrigo says that deconstruction or "trashing" of a text (or a discourse whether it is written or spoken) involves a careful critical reading designed "to unveil the implicit assumptions and hidden values . . . embedded within a particular narrative" (2003, 48).

> Deconstruction shows us how certain truth claims are privileged within a given story while certain others are disguised or dismissed altogether. Because deconstruction focuses on the actual words people use to convey their thoughts, it attempts to uncover the unconscious intent behind the grammar people employ when writing or speaking. Thus language or entire systems of communication are put under the microscope for closer inspection. In a sense, then, trashing a text entails reading between the lines to ascertain the meanings (ideology) given preferred status in a particular language system. (Arrigo 2003, 48)

Part of the postmodern critique involves the "resurrection of subjugated knowledges," the excluded, neglected, and marginal knowledges discounted by dominant social constructions. It involves including other voices: "The postmodern challenge invites us to embrace articulated differences, making them part of the social fabric of ongoing civic interaction . . . of evolving possibilities" (Arrigo 2003, 49).

Commentators have argued that there are numerous versions of postmodernism (Schwartz and Friedrichs 1994). For example, Peter McLaren (1994) offers resistance postmodernism, in which difference is the "recognition that knowledges are forged in histories that are riven with differentially constituted relations of power" (cited in Kraidy 2002, 15). For the sake of brevity, it is helpful to distinguish two broad types of postmodernist thought: skeptical and affirmative (Rosenau 1992; Einstadter and Henry 1995).

Skeptical postmodernism refers to the work of those who believe there is no basis for objectivity and no way truth either exists or can be discovered. They use deconstruction simply to undermine all claims to truth, revealing their underlying assumptions and disrupting their acceptance as fact. In some cases, skeptical postmodernists imply an extreme relativism that has no standards and accepts anything as valid. They do not believe in suggesting alternatives because they would themselves then be making truth claims and be subject to their own criticism (hence skeptics are also called nihilists).

Affirmative postmodernism, in contrast, refers to those who believe deconstruction also implies reconstruction, or rebuilding: "Exposing how an edifice is built, and how it stands, in spite of opposition, also implies how it can be rebuilt or built differently" (Einstadter and Henry 1995, 280–281). In deconstruction, affirmative postmodernists show how humans actively build their social world, rather than being passive subjects of external forces. They also show how people could invest their energies to build new social worlds. To understand the relevance of postmodernism to criminology, we shall briefly illustrate how postmodernism has been applied in criminology through Henry and Milovanovic's (1996) affirmative version known as constitutive criminology.

Constitutive Criminology

According to its founders, "Constitutive Criminology is a broad sweeping, wide-ranging holistic perspective on crime, criminals and criminal justice . . . whose objective is to help build a less harmful society" (Henry and Milovanovic 2003, 57). The core of the constitutive argument is that crime and its control cannot be separated from the totality of the structural and cultural contexts in which it is produced (Henry and Milovanovic 1994, 1996, 1999, 2003). It rejects the argument of traditional criminology that crime can be separated from that process and analyzed and corrected apart from it. Crime is an integral part of the total production of society, and insofar as societies are interconnected through globalization processes, crime is a global production. It is a coproduced outcome of humans and the social and organizational structures that people develop and endlessly (re)build. Therefore, criminological analysis of crime must relate crime to the total social and ultimately global picture, rather than to any single part of it. This is not an easy task.

To accomplish their project, constitutive theorists start by redefining crime, victims, and criminals (Milovanovic and Henry 2001; Henry and

Lanier 2001). They argue that unequal power relations, built on the constructions of difference, provide the conditions that define crime as harm. Thus constitutive criminology redefines crime as the harm resulting from humans investing energy in harm-producing relations of power. Humans suffering such "crimes" are in relations of inequality. Crimes are people being disrespected. People are disrespected in several ways, but all have to do with denying or preventing our becoming fully social beings (and in this the theory is similar to Marx's assumptions about human nature). What is human is to make a difference to the world, to act on it, to interact with others, and together to transform environment and ourselves. If this process is prevented, we become less than human; we are harmed. This is similar to the difference in the well-being of caged animals (e.g., rabbits) if allowed the freedom to engage their world and be stimulated by it and by their interaction with other animals. Thus Henry and Milovanovic define crime as "the power to deny others their ability to make a difference" (1996, 116).

Constitutive criminologists find it helpful to identify crime in relation to power differentials and hierarchical relations. They distinguish between "crimes of reduction" and "crimes of repression." Harms of reduction occur when offended parties experience a loss of some quality relative to their present standing. They could have property stolen from them, but they could also have dignity stripped from them, as in hate crimes. Harms of repression occur when people experience a limit, or restriction, preventing them from achieving a desired position or standing. They could be prevented from achieving a career goal because of sexism or racism or meet a promotional "glass ceiling." Considered along a continuum of deprivation, harms of reduction or repression may be based on any number of constructed differences. At present, in Western industrial societies harms cluster around the following constructed differences: economic (class, property), gender (sexism), race and ethnicity (racism, hate), political (power, corruption), morality, ethics ("avowal of desire"), human rights, social position (status/prestige, inequality), psychological state (security, well being), self-realization/actualization, biological integrity, ("physically injured"), and others (Milovanovic and Henry 2001). Whatever the construction, actions are harms either because they move the offended away from a position or state they currently occupy or because they prevent them from occupying a position or state that they desire, whose achievement does not deny/deprive another.

Constitutive criminology also has a different definition of criminals and victims. The offender is viewed as an "excessive investor" in the power to dominate others. Such "investors" put energy into creating and magnifying differences between themselves and others, in order to gain some advantage over others (again the dimensions of what qualities are differentiated range from physical appearance to race, ethnicity, ability, wealth, beauty, intelligence, morality, etc.). This investment of energy disadvantages, disables, and destroys the human potentialities of others.

The victim is viewed as a "recovering subject," still with untapped human potential but with a damaged faith in humanity. Victims are more entrenched, more disabled, and suffer loss. Victims "suffer the pain of being denied their own humanity, the power to make a difference. The victim of crime is thus rendered a non-person, a non-human, or less complete being" (Henry and Milovanovic 1996, 116). This reconception of crime, offender, and victim locates criminality not in the person, structure, or culture but in the ongoing creation of social identities through discourse and discursive distinctions that are reinforced by social actions and institutions.

Not surprisingly, the constitutive analysis leads to a different notion of crime causation. To the constitutive theorist, crime is not so much caused as discursively constructed through human processes. Put simply, crime is the coproduced outcome not only of individuals and their environment but of human agents and the wider, increasingly global society through its excessive, even obsessive investment in crime through crime shows, crime drama, crime documentaries, crime news, crime books, crime films, crime precautions, criminal justice agencies, criminal lawyers, and, yes, even criminologists. All, as Marx noted, are parasitic on the crime problem, but as constitutive criminology suggests, they also contribute to its ongoing social and cultural production. They are the sustenance on which individual offenders feed and thrive.

If conventionally understood linear causality is rejected, what takes its place to explain how crime happens? Constitutive theorists, due to their observations about the "indeterminacy of causal relations," look to chaos theory to help reveal alternative ways of knowing. Chaos theory (also known as "nonlinear dynamics") argues that "orderly disorder governs the behavior of all natural systems." While exhibiting patterned regularity, they are simultaneously random and unpredictable (Arrigo 2003, 50; Henry and Milovanovic 1996; Milovanovic 1997; Williams and Arrigo 2001). Constitutive theorists argue that the complexity of social relations needs an explanation framed in terms of dialectical causality, such as interrelationships or coproduction rather than the "linear and deterministic concept of single or multiple causality" (Henry and Milovanovic 2003, 65). Indeed,

> these processes comprise relationships that are not deterministic but dialectical, a dialectic that assumes nonlinear development and a movement, through human agency, toward instability of social forms. . . . Whether a particular situation or interrelationship will result in criminality cannot be determined with any precision since the dynamics of human relations are

indeterminate, can be altered by seemingly small events, and are part of a historically situated, ongoing process that is also indeterminate. (Colvin 1997, 1449)

Given this interrelated yet indeterminate nature of social structures and humans, the question remains as to how these affirmative postmodernists recommend reducing harms that are crime. Constitutive criminology calls for a justice policy of replacement discourse "directed toward the dual process of deconstructing prevailing structures of meaning and displacing them with new conceptions, distinctions, words and phrases, which convey alternative meanings. . . . Replacement discourse, then, is not simply critical and oppositional, but provides both a critique and an alternative vision" (Henry and Milovanovic 1996, 204–205). In terms of diminishing the harm experienced from all types of crime (street, corporate, state, hate, etc.), constitutive criminology talks of "liberating" discourses that seek transformation of both the prevailing political economies and the associated practices of crime and social control.

Replacement discourse can be implemented through attempts by constitutive criminologists to reconstruct popular images of crime in the mass media through engaging in newsmaking criminology (Barak 1988, 1994). It can also be induced through narrative therapy (Parry and Doan 1994). Developed as part of family therapy, narrative therapy enables offenders (excessive investors in power) to construct more liberating life narratives and reconstitute themselves through them. As we shall see later, another form of replacement discourse comes in the form of peacemaking approaches to conflict. Although narrative therapy and abolitionism developed independently from postmodernism, they resonate.

Edgework Studies

"Edgework" is the term coined by Steven Lyng (1990) to describe and explain the high-risk behavior of those who engage in a variety of deviant activities such as skydiving, base-jumping, hang-gliding, surfboarding, downhill skiing, and other extreme sports. He is particularly interested in how and why these edgeworkers invoke a high degree of control and skill to avoid extreme danger, possibly death, in order to reap the "pleasures of sensation and emotion" of the body. We saw in Chapters 4 and 5 that biological and psychological explanations for such behaviors describe them as "sensation seeking." The central issue is what motivates people to pursue dangerous and risky behaviors?

Edgework theorists reject biopsychological arguments and rational choice explanations. Instead they develop a nonmaterial explanation for deviant motivation as an end in itself, as a place of freedom from constructed limits and borders, in which humans experience their own humanity enjoyed near "the invitational edge" that most control systems prevent humans from approaching (Matza 1969). Katz (1988) explored the phenomenology of subjective experience and emotions in his book *Seductions of Crime*. He focused on the idea that a significant dimension of the person's experience was emotional excitement, the adrenalin rushes, the sensual, the visceral experienced through the body. Katz explained the attraction to crime, from "sneaky thrills" to murder as an attempt to overcome what is perceived as an intolerable moral challenge/dilemma, typically a humiliation, in order to a reestablish a sense of humanism and self-respect. Paradoxically, murder becomes seen as "righteous slaughter" as a subject attempts to reassert control over his or her own moral dilemma through "moral transcendence." The subject regains their humanity though the sense of righteousness provided by rage that justifies the act, only to lose control to the consequences of the act as he crosses the edge. Yet it is approaching the edge that attracts. The edge is the borderline of order and disorder. Here the body experiences the "rush," the sensation of intense bodily pleasures: "It is the play of being in and out of control at the edge that provides the moments for the expression of bodily desires" (Milovanovic 2003, 8). The edge may be a moment in time, an event, but it is experienced as more real than everyday reality. Experiencing a car wreck, fighting a house fire, high-speed lane splitting on a motorcycle, and other such events provide an example of this sensation.

Lyng (1990) suggested that the structural context for such a search for meaning is the meaninglessness of the mundane, routine, alienated life of capitalism, although this was not consistent in the research (Ferrell, Milovanovic, and Lyng 2001). O'Malley and Mugford (1994) related these ideas to the structural context of late capitalist society, seeing a "phenomenology of pleasure" rooted in the nineteenth-century Romantic period in history (eventually replaced by the material rationality of capitalism). A second force was the civilizing process that laid down moral boundaries for appropriate action, orderly, rational behavior that creates barriers to spontaneous emotional expression. "Within modern cultures there is a steady and increasing pressure toward emotionally exciting activities, including leisure activities, as a source of transcendence and authenticity with which to offset the suffocation of an over controlled, alienated existence within the mundane reality of modern life" (O'Malley and Mugford 1994, 206). O'Malley and Mugford see Lyng's work as describing situations approaching but not crossing the limit, whereas Katz's study describes situations of going beyond the limit.

Drawing on earlier postmodern thought, particularly Lacanian and constitutive theory, Milovanovic, together with Lyng and Jeff Ferrell

(Ferrell, Milovanovic, and Lyng 2001; Milovanovic 2003) developed these ideas into a postmodernist informed study of desire that situates sensation seeking in the context of meaning construction, framed by wider cultural production, information technology, and mass media.

The attempt by some postmodernist and constitutive theorists to locate the motivation for crime and deviance between the human desire for pleasure framed in a historical and cultural period illustrates again how this perspective seeks to show the connectedness of people to each other that transcends the simple reductionist accounts of earlier theories. Before we examine other approaches that work from within this interconnectedness perspective, we will review some of the many criticisms of postmodernist/constitutive criminology.

The Limits of Postmodernist Criminology

Postmodernism has been sharply criticized by mainstream criminologists and even critical criminologists (Schwartz and Friedrichs 1994). It is criticized for being (1) difficult to understand, not least because of its complex language (Schwartz 1991); (2) nihilistic and relativistic, having no standards to judge anything as good or bad, thus fostering an "ideology of despair" (Melichar 1988, 366; Hunt 1990; Cohen 1990, 1993; Handler 1992); and (3) impractical and even dangerous to disempowered groups (Currie 1992; Jackson 1992).

In one specific example of how the disempowered may need more than a change in the discourse to protect their interests, Miller found over fifty local organizations in Seattle opposed the federally funded Weed and Seed operation, since it had the potential to further empower police to target and harass minorities while also deflecting "attention from underlying economic issues" (1992, 177). At the same time Weed and Seed illustrates the way official agencies can replace the discourse of, say, "rehabilitation" with the more punitive concept of Weed and Seed (see Kappeler and Kraska 1999 on how this was also done with the concept of "community policing"). The criticism that disempowered groups are not helped in postmodernist thinking has been made by socialist feminists and radical feminists. For example, Jackson (1992) and Lovibond (1989) argue that deconstructing gender categories may result in women being denied a position from which to speak, allowing men to continue to dominate through their control. Yet postmodernist feminists "insist that the challenge women confront is to construct a contingent method of communicating feminine ways of knowing freed from the trappings of masculine logic, sensibility and discourse" (Arrigo 2003, 52). Constitutive criminology offers a solution to these problems, but its ideas have not yet withstood the test of critical assessment and practical application.

Finally, postmodernism has not been well understood or received by practitioners working in criminal justice. It has most often been applied to correctional issues, where it refers to the discursive transformation of the penal process away from rehabilitation and toward a "new penology," designed to control the "risk society" through the use of actuarial techniques to target offenders as social types who represent different amounts of risk (Simon 1993; Feeley and Simon 1998; Garland 1996; Lucken 1998). Yet even in the corrections arena, "postmodern penal trends remain subordinate to modern penal trends that are still in place" (Hallsworth 2002, 145). It is less often mentioned with regard to law enforcement (but see Kappeler and Kraska 1999). Lisa Miller (2001) did provide an excellent yet simple (simplicity is greatly needed in this area of study!) example of the critical power of postmodernist criminology in her analysis of the Seattle Weed and Seed program, which deals with crime, politics, law enforcement, and neighbors.

Perhaps the greatest affinity of postmodern and constitutive theory is with the theorists who have developed an approach that not only recognizes the general interconnection of people but seeks to redesign the criminal justice system to address this. This field comprises three related humanitarian ideas: abolitionism, peacemaking, and restorative justice. In each case the idea is to develop a response to crime that brings offenders and victims together in a peaceful, community-oriented context to resolve the conflict and mitigate the harm caused by their crimes.

Making Peace, Not War

The theories considered in this section, like those of postmodernism and constitutive theory, take a holistic approach to the problems of crime, connecting crime, offenders, victims, the community, and the wider structural issues of societies in their global contexts. They include: 1) peacemaking, which advocates nonviolent approaches to resolving the conflict of crime; 2) restorative justice, which advocates adopting practices that integrate offenders with victims and their community; and 3) left realism, which sees crime and its victims connected to the criminal justice system and the structures of inequality in society.

There are several common threads linking the theories covered here. First, each views the victim(s) as an integral part of the process of crime production and control. Crime is no longer an individualized event with an easily identified victim. Barak (2000, xvi) has identified crimes of: domination, control, accommodation, interpersonal violence, resistance/rebellion, and crimes of survival. Each has a different type of victim. Some are raped. Others are not allowed equal participation in work, home, or society. Yet others are denied a healthy life. Many are not aware they are victims. Crime, by any definition, has a victim or victims (excluding crimes without victims). As we argued in Chapter 2, under contemporary American criminal justice practice the victim is often left out of the enforcement, judicial, and punishment processes (except to file a report or testify). Each of these theories explicitly addresses that omission.

Second, crime is a larger problem than the criminal justice system alone can address. Crime, like industry and disease, is now worldwide and part of globalization. In fact, opportunities for crime are increasing due to globalization. Barak found, "as part of the process of globalization, both legitimate and illegitimate fields of 'criminal enterprise' have been freed-up for the greater exploitation of humankind" (Barak, 2000, xvii). "Traditional" criminological theories are ill equipped to address these modern changes. Peacemaking, restorative justice, and left realism are able to provide solutions to the emerging problems associated with globalization because they recognize its wider complexity and the interconnectedness of people globally.

Third, the basic premises drawn on existing conceptualizations. For example, peacemaking grew out of the long-existing religious and philosophical traditions as well as the justice practices of indigenous populations, such as Native Americans. In the1970s, victims' advocates and abolitionists proposed similar models (see Chapter 10). Similarly, restorative justice is based on the early arguments of victimologists, Aboriginal people's justice, and Mennonite traditions. In criminal justice it appeared under calls for restitution and reparation. Finally, left realism draws on similar principles as 1930s strain theory, but frames this in a global context.

Peacemaking Criminology

We began this chapter mentioning the problems facing the continent of Africa. Ironically and fittingly, a model of a solution came from Africa itself in the form of Nelson Mandela. Jesus Christ, Mahatma Gandhi, Martin Luther King Jr., and Mandela were all responsible for significant social change through the application of what has come to be called "peacemaking." They facilitated this social change without the use of an army or organized police presence—indeed they often achieved their objectives *despite* law enforcement efforts. Clearly peacemaking is nothing new. Peacemaking, as articulated in the teachings of Buddhism, Christianity, Judaism, Islam, Taoism, and Native American religions, is thousands of years old. Yet there are interesting parallels with the ideas of postmodernism.

Science and the age of enlightenment generally relegated religion to a secondary status as a means of creating knowledge. Empiricism became the new god, with objectivity, determinism, and causality the new mantras. Postmodernism questioned this and opened the door for a reconsideration, if not reconceptualization, of ancient means of dispute resolution. According to Mason, "postmodernism is a useful tool for expanding our conceptualization and application of peace studies. In particular, as a system of ideas that stresses the unavoidable ethnocentric and normative character of Western assumptions about conflict resolution, postmodernism offers us a means to adjust planning and expectations to different societal conditions" (1995). Mason considers the conflict resolution measures used by several cultural groups to provide some insight. Contrasting the United States with Japan, for example, reveals that Americans value individuality over age and even status. Americans are highly verbal, precise, and litigious while the Japanese focus on expression and body language. The Hawaiian model of peacemaking focuses on a religious context, conciliation, and achieving harmony; in rural China the village as a whole resolves conflict (Mason 1995). Native Americans rely on restorative justice grounded in cultural beliefs (Winfree 2002). Each method is culturally specific, yet, if adaptation is possible and if the human state is malleable, then each offers lessons for peacemaking. Yet if we are serious about respecting diversity, we may have to tolerate that which may offend our cultural or religious sensitivities. This would be a small price to pay for peace—much cheaper than the wars we wage. Can peacemaking replace the war on crime?

Based on a spiritual humanistic critique of Western civilizations, the peacemaking criminologists Hal Pepinsky and Richard Quinney want to replace making war on crime with the idea of making peace on crime (Pepinsky and Quinney 1991). Like crimes, penal sanctions are intended harms and, as Harris noted, we "need to reject the idea that those who cause injury or harm to others should suffer severance of the common bonds of respect and concern that bind members of a community. We should relinquish the notion that it is acceptable to try to 'get rid of' another person, whether through execution, banishment, or caging away people about whom we do not care" (1991, 93). Peacemaking criminologists argue that instead of escalating the violence in our already violent society by responding to violence and conflict with state violence and conflict in the form of penal sanctions such as death and prison, we need to de-escalate violence by responding to it through forms of conciliation, mediation, and dispute settlement: "The only path to peace is peace itself. Punishment merely adds heat. . . . Relief from violence requires people to indulge in democracy, in making music together" (Pepinsky 1991b,

109–110). By democracy, Pepinsky means a genuine participation by all in life decisions that is only achievable in a decentralized, nonhierarchical social structure.

Bracewell (1990) articulates the central themes of peacemaking as (1) connectedness to each other and to our environment and the need for reconciliation; (2) caring for each other in a nurturing way as a primary objective in corrections; and (3) mindfulness, meaning the cultivation of inner peace. To promote such a vision of justice, according to Quinney (1991), it is necessary to recognize connectedness, or "oneness," with other beings in the world, the inseparable connection between our personal suffering and the suffering in the world. To change the world, we must first change ourselves. This means not retaliating against others when we are hurt by them and not classifying others in ways that deny them freedom.

Inspired by the work of Pepinsky and Quinney, John Fuller (1998, 2003) contrasts the peacemaking perspective with the war on crime perspective. He shows how "peacemaking criminology is part of a larger intellectual enterprise that spanned the range from interpersonal issues to global concerns, thus demonstrating the interconnectedness of criminal justice to larger areas of social justice" (Fuller 2003, 86). In *Criminal Justice: A Peacemaking Perspective* Fuller (1998) outlines six components: (1) Advocating nonviolence in criminal justice responses, particularly opposing the premeditated violence of the death penalty. (2) Social justice issues, such as sexism, racism, and inequality, need to be incorporated and corrected in criminal justice responses. (3) Inclusion means that every stakeholder affected by and connected with a crime, such as victim, families of victim and offender, neighbors, and so on, need to be involved in its solution, instead of restricting criminal justice to the offender and the state. (4) Correct means involving the offenders in the settlement of their cases, rather than having it imposed, and removing mechanisms of enforcement, such as racial profiling, that contribute to further crimes rather than those that reduce tensions. (5) Ascertainable criteria means that victims, offenders, and community members fully understand the criminal justice process that they participate in, restricting the use of legalese and technical jargon. (6) Categorical imperative means that all participants in the criminal justice system should be treated with respect and dignity. Fuller argues:

> As opposed to the war on crime perspective, the peacemaking perspective has the potential to provide lasting solutions to the problems that lead individuals to commit violations of law. The war on crime perspective, with its emphasis on punishment and retribution ensures that offenders will strive only to commit their crimes in a more efficient manner so as not to get caught. The peacemaking perspective on the other hand, seeks to address the

conditions of society that foster crime and to address the problems of the individual offender. Additionally the peacemaking perspective seeks to understand and respond to the concerns of the victims. (Fuller 2003, 88)

The Limits of Peacemaking Criminology

Not surprisingly, these ideas have met with considerable criticism from commentators who point out that "being nice" is not enough to stop others from committing harm, that peacemaking is unrealistic, and that it can extend the power of the state, thus widening the net of social control (Cohen 1985). Others have suggested that its value lies in sensitizing us to alternatives to accepting violence (DeKeseredy and Schwartz 1996). One of the most extensive criticisms of peacemaking is offered by Akers (2000), who claims that the perspective is not open to empirical scrutiny, is contradictory to Marxist and feminist ideas that claim to inform it, offers nothing new that has not been offered by traditional mainstream criminology, and does not offer a solution to address wider structural causes of violence. Advocates such as Fuller (2003) accept that the theory needs to be developed to be testable and agrees that although peacemaking policies "such as non-punitive treatment of offenders, mediation, restitution, offender reintegration, rehabilitation, and so on have been advocated by traditional criminology, unfortunately, with the war on crime mentality that dominates the criminal justice system today, these policies have fallen into disuse. . . . The peacemaking perspective provides a coherent web to weave together all of these progressive policies" (2003, 94).

Constitutive criminologists have developed a way of peacemaking that avoids some of the more obvious pitfalls. It is called social judo: "Judo means 'gentle way' and is based on the seeming paradox that the best defense is non-fighting and that one gains victory over an opponent by yielding—gentle turns away the sturdy opponent. . . . It is a method whereby the energy of the violent is redirected against the opponent to diffuse the violence" (Einstadter and Henry 1995, 315; Henry and Milovanovic 1996). As Bohm (1997, 16) says, "the judo metaphor is apt here because, on the one hand . . . using power to reduce the power of others only replaces one excessive investor with another. On the other hand, when using judo as a means of self-defence, the power of the aggressor is turned back against the aggressor." Although this model might release us from the punitive trap, as yet it remains underdeveloped, particularly as to how in practice energy invested by offenders can be turned back on them in peaceful ways.

Gregg Barak suggests explicit ways of achieving peace (2003). In American society, for example, the media plays a huge role in influencing perceptions. Unfortunately, rather than a positive force for peace, "organizationally and managerially, mass media overemphasizes interpersonal violence . . . while it ignores or downplays institutional and structural violence" (Barak 2003, 11). He continues to make a strong case for conflict resolution and peacemaking based on mutuality, human rights, and a "need-based justice."

Overall, peacemaking approaches have one common theme that is consistent with several of the critical approaches that we have examined: connections and the social nature of humans and the world we construct. All agree that the analytical approaches that separate individuals from their social context leave out much of what is important. The restorative justice approach has been most developed in this regard.

Restorative Justice

Restorative justice has its roots in several different approaches, including restitution practices of the first-century Anglo-Saxons, Native American and Aboriginal justice, Mennonite activism, victim movements, abolitionist and peacemaking criminology, and Braithwaite's ideas about reintegrative shaming (Sarre 2003). The term "restorative justice" was coined by psychologist Albert Eglash in writing about reparation (Eglash 1977, 95; Sarre 2003, 100–101). Like peacemaking, restorative justice is concerned with rebuilding relationships after an offense, rather than driving a wedge between offenders and their communities, which is the hallmark of modern criminal justice systems (Sarre 2003). Restorative justice is a "victim-centered response to crime that allows the victim, the offender, their families, and representatives of the community to address the harm caused by the crime" (Umbreit 2001). It focuses on "repairing the harm caused by the crime" (Daly 2000) and, like restitution, "seeks to restore losses suffered by crime victims and facilitate peace" (Coward-Yaskiw 2002). Rather than impose decisions about winners and losers through an adversarial system, "restorative justice seeks a facilitate dialog between all agents affected by the crime . . . including the victim, offender, their supporters, and the community at large" (Brennan 2003, 6). It involves "a process whereby all parties with a stake in a particular offence come together to resolve collectively how to deal with the aftermath of the offence and its implications for the future" (Marshall 2002, 11). In the process of coming together,

> Victims speak of how the crime affected them; offenders may be able to explain why they committed the offense, and community members can offer narratives on how the community may have been changed because of the crime. Supporters of both the victim and offender may offer their stories as well. By giving a voice to all parties involved it may help the victim under-

stand why the offense was committed (perhaps the offender had a substance abuse problem and needed money for drugs) and find the compassion to forgive and find treatment. (Brennan 2003, 7)

According to one of the founders of this approach, "restorative justice is about healing rather than hurting, moral learning, community participation and community caring, respectful dialogue, forgiveness, responsibility, apology, and making amends." Moreover, it "mostly works well in granting justice, closure, restoration of dignity, transcendence of shame, and healing for victim" (Braithwaite 2002, 11, 69). The approach is well summarized by Sarre:

> A restorative system of criminal justice endeavors to listen to, and appease, aggrieved parties to conflict and to restore, as far as possible, right relationships between antagonists. In restorative models crime is defined as a violation of one person by another, the focus is on problem solving, dialogue and restitution (where possible), mutuality, the repair of social injury and the possibilities of repentance and forgiveness." (2003, 98)

In practice, restorative justice includes a whole host of forums that include family conferencing for juveniles (Braithwaite and Mugford 1994; Strang 2000), family violence court, victim-offender mediation conferences and programs (VOM, VORP), family group counseling, sentencing circles, healing circles, and "other practices such as 'reparation boards' in Vermont, services to crime victims, meetings between imprisoned offenders and victims (or their family members)" (Daly 2000).

Unlike conventional criminal justice that focuses on the offense to the state by individuals but does nothing to deal with the consequences of the harm to the victims and the community, restorative justice builds community trust and adds to a community's "social capital," thereby providing protection against future crimes (Coleman 1988). "Restorative justice builds on social capital because it decentralizes the offense from merely the act of an offender breaking the law, to a breach in a community's trust in its members. This in turn allows the community along with the offender and victim to *collectively* look for a resolution" (Brennan 2003, 8). Many religious groups have long advocated for this type of solution.

The Limits of Restorative Justice

Sarre (2003, 101–102) identifies several criticisms that have been leveled at restorative justice that he says explain a reluctance to adopt it more widely. These include the views that it (1) is really rehabilitation in disguise, (2) excuses violence, particularly against women and children, (3) contradicts the principle of public open justice and legal protections by use of private forums and cooptation techniques on participants, (4) is soft on crime and ignores public retributive attitudes, (5) undermines, through community justice and informal judgments, the standards of traditional legal reasoning, (6) contradicts the legal notion of equal treatment of like cases and the certainty and consistency of outcomes (which under restorative justice are necessarily variable), and (7) assumes the status quo is a desired outcome, rather than striving for a transformative outcome that changes the situation of those offending and those harmed. In addition, restorative programs deal with less serious offenses. At the same time, there is an emerging set of principles that mitigate against some of the problems that have been identified:

All parties are present voluntarily.
Victims are treated with sensitivity and have the control lost through the crime restored.
Offenders are sufficiently coerced to not use the system for self-preservation but to help solve the problems created by their offense.
Trained and unbiased facilitators are used.
Facilitators are flexible toward the solutions proposed by the participants. (Umbreit 2001; Umbreit and Coates 1998)

There is growing evidence that restorative justice approaches are being increasingly adopted even for violent offenders. Ironically, Texas, one of the most punitive states, developed a victim-offender protocol for violent offenses in 1993 and similar ones have since been adopted by twelve other states (Umbreit, Coates, Vos, and Brown 2002). Umbreit and his colleagues suggest that "many of the principles of restorative justice can be applied in crimes of severe violence, including murder, with clear effectiveness in supporting both the process of victim healing and offender accountability" (2002, 2). However, although evidence is building, at present "there is a lack of definition and a lack of data" and "we need to find out about the performance of each restorative model in order to determine whether it can 'support the hopes of its proponents . . . or succumb to the criticisms of its detractors'" (Strang 2000; cited in Sarre 2003, 107).

In the final section of this chapter we examine left realism, a critical approach that, like peacemaking and restorative justice, seeks to work from the assumption that crime is interconnected with the wider society, that victims and the harm done to them need to be taken seriously, and that crime needs to be addressed from the wider perspective, not just theoretically but pragmatically.

Left Realism

Left realism took form in the 1980s when Jock Young, one of the coauthors of *The New Criminology* (Taylor et al. 1973), and his colleagues began to analyze the results of a local area victimization study (see, especially, Jones, MacLean, and Young 1986; Matthews and Young 1986, 1992; Young and Matthews 1992; MacLean 1991). Young had earlier criticized criminology "of the left" for being too idealistic and termed it "left idealism" (Young 1979; Lea and Young 1984). It was idealistic because it started from abstract concepts rather than concrete realities (MacLean 1991, 11). Lea and Young (1984) argued that left idealism's exclusive focus on corporate and white-collar crime, its romantic celebrations of street criminals as working-class revolutionaries, and its assertions about the need for broad revolutionary policies ignored the feelings of most working-class crime victims—who most feared criminal attack by members of their own class. By contrast, left realism takes victims seriously, arguing that crime destroys the quality of urban community life (Matthews 1987). But left realists are also acutely aware of the harm caused to victims suffering from crimes of inequality.

To complete the picture of crime, left realism argues that it is essential to include both victims and offenders in their relationships to each other, to the state's criminal justice agencies, and to the general public. Left realists call this set of relationships the "square of crime" (Young and Matthews 1992). More like strain theorists (discussed in Chapter 9) than Marxists, they argue that the capitalist system promotes competitive individualism and feeds off patriarchy and racism, creating inequalities among people that lead to relative deprivation (Young 1999). Those at the bottom of the heap experience relative deprivation because they cannot afford the pleasures of life enjoyed by others: "These are people who watch the same TV ads as everyone else and who are hustling to obtain products and status symbols such as color TVs, fancy cars, and expensive gold jewelry—desires created almost solely by capitalism" (DeKeseredy and Schwartz 1996, 250). Capitalism is the source of discontent. Young (1999) argues that many Americans and Europeans now live in "exclusive societies" "where an alarming number of people are excluded from the formal labor market, where thousands of people have to live on the street or in dilapidated public housing estates, and where inner-city violence is endemic" (DeKeseredy 2003, 39). These ghettos and ghost towns were produced by capital concentrations but were abandoned as it "winged its way elsewhere" to new global locations "where labor was cheaper and expectations lower" (Young 1999, 20). Since those isolated at the bottom of the heap are politically powerless to change their situation, they become angry and violent and abuse each other, producing violent crime incidents. Some of their number also turn to stealing the very symbols (TVs, etc.) they cannot afford to buy. In this context, crime is an unjust individualistic solution to the experience of injustice among people who lack legitimate means of solving the problem of relative depravation (Young 1999; DeKeseredy 2003).

Rather than protect them from crime, police agencies tend to reinforce the inequalities, and the criminal justice system produces its own casualties within already impoverished neighborhoods. Thus the "excluded" become victimized from all directions, by their oppression in the society, the crimes of their fellow oppressed, the crimes and injustices of corporations, and punitive actions of the criminal justice system.

Left realism, as its name suggests, is therefore critical of capitalism for creating and sustaining the inequalities and divisions that turn people against one another, favoring instead some form of socialist society (hence the term "left"). Rather than waiting for the revolution, they propose to do something immediate, practical, and concrete to alleviate the suffering (this accounts for "realism"). Unlike the "left idealists" who romanticize the crimes of the poor, or "progressive minimalists" who downplay the problems of the poor (Currie 1992; left realists seem to like to negatively label those they oppose!), left realists do not believe in waiting for a socialist revolution before implementing policies that reduce the suffering from crime caused by the capitalist system and its agencies of social control. They argue that to do so is irresponsible because it allows the sole voice in the policy debate to be the right realist "law and order" lobby (Matthews 1987). By contrast, right realists tend to view crime as the result of individual choice and include many of the ideas and policy recommendations we discussed in Chapter 3.

Instead of tougher sentences and more prisons, left realists prefer alternative practical policy interventions, not dissimilar to the others we have seen in this chapter, that deal with both the immediacy of the crime problem and people's fear of it (Lea and Young 1984). These include preventive policies that (1) introduce problem solvers into working-class neighborhoods to defuse problems and to address residents' concerns through local crime surveys, (2) use alternative sanctions such as restitution and community service to "demarginalize" offenders and integrate them back into the community, and (3) encourage community involvement and democratically accountable control of the police by community citizens. In general, left realists "seek short-term gains while remaining committed to long-term change. That is why they propose practical initiatives that can be implemented immediately and that 'chip away' at patriarchal capitalism" (DeKeseredy 2003, 36). These include efforts aimed at "reducing poverty and unemployment, curbing violence against women, and building strong communities" (2003, 37). In this regard, left realists are increasingly acknowledging the value of "collective efficacy" or "social capital" in which strong community networks of social support and informal social control ideas emerged from the ecology perspective (Chapter 8), while also paying attention to meaningful employment and effective social programs (2003, 39).

Limits of Left Realism

Left realism has been subject to several criticisms, not least the charge that it lacks originality and takes us little further than previous theory with regard to causation. As both Gibbons (1994, 170) and Shoemaker (1996, 219) pointed out, left realist policy proposals are similar to those that emerged from social ecology theory (discussed in Chapter 8), strain theory (discussed in Chapter 9), and mainstream sociological criminology in general. Michalowski (1991) also cautioned that left realists use a loose concept of community that could result in right-wing populist and racist control of the police. He warned of the contradictions in pursuing criminal justice reform without accompanying structural changes from the capitalist system to a socialist form.

Another major criticism of left realism is that it excludes feminist concerns, remaining "gender blind" and "gender biased." It makes no attempt to explain women's experiences of crime, victimization, or justice (Carlen 1992). Some argue that its policies call for a strengthening of the power of the oppressive state and have the effect of strengthening patriarchy and defeating women's interests (Schwartz and DeKeseredy 1991; DeKeseredy and Schwartz 1991).

Finally, left realists have been criticized for ignoring crimes of the powerful, such as corporate or white-collar crime (Henry 1999), and advocating so-called progressive policies that include reinforcing the very structures of capitalist oppression that they are critiquing, such as "job creation programs," "entrepreneurial skills training in schools and linking schools and private businesses" (DeKeseredy 2003, 37).

Conclusion

We began this chapter by reviewing major changes in the world that have occurred during the past twenty years, which have involved a globalization of economics, politics, and social and cultural life. We showed how this change has impacted production, consumption and distribution, communications, technology, and transportation. We showed how the world's societies now face changing kinds of threats. Underlying these changes is an increased interdependence with others in societies across the world. We argued that traditional criminological approaches that fail to acknowledge this global interconnectedness, and criminal justice approaches that adopt a war metaphor against crime, are inadequate to address the emerging problems, harms, and crimes of the twenty-first century. We explored new approaches, postmodernism and constitutive theory, peacemaking criminology and restorative justice, and left realism that have in common the view that criminology needs to take a holistic, integrative approach that brings offenders, victims, and the community back together. While these hold much promise for the future, others believe that in order to fully comprehend the complexity of the individual's relationship with global society we need first to incorporate and integrate the divisions in criminological thinking. In view of this, several criminologists have begun to examine the reconnection of criminology to itself under the umbrella term "integrated theory." We conclude with a discussion of this movement.

Summary Chart: Critical Criminologies

1. Postmodern/Constitutive

Human Nature and Society: Interrelated and coproductive of each other. Humans are socially constructed "subjects" whose energy and active agency build the very social structures that limit and channel their actions and transform them and thereby change society in an ongoing dialectical fashion. Both are socially constructed, although treated as if real.

Crime: Crime is harm produced through the exercise of power that denies others the ability to make a difference. Crimes of repression keep people from becoming what they might have been; crimes of reduction undermine what they already have become (e.g., by removing something from them, whether physically through violence; material assets through theft; or status, identity, belief, etc.).

Law: Law is myth: an exaggeration of one narrowly defined kind of rule to the exclusion of others, such as informal norms, customs, and so on.

Criminals: Criminals are "excessive investors" in the use of power to dominate others; expropriate the ability to make a difference by denying others. Victims are "recovering subjects" contingent on becoming fulfilled but never completing the process, damaged through having that progress interrupted.

Causal Logic: Crime is not so much caused as coproduced by the whole society through its investment in social construction of difference and expert knowledge and in building power based on this. The process of crime production is manifest through symbolic and harmful discourse that imbues social constructions with the appearance of objective realities and then treats them as such.

Criminal Justice Policy: Deconstruction of existing truth claims through exposing their arbitrary constitution; reconstruction of less harmful discourses; work toward decentralized superliberal democratic structure that accommodates a diversity of voices.

Criminal Justice Practice: Replacement discourse, through media; nonviolent settlement-directed talking; peacemaking alternatives such as mediation; restorative justice; and narrative therapy. Empowering ordinary people through
accepting their voice.

Evaluation: Unclear and complex; excludes others through use of highly abstract
jargon; nihilistic, lacking standards; not open to conventional empirical testing;
romantic about possibility of transformation.

2. Peacemaking/Restorative

Human Nature: Humans are products of power structures, repressed from being
their true humanistic cooperative selves and encouraged by hierarchical divisions to be competitive individualists. Can restore their humanity by reconnecting with others.

Society and the Social Order: A hierarchical system of power and authority regardless of the basis; socialist and even communist society as bad as capitalist
as each is dominated by a powerful centralized bureaucratic state. All hierarchical societies feed off and exploit divisions of class, race, and gender. Crime is
a reflection and an expression of broken social relations, and it harms other individuals and communities.

Law: The enforcement arm of state; itself a force of conflict that divides rather
than unites communities.

Criminals: The distorted product of power structures who can be reintegrated to
the community provided they are treated with respect and allowed to actively
make amends for their harms.

Causal Logic: Concentration of power creates hierarchies that divide people and
pit them against one another in an unnatural competitive struggle in which
they lose respect and see each other as objects and obstacles in the way of personal, often material, goals. The hierarchical system of power/authority is the
cause of crime.

Criminal Justice Policy: Replace systems of hierarchical power; abolish state coercion, especially prisons; and replace with fully participatory genuine democracy based on consensual decision making. Achieved through a spiritual
awakening. Philosophy is to reintegrate offender, victim, and community,
which provides an opportunity to correct problems in wider social relations.
Encourage diversity and difference and leave ambiguities of meaning unresolved.

Criminal Justice Practice: Replace existing form of justice with a peacemaking,
restorative, decentralized system of negotiated face-to-face informal justice in
which all members participate and share their decisions as fully responsible
members. Justice should be about peacemaking, healing wrongs through mediation and negotiation, with sanctions of collective persuasion and shaming. Responsibility for offense is shared with community.

Evaluation: Seen as untestable and having an air of conspiracy theory by mainstream critics; seen as supporting rather than challenging status quo by radical
critics, but as part of an overall solution by moderate supporters.

3. Left Realism

Human Nature: Humans are shaped by hierarchical power structures of class, race, and gender, which produce differentials in wealth and relative deprivation. Humans are repressed and coopted for the benefit of dominant interests.

Society and the Social Order: Capitalist class hierarchy uses the state to resolve contradictions; gains legitimacy by coopting the powerless.

Crime: Crime is harm to others; it is divisive and undermines community, which helps maintain the capitalist system.

Law: Law is a system of maintaining power that provides genuine protection against harm in order to gain legitimation for wider capitalist system. Law represents a history of victories over the powerful curbing their crude, arbitrary, and coercive will.

Criminals: Criminals are structurally powerless, commit genuine harm, and create real fear through victimizing others, especially others who are powerless; criminals are also victims of capitalism's structural contradictions and of the state via the criminal justice system.

Causal Logic: Relative deprivation from conspiring forces of class inequality, racism, and patriarchy causes crime as people feel injustice and anger and take this out on those closest to them. Other crime results from state inequities in justice and labeling of offenders.

Criminal Justice Policy: Ultimately should work toward democratic socialist society, but until then pragmatic approach to do something now to prevent suffering from crime rather than waiting for the revolution. Restructure rather than replace criminal justice. Strengthen and control the criminal justice system of capitalist society and correct bias that leaves structurally powerless more vulnerable to street crime. Belief that law can provide the structurally powerless with real gains, if not ideal victories. Protecting the structurally weak through improving social justice helps re-create community necessary to replace the existing capitalist system with decentralized socialism.

Criminal Justice Practice: Protects rights of victims. Essential to provide equal justice to powerless through state protection, community policing, neighborhood watch. Democratize police and subject them to community controls. Defends treatment, rehabilitation, and welfare against attacks from the political right.

Evaluation: Criticized by radical left for abandoning socialist cause, being reformist, and being coopted by capitalist system, which its policies seek to strengthen, particularly its bureaucratic apparatus. In supporting working-class victimology, it distracts from crimes of the powerful. Focus little different from mainstream criminology. Feminists argue it is gender blind, treating women as victims rather than active human agents.

Conclusion:
Integrative Theory

The Future of Criminology?

Stuart has a fifteen-year-old Toyota and lives in Michigan. He likes the design, convenience, and reliability of the car (like U.S. society), but it has a serious rust problem (like crime). The rust is a real threat to the car, since it can lead to the rotting of fuel or brake lines or even the driveshaft; it also makes the car and the author look worn out! How will he deal with the rust problem? He could fill in the body where the rust comes through (resocialization, education, skills training), but the rust will shortly reappear (recidivism). He could use better filler materials, but then the rust would come through elsewhere (crime displacement). He could hire someone to continually perform body repair work (the criminal justice system). He could replace broken and damaged parts with new ones, but soon they too would wear and break. He could take a broader approach and explore the structural causes of this rust and look to the environment. Michigan gets a lot of snow in winter and road crews use a lot of salt on the roads, which corrodes steel when mixed with melted snow. He could choose not to drive the car on winter roads (routine activities) or keep it in the garage, but that only seems to delay the problem. Why is it that other car owners in the state and car owners in other states do not seem to have the same rust problem (comparative crime data)?

Perhaps the problem is in the whole concept of the car and in the details of its local use, storage, and so on. Car manufacturers in competition with other manufacturers want to cut costs but not product performance; one way of doing so is to reduce the gauge of steel that is used in body manufacture. Lighter-gauge steel, in an environment of water vapor and carbon monoxide, as occurs in a garage, plus salt from the roads and a driver who takes little care to wash off the salt, combine to produce rust. If we lived in a culture that emphasized longevity of products rather than consumption, and if we recycled, and if body image (human and auto) were less hyped via the media, we might design cars for a lifetime rather than for obsolescence. What causes rust (crime)? Clearly, a combination of each of the dimensions is included in this illustration.

Since 1979, a trend in criminology has emerged that many find exciting and fitting with our changing global situation, which we discussed in the previous chapter. Instead of developing new theories that compete to supersede previous ones, some theorists have attempted to combine what they see as the best elements of these diverse positions (Johnson 1979; Elliott et al. 1985). Those engaging in integration have done so for a variety of reasons, not least because of a desire to arrive at central anchoring notions in theory, to provide coherence to a bewildering array of fragmented theories, to achieve comprehensiveness and completeness to advance scientific progress, and to synthesize causation and social control (Barak 1998). In this conclusion, we want to briefly explore integration of criminological theories, beginning with a simple definition, critically exploring some of the issues in integration, and then illustrating integration. We provide two examples of different kinds of integration: modernist and holistic.

Theoretical integration has been defined as the "combination of two or more preexisting theories, selected on the basis of their perceived commonalities, into a single reformulated theoretical model with greater comprehensiveness and explanatory value than any one of its component theories" (Farnworth 1989, 95). For example, one component of integrated theory may focus on the learning process, another on the impact of social control, and a third on the effects on class structure or social ecology. This sounds relatively straightforward and logical; it may even be, as students often tell us, plain common sense. But it is fraught with difficulty. Let us see why.

First is the issue of what precisely is integrated. Do we integrate theoretical concepts or propositions? Integrating concepts involves finding those that have similar meanings in different theories and merging them into a common language, as was done in Akers's ([1977] 1985, 1994) conceptual absorption approach. Akers merged concepts from social learning and social control theory (among others). For example, "belief," which in control theory refers to moral convictions for or against delinquency, is equated to "definitions favorable or unfavorable to crime," taken from differential association theory, and so on. Since this can reduce or absorb one or another concept to the other (Thornberry 1989; Hirschi 1979), even Akers asks whether it is integration or simply a "hostile takeover" (Akers 1994, 186).

Comprehensive attempts at conceptual integration can distort and even transform the original concepts, as in Pearson and Weiner's (1985) attempt to integrate every theory. For example, "commitment," which in control theory refers to the potential loss that crime may produce to those with whom one is bonded, is combined with more simplistic classical and learning ideas of rewards and punishment to become the new concept of "utility demand and reception." But if the integrated concepts are not reduced, then simply including all the major concepts becomes impracticably cumbersome.

If we do not integrate concepts, but merely their propositions, the problems can be worse. Propositional integration refers to combining propositions from theories or placing them in some causal order or sequence. As Shoemaker (1996, 254) observes in considering the integration of differential association and social control theories, "If one were to include all major components of these two theories in one comprehensive model, there would be at least 13 variables, and most likely more than double that amount. If other theoretical explanations were included, such as anomie, social disorganization, psychological and biological theories, the number of potential variables in the analysis would soon approach 50!" Testing such an integrated theory would be impractical on account of the difficulty of the large sample size required—that is, if we rely on positivistic principles of testing.

Beyond what is integrated is the issue of how propositions are logically related. Propositions may be related (1) end to end, which implies a sequential causal order, (2) side by side, which implies overlapping influences, or (3) up and down, which suggests that the propositions from one can be derived from a more abstract form (Hirschi 1979; Bernard and Snipes 1996).

A third related issue is the nature of causality that is assumed in the formal structure of any integrated theory. Does the integrated theory use linear causality, which takes the form of a sequential chain of events? Does it employ multiple causality, in which a crime is the outcome of several different causes or a combination of them together? Might interactive or reciprocal causality, in which the effects of one event, in turn, influence its cause(s), which then influence the event, be most appropriate? Alternatively, should the integrative theory use dialectical or reciprocal causality, such that causes and events are not discrete entities but are overlapping and interrelated, being codetermining (Einstadter and Henry 1995; Henry and Milovanovic 1996; Barak 1998)? Clearly the interactive and dialectical models of causality suggest a dynamic rather than static form of integration (Einstadter and Henry 1995). Should different causalities be integrated, some dynamic and some static?

A fourth issue is the level of concepts and theories that are integrated. Should these be of the same level or across levels? In other words, should only theories relating to the individual level be combined with others at the individual level (micro-level integration), as in Wilson and Herrnstein's (1985) combination of biological and rational choice; and structural cultural level with structural cultural (macro-level integration), as in Hagan and colleagues' (1987) power-control integration of Marxism and feminism? Should integrationists cross levels (macro-micro integration), as in Colvin and Pauly's (1983) attempt to combine Marxist, conflict, strain subculture, social learning, and social control theories? Integration levels to be considered, then, include (1) kinds of people, their human agency, and their interactive social processes; (2) kinds of organization, their collective agency, and their organizational processes; and (3) kinds of culture, structure, and context (Akers 1994; Barak 1998).

The level of integration may depend on what is to be explained, or the scope of integration, which is a fifth consideration. Is the integration intended to explain crime in general or a specific type of crime? Is it intended to apply to the population in general or only certain sectors of it (e.g., young, old, men, women, African American, Hispanic, etc.)?

Some have argued that by combining theories we lose more than we gain—that "theory competition" and "competitive isolation" are preferable to "integration." They point out that criminology shows a "considerable indifference and healthy skepticism toward theoretical integration" (Akers 1994, 195; Gibbons 1994). Yet others see "knowledge integration" as valuable (Shoemaker 1996; Bernard and Snipes 1996; Barak 1998; Robinson 2004).

Clearly, these are complex issues to resolve. The result, as Einstadter and Henry (1995) argue, may be that the original goal of reducing competitive theories is replaced by competition between different types of integrative theory as integrationists argue for their particular model as the best combination: "Since each integration theorist may use different criteria to construct his or her own comprehensive approach, what emerges is integrational chaos" (1995, 309). Indeed, there is a danger that all new developments in a particular tradition that draw on aspects of the earlier tradition are now labeled as "integrated." For example, Hunter and Dantzker (2002, 135) construct a typology of four types of integrated theories: (1) integrated classical theories—routine activities (Cohen and Felson 1979), rational choice (Cornish and Clarke 1986), criminal personality (Yockelson and Samenow (1976); (2) integrated biological theories—bioconditioning (Eysenck and Gudjonsson 1989), human nature (Wilson and Herrnstein 1985); (3) integrated psychological theories—delinquency development (Farrington 1988), age-graded (Sampson and Laub 1993), self-derogation (Kaplan 1975); and (4) integrated sociological theories. The last category is further divided into four subtypes: (a) integrated learning—composed of network analysis theory (Krohn 1986) and interactional theory (Thornberry 1987); (b) integrated control theory—composed of control balance theory (Tittle 1995), social developmental theory (Weis and Hawkins 1981), and reintegrative shaming theory (Braithwaite 1989); (c) integrated strain theory— composed of integrated theory (Elliott, Huizinga and Agerton 1985) and general strain theory (Agnew 1985); and (d) integrated conflict theory—composed of power control theory (Hagan, Simpson, and Gillis 1987) and integrated structural Marxist theory (Colvin and Pauly 1983). Hunter and Dantzker include fourteen different theories labeled "integrated." They go on to describe approaches beyond integration that they call "holistic theories" by which they mean general explanations of crime, which "combine multifactor perspectives" allowing "criminologists to see the entire panorama" rather than a one-dimensional picture (2002, 150). Here they include another seven theories (making 21 in all): bioenvironmental theory (Jeffrey 1977), conceptual absorption theory (Akers 2000), conceptual integration theory (Pearson and Weiner 1985), general paradigm theory (Vila 1994), self-control theory and integrative delinquency theory (Gottfredson and Hirschi 1990), and their own identity theory (Hunter and Dantzka 2003, 155–157).

In an effort to bring some clarity to the integrated picture, Einstadter and Henry (1995, 303) developed an analysis of the various "integrated theories" showing which original theories they explicitly drew together. Below we have extended and adapted this table, including only the theories that explicitly attempt integration. We also include a brief description of the approach taken by the integrated theory, since space precludes a more extensive treatment.

Although this table does not exhaust the range of integrative theories and it conflates similar ones, while leaving out others that are no more than developments of earlier theories, it indicates that the theories most frequently included in integrated paradigms are social learning and social control, followed by anomie, conflict, then Marxist, ecology, psychology/personality, and rational choice. With social learning most frequently incorporated, there is some justification to Aker's (2000) claim that all criminal behavior is based on social learning because almost all theories draw on social learning as a component. The relatively low number of inclusions of feminist theory does little to challenge feminist views that gender has been left out of criminological theorizing. Regardless, the above analysis suggests that the array of integrated theories is now as vast as the array of original theories, as Einstadter and Henry (1995) predicted, which leads to considerable confusion.

Recently some have begun to suggest ways out of this theoretical quagmire: (1) identifying two broad approaches to integration: modernist and postmodernist and (2) providing an integration of integrated theory. We might call this hyperintegration.

Barak's book *Integrating Criminologies* (1998) provides the most comprehensive review of integration to date, suggests that modernist integration, in all its different guises, really aims at the "questionable objective of delivering some kind of positivist prediction of 'what causes criminal behavior.'" In postmodernist integration, however, "everything,

TABLE C.1—Integrative Theories

Theory (ordered by year idea first introduced)	Theorists	Core Idea	Classical/ Rational Choice	Biological	Psychological Personality	Learning	Control Social Bonding	Labeling/social contructionism	Ecology/ cultural	Subcultural	Strain Anomie	Conflict	Marxist Radical	Feminist	Post-modernist	Peacemaking Restorative
Integrated theory social	Elliott, Huizinga and Agerton, 1979, 1985	Strain in family, school, community weakens social bonds, increases bonds with delinquent peers				X	X				X					
Social developmental model/ theory	Weis and Hawkins, 1981; Weis and Sederstrom, 1979	Socialization in poorly bonded families reduces resistance to delinquency via peer subculture				X	X			X	X					
Integrated structural Marxist theory/ differential coercion theory	Colvin and Pauly, 1983; Colvin, 2000	Capitalist exploitation produces coercive family environment, strains family, weakens bonds, aggravated by coercive school				X	X			X	X	X	X			

Theory	Authors	Description													
Left realist/exclusion theory	Mathews and Young, 1986; Young 1999	Capitalist market economy creates poor underclass, excluded from share of wealth, experience relative deprivation and subcultural conflict								X	X	X			
Conceptual integration theory	Pearson and Weiner, 1985	Primarily considers all the factors that can affect social learning and lead to crime	X			X	X	X	X	X	X	X			
Human nature	Wilson and Herrnstein, 1985	Humans make decisions shaped by biological, psychological, and environmental interactive factors	X	X	X	X									
Power control theory	Hagan, Simpson, and Gillis, 1987	Capitalism and patriarchy affect men and women in workplace, resulting in differential control over girls and boys at home with different delinquency outcomes	X			X				X	X	X			

(continues)

TABLE C.1—Integrative Theories (continued)

Theory (ordered by year idea first introduced)	Theorists	Core Idea	Classical/ Rational Choice	Biological	Psychological Personality	Learning	Control Social Bonding	Labeling/social contructionism	Ecology/ cultural	Subcultural	Strain Anomie	Conflict	Marxist Radical	Feminist	Post-modernist	Peacemaking Restorative
Network analysis theory	Krohn, 1986	Differential reinforcement of convention or deviant acts depending on extent and density of network contacts				X	X									
Interactional theory	Thornberry, 1987	Adolescence weakens conventional bonds, peers in disorganized communities become influential, but diminish with work and marriage			X	X	X		X							
Delinquency development/ age-graded/life course/ pathways	Farrington, 1988; Loeber and LeBlanc, 1990; Sampson and Laub, 1993	Poor parental interaction, poor role models shape criminal personality, reinforced by criminal career, or limited by social capital			X	X	X		X							

Theory	Citation	Description															
Reintegrative shaming theory	Braithwaite, 1989	Strain affects bonding, which if weakened makes labeling a shaming and excluding process, rather than reintegrating and normalizing					X		X	X				X			X
Edgework Theory	Lyng, 1990; O'Malley and Mugford, 1994 Milovanovic, 2002	Historical and cultural limits on the expression of human desire lead to pursuit of emotional expression via approaching the edge							X								
Constitutive theory	Henry and Milovanovic, 1991, 1996	Power and inequality build socially constructed differences through which harm deprivations imposed on the subordinated	X		X	X				X			X	X	X	X	
General ecology theory	Vila, 1994	Desire for resources interacts with socio-cultural & ecological factors, in a chaotic nonlinear way	X	X	X		X				X						

(continues)

TABLE C.1—Integrative Theories (continued)

Theory (ordered by year idea first introduced)	Theorists	Core Idea	Classical/ Rational Choice	Biological	Psychological Personality	Learning	Control Social Bonding	Labeling/social contructionism	Ecology/ cultural	Subcultural	Strain Anomie	Conflict	Marxist Radical	Feminist	Post-modernist	Peacemaking Restorative
Control balance theory	Tittle, 1995	Imbalance between amount of control exercised relative to amount subjected to leads to crime	X		X	X	X		X			X			X	
Integrated systems theory	Robinson, 2004	Crime is the outcome of a combination of risk factors, from biological through organism, group, community, and societal	X	X	X	X	X	X	X	X	X	X				
Total Number of inclusions by Integrated Theorists			6	3	6	12	11	5	6	5	7	7	6	2	3	2

at both the micro and macro levels, affects everything else, and where these effects are continuously changing over time" (1998, 188). The clash between modernist and postmodernist approaches is reminiscent of the old criminological division between functionalist and conflict theories (Henry and Milovanovic 1996; Milovanovic 1995).

This division is now applied to integration. Modernist integrative schemes, of the kind discussed so far, whatever form they take, are propositional and predictive, use linear or multiple causality, and are particularistic and static. Postmodernist integrative schemes, in contrast, are conceptual and interpretive, use interactive or reciprocal causality, and are holistic and dynamic. Barak argues that these holistic integrative models (e.g., "interactional," "ecological," "constitutive") of crime and crime control hold out the most promise for developing criminology. But rather than stopping there, Barak's hyperintegration model attempts to integrate these integrations, arguing that bringing together both modernist and postmodernist sensibilities is necessary to capture the "whole picture" of the social reality of crime.

The most recent advance in integrated theory by Matthew Robinson (2004) attempts to integrate all the factors from human "cell to society" (clustered in 22 groups) in a developmental interactive sequence to show how antisocial behavior is more or less likely. Robinson states, "The integrated systems theory of antisocial behavior attempts to advance the state of theories . . . past its myopic state by illustrating how risk factors at different levels of analysis from different academic disciplines interact to increase the probability that a person will commit antisocial behavior" (2004, 271). Instead of discussing theories in historical sequence (he believes criminology is "stuck in the past") and instead of dividing them by disciplines (which he says reinforces "artificial boundaries in knowledge about crime" and "limits our understanding of it") and instead of discussing the merits of different theories (which he believes creates false divisions), he examines the meaningful (tested) contribution to our understanding of crime made by each discipline (2004, x–xi). How this theory stands up to empirical testing remains to be seen, but this is perhaps the most ambitious, comprehensive interdisciplinary attempt so far to move integration of criminological theory to new heights.

Conclusion

At the beginning of the twentieth century, criminology had two very different paradigms to rub together, classical (free will) versus positivism (determinism). As the twentieth century progressed, the number and diversity of theories proliferated and calls for integration were issued. As the twenty-first century begins, we are invited to reconstitute the criminological enterprise anew from the perspective of a post-postmodernist hyperintegrative theory. How far this will take hold remains to be seen. As to what causes crime, we leave that for you to ponder, but each of the theories presented in this book makes a contribution. Now that you have read them, you will have an enhanced understanding of the complexity of crime and criminality.

We do not conclude this book with a solution to the crime problem. There is no single policy solution and there are no easy answers. As should be apparent from reading the often contradictory theories we have presented, there is no consensus on how to address crime. Even if a consensus did exist, it would be problematic, since without conflict and differences of opinion, evolutionary progress is not possible. This book is descriptive, not prescriptive. It is ultimately up to readers—the future criminological scholars and policymakers—to arrive at future crime solutions. Our goal has been to show what has transpired and where future directions in theory are leading us. Good luck!

References

Abbott, Jack Henry. 1981. *In the Belly of the Beast*. London: Hutchinson.

Abrahamsen, David. 1944. *Crime and the Human Mind*. New York: Columbia University Press.

_____. 1960. *The Psychology of Crime*. New York: Columbia University Press.

_____. 1973. *The Murdering Mind*. New York: Harper & Row.

Acker, James R. 1991. "Social Science in Supreme Court Death Penalty Cases: Citation Practices and Their Implications." *Justice Quarterly* 8:421–446.

Adams, A. Troy. 2000. "The Status of School Discipline and Violence." In W. Hinkle and S. Henry, eds., *School Violence*, Vol 567 *ANNALS of the American Academy of Political and Social Science*. Thousand Oaks, Calif.: Sage.

Adler, Alfred. 1931. *What Life Should Mean to You*. London: Allen & Unwin.

Adler, Freda. 1975. *Sisters in Crime: The Rise of the New Female Criminal*. New York: McGraw-Hill.

Adler, Freda, and William S. Laufer, eds. 1995. *The Legacy of Anomie Theory*. Vol. 6 of *Advances in Criminological Theory*. New Brunswick, N.J.: Transaction.

Adler, Freda, Gerhard O.W. Mueller, and William S. Laufer. 1995. *Criminology*. 2nd ed. New York: McGraw-Hill.

Ageton, Suzanne S., and Delbert S. Elliott. 1974. "The Effects of Legal Processing on Delinquent Orientations." *Social Problems* 22:87–100.

Agnew, Robert S. 1984. "Goal Achievement and Delinquency." *Sociology and Social Research* 68:435–451.

_____. 1985. "A Revised Strain Theory of Delinquency." *Social Forces* 64:151–167.

_____. 1989. "A Longitudinal Test of Revised Strain Theory." *Journal of Quantitative Criminology* 5:373–387.

_____. 1991. "The Interactive Effects of Peer Variables on Delinquency." *Criminology* 29:47–72.

_____. 1992. "Foundation for a General Strain Theory of Crime and Delinquency." *Criminology* 30:47–87.

_____. 1994. "The Techniques of Neutralization and Violence." *Criminology* 32:555–580.

_____. 1995a. "The Contribution of Social-Psychological Strain Theory to the Explanation of Crime and Delinquency." In Freda Adler and William S. Laufer, eds., *The Legacy of Anomie Theory*. Vol. 6 of *Advances in Criminological Theory*. New Brunswick, N.J.: Transaction.

_____. 1995b. "Controlling Delinquency: Recommendations from General Strain Theory." In Hugh D. Barlow, ed., *Crime and Public Policy: Putting Theory to Work*. Boulder: Westview.

_____. 2001. "Building on the Foundation of Generalized Stain Theory: Specifying the Types of Strain Most Likely to Lead to Crime and Delinquency." Unpublished manuscript, Emory University, Atlanta.

_____. 2002. "Experienced, Vicarious, and Anticipated Strain: An Exploratory Study on Physical Victimization and Delinquency." *Justice Quarterly* 19:603–629.

Agnew, Robert, and Helen Raskin White. 1992. "An Empirical Test of General Strain Theory." *Criminology* 30:475–499.

Agnew, Robert, Timothy Brezina, John Paul Wright, and Frances Cullen. 2002. "Strain, Personality Traits, and Delinquency: Extending General Strain Theory." *Criminology* 40:43–72.

Ahluwalia, Seema. 1991. "Currents in British Feminist Thought: The Study of Male Violence." *Critical Criminologist* 3:5–6, 12–14.

Aichhorn, August. 1935. *Wayward Youth.* New York: Viking.

Akers, Ronald. 2000. *Criminological Theories: Introduction, Evaluation, and Application.* 3rd ed. Los Angeles: Roxbury.

Akers, Ronald L. 1968. "Problems in the Sociology of Deviance: Social Definitions and Behavior." *Social Forces* 46:455–465.

_____. [1977] 1985. *Deviant Behavior: A Social Learning Approach.* Belmont, Calif.: Wadsworth.

_____. 1990. "Rational Choice, Deterrence, and Social Learning Theory: The Path Not Taken." *Journal of Criminal Law and Criminology* 81:653–676.

_____. 1994. *Criminological Theories: Introduction and Evaluation.* Los Angeles: Roxbury.

_____. 1998a. "Is Differential Association/Social Learning Cultural Deviance Theory?" In Stuart Henry and Werner Einstadter, eds., *The Criminology Theory Reader,* 228–242. New York: New York University Press.

_____. 1998b. *Social Learning and Social Structure: A General Theory of Crime And Deviance.* Boston: Northeastern University Press.

Akers, Ronald L., Marvin D. Krohn, Lonn Lanza-Kaduce, and Marcia Radosevich. 1979. "Social Learning and Deviant Behavior: A Specific Test of a General Theory." *American Sociological Review* 44:635–655.

Alarid, Leanne Fiftal, Velmer Burton, and Francis Cullen. 2000. "Gender and Crime Among Felony Offenders: Assessing the Generality of Social Control." *Journal of Research in Crime and Delinquency* 37:171–199.

Albonetti, Celesta A., Robert M. Hauser, John Hagan, and Ilene H. Nagel. 1989. "Criminal Justice Decision Making as a Stratification Process: The Role of Race and Stratification Resources in Pretrial Release." *Journal of Quantitative Criminology* 5:57–82.

Albrow, Martin. 1990. Introduction to M. Albrow and E. King, eds., *Globalization, Knowledge, and Society,* 3–13. London: Sage.

Alexander, Franz, and William Healy. 1935. *Roots of Crime.* New York: Knopf.

Alihan, M. A. 1938. *Social Ecology: A Critical Analysis.* New York: Columbia University Press.

Alleman, Ted. 1993. "Varieties of Feminist Thought and Their Application to Crime and Criminal Justice." In Roslyn Muraskin and Ted Alleman, eds., *It's a Crime: Women and Justice.* Englewood Cliffs, N.J.: Prentice Hall.

Allen, Craig M., and Henry L. Pothast. 1994. "Distinguishing Characteristics of Male and Female Child Sex Abusers." *Journal of Offender Rehabilitation* 21:73–88.

Allport, Gordon, W. 1937. *Personality: A Psychological Explanation.* New York: Holt.

_____. 1961. *The Person in Psychology.* Boston: Beacon.

Al-Talib, Nadhim I., and Christine Griffin. 1994. "Labelling Effect on Adolescents' Self-Concept." *International Journal of Offender Therapy and Comparative Criminology* 38:47–57.

American Friends Service Committee. 1971. *Struggle for Justice.* New York: Hill & Wang.

Anderson, Elijah. 1990. *Streetwise: Race, Class, and Change in an Urban Community.* Chicago: University of Chicage Press.

_____. 1999. *Code of Streets: Decency, Violence, and the Moral Life of the Inner City.* New York: Norton.

Arrigo, Bruce, ed. 1999. *Social Justice/Criminal Justice: The Maturation of Critical Theory in Crime, Law, and Deviance.* Belmont, Calif.: West/Wadsworth.

_____. 2000. *Introduction to Forensic Psychology: Issues and Controversies in Crime and Justice.* New York: Academic.

_____. 2003. "Postmodern Justice and Critical Criminology: Postitional, Relational, and Provisional Science." In Martin D. Schwartz and Suzanne E. Hatty, eds., *Controversies in Critical Criminology,* 43–55. Cincinnati: Anderson.

Arrigo, Bruce, and T. R. Young. 1996. *Postmodern Criminology: Theories of Crime and Crimes of Theorists.* Red Feather Institute Transforming Sociology. Weidman, Mich.: Red Feather Institute.

Aultman, Madeline G., and Charles F. Wellford. 1979. "Towards an Integrated Model of Delinquency Causation: An Empirical Analysis." *Sociology and Social Research* 63:316–327.

Bachman, Ronet, Raymond Paternoster, and Sally Ward. 1992. "The Rationality of Sexual Offending: Testing a Deterrence/Rational Choice Conception of Sexual Assault." *Law and Society Review* 26:343–372.

"Bad Vibrations." 2002. *People,* September 2, 95–97.

Baier, Colin J., and Bradley R.E. Wright. 2001. "If You Love Me, Keep My Commandments: A Meta-Analysis of the Effect of Religion on Crime." *Journal of Research in Crime and Delinquency* 38:3–21.

Bailey, W. C., and R. D. Peterson. 1989. "Murder and Capital Punishment: A Monthly Time Series Analysis of Execution Publicity." *American Sociological Review* 54:722–742.

Baker, Laura A., Wendy Mack, Terry E. Moffitt, and Sarnoff A. Mednick. 1989. "Sex Differences in Property Crime in a Danish Adoption Cohort." *Behavior Genetics* 19:355–370.

Baker, Paul J., and Louis E. Anderson. 1987. *Social Problems: A Critical Thinking Approach.* Belmont, Calif.: Wadsworth.

Balkan, Sheila, Ronald Berger, and Janet Schmidt. 1980. *Crime and Deviance in America: A Critical Approach.* Belmont, Calif.: Wadsworth.

Ball, Richard A. 1966. "An Empirical Exploration of Neutralization Theory." *Criminologica* 4:22–32.

Ball, Richard A., and J. Robert Lilly. 1971. "Juvenile Delinquency in an Urban County." *Criminology* 9:69–85.

Bandura, Albert. 1969. *Principles of Behavior Modification.* New York: Holt, Rinehart & Winston.

_____. 1973. *Aggression: A Social Learning Analysis.* Englewood Cliffs, N.J.: Prentice Hall.

_____. 1977. *Social Learning Theory.* Englewood Cliffs, N.J.: Prentice Hall.

Bandura, Albert, and R. Walters. 1963. *Social Learning and Personality Development.* New York: Holt, Rinehart & Winston.

Barak, Gregg. 1988. "Newsmaking Criminology: Reflections on the Media, Intellectuals, and Crime." *Justice Quarterly* 5:565–587.

_____. 1998. *Integrating Criminologies.* Boston: Allyn & Bacon.

_____. 2003. *Violence and Nonviolence: Pathways to Understanding.* Thousand Oaks, Calif.: Sage.

Barak, Gregg, ed. 1991a. *Crimes by the Capitalist State: An Introduction to State Criminality.* Albany: State University of New York Press.

_____. 1991b. *Gimme Shelter: A Social History of Homelessness in America.* Westport, Conn: Praeger.

_____. 1994. *Media, Process, and the Social Construction of Crime: Studies in Newsmaking Criminology.* New York: Garland.

_____. 1996. *Representing O.J.: Murder, Criminal Justice, and Mass Culture.* Albany, N.Y.: Harrow & Heston.

Barkow, J. H., L. Cosmides, and J. Tooby. 1992. *The Adapted Mind: Evolutionary Psychology and the Generation of Culture.* New York: Oxford University Press.

Barlow, David, and Melissa Hickman Barlow. 2002. "A Survey of African American Police Officers." *Police Quarterly* 5:334–358.

Barrett, Michele, and Mary McIntosh. 1985. "Ethnocentrism and Socialist Feminism Theory." *Feminist Review* 20:23–47.

Barry, Kathleen. 1979. *Female Sexual Slavery.* Englewood Cliffs, N.J.: Prentice Hall.

Bartlett, K. 1991. "Feminist Legal Methods." In K. Bartlett and R. Kennedy, eds., *Feminist Legal Theory.* Boulder: Westview.

Bartol, Curt R. 1991. *Criminal Behavior: A Psychological Approach.* 3rd ed. Englewood Cliffs, N.J.: Prentice Hall.

_____. 1999. *Criminal Behavior: A Psychological Approach.* Upper Saddle River, N.J.: Prentice Hall.

Bartol, Curt, and A. M. Bartol. 1994. *Psychology and Law: Research and Application.* Pacific Grove, Calif.: Brooks/Cole.

Bartusch, Dawn Jeglum, and Ross L. Matsueda. 1996. "Gender, Reflected Appraisals, and Labeling: A Cross-Group Test of an Interactionist Theory of Delinquency." *Social Forces* 75:145–176.

Baskin, Deborah, Ira Sommers, and Henry Steadman. 1991. "Assessing the Impact of Psychiatric Impairment on Prison Violence." *Journal of Criminal Justice* 19:271–280.

Beccaria, Cesare. [1764] 1963. *On Crimes and Punishments.* Translated by Henry Paolucci. Indianapolis: Bobbs-Merrill.

Beck, Aaron T. 1999. *Prisoners of Hate: The Cognitive Basis of Anger, Hostility, and Violence.* New York: Perenial.

Becker, Gary S. 1968. "Crime and Punishment: An Economic Approach." *Journal of Political Economy* 76:169–217.

Becker, Paul J., Arthur J. Jipson, and Alan S. Bruce. 2002. "State of Indiana v. Ford Motor Company Revisited." *American Journal of Criminal Justice* 26, 2:181–202.

Becker, Howard. [1963] 1973. *Outsiders: Studies in the Sociology of Deviance.* New York: Free Press.

Beirne, Piers. 1979. "Empiricism and the Critique of Marxism on Law and Crime." *Social Problems* 26:373–385.

_____. 1991. "Inventing Criminology: The 'Science of Man' in Cesare Beccaria's Dei Delitti e Delle Pene (1764)." *Criminology* 29:777–820.

_____. 1993. *Inventing Criminology: Essays on the Rise of "Homo Criminalis."* Albany: State University of New York Press.

_____. 1994. "The Law Is an Ass: Reading E. P. Evans' The Medieval Prosecution and Capital Punishment of Animals." *Animals and Society* 2:27–46.

Beirne, Piers, and James Messerschmidt. [1991] 1995. *Criminology.* 2nd ed. Fort Worth, TX: Harcourt Brace College.

_____. 2000. *Criminology.* 3rd ed. Boulder: Westview.

Bellair, Paul E. 2000. "Informal Surveillance and Street Crime: A Complex Relationship." *Criminology* 38:137–169.

Benda, Brent B., and Leanne Whiteside. 1995. "Testing an Integrated Model of Delinquency Using LISREL." *Journal of Social Service Research* 21:1–32.

Bender, Frederic. 1986. *Karl Marx: The Essential Writings.* Boulder: Westview.

Bennett, Richard R. 1991. "Routine Activities: A Cross-National Assessment of a Criminological Perspective." *Social Forces* 70:147–163.

Bennett, Richard R., and Jeanne M. Flavin. 1994. "Determinants of Fear of Crime: The Effect of Cultural Setting." *Justice Quarterly* 11:357–381.

Bennett, Trevor. 1986. "A Decision-making Approach to Opioid Addiction." In Derek B. Cornish and Ronald V. Clarke, eds., *The Reasoning Criminal.* New York: Springer-Verlag.

Bennett, Trevor, and Richard Wright. 1984. *Burglars on Burglary.* Aldershot, U.K.: Gower.

Bentham, Jeremy. [1765] 1970. *An Introduction to the Principles of Morals and Legislation.* Edited by J. H. Burns and H. L. A. Hart. London: Athlone.

Berg, Bruce. [1989] 2000. *Qualitative Research Methods for the Social Sciences.* Boston: Allyn & Bacon.

Bernard, Thomas J., and Jeffrey B. Snipes. 1996. In Michael Tonry, ed., *Crime and Justice: A Review of Research.* Vol. 20. Chicago: University of Chicago Press.

Bernburg, Jon Gunnar. 2002. "Anomie, Social Change, and Crime: A Theoretical Examination of Institutional-Anomie Theory." *British Journal of Criminology* 42:729–742.

Best, Steven, and Douglas Kellner. 1991. *Postmodern Theory: Critical Interrogations.* Basingstoke, U.K.: Macmillan.

Bianchi, Herman, and Rene Van Swaaningen, eds. 1986. *Abolitionism: Toward a Nonrepressive Approach to Crime.* Amsterdam: Free University Press.

Biderman, Albert, and Albert J. Reiss Jr. 1980. *Data Sources on White-Collar Law-Breaking.* Washington, D.C.: Government Printing Office.

Blatier, Catherine. 2000. "Locus of Control, Causal Attributions, and Self-Esteem: A Comparison Between Prisoners." *International Journal of Offender Therapy and Comparative Criminology* 44:97–110.

Blomberg, Thomas, and Stanley Cohen, eds. 1995. *Punishment and Social Control.* Hawthorne, N.Y.: Aldine de Gruyter.

Blumer, Herbert. 1969. *Symbolic Interactionism: Perspective and Method.* Englewood Cliffs, N.J.: Prentice Hall.

Blumstein, Alfred, Jacqueline Cohen, Susan E. Martin, and Martin H. Tonry, eds. 1983. *Research on Sentencing: The Search for Reform.* Vol. 1. Washington, D.C.: National Academy Press.

Blumstein, Alfred, Jacqueline Cohen, and Richard Rosenfeld. 1991. "Trend and Deviation in Crime Rates: A Comparison of UCR and NCS Data for Burglary and Robbery." *Criminology* 29:237–264.

_____. 1992. "The UCR-NCS Relationship Revisited: A Reply to Menard." *Criminology* 30:115–124.

Bogan, Kathleen M. 1990. "Constructing Felony Sentencing Guidelines in an Already Crowded State: Oregon Breaks New Ground." *Crime and Delinquency* 36:467–487.

Bohm, Robert. 1982. "Radical Criminology: An Explication." *Criminology* 19:565–589.

_____. 1989. "Humanism and the Death Penalty, with Special Emphasis on the Post-Furman Experience." *Justice Quarterly* 6:173–195.

_____. 1991. "American Death Penalty Opinion, 1936–1986: A Critical Examination of the Gallup Polls." In Robert Bohm, ed., *The Death Penalty in America: Current Research.* Cincinnati: Anderson.

_____. 1993. "Social Relationships That Arguably Should Be Criminal Although They Are Not: On the Political Economy of Crime." In Kenneth Tunnell, ed., *Political Crime in Contemporary America: A Critical Approach.* New York: Garland.

_____. 1997a. *A Primer on Crime and Delinquency.* Belmont, Calif.: Wadsworth.

_____. 1997b. "Review of Stuart Henry and Dragan Milovanovic's Constitutive Criminology." *Criminologist* 22:15–16.

Bohm, Robert M., and Keith N. Haley. 1999. *Introduction to Criminal Justice.* 2nd ed. New York: Glencoe/McGraw-Hill.

Boies, Henry M. 1893. *Prisoners and Paupers.* New York: Putnam.

Boland, Barbara. 1996. "What Is Community Prosecution?" *National Institute of Justice Journal* 231 (August):35–40.

Bonger, Willem. [1905] 1916. *Criminality and Economic Conditions.* Boston: Little, Brown.

Bonta, James, Moira Law, and Karl Hanson. 1998. "The Prediction of Criminal and Violent Recidivism among Mentally Disordered Offenders: A Meta Analysis." *Psychological Bulletin* 123:123–142.

Booth, Alan, and D. Wayne Osgood. 1993. "The Influence of Testosterone on Deviance in Adulthood: Assessing and Explaining the Relationship." *Criminology* 31:93–117.

Bordo, Susan. 1990. "Feminism, Postmodernism, and Gender Scepticism." In Linda J. Nicholson, ed., *Feminism/Postmodernism.* New York: Routledge.

Borgmann, Albert. 1992. *Crossing the Postmodern Divide.* Chicago: University of Chicago Press.

Bottomley, A. Keith. 1979. *Criminology in Focus.* London: Martin Robertson.

Bourdieu, Pierre. 1977. *Outline of a Theory of Practice*. Cambridge: Cambridge University Press.

Bowers, William, and Glenn Pierce. 1975. "The Illusion of Deterrence in Issac Ehrlich's Research on Capital Punishment." *Yale Law Journal* 85:187–208.

_____. 1980. "Deterrence or Brutalization? What Is the Effect of Executions?" *Crime and Delinquency* 26:453–484.

Bowlby, John. 1946. *Forty-Four Juvenile Thieves: Their Characters and Home-Life*. London: Bailliere, Tindall & Cox.

_____. 1951. *Maternal Care and Mental Health*. Geneva: World Health Organization.

_____. 1988. *A Secure Base: Clinical Applications of Attachment Theory*. London: Routledge.

Box, Steven. 1977. "Hyperactivity: The Scandalous Silence." *New Society* 42:458–460.

_____. [1971] 1981. *Deviance, Reality and Society*. New York: Holt, Rinehart & Winston.

_____. 1983. *Power, Crime, and Mystification*. London: Tavistock.

Box, Steven, and Chris Hale. 1983. "Liberation and Female Delinquency in England and Wales." *British Journal of Criminology* 23:35–49.

_____. 1985. "Unemployment, Imprisonment, and Prison Overcrowding." *Contemporary Crises* 9:209–228.

_____. 1986. "Unemployment, Crime, and Imprisonment and the Enduring Problem of Prison Overcrowding." In Roger Matthews and Jock Young, eds., *Confronting Crime*. London: Sage.

Bracewell, Michael C. 1990. "Peacemaking: A Missing Link in Criminology." *Criminologist* 15:3–5.

Braithwaite, John. 1989. *Crime, Shame, and Reintegration*. Cambridge: Cambridge University Press.

_____. 1995. "Reintegrative Shaming, Republicanism, and Public Policy." In Hugh D. Barlow, ed., *Crime and Public Policy: Putting Theory to Work*. Boulder: Westview.

_____. 2002. *Restorative Justice and Responsive Regulation*. New York: Oxford University Press.

Braithwaite, John, and Steve Mugford. 1994. "Conditions of Successful Reintegration Ceremonies: Dealing with Young Offenders." *British Journal of Criminology* 342:139–171.

Braukmann, Curtis J., and Montrose Wolf. 1987. "Behaviorally Based Group Homes for Juvenile Offenders." In Edward K. Morris and Curtis J. Braukmann, eds., *Behavioral Approaches to Crime and Delinquency: A Handbook of Applications Research and Concepts*. New York: Plenum.

Brayton, Steven. 2002. "Outsourcing War: Mercenaries and the Privatization of Peacekeeping." *Journal of International Affairs* 55:303–330.

Brennan, Luann. 2003. *Restoring the Justice in Criminal Justice*. Detroit: Wayne State University, Department of Interdisciplinary Studies.

Brezina, Timothy. 1996. "Adapting to Strain: An Examination of Delinquent Coping Responses." *Criminology* 34:39–60.

Brezina, Timothy, Paul Mazerolle, and Alex P. Piquero. 2001. "Student Anger and Aggressive Behavior in School: An Intial Test of Agnew's Macro-level Strain Theory." *Journal of Research in Crime and Delinquency* 38:362–386.

Broidy, Lisa M. 2001. "A Test of General Strain Theory." *Criminology* 39:9–35.

Bromberg, Walter. 1965. *Crime and the Mind: A Psychiatric Analysis of Crime and Punishment.* New York: Macmillan.

Brown, Beverly. 1988. "Review of Capitalism, Patriarchy and Crime." *International Journal of the Sociology of Law* 16:408–412.

_____. 1990. "Reassessing the Critique of Biologism." In Loraine Gelsthorpe and Allison Morris, eds., *Feminist Perspectives in Criminology.* Milton Keynes, U.K.: Open University Press.

Brownfield, David, and Ann Marie Sorenson. 1994. "Sibship Size and Sibling Delinquency." *Deviant Behavior* 15:45–61.

Brownmiller, Susan. 1975. *Against Our Will: Men, Women, and Rape.* London: Secker & Warburg.

Bruinsma, Gerben J.N. 1992. "Differential Association Theory Reconsidered: An Extension and Its Empirical Test." *Journal of Quantitative Criminology* 8:29–49.

Buckley, Walter. 1967. *Sociology and Modern Systems Theory.* Englewood Cliffs, N.J.: Prentice Hall.

Bureau of Justice Statistics (BJS). 1981. *Dictionary of Criminal Justice Data Terminology.* Washington, D.C.: U.S. Department of Justice.

_____. 1983. "The Seriousness of Crime: Results of a National Survey." In *Report to the Nation on Crime and Justice.* Washington, D.C.: U.S. Department of Justice.

_____. 1988. *Report to the Nation on Crime and Justice.* Washington, D.C.: U.S. Department of Justice.

_____. 1993. *Highlights from 20 Years of Surveying Crime Victims: The National Crime Victimization Survey, 1973–92.* Washington, D.C.: U.S. Department of Justice.

_____. 1994. *Sourcebook of Criminal Justice Statistics—1993.* Washington, D.C.: U.S. Department of Justice.

_____. 1995. *Sourcebook of Criminal Justice Statistics—1994.* Washington, D.C.: U.S. Department of Justice.

_____. 1996. *Sourcebook of Criminal Justice Statistics—1995.* Washington, D.C.: U.S. Department of Justice.

_____. 1998. *School Crime Supplement to the National Crime Victimization Survey, 1989 and 1995.* Washington, D.C.: U.S. Department of Justice, Office of Justice Programs.

Burgess, Ernest W. 1925. "The Growth of the City." In Robert E. Park, Ernest W. Burgess, and Roderick D. McKenzie, eds., *The City.* Chicago: University of Chicago Press.

_____. 1950. "Comment to Hartung." *American Journal of Sociology* 56:25–34.

Burgess, P. K. 1972. "Eysenck's Theory of Criminality: A New Approach." *British Journal of Criminology* 12:74–82.

Burgess, Robert L., and Ronald L. Akers. 1966. "A Differential Association-Reinforcement Theory of Criminal Behavior." *Social Problems* 14:128–147.

Burkett, Steven R., and Mervin White. 1974. "Hellfire and Delinquency: Another Look." *Journal for the Scientific Study of Religion* 13:455–462.

Bursik, Robert J., Jr. 1988. "Social Disorganization and Theories of Crime and Delinquency: Problems and Prospects." *Criminology* 26:519–551.

_____. 1989. "Political Decision-making and Ecological Models of Delinquency: Conflict and Consensus." In S. F. Messner, M. D. Krohn, and A. E. Liska, eds., *Theoretical Integration in the Study of Deviance and Crime*. Albany: State University of New York Press.

_____. 1999. "The Informal Control of Crime Through Neighborhood Networks." *Sociological Focus* 32:85–97.

Bursik, Robert J., Jr., and Harold G. Grasmick. 1993a. "Economic Deprivation and Neighborhood Crime Rates, 1960–1980." *Law and Society Review* 27:263–283.

_____. 1993b. *Neighborhoods and Crime: The Dimensions of Effective Community Control*. New York: Lexington.

_____. 1995. "Neighborhood-Based Networks and the Control of Crime and Delinquency." In Hugh D. Barlow, ed., *Crime and Public Policy: Putting Theory to Work*. Boulder: Westview.

Bursik, Robert J., Jr., and Jim Webb. 1982. "Community Change and Patterns of Delinquency." *American Journal of Sociology* 88:24–42.

Burton, Velmer S., Frances T. Cullen, David Evans, and R. Gregory Dunaway. 1994. "Reconsidering Strain Theory: Operationalization, Rival Theories and Adult Criminality." *Journal of Quantitative Criminology* 10:213–239.

Cadoret, R. J. 1978. "Psychopathology in Adopted-away Offspring of Biologic Parents with Antisocial Behavior." *Archives of General Psychiatry* 35:176–184.

Cadoret, R. J., W. R. Yates, E. Troughton, G. Woodworth, and M. Stewart. 1995. "Adoption Study Demonstrating Two Genetic Pathways to Drug Use." *Archives of General Psychiatry* 52:42-52.

Cain, Maureen. 1989. *Growing Up Good: Policing the Behavior of Girls in Europe*. London: Sage.

Calavita, Kitty, and Henry Pontell. 1993. "Savings and Loan Fraud as Organized Crime: Toward a Conceptual Typology of Corporate Illegality." *Criminology* 31:519–548.

Calhoun, Craig, and Henryk Hiller. 1986. "Coping with Insidious Injuries: The Case of Johns-Manville Corporation and Asbestos Exposure." *Social Problems* 35:162–181.

Calley, William L. 1974. "So This Is What War Is." In Charles H. McCaghy, James K. Skipper Jr., and Mark Lefton, eds., *In Their Own Behalf: Voices from the Margin*. Englewood Cliffs, N.J.: Prentice Hall.

Campaign for an Effective Crime Policy (CECP). 1997. *The Impact of Three Strikes and You're Out Laws: What Have We Learned?* Washington, D.C.: CEPC.

Campbell, Anne. 1981. *Girl Delinquents*. Oxford, U.K.: Basil Blackwell.

_____. 1984. *The Girls in the Gang*. Cambridge, U.K.: Basil Blackwell.

_____. 1993. *Men, Women, and Aggression*. New York: Basic.

Campbell, Anne, Steven Muncer, and Daniel Bibel. 1998. "Female-Female Criminal Assault: An Evolutionary Perspective." *Journal of Research in Crime and Delinquency* 35:413-428.

Canadian Law Commission. 2003. *What Is a Crime?* Ottawa: Canadian Law Commission.

Capowich, George E. 2003. "The Conditioning Effects of Neighborhood Ecology on Burglary Victimization." *Criminal Justice and Behavior* 30:39–61.

Capowich, George E., Paul Mazerolle, and Alex Piquero. 2001. "General Strain Theory, Situational Anger, and Social Networks: An Assessment of Conditioning Influences." *Journal of Criminal Justice* 29:445–461.

Caputo Alicia A., Paul J. Frick, and Stanley L. Brodsky. 1999. "Family Violence and Juvenile Sex Offending." *Criminal Justice and Behavior* 26:338–356.

Carey, Gregory. 1992. "Twin Imitation for Antisocial Behavior: Implications for Genetic and Family Research." *Journal of Abnormal Psychology* 101:18–25.

Carlen, Pat. 1992. "Women, Crime, Feminism and Realism." In John Lowman and Brian D. MacLean eds., *Realist Criminology: Crime Control and Policing in the 1990s,* 203–220. Toronto: University of Toronto Press.

Carmin, Cheryl, Fred Wallbrown, Raymond Ownby, and Robert Barnett. 1989. "A Factor Analysis of the MMPI in an Offender Population." *Criminal Justice and Behavior* 16:486–494.

Carrabine, Eamonn. 2001. "Incapacitation." In E. McLaughlin and J. Muncie, eds., *The Sage Dictionary of Criminology,* 146–147. London: Sage.

Carver, Terrell. 1987. *A Marx Dictionary.* Cambridge, U.K.: Polity.

Caspi, Avshalom, Terrie E. Moffitt, Phil A. Silva, Magda Stouthamer-Loeber, Robert F. Kruega, and Pamela S. Schmutte. 1994. "Are Some People Crime-Prone? Replications of the Personality Crime Relationship Across Countries, Genders, Races, and Methods." *Criminology* 32:163–195.

Caulfield, Susan L. 2000. "Creating Peaceable Schools." In W. Hinkle and S. Henry, eds., *School Violence.* Vol. 567 of *Annals of the American Academy of Political and Social Science.* Thousand Oaks, Calif.: Sage.

Caulfield, Susan, and Nancy Wonders. 1994. "Gender and Justice: Feminist Contributions to Criminology." In Gregg Barak, ed., *Varieties of Criminology: Readings from a Dynamic Discipline.* Westport, Conn.: Praeger.

Cernkovich, Stephen A., and Peggy C. Giordano. 1987. "Family Relationships and Delinquency." *Criminology* 25:295–319.

Cernkovich, Stephen, Peggy Giordano, and Jennifer Rudolph. 2000. "Race, Crime and the American Dream." *Journal of Research in Crime and Delinquency* 37:131–170.

Chambliss, William J. 1973. "The Saints and the Roughnecks." *Society* 11:24–31.

———. 1975. "Toward a Political Economy of Crime." *Theory and Society* 2:149–170.

———. 1988. *Exploring Criminology.* New York: Macmillan.

———. 1989. "On Trashing Marxist Criminology." *Criminology* 27:231–238.

Chambliss, William J., and Robert B. Seidman. [1971] 1982. *Law, Order, and Power.* 2nd ed. Reading, Mass.: Addison-Wesley.

Chamlin, Mitchell B. 1989. "A Macro Social Analysis of the Change in Robbery and Homicide Rates: Controlling for Static and Dynamic Effects." *Sociological Focus* 22:275–286.

Chamlin, Mitchell B., and John Cochran. 1995. "Assessing Messner and Rosenfeld's Institutional Anomie Theory: A Partial Test." *Criminology* 33:411–429.

Champion, Dean, J. 1997. *The Roxbury Dictionary of Criminal Justice.* Los Angeles: Roxbury Publishing.

Chappell, Duncan, Gilbert Geis, Stephen Schafer, and Larry Siegel. 1971. "Forcible Rape: A Comparative Study of Offenses Known to the Police in Boston and Los Angeles." In James Henslin, ed., *Studies in the Sociology of Sex.* New York: Appleton Century Crofts.

Chermak, Steven. 1994. "Body Count News: How Crime Is Presented in the News Media." *Justice Quarterly* 11:561–582.

Chesney-Lind, Meda. 1986. "Women and Crime: The Female Offender." *Signs* 12:78–96.

———. 1989. "Girl's Crime and Woman's Place: Toward a Feminist Model of Female Delinquency." *Crime and Delinquency* 35:5–29.

———. 1997. *The Female Offender: Girls, Women and Crime.* Thousand Oaks, Calif.: Sage.

Chesney-Lind, Meda, and Randall G. Sheldon. 1992. *Girls, Delinquency, and Juvenile Justice.* Pacific Grove, Calif.: Brooks/Cole.

Chin, Ko-lin. 1990. *Chinese Subculture and Criminality: Non-Traditional Crime Groups in America.* Westport, Conn.: Greenwood.

Chiricos, Theodore G., and Gordon P. Waldo. 1975. "Socioeconomic Status and Criminal Sentencing: An Empirical Assessment of a Conflict Proposition." *American Sociological Review* 40:753–772.

Christiansen, Karl O. 1977. "A Preliminary Study of Criminality Among Twins." In Sarnoff A. Mednick and Karl O. Christiansen, eds., *Biological Basis of Criminal Behavior.* New York: Gardner.

Christie, Nils. 1977. "Conflicts as Property." *British Journal of Criminology* 17:1–19.

———. 1981. *The Limits to Pain.* Oxford, U.K.: Martin Robertson.

Cilliers, Jakkie. 2003. "Peacekeeping, Africa and the Emerging Global Security Architecture." *African Security Review* 12:111–114.

Cintron, Ralph. 2000. "Listening to What the Streets Say: Vengeance as Ideology?" In W. Hinkle and S. Henry, eds., *School Violence.* Vol. 567 of *Annals of the American Academy of Political and Social Science.* Thousand Oaks, Calif.: Sage.

Clark, William L., and William L. Marshall. 1978. "Legal Definitions of Crime, Criminal, and Rape." In Leonard D. Savitz and Norman Johnston, eds., *Crime in Society.* New York: John Wiley.

Clarke, Ronald V., and Derek B. Cornish, eds. 1983. *Crime Control in Britain: A Review of Policy and Research.* Albany: State University of New York Press.

———. 1985. "Modeling Offenders' Decisions: A Framework for Research and Policy." In Michael Tonry and Norval Morris, eds., *Crime and Justice and Annual Review of Research.* Vol. 6. Chicago: University of Chicago Press.

Clarke, Ronald V., and Marcus Felson, eds. 1993. *Routine Activity and Rational Choice: Advances in Criminological Theory.* New Brunswick, N.J.: Transaction Publishers.

Clarke, Ronald V., and Patricia Mayhew. 1980. *Designing Out Crime.* London: Her Majesty's Printing Office.

Clear, Todd R. 1996. "Towards a Correction of 'Place': The Challenge of 'Community' in Corrections." *National Institute of Justice Journal* 231 (August):52–56.

Cleckly, Hervey. 1941. *The Mask of Insanity.* St. Louis, Mo.: Mosby.

Clinard, Marshall B. 1983. *Corporate Ethics and Crime: The Role of Management.* Beverly Hills, Calif.: Sage.

Clinard, Marshall B., and Richard Quinney. 1973. *Criminal Behavior Systems.* New York: Holt, Rinehart & Winston.

Clinard, Marshall B., and Peter C. Yeager. 1980. *Corporate Crime.* New York: Free Press.

Cloward, Richard A. 1959. "Illegitimate Means, Anomie, and Deviant Behavior." *American Sociological Review* 24:164–176.

Cloward, Richard A., and Lloyd Ohlin. 1960. *Delinquency and Opportunity.* New York: Free Press.

Cochran, John K., and Mitchell B. Chamlin. 2000. "Deterrence and Brutalization: The Dual Effects of Executions." *Justice Quarterly* 17, 4:685–706.

Cochran, John K., Mitchell B. Chamlin, and Mark Seth. 1994. "Deterrence or Brutalization? An Impact Assessment of Oklahoma's Return to Capital Punishment." *Criminology* 32:107–134.

Cochrane, Raymond. 1974. "Crime and Personality: Theory and Evidence." *Bulletin of the British Psychological Society* 27:19–22.

Cohen, Albert. 1955. *Delinquent Boys.* New York: Free Press.

_____. 1965. "The Sociology of the Deviant Act: Anomie Theory and Beyond." *American Sociological Review* 30:5–14.

_____. 1966. *Deviance and Control.* Englewood Cliffs, N.J.: Prentice Hall.

Cohen, Albert K., Alfred Lindesmith, and Karl Schuessler, eds. 1956. *The Sutherland Papers.* Bloomington: Indiana University Press.

Cohen, Deborah Vidaver. 1995. "Ethics and Crime in Business Firms: Organizational Culture and the Impact of Anomie." In Freda Adler and William S. Laufer, eds., *The Legacy of Anomie Theory.* Vol. 6 of *Advances in Criminological Theory.* New Brunswick, N.J.: Transaction.

Cohen, Gary. 1998. *Bhopal and the New World Order.* http://www.simplelife.com/FINDORGANICCOTTON/31LINKSBHOPAL.html.

Cohen, Jacqueline, and Michael H. Tonry. 1983. "Sentencing Reform Impacts." In A. Blumstein, J. Cohen, S. E. Martin, and M. H. Tonry, eds., *Research on Sentencing: The Search for Reform.* Vol. 2. Washington, D.C.: National Academy Press.

Cohen, Lawrence E., and Marcus Felson. 1979. "Social Change and Crime Rate Trends: A Routine Activities Approach." *American Sociological Review* 44:588–608.

Cohen, Lawrence E., and Richard Machalek. 1988. "A General Theory of Expropriative Crime: An Evolutionary Ecological Approach." *American Journal of Sociology* 94:465–501.

Cohen, Stanley. 1985. *Visions of Social Control.* Cambridge, U.K.: Polity.

_____. 1988. *Against Criminology.* New Brunswick, N.J.: Transaction.

_____. 1990. "Intellectual Scepticism and Political Commitment: The Case of Radical Criminology." Bonger Memorial Lecture (May 14), University of Amsterdam.

_____. 1993. "Human Rights and Crimes of the State: The Culture of Denial." *Australian and New Zealand Journal of Criminology* 26:97–115.

Cohn, E. G., and D. P. Farrington. 1998. "Changes in the Most Cited Scholars in Major American Criminology and Criminal Justice Journals between 1986–1990 and 1991–1995." *Journal of Criminal Justice* 26:99–116.

Coleman, J. W. 1987. "Toward an Integrated Theory of White-Collar Crime." *American Journal of Sociology* 93:406–439.

Coleman, James. 1988. "Social Capital in the Creation of Human Capital." *American Journal of Sociology* 94:95–121.

Collins, Hugh. 1987. "Roberto Unger and the Critical Legal Studies Movement." *Journal of Law and Society* 14:387–410.

Colvin, Mark. 1997. "Review of Stuart Henry and Dragan Milovanovic's Constitutive Criminology." *American Journal of Sociology* 102:1448–1450.

_____. 2000. *Crime and Coercion: An Integrated Theory of Chronic Criminality*. New York: Palgrave.

Colvin, Mark, and John Pauly. 1983. "A Critique of Criminology: Toward an Integrated Structural-Marxist Theory of Delinquency Production." *American Journal of Sociology* 89:513–551.

Comby, Henry B., III. 1982. "Status Offender Treatment in the Juvenile Court: A Conflict Theory Approach." *Free Inquiry in Creative Sociology* 10:105–107.

Conklin, John E. 1977. *Illegal but Not Criminal: Business Crime in America*. Englewood Cliffs, N.J.: Prentice Hall.

Conly, Catherine, and Daniel McGillis. 1996. "The Federal Role in Revitalizing Communities and Preventing and Controlling Crime and Violence." *National Institute of Justice Journal* 231 (August):24–30.

Cooley, Charles Horton. [1902] 1964. *Social Organization: A Study of the Larger Mind*. New York: Schocken.

Corbett, Claire, and Frances Simon. 1992. "Decisions to Break or Adhere to the Rules of the Road, Viewed from the Rational Choice Perspective." *British Journal of Criminology* 32:537–549.

Cordella, Peter, and Larry Siegel, eds. 1996. *Readings in Contemporary Criminological Theory*. Boston: Northeastern University Press.

Cordner, Gary. 1981. "The Effects of Directed Patrol: A Natural Quasi-Experiment in Pontiac." In J. Fyfe, ed., *Contemporary Issues in Law Enforcement*, 37–58. Beverly Hills, Calif.: Sage.

_____. 1998. "Problem Oriented Policing vs. Zero Tolerance." In T. Shelly and A. Grant, eds., *Problem Oriented Policing*, 303–329. Washington D.C.: Police Executive Research Forum (PERF).

Cornish, Derek B., and Ronald V. Clarke, eds. 1986. *The Reasoning Criminal*. New York: Springer-Verlag.

_____. 1987. "Understanding Crime Displacement: An Application of Rational Choice Theory." *Criminology* 25:933–947.

Cortes, J. B., and F. M. Gatti. 1972. *Delinquency and Crime: A Biopsychosocial Approach*. New York: Seminar Press.

Coser, Lewis. 1956. *The Functions of Social Conflict*. New York: Macmillan.

_____. 1968. "Conflict: Social Aspects." In David L. Sills, ed., *The International Encyclopedia of the Social Sciences*. Vol. 3. New York: Macmillan/Free Press.

Costanza, S. E., William B. Bankstona, and Edward Shihadeh. 1999. "Alcohol Availability and Violent Crime Rates: A Spatial Analysis." *Journal of Crime and Justice* 24:71–83.

Costello, Barbara J., and Paul R. Vowell. 1999. "Testing Control Theory and Differential Association: A Reanalysis of the Richmond Youth Project Data." *Criminology* 37:815–837.

Coward-Yaskiw, Stephanie. 2002. "Restorative Justice: What Is It? Can It Work? What Do Women Think?" *Horizons* 15 (Spring). http://web2.infotrac.galegroup.com.

Cressey, Donald R. 1953. *Other People's Money*. Glencoe, Ill.: Free Press.

_____. 1962. "The Development of a Theory: Differential Association." In M. E. Wolfgang, L. Savitz, and N. Johnston, eds., *The Sociology of Crime and Delinquency.* New York: John Wiley.

_____. 1970. "The Respectable Criminal." In James Short, ed., *Modern Criminals.* New York: Transaction-Aldine.

_____. [1965] 1987. "The Respectable Criminal." In Paul J. Baker and Louis E. Anderson, eds., *Social Problems: A Critical Thinking Approach.* Belmont, Calif.: Wadsworth.

Crews, Gordon A., and Jeffrey A. Tipton. 2002. "A Comparison of Public School and Prison Security Measures: Too Much of a Good Thing?" http://www.kci.org/publication/articles/school_security_measures.htm.

Crowe, R. R. 1974. "An Adoption Study of Antisocial Personality." *Archives of General Psychiatry* 31:785–791.

_____. 1975. "An Adoptive Study of Psychopathy: Preliminary Results from Arrest Records and Psychiatric Hospital Records." In R. R. Fieve, D. Rosenthal, and H. Brill, eds., *Genetic Research in Psychiatry.* Baltimore: Johns Hopkins University Press.

Cullen, Francis T. 1994. "Social Support as an Organizing Concept for Criminology." *Justice Quarterly* 11:527–559.

Cullen, Francis T., William J. Maakestad, and Gray Cavender. 1987. *Corporate Crime Under Attack.* Cincinnati: Anderson.

Curran, Daniel J., and Claire M. Renzetti. 1994. *Theories of Crime.* Boston: Allyn & Bacon.

Currie, Dawn H. 1989. "Women and the State: A Statement on Feminist Theory." *Critical Criminologist* 1:4–5.

_____. 1992. "Feminist Encounters with Postmodernism: Exploring the Impasse of the Debates on Patriarchy and Law." *Canadian Journal of Women and the Law* 5:63–86.

Currie, Elliott. 1985. *Confronting Crime: An American Challenge.* New York: Pantheon.

_____. 1992. "Reatreatism, Minimalism, Realism: Three Styles of Reasoning on Crime and Drugs in the United States." In John Lowman and Brian D. MacLean, eds., *Realist Criminology: Crime Control and Policing in the 1990s,* 88–97. Toronto: University of Toronto Press.

_____. 1997. "Market, Crime, and Community: Toward a Mid-Range Theory of Post-Industrial Violence." *Theoretical Criminology* 1:147–172.

_____. 1998. *Crime and Punishment in America.* New York: Metropolitan Books.

Dabbs, James M., and Robin Morris. 1990. "Testosterone and Antisocial Behavior in a Sample of 4,462 Men." *Psychological Science* 1:209–211.

Dabbs, James M., Jasmin K. Riad, and Susan E. Chance. 2001. "Testosterone and Ruthless Homicide." *Personality and Individual Differences* 31:599–603.

Dahrendorf, Ralf. 1958. "Out of Utopia: Toward a Reconstruction of Sociological Analysis." *American Journal of Sociology* 67:115–127.

_____. 1959. *Class and Class Conflict in an Industrial Society.* London: Routledge & Kegan Paul.

D'Alessio, Stewart J., and Lisa Stolzenberg. 1995. "The Impact of Sentencing Guidelines on Jail Incarceration in Minnesota." *Criminology* 33:283–302.

Dalgard, Odd S., and Einar Kringlen. 1976. "A Norwegian Twin Study of Criminology." *British Journal of Criminology* 16:213–232.

Dallek, Robert. 2003. *An Unfinished Life: John F. Kennedy 1917–1963.* Boston, Mass.: Little, Brown.

Dalton, Katharina. 1961. "Menstruation and Crime." *British Medical Journal* 3:1752–1753.

_____. 1971. *The Premenstrual Syndrome.* Springfield, Ill.: Charles C. Thomas.

Daly, Kathleen. 1992. "Women's Pathways to Felony Court: Feminist Theories of Lawbreaking and Problems of Representation." *Review of Law and Women's Studies* 2:1–42.

_____. 2000. "Restorative Justice in Diverse and Unequal Societies." *Law in Context* 17, 1:167–190.

Daly, Kathleen, and Lisa Maher. 1998. *Criminology at the Crossroads: Feminist Readings in Crime and Justice.* New York: Oxford University Press.

Daly, Kathleen, and Meda Chesney-Lind. 1988. "Feminism and Criminology." *Justice Quarterly* 5:497–538.

Dann, Robert. 1935. "The Deterrent Effect of Capital Punishment." *Friends Social Service* Series 29. Cited in Larry Siegel. 1995. *Criminology: Theories, Patterns, and Typologies.* 5th ed. Minneapolis: West.

Danner, Mona J.E. 1991. "Socialist Feminism: A Brief Introduction." In Brian D. MacLean and Dragan Milovanovic, eds., *New Directions in Critical Criminology.* Vancouver: Collective.

Danzig, Richard. 1973. "Toward the Creation of a Complementary Decentralized System of Criminal Justice." *Stanford Law Review* 26:1–54.

Darwin, Charles R. 1871. *Descent of Man: Selection in Relation to Sex.* London: John Murray.

_____. [1859] 1968. *On the Origin of Species.* New York: Penguin.

Debro, Julius. 1970. "Dialogue with Howard S. Becker." *Issues in Criminology* 5:159–179.

DeCoster, Stacy, and Karen Heimer. 2001. "The Relationship Between Law Violation and Depression: An Interactionist Analysis." *Criminology* 39:799–836.

Deflem, Mathiew. 1999. "Review of 'The Future of Anomie Theory.'" Edited by Nikos Passas and Robert Agnew. *Social Forces* 78:364–366.

DeFleur, Lois B. 1967. "Ecological Variables in the Cross-Cultural Study of Delinquency, and Community." *Social Forces* 45:556–570.

DeFleur, Melvin, and Richard Quinney. 1966. "A Reformulation of Sutherland's Differential Association Theory and a Strategy for Empirical Verification." *Journal of Research in Crime and Delinquency* 2:1–22.

De Haan, Willem. 1990. *The Politics of Redress.* Boston: Unwin Hyman.

DeKeseredy, Walter S. 1993. *Four Variations of Family Violence: A Review of Sociological Research.* Ottawa: Health Canada.

_____. 2003. "Left Realism and Inner City Violence." In Martin D. Schwartz and Suzanne E. Hatty, eds., *Controversies in Critical Criminology,* 29–41. Cincinnati: Anderson.

DeKeseredy, Walter S., and Martin D. Schwartz. 1991. "British and U.S. Left Realism: A Critical Comparison." *International Journal of Offender Therapy and Comparative Criminology* 35:248–262.

_____. 1996. *Contemporary Criminology.* Belmont, Calif.: Wadsworth.

DeLisi, Matt. 2001. "It's All in the Record: Assessing Self-Control Theory with an Offender Sample." *Criminal Justice Review* 26:1–16.

Dembo, Richard, Gary Grandon, Lawrence La Voie, James Schmeidler, and William Burgos. 1986. "Parents and Drugs Revisited: Some Further Evidence in Support of Social Learning Theory." *Criminology* 24:85–104.

Denno, Deborah. 1985. "Sociological and Human Developmental Explanations of Crime: Conflict or Consensus." *Criminology* 23:711–741.

———. 1989. *Biology, Crime, and Violence: New Evidence.* Cambridge: Cambridge University Press.

Derrida, Jacques. 1970. "Structure, Sign, and Play in the Discourse of Human Sciences." In Richard Macksey and Eugenio Donato, eds., *The Languages of Criticism and the Sciences of Man.* Baltimore: Johns Hopkins University Press.

———. 1981. *Positions.* Chicago: University of Chicago Press.

Ditton, Jason. 1977. *Part-Time Crime: An Ethnography of Fiddling and Pilferage.* London: Macmillan.

Dobash, R., R. E. Dobash, M. Wilson, and M. Daly. 1992. "The Myth of Sexual Symmetry in Marital Violence." *Social Problems* 39:71–91.

Dodge, K. A. 1993. "Social Cognitive Mechanism in the Development of Conduct Disorders and Depression." *Annual Review of Psychology* 44:559–584.

Dollard, J., L. W. Doob, N. E. Miller, O. H. Mowrer, and R. R. Sears. 1939. *Frustration and Aggression.* New Haven, Conn.: Yale University Press.

Douglas, Jack D., and Paul K. Rasmussen. 1977. *The Nude Beach.* Beverly Hills, Calif.: Sage.

Douglas, Mary. 1970. *Natural Symbols.* London: Crescent.

———. 1978. *Cultural Bias.* London: Royal Anthropological Institute.

Dowie, Mark. [1977] 1979. "Pinto Madness." *Mother Jones* 2 (September-October):18–34. Reprinted in Jerome Skolnick and Elliot Currie, eds., *Crisis in American Institutions.* 4th ed. Boston: Little, Brown.

Drahms, August. [1900] 1971. *The Criminal: His Personnel and Environment—A Scientific Study, with an Introduction by Cesare Lombroso.* Montclair, N.J.: Patterson Smith.

Dugdale, Richard Louis. [1877] 1895. *The Jukes: A Study in Crime, Pauperism, Disease and Heredity.* 3rd ed. New York: Putnam.

Durkheim, Emile. [1895] 1950. *The Rules of Sociological Method.* Edited by G. E. G. Catlin. Translated by S. A. Solovay and J. H. Mueller. Glencoe, Ill.: Free Press.

———. [1897] 1951. *Suicide: A Study in Sociology.* New York: Free Press.

———. [1895] 1982. *The Rules of Sociological Method and Selected Texts on Sociology and Its Method.* Edited by Steven Lukes. Translated by W. D. Halls. London: Macmillan.

———. [1893] 1984. *The Division of Labor in Society.* New York: Free Press.

Duster, Troy. 1970. *The Legislation of Morality.* New York: Free Press.

Ebbe, Obi N.I. 1989. "Crime and Delinquency in Metropolitan Lagos: A Study of 'Crime and Delinquency' Theory." *Social Forces* 67:751–765.

Edelhertz, Herbert. 1970. *The Nature, Impact, and Prosecution of White-Collar Crime.* Washington, D.C.: U.S. Government Printing Office.

Edwards, Susan. 1990. "Violence Against Women: Feminism and the Law." In Loraine Gelsthorpe and Allison Morris, eds., *Feminist Perspectives in Criminology,* 144–159. Milton Keynes, UK: Open University Press.

Eglash, Albert. 1977. "Beyond Restitution: Creative Restitution." In J. Hudson and B. Galaway, eds., *Restitution in Criminal Justice.* Lexington, Mass.: Lexington.

Ehrenkranz, Joel, Eugene Bliss, and Michael Sheard. 1974. "Plasma Testosterone: Correlation with Aggressive Behavior and Social Dominance in Man." *Psychosomatic Medicine* 35:469–475.

Ehrenreich, Barbara, and Annette Fuentes. 1994. "Life on the Global Assembly Line." In Jerome H. Skolnick and Elliot Currie, eds., *Crisis in American Institutions,* 326–340. 9th ed. New York: HarperCollins.

Ehrlich, Isaac. 1973. "Participation in Illegitimate Activities: An Economic Analysis." *Journal of Political Economy* 81:521–567.

_____. 1975. "The Deterrent Effect of Capital Punishment: A Question of Life or Death." *American Economic Review* 65:397–417.

_____. 1982. "The Market for Offenses and the Public Enforcement of Laws: An Equilibrium Analysis." *British Journal of Social Psychology* 21:107–120.

Einstadter, Werner, and Stuart Henry. 1995. *Criminological Theory: An Analysis of Its Underlying Assumptions.* Fort Worth, Tex.: Harcourt Brace College.

Eisenstein, Zillah. 1979. *Capitalist Patriarchy and the Case for Socialist Feminism.* New York: Monthly Review Press.

Elias, Robert. 1986. *The Politics of Victimization: Victims, Victimology, and Human Rights.* New York: Oxford University Press.

Elliott, Delbert S., and Susan S. Ageton. 1980. "Reconciling Race and Class Differences in Self-Reported and Official Estimates of Delinquency." *American Sociological Review* 45:95–110.

_____. 1983. *National Youth Survey, 1976.* Ann Arbor, Mich.: ICPSR.

Elliott, Delbert S., Susan S. Ageton, and R. Canter. 1979. "An Integrated Theoretical Perspective on Delinquent Behavior." *Journal of Research on Crime and Delinquency* 16:3–27.

Elliott, Delbert. S., Beatrice A. Hamburg, and K. R. Williams. 1998. *Violence in American Schools.* Cambridge: Cambridge University Press.

Elliott, Delbert S., and David Huizinga. 1983. "Social Class and Delinquent Behavior in a National Youth Panel: 1976–1980." *Criminology* 21:149–177.

Elliott, Delbert, David Huizinga, and Susan Ageton. 1985. *Explaining Delinquency and Drug Use.* Beverly Hills, Calif.: Sage.

Elliott, Delbert S., and Harwin L. Voss. 1974. *Delinquency and Dropout.* Lexington, Mass.: Lexington.

Ellis, Lee. 1987. "Criminal Behavior and r/K Selection: An Extension of Gene Based Evolutionary Theory." *Deviant Behavior* 8:149–176.

_____. 1988. "Neurohormonal Bases of Varying Tendencies to Learn Delinquent and Criminal Behavior." In E. K. Morris and C. J. Braukmann, eds., *Behavioral Approaches to Crime and Delinquency.* New York: Plenum.

_____. 1989. *Theories of Rape: Inquiries into the Causes of Sexual Aggression.* New York: Hemisphere.

_____. 1990. "Introduction: The Nature of the Biosocial Perspective." In L. Ellis and H. Hoffman, eds., *Crime in Biological, Social, and Moral Contexts.* New York: Praeger.

_____. 1995. "Arousal Theory and the Religiosity-Criminality Relationship." In Peter Cordella and Larry Siegel, eds., *Contemporary Criminological Theory.* Boston: Northeastern University Press.

Ellis, Lee, and H. Hoffman, eds. *Crime in Biological, Social and Moral Contexts.* New York: Praeger.

Ellis, Lee, and Anthony Walsh. 1997. "Gene Based Evolutionary Theories in Criminology." *Criminology* 35:229–267.

Ellis, Lee, and Anthony Walsh. 2000. *Criminology: A Global Perspective.* Boston: Allyn & Bacon.

Ellsworth, M. J. 1927. *The Bath School Disaster.* Bath, Mich.: Bath School Museum.

Emory, L. E., C. M. Cole, and W. J. Meyer. 1992. "The Texas Experience with DepoProvera: 1980–1990." *Journal of Offender Rehabilitation* 18:125–139.

Empey, Lamar T., and Steven G. Lubeck. 1971a. *Explaining Delinquency.* Lexington, Mass.: D. C. Heath.

_____. 1971b. *The Silverlake Experiment.* Chicago: Aldine.

Empey, Lamar T., and Mark C. Stafford. 1991. *American Delinquency: Its Meaning and Construction.* 3rd ed. Belmont, Calif.: Wadsworth.

Engel, Robin Shepard, Jennifer M. Calnon, and Thomas J. Bernard. 2002. "Theory and Racial Profiling: Shortcomings and Future Directions in Research." *Justice Quarterly* 19:249–273.

Engels, Friedrich. 1884. "The Origin of the Family, Private Property and the State." In Karl Marx and Friedrich Engels, *Selected Works.* Moscow: Progress.

_____. [1845] 1958. *The Condition of the Working Class in England.* Oxford, U.K.: Blackwell.

Enzmann, Dirk, Werner Greve, and Daniela Hosser. 2001. "The Stabilization of Self-Esteem Among Incarcerated Adolescents: Accommodative and Immunizing Processes." *International Journal of Offender Therapy and Comparative Criminology* 45:749–768.

Ericson, Richard, and Kevin Carriere. 1994. "The Fragmentation of *Criminology.*" In D. Nelken, ed., *The Futures of Criminology.* London: Sage.

Ermann, M. David, and William H. Clements. 1984. "The Interfaith Center on Corporate Responsibility and Its Campaign Against Marketing Infant Formula in the Third World." *Social Problems* 32:185–196.

Ermann, M. David, and Richard J. Lundman. [1992] 1996. *Corporate and Governmental Deviance.* 4th ed. New York: Oxford University Press.

Estabrook, Arthur H. 1916. *The Jukes in 1915.* Washington, D.C.: Carnegie Institute.

Evans, T. Davis, Francis Cullen, Gregory Dunaway, and Velmer Burton. 1995. "Religion and Crime Reexamined: The Impact of Religion, Secular Controls and Social Ecology on Adult Criminality." *Criminology* 33:195–224.

Eysenck, Hans J. [1964] 1977. *Crime and Personality.* 2nd ed. London: Routledge & Kegan Paul.

_____. 1983. "Personality, Conditioning and Anti-social Behavior." In S. Laufer and J. M. Day, eds., *Personality Theory, Moral Development, and Criminal Behavior.* Lexington, Mass.: Lexington.

Eysenck, Hans J., and G. H. Gudjonsson. 1989. *The Causes and Cures of Criminality.* New York: Plenum.

Fagan, Jeffrey. 1991. "Drug Selling and Licit Income in Distressed Neighborhoods: The Economic Lives of Street-Level Drug Users and Dealers." In Adele V. Harrell and George E. Peterson, eds., *Drugs, Crime, and Social Isolation.* Washington, D.C.: Urban Institute Press.

Farnworth, Margaret. 1989. "Theory Integration Versus Model Building." In Stephen F. Messner, Marvin D. Krohn, and Allen Liska, eds., *Theoretical Integration in the Study of Deviance and Crime.* Albany: State University of New York Press.

Farnworth, Margaret, and Michael J. Leiber. 1989. "Strain Theory Revisited: Educational Goals, Educational Means, and Delinquency." *American Sociological Review* 54:263–274.

Farrell, Ronald A., and Victoria Lynn Swigert. 1988. *Social Deviance.* 3rd ed. Belmont, Calif.: Wadsworth.

Farrington, David P. 1998. "Psychological Factors in the Explanation and Reduction of Delinquency." *Today's Delinquent* 7:44–46.

Farrington, David, and Brandon Welsh. 2002. "Improved Street Lighting and Crime Prevention." *Justice Quarterly* 19, 2:313–342.

Farrington, David, and Donald J. West. 1995. "Criminal, Penal and Life Histories of Chronic Offenders: Risk and Protective Factors and Early Identification." *Criminal Behavior and Mental Health* 3:492–523.

Fattah, Ezzat A. 1992. *Towards a Critical Victimology.* New York: St. Martin's.

Faust, Frederic L. 1995. "Review of 'A Primer in the Psychology of Crime' by S. Giora Shoham and Mark C. Seis." *Social Pathology* 1:48–61.

Feder, Lynette. 1995. "Psychiatric History, Due Procedural Safeguards, and the Use of Discretion in the Criminal Justice Process." *Justice Quarterly* 12:279–305.

Federal Bureau of Investigation (FBI). 1992. *Uniform Crime Reporting Handbook: NIBRS Edition.* Washington, D.C.: Government Printing Office.

———. 1993. *Uniform Crime Reports.* Washington, D.C.: Government Printing Office.

Feeley, Malcom, and Jonathan Simon. 1992. "The New Penology: Notes on the Emerging Strategy of Corrections and Its Implications" *Criminology* 30:449–470.

———. 1998. "The New Penology: Notes on the Emerging Strategy of Corrections and Its Implications." In Stuart Henry and Werner Einstader, eds., *The Criminology Theory Reader.* New York: New York University Press.

Feinberg, Todd. 2001. *Altered Egos: How the Brain Creates the Self.* Oxford: Oxford University Press.

Feldman, M. P. 1977. *Criminal Behavior: A Psychological Analysis.* London: John Wiley.

Felson, Marcus. 1986. "Routine Activities and Crime Prevention in the Developing Metropolis." In Derek B. Cornish and Ronald V. Clarke, eds., *The Reasoning Criminal.* New York: Springer-Verlag.

———. 1987. "Routine Activities, Social Controls, Rational Decisions, and Criminal Outcomes." *Criminology* 25:911–931.

Felson, Marcus, and Lawrence E. Cohen. 1981. "Molding Crime Rate Trends: A Criminal Opportunity Perspective." *Journal of Research in Crime and Delinquency* 18:138–164.

Felson, Richard B. 1992. "'Kick 'em When They're Down': Explanations of the Relationship Between Stress and Interpersonal Aggression and Violence." *Sociological Quarterly* 33:1–16.

Ferman, A. Louis, Stuart Henry, and Michele Hoyman, eds. 1987. *The Informal Economy*. Vol. 493 of *Annals of the American Academy of Political and Social Science*. Thousand Oaks, Calif.: Sage.

Ferrell, Jeff. 1994. "Confronting the Agenda of Authority: Critical Criminology, Anarchism." In Gregg Barak, ed., *Varieties of Criminology: Readings from a Dynamic Discipline*. Westport, Conn.: Praeger.

_____. 2003. "Cultural Criminology." In Martin D. Schwartz and Suzanne E. Hatty, eds., *Controversies in Critical Criminology*, 71–84. Cincinnati, Ohio: Anderson.

Ferrell, Jeff, and Clinton R. Saunders, eds. 1994. *Cultural Criminology*. Boston: Northeastern University Press.

Ferrell, Jeff, Dragan Milovanovic, and Steven Lyng. 2001. "Edgework, Media Practices, and the Elongation of Meaning." *Theoretical Criminology* 5, 2:177–202.

Ferri, Enrico. 1901. *Criminal Sociology*. New York: D. Appleton.

Fiero, John W. 1996. "Roe v Wade." In Joseph M. Bessette, ed., *Ready Reference: American Justice*. Englewood Cliffs, N.J.: Salem Press.

Figueira-McDonough, Josephina. 1980. "A Reformulation of the Equal Opportunity Explanation of Female Delinquency." *Crime and Delinquency* 26:333–343.

_____. 1983. "On the Usefulness of Merton's Anomie Theory: Academic Failure and Deviance Among High School Students." *Youth and Society* 14:259–279.

Finestone, Harold. 1976. *Victims of Change*. Westport, Conn.: Greenwood.

Fishbein, Diana H. 1990. "Biological Perspectives in Criminology." *Criminology* 28:27–72.

_____. 1998. "Biological Perspectives in *Criminology*." In Stuart Henry and Werner Einstadter, eds., *The Criminology Theory Reader*. New York: New York University Press.

Fishbein, Diana H., and Susan E. Pease. 1988. "The Effects of Diet on Behavior: The Implications for Criminology and Corrections." *Research in Corrections* 1:1–44.

Fishbein, Diana H., and Melissa Reuland. 1994. "Psychological Correlates of Frequency and Type of Drug Use Among Jail Inmates." *Addictive Behaviors* 19:583–598.

Fishbein, Diana H., and Robert W. Thatcher. 1986. "New Diagnostic Methods in *Criminology*: Assessing Organic Sources of Behavioral Disorders." *Journal of Research in Crime and Delinquency* 23:240–267.

Fisher, Eric. 1975. "Community Courts: An Alternative to Criminal Adjudication." *American University Law Review* 24:1253–1274.

Flavin, Jeanne. 2001. "Feminism for the Mainstream Criminologist: An Invitation." *Journal of Criminal Justice* 29:271–285.

Fogel, David. 1975. *We Are the Living Proof: The Justice Model for Corrections*. Cincinnati: Anderson.

Forst, M. 1983. "Capital Punishment and Deterrence: Conflicting Evidence?" *Journal of Criminal Law and Criminology* 74:927–942.

Foster, Jack D., Simon Dinitz, and Walter C. Reckless. 1972. "Perceptions of Stigma Following Public Intervention for Delinquent Behavior." *Social Problems* 20:202–209.

Foster, Janet. 1990. *Villains: Crime and Community in the Inner City.* New York: Routledge.

Foucault, Michel. 1977. *Discipline and Punish.* Harmondsworth, U.K.: Allen Lane.

———. 1980. *Power/Knowledge: Selected Interviews and Other Writings 1972–1977.* Edited by Colin Gordon. Brighton, U.K.: Harvester.

Fox, James Alan, and Jack Levin. 1994. "Firing Back: The Growing Threat of Workplace Homicide." *Annals of the American Academy of Political and Social Science* 563:16–30.

Fox, Richard, G. 1971. "The XYY Offender: A Modern Myth." *Journal of Criminal Law, Criminology, and Police Science* 62:59–73.

Frazier, Charles E., Donna M. Bishop, and John C. Henretta. 1992. "The Social Context of Race Differentials in Juvenile Justice Dispositions." *Sociological Quarterly* 33:447–458.

Frazier, Charles E., and John K. Cochran. 1986. "Official Intervention, Diversion from the Juvenile Justice System, and Dynamics of Human Services Work: Effects of a Reform Goal Based on Labeling Theory." *Crime and Delinquency* 32:157–176.

Free, Marvin D., Jr. 1994. "Religiosity, Religious Conservatism, Bonds to School, and Juvenile Delinquency Among Three Categories of Drug Users." *Deviant Behavior* 15:151–170.

Freud, Sigmund. 1915. *Der Verbrecher aus Schuldbewusstsein.* Vol. 10 of *Gesammelte Schriften.* Vienna: Internationaler Psychoanalytsischer Verlag.

———. 1950. "Criminals from a Sense of Guilt." In *Gesammelte Werke,* 14:332–333. London: Imago.

Friedlander, Kate. 1947. *The Psychoanalytical Approach to Juvenile Delinquency.* London: International Universities Press.

Friedman, Jennifer, and Dennis P. Rosenbaum. 1988. "Social Control Theory: The Salience of Components by Age, Gender, and Type of Crime." *Journal of Quantitative Criminology* 4:363–381.

Friedrichs, David O. 1991. "Peacemaking Criminology in a World Filled with Conflict." In Brian D. MacLean and Dragan Milovanovic, eds., *New Directions in Critical Criminology.* Vancouver: Collective.

———. 1996. *Trusted Criminals: White Collar Crime in Contemporary Society.* Belmont, Calif.: Wadsworth.

Fuller, John. 1998. *Criminal Justice: A Peacemaking Perspective.* Boston: Allyn & Bacon.

———. 2003. "Peacemaking Criminology." In Martin D. Schwartz and Suzanne E. Hatty, eds., *Controversies in Critical Criminology,* 85–95. Cincinnati: Anderson.

Gaarder, Emily, and Joanne Belknap. 2002. "Tenuous Borders: Girls Transferred to Adult Court." *Criminology* 40:481–517.

Gabor, Thomas. 1994. *Everybody Does It! Crimes by the Public.* Toronto: University of Toronto Press.

Gacono, Carl, and J. Reid Meloy. 1994. *The Rorschach Assessment of Aggressive and Psychopathic Personalities.* Hillsdale, N.J.: Lawrence Erlbaum.

Gado, Mark. 2002. "Hell Comes to Bath: America's Worst School Violence Ever Hell Comes to Bath." http://www.crimelibrary.com/serial7/bath.

Gans, Herbert J. 1997. "Best-Sellers by Sociologists: An Exploratory Study." *Contemporary Sociology* 26:131–135.

Gardiner, Richard A. 1978. *Design for Safe Neighborhoods: The Environmental Security Planning and Design Process.* Washington, D.C.: LEAA–U.S. Department of Justice.

Garland, Allen E. 2001. "The Biological Basis of Crime: An Historical and Methodological Study." *Historical Studies in the Physical and Biological Sciences* 31:183–223.

Garland, David. 1985. *Punishment and Welfare: A History of Penal Strategies.* Brookfield, Vt.: Gower.

_____. 1996. "The Limits of the Sovereign State: Strategies of Crime Control in Contemporary Society." *The British Journal of Criminology* 36:445–471.

_____. 1997. "'Governmentality' and the Problem of Crime: Foucault, Criminology, Sociology. *Theoretical Criminology* 1, no. 2:173–214.

Garofalo, James, Leslie Siegel, and John Laub. 1987. "School-Related Victimizations Among Adolescents: An Analysis of National Crime Survey (NCS) Narratives." *Journal of Quantitative Criminology* 3:321–338.

Garofalo, Raffaele. 1914. *Criminology.* Translated by Robert Wyness Millar. Boston: Little, Brown.

Geerken, Michael, and Walter Gove. 1975. "Deterrence: Some Theoretical Considerations." *Law and Society Review* 9:497–514.

Geis, Gilbert. 1995. "The Limits of Academic Tolerance: The Discontinuance of the School of Criminology at Berkeley." In Thomas G. Blomberg and Stanley Cohen, eds., *Punishment and Social Control: Essays in Honor of Sheldon L. Messinger.* Hawthorn, N.Y.: Aldine de Gruyter.

Gelsthorpe, Loraine, and Allison Morris. 1988. "Feminism and Criminology in Britain." In Paul Rock, ed., *A History of British Criminology.* Oxford: Clarendon.

Gelsthorpe, Loraine, and Allison Morris, eds. 1990. *Feminist Perspectives in Criminology.* Philadelphia: Open University Press.

Gerlach, Neil. 2001. "From Disciplinary Gaze to Biological Gaze: Genetic Crime Thrillers and Biogovernance." *Canadian Review of American Studies* 31:95–118.

Gibbons, Don C. 1979. *The Criminological Enterprise: Theories and Perspectives.* Englewood Cliffs, N.J.: Prentice Hall.

_____. 1994. *Talking About Crime and Criminals: Problems and Issues in Theory Development in Criminology.* Englewood Cliffs, N.J.: Prentice Hall.

Gibbs, Jack P. 1966. "Conceptions of Deviant Behavior: The Old and the New." *Pacific Sociological Review* 14:20–37.

Gibbs, Leonard. 1974. "Effects of Juvenile Legal Procedures on Juvenile Offenders' Self-Attitudes." *Journal of Research in Crime and Delinquency* 11:51–55.

Gibbs, W. Wayt. 1995. "Seeking the Criminal Element." *Scientific American* 272:100–107.

Gilbert P. 1998. "Evolutionary Psychopathology: Why Isn't the Mind Designed Better Than It Is?" *British Journal of Medical Psychology* 71:353–373.

Gill, O. 1977. *Luke Street: Housing Policy, Conflict, and the Creation of the Delinquency Area.* London: Macmillan.

Gilsinan, James F. 1990. *Criminology and Public Policy.* Englewood Cliffs, N.J.: Prentice Hall.

Glaser, Brian A., Georgia B. Calhoun, and John V. Petrocelli. 2002. "Personality Characteristics of Male Juvenile Offenders by Adjudicated Offenses as Indicated by the MMPI-A." *Criminal Justice and Behavior* 29:183–201.

Glaser, Daniel. 1956. "Criminality Theories and Behavioral Images." *American Journal of Sociology* 61:433–444.

_____. 1978. *Crime in Our Changing Society.* New York: Holt, Rinehart & Winston.

Glueck, Sheldon. 1956. "Theory and Fact in Criminology: A Criticism of Differential Association." *British Journal of Delinquency* 7:92–109.

Glueck, Sheldon, and Elinor Glueck. 1950. *Unraveling Juvenile Delinquency.* New York: Commonwealth Fund.

_____. 1956. *Physique and Delinquency.* New York: Harper & Brothers.

_____. 1968. *Delinquents and Nondelinquents in Perspective.* Cambridge: Harvard University Press.

Goddard, Henry H. 1912. *The Kallikak Family: A Study in the Heredity of Feeblemindedness.* London: Macmillan.

Goffman, Erving. 1961. *Asylums.* New York: Doubleday Anchor.

_____. 1963. *Stigma: Notes on the Management of Spoiled Identity.* Englewood Cliffs, N.J.: Prentice Hall.

Gold, Martin. 1970. *Delinquent Behavior in an American City.* Belmont, Calif.: Wadsworth.

Goldstein, Arnold P., Leonard Krasner, and Sol L. Garfield. 1989. *Reducing Delinquency: Intervention in the Community.* New York: Pergamon.

Goodstein, Lynne, and John R. Hepburn. 1986. "Determinate Sentencing in Illinois: An Assessment of Its Development and Implementation." *Criminal Justice Policy Review* 1:305–328.

Goring, Charles. [1913] 1972. *The English Convict: A Statistical Study, 1913.* Montclair, N.J.: Patterson Smith.

Gorman, D. M., and Helene Raskin White. 1995. "You Can Choose Your Friends, but Do They Choose Your Crime? Implications of Differential Association Theories for Crime Prevention Policy." In Hugh D. Barlow, ed., *Crime and Public Policy: Putting Theory to Work.* Boulder: Westview.

Gottfredson, Michael R., and Travis Hirschi. 1990. *A General Theory of Crime.* Stanford, Calif.: Stanford University Press.

Gould, Leroy, Gary Kleck, and Marc Gertz. 1992. "The Concept of 'Crime' in Criminological Theory and Practice." *Criminologist* 17:1–6.

Gove, Walter, ed. 1975. *The Labeling of Deviance: Evaluating a Perspective.* New York: John Wiley.

Gove, Walter, and C. Wilmoth. 1990. "Risk, Crime, and Neurophysiological Highs: A Consideration of Brain Processes That May Reinforce Delinquent and Criminal Behavior." In L. Ellis and H. Hoffman, eds., *Crime in Biological, Social, and Moral Contexts.* New York: Praeger.

Grant, J. 1993. *Fundamental Feminism: Contesting the Core Concepts of Feminist Theory.* New York: Routledge.

Grasmick, Harold G., and Robert J. Bursik Jr. 1990. "Conscience, Significant Others, and Rational Choice: Extending the Deterrence Model." *Law and Society Review* 24:837–861.

Grasmick, Harold G., Robert J. Bursik Jr., and John K. Cochran. 1991. "'Render unto Caesar What Is Caesar's: Religiosity and Taxpayers' Inclinations to Cheat." *Sociological Quarterly* 32:251–266.

Grasmick, Harold G., Charles Tittle, Robert Bursik, and Bruce Arneklev. 1993. "Testing the Core Empirical Implications of Gottfredson and Hirschi's General Theory of Crime." *Journal of Research on Crime and Delinquency* 30:5–29.

Green, Gary S. 1990. *Occupational Crime.* Chicago: Nelson-Hall.

_____. [1990] 1997. *Occupational Crime.* 2nd ed. Chicago: Nelson-Hall.

Greenberg, David F. ed. [1981] 1993. *Crime and Capitalism: Readings in Marxist Criminology.* Palo Alto, Calif.: Mayfield.

Greenberg, Jerald. 1990. "Employee Theft as a Reaction to Underpayment Inequity: The Hidden Cost of Pay Cuts." *Journal of Applied Psychology* 75:561–568.

Greenwood, Peter W. 1983. "Controlling the Crime Rate through Imprisonment." In J. Q. Wilson, ed., *Crime and Public Policy.* San Francisco: Institute for Contemporary Studies.

_____. 1996. *Diverting Children from a Life of Crime: What Are the Costs?* Santa Monica, Calif.: RAND.

Griffin, Susan. 1979. *Rape: The Power of Consciousness.* San Francisco: Harper & Row.

Gross, Edward. 1978. "Organizational Sources of Crime: A Theoretical Perspective." In Norman K. Denzin, ed., *Studies in Symbolic Interaction.* Greenwich, Conn.: JAI.

Grossman, Dave. 1998. "Trained to Kill: Are We Teaching Our Children to Commit Murder." *Christianity Today,* August 10.

Grossman, Dave, and G. DeGaetano. 1999. *Stop Teaching Our Kids to Kill: A Call to Action Against TV, Movie, and Video Game Violence.* New York: Crown.

Gusfield, Joseph R. 1963. *Symbolic Crusade.* Urbana: University of Illinois Press.

Hagan, Frank E. 1986. *Introduction to Criminology.* Chicago: Nelson-Hall.

_____. 1993. *Research Methods in Criminal Justice and Criminology.* New York: Macmillan.

Hagan, John. 1977. *The Disreputable Pleasures.* Toronto: McGraw-Hill Ryerson.

_____. 1985. *Modern Criminology: Crime, Criminal Behavior, and Its Control.* New York: McGraw-Hill.

_____. 1993. "The Social Embeddedness of Crime and Unemployment." *Criminology* 31:465–492.

_____. 1994. *Crime and Disrepute.* Thousand Oaks, Calif.: Pine Forge Press.

Hagan, John, and Alberto Palloni. 1990. "The Social Reproduction of a Criminal Class in Working-Class London, Circa 1950–1980." *American Journal of Sociology* 96:265–299.

Hagan, John, John Simpson, and A. R. Gillis. 1987. "Class in the Household: A Power-Control Theory of Gender and Delinquency." *American Journal of Sociology* 92:788–816.

Hagedorn, John M. 1988. *People and Folks: Gangs, Crime, and the Underclass in a Rustbelt City.* Chicago: Lake View.

_____. 1994. "Homeboys, Dope Fiends, Legits and New Jacks." *Criminology* 32:197–220.

Hale, Robert. 1992. "Arrest Rates and Community Characteristics: Social Ecology Theory Applied to a Southern City." *American Journal of Criminal Justice* 16:17–32.

Hall, Jerome. 1952. *Theft, Law, and Society.* 2nd ed. Indianapolis: Bobbs Merrill.

Halleck, Seymour. 1971. *Psychiatry and the Dilemmas of Crime.* Berkeley: University of California Press.

Hallsworth, Simon. 2002. "Case for a Postmodern Penality." *Theoretical Criminology* 6:145–163.

Hamlin, John E. 1988. "The Misplaced Role of Rational Choice in Neutralization Theory." *Criminology* 26:425–438.

Handler, Joel. 1992. "The Presidential Address, 1992 Law and Society: Postmodernism, Protest, and the New Social Movement." *Law and Society Review* 26:697–731.

Harris, Anthony R. 1976. "Race, Commitment to Deviance, and Spoiled Identity." *American Sociological Review* 41:432–442.

Harris, Kay M. 1991. "Moving into the New Millennium: Toward a Feminist View of Justice." In Harold E. Pepinsky and Richard Quinney, eds., *Criminology as Peacemaking.* Bloomington: Indiana University Press.

Harris, Melissa, and Sandra Mathers. 2002. "Orlando Restricts Homeless." *Orlando Sentinel,* August 6.

Hartmann, Heidi. 1981. "The Unhappy Marriage of Marxism and Feminism: Towards a More Progressive Union." In Lydia Sargent, ed., *Women and Revolution.* Boston: South End.

Hartung, Frank. 1950. "White-Collar Offenses in the Wholesale Meat Industry in Detroit." *American Journal of Sociology* 56:25–34.

Hathaway, Starke. 1939. "The Personality Inventory as an Aid in the Diagnosis of Psychopathic Inferiors." *Journal of Consulting Psychology* 3:112–117.

Hatty, Suzanne E. 2000. *Masculinities, Violence, and Culture.* Thousand Oaks, Calif.: Sage.

Hawley, Amos H. 1950. *Human Ecology: A Theory of Community Structure.* New York: Ronald.

Hay, Carter. 2001. "Parenting, Self-Control, and Delinquency: A Test of Self-Control Theory." *Criminology* 39:707–735.

Hayner, Norman S. 1933. "Delinquency Areas in the Puget Sound Region." *American Journal of Sociology* 22:314–328.

Haynes, Roger, Kevin Cole, and Jennifer Woll. 1994. *Federal Sentencing Guidebook.* New York: McGraw-Hill.

Healy, William, and Augusta Bronner. 1926. *Delinquents and Criminals: Their Making and Unmaking.* New York: Macmillan.

———. 1936. *New Light on Delinquency and Its Treatment.* New Haven, Conn.: Yale University Press.

Heidensohn, Frances. 1985. *Women and Crime.* Basingstoke, U.K.: Macmillan.

Heimer, K., and S. De Coster. 1999. "The Gendering of Violent Delinquency." *Criminology* 37:27–317.

Heineke, John M., ed. 1978. *Economic Models of Criminal Behavior.* New York: North-Holland.

———. 1988. "Crime, Deterrence, and Choice: Testing the Rational Behavior Hypothesis." *American Sociological Review* 53:303–305.

Heinlein, Gary. 2002. "Michigan Eases Drug Sentences: Judges' Discretion Replaces Mandatory Terms for Offenders." *Detroit News and Free Press,* December 29, pp. A1, A9.

Heitgerd, Janet L., and Robert J. Bursik Jr. 1987. "Extracommunity Dynamics and the Ecology of Delinquency." *American Journal of Sociology* 92:775–787.

Henderson, Charles R. 1893. *An Introduction to the Study of the Dependent, Defective, and Delinquent Classes.* Boston: D. C. Heath.

Henning, K. R., and B. C. Frueh 1996. "Cognitive-Behaviorial Treatment of Incarcerated Offenders: An Evaluation of the Vermont Department of Corrections' Cognitive Self-change Program." *Criminal Justice and Behavior* 23, 4:523–541.

Henry, Stuart. 1976. "Fencing with Accounts: The Language of Moral Bridging." *British Journal of Law and Society* 3:91–100.

_____. 1977. "On the Fence." *British Journal of Law and Society* 4:124–133.

_____. 1983. *Private Justice.* London: Routledge & Kegan Paul.

_____. 1984. "Contradictions of Collective Justice: The Case of the Co-op Cops." *Howard Journal of Criminal Justice* 23:158–169.

_____. 1985. "Community Justice, Capitalist Society, and Human Agency: The Dialectics of Collective Law in the Co-operative." *Law and Society Review* 19:303–327.

_____. [1978] 1988. *The Hidden Economy: The Context and Control of Borderline Crime.* Oxford, U.K.: Martin Robertson; Port Townsend, Wash.: Loompanics Unlimited.

_____. 1991. "The Informal Economy: A Crime of Omission by the State." In Gregg Barak, ed., *Crimes by the Capitalist State: An Introduction to State Criminality.* Albany: State University of New York Press.

_____. 1999. "Is Left Realism a Useful Theory for Addressing the Problems of Crime? No?" In John R. Fuller and Eric W. Hickey, eds., *Controversial Issues in Criminology,* 137–144. Boston: Allyn & Bacon.

Henry, Stuart, ed. 1981. *Informal Institutions.* New York: St. Martin's.

_____. 1990. *Degrees of Deviance: Student Accounts of Their Deviant Behavior.* Aldershot, U.K.: Avebury; Salem, Wis.: Sheffield.

_____. 1994. *Employee Dismissal: Justice at Work.* Vol. 536 of *Annals of the American Academy of Political and Social Science.* Thousand Oaks, Calif.: Sage.

Henry, Stuart, and Roger Eaton, eds. 1999. *Degrees of Deviance: Students' Accounts of Their Deviant Behavior.* Salem, Wis.: Sheffield.

Henry, Stuart, and Mark M. Lanier. 1998. "The Prism of Crime: Arguments for an Integrated Definition of Crime." *Justice Quarterly* 15, no. 4:609–627.

Henry, Stuart, and Mark Lanier, eds. 2001. *What Is Crime?* Boulder: Rowman & Littlefield.

Henry, Stuart, and Dragan Milovanovic. 1991. "Constitutive Criminology: The Maturation of Critical Theory." *Criminology* 29:293–316.

_____. 1994. "The Constitution of Constitutive *Criminology*: A Postmodern Approach to Criminological Theory." In David Nelken, ed., *The Futures of Criminology.* London: Sage.

_____. 1996. *Constitutive Criminology: Beyond Postmodernism.* London: Sage.

_____. 1999. *Constitutive Criminology at Work: Applications to Crime and Justice.* Albany, N.Y.: SUNY Press.

_____. 2003. "Constitutive *Criminology*." In Martin D. Schwartz and Suzanne E. Hatty, eds., *Controversies in Critical Criminology,* 57–70. Cincinnati: Anderson.

Hepburn, John R. 1977. "The Impact of Police Intervention upon Juvenile Delinquents." *Criminology* 18:121–129.

Hepburn, John R., and Lynne Goodstein. 1986. "Organizational Imperatives and Sentencing Reform Implementation: The Impact of Prison Practices and Priorities on the Attainment of the Objective of Determinate Sentencing." *Crime and Delinquency* 32:329–365.

Heumann, Milton, and Colin Loftin. 1979. "Mandatory Sentencing and the Abolition of Plea Bargaining: The Michigan Felony Firearm Statute." *Law and Society Review* 13:393–430.

Hibbert, Christopher. [1963] 1966. *The Roots of Evil: A Social History of Crime and Punishment.* London: Weidenfeld & Nicolson.

Hil, Richard. 2002. "Facing Change: New Directions for Critical Criminology in the Early New Millennium?" *Western Criminology Review* 3, no. 2. http://wcr.sonoma.edu/v3n2/hil.html.

Hills, Stuart L. 1971. *Crime, Power, and Morality.* Scranton, Pa.: Chandler.

Hinckeldey, Christoph, ed. 1981. *Criminal Justice Through The Ages: From Divine Judgement to Modern German Legislation.* Translated by John Fosberry. Medieval Crime Museum, Rothenburg ob der Tauber, 4. Heilsbronn, Germany: Druckerei Schulist.

Hindelang, Michael J. 1970. "The Commitment of Delinquents to Their Misdeeds: Do Delinquents Drift?" *Social Problems* 17:502–509.

_____. 1973. "Causes of Delinquency: A Partial Replication and Extension." *Social Problems* 20:471–487.

_____. 1974. "Moral Evaluations of Illegal Behaviors." *Social Problems* 21:370–385.

Hinkle, William, and Stuart Henry, eds. 2000. *School Violence.* Vol. 567 of *Annals of the American Academy of Political and Social Science.* Thousand Oaks, Calif.: Sage.

Hirschi, Travis. 1969. *Causes of Delinquency.* Berkeley: University of California Press.

_____. 1979. "Separate and Equal Is Better." *Journal of Research in Crime and Delinquency* 16:34–38.

Hirschi, Travis, and Michael Hindelang. 1977. "Intelligence and Delinquency: A Revisionist Review." *American Sociological Review* 42:471–586.

Hirschi, Travis, and Rodney Stark. 1969. "Hellfire and Delinquency." *Social Problems* 17:202–213.

Hoffman-Bustamente, Dale. 1973. "The Nature of Female Criminality." *Issues in Criminology* 8:117–136.

Hoffmann, John P., and Timothy Ireland. 1995. "Cloward and Ohlin's Strain Theory Reexamined: An Elaborated Theoretical Model." In Freda Adler and William S. Laufer, eds., *The Legacy of Anomie Theory.* Vol. 6 of *Advances in Criminological Theory.* New Brunswick, N.J.: Transaction.

Hoge, Robert D. 1999. "An Expanded Role for Psychological Assessments in Juvenile Justice Systems." *Criminal Justice and Behavior* 26:251–266.

Hollin, Clive R. 1990. *Cognitive Behavioral Interventions with Young Offenders.* New York: Pergamon.

Hollinger, Richard C. 1991. "Neutralizing in the Workplace: An Empirical Analysis of Property Theft and Production Deviance." *Deviant Behavior* 12:169–202.

Hollinger, Richard C., and John P. Clark. 1983. *Theft by Employees.* Lexington, Mass.: D. C. Heath.

Holman, John E., and James F. Quinn. 1992. *Criminology: Applying Theory.* St. Paul, Minn.: West.

Hood-Williams, John. 2001. "Gender, Masculinities, and Crime: From Structures to Psyches." *Theoretical Criminology* 5:37–60.

Hooton, Ernest A. 1939. *The American Criminal: An Anthropological Study.* Cambridge: Harvard University Press.

Horney, Julie. 1978. "Menstrual Cycles and Criminal Responsibility." *Law and Human Nature* 2:25–36.

Horowitz, Donald. 1977. *Courts and Social Policy.* Washington, D.C.: Brookings Institute.

Horwitz, Allan, and Michael Wasserman. 1979. "The Effect of Social Control on Delinquent Behavior: A Longitudinal Test." *Sociological Focus* 12:53–70.

Huesmann, L. Rowell, Jessica Moise-titus, Cheryl-Lynn Podolski, and Leonard D. Eron. 2003. "Longitudinal Relations Between Children's Exposure to TV Violence and their Aggressive and Violent Behavior in Young Adulthood: 1977–1992." *Developmental Psychology* 39:201–221.

Howe, Adrian. 1994. *Punish and Critique: Towards a Feminist Analysis of Penality.* London: Routledge.

Hughes, S. P., and Ann L. Schneider. 1989. "Victim-Offender Mediation: A Survey of Program Characteristics and Perceptions of Effectiveness." *Crime and Delinquency* 35:217–233.

Huizinga, David, and Delbert S. Elliott. 1987. "Juvenile Offenders: Prevalence, Offender Incidence, and Arrest Rates by Race." *Crime and Delinquency* 33:206–223.

Humphries, Laud. 1970. *Tearoom Trade: Impersonal Sex in Public Places.* Chicago: Aldine.

Hunt, Alan. 1990. "The Big Fear: Law Confronts Postmodernism." *McGill Law Journal* 35:507–540.

———. 1991. "Postmodernism and Critical *Criminology.*" In Brian D. MacLean and Dragan Milovanovic, eds., *New Directions in Critical Criminology.* Vancouver: Collective.

Hunter, Albert J. 1985. "Private, Parochial, and Public Orders: The Problem of Crime and Incivility in Urban Communities." In Gerald D. Suttles and Mayer N. Zald, eds., *The Challenge of Social Control: Citizenship and Institution Building in Modern Society.* Norwood, N.J.: Ablex.

Hunter, Ronald D., and Mark L. Dantzker. 2002. *Crime and Criminality: Causes and Consequences.* Upper Saddle River, N.J.: Prentice Hall.

Hurwitz, Stephan, and Karl O. Christiansen. 1983. *Criminology.* London: George Allen & Unwin.

Hussey, Ann C. 1997. "Incapacitation." In F. Schmalleger, ed., *Crime and the Justice System in America,* 120–121. Westport, Conn.: Greenwood.

Hutchings, Barry, and Sarnoff A. Mednick. 1975. "Registered Criminality in the Adoptive and Biological Parents of Registered Male Criminal Adoptees." In

R. R. Fieve, D. Rosenthal, and H. Brill, eds., *Genetic Research in Psychiatry.* Baltimore: Johns Hopkins University Press.

Hutchinson, Thomas W., David Yellen, Debra Young, and Matthew R. Kip. 1994. *Federal Sentencing Law and Practice.* 2nd ed. St. Paul, Minn.: West.

In re Winship, 397 U.S. 358, 90 S.Ct. 1068 (1970).

Institute for Social Research (ISR). 1994. *Monitoring the Future, 1992.* Ann Arbor: ICPSR.

Jackson, Elton F., Charles R. Tittle, and Mary Jean Burke. 1986. "Offense-Specific Models of the Differential Association Process." *Social Problems* 33:335–356.

Jackson, Stevi. 1992. "The Amazing Deconstructing Woman Suggests Some Problems with Postmodern Feminism." *Trouble and Strife* 25:25–31.

Jacobs, David. 1978. "Inequality and the Legal Order: An Ecological Test of the Conflict Model." *Social Problems* 25:515–525.

Jacobs, Patricia A., M. Brunton, M. M. Melville, R. P. Brittain, and W. McClemont. 1965. "Aggressive Behavior: Mental Subnormality and the XYY Male." *Nature* 208:1351–1352.

Jacoby, Joseph E. 1994. Classics of *Criminology.* 2nd ed. Prospect Heights, Ill.: Waveland.

Jaggar, Alison. 1983. *Feminist Politics and Human Nature.* New Jersey: Rowman & Allanheld.

James, Leon, and Diane Nahl. 2001. *Road Rage and Aggressive Driving: Steering Clear of Highway Warfare.* New York: Prometheus Books.

Jaquith, Susan M. 1981. "Adolescent Marijuana and Alcohol Use: An Empirical Test of Differential Association Theory." *Criminology* 19:271–280.

Jarjoura, G. Roger. 1996. "The Conditional Effect of Social Class on the Dropout-Delinquency Relationship." *Journal of Research in Crime and Delinquency* 33:232–255.

Jeffery, C. Ray. 1965. "Criminal Behavior and Learning Theory." *Journal of Criminal Law, Criminology, and Police Science* 56:294–300.

_____. 1977. "Criminology as an Interdisciplinary Behavioral Science." *Criminology* 16:153–156.

_____. 1971. *Crime Prevention Through Environmental Design.* Beverly Hills, Calif.: Sage.

Jensen, Gary F. 1972a. "Delinquency and Adolescent Self-Conceptions: A Study of the Personal Relevance of Infraction." *Social Problems* 20:84–103.

_____. 1972b. "Parents, Peers, and Delinquent Action: A Test of the Differential Association Perspective." *American Journal of Sociology* 78:562–575.

_____. 1980. "Labeling and Identity: Toward a Reconciliation of Divergent Findings." *Criminology* 18:121–129.

_____. 1993. "Biological Perspectives." *Journal of Criminal Justice Education* 4:292–293.

_____. 1994. "Biological and Neuropsychiatric Approaches to Criminal Behavior." In Gregg Barak, ed., *Varieties of Criminology: Readings from a Dynamic Discipline.* Westport, Conn.: Praeger.

Jensen, Gary F., and David Brownfield. 1986. "Gender, Lifestyles, and Victimization: Beyond Routine Activity." *Violence and Victims* 1:85–99.

Johns, Christina. 1992. *The War on Drugs.* Westport, Conn.: Greenwood.

Johnson, Richard E. 1979. *Juvenile Delinquency and Its Origins.* Cambridge: Cambridge University Press.

Johnson, Richard E., Anastasios C. Marcos, and Stephen J. Bahr. 1987. "The Role of Peers in the Complex Etiology of Adolescent Drug Use." *Criminology* 25:323–340.

Johnson, Valerie. 1985. "Adolescent Alcohol and Marijuana Use: A Social Learning Perspective." Paper presented at the annual meeting of the Society for the Study of Social Problems, Washington, D.C., August.

_____. 1988. "Adolescent Alcohol and Marijuana Use: A Longitudinal Assessment of a Social Learning Perspective." *American Journal of Drug and Alcohol Abuse* 14:419–439.

Johnstone, John W. 1978. "Social Class, Social Areas, and Delinquency." *Sociology and Social Research* 63:49–72.

Jonassen, Christen T. 1949. "A Re-Evaluation and Critique of the Logic and Some Methods of Shaw and McKay." *American Sociological Review* 14:608–614.

Jones, T., Brian D. MacLean, and Jock Young. 1986. *The Islington Crime Survey: Crime Policing and Victimization in Inner-City London.* Aldershot, U.K.: Gower.

Joutsen, Matti. 1994. "Victimology and Victim Policy in Europe." *Criminologist* 19:1–6.

Kamin, L. J. 1985. "Criminality and Adoption." *Science* 227:982.

Kaplan, Howard B. 1975. *Self-Attitudes and Deviant Behavior.* Pacific Palisades, Calif.: Goodyear.

Kappeler, Victor E., and Peter B. Kraska. 1999. "Policing Modernity: Scientific and Community Based Violence on Symbolic Playing Fields." In Stuart Henry and Dragan Milovanovic, eds., *Constitutive Criminology at Work: Applications to Crime and Justice.* Albany: SUNY Press.

Karmen, Andrew. 1990. *Crime Victims: An Introduction to Victimology.* 2nd ed. Pacific Grove, Calif.: Brooks/Cole.

Karmen, Andrew. 2001. *Crime Victims.* 4th ed. Belmont, Calif.: Wadsworth.

Kasindorf, Martin. 2002. "Three Strikes Laws Fall Out of Favor." *USA Today*, February 2, p. 3A.

Katz, Charles M., Vincent J. Webb, and David R. Schaefer. 2001. "An Assessment of the Impact of Quality-of-Life Policing on Crime and Disorder." *Justice Quarterly* 18:825–876.

Katz, Jack. 1988. *Seductions of Crime: Moral and Sensual Attractions of Doing Evil.* New York: Basic.

Katz, Janet, and William J. Chambliss. 1991. "Biology and Crime." In Joseph F. Sheley, ed., *Criminology: A Contemporary Handbook.* Belmont, Calif.: Wadsworth.

Katz, John. 1999. "Voices from Hellmouth." http://slashdot.org.

Kelling, G., and C. Coles. 1996. *Fixing Broken Windows.* New York: Free Press.

Kennedy, David M. 1996. "Neighborhood Revitalization: Lessons from Savannah and Baltimore." *National Institute of Justice Journal* 231 (August):13–17.

Kennedy, Leslie W., and David R. Forde. 1990a. "Risky Lifestyles and Dangerous Results: Routine Activities and Exposure to Crime." *Sociology and Social Research* 74:208–211.

_____. 1990b. "Routine Activities and Crime: An Analysis of Victimization in Canada." *Criminology* 28:101–115.

Kilcher, Jewel. 1994. *Pieces of You*. New York: Atlantic Records.

Kinsey, Richard. 1979. "Despotism and Legality." In Bob Fine, Richard Kinsey, John Lea, Sol Picciotto, and Jock Young, eds., *Capitalism and the Rule of Law: From Deviancy Theory to Marxism*. London: Hutchinson.

Klein, Dorie. [1973] 1980. "The Etiology of Female Crime: A Review of the Literature." In Susan K. Datesman and Frank R. Scarpitti, eds., *Women, Crime, and Justice*. New York: Oxford University Press.

Klinger, David. 1997. "Negotiating Order in Patrol Work: An Ecological Theory of Police Response to Crime." *Criminology* 35:277–306.

Klockars, Carl. 1974. *The Professional Fence*. New York: Free Press.

_____. 1980. "The Contemporary Crisis of Marxist Criminology." In James Inciardi, ed., *Radical Criminology: The Coming Crisis*. Beverly Hills, Calif.: Sage.

Knoblich, Guenther, and Roy King. 1992. "Biological Correlates of Criminal Behavior." In Joan McCord, ed., *Facts, Frameworks, and Forecasts*. Vol. 3 of *Advances in Criminological Theory*. New Brunswick, N.J.: Transaction.

Knopp, Fay Honey. 1991. "Community Solutions to Sexual Violence: Feminist/ Abolitionist Perspectives." In Harold Pepinsky and Richard Quinney, eds., *Criminology as Peacemaking*. Bloomington: Indiana University Press.

Knox, Colin. 2001. "The 'Deserving' Victims of Political Violence: Punishment Attacks in Northern Ireland." *International Journal of Policy and Pratice* 1, 2:181–199.

Kobrin, Solomon. 1959. "The Chicago Area Project: A 25-year Assessment." *Annals of the American Academy of Political and Social Science* 322:20–29.

_____. 1971. "The Formal Legal Properties of the Shaw-McKay Delinquency Theory." In Harwin L. Voss and David M. Peterson, eds., *Ecology, Crime, and Delinquency*. New York: Appleton, Century, Crofts.

Kohlberg, Lawrence. 1969. "Stage and Sequence: The Cognitive-Developmental Approach to Socialization." In D. A. Goslin, ed., *Handbook of Socialization Theory and Research*. Chicago: Rand McNally.

Kornhauser, Ruth. 1978. *Social Sources of Delinquency*. 2nd ed. Chicago: University of Chicago Press.

_____. 1984. *Social Sources of Delinquency*. 3rd. ed. Chicago: University of Chicago Press.

Kraidy, Ute Sartorius. 2002. "Sunny Days on Sesame Street? Multiculturalism and Resistance Postmodernism." *Journal of Communication Inquiry* 26:9–25.

Kramer, John H., and Robin L. Lubitz. 1985. "Pennsylvania's Sentencing Reform: The Impact of Commission-Established Guidelines." *Crime and Delinquency* 31:481–500.

Kramer, John H., Robin L. Lubitz, and Cynthia A. Kempinen. 1989. "Sentencing Guidelines: A Quantitative Comparison of Sentencing Policy in Minnesota, Pennsylvania, and Washington." *Justice Quarterly* 6:565–587.

Kramer, Ronald C. 1982. "The Debate Over the Definition of Crime: Paradigms, Value Judgements, and Criminological Work." In Frederick Elliston and Norm Bowie, eds., *Ethics, Public Policy, and Criminal Justice*, 33–58. Cambridge, Mass: Oelgeschlager, Gunn, and Hain.

_____. 1984. "Corporate Criminality: The Development of an Idea." In Ellen Hochstedler, ed., *Corporations as Criminals*. Beverly Hills, Calif.: Sage.

_____. 2000. "The Role of Poverty, Inequality and Social Exclusion in Shaping the Problem of Youth Violence." In W. Hinkle and S. Henry, eds., *School Violence.* Vol. 567 of *Annals of the American Academy of Political and Social Science.* Thousand Oaks, Calif.: Sage.

Kretschmer, Ernest. [1921] 1925. *Physique and Character.* New York: Harcourt, Brace.

Krisberg, Barry. 1975. *Crime and Privilege: Towards a New Criminology.* Englewood Cliffs, N.J.: Prentice Hall.

Krohn, Marvin D. 1986. "The Web of Conformity: A Network Approach to the Explanation of Delinquent Behavior." *Social Problems* 33:581–93.

_____. 1991. "Control and Deterrence Theories." In Joseph F. Sheley, ed., *Criminology: A Contemporary Handbook.* Belmont, Calif.: Wadsworth.

Krohn, Marvin D., and James L. Massey. 1980. "Social Control and Delinquent Behavior: An Examination of the Elements of the Social Bond." *Sociological Quarterly* 21:529–543.

Krohn, Marvin D., William Skinner, James Massey, and Ronald Akers. 1985. "Social Learning Theory and Adolescent Cigarette Smoking: A Longitudinal Study." *Social Problems* 32:455–471.

Krueger, Robert, Pamela Schmutte, Avshalom Caspi, Terrie Moffitt, Kathleen Campbell, and Phil Silva. 1994. "Personality Traits Are Linked to Crime Among Men and Women: Evidence from a Birth Cohort." *Journal of Abnormal Psychology* 103:328–338.

LaFree, Gary, Kriss A. Drass, and Patrick O'Day. 1992. "Race and Crime in Postwar America: Determinants of African-American and White Rates, 1957–1988." *Criminology* 30:157–188.

LaGrange, Randy L., and Helene Raskin White. 1985. "Age Differences in Delinquency: A Test of Theory." *Criminology* 23:19–45.

LaGrange, T., and R. Silverman. 1999. "Low Self-Control and Opportunity: Testing the General Theory of Crime as an Explanation for Gender Differences in Delinquency." *Criminology* 37:41–72.

Landsheer, J. A., H't Hart, and W. Kox. 1994. "Delinquent Values and Victim Damage: Exploring the Limits of Neutralization Theory." *British Journal of Criminology* 34:44–53.

Laner, Mary Riege, and Jeanine Thompson. 1982. "Abuse and Aggression in Courting Couples." *Deviant Behavior* 3:229–244.

Lanier, Mark M. 1993. "Explication and Measurement of the Theoretical Constructs Underlying Community Policing." Ph.D. diss., Michigan State University.

_____. 1994. "Preparing for Jobs in Academia and Research" and "Experiences of Graduate School." In Stuart Henry, ed., *Inside Jobs: A Realistic Guide to Criminal Justice Careers for College Graduates.* Salem, Wis.: Sheffield.

_____. 1996a. "An Evolutionary Typology of Women Police Officers." *Women and Criminal Justice* 8:35–57.

_____. 1996b. "Justice for Incarcerated Women with HIV in the Twenty-First Century." In Roslyn Muraskin and Albert R. Roberts, eds., *Visions for Change: Criminal Justice in the Twenty-First Century.* Englewood Cliffs, N.J.: Prentice Hall.

Lanier, Mark, and William Davidson II. 1995. "Methodological Issues Related to Instrument Development for Community Policing Assessments." *Police Studies* 17:21–40.

Lanier, Mark, Ralph DiClemente, and P. F. Horan. 1991. "HIV Knowledge and Behaviors of Incarcerated Youth: A Comparison of High and Low Risk Locales." *Journal of Criminal Justice* 19:257–262.

Lanier, Mark, and Belinda McCarthy. 1989. "AIDS Awareness and the Impact of AIDS Education in Juvenile Corrections." *Criminal Justice and Behavior* 16:395–411.

Lanier, Mark, and Cloud H. Miller. 1995. "Attitudes and Practices of Federal Probation Officers Toward Pre-Plea/Trial Investigative Report Policy." *Crime and Delinquency* 41:364–377.

Lanier, Mark, and John P. Sloan. 1996. "Cynicism, Fear, Communication, and Knowledge of Acquired Immunodeficiency Syndrome (AIDS) Among Juvenile Delinquents." *Crime and Delinquency* 42:231–243.

Lasley, James R. 1988. "Toward a Control Theory of White-Collar Offending." *Journal of Quantitative Criminology* 4:347–362.

Lasley, James R., and Jill Leslie Rosenbaum. 1988. "Routine Activities and Multiple Personal Victimization." *Sociology and Social Research* 73:47–50.

Lauritsen, Janet L., John H. Laub, and Robert J. Sampson. 1992. "Conventional and Delinquent Activities: Implications for the Prevention of Violent Victimization Among Adolescents." *Violence and Victims* 7:91–108.

Lawrence, Richard. 1998. *School Crime and Juvenile Justice.* New York: Oxford University Press.

Lea, John, and Jock Young. 1984. *What Is to Be Done About Law and Order?* Harmondsworth, U.K.: Penguin.

Leiber, Michael J., Margaret Farnworth, Katherine M. Jamieson, and Mahesh K. Nalla. 1994. "Bridging the Gender Gap in Criminology: Liberation and Gender-Specific Strain Effects on Delinquency." *Sociological Inquiry* 64:56–68.

Leiber, Michael J., and Katherine M. Jamieson. 1995. "Race and Decision Making Within Juvenile Justice: The Importance of Context." *Journal of Quantitative Criminology* 11:363–388.

Leiber, Michael J., and Tina Mawhorr. 1995. "Evaluating the Use of Social Skills Training and Employment with Delinquent Youth." *Journal of Criminal Justice* 23:127–141.

Lejins, Peter P. 1987. "Thorsten Sellin: A Life Dedicated to Criminology." *Criminology* 25:975–988.

Lemert, Edwin M. 1951. *Social Pathology.* New York: McGraw-Hill.

_____. 1967. *Human Deviance, Social Problems, and Social Control.* Englewood Cliffs, N.J.: Prentice Hall.

Leonard, Eileen B. 1982. *Women, Crime, and Society: A Critique of Criminological Theory.* New York: Longman.

Levine, Murray, and David Perkins. 1987. *Principles of Community Psychology.* New York: Oxford University Press.

Liazos, Alexander. 1972. "The Poverty of the Sociology of Deviance: Nuts, Sluts and Perverts." *Social Problems* 20:103–120.

Lilly, J. Robert, Francis T. Cullen, and Richard A. Ball. [1989] 1995. *Criminological Theory: Context and Consequences.* Thousand Oaks, Calif.: Sage.

_____. 2002. *Criminological Theory: Context and Consequences.* 3rd ed. Thousand Oaks, Calif.: Sage.

Liska, Allen E., and Mitchell B. Chamlin. 1984. "Social Structure and Crime Control Among Macrosocial Units." *American Journal of Sociology* 90:383–395.

Liska, Allen E., and Mark D. Reed. 1985. "Ties to Conventional Institutions and Delinquency: Estimating Reciprocal Effects." *American Sociological Review* 50:547–560.

Lizotte, Alan. 1985. "The Uniqueness of Rape: Reporting Assaultive Violence to the Police." *Crime and Delinquency* 32:169–191.

Loeber, Ralph, and Marc LeBlanc. 1990. "Toward a Developmental Criminology." In Norval Morris and Michael Tonry, eds., *Crime and Justice.* Vol. 23. Chicago: University of Chicago Press.

Lofland, John H. 1969. *Deviance and Identity.* Englewood Cliffs, N.J.: Prentice Hall.

Lombroso, Cesare. 1876. *L'Uomo Delinquente.* Milan: Hoepli.

_____. 1911. Introduction to Gina Lombroso-Ferrero, ed., *Criminal Man According to the Classification of Cesare Lombroso.* New York: Putnam.

_____. [1912] 1968. *Crime: Its Causes and Remedies.* Montclair, N.J.: Patterson Smith.

Lombroso, Cesare, and William Ferrero. 1900. *The Female Offender.* New York: D. Appleton.

Lombroso-Ferrero, Gina. 1994. "Criminal Man." In Joseph E. Jacoby, ed., *Classics of Criminology.* 2nd ed. Prospect Heights, Ill.: Waveland.

Longstreet, Wilma S. 2003. "Early Postmodernism in Social Education—Revisiting 'Decision Making: The Heart of Social Studies Instruction!'" *Social Studies* 94:11–15.

Lorber, Judith. 1996. "Beyond the Binaries: Depolarizing the Categories of Sex, Sexuality, and Gender." *Sociological Inquiry* 66:143–159.

Lotke, Eric. 1993. "Sentencing Disparity Among Co-Defendants: The Equalization Debate." *Federal Sentencing Reporter* 6:116–119. Berkeley: University of California Press.

Love, Barbara, and Elizabeth Shanklin. 1978. "The Answer Is Matriarchy." In Ginny Vida, ed., *Our Right to Love.* Englewood Cliffs, N.J.: Prentice Hall.

Lovibond, Sabina. 1989. "Feminism and Postmodernism." *New Left Review* 178:5–28.

Lucken, Karol. 1998. "Contemporary Penal Trends: Modern or Postmodern?" *The British Journal of Criminology* 38:106–123.

Lydston, George F. 1904. *The Diseases of Society (The Vice and Crime Problem).* Philadelphia: J. B. Lippincott.

Lykken, D. 1995. *The Antisocial Personalities.* Hillsdale, N.J.: Lawrence Erlbaum.

Lynch, Michael. 2000. "J. Phillippe on Crime: An Examination and Critique of the Explanation of Crime and Race." *Social Pathology* 6:228–244.

Lynch, Michael J., and W. Byron Groves. 1986. *A Primer in Radical Criminology.* New York: Harrow & Heston.

Lyng, Steve. 1990. "Edgework." *American Journal of Sociology* 95, 4:876–921.

Lyng, Steve, ed. 2003. *Edgework.* Albany: SUNY Press.

MacCoun, Robert, and Peter Router. 1992. "Are the Wages of Sin $30 an Hour? Economic Aspects of Street-Level Drug Dealing." *Crime and Delinquency* 38:477–491.

MacDonald, Arthur. 1893. *Criminology.* With an introduction by Dr. Cesare Lombroso. New York: Funk & Wagnalls.

Mack, Dorothy, and Laura Weinland. 1989. "Not Guilty by Reason of Insanity Evaluations: A Study of Defendants and Examiners." *Journal of Criminal Justice* 17:39–45.

MacKinnon, Catharine. 1987. *Feminism Unmodified: Discourses on Life and Law.* Cambridge: Harvard University Press.

_____. 1989. *Toward a Feminist Theory of the State.* Cambridge: Harvard University Press.

MacLean, Brian D. 1991. "The Origins of Left Realism." In Brian D. MacLean and Dragan Milovanovic, eds., *New Directions in Critical Criminology.* Vancouver: Collective.

_____. 1996. "Crime, Criminology, and Society: A Short but Critical Introduction." In Brian D. MacLean, ed., *Crime and Society: Readings in Critical Criminology.* Mississauga, Ont.: Copp Clark.

MacLean, Brian D., and Dragan Milovanovic, eds. 1991. *New Directions in Critical Criminology.* Vancouver: Collective.

_____. 1997. *Thinking Critically About Crime.* Vancouver: Collective.

Maedor, Thomas. 1985. *Crime and Madness.* New York: Harper & Row.

Magnusson, David, Britt Klinteberg, and Hakan Stattin. 1992. "Autonomic Activity/Reactivity, Behavior, and Crime in a Longitudinal Perspective." In Joan McCord, ed., *Facts, Frameworks, and Forecasts.* Vol. 3 of *Advances in Criminological Theory.* New Brunswick, N.J.: Transaction.

Maguire, Mike, and Trevor Bennett. 1982. *Burglary in a Dwelling.* London: Heinemann.

Maher, Lisa. 1997. *Sexed Work: Gender, Race and Resistance in a Brooklyn Drug Market.* Oxford: Clarendon Press.

Mama, Amina. 1989. "Violence Against Black Women: Gender, Race, and State Responses." *Feminist Review* 32:30–48.

Mankoff, Milton. 1971. "Societal Reaction and Career Deviance: A Critical Analysis." *Sociological Quarterly* 12:204–218.

_____. 1978. "On the Responsibility of Marxist Criminology: A Reply to Quinney." *Contemporary Crisis* 2:293–301.

Mannheim, Hermann. 1965. *Comparative Criminology.* Boston: Houghton Mifflin.

Manning, Peter K. 1988. *Symbolic Communications: Signifying Calls and the Police Response.* Cambridge: MIT Press.

_____. 1989. "On the Phenomenology of Violence." *Criminologist* 14:1–22.

Marcos, Anastasios C., Stephen J. Bahr, and Richard E. Johnson. 1986. "Test of a Bonding/Association Theory of Adolescent Drug Use." *Social Forces* 65:135–161.

Markle, Gerald E., and R. J. Troyer. 1979. "Smoke Gets in Your Eyes: Cigarette Smoking as Deviant Behavior." *Social Problems* 26:611–625.

Markowitz, Fred E., Paul E. Bellair, Allen E. Liska, and Jianhong Liu. 2001. "Extending Social Disorganization Theory: Modeling Relationships Between Cohesion, Disorder, and Fear." *Criminology* 39:293–320.

Mars, Gerald. 1982. *Cheats at Work: An Anthropology of Workplace Crime.* London: Allen & Unwin.

Marshall, Tony. 1999. *Restorative Justice: An Overview*. London: Home Office Research Development and Statistics.

Martens, Willem H.J. 1997. "Psychopathy and Maturation." Master's thesis, Tilburg University, The Netherlands.

_____. 2000. "Antisocial and Psychopathic Personality Disorders: Causes, Course, and Remission: A Review Article." *International Journal of Offender Therapy and Comparative Criminology* 44:406–430.

_____. 2002. "Criminality and Moral Dysfunctions: Neurological, Biochemical, and Genetic Dimensions." *International Journal of Offender Therapy and Comparative Criminology* 46:170–182.

Martin, Randy, Robert J. Mutchnick, and Timothy W. Austin. 1990. *Criminological Thought: Pioneers Past and Present*. New York: Macmillan.

Martinson, Robert. 1974. "What Works? Questions and Answers About Prison Reform." *Public Interest* 35:22–54.

Maruna, Shadd. 2003. "Excuses, Excuses: What Have We Learned in 50 Years of Testing 'Neutralization Theory'?" Lecture to Cambridge University's Institute of Criminology, May 8.

Marx, Karl. [1844] 1975. *The Economic and Philosophical Manuscripts of 1844*. New York: International.

_____. [1859] 1975. "'Preface' to a Contribution to the Critique of Political Economy." In Lucio Colletti, ed., *Karl Marx: Early Writings*. Harmondsworth, U.K.: Penguin.

_____. [1862] 1964. "Theories of Surplus Value." In Tomas B. Bottomore and Maximilien Rubel, eds., *Karl Marx: Selected Writings in Sociology and Social Philosophy*. Vol. 1. New York: McGraw-Hill.

Marx, Karl, and Friedrich Engels. [1845] 1964. *The German Ideology*. London: Lawrence & Wishart.

Mason, Gregory H. 1995. "Some Implications of Postmodernism for the Field of Peace Studies." *Peace and Change* 20:120–132.

Mathiesen, Thomas. 1974. *The Politics of Abolition: Essays in Political Action Theory*. London: Martin Robertson.

_____. 1986. "The Politics of Abolition." *Contemporary Crisis* 10:81–94.

Matsueda, Ross L. 1992. "Reflected Appraisals, Parental Labeling, and Delinquency: Specifying a Symbolic Interactionist Theory." *American Journal of Sociology* 97:1577–1611.

Matthews, Rick A. 2003. "Marxist Criminology." In Martin D. Schwatrz and Suzanne E. Hatty, eds., *Controversies in Critical Criminology*, 1–13. Cincinnati, Ohio: Anderson.

Matthews, Roger. 1987. "Taking Realist Criminology Seriously." *Contemporary Crisis* 11:371–401.

Matthews, Roger, and Jock Young, eds. 1986. *Confronting Crime*. Beverly Hills, Calif.: Sage.

_____. 1992. *Issues in Realist Criminology*. Beverly Hills, Calif.: Sage.

Matza, David. 1964. *Delinquency and Drift*. New York: John Wiley.

_____. 1969. *Becoming Deviant*. Englewood Cliffs, N.J.: Prentice Hall.

Matza, David, and Gresham Sykes. 1961. "Juvenile Delinquency and Subterranean Values." *American Sociological Review* 26:712–719.

Maurer, M. 1997. *Intended and Unintended Consequences: State Racial Disparities in Imprisonment*. Washington, D.C.: The Sentencing Project.

Maxfield, Michael. 1987. "Household Composition, Routine Activities, and Victimization: A Comparative Analysis." *Journal of Quantitative Criminology* 3:301–320.

Mayhew, Henry. [1861] 1981. "A Visit to the Rookery of St. Giles and Its Neighbourhood." In Mike Fitzgerald, Gregor McLennan, and Jennie Pawson, eds., *Crime and Society: Readings in History and Society*. London: Routledge & Kegan Paul.

Mayhew, Pat, and Mike Hough. 1991. "The British Crime Survey: The First Ten Years." In G. Kaiser, H. Kury, and H.-J. Albrecht, eds., *Victims and Criminal Justice*. Freiberg, Germany: Max Planck Institute.

Mays, G. Larry. 1989. "The Impact of Federal Sentencing Guidelines on Jail and Prison Overcrowding and Early Release." In Dean Champion, ed., *The U.S. Sentencing Guidelines: Implications for Criminal Justice*. New York: Praeger.

McCarthy, Bill. 1996. "The Attitudes and Actions of Others: Tutelage and Sutherland's Theory of Differential Association." *British Journal of Criminology* 36:135–147.

McLaren, Peter. 1994. "Postmodernism and the Death of Politics: A Brazilian Reprieve." In Peter McLaren and C. Lankshear, eds., *Politics of Liberation: Paths from Freire*, 193–215. New York: Routledge.

McCord, William, and Joan McCord. 1964. *The Psychopath: An Essay on the Criminal Mind*. New York: Van Nostrand.

McDowall, David, and Colin Loftin. 1992. "Comparing the UCR and NCS over Time." *Criminology* 30:125–132.

McFadden, Gerald S., Judy Clarke, and Jeffery L. Staniels. 1991. *Federal Sentencing Manual*. New York: Matthew Bender.

McGee, Zina T. 1992. "Social Class Differences in Parental and Peer Influence on Adolescent Drug Use." *Deviant Behavior* 13:349–372.

McKim, W. Duncan. 1900. *Heredity and Human Progress*. New York: Putnam.

McLaughlin, Eugene. 2001. "Deterrence." In Eugene McLaughlin and John Muncie, eds., *The Sage Dictionary of Criminology*. London: Sage.

Mead, George Herbert. 1934. *Mind, Self, and Society*. Edited by C. W. Morris. Chicago: University of Chicago Press.

Mednick, Sarnoff A. 1977. "A Bio-Social Theory of the Learning of Law-Abiding Behavior." In Sarnoff A. Mednick and Karl O. Christiansen, eds., *Biosocial Bases of Criminal Behavior*. New York: Gardner.

———. 1985. "Crime in the Family Tree." *Psychology Today*, March, 58–61.

Mednick, Sarnoff A., and Karl O. Christiansen. 1977. *Biosocial Bases of Criminal Behavior*. New York: Gardiner.

Mednick, Sarnoff A., W. F. Gabrielli, and Barry Hutchings. 1984. "Genetic Influences in Criminal Convictions: Evidence from an Adoption Cohort." *Science* 224:891–894.

———. 1987. "Genetic Factors in the Etiology of Criminal Behavior." In Sarnoff A. Mednick, Terrie Moffitt, and Susan Stack, eds., *The Causes of Crime: New Biological Approaches*. Cambridge: Cambridge University Press.

Mednick, Sarnoff A., and J. Volavka. 1980. "Biology and Crime." In Norvil Morris and Michael Tonry, eds., *Crime and Justice: An Annual Review of Research.* Chicago: University of Chicago Press.

Meehan, Albert J., and Micheal C. Ponder. 2002. "Race and Place: The Ecology of Racial Profiling African American Motorists." *Justice Quarterly* 19:399–430.

Meiczkowski, Thomas. 1992. "Crack Dealing on the Street: The Crew System and the Crack House." *Justice Quarterly* 9:151–163.

Melichar, Kenneth E. 1988. "Deconstruction: Critical Theory or an Ideology of Despair?" *Humanity and Society* 12:366–385.

Menard, Scott. 1987. "Short-Term Trends in Crime and Delinquency: A Comparison of UCR, NCS and Self-Report Data." *Justice Quarterly* 4:455–474.

Menard, Scott, and Herbert Covey. 1988. "UCR and NCS: Comparisons over Space and Time." *Journal of Criminal Justice* 16:371–384.

Mendelsohn, Benjamin. 1963. "The Origin of the Doctrine of Victimology." *Excerpta Criminologica* 3:239–244.

Menzies, Robert, and Dorothy Chunn. 1991. "Kicking Against the Pricks: The Dilemmas of Feminist Teaching in Criminology." *Critical Criminologist* 3:7–8, 14–15.

Merton, Robert K. 1938. "Social Structure and Anomie." *American Sociological Review* 3:672–682.

_____. 1964. "Anomie, Anomia, and Social Interaction: Contexts of Deviant Behavior." In Marshall B. Clinard, ed., *Anomie and Deviant Behavior: A Discussion and Critique.* New York: Free Press.

_____. [1957] 1968. *Social Theory and Social Structure.* New York: Free Press.

_____. 1995. "Opportunity Structure: The Emergence, Diffusion, and Differentiation of a Sociological Concept, 1930s–1950s." In Freda Adler and William S. Laufer, eds., *The Legacy of Anomie Theory.* Vol. 6 of *Advances in Criminological Theory.* New Brunswick, N.J.: Transaction.

Messerschmidt, James W. 1986. *Capitalism, Patriarchy, and Crime: Toward a Socialist Feminist Criminology.* Totowa, N.J.: Rowman & Littlefield.

_____. 1993. *Masculinities and Crime: Critique and Reconceptualization of Theory.* Boston: Rowman & Littlefield.

Messner, Stephen, and Judith R. Blau. 1987. "Routine Leisure Activities and Rates of Crime: A Macro-Level Analysis." *Social Forces* 65:1035–1051.

Messner, Steven. 1984. "The 'Dark Figure' and Composite Indexes of Crime: Some Empirical Explorations of Alternative Data Sources." *Journal of Criminal Justice* 12:435–444.

Messner, Steven, Marvin D. Krohn, and Allen E. Liska, eds. 1989. *Theoretical Integration in the Study of Deviance and Crime: Problems and Prospects.* Albany: SUNY Press.

Messner, Steven, and Richard Rosenfeld. 1994. *Crime and the American Dream.* Belmont, Calif.: Wadsworth.

Messner, Steven, and Kenneth Tardiff. 1985. "The Social Ecology of Urban Homicide: An Application of the Routine Activities Approach." *Criminology* 23:241–267.

Michael, Jerome, and Mortimer J. Adler. 1933. *Crime, Law, and Social Science.* New York: Harcourt Brace Jovanovich.

Michalowski, Raymond. 1985. *Order, Law, and Crime.* New York: Random House.

_____. 1991. "'Niggers, Welfare Scum, and Homeless Assholes': The Problems of Idealism, Consciousness, and Context in Left Realism." In Brian D. MacLean and Dragan Milovanovic, eds., *New Directions in Critical Criminology.* Vancouver: Collective.

Miethe, Terance D. 1987. "Charging and Plea Bargaining Practices Under Determinate Sentencing: An Investigation of the Hydraulic Displacement of Discretion." *Journal of Criminal Law and Criminology* 78:101–122.

Miethe, Terance D., and Charles A. Moore. 1985. "Socioeconomic Disparities Under Determinate Sentencing Systems: A Comparison of Pre-Guideline and Post-Guideline Practices in Minnesota." *Criminology* 23:337–363.

_____. 1989. *Sentencing Guidelines: Their Effect in Minnesota.* Washington, D.C.: National Institute of Justice.

Miethe, Terance D., Mark C. Stafford, and J. Scott Long. 1987. "Social Differentiation in Criminal Victimization: A Test of Routine Activities/Lifestyle Theories." *American Sociological Review* 52:184–194.

Miller, Jody. 2003. "Feminist Criminology." In Martin D. Schwartz and Suzanne E. Hatty, eds., *Controversies in Critical Criminology,* 15–28. Cincinnati: Anderson.

Miller, Joshua D., and Donald Lynam. 2001. "Structural Models of Personality and their Relation to Antisocial Behavior: A Meta-Analytical Review." *Criminology* 39:765–787.

Miller, Lisa L. 2001. "Looking for Postmodernism in All the Wrong Places." *British Journal of Criminology* 41:168–184.

Miller, Walter B. 1958. "Lower Class Culture as a Generating Milieu of Gang Delinquency." *Journal of Social Issues* 14:5–19.

_____. 1962. "The Impact of a Total-Community Delinquency Control Project." *Social Problems* 10:168–191.

Mills, C. Wright. 1940. "Situated Actions and Vocabularies of Motive." *American Sociological Review* 5:904–913.

_____. 1959. *The Sociological Imagination.* New York: Oxford University Press.

Milovanovic, Dragan. 1995. "Dueling Paradigms: Modernist Versus Postmodernist." *Humanity and Society* 19:1–22.

_____. 2002. *Critical Criminology at the Edge.* Monsey, New York: Criminal Justice Press.

_____. 2003. Introduction to S. Lyng, ed., *Edgework.* Albany: SUNY Press.

_____. 1997. *Chaos, Criminology, and Social Justice.* New York: Praeger.

Milovanovic, Dragan, and Stuart Henry. 2001. "Constitutive Definition of Crime as Harm." In Stuart Henry and Mark Lanier, eds., *What Is Crime? Controversies over the Nature of Crime and What to Do About It.* Boulder: Rowman & Littlefield.

Milovanovic, Dragan, and Stuart Henry. 2003. "Constitutive Penology." In Mary Bosworth, ed. *The Encyclopedia of Prisons and Corrections.* Thousand Oaks, Calif.: Sage.

Minor, W. William. 1980. "The Neutralization of Criminal Offense." *Criminology* 18:103–120.

_____. 1981. "Techniques of Neutralization: A Reconceptualization and Empirical Examination." *Journal of Research in Crime and Delinquency* 18:295–318.

_____. 1984. "Neutralization as a Hardening Process: Considerations in the Modeling of Change." *Social Forces* 62:995–1019.

Mitchell, Jim, and Richard A. Dodder. 1983. "Types of Neutralization and Types of Delinquency." *Journal of Youth and Adolescence* 12:307–318.

Moffitt, Terrie, Donald Lynam, and Phil Silva. 1994. "Neuropsychological Tests Predicting Male Delinquency." *Criminology* 32:277–300.

Moffitt, Terrie, and Phil Silva. 1988. "Self-Reported Delinquency, Neuropsychological Deficit, and History of Attention Deficit Disorder." *Journal of Abnormal Psychology* 16:553–569.

Mokhiber, Russell. 1988. *Corporate Crime and Violence—Big Business Power and the Abuse of the Public Trust*. San Francisco: Sierra Club Books.

Monahan, John. 1992. "Mental Disorder and Violent Behavior: Perceptions and Evidence." *American Psychologist* 47:511–521.

Monahan, John, and Henry Steadman. 1984. "Crime and Mental Disorder." *Research in Brief*. Washington, D.C.: National Institute of Justice.

Morash, Merry. 1982. "Juvenile Reaction to Labels: An Experiment and an Exploratory Study." *Sociology and Social Research* 67:76–88.

Morash, Merry, and L. Rucker. 1998. "A Critical Look at the Idea of Boot Camps as a Correctional Reform." In S. L. Miller, ed., *Crime Control and Women*, 32–51. Thousand Oaks, Calif.: Sage.

Morgan, H. Wayne. 1981. *Drugs in America: A Social History, 1800–1980*. New York: Syracuse University Press.

Morgan, J., and L. Zedner. 1992. "The Victim's Charter: A New Deal for Child Victims?" *Howard Journal of Criminal Justice* 1:294–307.

Moriarty, Laura J., and James E. Williams. 1996. "Examining the Relationship Between Routine Activities Theory and Social Disorganization: An Analysis of Property Crime Victimization." *American Journal of Criminal Justice* 12, 1:43–59.

Morris, Allison. 1987. *Women, Crime, and Criminal Justice*. Oxford, U.K.: Blackwell.

Morris, Terrence P. 1957. *The Criminal Area: A Study in Social Ecology*. London: Routledge & Kegan Paul.

Morrisey, Belinda. 2003. *When Women Kill: Questions of Agency and Subjectivity*. New York: Routledge.

Morton, Teru L., and Linda S. Ewald. 1987. "Family-Based Interventions for Crime and Delinquency." In Edward K. Morris and Curtis J. Braukmann, eds., *Behavioral Approaches to Crime and Delinquency: A Handbook of Applications Research and Concepts*. New York: Plenum.

Moyer, Imogene L. 2001. *Criminological Theories: Traditional and Nontraditional Voices and Themes*. Thousand Oaks, Calif.: Sage.

Muncie, John. 2000. "Decriminalizing Criminology." In George Mair and Roger Tarling, eds., *The British Criminology Conference: Selected Proceedings Volume 3* (http://www.britsoccrim.org/bccsp/vol03/muncie.html).

Munro, Vanessa E. 2003. "On Power and Domination: Feminism and the Final Foucault." *European Journal of Political Theory* 2:79–99.

Murray, C. 1997. *Does Prison Work?* London: Institute for Economic Affairs.

Myers, Wade, Kerrilyn Scott, Ann Burgess, and Allen Burgess. 1995. "Psychopathy, Biopsychosocial Factors, Crime Characteristics, and Classification of 25 Homicidal Youths." *Journal of the American Academy of Child Adolescent Psychiatry* 34:1483–1489.

Naffine, Ngaire. 1987. *Female Crime: The Construction of Women in Criminology.* London: Allen & Unwin.

Nagin, Daniel S., and Raymond Paternoster. 1993. "Enduring Individual Differences and Rational Choice Theories of Crime." *Law and Society Review* 27:467–496.

National Advisory Commission on Criminal Justice Standards and Goals. 1971. *A National Strategy to Reduce Crime.* Washington, D.C.: Government Printing Office.

Nee, C., and M. Taylor. 1988. "Residential Burglary in the Republic of Ireland: A Situational Perspective." *Howard Journal of Criminal Justice* 27:105–116.

Nelken, David. 1994. *The Futures of Criminology.* London: Sage.

Nelken, David, ed. 1994. "Whom Can You Trust? The Future of Comparative Criminology." In David Nelken, ed., The Futures of Criminology. London: Sage.

Nelkin, Dorothy. 1993. "The Grandiose Claims of Geneticists." *Chronicle of Higher Education,* March 3, B1–B3.

Nelkin, Dorothy, and Lawrence Tancredi. 1994. "Dangerous Diagnostics and Their Social Consequences." *Scientist* 12:12.

Nettler, Gwynn. 1984. *Explaining Crime.* 3rd ed. New York: McGraw-Hill.

Newman, Oscar. 1972. *Defensible Space.* New York: Macmillan.

_____. 1973. *Architectural Design for Crime Prevention.* Washington, D.C.: U.S. Department of Justice, National Institute of Law Enforcement and Justice.

_____. 1996. *Creating Defensible Space.* Rockville, Md.: U.S. Department of Housing and Urban Development, Office of Policy Development and Research.

Nicholson, Jane. 2000. "Reconciliations: Prevention and Recovery for School Violence." In W. Hinkle and S. Henry, eds., *School Violence.* Vol. 567 of *Annals of the American Academy of Political and Social Science.* Thousand Oaks, Calif.: Sage.

Nye, Ivan F. 1958. *Family Relationships and Delinquent Behavior.* New York: John Wiley.

O'Donoghue, Edward Geoffrey. 1923. *Bridewell Hospital: Palace, Prison, Schools, from the Earliest Times to the End of the Reign of Elizabeth.* London: Lane.

Olweus, Dan. 1987. "Testosterone and Adrenaline: Aggressive Antisocial Behavior in Normal Adolescent Males." In Sarnoff A. Mednick, Terrie Moffitt, and Susan Stack, eds., *The Causes of Crime: New Biological Approaches.* Cambridge: Cambridge University Press.

Olweus, Dan, Ake Mattsson, Daisy Schalling, and Hans Low. 1980. "Testosterone, Aggression, Physical and Personality Dimensions in Normal Adolescent Males." *Psychosomatic Medicine* 42:253–269.

O'Malley, Pat, and Steve Mugford. 1994. "Crime, Excitement, and Modernity." In Gregg Barak, ed., *Varieties of Criminology.* Westport, Conn.: Praeger.

Orcutt, James D. 1987. "Differential Association and Marijuana Use: A Closer Look at Sutherland (with a Little Help from Becker)." *Criminology* 25:341–358.

Orozco-Truong, Rosalie. 1996. "Empathy, Guilt, and Techniques of Neutralization: Their Role in a Conceptual Model of Delinquent Behavior." Ph.D. diss., University of Colorado.

Orru, Marco. 1987. *Anomie: History and Meanings.* Boston: Allen & Unwin.

_____. 1990. "Merton's Instrumental Theory of Anomie." In J. Clark, C. Modgil, and S. Modgil, eds., *Robert K. Merton: Consensus and Controversy.* London: Falmer.

O'Shea, Timothy. 2000. "The Efficacy of Home Security Measures." *American Journal of Criminal Justice* 24, 2:155–167.

Osgood, D. Wayne, Janet K. Wilson, Patrick M. O'Malley, Jerald G. Bachman, and Lloyd D. Johnston. 1996. "Routine Activities and Individual Deviant Behavior." *American Sociological Review* 61:635–655.

Packer, Herbert L. 1968. *The Limits of Criminal Sanction.* Stanford, Calif.: Stanford University Press.

Palamara, Frances, Francis T. Cullen, and Joanne C. Gersten. 1986. "The Effect of Police and Mental Health Intervention on Juvenile Deviance: Specifying Contingencies in the Impact of Formal Reaction." *Journal of Health and Social Behavior* 27:90–105.

Palen, J. J. 1981. *The Urban World.* 3rd ed. New York: McGraw-Hill.

Pallone, Nathaniel J., and James J. Hennessy. 1992. *Criminal Behavior: A Process Psychology Analysis.* New Brunswick, N.J.: Transaction.

Paolucci, Henry. 1963. Introduction to Cesare Beccaria, *On Crimes and Punishments.* Translated by Henry Paolucci. Indianapolis: Bobbs-Merrill.

Pape, Eric. 1999. "You're Out! (The Three-Strikes Law in California)." *Los Angeles Magazine*, August.

Park, Robert E. 1926. "The Urban Community as a Special Pattern and a Moral Order." In Ernest W. Burgess, ed., *The Urban Community.* Chicago: University of Chicago Press.

Park, Robert E., and Ernest W. Burgess. 1920. *Introduction to the Science of Sociology.* Chicago: University of Chicago Press.

Park, Robert E., Ernest W. Burgess, and Roderick McKenzie. 1925. *The City.* Chicago: University of Chicago Press.

Parker, Robert Nash. 1998. "Alcohol, Homicide, and Cultural Context." *Homicide Studies* 2:6–30.

Parry, Alan, and Robert E. Doan. 1994. *Story Re-Visions: Narrative Therapy in the Postmodern World.* New York: Guilford.

Passas, Nikos. 1990. "Anomie and Corporate Deviance." *Contemporary Crisis* 14:157–158.

_____. 1993. "I Cheat Therefore I Exist: The BCCI Scandal in Context." In W. M. Hoffman, S. Kamm, R. E. Frederick, and E. Petry, eds., *Emerging Global Business Ethics.* New York: Quorum.

_____. 1995. "Continuities in the Anomie Tradition." In Freda Adler and William S. Laufer, eds., *The Legacy of Anomie Theory.* Vol. 6 of *Advances in Criminological Theory.* New Brunswick, N.J.: Transaction.

_____. 2000. "Global Anomie, Dysnomie, and Economic Crime: Hidden Consequences of Neoliberalism and Globalization in Russia and Around the World." *Social Justice* 27, 2:16–44.

Passingham, R. E. 1972. "Crime and Personality: A Review of Eysenck's Theory." In V. D. Nebylitsyn and J. A. Gray, eds., *Biological Bases of Individual Behavior.* London: Academic.

Paternoster, Raymond. 1987. "The Deterrent Effect of the Perceived Certainty and Severity of Punishment: A Review of the Evidence and Issues." *Justice Quarterly* 4:173–217.

_____. 1989. "Decisions to Participate in and Desist from Four Types of Common Delinquency: Deterrence and Rational Choice Perspective." *Law and Society Review* 23:7–40.

Paternoster, Raymond, and Lee Ann Iovanni. 1989. "The Labeling Perspective and Delinquency: An Elaboration of the Theory and an Assessment of the Evidence." *Justice Quarterly* 6:359–394.

Paternoster, Raymond, and Paul Mazerolle. 1994. "General Strain Theory and Delinquency: A Replication and Extension." *Journal of Research on Crime and Delinquency* 31:235–263.

Paternoster, Raymond, Linda E. Saltzman, Gordon P. Waldo, and Theodore G. Chiricos. 1983. "Perceived Risk and Social Control: Do Sanctions Really Deter?" *Law and Society Review* 17:457–480.

_____. 1985. "Assessments of Risk and Behavioral Experience: An Exploratory Study of Change." *Criminology* 23:417–436.

Paternoster, Raymond, and Sally Simpson. 1993. "A Rational Choice Theory of Corporate Crime." In Ronald V. Clarke and Marcus Felson, eds., *Routine Activity and Rational Choice: Advances in Criminological Theory*. New Brunswick, N.J.: Transaction Publishers.

_____. 1996. "Sanction Threats and Appeals to Morality: Testing a Rational Choice Model of Corporate Crime." *Law and Society Review* 30:549–583.

Patterson, Gerald R. 1997. *Performance Models for Parenting: A Social Interactional Perspective*. New York: John Wiley.

Pavarini, M. 1994. "Is Criminology Worth Saving?" In David Nelken, ed., *The Futures of Criminology*. London: Sage.

Pavlov, Ivan P. [1906] 1967. *Lectures on Conditioned Reflexes: Twenty-Five Years of Objective Study of the Higher Nervous Activity (Behavior) of Animals*. New York: International.

Pearson, Frank S., and Neil A. Weiner. 1985. "Toward an Integration of Criminological Theories." *Journal of Criminal Law and Criminology* 76:116–150.

Pepinsky, Hal. 2000. "Educating for Peace." In W. Hinkle and S. Henry, eds., *School Violence*. Vol. 567 of *Annals of the American Academy of Political and Social Science*. Thousand Oaks, Calif.: Sage.

Pepinsky, Harold. 1976. *Crime and Conflict: A Study of Law and Society*. Oxford, U.K.: Martin Robertson.

_____. 1978. "Communist Anarchism as an Alternative to the Rule of Criminal Law." *Contemporary Crisis* 2:315–327.

_____. 1983. "Crime Causation: Political Theories." In Sanford E. Kadish, ed., *Encyclopedia of Crime and Justice*. New York: Free Press.

_____. 1991a. *The Geometry of Violence and Democracy*. Bloomington: Indiana University Press.

_____. 1991b. "Peacemaking in Criminology." In Brian D. MacLean and Dragan Milovanovic, eds., *New Directions in Critical Criminology*. Vancouver: Collective.

Pepinsky, Harold, and Richard Quinney, eds. 1991. *Criminology as Peacemaking*. Bloomington: Indiana University Press.

Perry, Ronald W. 1980. "Social Status and the Black Violence Hypothesis." *Journal of Social Psychology* 111:131–137.

Petee, Thomas, Gregory Kowalski, and Don Duffield. 1994. "Crime, Social Disorganization, and Social Structure: A Research Note on the Use of Interurban Ecological Models." *American Journal of Criminal Justice* 19:117–132.

Peterson, Ruth, Lauren Krivo, and Mark Harris. 2000. "Disadvantage and Neighborhood Violent Crime: Do Local Institutions Matter?" *Journal of Research on Crime and Delinquency* 37:31–63.

Pettiway, Leon E., Sergey Dolinsky, and Alexander Grigoryan. 1994. "The Drug and Criminal Activity Patterns of Urban Offenders: A Markov Chain Analysis." *Journal of Quantitative Criminology* 10:79–107.

Pfuhl, Erdwin H., and Stuart Henry. 1993. *The Deviance Process.* 3rd ed. Hawthorn, N.Y.: Aldine De Gruyter.

Phillips, Llad, and Harold L. Votey Jr. 1987. "The Influence of Police Interventions and Alternative Income Sources on the Dynamic Process of Choosing Crime as a Career." *Journal of Quantitative Criminology* 3:251–273.

Piaget, Jean. [1937] 1954. *The Construction of Reality in the Child.* New York: Basic.

_____. [1932] 1965. *The Moral Judgement of the Child.* New York: Free Press.

_____. [1923] 1969. *The Language and Thought of the Child.* New York: Meridian.

Piliavin, Irving, Rosemary Irene Gartner, Craig Thornton, and Ross L. Matsueda. 1986. "Crime, Deterrence, and Rational Choice." *American Sociological Review* 51:101–119.

Piquero, Alex R. 2000. "Assessing the Relationships between Gender, Chronicity, Seriousness, and Offense Skewness in Criminal Offending." *Journal of Criminal Justice* 28:103–115.

Piquero, Alex R., Nicole Leeper, and Miriam D. Sealock. 2000. "Generalizing General Strain Theory: An Examination of an Offending Population." *Justice Quarterly* 17:449–475.

Pitch, Tamar. 1985. "Critical Criminology and the Construction of Social Problems and the Question of Rape." *International Journal of the Sociology of Law* 13:35–46.

Platt, Tony. 1974. "Prospects for a Radical Criminology in the United States." *Crime and Social Justice* 1:2–10.

Platt, Tony, and Paul Takagi. 1979. "Biosocial Criminology: A Critique." *Crime and Social Justice* 11 (Spring/Summer):5–13.

Plummer, Ken. 1979. "Misunderstanding Labelling Perspectives." In David Downes and Paul Rock, eds., *Deviant Interpretations.* Oxford: Oxford University Press.

Pogarsky, Greg. 2002. "Identifying 'Deterrable' Offenders: Implications for Research on Deterrence." *Justice Quarterly* 19, 3:431–452.

Polakowski, Michael. 1994. "Linking Self and Social Control with Deviance: Illuminating the Structure Underlying a General Theory of Crime and Its Relation to Deviant Activity." *Journal of Quantitative Criminology* 10:41–78.

Polding, Brian Earl. 1995. "Dishonesty of College Students." Ph.D. diss., University of Florida.

Polk, Kenneth. 2003. "Masculinities, Femininities, and Homicide: Competing Explanations for Male Violence." In Martin D. Schwartz and Suzanne E. Hatty, eds., *Controversies in Critical Criminology,* 133–145. Cincinnati: Anderson.

Pollack, William. 1998. *Real Boys: Rescuing Our Sons from the Myths of Boyhood.* New York: Random House.

Pollak, Otto. 1950. *The Criminality of Women*. Philadelphia: University of Pennsylvania Press.

Popper, Karl. 1959. *The Logic of Scientific Discovery*. New York: Basic.

Potter, Gary, and Terry Cox. 1990. "A Community Paradigm of Organized Crime." *American Journal of Criminal Justice* 15:1–23.

Pratt, Travis C., and Francis Cullen. 2000. "The Empirical Status of Gottfredson and Hirschi's General Theory of Crime: A Meta-Analysis." *Criminology* 38:931–954.

Putnam, Robert D. 1995. "Bowling Alone: America's Declining Social Capital." *Journal of Democracy* 6, 1:65–78.

Quinney, Richard. 1970. *The Social Reality of Crime*. Boston: Little, Brown.

_____. 1974. *Critique of the Legal Order: Crime Control in a Capitalist Society*. Boston: Little, Brown.

_____. 1975a. "Crime Control in a Capitalist Society." In Ian Taylor, Paul Walton, and Jock Young, eds., *Critical Criminology*. London: Routledge & Kegan Paul.

_____. 1975b. *Criminology*. Boston: Little, Brown.

_____. 1977. *Class, State, and Crime*. New York: David McKay.

_____. 1991. "Oneness of All: The Mystical Nature of Humanism." In Brian D. MacLean and Dragan Milovanovic, eds., *New Directions in Critical Criminology*. Vancouver: Collective.

Quinney, Richard, and John Wildeman. 1991. *The Problem of Crime: A Peace and Social Justice Perspective*. 3rd ed. London: Mayfield.

Rada, R. T., D. R. Laws, and R. Kellner. 1976. "Plasma Testosterone Levels in the Rapist." *Psychosomatic Medicine* 38:257–268.

Rafter, Nicole Hahn. 1992. "Criminal Anthropology in the United States." *Criminology* 30:525–545.

_____. 1998. *Creating Born Criminals*. Champaign: University of Illinois Press.

Randall, Teri. 1993. "A Novel, Unstable DNA Mutation Cracks Decades-Old Clinical Enigma." *Journal of the American Medical Association* 269:557–558.

Rankin, Joseph H. 1980. "School Factors and Delinquency: Interaction by Age and Sex." *Sociology and Social Research* 64:420–434.

Rankin, Joseph H., and Roger Kern. 1994. "Parental Attachments and Delinquency." *Criminology* 32:495–515.

Rankin, Joseph H., and Edward L. Wells. 1990. "The Effect of Parental Attachments and Direct Controls of Delinquency." *Journal of Research on Crime and Delinquency* 27:140–165.

_____. 1994. "Social Control, Broken Homes, and Delinquency." In Gregg Barak, ed., *Varieties of Criminology*. Westport, Conn.: Praeger.

Rappaport, J. 1977. *Community Psychology: Values, Research, and Action*. New York: Holt, Rinehart & Winston.

Ray, Melvin C., and William R. Downs. 1986. "An Empirical Test of Labeling Theory Using Longitudinal Data." *Journal of Research in Crime and Delinquency* 23:169–194.

Reckless, Walter C. 1940. *Criminal Behavior*. New York: McGraw-Hill.

_____. 1961. "A New Theory of Delinquency and Crime." *Federal Probation* 25:42–46.

_____. [1950] 1973. *The Crime Problem*. Englewood Cliffs, N.J.: Prentice Hall.

Redl, Fritz, and Hans Toch. 1979. "The Psychoanalytical Explanation of Crime." In H. Toch, ed., *Psychology of Crime and Criminal Justice.* New York: Holt, Rinehart & Winston.

Redl, Fritz, and David Wineman. 1951. *Children Who Hate.* New York: Free Press.

_____. 1952. *Controls from Within.* New York: Free Press.

Reed-Sanders, Delores, and Richard A. Dodder. 1979. "Labeling Versus Containment Theory: An Empirical Test with Delinquency." *Free Inquiry in Creative Sociology* 7:18–22.

Regoli, Robert, and Eric Poole. 1978. "The Commitment of Delinquents to Their Misdeeds: A Reexamination." *Journal of Criminal Justice* 6:261–269.

Reiman, Jeffrey. [1979] 1995. *The Rich Get Richer and the Poor Get Prison.* New York: John Wiley.

Reiss, Albert J., Jr. 1951. "Delinquency as the Failure of Personal and Social Controls." *American Sociological Review* 16:196–207.

Reiss, Albert J., Jr., and A. Lewis Rhodes. 1964. "An Empirical Test of Differential Association Theory." *Journal of Research on Crime and Delinquency* 1:5–18.

Rengert, G., and J. Wasilchick. 1985. *Suburban Burglary: A Time and Place for Everything.* Springfield, Ill.: Charles C. Thomas.

Rice, Marcia. 1990. "Challenging Orthodoxies in Feminist Theory: A Black Feminist Critique." In Loraine Gelsthorpe and Allison Morris, eds., *Feminist Perspectives in Criminology.* Milton Keynes, U.K.: Open University.

Riggs, David, Barbara Rothman, and Edna Foa. 1995. "A Prospective Examination of Symptoms of Posttraumatic Stress Disorder in Victims of Nonsexual Assault." *Journal of Interpersonal Violence* 10:201–214.

Robinson, David, and Stuart Henry. 1977. *Self-help and Health: Mutual Aid for Modern Problems.* Oxford, U.K.: Martin Robertson.

Robinson, Laurie. 1996. "Linking Community-Based Initiatives and Community Justice: The Office of Justice Programs." *National Institute of Justice Journal* 231 (August) 4–7.

Robinson, Matthew B. 2000. "Preventing Residential Burglary." *American Journal of Criminal Justice* 24, 2:169–179.

_____. 2004. *Why Crime? An Integrated Systems Theory of Antisocial Behavior.* Upper Saddle River, N.J.: Pearson Prentice Hall.

Robison, Sophia M. 1936. *Can Delinquency Be Measured?* New York: Columbia University Press.

Rodgers, Karen, and Georgia Roberts. 1995. "Women's Non-Spousal Multiple Victimization: A Test of the Routine Activities Theory." *Canadian Journal of Criminology* 37:363–391.

Roe v. Wade, 410 U.S. 113, 93 S.Ct. 705 (1973).

Rose, Nikolas. 2000. "The Biology of Culpability: Pathological Identity and Crime Control in a Biological Culture." *Theoretical Criminology* 4:5–34.

Rosen, Lawrence, Leonard Savitz, Michael Lalli, and Stanley Turner. 1991. "Early Delinquency, High School Graduation, and Adult Criminality." *Sociological Viewpoints* 7:37–60.

Rosenau, Pauline M. 1992. *Postmodernism and the Social Sciences—Insights, Inroads, and Intrusions.* Princeton, N.J.: Princeton University Press.

Rosenfeld, Richard, and Steven Messner. 1995a. "Consumption and Crime: An Institutional Inquiry." Paper presented at the annual meeting of the Academy of Criminal Justice Sciences Boston, March.

_____. 1995b. "Crime and the American Dream: An Institutional Analysis." In Freda Adler and William S. Laufer, eds., *The Legacy of Anomie Theory*. Vol. 6 of *Advances in Criminological Theory*. New Brunswick, N.J.: Transaction.

Roshier, Bob. 1989. *Controlling Crime: The Classical Perspective in Criminology*. Philadelphia: Open University Press.

Rottman, David B. 1996. "Community Courts: Prospects and Limits." *National Institute of Justice Journal* 231 (August):46–51.

Rountree, Pamela Wilcox, and Kenneth C. Land. 1996. "Perceived Risk Versus Fear of Crime: Empirical Evidence of Conceptually Distinct Reactions in Survey Data." *Social Forces* 74:1353–1376.

Rowe, David C. 1986. "Genetic and Environmental Components of Antisocial Behavior: A Study of 265 Twin Pairs." *Criminology* 24:513–532.

Rowe, David C., and David Farrington. 1997. "The Familial Transmission of Criminal Convictions." *Criminology* 35:177–201.

Rubin, R. T. 1987. "The Neuroendocrinology and Neurochemistry of Antisocial Behavior." In Sarnoff A. Mednick, Terrie Moffitt, and Susan Stack, eds., *The Causes of Crime: New Biological Approaches*. Cambridge: Cambridge University Press.

Rush, George E. 1994. *The Dictionary of Criminal Justice*. 4th ed. Guilford, Conn.: Dushkin Publishing Group.

_____. 2000. *The Dictionary of Criminal Justice*. 5th ed. London: Dushkin/McGraw-Hill.

Rushton, J. Phillippe. 1995. *Race, Evolution, and Behavior: A Life History Perspective*. New Brunswick, N.J.: Transaction.

_____. 1990. "Race and Crime: A Reply to Roberts and Gabor." *Canadian Journal of Criminology* 32:315–334.

_____. 1999. *Race Evolution and Behavior*. New Brunswick, N.J.: Transaction.

Russell, Stuart. 1997. "The Failure of Postmodern Criminology." *Critical Criminology* 8:61–90.

Ryan, Kevin, and Jeff Ferrell. 1986. "Knowledge, Power, and the Process of Justice." *Crime and Social Justice* 25:178–195.

Sacco, Vincent E., and Leslie W. Kennedy. 1996. *The Criminal Event: An Introduction to Criminology*. Belmont, Calif.: Wadsworth.

Sagarin, Edward. 1969. *Odd Man In: Societies of Deviants in America*. Chicago: Quadrangle.

Sagarin, Edward, and Jose Sanchez. 1988. "Ideology and Deviance: The Case of the Debate over the Biological Factor." *Deviant Behavior* 9:87–99.

Salgado, Gamini. 1972. *Cony-Catchers and Bawdy Baskets*. Harmondsworth, UK: Penguin Books.

Samenow, Stanton E. 1984. *Inside the Criminal Mind*. New York: Times Books.

Sampson, Robert J. 1986. "Effects of Socioeconomic Context on Official Reactions to Juvenile Delinquency." *American Sociological Review* 51:876–885.

_____. 1999. "Techniques of Research Neutralization." *Theoretical Criminology* 3:438–451.

Sampson, Robert J., Stephen W. Raudenbush, and Felton Earls. 1997. "Neighborhoods and Violent Crime: A Multi-level Study of Collective Efficacy." *Science* 277:918–924.

Sampson, Robert J., and W. Byron Groves. 1989. "Community Structures and Crime: Testing Social Disorganization Theory." *American Journal of Sociology* 94:774–802.

Sampson, Robert J., and William Julius Wilson. 1993. "Toward a Theory of Race, Crime, and Urban Inequality." In John Hagan and Ruth Peterson, eds., *Crime and Inequality.* Stanford, Calif.: Stanford University Press.

Sampson, Robert J., and John D. Wooldredge. 1987. "Linking the Micro- and Macro-Level Dimensions of Lifestyle–Routine Activity and Opportunity Models of Predatory Victimization." *Journal of Quantitative Criminology* 3:371–393.

Sampson, Robert J., and John H. Laub. 1993. *Crime in the Making: Pathways and Turning Points Through Life.* Cambridge: Cambridge University Press.

Sanday, Peggy Reeves. 1981. "The Socio-Cultural Context of Rape: A Cross-Cultural Study." *Journal of Social Issues* 37:5–27.

_____. 2002. *Women in the Center.* Philadelphia: University of Pennsylvania Press.

_____. 2003. "Matriarchal, Islamic and Peace-Builders: The Minangkabau of Indonesia Offer an Alternative Social System." http://www.museum.upenn. edu/new/research/Exp_Rese_Disc/Asia/sanday-research.shtml.

Sanders, William B. 1983. *Criminology.* Reading, Mass.: Addison-Wesley.

Sandys, Marla, and Edmund F. McGarrell. 1994. "Attitudes Toward Capital Punishment Among Indiana Legislators: Diminished Support in Light of Alternative Sentencing Options." *Justice Quarterly* 11:651–677.

Saranson, S. B. 1981. "An Asocial Psychology and a Misdirected Clinical Psychology." *American Psychologist* 36:827–836.

Sarat, Austin. 1978. "Understanding Trial Courts: A Critique of Social Science Approaches." *Judicature* 61:318–326.

Sarbin, T. R., and L. E. Miller. 1970. "Demonism Revisited: The XYY Chromosome Anomaly." *Issues in Criminology* 5:195–207.

Sarre, Rick. 2003. "Restorative Justice: A Paradigm of Possibility." In Martin D. Schwartz and Suzanne E. Hatty, eds., *Controversies in Critical Criminology,* 97–108. Cincinnati: Anderson.

Saunders, D. 1988. "Wife Abuse, Husband Abuse, or Mutual Combat? A Feminist Perspective on the Empirical Findings." In K. Yllo and M. Bograd, eds., *Feminist Perspectives on Wife Abuse.* Newbury Park, Calif.: Sage.

Savitz, L., S. H. Turner, and T. Dickman. 1977. "The Origins of Scientific Criminology: Franz Joseph Gall as the First Criminologist." In Robert F. Meier, ed., *Theory in Criminology.* Beverly Hills, Calif.: Sage.

Savolainen, Jukka. 2000. "Inequality, Welfare State, and Homicide: Further Support for the Instituational Anomie Theory." *Criminology* 38:1021–1042.

Schafer, Stephen. 1968. *The Victim and His Criminal: A Study in Functional Responsibility.* New York: Random House.

_____. 1976. *Introduction to Criminology.* Reston, Va.: Reston.

_____. 1977. *Victimology: The Victim and His Criminal.* Reston, Va.: Reston.

Schlegel, Kip, and David Weisburd, eds. 1992. *White-Collar Crime Reconsidered.* Boston: Northeastern University Press.

Schlossman, S., G. Zellman, R. Shavelson, M. Sedlak, and J. Cobb. 1984. *Delinquency Prevention in South Chicago: A Fifty-Year Assessment of the Chicago Area Project.* Santa Monica, Calif.: Rand.

Schmalleger, Frank. 1999. *Criminology Today.* 2nd ed. Upper Saddle River, N.J.: Prentice-Hall.

_____. [1999] 2002. *Criminology Today: An Integrative Introduction.* 3rd ed. Upper Saddle River, N.J.: Prentice Hall.

Schmidt, Peter, and Ann D. Witte. 1984. *An Economic Analysis of Crime and Justice: Theory, Methods, and Applications.* Orlando, Fla.: Academic.

Schneider, Anne L., and Laurie Ervin. 1990. "Specific Deterrence, Rational Choice, and Decision Heuristics: Applications in Juvenile Justice." *Social Science Quarterly* 71:585–601.

Schrager, Laura S., and James F. Short. 1978. "Toward a Sociology of Organizational Crime." *Social Problems* 25:407–419.

Schuessler, Karl, and Donald Cressey. 1950. "Personality Characteristics of Criminals." *American Journal of Sociology* 55:476–484.

Schulhofer, Stephen J., and Ilene H. Nagel. 1989. "Negotiating Pleas Under Federal Sentencing Guidelines: The First Fifteen Months." *American Criminal Law Review* 27:231–288.

Schur, Edwin M. 1965. *Crimes Without Victims: Deviant Behavior and Public Policy.* Englewood Cliffs, N.J.: Prentice Hall.

_____. 1973. *Radical Non-Intervention: Rethinking the Delinquency Problem.* Englewood Cliffs, N.J.: Prentice Hall.

Schur, Edwin M., and Hugo Adam Bedau. 1974. *Victimless Crimes.* Englewood Cliffs, N.J.: Prentice Hall.

Schwartz, Gary. 1987. *Beyond Conformity or Rebellion: Youth and Authority.* Chicago: University of Chicago Press.

Schwartz, Martin D. 1991. "The Future of Criminology." In Brian MacLean and Dragan Milovanovic, eds., *New Directions in Critical Criminology.* Vancouver: Collective.

Schwartz, Martin D., and David O. Friedrichs. 1994. "Postmodern Thought and Criminological Discontent: New Metaphors for Understanding Violence." *Criminology* 32:221–246.

Schwartz, Martin D., and Dragan Milovanovic, eds. 1996. *Race, Gender, and Class in Criminology: The Intersection.* New York: Garland.

Schwartz, Martin D., and Walter S. DeKeseredy. 1991. "Left Realist Criminology: Strengths, Weaknesses, and Feminist Critique." *Crime, Law, and Social Change* 15:51–72.

Schwendinger, Herman, and Julia Schwendinger. 1970. "Defenders of Order or Guardians of Human Rights?" *Issues in Criminology* 5:123–157.

Schwendinger, Julia, and Herman Schwendinger. 1983. *Rape and Inequality.* Beverly Hills, Calif.: Sage.

Schwitzgebel, R. K. 1974. "The Right to Effective Treatment." *California Law Review* 62:936–956.

Seis, Mark C., and Kenneth L. Elbe. 1991. "The Death Penalty for Juveniles: Bridging the Gap Between an Evolving Standard of Decency and Legislative Policy." *Justice Quarterly* 8:465–487.

Sellers, Christine. 1999. "Self-Control and Intimate Violence: An Examination of the Scope and Specification of the General Theory of Crime." *Criminology* 37:375–404.

Sellers, Christine, Travis C. Pratt, L. Thomas Winfree, and Francis T. Cullen. 2000. "The Empirical Status of Social Learning Theory: A Meta-Analysis." Paper presented at the annual meeting of the American society of Criminology Annual Meeting, San Francisco (November).

Sellin, Thorsten. 1938. *Culture Conflict and Crime.* New York: Social Science Research Council.

Severance, Lawrence, Jane Goodman, and Elizabeth Loftus. 1992. "Inferring the Criminal Mind: Toward a Bridge Between Legal Doctrine and Psychological Understanding." *Journal of Criminal Justice* 20:107–120.

Shaw, Clifford R., and Henry D. McKay. 1931. *Social Factors in Juvenile Delinquency. Report of the Causes of Crime.* National Commission on Law Observance and Enforcement, Report no. 13. Washington, D.C.: Government Printing Office.

_____. [1942] 1969. *Juvenile Delinquency and Urban Areas: A Study of Delinquents in Relation to Differential Characteristics of Local Communities in American Cities.* Chicago: University of Chicago Press.

Shein, Marcia G., and Cloud Miller. 1995. "A Knowing, Intelligent, and Voluntary Plea: The Justice Department's Latest Oxymoron." *Champion* 19 (January-February):10–15. Washington, D.C.: National Association of Criminal Defense Lawyers.

Sheldon, William H., Emil M. Hastl, and Eugene McDermott. 1949. *Varieties of Delinquent Youth.* New York: Harper.

Shoemaker, Donald J. 1996. *Theories of Delinquency: An Examination of Explanations of Delinquent Behavior.* 3rd ed. New York: Oxford University Press.

Shoham, S. Giora. 1979. *Salvation Through the Gutters: Deviance and Transcendence.* New York: Harper.

Shoham, S. Giora, and Mark C. Seis. 1993. *A Primer in the Psychology of Crime.* New York: Harrow & Heston.

Short, James F., Jr. 1957. "Differential Association and Delinquency." *Social Problems* 4:233–239.

_____. 1960. "Differential Association as a Hypothesis: Problems of Empirical Testing." *Social Problems* 8:14–25.

_____. 2002. "Criminology, the Chicago School, and Sociological Theory." *Crime, Law, and Social Change* 37:107–115.

Short, James F., Jr., and Fred L. Stodtbeck. 1965. *Group Process and Gang Delinquency.* Chicago: University of Chicago Press.

Shover, Neal, and Werner J. Einstadter. 1988. *Analyzing Corrections.* Belmont, Calif.: Wadsworth.

Shover, Neal, and David Honaker. 1992. "The Socially Bounded Decision Making of Persistent Property Offenders." *Howard Journal of Criminal Justice* 31:276–293.

Shover, Neal, and John Paul Wright, eds. 2001. *Crimes of Privilege.* New York: Oxford University Press.

Siegel, Larry J. 1989. *Criminology.* Minneapolis: West.

_____. 1995. *Criminology: Theories, Patterns and Typologies.* 5th ed. Minneapolis: West.

_____. 1998. *Criminology: Theories, Patterns and Typologies.* 6th ed. Belmont, Calif.: West/Wadsworth.

_____. 2004. *Criminology: Theories, Patterns, and Typologies.* 8th ed. Belmont, Calif.: Wadsworth.

Simcha-Fagan, Ora, and Joseph E. Schwartz. 1986. "Neighborhood and Delinquency: An Assessment of Contextual Effects." *Criminology* 24:667–704.

Simmel, Georg. [1908] 1955. *The Sociology of Conflict.* Translated Kurt H. Wolff, and *The Web of Group Affiliations*, trans. Reinhard Bendix. Glencoe, Ill.: Free Press.

Simon, David R. 2002. *Elite Deviance.* 7th ed. Boston: Allyn & Bacon.

Simon, David R., and D. Stanley Eitzen. 1982. *Elite Deviance.* Boston: Allyn & Bacon.

Simon, Jonathan. 1993. *Poor Discipline: Parole and the Social Control of the Underclass, 1890–1900.* Chicago: University of Chicago Press.

Simon, Rita. 1975. *Women and Crime.* Lexington, Mass.: D. C. Heath.

Simpson, Sally S. 1989. "Feminist Theory, Crime, and Justice." *Criminology* 27:605–631.

Simpson, Sally S., and Lori Elis. 1994. "Is Gender Subordinate to Class? An Empirical Assessment of Colvin and Pauly's Structural Marxist Theory of Delinquency." *Journal of Criminal Law and Criminology* 85:453–480.

_____. 1995. "Doing Gender: Sorting Out the Caste and Crime Conundrum." *Criminology* 33:47–81.

Skinner, B. F. 1953. *Science and Human Behavior.* New York: Macmillan.

_____. 1971. *Beyond Freedom and Dignity.* New York: Knopf.

Skogan, Wesley. 1986. "Fear of Crime and Neighborhood Change." In Albert J. Reiss Jr., and Michael Tonry, eds., *Communities and Crime.* Chicago: University of Chicago Press.

_____. 1996. "The Community's Role in Community Policing." *National Institute of Justice Journal* 231 (August):31–34.

Skolnick, Jerome. 1995. "Sheldon L. Messinger: The Man, His Work and the Carceral Society." In Thomas Blomberg and Stanley Cohen, eds., *Punishment and Social Control.* Hawthorne, N.Y.: Aldine de Gruyter.

Smart, Carol. 1976. *Women, Crime, and Criminology: A Feminist Critique.* London: Routledge & Kegan Paul.

_____. 1979. "The New Female Criminal: Reality or Myth?" *British Journal of Criminology* 19:50–59.

_____. 1987. "Review of Capitalism, Patriarchy and Crime." *Contemporary Crisis* 11:327–329.

_____. 1989. *Feminism and the Power of Law.* London: Routledge.

_____. 1990. "Feminist Approaches to Criminology or Postmodern Woman Meets Atavistic Man." In Loraine Gelsthorpe and Allison Morris, eds., *Feminist Perspectives in Criminology.* Milton Keynes, U.K.: Open University Press.

_____. 1992. "The Women of Legal Discourse." *Social and Legal Studies: An International Journal* 1:29–44.

Smith, Brent, and Gregory Orvis. 1993. "America's Response to Terrorism: An Empirical Analysis of Federal Intervention Strategies During the 1980s." *Justice Quarterly* 10:661–681.

Smith, Carolyn, and Terence Thornberry. 1995. "The Relationship Between Childhood Maltreatment and Adolescent Involvement in Delinquency." *Criminology* 33:451–481.

Smith, Lacey Baldwin. 1967. *Elizabethan World*. New York: American Heritage.

Smith, Michael R., and Matthew Petrocelli. 2001. "Racial Profiling? A Multivariate Analysis of Police Traffic Stop Data." *Police Quarterly* 4:4–27.

Snodgrass, Jon. 1976. "Clifford R. Shaw and Henry D. McKay: Chicago Sociologists." *British Journal of Criminology* 16:1–19.

Soroka, Michael P., and George J. Bryjak. 1999. *Social Problems: A World at Risk*. 2nd ed. Boston: Allyn & Bacon.

South, Scott J., and Richard B. Felson. 1990. "The Racial Patterning of Rape." *Social Forces* 69:71–93.

Sparks, Richard F. 1981. "Surveys of Victimization: An Optimistic Assessment." *Crime and Justice: An Annual Review of Research* 3:1–60.

Spergel, Irving. 1964. *Racketville, Slumtown, Haulburg: An Exploratory Study of Delinquent Subcultures*. Chicago: University of Chicago Press.

Spitzer, Steven. 1975. "Towards a Marxian Theory of Deviance." *Social Problems* 22:638–651.

Stahura, John M., and Richard C. Hollinger. 1988. "A Routine Activities Approach to Suburban Arson Rates." *Sociological Spectrum* 8:349–369.

Stahura, John M., and John J. Sloan III. 1988. "Urban Stratification of Places, Routine Activities, and Suburban Crime Rates." *Social Forces* 66:1102–1118.

Staples, J. Scott. 2000. "The Meaning of Violence in Our Schools: Rage Against a Broken World." In W. Hinkle and S. Henry, eds., *School Violence*. Vol. 567 of *Annals of the American Academy of Political and Social Science*. Thousand Oaks, Calif.: Sage.

Stark, Rodney. 1987. "Deviant Places: A Theory of the Ecology of Crime." *Criminology* 25:893–909.

Stattin, Hakan, and Ingrid Klackenberg-Larsson. 1993. "Early Language and Intelligence Development and Their Relationship to Future Criminal Behavior." *Journal of Abnormal Psychology* 102:369–378.

Steffensmeier, Darrell. 1978. "Crime and the Contemporary Woman: An Analysis of Changing Levels of Female Property Crime, 1960–75." *Social Forces* 57:566–584.

_____. 1980. "Sex Differences in Patterns of Adult Crime, 1965–77: A Review and Assessment." *Social Forces* 58:1080–1108.

_____. 1986. *The Fence*. Langham, Md.: Rowman & Littlefield.

Stitt, B. Grant, and David J. Giacopassi. 1992. "Trends in the Connectivity of Theory and Research in Criminology." *Criminologist* 17, 1:3–6.

Stolzenberg, Lisa, and Stewart J. D'Alessio. 1994. "Sentencing and Unwarranted Disparity: An Empirical Assessment of the Long-Term Impact of Sentencing Guidelines in Minnesota." *Criminology* 32:301–310.

Stone, Christopher. 1996. "Community Defense and the Challenge of Community Justice." *National Institute of Justice Journal* 231 (August):41–45.

Strang, Heather. 2000. "The Future of Restorative Justice." In D. Chappell and P. Wilson, eds., *Crime and the Criminal Justice System in Australia: 2000 and Beyond*, 22–23. Sydney, Australia: Butterworths.

Suchar, Charles S. 1978. *Social Deviance: Perspectives and Prospects*. New York: Holt, Rinehart & Winston.

Sundquist, James L., ed. 1969. *On Fighting Poverty*. New York: Basic.

Surette, Ray. 1997. *Media, Crime, and Criminal Justice*. 2nd ed. Pacific Grove, Calif.: Brooks/Cole.

Sutherland, Edwin H. 1924. *Criminology*. Philadelphia: J. B. Lippincott.

_____. 1937. *The Professional Thief: By a Professional Thief*. Chicago: University of Chicago Press.

_____. [1939] 1947. *Principles of Criminology*. Philadelphia: J. B. Lippincott.

_____. 1949a. *White Collar Crime*. New York: Holt, Rinehart & Winston.

_____. 1949b. "The White Collar Criminal." In Vernon C. Branham and Samuel B. Kutash, eds., *Encyclopedia of Criminology*. New York: Philosophical Library.

Sutherland, Edwin H., and Donald R. Cressey. 1966. *Principles of Criminology*. Philadelphia: J. B. Lippincott.

Sutherland, Grant R., and Robert Richards. 1994. "Dynamic Mutations." *American Scientist* 82:157–163.

Sutherland, I., and J. P. Shepherd. 2002. "A Personality-Based Model of Adolescent Violence." *British Journal of Criminology* 42:433–441.

Suttles, Gerald. 1972. *The Social Construction of Communities*. Chicago: University of Chicago Press.

Syed, Fariya. 1996. *Case Studies of Female Sex Offenders*. Correctional Services of Canada.

Sykes, Gresham. 1974. "Critical Criminology." *Journal of Criminal Law and Criminology* 65:206–213.

Sykes, Gresham, and David Matza. 1957. "Techniques of Neutralization: A Theory of Delinquency." *American Sociological Review* 22:664–670.

Tame, Chris R. 1995. "Freedom, Responsibility, and Justice: The *Criminology* of the 'New Right.'" In Kevin Stenson and David Cowell, eds., *The Politics of Crime Control*. Thousand Oaks, Calif.: Sage.

Tannenbaum, Frank. 1938. *Crime and the Community*. Boston: Ginn.

Tappan, Paul W. 1947. "Who Is the Criminal?" *American Sociological Review* 12:96–102.

Tarde, Gabriel. [1890] 1903. *Gabriel Tarde's Laws of Imitation*. Translated by E. Parsons. New York: Henry Holt.

Taylor, Ian. 1981. *Law and Order: Arguments for Socialism*. London: Macmillan.

Taylor, Ian, Paul Walton, and Jock Young. 1973. *The New Criminology: For a Social Theory of Deviance*. London: Routledge & Kegan Paul.

_____. 1975. *Critical Criminology*. London: Routledge & Kegan Paul.

Taylor, Laurie. 1972. "The Significance and Interpretation of Motivational Questions: The Case of Sex Offenders." *Sociology* 6:23–29.

Taylor, Lawrence. 1984. *Born to Crime: The Genetic Causes of Criminal Behavior*. Boulder: Westview.

Taylor, Lawrence, and Katharina Dalton. 1983. "Premenstrual Syndrome: A New Criminal Defense?" *California Western Law Review* 19:269–287.

Taylor, Ralph B. 1988. *Human Territorial Functioning*. Cambridge: Cambridge University Press.

Taylor, Ralph B., and Jeanette Covington. 1988. "Neighborhood Changes in Ecology and Violence." *Criminology* 26:553–589.

Taylor, Ralph B., and Adele V. Harrell. 1996. *Physical Environment and Crime*. Washington, D.C.: U.S. Department of Justice, National Institute of Justice.

Telfer, Mary A., David Baker, and Gerald R. Clark. 1968. "Incidence of Gross Chromosomal Errors Among Tall Criminal American Males." *Science* 159:1249–1250.

Thomas, Jim, and Sharon Boehlefeld. 1991. "Rethinking Abolitionism: 'What Do We Do with Henry?' Review of de Haan, The Politics of Redress." *Social Justice* 18:239–251.

Thomas, William I., and Florian Znaniecki. 1920. *The Polish Peasant in Europe and America*. Vol. 2. Boston: Gorham.

Thompkins, Douglas E. 2000. "School Violence: Gangs and a Culture of Fear." In W. Hinkle and S. Henry, eds., *School Violence*. Vol. 567 of *Annals of the American Academy of Political and Social Science*. Thousand Oaks, Calif.: Sage.

Thompson, William E., Jim Mitchell, and Richard A. Dodder. 1984. "An Empirical Test of Hirschi's Control Theory of Delinquency." *Deviant Behavior* 5:11–22.

Thornberry, Terence P. 1987. "Toward an Interactional Theory of Delinquency." *Criminology* 25:863–891.

_____. 1989. "Reflections on the Advantages and Disadvantages of Theoretical Integration." In Stephen F. Messner, Marvin D. Krohn, and Allen Liska, eds., *Theoretical Integration in the Study of Deviance and Crime*. Albany: State University of New York Press.

Thornberry, Terence P., Melanie Moore, and R. L. Christenson. 1985. "The Effect of Dropping Out of High School on Subsequent Criminal Behavior." *Criminology* 23:3–18.

Thornhill, Randy, and Craig Palmer. 2000. *A Natural History of Rape: Biological Bases of Sexual Coercion*. Cambridge: MIT Press.

Thrasher, Frederick M. 1927. *The Gang*. Chicago: University of Chicago Press.

Tifft, Larry L. 1979. "The Coming Redefinitions of Crime: An Anarchist Perspective." *Social Problems* 26:392–402.

Tifft, Larry L., and Dennis Sullivan. 1980. *The Struggle to Be Human: Crime, Criminology, and Anarchism*. Sanday, U.K.: Cienfuegos.

_____. 2001. "A Needs Based, Social Harm Definition of Crime." In Stuart Henry and Mark M. Lanier, eds., *What Is Crime?* Boulder, Colo.: Rowman & Littlefield.

Timmer, Doug A., and Stanley D. Eitzen. 1989. *Crime in the Streets and Crime in the Suites: Perspectives on Crime and Criminal Justice*. Boston: Allyn & Bacon.

Tittle, Charles. 1991. "Being Labeled a Criminologist." *Criminologist*, May-June, 1, 3–4.

_____. 1995. *Control Balance: Toward a General Theory of Deviance*. Boulder: Westview Press.

Tittle, Charles R., Wayne J. Villemez, and Douglas A. Smith. 1978. "The Myth of Social Class and Criminality: An Empirical Assessment of the Empirical Evidence." *American Sociological Review* 43:643–656.

Toby, Jackson. 1957. "Social Disorganization and Stake in Conformity: Complementary Factors in the Predatory Behavior of Hoodlums." *Journal of Criminal Law, Criminology, and Police Science* 48:12–17.

Tong, Rosemary. 1998. *Feminist Thought.* 2nd ed. Boulder: Westview.

Tonry, Michael. 1988. "Structuring Sentencing." In Michael Tonry and Norvil Morris, eds., *Crime and Justice: A Review of Research.* Chicago: University of Chicago Press.

_____. 1995. *Malign Neglect: Race, Crime, and Punishment in America.* New York: Oxford University Press.

Tooby, J., and L. Cosmides. 1992. "The Psychological Foundations of Culture." In J. H. Barkow, L. Cosmides, and J. Tooby, eds., *The Adapted Mind: Evolutionary Psychology and the Generation of Culture,* 19–136. New York: Oxford University Press.

Torstensson, Marie. 1990. "Female Delinquents in a Birth Cohort: Tests of Some Aspects of Control Theory." *Journal of Quantitative Criminology* 6:101–115.

Tracy, Paul E., Marvin E. Wolfgang, and Robert M. Figlio. 1985. *Delinquency in Two Birth Cohorts: Executive Summary.* Washington, D.C.: U.S. Department of Justice.

_____. 1990. *Delinquency Careers in Two Birth Cohorts.* New York: Plenum.

Trice, Harrison M., and Paul M. Roman. 1970. "Delabeling, Relabeling and Alcoholics Anonymous." *Social Problems* 17:538–546.

Trojanowicz, Robert, and Bonnie Bucqueroux. 1990. *Community Policing: A Contemporary Perspective.* Cincinnati: Anderson.

Tucker, Robert. 1978. *The Marx-Engels Reader.* New York: Norton.

Tunnell, Kenneth. 1992. *Choosing Crime: The Criminal Calculus of Property Offenders.* Chicago: Nelson-Hall.

Turk, Austin. T. 1964. "Prospects for Theories of Criminal Behavior." *Journal of Criminal Law, Criminology, and Police Science* 55:454–461.

_____. 1966. "Conflict and Criminality." *American Sociological Review* 31:338–352.

_____. 1969. *Criminality and the Legal Order.* Chicago: Rand McNally.

_____. 1976. "Law as a Weapon in Social Conflict." *Social Problems* 23:276–291.

_____. 1980. "Analyzing Official Deviance: For Nonpartisan Conflict Analysis in Criminology." In James A. Inciardi, ed., *Radical Criminology: The Coming Crisis.* Beverly Hills, Calif.: Sage.

_____. 1982. *Political Criminality: The Defiance and Defense of Authority.* Beverly Hills, Calif.: Sage.

_____. 1995. "Transformation Versus Revolutionism and Reformism: Policy Implications of Conflict Theory." In Hugh Barlow, ed., *Crime and Public Policy.* Boulder: Westview.

Turner, Jonathan H. 1986. *The Structure of Sociological Theory.* 4th ed. Chicago: Dorsey.

Tygart, Clarence E. 1988. "Strain Theory and Public School Vandalism: Academic Tracking, School Social Status, and Students' Academic Achievement." *Youth and Society* 20:106–118.

Umbreit, Mark. 1994. *Victim Meets Offender: The Impact of Restorative Justice and Mediation.* Monsey, N.Y.: Criminal Justice Press.

_____. 2001. "Family Group Conferencing: Implications for Crime Victims." The Center for Restorative Justice, University of Minnesota. http://www.ojp.us-

doj.gov/ovc/publications/infores/restorative_justice/96523-family_group/
family3.html.

Umbreit, Mark S., and Robert B. Coates. 1998. *Multi-Cultural Implications of Restorative Justice: Potential Pitfalls and Dangers*. Washington, D.C.: U.S. Department of Justice, Office for Victims of Crime.

Umbreit, Mark S., Robert B. Coates, Betty Vos, and Kathy Brown. 2002. *Victim Offender Dialogue in Crimes of Severe Violence: A Multi-Site Study of Programs in Texas and Ohio*. Minneapolis, Minn.: Center for Restorative Justice, University of Minnesota.

Unger, Robert M. 1976. *Law in Modern Society*. New York: Free Press.

U.S. Sentencing Commission. 1994. *Federal Sentencing Guidelines Manual*. 1994–1995 ed. St. Paul, Minn.: West.

van Swaaningen, Rene. 1997. *Critical Criminology: Visions from Europe*. London: Sage.

Vaughan, Diane. 1983. *Controlling Unlawful Organization Behavior: Social Structure and Corporate Misconduct*. Chicago: University of Chicago Press.

_____. 1998. "Rational Choice, Situated Action and the Social Control of Organizations." *Law and Society Review* 32:23–61.

Vazsonyi, Alexander T., Lloyd E. Pickering, Marianne Junger, and Dick Hessing. 2001. "An Empirical Test of a General Theory of Crime: A Four Nation Comparative Study of Self-Control and the Prediction of Deviance." *Journal of Research in Crime and Delinquency* 38:91–131.

Venturelli, Peter J. 2000. "Drugs in Schools: Myths and Realities." In W. Hinkle and S. Henry, eds., *School Violence*. Vol. 567 of *Annals of the American Academy of Political and Social Science*. Thousand Oaks, Calif.: Sage.

Vila, Bryan. 1994. "A General Paradigm for Understanding Criminal Behavior: Extending Evolutionary Ecological Theory." *Criminology* 32:311–359.

Virkkunen, M.J. DeJong, J. Bartkko, F. K. Goodwin, and M. Linnoila. 1989. "Relationship of Psychobiological Variables to Recidivism in Violent Offenders and Impulsive Fire Setters." *Archives of General Psychiatry* 46:600–603.

Vito, G. F., Edward Latessa, and D. G. Wilson. 1988. *Introduction to Criminal Justice Research Methods*. Springfield, Ill.: Charles C. Thomas.

Vold, George B. [1958] 1979. *Theoretical Criminology*. New York: Oxford University Press.

Vold, George B., and Thomas J. Bernard. 1986. *Theoretical Criminology*. 3rd ed. New York: Oxford University Press.

Vold, George B., Thomas J. Bernard, and J. B. Snipes. 1998. *Theoretical Criminology*. 4th ed. New York: Oxford University Press.

Von Hentig, H. 1948. *The Criminal and His Victim*. New Haven, Conn.: Yale University Press.

Von Hirsch, Andrew. 1976. *Doing Justice: The Choice of Punishments*. New York: Hill & Wang.

Von Hirsch, Andrew, and Nils Jareborg. 1991. "Gauging Criminal Harm: A Living Standard Analysis." *Oxford Journal of Legal Studies* 2:1–38.

Waldo, Gordon, and Simon Dinitz. 1967. "Personality Attributes of the Criminal: An Analysis of Research Studies, 1950–1965." *Journal of Research in Crime and Delinquency* 4:185–202.

Walker, Jeffrey T. 1994. "Human Ecology and Social Disorganization Revisit Delinquency in Little Rock." In Gregg Barak, ed., *Varieties of Criminology: Readings from a Dynamic Discipline*. Westport, Conn.: Praeger.

Walklate, Sandra. 1989. *Victimology: The Victim and the Criminal Justice Process*. London: Unwin Hyman.

Wallerstein, James S., and Clement E. Wyle. 1947. "Our Law-abiding and Law-breakers." *Probation* 25:107–112.

Walsh, Anthony. 2000. "Behavior Genetics and Anomie/Strain Theory." *Criminology* 38:1075-1108.

Walsh, Dermot. 1980. *Break-Ins: Burglary from Private Houses*. London: Constable.

Walters, Glenn. 1992. "A Meta-Analysis of the Gene-Crime Relationship." *Criminology* 30:595–613.

_____. 1995. "The Psychological Inventory of Criminal Thinking Styles." *Criminal Justice and Behavior* 22:307–325.

Walters, Glenn, and Thomas White. 1989. "Heredity and Crime: Bad Genes or Bad Research." *Criminology* 27:455–486.

Walton, Paul, and Jock Young. 1998. *The New Criminology Revisited*. London: Macmillan.

Ward, Tony, and Richard Siegert. 2002. "Rape and Evolutionary Psychology: A Critique of Thornhill and Palmer's Theory." *Aggression and Behavior* 7:145–168.

Ward, Tony, T. Keenan, and S. Hudson. 2000. "Understanding Cognitive, Affective, and Intimacy Deficits in Sexual Offenders: A Developmental Perspective." *Aggression and Behavior* 5:41–62.

Waring, Elin, David Weisburd, and Ellen Chayet. 1995. "White-Collar Crime and Anomie." In Freda Adler and William S. Laufer, eds., *The Legacy of Anomie Theory*. Vol. 6 of *Advances in Criminological Theory*. New Brunswick, N.J.: Transaction.

Warner, Barbara D. 2003. "The Role of Attenuate Culture in Social Disorganization Theory." *Criminology* 41:73–97.

Warr, Mark, and Mark Stafford. 1991. "The Influence of Delinquent Peers: What They Think or What They Do?" *Criminology* 29:851–866.

Weber, Max. [1922] 1966. *The Theory of Social and Economic Organization*. New York: Free Press.

Weed, Frank J. 1995. *Certainty of Justice: Reform in the Crime Victim Movement*. Hawthorne, N.Y.: Aldine de Gruyter.

Weinstein, Jay, Werner Einstadter, Joseph Rankin, Stuart Henry, and Peggy Wiencek. 1991. *Taylor Community Action Study: Survey and Needs Assessment*. Ypsilanti: Eastern Michigan University, Department of Sociology.

Weisel, Deborah Lamm, and Adele Harrell. 1996. "Crime Prevention Through Neighborhood Revitalization: Does Practice Reflect Theory?" *National Institute of Justice Journal* 231 (August):18–23.

Weis, Robert. 1983. "Radical Criminology: A Recent Development." In Elmer H. Johnson, ed., *International Handbook of Contemporary Developments in Criminology: General Issues and the Americas*. Westport, Conn.: Greenwood.

Weis, Joseph, and J. David Hawkins. 1981. *Reports of the National Juvenile Justice Assessment Centers, Preventing Delinquency*. Washington, D.C.: U.S. Department of Justice.

Weis, Joseph, and John Sederstrom. 1981. *Reports of the National Juvenile Justice Assessment Centers, The Prevention of Serious Delinquency: What to Do.* Washington, D.C.: U.S. Department of Justice.

Weisburd, David. 1997. "Reorienting Crime Prevention Research and Policy: From the Causes of Criminality to the Context of Crime." *NIJ Research Report* (June).

Wellford, Charles. 1975. "Labeling Theory and Criminology: An Assessment." *Social Problems* 22:313–332.

Wells, Edward L., and Joseph H. Rankin. 1988. "Direct Parental Controls and Delinquency." *Criminology* 26:263–285.

Wells, Edward L., and Joseph H. Rankin. 1991. "Families and Delinquency: A Meta-Analysis of the Impact of Broken Homes." *Social Problems* 38:71–93.

Welsh, Wayne N. 2000. "The Effects of School Climate on School Disorder." In W. Hinkle and S. Henry, eds., *School Violence.* Vol. 567 of *Annals of the American Academy of Political and Social Science.* Thousand Oaks, Calif.: Sage.

White, Helene Raskin, and Randy L. LaGrange. 1987. "An Assessment of Gender Effects in Self Report Delinquency." *Sociological Focus* 20:195–213.

Wiatrowski, Michael, and Kristine L. Anderson. 1987. "The Dimensionality of the Social Bond." *Journal of Quantitative Criminology* 3:65–81.

Wieck, D. 1978. "Anarchist Justice." In J. R. Pennock and J. W. Chapman, eds., *Anarchism.* New York: New York University Press.

Wilkins, Leslie. 1965. *Social Deviance: Social Policy, Action, and Research.* London: Tavistock.

Williams, Christopher R., and Bruce A. Arrigo. 2001. *Law, Psychology, and Justice: Chaos Theory and the New (dis)Order.* Albany, N.Y.: SUNY Press.

Williams, Frank P., III, and Marilyn D. McShane. 1988. *Criminological Theory.* Englewood Cliffs, N.J.: Prentice Hall.

Williams, Juan. 1994. "Violence, Genes, and Prejudice." *Discover* 15:92–102.

Williams, Kirk, and Richard Hawkins. 1989. "The Meaning of Arrest for Wife Assault." *Criminology* 27:163–181.

Williams, Terry. 1989. *The Cocaine Kids.* Reading, Mass.: Addison-Wesley.

_____. 1992. *Crack House: Notes from the End of the Line.* Reading, Mass.: Addison-Wesley.

Wills, Garry. 1978. *Inventing America: Jefferson's Declaration of Independence.* Garden City, N.Y.: Doubleday.

Wilson, Edmund O. 1975. *Sociobiology.* Cambridge: Harvard University Press.

Wilson, James Q., and Richard Herrnstein. 1985. *Crime and Human Nature.* New York: Simon & Schuster.

Wilson, James Q., and George Kelling. 1982. "Broken Windows: The Police and Neighborhood Safety." *Atlantic Monthly* (March):29–38.

Wilson, William Julius. 1996. *When Work Disappears: The World of the New Urban Poor.* New York: Alfred A. Knopf.

Winfree, L. Thomas, Jr. 2002. "Peacemaking and Community Harmony: Lessons (and Admonitions) from the Navajo Peacemaking Courts." In Elmar G. M. Weitekamp and Hans-Jurgen Kerner, eds., *Resoratative Justice: Theoretical Foundations.* Portland, Ore.: Willan.

Wolfgang, Marvin E., and F. Ferracuti. 1982. *The Subculture of Violence: Toward an Integrated Theory in Criminology.* Beverly Hills, Calif.: Sage.

Wolfgang, Marvin, Robert Figlio, and Thorsten Sellin. 1972. *Delinquency in a Birth Cohort*. Chicago: University of Chicago Press.

Wolfgang, Marvin, Terence Thornberry, and Robert Figlio. 1987. *From Boy to Man, from Birth to Crime*. Chicago: University of Chicago Press.

Wood, Peter B., John K. Cochran, Betty Pfefferbaum, and Bruce J. Arneklev. 1995. "Sensation Seeking and Delinquent Substance Abuse: An Extension of Learning Theory." *Journal of Drug Issues* 25:173–193.

Wood, Peter B., Walter R. Gove, and John K. Cochran. 1994. "Motivations for Violent Crime Among Incarcerated Adults: A Consideration of Reinforcement Processes." *Journal of the Oklahoma Criminal Justice Consortium* 1:63–80.

Woodcock, George. 1963. *Anarchism: A History of Libertarian Ideas and Movements*. Harmondsworth, U.K.: Penguin.

_____. 1977. *The Anarchist Reader*. London: Fontana.

Wright, Bradley R. E., Avshalom Caspi, Terrie E. Moffitt, and Phil Silva. 1999. "Low Self-Control, Social Bonds, and Crime: Social Causation, Social Selection or Both?" *Criminology* 37:479–514.

Wright, John P., Francis T. Cullen, and Michael B. Blankenship. 1996. "Chained Factory Fire Exits: Media Coverage of a Corporate Crime That Killed 25 Workers." In M. David Ermann and Richard J. Lundman, eds., *Corporate and Governmental Deviance*. 5th ed. New York: Oxford University Press.

Wright, Richard A., and J. Mitchell Miller. 1998. "Taboo until Today? The Coverage of Biological Arguments in Criminology Textbooks, 1961 to 1970 and 1987 to 1996." *Journal of Criminal Justice* 26:1–19.

Wylie, Sarah E., ed. 1994. "Georgetown Law Journal Project. Twenty-third Annual Review of Criminal Procedure: United States Supreme Court and Courts of Appeal 1992–1993." *Georgetown Law Journal* 82, no. 3. Washington, D.C.: Georgetown University Law Center.

Yochelson, Samuel, and Stanton Samenow. 1976. *The Criminal Personality*. Vol. 1. New York: Jason Aronson.

_____. 1977. *The Criminal Personality*. Vol. 2. New York: Jason Aronson.

Yogan, Lissa J. 2000. "School Tracking and Student Violence." In W. Hinkle and S. Henry, eds., *School Violence*. Vol. 567 of *Annals of the American Academy of Political and Social Science*. Thousand Oaks, Calif.: Sage.

Yogan, Lissa, and Stuart Henry. 2000. "Masculine Thinking and School Violence: Issues of Gender and Race." In D. S. Sandhu and C.B. Aspey, eds., *School Violence: A Practical Guide for Counselors*. Washington, D.C.: American Counseling Association.

Young, Alison. 1990. *Femininity in Dissent*. London: Routledge.

_____. 1996. *Imagining Crime*. London: Sage.

Young, Jock. 1971. "The Role of Police as Amplifiers of Deviancy, Negotiators of Reality and Translators of Fantasy." In Stan Cohen, ed., *Images of Deviance*. Harmondsworth, U.K.: Penguin.

_____. 1979. "Left Idealism, Reformism and Beyond." In Bob Fine, Richard Kinsey, John Lea, Sol Picciotto, and Jock Young, eds., *Capitalism and the Rule of Law*. London: Hutchinson.

_____. 1981. "Thinking Seriously About Crime: Some Models of Criminology." In Mike Fitzgerald, Gregor McLennan, and Jennie Pawson, eds., *Crime and Society: Readings in History and Society*. London: Routledge & Kegan Paul.

_____. 1987. "The Tasks Facing a Realist Criminology." *Contemporary Crisis* 11:337–356.

Young, Jock, and Roger Matthews, eds. 1992. *Rethinking Criminology: The Realist Debate.* Newbury Park, Calif.: Sage.

_____. 1999. *The Exclusive Society.* London: Sage.

Young, T. R. 1995. *The Red Feather Dictionary of Critical Social Science.* Boulder: Red Feather Institute.

Zaubermann, Renne, R. Philip, C. Perez-Diaz, and R. Levy. 1990. *Les victimes, comportements et attitudes; enquete nationale de victimisation.* Paris: CESDIP.

Zhang, Lening, John W. Welte and William F. Wieczorek. 2002. "Underlying Common Factors of Adolescent Problem Behaviors." *Criminal Justice and Behavior* 29:161–182.

Zietz, Dorothy. 1981. *Women Who Embezzle or Defraud: A Study of Convicted Felons.* New York: Praeger.

Zuckerman, Marvin. 1979. *Sensation-Seeking: Beyond the Optimal Level of Arousal.* Hillsdale, N.J.: Lawrence Erlbaum.

_____. 1989. "Personality in the Third Dimension: A Psychobiological Approach." *Personality and Individual Differences* 10:391–418.

_____. 1994. *Behavioral Expressions and Biosocial Bases of Sensation Seeking.* Cambridge: Cambridge University Press.

Index